# iPad Made Simple

Martin Trautschold
and
Gary Mazo

Apress®

**iPad Made Simple**



ISBN-13 (pbk): 978-1-4302-3129-5

ISBN-13 (electronic): 978-1-4302-3130-1

Printed and bound in the United States of America 9 8 7 6 5 4 3 2 1



Distributed to the book trade worldwide by Springer Science+Business Media, LLC., 233 Spring Street, 6th Floor, New York, NY 10013. Phone 1-800-SPRINGER, fax (201) 348-4505, e-mail orders-ny@springer-sbm.com, or visit www.springeronline.com.

For information on translations, please e-mail rights@apress.com, or visit www.apress.com.

Apress and friends of ED books may be purchased in bulk for academic, corporate, or promotional use. eBook versions and licenses are also available for most titles. For more information, reference our Special Bulk Sales–eBook Licensing web page at www.apress.com/info/bulksales.

*This book is dedicated to our families—to our wives, Julie and Gloria, and to our kids, Sophie, Livvie and Cece, and Ari, Dan, Sara, Billy, Elise and Jonah.*

*Without their love, support, and understanding, we could never take on projects like this one. Now that the book is done, we will gladly share our iPads with them – for a little while!*

# Contents at a Glance

# Contents

# About the Authors

**Martin Trautschold** is the founder and CEO of Made Simple Learning, a leading provider of Apple iPad, iPhone, iPod touch, BlackBerry, and Palm webOS books and video tutorials. He has been a successful entrepreneur in the mobile device training and software business since 2001. With Made Simple Learning, he helped to train thousands of BlackBerry Smartphone users with short, to-the-point video tutorials. Martin has now co-authored fifteen "Made Simple" guide books. He also co-founded, ran for 3 years, and then sold a mobile device software company. Prior to this, Martin spent 15 years in technology and business consulting in the US and Japan. He holds an engineering degree from Princeton University and an MBA from the Kellogg School at Northwestern University. Martin and his wife, Julia, have three daughters. He enjoys rowing and cycling. Martin can be reached at `martin@madesimplelearning.com`.

**Gary Mazo** is Vice President of Made Simple Learning and is a writer, a college professor, a gadget nut, and an ordained rabbi. Gary joined Made Simple Learning in 2007 and has co-authored the last thirteen books in the Made Simple series. Along with Martin, and Kevin Michaluk from CrackBerry.com, Gary co-wrote *CrackBerry: True Tales of BlackBerry Use and Abuse*—a book about BlackBerry addiction and how to get a grip on one's BlackBerry use. Gary also teaches writing, philosophy, technical writing, and more at the University of Phoenix. Gary is a regular contributor to CrackBerry.com—writing product reviews and adding editorial content. He holds a BA in anthropology from Brandeis University. Gary earned his M.A.H.L (Masters in Hebrew Letters) as well as ordination as Rabbi from the Hebrew Union College-Jewish Institute of Religion in Cincinnati, Ohio. He has served congregations in Dayton, Ohio, Cherry Hill, New Jersey and Cape Cod, Massachusetts. Gary is married to Gloria Schwartz Mazo; they have six children. Gary can be reached at: `gary@madesimplelearning.com`.

# About the Technical Reviewer

**Rene Ritchie** is editor of `TiPb.com`, the iPhone and iPad blog, which covers the full range of news, how-tos and app, game, and accessory reviews. Part of the Smartphone Experts network, TiPb also provides a full range of help and community forums and has a thriving YouTube channel (`http://www.youtube.com/theiphoneblog/`), Facebook page (`http://www.facebook.com/tipbcom/`) and Twitter following (`http://twitter.com/tipb`). A graphic designer, web developer, and author, Rene lives and works in Montreal. He can be reached via `rene@tipb.com` or `@reneritchie` on Twitter.

# Acknowledgments

A book like this takes many people to successfully complete. We would like to thank Apress for believing in us and our unique style of writing.

We would like to thank our Editors, Jim and Laurin, and the entire editorial team at Apress.

We would also like to thank our Technical Editor, Rene Ritchie from tipb.com. His expertise and suggestions helped to make this a better book.

Lastly, although mentioned before, we would like to thank our families for their patience and support in allowing us to pursue projects such as this one.

Part I

# Quick Start Guide

In your hands is one of the most exciting devices to hit the market in quite some time: the iPad. This Quick Start Guide will help get you and your new iPad up and running in a hurry. You'll learn all about the buttons, switches, and ports, and how to use the innovative and responsive touch screen. Our App Reference Tables introduce you to the apps on your iPad—and serve as a quick way to find out how to accomplish a task. We finish up with some cool accessories to make your iPad even more useful.

# Quick Start Guide

This Quick Start Guide is meant to be just that—a tool that can help you jump right in and find information in this book—and learn the basics of how to get around and enjoy your iPad right away.

We start with the nuts and bolts in our “Learning Your Way Around” section—what all the keys, buttons, switches, and symbols mean and do on your iPad. You’ll see some handy features like the screen rotation lock and learn how to interact with the menus, submenus, and set switches—which you do in almost every application on your iPad. You’ll also find out how to read your connectivity status and what to do when you travel on an airplane.

**TIP:** Check out Chapter 2, “Typing Tips, Copy/Paste & Search” for great typing tips and more.

In “Touch Screen Basics,” we help you learn how to touch, swipe, flick, zoom, and more.

In “App Reference Tables,” we’ve organized the app icons into general categories so you can quickly browse the icons and jump to a section in the book to learn more about the app a particular icon represents. Here are the tables:

- Getting Started (Table 2)
- Stay Organized (Table 3)
- Be Entertained (Table 4)
- Stay Informed (Table 5)
- Network Socially (Table 6)
- Be Productive (Table 7)

In “Other Fun Stuff,” we show you the electronic Picture Frame and how to enjoy videos on your iPad.

In "iPad Accessories," we give you a brief overview of some of the more common accessories you might find interesting.

So let's get started!

# Learning Your Way Around

To help you get comfortable with your iPad, we start with the basics—what the buttons, keys, and switches do—then we move into how you start apps and navigate the menus. Probably the most important status indicator on your iPad, besides the battery, is the one that shows network status in the upper right corner. You'll see how to quickly read the network status icons.

## Keys, Buttons, and Switches

Figure 1 shows all the things you can do with the buttons, keys, switches, ports on your iPad. Go ahead and try out a few things to see what happens. Try pressing the **Volume Down** key for 2 seconds, double-click the **Home** button, try the **Screen Rotation Lock** switch, and press and hold the **Power/Sleep** key. Have some fun getting acquainted with your device.

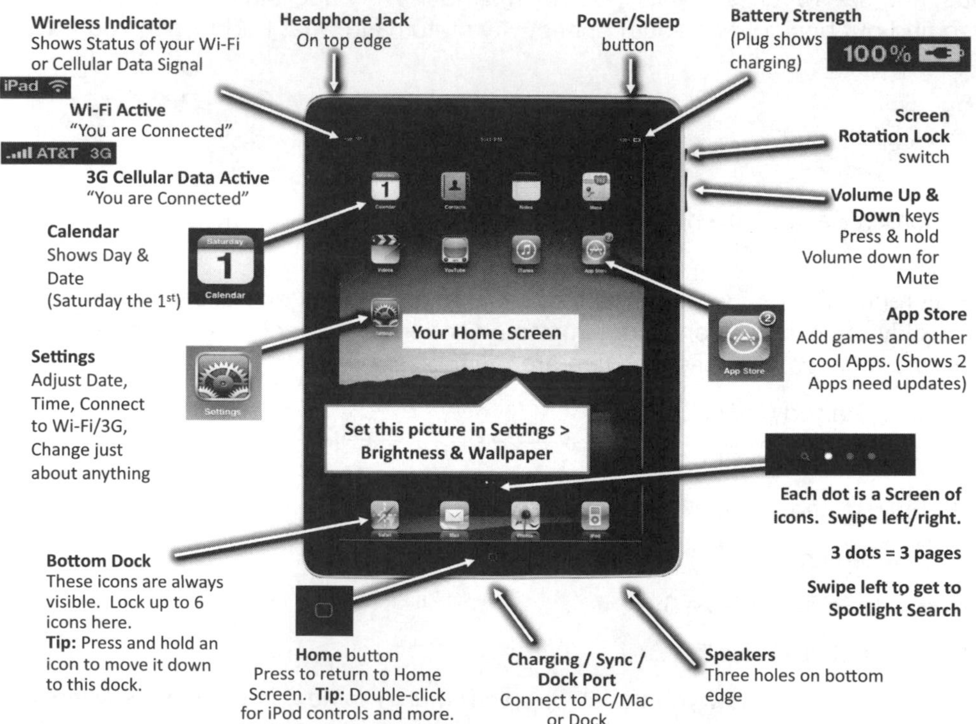


**Figure 1.** *iPad buttons, ports, switches and keys*

## Locking the Screen

As soon as you start touching the iPad, you'll notice the screen rotates amazingly fast. There are times when you don't want it to rotate—for example, when you have it in your lap or on the table. In such cases, you need to move the **Screen Rotation Lock** switch (just above the volume keys on the right side) down to lock the screen. See Figure 2.

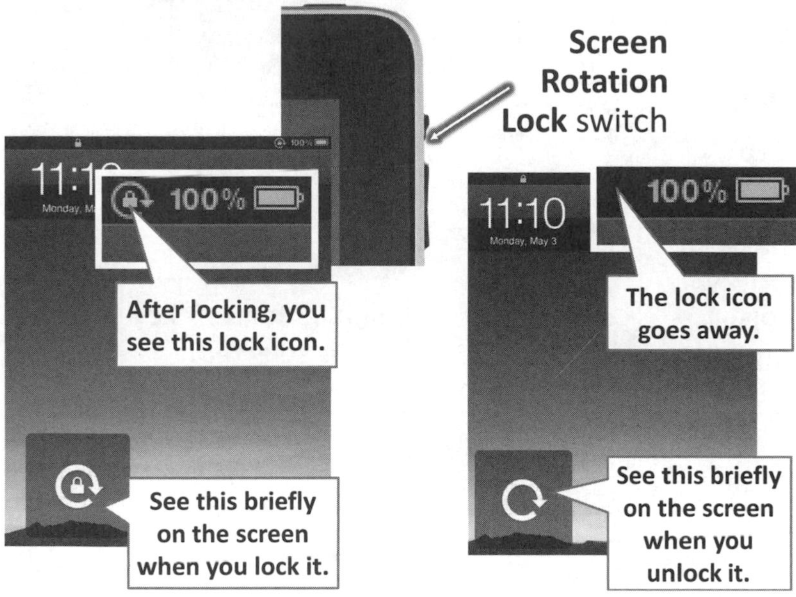
Screen Rotation Lock switch
11:10
100%
After locking, you see this lock icon.
See this briefly on the screen when you lock it.
11:10
Monday, May 3
100%
The lock icon goes away.
See this briefly on the screen when you unlock it.

**Figure 2.** *Locking or unlocking the screen*

## Starting Apps and Using Soft Keys

Some apps have soft keys at the bottom of the screen, such as the **iPod** app shown in Figure 3.

For the soft keys to work in the **iPod** app, you must have some content (music, videos, podcasts, etc.) on your iPad. See Chapter 3, "Sync with iTunes," for help syncing your music, videos, and more.

1. Tap the **iPod** icon to start the **iPod** app.
2. Touch the **Albums** soft key at the bottom to view your albums.
3. Touch the **Artists** soft key to view a list of your artists.
4. Try all the soft keys in **iPod** and other apps.

> **TIP:** You know which soft key is selected because it is highlighted—usually with a color. The other soft keys are gray but can still be touched.

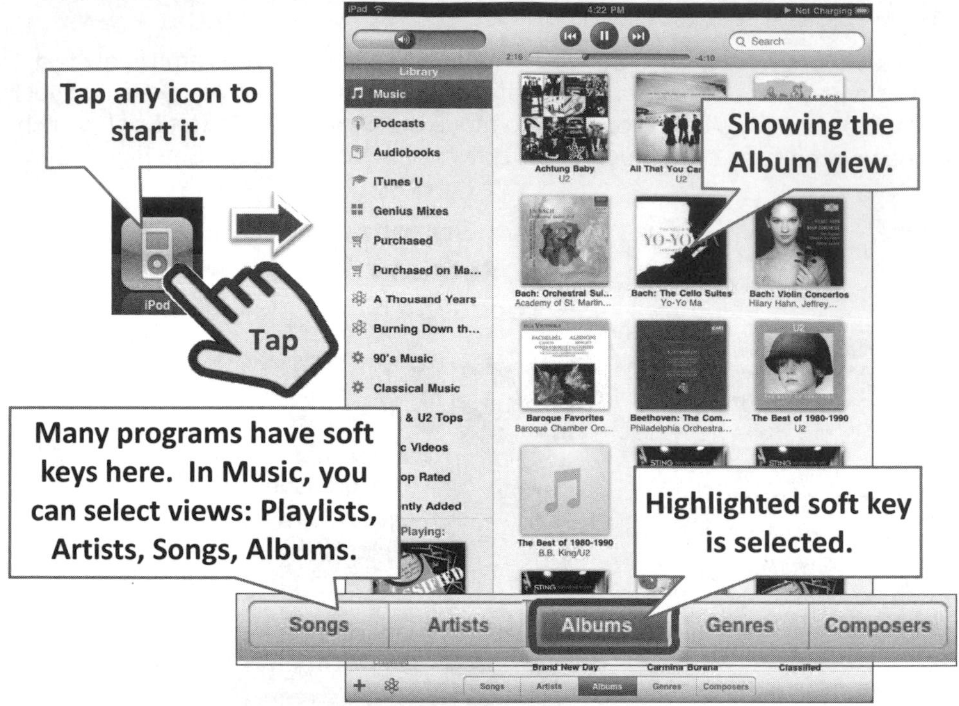


**Figure 3.** *Working with soft keys in apps*

## Menus, Submenus, and Switches

Once you are in a program, you can select any menu item by simply touching it. Just tap on the menu name, such as **Auto-Lock**, as shown in Figure 4.

Submenus are any menus below the main menu.

> **TIP:** You know there is a submenu or another screen if you see the greater than symbol next to the menu item (**>**).

How do you get back up to the previous screen or menu? Tap the button in the top of the menu. If you're in the **Auto-Lock** menu, for example, you'd touch the **General** button.

You'll see a number of switches on the iPad, such as the one next to **Battery Percentage** shown in Figure 4. To set a switch (e.g., from **ON** to **OFF**), just touch it.

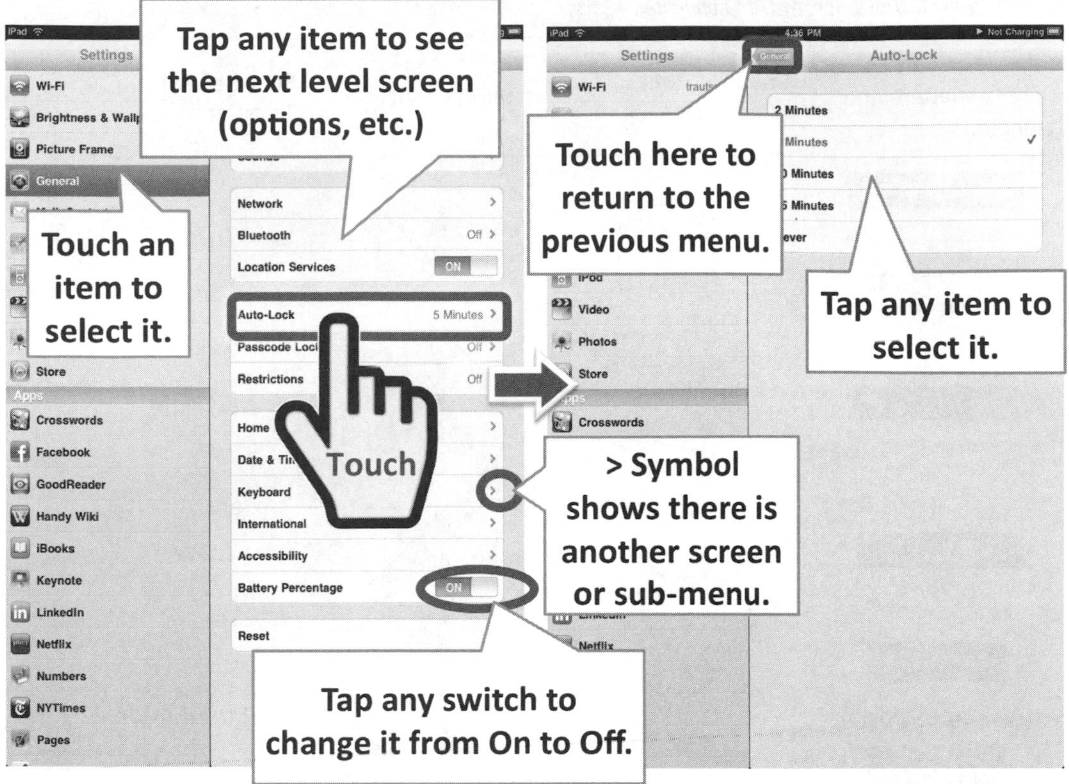


**Figure 4.** *Selecting menu items, navigating submenus, and setting switches*

## Reading the Connectivity Status Icons

Since most of the functions on your iPad work only when you are connected to the Internet (e-mail, Web, App Store, iTunes, etc.), you need to know when you're connected. Understanding how to read the status bar can save you time and frustration.

**Cellular Data Signal Strength (1-5 bars):**

Strong Weak Radio Off – Airplane Mode

**Wi-Fi Network Signal Strength (1-3 symbols):**

**Strong** **Weak** **Off**

You can tell if you are connected to a network, and the general speed of the connection, by looking at the left end of your iPad top status bar. Table 1 shows what you may see.

**Table 1.** *How to Tell When You Are Connected*

| In the upper left corner, if you see letters and symbols... | Cellular Data Connection | Wi-Fi Connection | Speed of Data Transfer |
|---|---|---|---|
| .ıll AT&T 3G or iPad | ✓ | ✓ | HIGH |
| .ıll AT&T E | ✓ | ✗ | MEDIUM |
| .ıll AT&T O | ✓ | ✗ | LOW |
| (Airplane Mode) iPad | ✗ | ✗ | No connection |

Chapter 4, "Wi-Fi and 3G Connectivity," shows you how to connect your iPad to a Wi-Fi or 3G Cellular Data Network.

## Traveling with your iPad—Airplane Mode and Wi-Fi

When you're flying on an airplane, the flight crew usually asks you to turn off all portable electronic devices for takeoff and landing. Then, when you get to altitude, they say "all approved electronic devices" can be turned back on.

You can turn off the iPad by pressing and holding the **Sleep/Wake** button on the top right edge until the slider appears, then **slide to power off** with your finger.

If you have a 3G/Cellular Data iPad, you can turn on **Airplane Mode** in the **Settings** icon as follows:

1. Tap the **Settings** icon.
2. Set the switch next to **Airplane Mode** in the top of the left column to **ON**.

> **TIP:** Some airlines do have in-flight Wi-Fi networks, so in this case you'll want to leave your Wi-Fi turned on.

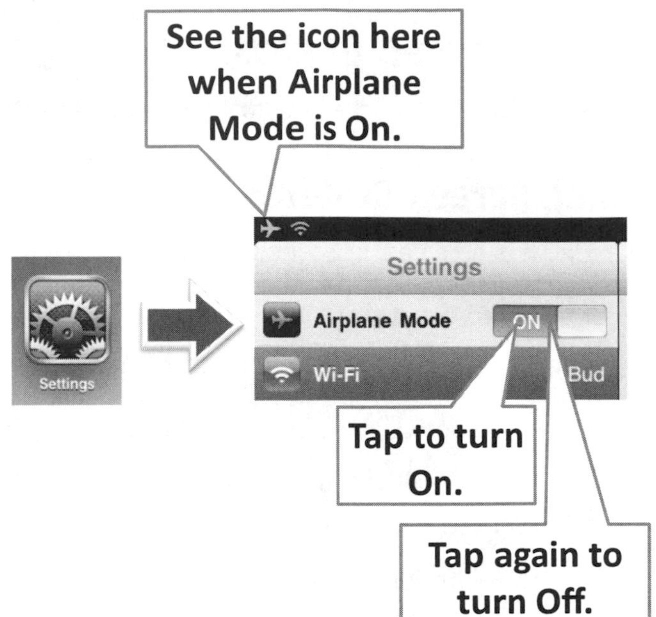


It's easy to turn off your Wi-Fi connection (see Figure 5):

3. Tap the **Settings** icon.
4. Tap **Wi-Fi** in the top of the left column.
5. Set the switch next to **Wi-Fi** in the top of the right column to **OFF**.

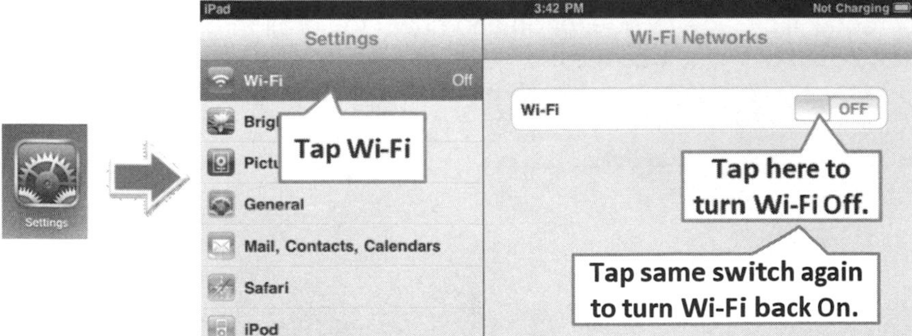


**Figure 5.** *Turning Wi-Fi off or on*

# Touch Screen Basics

In this section we describe how to interact with the iPad touch screen.

## Touch Screen Gestures

The iPad has an amazingly sensitive and intuitive touch screen. Apple, renowned for making the iPhone, iPod touch and iPods easy to use, has come up with an excellent, larger touch-screen device.

If you are used to a physical keyboard and a trackball or trackpad, or an iPod's intuitive scroll wheel, this touch screen will take a little effort to master. With a little practice, though, you'll soon become comfortable interacting with your iPad.

You can do almost anything on your iPad by using a combination of:

- Touch screen "gestures"
- Touching icons or soft keys on the screen
- Tapping the **Home** button at the bottom

The following section describe the various gestures.

# Touching and Flicking

To start an app, confirm a selection, select a menu item, or select an answer, simply touch the screen. To move quickly through contacts, lists, and the music library in list mode, flick side to side, or up and down to scroll through items. Figure 6 shows both of these gestures.

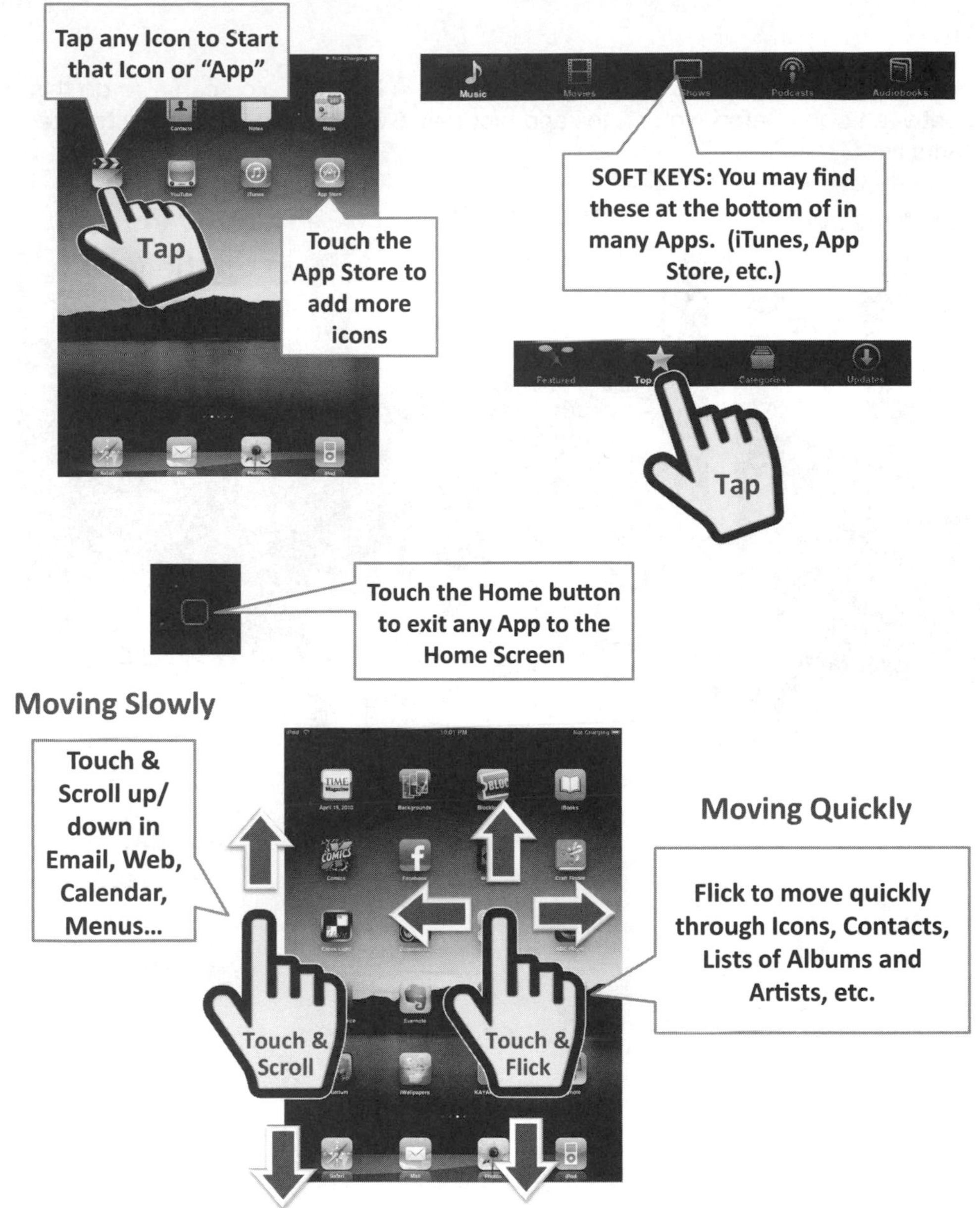
Tap any Icon to Start that Icon or "App"
Tap
Touch the App Store to add more icons
Music
Movies
Podcasts
Audiobooks
SOFT KEYS: You may find these at the bottom of in many Apps. (iTunes, App Store, etc.)
Featured
Top
Categories
Updates
Tap
Touch the Home button to exit any App to the Home Screen
Moving Slowly
Touch & Scroll up/ down in Email, Web, Calendar, Menus...
Moving Quickly
Flick to move quickly through Icons, Contacts, Lists of Albums and Artists, etc.
Touch & Scroll
Touch & Flick

**Figure 6.** *Basic touch-screen gestures*

## Swiping

To swipe, gently touch and move your finger as shown in Figure 7. You can also do this to move between open **Safari** web pages and pictures. Swiping also works in lists, like the Contacts list.

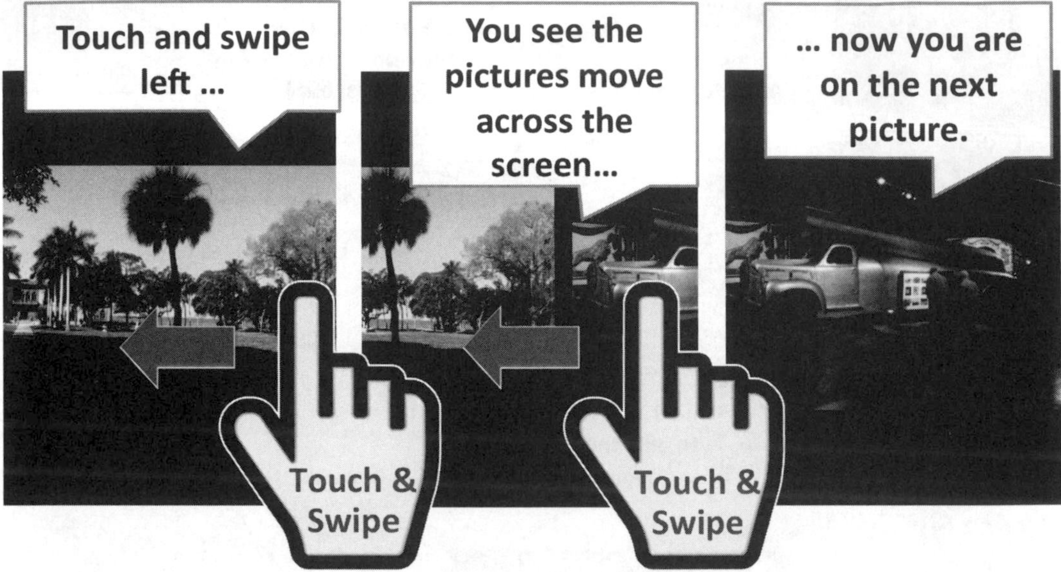


**Figure 7.** *Touch and swipe to move between pictures and web pages.*

## Scrolling

Simply tap and slide your finger to move or scroll around the screen, as shown in Figure 8. Use in messages (e-mail), web browser, menus, and more.

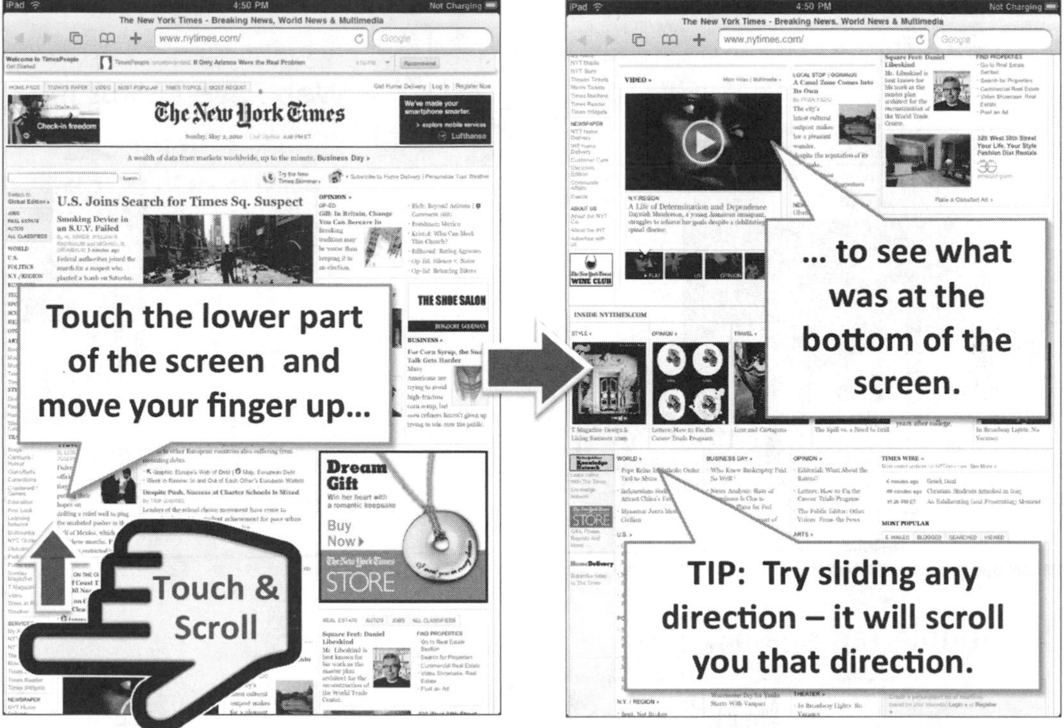


**Figure 8.** *Touch and slide your finger to scroll around a web page, a zoomed picture, and more.*

## Double-Tapping

You can double-tap the screen to zoom in and then double-tap again to zoom back out. This works in many places, such as web pages, mail messages, and pictures (Figure 9).

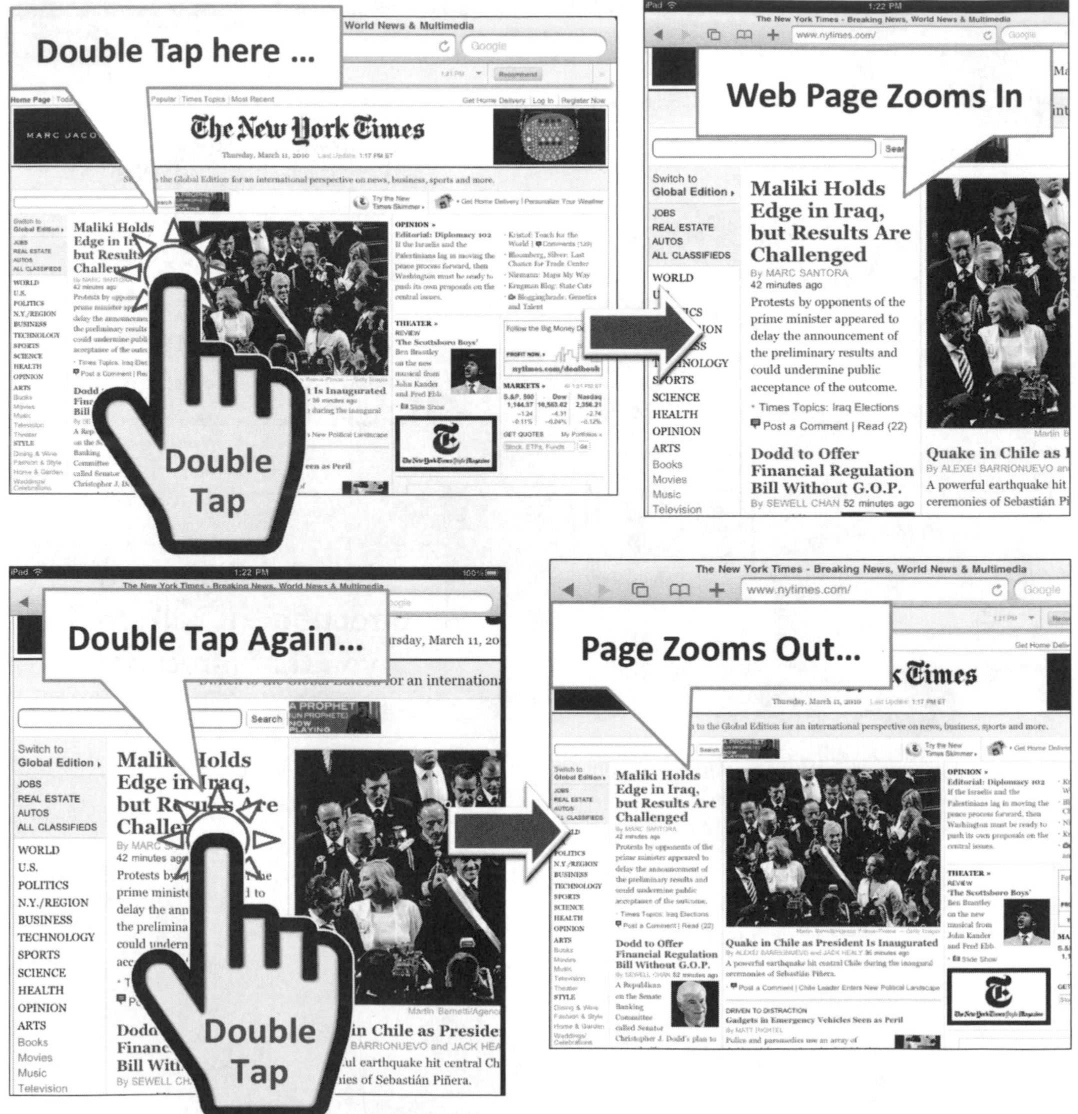


**Figure 9.** *Double-tapping to zoom in or out.*

## Pinching

You can also pinch open or closed to zoom in or out. This works in many places, such as web pages, mail messages, and pictures (Figure 10).

1. To zoom in, place two fingers touching on the screen.
2. Gradually slide your fingers open. The screen zooms in.
3. To zoom out, place to fingers with space between them on the screen.
4. Gradually slide your fingers closed so they touch. The screen zooms out.

**Figure 10.** *Pinch open to zoom in and pinch closed to zoom out.*

## Two-Finger Twist

This trick works in all the **iWork** apps (**Pages**, **Numbers**, and **Keynote**). Touch an image with two fingers at the same time, then rotate your hand on the screen to rotate the image (see Figure 11). It works temporarily in the **Photos** app, but the images rotate back to their previous orientation when you let go.

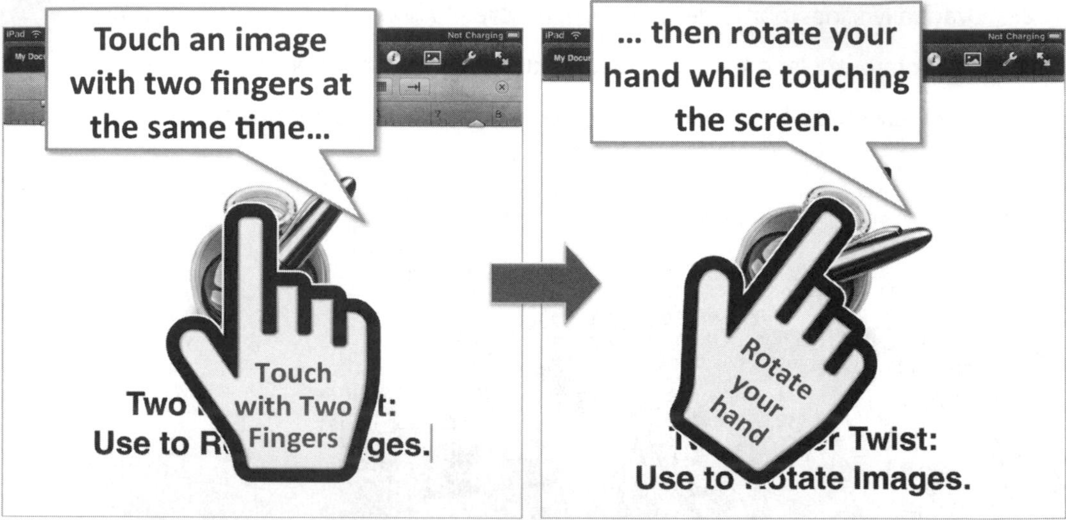


**Figure 11.** *Twist with two fingures to rotate an image.*

# App Reference Tables

This section gives you a number of tables that group the apps on your iPad, as well as other apps you can download, into handy reference tables. Each table gives you a brief description of the app and tells where to find more information in this book.

## Getting Started

Table 2 provides some quick links to help you connect your iPad to the Web (using **Wi-Fi** or **3G**), buy and enjoy songs or videos (**iTunes**, **iPod**, and **Videos**), get out of apps, sleep, power off, unlock your iPad, use the electronic **Picture Frame**, and more.

**Table 2.** *Getting Started*

| To Do This... | Use This... | | Where to Learn More |
|---|---|---|---|
| Turn the iPad on or off |  | **Power/Sleep** button. Press and hold this key on the top. | Getting Started–Ch. 1 |
| Adjust settings and connect to the Internet (via Wi-Fi or 3G) |  | **Settings > Wi-Fi Network/ Cellular Data** | Wi-Fi & 3G - Ch. 4 |
| Return to Home Screen |  | **Home Button** | Getting Started - Ch. 1 |
| Unlock the iPad |  | Slide your finger to unlock your iPad | Getting Started - Ch. 1 |
| Enable Picture Frame |  | Tap the Flower icon when locked | Personalize - Ch. 6 |
| Completely power down your iPad | Press and hold power key | Then slide  | Getting Started - Ch. 1 |
| Sync music, videos, pictures, addresses, calendar, e-mail, and notes with your computer | **iTunes (for Windows)** and **Apple Mac)**<br>**MobileMe Sync Service**<br>**Google/Exchange Sync** | | iTunes Sync - Ch. 3<br>Other Sync Methods - Ch. 24 |
| Surf the Web |  | **Safari** | Safari - Ch. 11 |

## Stay Organized

Table 3 gives you links to everything from organizing and finding your contacts to managing your calendar, from reading and responding to your e-mail to getting driving directions, and more.

**Table 3.** *Staying Organized*

| To Do This... | Use This... | | Where to Learn More |
|---|---|---|---|
| Manage your contact names and numbers | Contacts | **Contacts** | Contacts – Ch. 13 |
| Manage your calendar | Wednesday 27 Calendar | **Calendar** | Calendar – Ch. 14 |
| View and send e-mail | 7 Mail | **Mail** | E-Mail – Ch. 12 |
| Find just about anything, get directions, avoid traffic, more | 280 Maps | **Maps** | Maps – Ch. 16 |

## Be Entertained

You can have lots of fun with your iPad; Table 4 shows you how. Buy or rent movies, check out free Internet radio with **Pandora**, buy a book and enjoy it in a whole new way using **iBooks**. If you already use a **Kindle**, you can sync all your Kindle books to your iPad and enjoy them right away. Choose from over 150,000 apps from the **App Store** to make your iPad even more amazing, fun, and useful. Rent a movie from **Netflix** or **iTunes**—download it immediately for later viewing (say on an airplane or train). If you have a favorite ABC TV show, chances are you can find and watch it using the **ABC** app.

**Table 4.** *Being Entertained*

| To Do This... | Use This... | | Where to Learn More |
|---|---|---|---|
| Buy music, videos, podcasts and more. | iTunes |  **Tunes** | iTunes on iPad – Ch. 19 |
| Browse and download apps right to your iPad |  App Store | **App Store** | App Store – Ch. 20 |
| See playlists, artists,songs, albums, audiobooks, and more. |  iPod | **iPod** | Music – Ch. 7 |
| Listen to free Internet radio | PANDORA Pandora |  **Pandora** | iBooks & E-Books – Ch. 8 |
| Read a book anytime, anywhere |  iBooks | **iBooks** | iBooks & E-Books – Ch. 8 |

| | | | |
|---|---|---|---|
| Read your Kindle Books |  | **Kindle** | Photos – Ch. 15 |
| Look at, zoom in on, and organize your pictures |  | **Photos** | Videos & TV – Ch. 9 |
| Watch movies and music videos |  | **Videos** | Videos & TV – Ch. 9 |
| Rent a movie |  | **Netflix** | Videos & TV – Ch. 9 |
| Watch a TV show (Most are free and look amazing on the iPad screen.) |  | **ABC Player** | Videos & TV – Ch. 9 |
| Play a game |  | **Games Icons** | Games – Ch.21 |
| Work on a crossword puzzle by tapping your finger |  | **Times Crosswords** | App Store – Ch. 20 |
| Interact with a comic in a whole new way |  | **Marvel Comics** | New Media – Ch. 23 |

## Stay Informed

Read your favorite magazine or newspaper with up-to-the-minute vibrant pictures and videos (Table 5). Check out the latest weather like never before. Do more than browse the Web—interact with it using Safari on your iPad.

**Table 5.** *Staying Informed*

| To Do This... | Use This... | Where to Learn More |
|---|---|---|
| Read a magazine | TIME Magazine April 19, 2010 **Time Magazine** | New Media – Ch. 23 |
| Read the newspaper | NYTimes **New York Times** | New Media – Ch. 23 |
| Check the weather | The Weather Channel TWC MAX+ **The Weather Channel** | App Store – Ch. 20 |
| Browse the Web | Safari **Safari** | Safari – Ch. 11 |

## Network Socially

Connect and stay up to date with friends, colleagues, and professional networks using the social networking tools on your iPad (Table 6).

**Table 6.** *Networking Socially*

| To Do This... | Use This... | Where to Learn More |
|---|---|---|
| Skype | **Skype** | Social Networking – Ch. 22 |
| Network on LinkedIn | **LinkedIn** | Social Networking – Ch. 22 |
| Stay connected with friends on Facebook | **Facebook** | Social Networking – Ch. 22 |
| Follow your favorites on Twitter | **TweetDeck** | Social Networking – Ch. 22 |

## Be Productive

Work with documents, spreadsheets, and presentation files using **Pages**, **Numbers,** and **Keynote**—and the touch screen interface on the iPad. Grab images to size them, rotate them, or move them around documents and presentations by just dragging, expanding them, or rotating them with your fingers. Access and read just about any PDF file or other document with the **GoodReader** app. Take notes with the basic **Notes** app, or step up to the advanced **Evernote** app, which has amazing capabilities to integrate audio, pictures, and text notes, and sync everything to a web site. See Table7.

**Table 7.** *Being Productive*

| To Do This... | Use This... | | Where to Learn More |
|---|---|---|---|
| Write a letter, paper, or book | Pages | **Pages** | iWork – Ch. 18 |
| Calculate using a spreadsheet | Numbers | **Numbers** | iWork – Ch. 18 |
| Develop and deliver a presentation | Keynote | **Keynote** | iWork – Ch. 18 |
| Access and read almost any document | GoodReader | **GoodReader** | New Media – Ch. 23 |
| Take notes, store your grocery list, and more | Notes | **Notes** | Notes – Ch. 17 |
| Take and organize your notes in a whole new way | Evernote | **Evernote** | Notes – Ch. 17 |

# Other Fun Stuff

The iPad can be used as a fantastic electronic **Picture Frame**—we show you the basics here. And you'll love your iPad as a video player! In this section we give you a few quick tips for getting around your video and music player, as well as getting the most out of videos you see embedded in web pages.

## iPad as Electronic Picture Frame

You may wonder what that little icon of the flower is next to **Slide to Unlock** when you lock your iPad. This starts your electronic **Picture Frame**—a great way to share your pictures with others or simply enjoy your own pictures. To enjoy the Picture Frame you need to:

1. Load up your iPad with your pictures using **iTunes** as we show in "Photos—Automatically Sync" section in Chapter 3, "Sync with iTunes."

2. Tap the Picture Frame icon to turn on the electronic picture frame.

3. Tap the icon again to turn it off.

The **Picture Frame** will cycle through all your pictures, or you can customize it to show only selected photo albums.

Tap this icon to turn your iPad into an Electornic Picture Frame..
slide to unlock

**TIP:** You can customize the way your picture frame operates, select specific albums and more. See the "Personalize Your Picture Frame" section in Chapter 6, "Personalize & Secure Your iPad."

## Navigating Around Your Music and Video Player

When playing a song or video, just tap anywhere in the middle of the screen to show or hide the controls at the top of the screen, as shown in Figure 12.

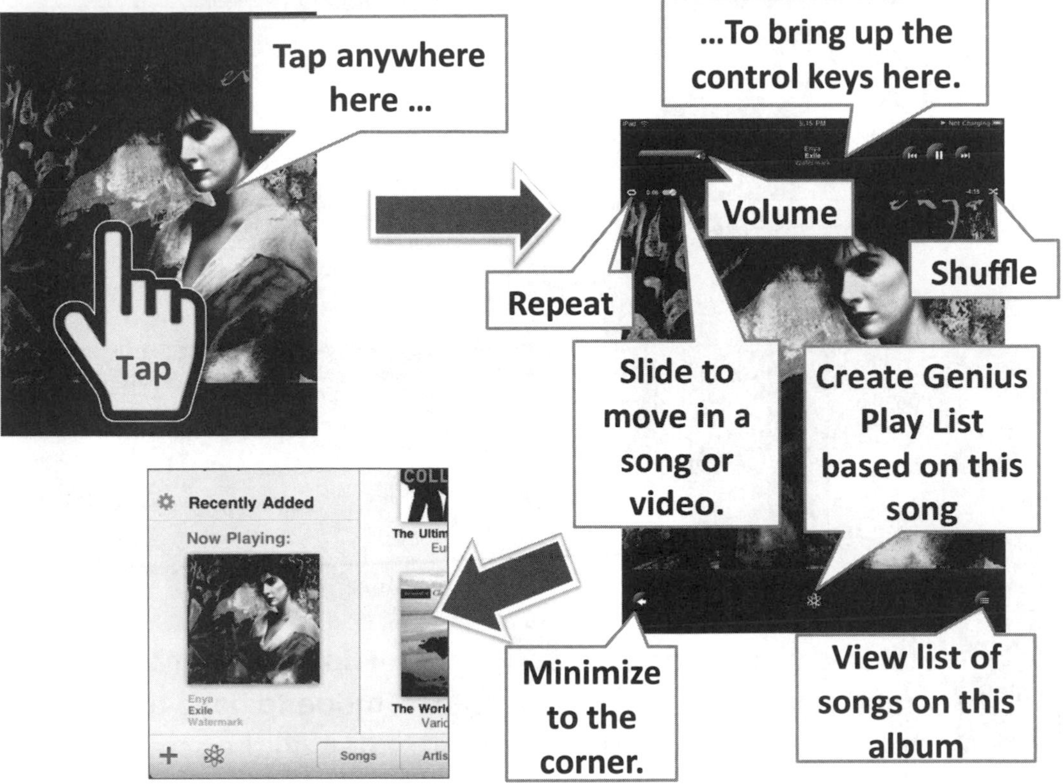


**Figure 12.** *Navigate around your music and video player.*

## Watching Videos in Web Pages

A really fun thing to do is watch supported video formats right in their web pages. Unfortunately, the iPad does not support the Adobe Flash video format, which is used by many web sites. But there are many you can watch, such as the video on the front page of the *New York Times* web page, as shown in Figure 13.

1. Tap the **Safari** icon.
2. Tap the address bar at the top and type in: `www.nytimes.com`.
3. Locate and tap any video; usually you'll see a play icon like this  in the middle of the picture.
4. The video will start playing right in the web page.

5. To expand the video to full screen, pinch open right inside the video. Put two fingers in the video and expand them while sliding them on the screen.
6. To watch the video in widescreen, tilt your iPad to horizontal mode.

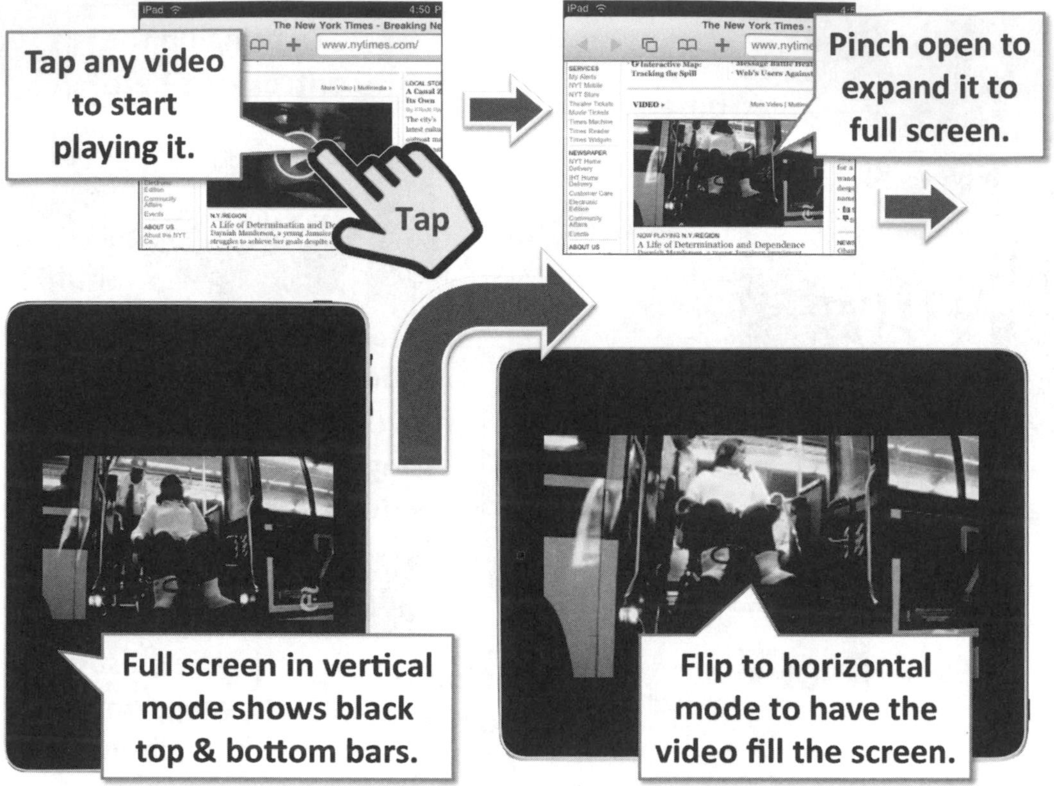

Tap any video to start playing it.
Tap
Pinch open to expand it to full screen.
Full screen in vertical mode shows black top & bottom bars.
Flip to horizontal mode to have the video fill the screen.

**Figure 13.** *How to enjoy videos in web pages*

# iPad Accessories

Now let's take a brief tour of some of the accessories you might purchase to enhance the functionality of your iPad. You can buy most of these from any Apple store, Apple.com, or other accessory stores.

> **NOTE:** We show you more accessories, such as cases, in Chapter 1, "Getting Started."

## Apple Keyboards

You should invest in one of these two keyboards if you plan on doing a lot of typing on your iPad (Figure 14). Each one costs about $70.00. We show you more about how to use these keyboards in Chapter 2, "Typing, Copy/Paste & Search."

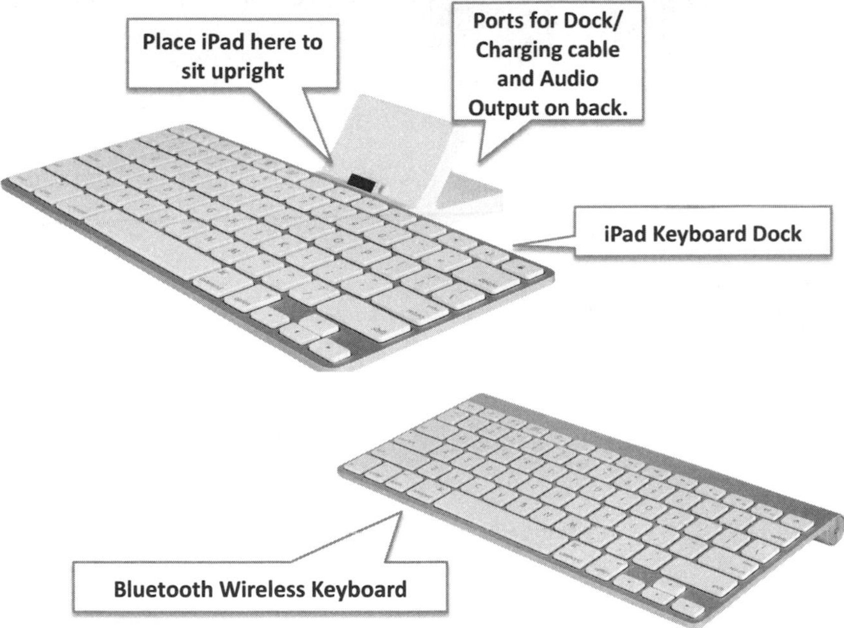


**Figure 14.** *Apple iPad Keyboard Dock and Apple Wireless Bluetooth Keyboard.*

## Apple iPad Dock

If you want to set your iPad up in a vertical orientation to use it as an electronic picture frame or have it held for you while you use it, check out the $29.00 **iPad Dock**. The **iPad Dock** also has a dock connector port in the back so you can connect it to your computer or charger while the iPad is in sitting in the dock. See Figure 15.

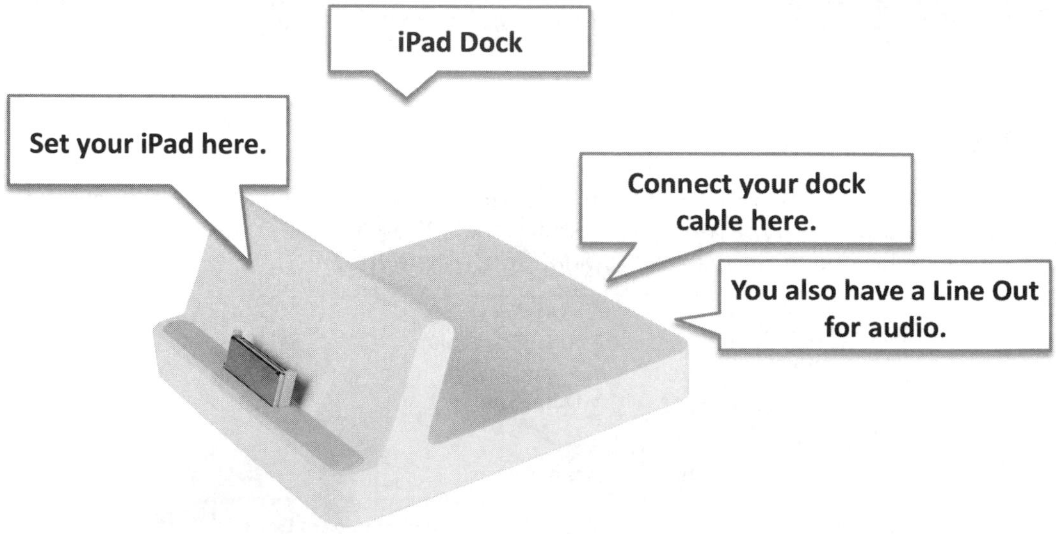

iPad Dock
Set your iPad here.
Connect your dock cable here.
You also have a Line Out for audio.

**Figure 15.** *Apple iPad Dock.*

## Apple Camera Connection Kit

If you want to transfer your pictures from your digital camera to your iPad directly, without first transferring them to your computer, you can do it with the **Camera Connection Kit** accessory. This $ 29.00 accessory gives you two small accessories—the one shown on the left of Figure 16 is the USB adapter; the other is the SD Card adapter. Both plug into the dock connector port on the bottom of your iPad.

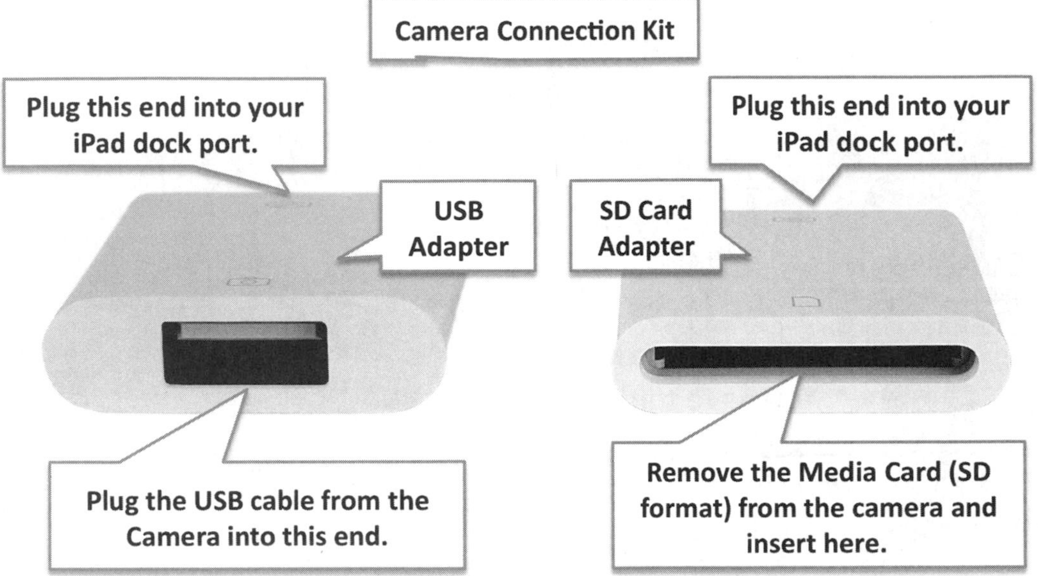

Camera Connection Kit
Plug this end into your iPad dock port.
Plug this end into your iPad dock port.
USB Adapter
SD Card Adapter
Plug the USB cable from the Camera into this end.
Remove the Media Card (SD format) from the camera and insert here.

**Figure 16.** *Apple Camera Connection Kit*

To import photos using these adapters, follow these steps:

1. Plug either the USB or the SD Card accessory into the dock port at the bottom of your iPad.
    a. If you are using the USB connector, plug the USB cable from your camera into the connector.
    b. If you are using the SD card connector, remove the SD memory card from your camera and insert it into the connector.
2. Your iPad should be turned on. If it is, it will immediately bring you to the **Import Photos** screen. See Figure 17.
3. To import all photos, tap the **Import All** button in the upper right corner.
4. To import selected photos, tap pictures to select them. Then, tap the **Import** button and choose **Import Selected**.
5. You then have the option to **Keep** or **Delete** the photos on the camera or SD card.

6. The most recent imported photos will show up in the **Last Import** photo album. All imported photos will show up in the **All Imported** photo album.

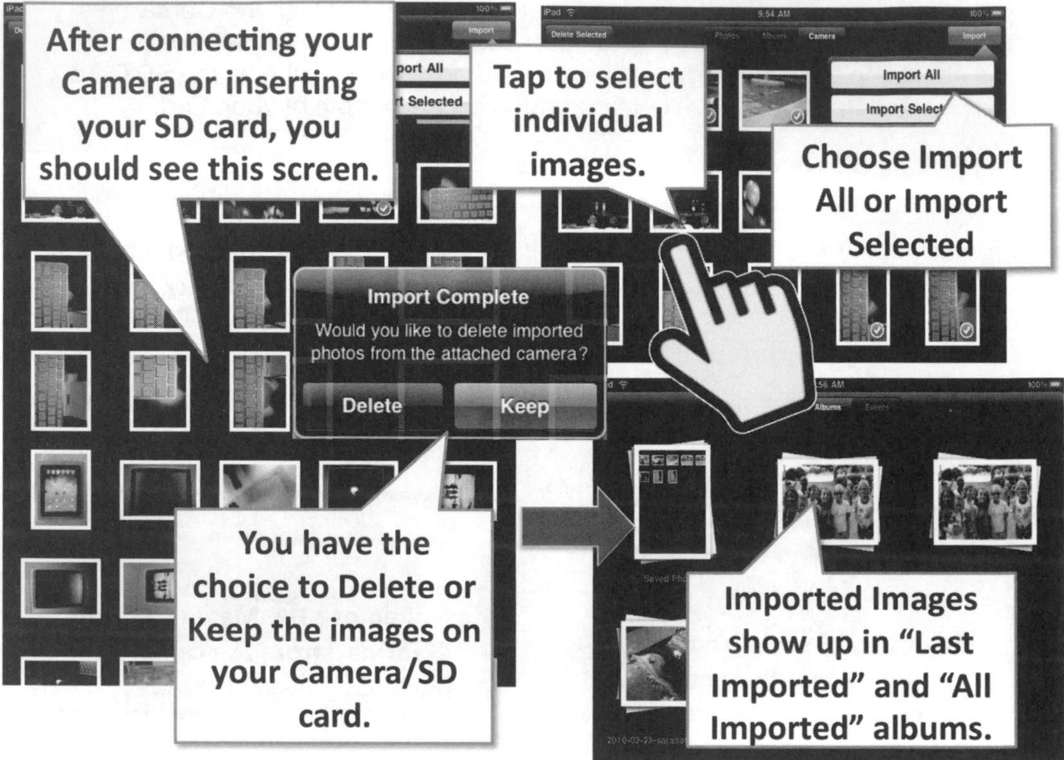


**Figure 17.** *Import photos using the Camera Connection Kit.*

## VGA Adapter Cable

If you are using the **Keynote** app and want to play a presentation on a larger external VGA monitor from your iPad, or want to play movies you rented or purchased from **iTunes**, this accessory is for you.

> **CAUTION:** As of publishing time, this accessory worked only in very limited apps and situations. It worked only for the **Keynote** app in **Play** mode, and for certain movies purchased or rented from **iTunes**. It did not display the iPad screen as soon as you plugged it in.

This VGA Adapter Cable costs $ 29.00. You plug one end into your dock connector on the bottom of your iPad, and the other end connects to the VGA cable going to the external monitor, as shown in Figure 18. When you **Play** your presentation in **Keynote**, you can advance slides or jump between slides using your iPad.

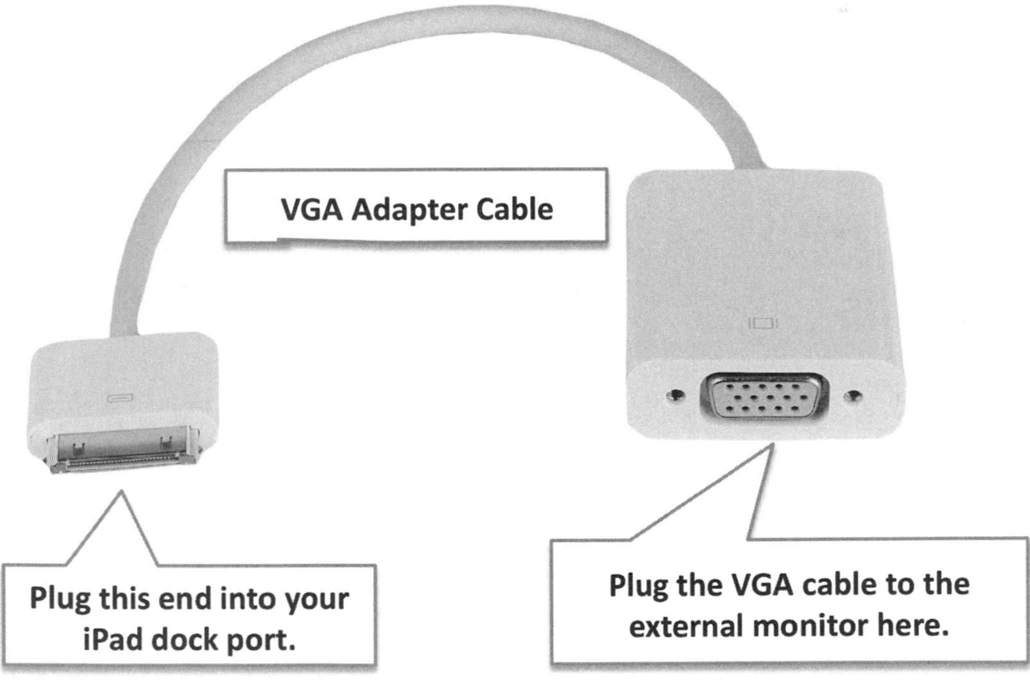
VGA Adapter Cable
Plug this end into your iPad dock port.
Plug the VGA cable to the external monitor here.

**Figure 18.** *VGA Adapter Cable for iPad*

Part I

# Introduction

Welcome to your new iPad—and to the book that tells you what you need to know to get the most out of it. In this part we show you how the book is organized and where to go to find what you need. We even show you how to get some great tips and tricks sent right to your iPad via short e-mail messages.

# Introduction

## Congratulations on Your iPad!

In your hands is perhaps the most powerful and elegant media player, E-Book reader, gaming machine, life organizer, and just about everything else available today—the iPad.

The iPad can do close to 90% of what you already do on your computer.... only better. The iPad can do virtually everything you can do on your smartphone. You can even make phone calls from your iPad with the **Skype** app. Yet, the iPad is neither computer nor smartphone—it is nestled somewhere in between, where most of us live.

> **NOTE:** Take a look at Chapter 22 where we show you how to use the Skype phone app on your iPad!

With your iPad you can view your photos and interact with them using the same touch-screen gestures as an iPhone or iPod touch. You can pinch and zoom, rotate and e-mail your photos all with simple gestures.

With your iPad you can interact with your content like never before. Newspapers look and read like newspapers and a web site all in one. Flip through stories, videos, and pictures, and interact with your news.

With your iPad you can, for the first time, really feel like you are reading a book when you read on an electronic device. Pages turn slowly or quickly (you can even see the words on the back of the pages when you turn them).

With your iPad you can manage your media library like never before. iTunes is a beautiful interface on the iPad. Choosing music, watching videos, organizing playlists, and more is effortless and fun on the large, high definition–quality screen.

Do you have a Netflix account? You can manage your content, organize your queue, and stream high-quality movies and TV shows right on the iPad.

No more updating your Facebook status on the tiny screen of your smartphone—with the iPad you can see the full web site and have access to all the features of your desktop version, yet also be able to "interact" with Facebook like never before, using the touch screen.

Stay connected to the web and your e-mail with the built-in Wi-Fi connection or the optional 3G connection of the iPad. All the latest high-speed protocols are supported, so you can always be in touch and get the latest content. There is even an almost "full-size" keyboard to type out e-mails when you turn the iPad into landscape mode.

## Getting the Most Out of *iPad Made Simple*

This book can be read cover-to-cover, but you can also peruse it in a modular fashion, by chapter or by topic within a chapter. Maybe you just want to check out the App store, try iBooks, get setup with your e-mail or contacts, or you might just want to load up your music. You can do all this and more with our book.

You will soon realize that your iPad is a very powerful device. There are, however, many secrets "locked" inside that we help you "unlock" throughout this book.

Take your time—this book can help you on your way to learning how to best use, work and have fun with your new iPad. Think back to when you tried to use your first Windows or Mac computer. It took a little while to get familiar with how to do things. It's the same with the iPad. Use this book to help you get up to speed and learn all the best tips and tricks more quickly.

Remember that devices this powerful are not always easy to grasp—at first.

You'll get the most out of your iPad if you read the book a section at a time and then try out what you read. We all know that reading and then doing an activity gives us a much higher retention rate than simply reading alone.

So, in order to learn and remember what you learn, we recommend to:

***Read a little, try a little on your iPad, and repeat!***

# How This Book Is Organized

Knowing how this book is organized will help you more quickly locate things that are important to you. Here we show you the main organization of this book. Remember to take advantage of our abridged table of contents, detailed table of contents, and our comprehensive index to help you quickly pinpoint items of interest.

## Day in the Life of an iPad User

Located inside the front and back cover, this is an excellent piece of information full of easy-to-access cross-reference chapter numbers. So if you see something you want to learn, simply thumb to that page and learn it—all in just a few minutes.

## Part 1: Quick Start Guide

**Touch Screen Basics:** Use many visual images to help you quickly learn how to touch, swipe, flick, zoom and more with your iPad touch screen.

**App Reference Tables**: Quickly peruse the icons or apps grouped by category. Get a thumbnail of what all the apps do on your iPad and Chapters to jump right to the details of how to get the most out of each app in this book.

**Other Fun Stuff:** Learn quickly about the iPad as music and video player and electronic picture frame.

**iPad Accessories:** Get a brief overview of some of the more common accessories, such as keyboards, camera and VGA adapter connectors.

## Part 2: Introduction

You are here now . . .

## Part 3: You and Your iPad . . .

This is the meat of the book, organized in 25 easy-to-understand chapters packed with loads of pictures to guide you every step of the way.

## Part 4: iPad's Soulmate: iTunes

As a special bonus for our readers, we have provided an extensive iTunes Bonus Guide in Chapter 26 which shows you how to really get around iTunes and explore all the possibilities of the desktop application. The more comfortable you can get with iTunes, the more you can arrange and use content from your computer on your iPad – making for a more enjoyable user experience.

# Quickly Locating Tips, Cautions, and Notes

If you flip through this book, you can instantly see these items based on their formatting. For example, if you wanted to find all the Calendar tips, you would flip to the Calendar chapter and quickly find them.

> **TIPS, CAUTIONS,** and **NOTES** are all formatted like this, with a gray background, to help you see them more quickly.

# Free iPad E-mail Tips

Check out the authors web site at `www.madesimplelearning.com` for a series of very useful "bite-size" chunks of iPad tips and tricks. We have taken a selection of great tips out of this book and even added a few new ones. Click on the "Free Tips" section and register for your tips in order to receive a tip right in your iPad inbox about once a week. Learning in small chunks is a great way to master your iPad!

Part III

# You and Your iPad . . .

This is the heart of *iPad Made Simple*. In this section, you'll find clearly labeled chapters—each explaining the key features of your iPad. You'll see that most chapters focus on an individual app or a specific type of application. Many of the chapters discuss applications that come with your iPad, but we also include some fun and useful apps you can download from the App Store. Sure, the iPad is for fun, but it's for a whole lot more as well, so you'll learn how to be productive with iWorks in this section, too. We finish with some handy troubleshooting tips that can help if your iPad isn't working quite right.

Chapter 1

# Getting Started

In this chapter, we will take you on a step-by-step tour of your iPad, from charging it to activating iTunes for the first time. In our iPad Basics section at the end of this chapter, we will show you the basics of how to maneuver around on your iPad so you can get up and running quickly.

## Setting Up your iPad

In this section, we give you some iPad battery and charging tips, then talk about how to tell if your iPad was already activated and the **Slide to Unlock** feature.

### Charging Your iPad and Battery Tips

Your device may already have some battery life, but you might want to charge it completely so you can enjoy uninterrupted hours of use after you get it set up. This charging time will give you a chance to check out the rest of this chapter, install or update iTunes, or check out all the cool iPad apps in the iTunes App Store (Chapter 20).

The charger cable is the same as the USB connection cable you use to connect your iPad to your computer. It is located under the little white booklet beneath your iPad in the box that says "Designed by Apple in California." Plug the wide end of the cable into the bottom of your iPad (next to the **Home** button) and the USB cable end into the small white box that has the fold out plug for the electrical socket.

To make sure your device is plugged in correctly and getting charged, look for the small plug icon inside the battery indicator in the upper right corner of the iPad screen. If the screen is blank, tap the **Home** button once to light up the screen.

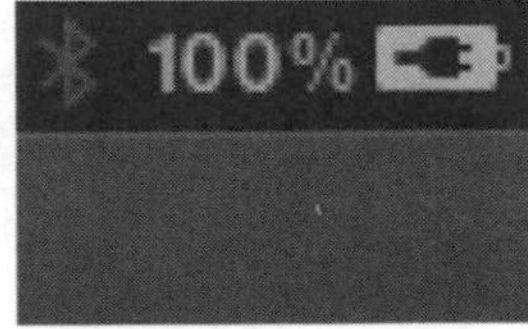

## Battery & Charging FAQ

**Will my iPad charge when connected to my computer?**

The answer is: "It depends."

Yes, if you see the plug icon inside the battery when you connect your iPad to your computer with the USB cable. Most Mac computers, some Windows computers, and some powered USB hubs (an accessory that you can purchase that is plugged into the wall and has USB ports), provide enough power to charge your iPad while it is "awake" (screen on).

Maybe, but only when the iPad is in "sleep" mode (screen off) when you see a "Not Charging" message next to the Battery icon on your iPad after you connect it to your computer. In this case, your iPad will probably be charging when it is in sleep mode. You will have to experiment with your computer and iPad. We discovered that with a Windows laptop, the iPad definitely charged fine in sleep mode, even though it said "Not Charging" when it was awake.

**How long will my iPad last on a full charge?** Apple says about 10 hours when you are watching movies, reading books, or listening to music. This should be plenty of time for a long flight or car ride. You will probably get another hour or so when your iPad is new and may get less time as your iPad gets older. According to Apple, the iPad has up to a month of stand-by power (when the device is in sleep mode).

**TIP**: Most airports have wall sockets available today where you can top-off your iPad while you are waiting for your flight. Some airports have labeled "Charging Stations," and others simply have wall sockets that may even be hidden behind chairs or other objects. You may have to do a bit of hunting to beat out all those other power-hungry travelers!

**TIP**: If you are taking a long car trip, you can buy a power inverter to convert your 12V car power outlets into a power outlet to which you can plug in your iPad charger. Do a web search for "power inverter for cars" to find many options for under US $50. A small price to pay for hours of enjoyment on your iPad!

## Your iPad Activation May Have Been Done at the Retail Store

You may not need to charge your iPad at first. When you turn on your iPad or tap the **Home** button (at the bottom of the device), if you see a **Slide to Unlock** screen or a screen of icons on your Home Screen (Figure 1–1) instead of the black screen showing the USB cable needing to be plugged into iTunes (Figure 1–2), then your iPad has already been activated. If so, then you can "slide to unlock."

## Slide to Unlock

When you first power on your iPad, you will see the **Slide to Unlock** screen. Just follow the path of the arrow and gently slide the **unlock** button to the right.

Once you do that, you will see your **Home** Screen.

You will see four icons locked in the **Bottom Dock** (Figure 1–1, bottom-right) while the rest of the icons can move back and forth in "pages" above this **Bottom Dock**. Learn how to move your favorite icons into the **Bottom Dock** in the "Moving Icons" section in Chapter 5.

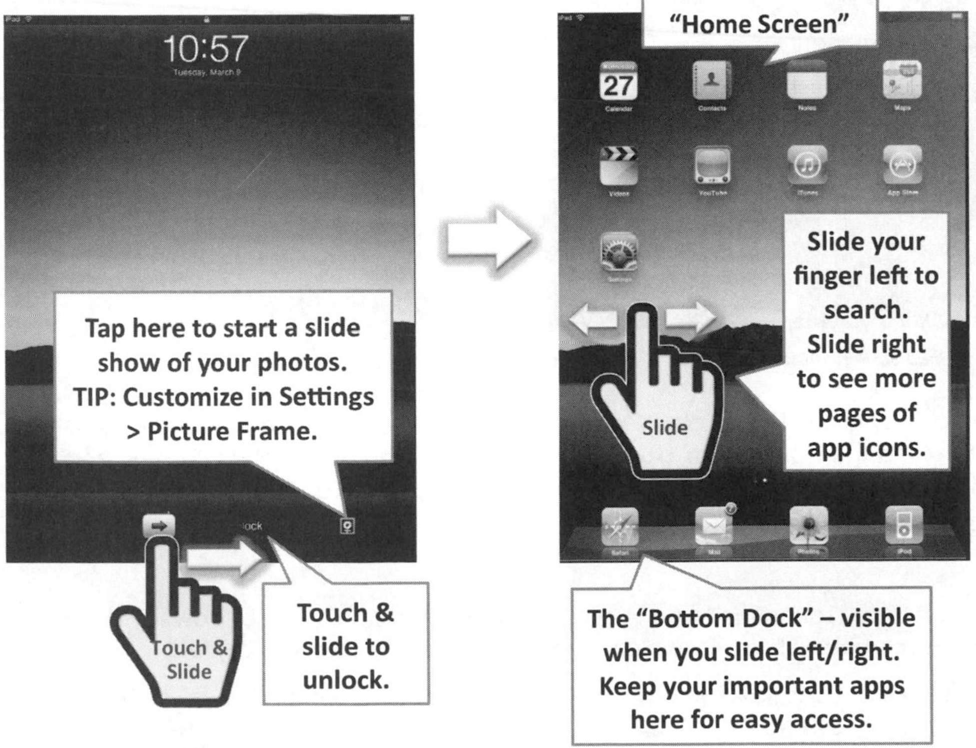


**Figure 1–1.** *Slide to Unlock, moving around your Home Screen and the Bottom Dock*

# iTunes and Your iPad

To activate your iPad and load up your music and videos, you will need to connect it to iTunes on your computer. iTunes is also required to backup your iPad and later restore it.

If you don't have iTunes, or are not sure if you have the latest version, then you will have to upgrade. Connecting your iPad to iTunes the first time will activate or tie your iPad to your Apple ID. Once you do that, you can buy songs, movies, books and just about anything else right from your iPad or in iTunes on your computer.

## Install or Upgrade iTunes on Your Computer

As you have seen from your iPad screen, you need to connect your iPad to iTunes (version 9.1 or higher) loaded on your computer Figure 1–2). This means you may need to upgrade to or install the latest version.

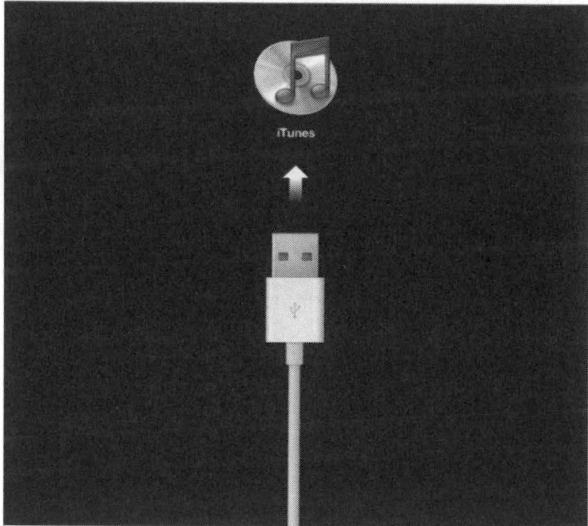


**Figure 1–2.** *iPad screen showing the need to connect to iTunes software to get started.*

If you need to upgrade iTunes to 9.1 or higher, start iTunes. If you are a Windows user, select **Help** and then **Check for Updates**; If you are a Mac user, select **iTunes**, and then **Check for Updates**. Follow the instructions to update iTunes.

Need detailed instructions? See our "iTunes Upgrade" section in Chapter 26: "iTunes Guide".

If you do not have iTunes loaded on your computer, then open a web browser and go to `www.itunes.com/download`. Download the software from the link provided.

Need detailed instructions? See our "How to Download and Install iTunes" section in Chapter 26: "iTunes Guide".

## Connecting Your iPad to iTunes the First Time

Once you have installed or upgraded to iTunes version 9.1 or higher, you are ready to connect your iPad to iTunes on your computer.

> **TIP**: Using the iTunes Home Sharing feature, you can share your purchased content from the same iTunes account (music, apps, videos, iBooks, and more) across authorized computers on your home network. Also, you can sync any of the same content to any iPod/iPhone/iPad under the same iTunes account. Learn more about syncing content using iTunes in Chapter 3: "Sync with iTunes" and learn about Home Sharing in Chapter 26: "iTunes Guide".

By connecting your iPad to iTunes, you will register or associate your iPad (via the device serial number) to a particular iTunes Account (Apple ID).

> **TIP:** The bonus of this approach is that if you have purchased apps for an iPhone or iPod touch and other content (music, videos, and more), then you can run all those apps on your iPad! Note that you can authorize an iPad on more than one iTunes account; however, all content you sync to that iPad has to originate from a single computer. So you need to select your "main" computer to sync with your iPad.

If you do not yet have an iTunes Account (Apple ID), we will show you how to create one later in this chapter.

## Start up iTunes

If iTunes is not already running, double-click the **iTunes** icon on your desktop.

Mac users may have to click the **Finder** icon, select the **Go** menu, and then **Applications** to look for iTunes. (The Mac shortcut is Shift+Command+A)

Windows users, click on the **Start** menu or Windows logo in the lower left corner, select **All Programs**, then **iTunes**.

After you start iTunes, it should open and have the left and main window nav bars look similar to the image shown on Figure 1–3. The main window content may look quite different.

**Figure 1–3.** *iTunes software main window (selections shown: iTunes Store and App Store)*

> **NOTE:** What is shown in the main window on your iTunes will look quite different depending on what you select in the left nav bar and the top nav bar. In Figure 1–3, the iTunes Store is selected in the left nav bar and the App Store is selected in the main nav bar so we see App Store related content in the main window.

## Registering or Activating your iPad the First Time

Once you have iTunes installed or updated and running on your computer, you are ready to connect your iPad for the first time and get it registered or activated so you can start using it.

> **NOTE:** You can skip this registration section and jump to the "Set Up Your iPad" section later in this chapter if your iPad has already been registered. You know if your iPad is already registered if you see either **Slide to Unlock** at the bottom of the screen or a screen of icons when you tap the **Home** button on the bottom of your device.

1. Plug in the white USB connection cable that was supplied with your iPad to an available USB port on your computer.

> **NOTE:** You need to use the USB cable instead of Bluetooth or Wi-Fi to connect your iPad to iTunes on your computer.

When you connect your iPad to your computer the first time, your Windows computer should automatically install the necessary drivers. If you are on a Mac computer, Apple recommends that you upgrade to the latest version of the operating system before using your iPad.

Then, iTunes will launch, if you have not already started it.

2. In order to see the **Setup** screen, you may need to click **iPad** under **DEVICES** in the left nav bar. Then you should see the new iPad setup screen, as shown in Figure 1–4.

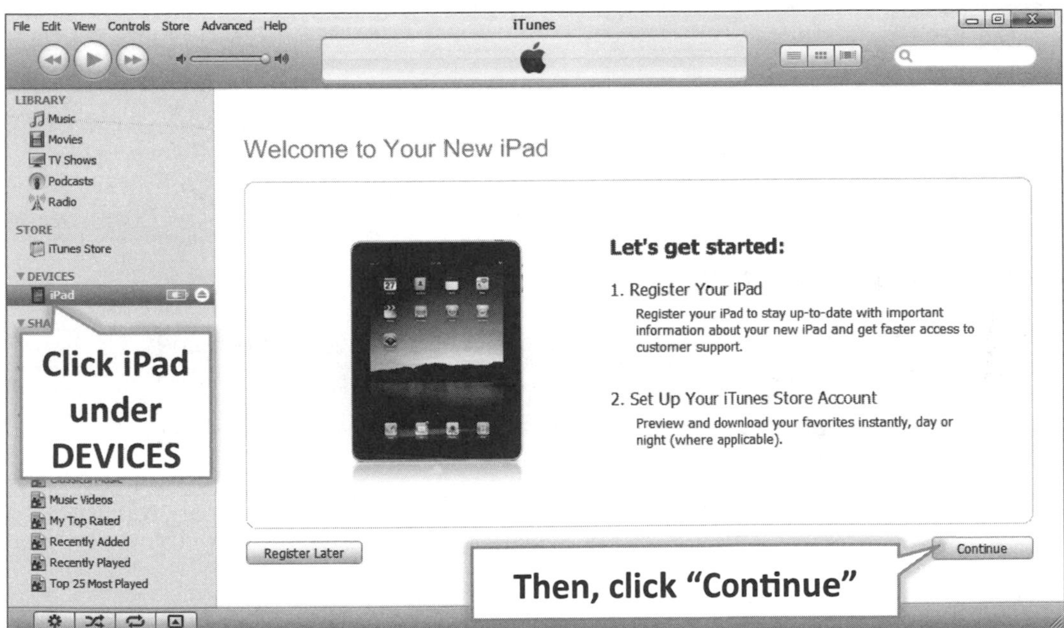


**Figure 1–4.** *iPad first time Setup window in iTunes after clicking on "iPad" in left nav bar*

3. Click the **Continue** button to see the Apple iPad License Agreement, as shown in Figure 1–5.

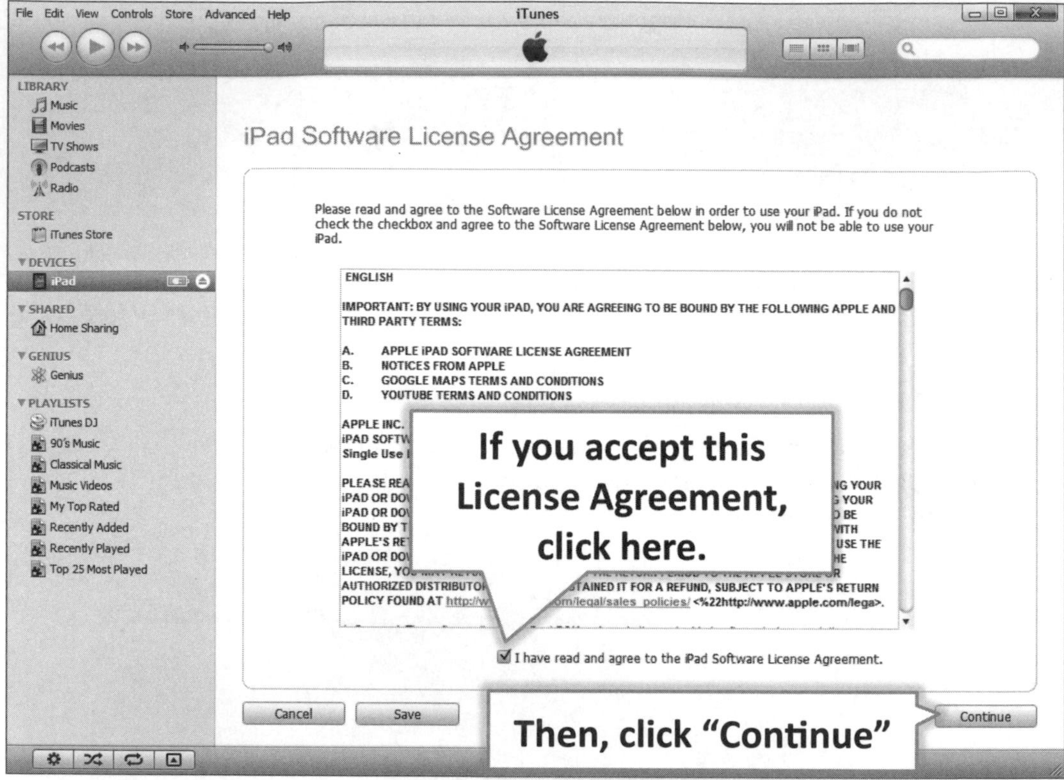


**Figure 1–5.** *iPad first time Setup License Agreement screen*

4. In order to continue, check the box under the License Agreement and click the **Continue** button.

5. You will then be given the opportunity to sign-in using your Apple ID or create a new Apple ID (Figure 1–6).

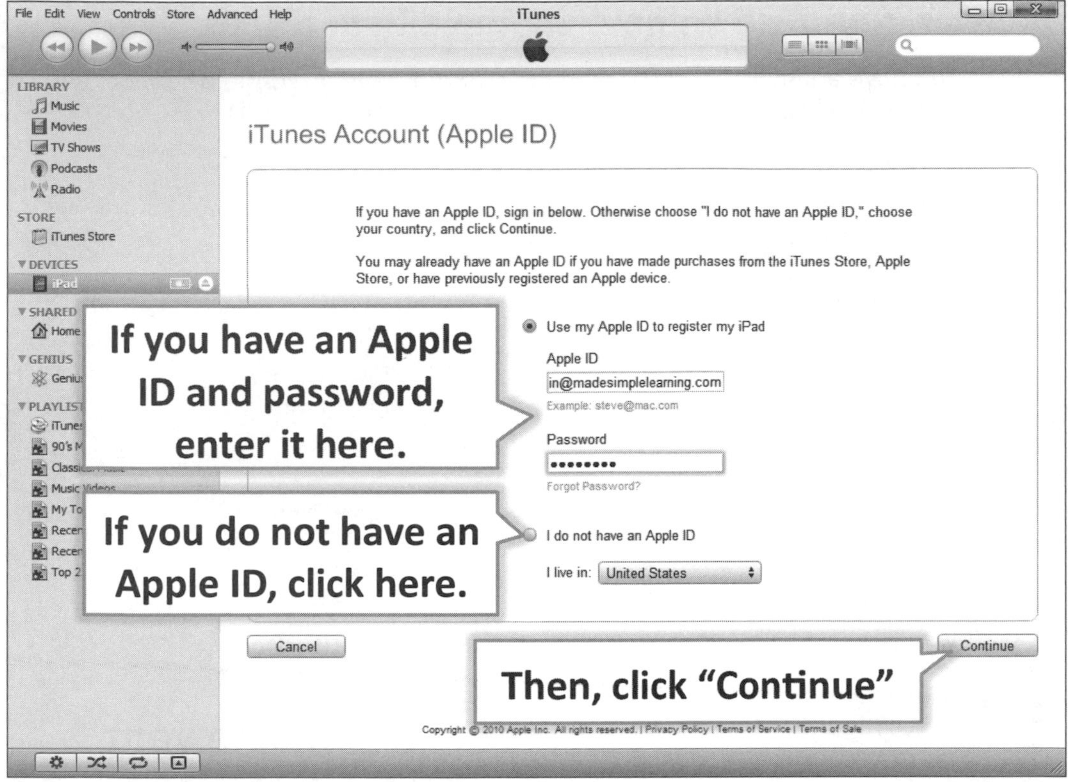


**Figure 1–6.** *iPad first time setup login or create Apple ID*

6. Enter your Apple ID and password or click **I do not have an Apple ID** and select your country.
7. Then click the **Continue** button And proceed as follows.
   - If you tried to enter your Apple ID and password and received an error message about "additional security information is required," then read our "Troubleshooting: Fixing the Apple ID Security Error" section in Chapter 26: "iTunes Guide."
   - If you successfully logged in with your Apple ID, then you will see either the main iTunes window or an ad promoting the MobileMe service. Skip to the "Successful iPad Registration" section in this chapter
   - If you do not have an Apple ID and need to create a new one, then read the next section.

# Register Your iPad Without an Apple ID in iTunes

If you do not have an Apple ID and clicked the **I do not have an Apple ID** option, shown in Figure 1–6, follow these steps to register your iPad and create an ID.

1. Click **Continue** (Figure 1–6) to see the registration screen shown in Figure 1–7.

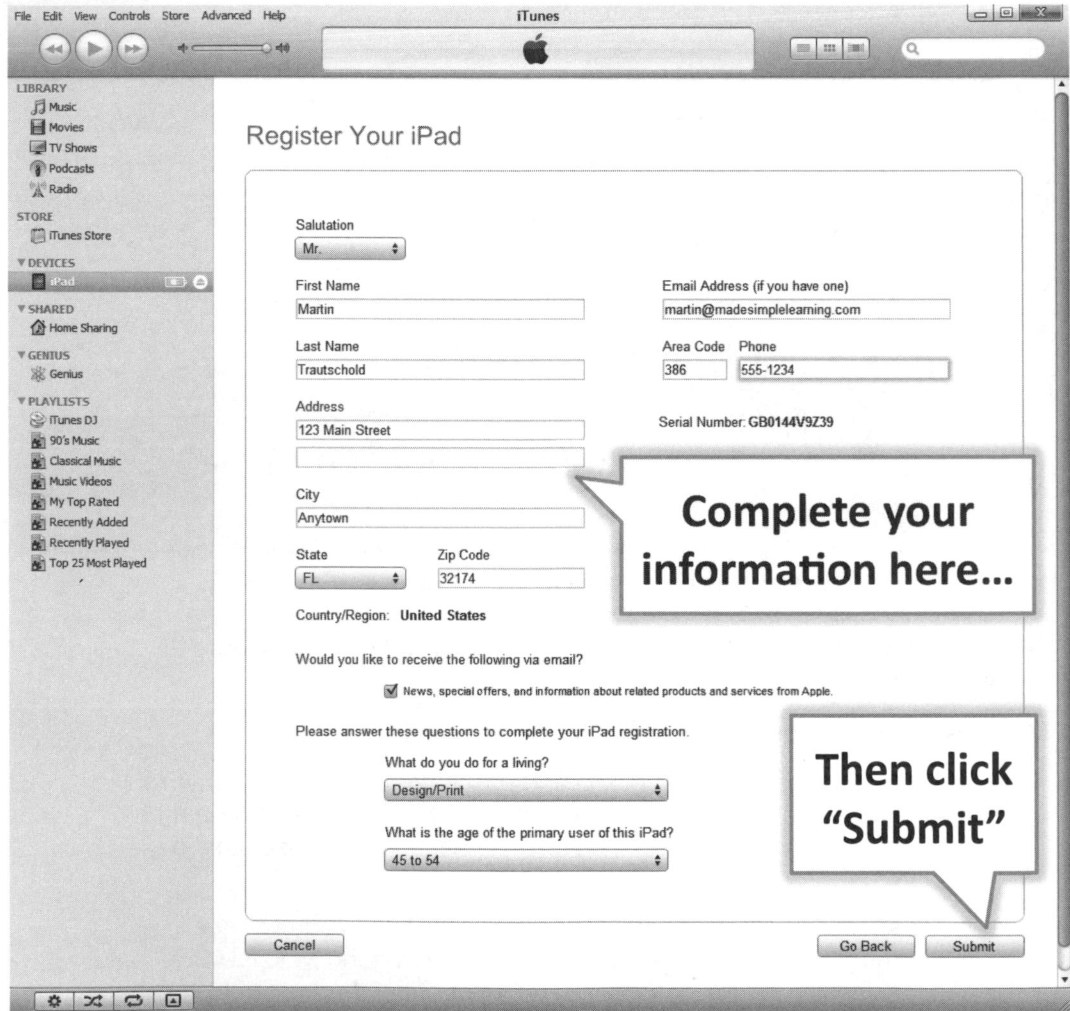


**Figure 1–7.** *iPad registration screen – without an Apple ID*

2. Type in your information and click **Submit** to complete your registration.

If everything has been entered correctly, you will see either the MobileMe ad (Figure 1–8) or the Set Up Your iPad screen (Figure 1–9).

## Apple's MobileMe Sync Service

After registering your iPad for the first time, you will probably see a screen advertising MobileMe as shown in Figure 1–8.

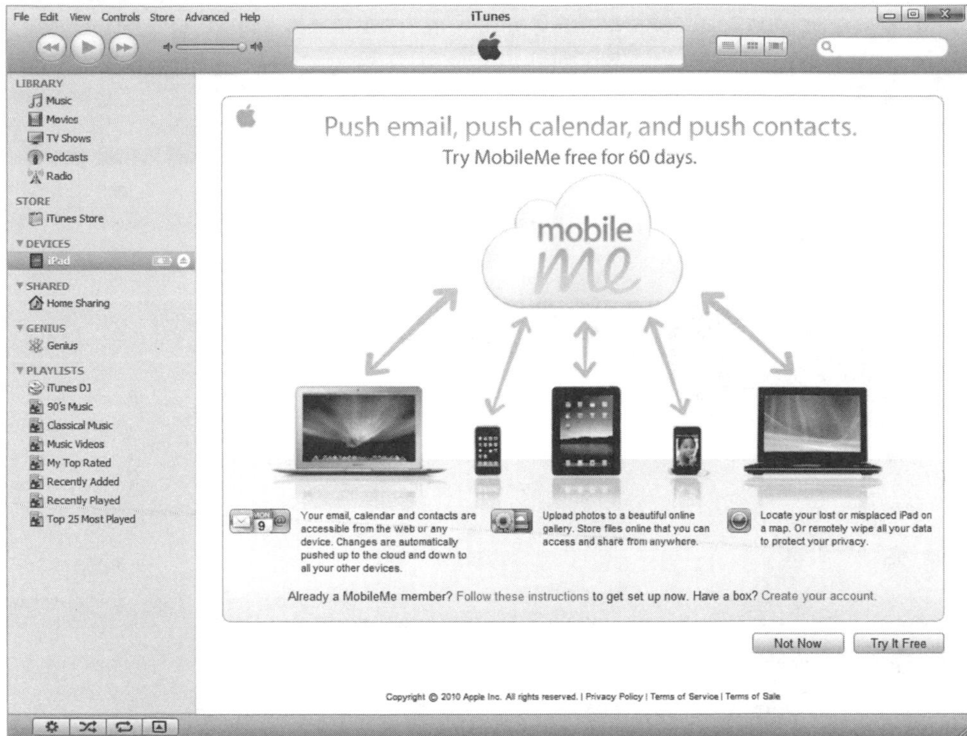


**Figure 1–8.** *iTunes MobileMe ad page (usually appears after registering your iPad)*

To keep moving with setting up your iPad, click the **Not Now** button to continue to the next screen shown on Figure 1–9.

If you would like to try MobileMe, Apple's wireless sync service, please follow the detailed instructions for the MobileMe service in Chapter 24: "Other Sync Methods."

### What is MobileMe?

MobileMe is free for a limited time (currently 60 days), then it costs US $99.00 for a single user or US $149.00 for a family plan. MobileMe provides a way to keep your e-mail, contacts, calendar, and web bookmarks shared across all your computers and mobile devices. You can even use MobileMe to locate a missing iPad! At publishing time, photo sharing is limited to Mac computers with MobileMe iPhoto folders. See our MobileMe Tour section in Chapter 24: "Other Sync Methods"

# Set Up Your iPad

The first time you connect your iPad, you have the chance to give it a name and select some other options, as shown in Figure 1–9.

If you instead see a screen that asks about **Restoring from a backup**, then skip to the "Setup or Restore from Backup" section later in this chapter.

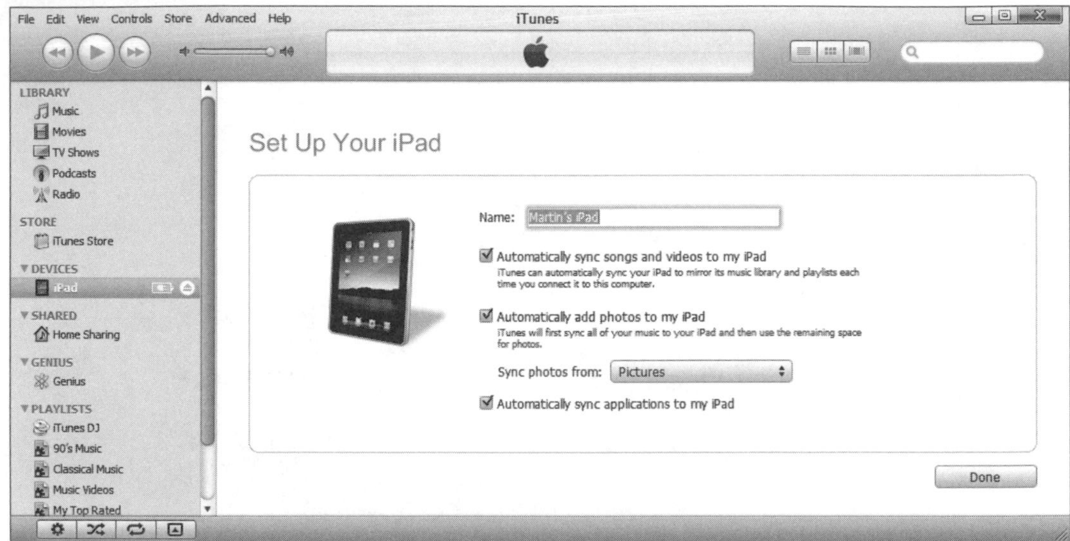


**Figure 1–9.** *Set Up Your iPad screen*

1. Give your iPad a **Name**. Each time you plug in your iPad—to this or any other computer—your iPad will show the name you choose here. In this case, we will call this one: **Martin's iPad**.

**TIP: For Quick Setup**

To get moving quickly, uncheck all three boxes on the screen shown in Figure 1–9 and click **Done**. You can check or uncheck these boxes within the tabs you find in iTunes later. We show you the details in Chapter 3: **Sync with iTunes**, and in Chapter 26: **iTunes Guide.**

2. Check the box next to **Automatically sync songs and videos to my iPad** if you want all of your music and videos stored in your computer's iTunes library on your new iPad.

**CAUTION:** Your iPad does not have as much memory as your computer, so be careful selecting automatically sync when you have thousands of songs, photos, or many videos in your computer iTunes library.

3. Check the box next to **Automatically add photos to my iPad** if you want all your photos in specific folders on your computer synced to your new iPad.

4. Check the box next to **Automatically sync applications to my iPad** if you would like applications you purchase on your iPad backed up to your computer. This option allows you to update Apps from iTunes on your computer and be able to manage and arrange your App icons and Home Screens using iTunes on your computer. We recommend you check this box.

5. Click **Done** to complete the Set Up screen.

# Setup or Restore from Backup

If you have already synced a similar device such as an iPhone or iPodTtouch to your iTunes, then you will probably see a screen similar to Figure 1–10.

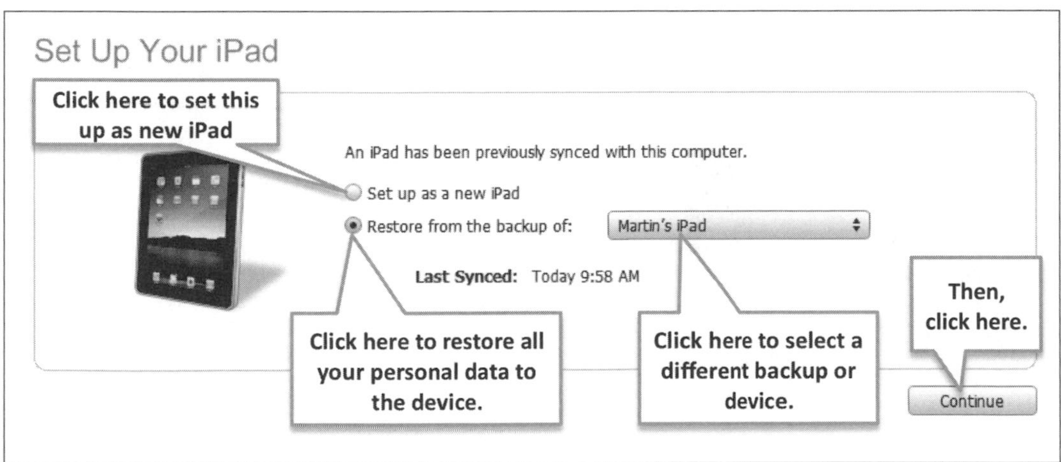


**Figure 1–10.** *Set Up or Restore iPad screen*

If you would like to set this up as a new iPad:

1. Click the selection next to Set up as a new iPad.

2. Click the Continue button.

3. You will then follow the steps in the section "Set Up Your iPad."

> **NOTE:** If you want to keep your existing iPhone and/or iPod Touch and set up your new iPad, then you should select **Set up a New iPad** as shown in Figure 1–10.

If you would like to restore from a backup of another iPad or device (iPhone/iPod touch):

1. Click the selection next to **Restore from the backup of:**.
2. Select the particular backup file from the drop-down menu.
3. Click the **Continue** button.

> **CAUTION:** We have heard of people experiencing problems (lock-ups, lower battery life,and so forth) when they restored a backup from a non-iPad (iPhone/iPod Touch) to the iPad. Also, selecting restore here assumes you have first made a backup of your old device (iPhone/iPod Touch) in order to restore the latest information to your new iPad.

## Setup Complete: The iPad Summary Screen

Once you confirm your choices and click **Done** (Figure 1–9), you will be taken to the main **Summary** screen (Figure 1–11).

**Figure 1–11.** *iPad Summary screen in iTunes*

# Maintaining Your iPad

Now that you have set up your iPad, you will want to know how to safely clean the screen and then keep it protected with various cases.

## Cleaning Your iPad Screen

After using your iPad a little while, you will see that your fingers (or other fingers besides yours) have left smudges and oil on the formerly pristine screen. You will want to know how to safely clean the screen. One way to keep the screen cleaner throughout the day is to place a protective screen cover on the iPad, which may also have the added benefit of cutting down on glare (discussed in the next section).

We also recommend the following:

1. Turn off your iPad by pressing and holding the **Sleep/Power** key on the top edge, then use the slider to turn it off.
2. Remove any cables, such as the USB Sync cable.
3. Rub the screen with a soft, dry lint-free cloth (such as a cloth supplied to clean eyeglasses or something similar).
4. If the dry cloth does not work, then try adding a very little bit of water to dampen the cloth. If you use a damp cloth, try not to get any water in the openings.

**CAUTION:** Never use household cleaners, abrasive cleaners such as SoftScrub, ammonia-based cleaners such as Windex, alcohol, aerosol sprays, or solvents.

## Cases and Protective Covers for Your iPad

Once you have your iPad in your hands, you will notice how beautifully it is constructed. You will also notice that it can be fairly slippery and could slip out of your hands or rock around a bit or have the back get scratched when you are typing on it.

We recommend buying a protective case for your iPad. Average cases run about US$10-$40 and fancy leather cases can run US$100 or more. Spending a little to protect your iPad that costs $500 or more makes good sense.

## Where to Buy Your Covers

You can purchase your iPad protective cover at any of the following locations.

- Amazon.com (`http://www.amazon.com`)
- The Apple Accessory Store: (`http://store.apple.com`)
- iLounge: (`http://ilounge.pricegrabber.com`)
- TiPB – The iPhone + iPad Blog Store (http://store.tipb.com/)

You could also do a web search for "iPad cases" or "iPad protective covers."

> **TIP**: You *may* be able to use a case designed for another type of computer, for example a netbook or small tablet computer, for your iPad. If you go this route to try and save some money, just make sure your iPad fits securely in the case or cover.

## What to Buy . . .

The following sections provide some types of cases and price ranges from which to choose.

### Rubber/Silicone Cases ($10-$30)

**What these do:** Provides a cushioned grip and should absorb iPad bumps and bruises

**Pros**: Inexpensive, colorful, and comfortable to hold

**Cons**: Not as professional as a leather case

### Waterproof Cases ($10-$40)

**What these do:** Provides waterproof protection for your iPad and allow you to safely use the iPad near water (in the rain, at the pool, at the beach, on the boat, an so forth)

**Pros**: Provides good water protection

**Cons**: May make the touch screen harder to use, usually does not protect from drops or bumps

### Hard Plastic/Metal Case ($20-$50)

**What these do:** Provides hard, solid protection against scratches, bumps, and short drops

**Pros**: Provides good protection

**Cons**: Adds some bulk and weight

### Leather Book or Flip Cases ($50-$100+)

**What these do:** Provides more of a luxury feel, protects the front and sides as well as the back

**Pros**: Leather luxury feel, protects the front and the back

**Cons**: More expensive, adds bulk and weight

### Screen and Back Cover Protectors ($5-$40)

**What these do:** Protects the screen and back of the iPad from scratches

**Pros**: Helps prolong life of your iPad, protects against scratches, most decrease screen glare

**Cons**: Some may increase glare or may affect touch sensitivity of the screen

# iPad Basics

Now that you have your iPad charged with a clean screen, registered, and decked out with a new protective case, let's take a look at some of the basics to help you get up and running.

## Powering On/Off and Sleep/Wake

To power on your iPad, press and hold the **Power/Sleep** button on the top edge of the iPad for a few seconds (Figure 1–12). Simply tapping this button quickly won't power on the iPad if it is completely off—you really need to hold it until you see the iPad power on.

When you are no longer using your iPad, you have two options: you can either put it into sleep mode or turn it off completely.

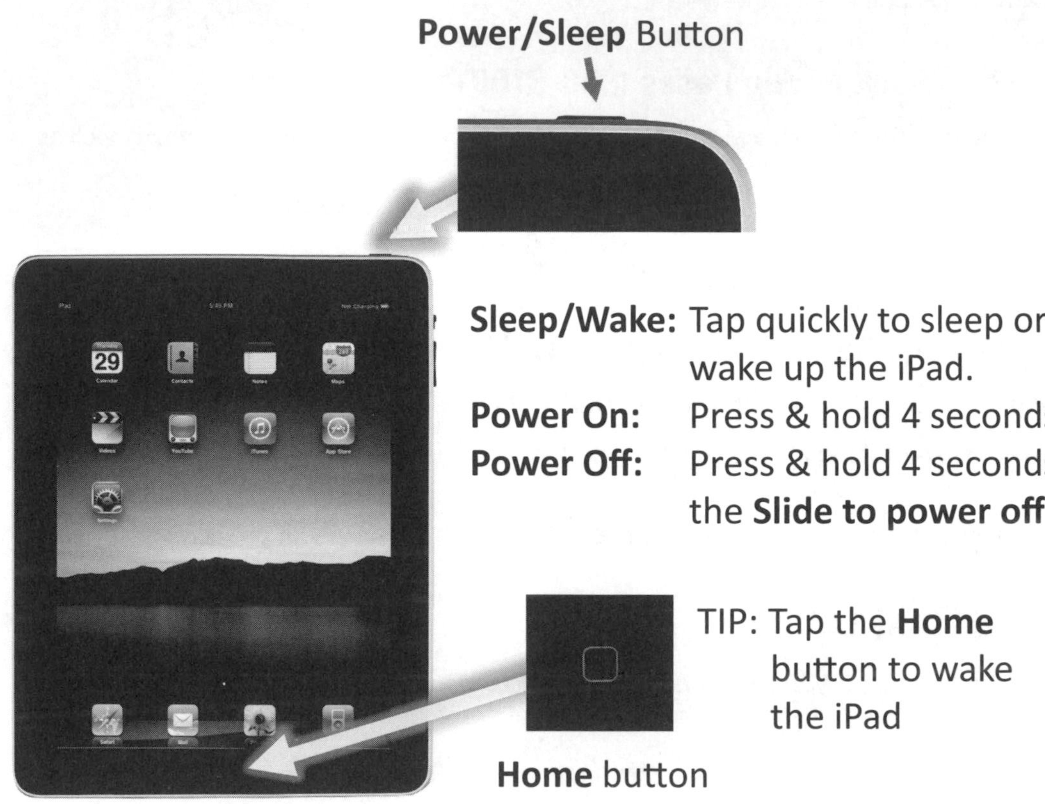
**Power/Sleep** Button
**Sleep/Wake:** Tap quickly to sleep or wake up the iPad.
**Power On:** Press & hold 4 seconds
**Power Off:** Press & hold 4 seconds the **Slide to power off**
TIP: Tap the **Home** button to wake the iPad
**Home** button

**Figure 1–12.** ***Power/Sleep*** *button and* ***Home*** *button*

The advantage of Sleep Mode is that when you want to use your iPad again, just a quick tap of the **Power/Sleep** button or the **Home** button will bring your iPad back awake. According to Apple, the iPad has up to a month of stand-by power.

If you want to maximize your battery or if you know you won't be using your iPad for quite some time—say, when you go to sleep—you might want to turn it off completely. The way to do this is to press and hold the **Power/Sleep** button until you see the **Slide to Power Off** bar appear. Just slide the bar to the right and the iPad will power off.

## The Home Button

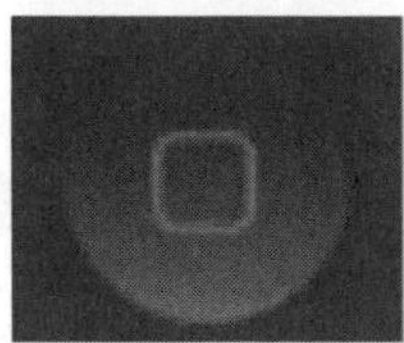

The main key you will use most often is your **Home** button (Figure 1–12). This button will begin everything you do with your iPad. Press it once to wake up your iPad (assuming it is in Sleep mode.)

Pressing the **Home** button will take you out of any application program and bring you back to your **Home** screen.

> **TIP:** Double-tapping your **Home** button can be set to do different things, such as starting the iPad function, Search, or more (see how to configure this in the section below).

## Double-Clicking the Home Button

You can customize what happens when you double-click (or double-tap) the **Home** button.

1. Just touch the **Settings** icon and touch the **General** tab (Figure 1–13).
2. Scroll down to and touch the **Home** tab.

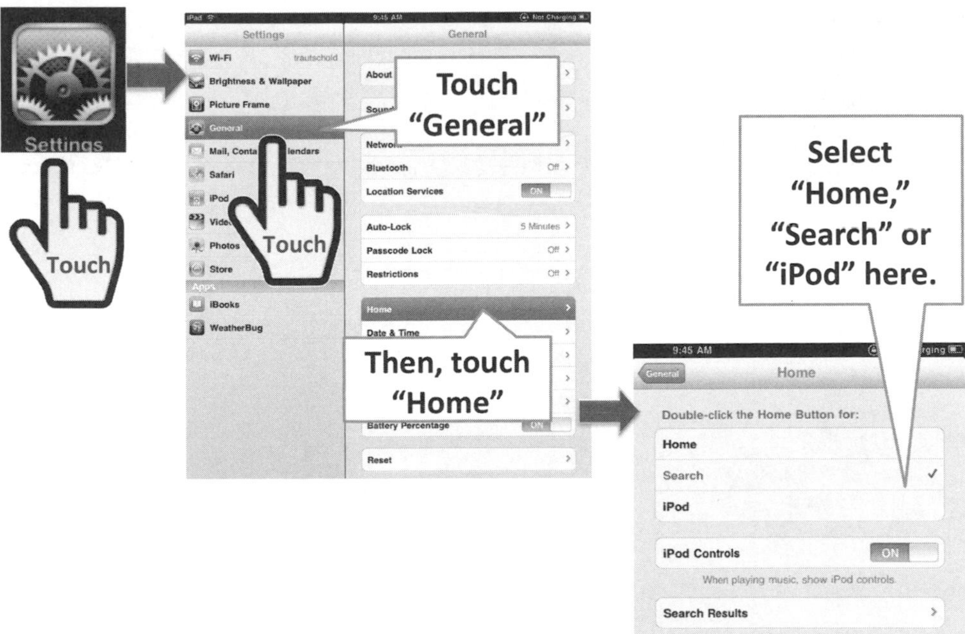


**Figure 1–13.** *Configuring the action when you double-click the* ***Home*** *button.*

3. You will then see several options under **Double-click the Home Button for:**.
4. **Home.** This is essentially the same thing as pressing the **Home** button once.
5. **Search.** Will bring up the Search icon to find anything on your iPad in **Contacts**, **Music**, **Email**, **Calendar**, and more.
6. **iPod.** Select this to bring up the iPod when you double-click the **Home** button. When you double-click **Home** while playing music (and your **iPod Controls** is set to **ON**), you will see the **iPod** controls appear.
7. Tap the selection you want for the **Home** button.
8. If **iPod Controls** is set to **Off,** then double-click **Home**, which automatically brings you into the iPod, whether or not you are listening to music. This is very helpful if you are in the midst of listening to music and want to quickly pause or change the song.

## Volume Keys

Located on the upper right-hand side of the iPad (Figure 1–14) are simple **Volume Up/Volume Down** keys that you will find very handy. In many places, you can also control the volume of the song, video, or podcast playing by sliding your finger on the screen volume control.

> **Tip**: Hold down the **Volume Down** Key for about two seconds to quickly mute the sound on the iPad.

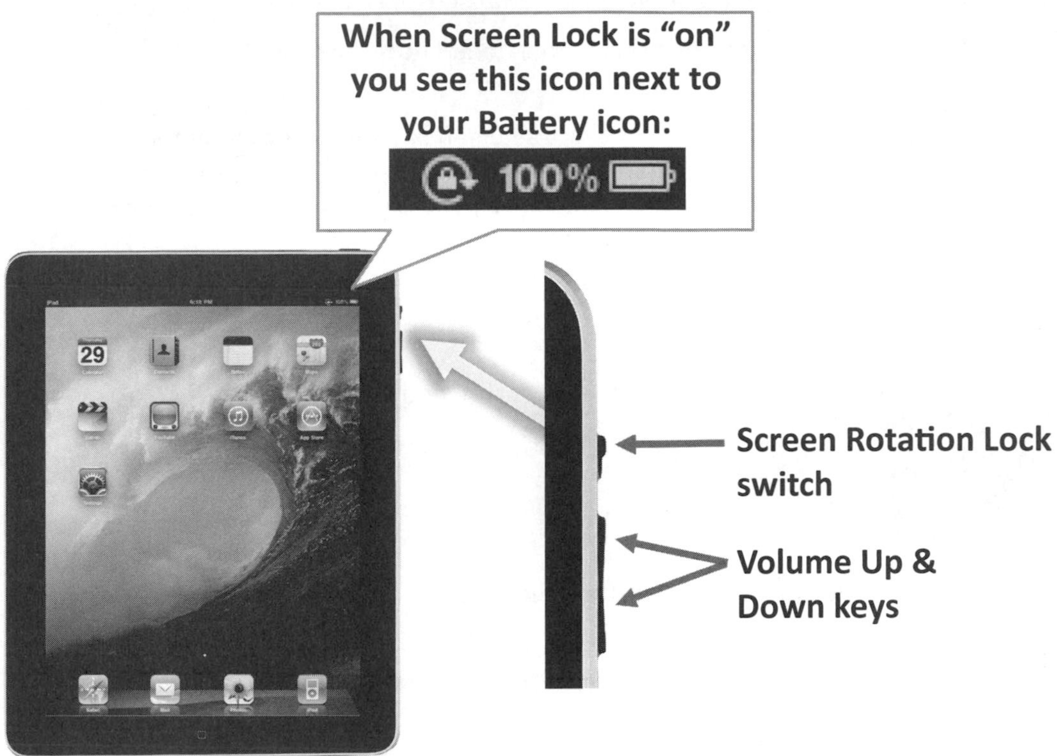


**Figure 1–14.** ***Screen Rotation Lock*** *switch and* ***Volume Up/Down*** *keys and* ***Home*** *button*

## Stopping the Screen Rotation Using Screen Rotation Lock Switch

Just above the **Volume** keys, you will find the **Screen Rotation Lock** switch (see Figure 1–14). Use this when you want to force the iPad to stop rotating the screen. This is useful when you have your iPad sitting flat on your desk or in your lap and want to force it to stay in either portrait or landscape rotation.

> **TIP:** This is a great way to read iBooks in bed. Turn your iPad to **Landscape** mode, lock the screen rotation switch, and read your book. Check out Chapter 8 "iBooks and e-Books" for more.

## Adjust or Disable the Auto-Lock Time Out Feature

You will notice that your iPad will Auto-Lock and go into **Sleep Mode** with the screen blank after a short amount of time. You can change this time or even disable this feature altogether using the **Settings** Icon.

1. Touch the **Settings** icon from your **Home** screen.
2. Touch **General** in the left column, then touch **Auto-Lock** in the right column.
3. You will see your current Auto-Lock setting next to **Auto-Lock** on this page (Figure 1–15). The default setting is that the iPad locks after **5** minutes of sitting idle (to save battery life.) The choices you have for this setting are **2**, **5**, **10**, **15** minutes, or **Never**.

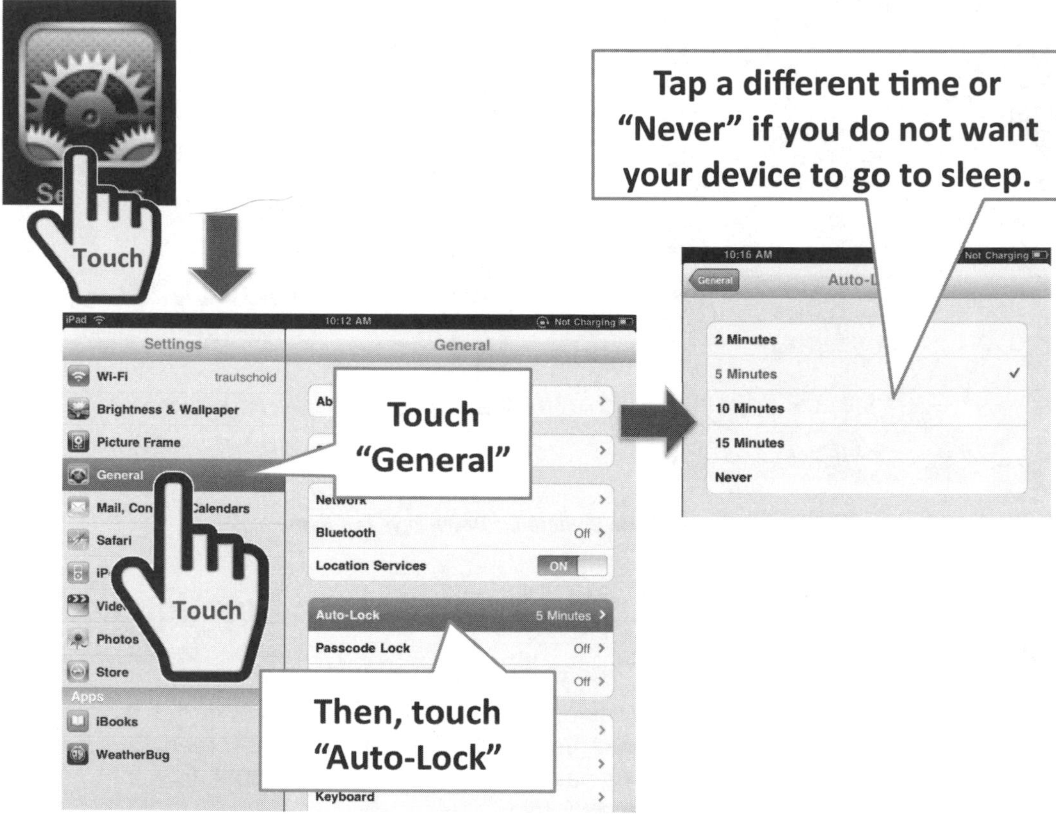


**Figure 1–15.** *Settings to adjust or remove the time-out for the **Auto-Lock** feature.*

4. Touch the desired setting to select it—you know it's selected when you see the check mark next to it.
5. Then, touch the **General** button in the upper left-hand corner to get back to the **General** screen. You should see your

**BATTERY LIFE TIP:**

Setting the **Auto-Lock** shorter (for example, 2 minutes) will help you

change now reflected next to **Auto- Lock**.

save battery life.

## Adjusting the Date and Time

Usually, the date and time is either set for you or adjusts when you connect your iPad to your computer, which we cover in Chapter 3: "Sync with iTunes." You can, however, manually adjust your date and time quite easily. You may want to do this when you are traveling with your iPad and need to adjust the time zone when you land.

1. Touch the **Settings** icon.
2. Touch **General** in the left column, and **Date & Time** in the right column to see the **Date & Time** settings screen (Figure 1–16).
3. If you prefer to see **09:30** and **14:30** instead of **9:30 AM** and **2:30 PM**, respectively, then tap the **24-Hour Time** setting switch to **ON**.

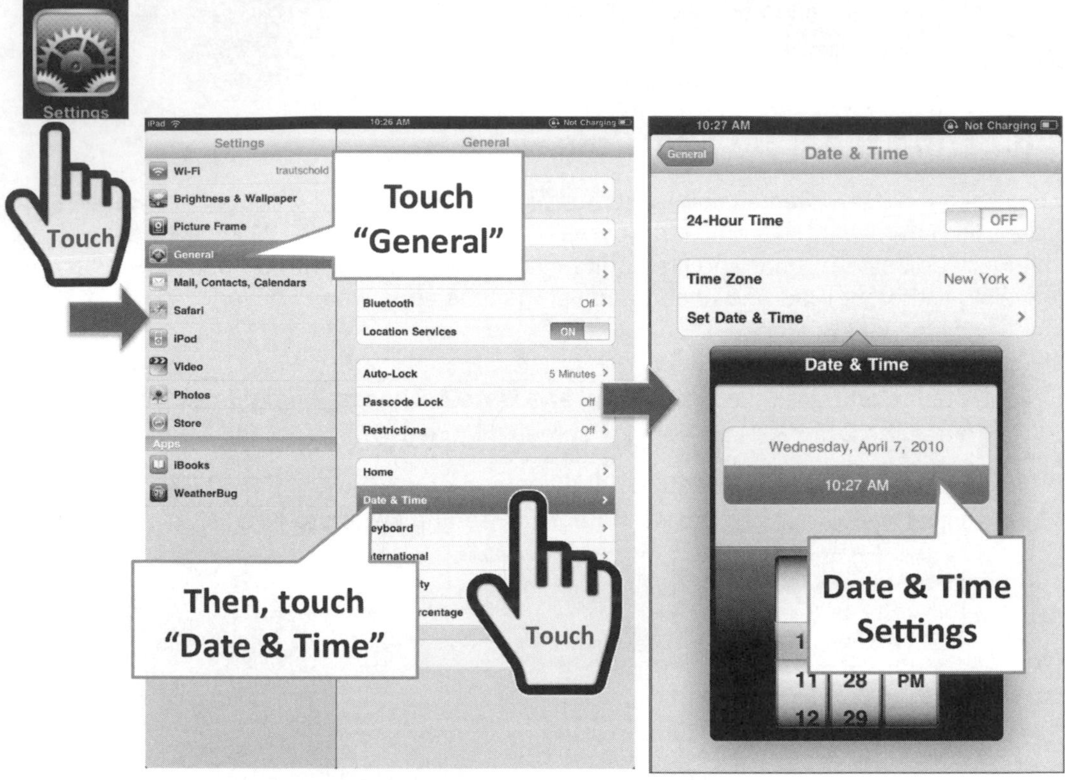


**Figure 1–16.** *Setting your date, time, time zone and 24-hour or 12-hour clock*

1. To set the date and time, touch the **Set Date & Time** button to see the pop-up window with the wheels that rotate as you touch and move them.
2. In Figure 1–17, you touch and slide the hour wheel and to move it upwards to change the time from 10 to 11.

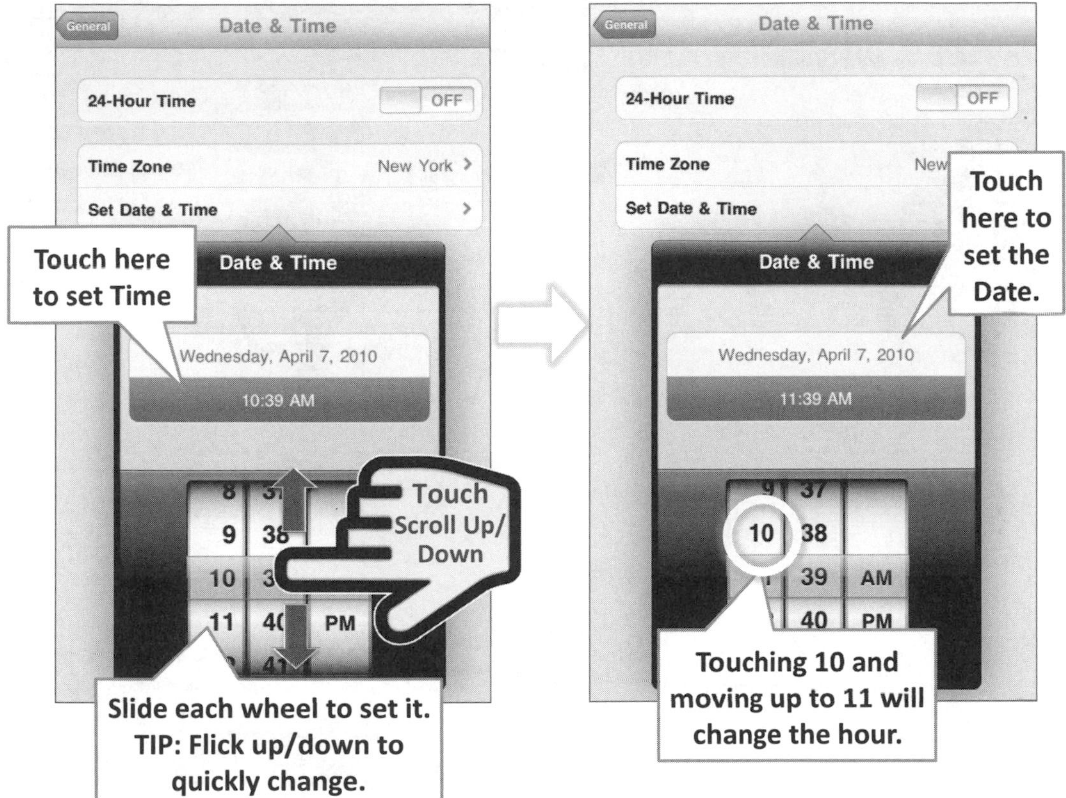


**Figure 1–17.** *Setting the date and time*

## Setting Your Time Zone

To set the time zone:

1. Touch **Time Zone** in the right column.
2. Start to type in the name of the desired city (Figure 1–18).
3. Touch the name of the city to select it and the screen will automatically move back to the **Date and Time** screen.

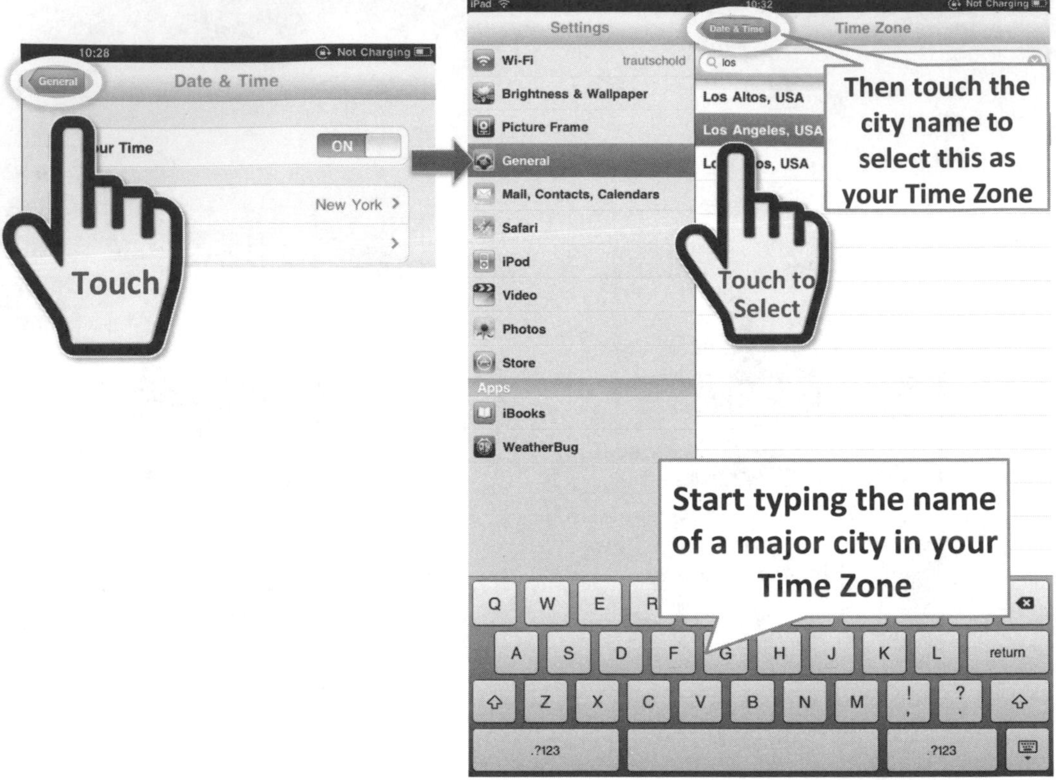


**Figure 1–18.** *Setting your time zone.*

## Adjusting the Brightness

Your iPad has an **Auto-Brightness** control available, which is usually the default (see Figure 1–19). This uses the built-in light sensor to adjust the brightness of the screen. Generally, we advise that you keep this set to **ON**.

If you want to adjust the brightness, you certainly can. From your **Home** screen, touch the **Settings** icon. Then touch the **Brightness & Wallpaper** tab, which is near the top of the left column (Figure 1–19), and move the slider control to adjust the brightness.

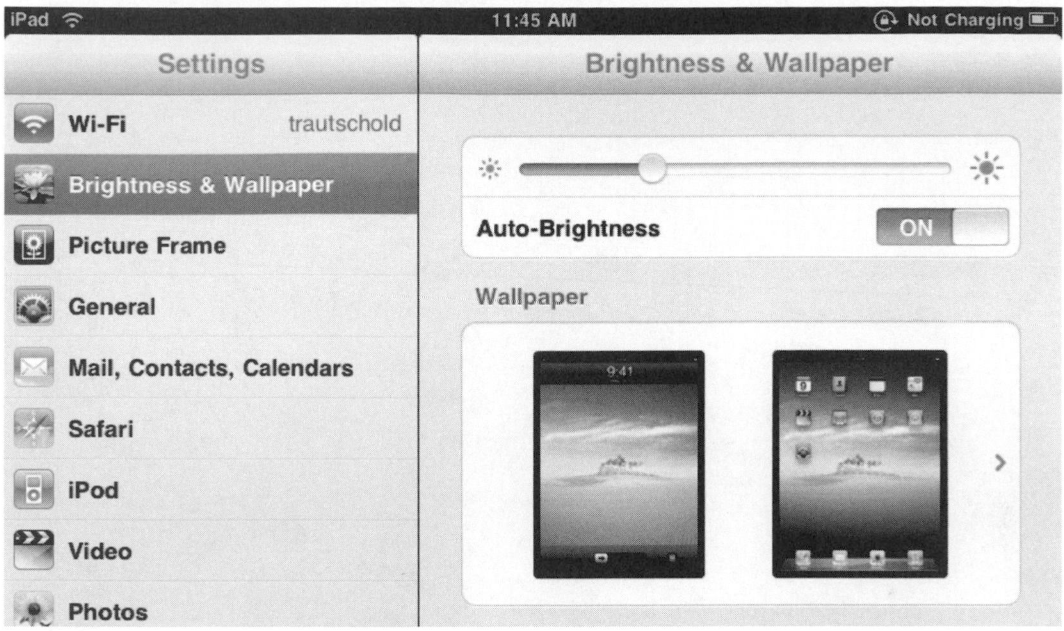


**Figure 1–19.** *Setting the brightness of your iPad*

> **TIP**: Setting the brightness lower will help you save battery life. A little less than 1/2 way across seems to work fine.

Chapter 2

# Typing Tips, Copy/Paste & Search

In this chapter, we show you some good ways to type and save valuable time typing on your iPad, whether you use the portrait (vertical/smaller) keyboard or the landscape (horizontal/larger) keyboard. You will learn how to select different language keyboards, how to type symbols, and other tips. We will also show you some tips and tricks when working with various external keyboard accessories for your iPad.

Later in this chapter, we will show you about the spotlight search and the Copy and Paste function. Copy and Paste will save you lots of time as well as increase accuracy when working with your iPad.

## Typing on Your iPad

You will quickly find two on-screen keyboards on your iPad: the smaller one visible when you hold your iPad in a vertical orientation, and the larger landscape keyboard when you hold the iPad in a horizontal orientation. The nice thing is that you can choose whichever keyboard works best for you. And if you prefer a physical keyboard, we show you the ins-and-outs of a couple of nice accessory keyboards as shown in Figure 2–1.

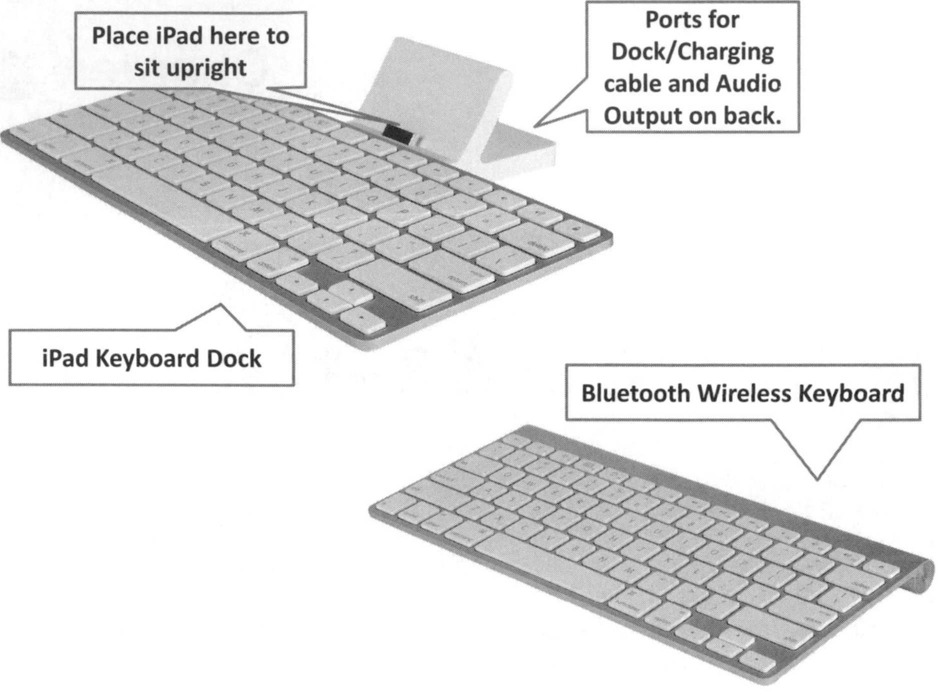


**Figure 2–1.** *Two optional keyboard accessories: The iPad Keyboard Dock and the Bluetooth Wireless Keyboard*

## Typing on the Screen with the Portrait Keyboard

You will find when you first start out with your iPad that you can most easily type with one finger—usually your index finger—while holding the iPad with the other hand.

After a little while, you should be able to experiment with thumb typing (like you see so many people doing with their iPhone or BlackBerry smartphones). Once you practice a little, typing with two thumbs instead of a single finger will really boost your speed. Just be patient, it does take practice to become proficient typing quickly with your two thumbs.

You will actually notice after a while that the keyboard touch sensitivity assumes you are typing with two thumbs. What this means is that the letters on the left side of your keyboard are meant to be pressed on their left side, and the keys on the right are meant to be touched/pressed on their right side (Figure 2–2).

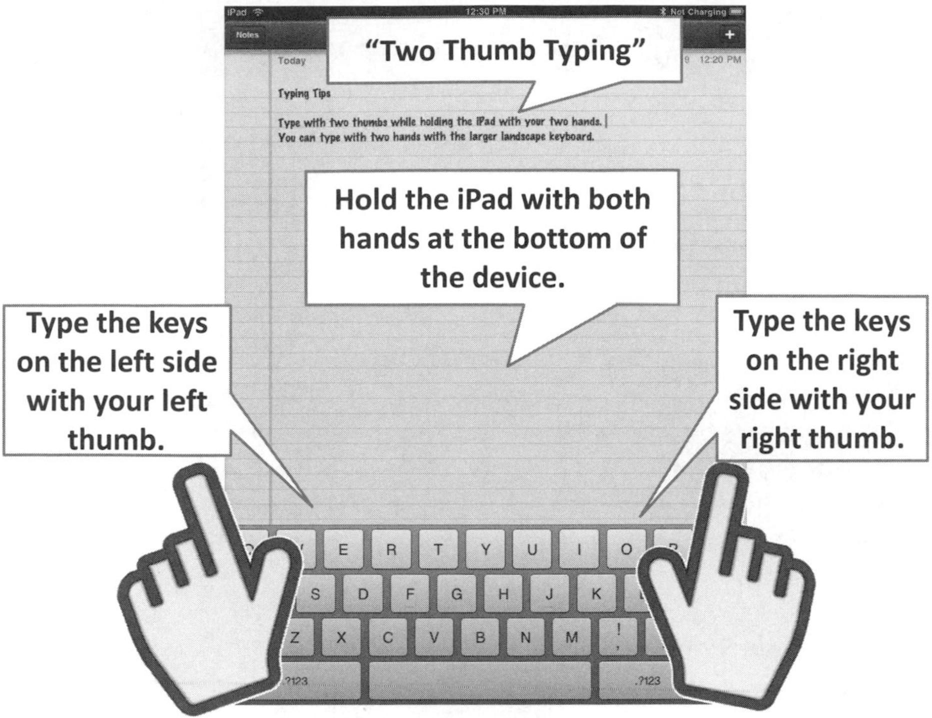


**Figure 2–2.** *Typing with two thumbs while holding the iPad vertically.*

**TIP:** If you have larger hands and find typing on the smaller vertical keyboard challenging, then flip your iPad on its side to get the larger, landscape keyboard (see Figure 2–3).

## Typing on the Screen with the Larger Landscape Keyboard

Simply turn the iPad sideways in almost any App and the keyboard will change to a larger, landscape keyboard to make it easier to type (see Figure 2–3).

1. Lay the iPad on a flat surface. It usually helps if you either have the iPad in a case (see Chapter 1, "Getting Started," to learn about various cases), or sitting on a soft surface so it does not rock while you are typing.
2. Type with two hands like you would on a normal computer keyboard. With some practice, you can almost type as fast on this larger keyboard as you do on a regular physical keyboard.

**TIP:** Try recycling an old mouse pad to use as a rest for your iPad while you type.

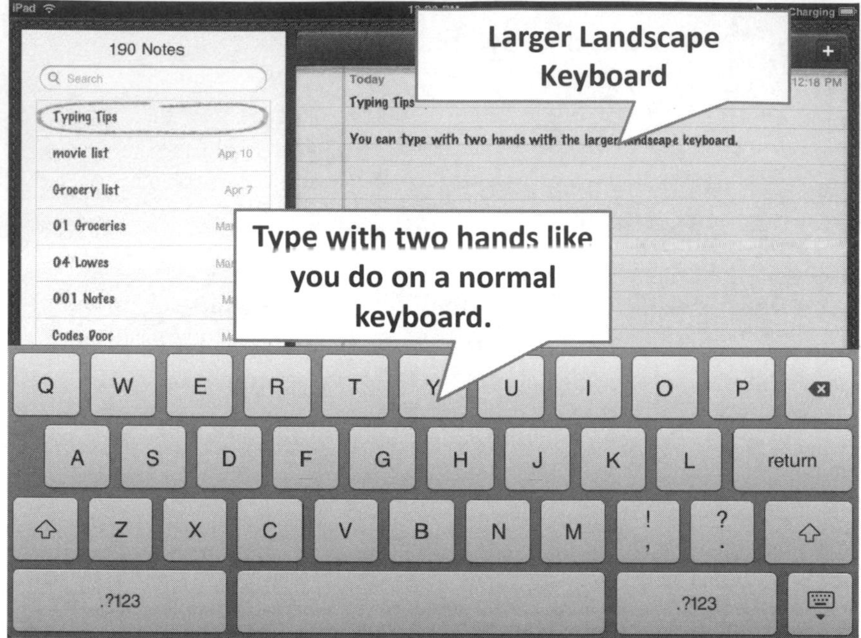


**Figure 2–3.** *Typing with two hands while letting the iPad rest on a flat surface.*

> **TIP:** For the frequent traveler, using the virtual keyboards on your iPad are perfect space savers in those cramped airline seats compared to any laptop computer!

## Typing with External Keyboards (Purchase as Separate Accessories)

If you need to do a lot of typing or are simply uncomfortable with the "typing on glass" feel of the virtual keyboards, you can buy external keyboards that work with the iPad. We have tested two from Apple, Inc., but we are sure there are more keyboard dock and Bluetooth options available. Check out the iPad/iPhone/iPod blogs or online stores to find keyboards and other accessories. You can also do a quick web search for "iPad external keyboard" to find options.

> **TIP:** If you plan to do a lot of typing on your iPad, investing some money in one of these external keyboards can be worth its weight in gold! In our testing, we preferred the Apple iPad Keyboard Dock because it held the iPad at a very nice angle for typing.

**CAUTION:** A few iPad apps only work in landscape orientation and will not work with the Keyboard Dock because the whole app will look sideways when in the vertical orientation—Apple Keynote is one prominent example.

## Apple Wireless Keyboard (Bluetooth) — About US $70

Besides being easier and faster to type on, external keyboards give you the added benefit of showing you more of the iPad screen since the virtual keyboard is gone.

**TIP:** If you own another Apple computer, you may already own the Wireless Keyboard—it is the same Wireless Keyboard that Apple has made for a while.

### Getting it Connected

Since it uses a wireless Bluetooth connection, you first have to connect, or "pair," this keyboard with your iPad. (See Chapter 10, "Bluetooth," for more help.)

1. Tap the **Settings** icon (refer to Figure 2–4).
2. Tap **General** in the left column.
3. Tap **Bluetooth** in the right column.
4. Make sure the Bluetooth receiver is set to **ON** by tapping the switch if it shows OFF.
5. Turn on your Apple Wireless Keyboard by pressing the **On/Off** button on the right edge of the round tube under the top of the keyboard. You will know when the keyboard is on and has batteries when the green light in the upper right corner is on or flashing.
6. Once the Wireless Keyboard is powered on, you should see it listed under **Devices** in the **Bluetooth** screen on the iPad. Tap the Keyboard listed under **Devices** to have the iPad generate a pairing number (see Figure 2–4).
7. Type in the pairing code number from the iPad on the Wireless Keyboard and press the **Enter/Return** key on the keyboard.
8. Sometimes it takes two or three tries to get the keyboard to pair with your iPad. Keep trying, it will work eventually!

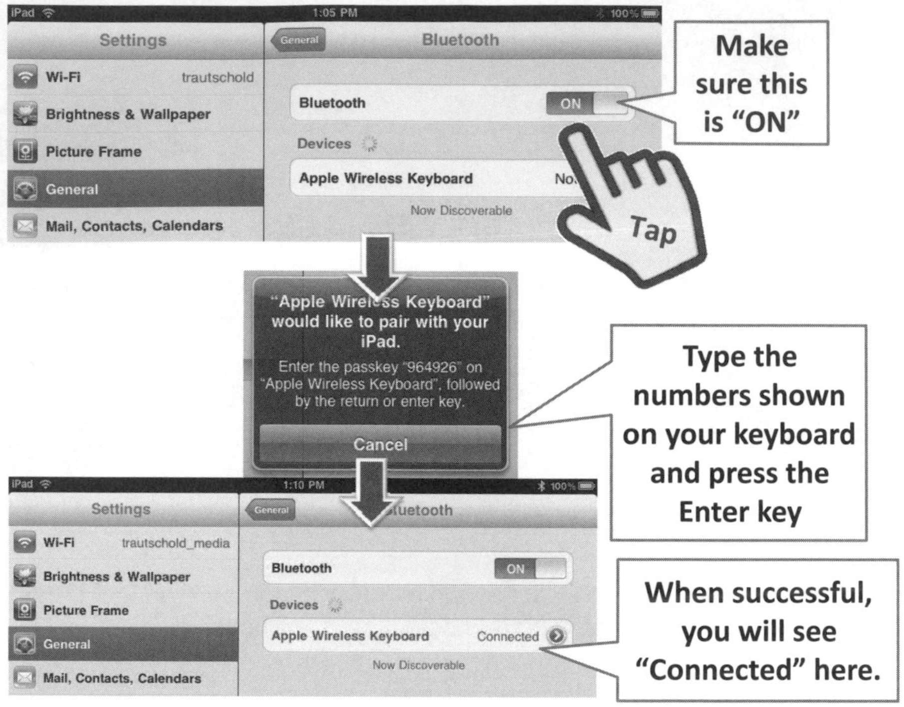


**Figure 2–4.** *Pairing a Bluetooth Wireless Keyboard to your iPad.*

### To Switch Between the Wireless Keyboard and the On-Screen Keyboard

Simply press the **Eject** key in the upper right corner of the keyboard to temporarily disconnect the Wireless Keyboard and see the on-screen keyboard.

Press the **Eject** key again to re-connect the wireless keyboard and make the on-screen keyboard disappear.

## Apple iPad Keyboard Dock—About US $70

Besides giving you the physical keyboard to type on, the Keyboard Dock also gives you the added benefit of holding your iPad up at an angle like a regular computer screen. It is very nice!

Other benefits of this keyboard are that it is designed by Apple specifically for the iPad so you have specially designed keys as shown in Figure 2–5. To the right of these keys, along the top, you also have media control keys: **Previous Track**, **Play/Pause**, **Next Track**, **Volume** keys, and a **Lock** key.

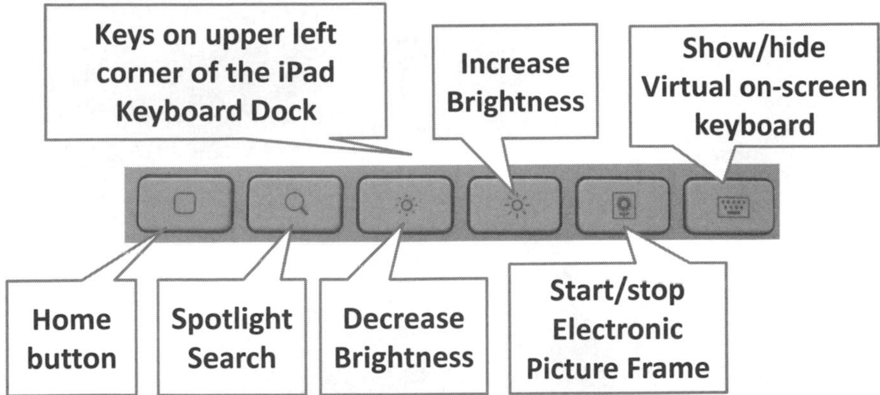


**Figure 2–5.** *Special keys on the iPad Keyboard Dock*

> **TIP:** To wake up the sleeping iPad, you can simply tap any key on the iPad Keyboard Dock.

Unlike a laptop computer, the angle at which the iPad sits in the dock is fixed and cannot be adjusted; however, this angle seemed to work perfectly for us when we tested it.

> **CAUTION:** The iPad can be a little unstable in the Keyboard Dock. We recommend a good flat, stable surface. Also, be careful if you have little people, or really big dogs, running around that could easily and accidentally knock the iPad off the dock.

## Connecting Your iPad to the Keyboard Dock

Connecting your iPad to the Keyboard Dock is very simple—just set it on the dock to plug it into the port on the bottom of the iPad, as shown in Figure 2–6.

**Figure 2–6.** *iPad sitting in Keyboard Dock—Great for typing long documents.*

> **NOTE:** If you have put your iPad in a case, you will most likely have to remove it before you connect the iPad to the Keyboard Dock. This has the added benefit of allowing the iPad to dissipate heat if you are charging it while it is in the dock.

You can then plug your USB sync and charging cable to the back of the Keyboard dock to simultaneously connect the iPad to your computer or charge it in the wall socket.

Simply pull the iPad up and out of the Keyboard Dock to disconnect it.

**CAUTION:** As of publishing time, standard keyboard tricks such as Command-C for Copy, Command-V for Paste, and the iPad Auto-Correction did work with the two keyboard accessories; however the iPad Auto-Capitalization and Double Space for Period shortcuts did not work.

### Connecting Two Keyboards at Once

If you happen to have both the Wireless Keyboard and the Keyboard Dock, we have discovered that you could simultaneously type with both keyboards on the iPad. Take turns typing on the same document? Dueling keyboards? Duet typing? In any case, a strange but true capability of these keyboards.

## Saving Time with Auto-Correction

When you are typing for a while, you will begin to notice a little pop-up window directly below some of the words you are typing—this is called Auto-Correction. (If you never see this pop-up window, then you will have to enable Auto-Correction in your **Settings** icon on your iPad) You can save yourself time when you see the correct word guessed by just pressing the **Space** key at the bottom of the keyboard to select that word.

In this example, we start typing the word "especially," and when we get to the c in the word, the correct word "especially" appears below in a pop-up. To select it, we simply press the **Space** key at the bottom (see Figure 2–7).

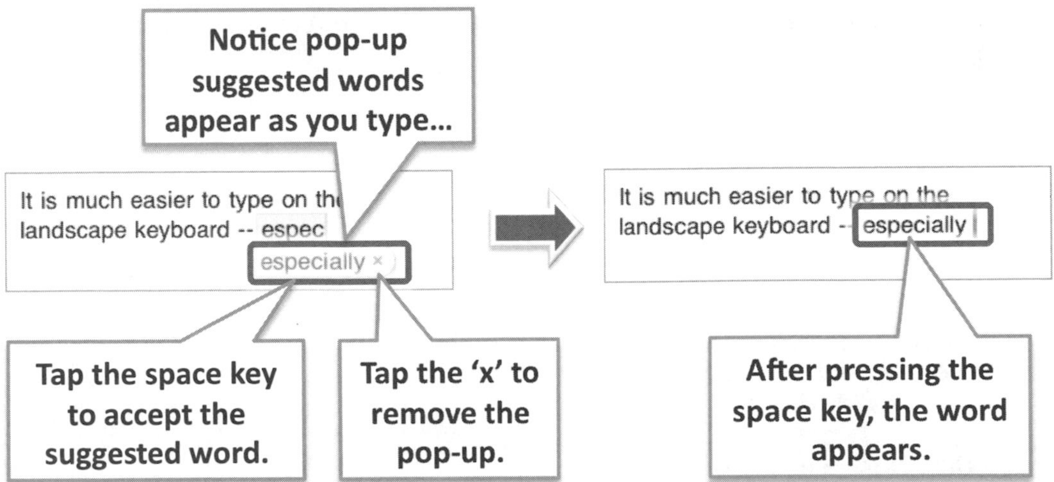


**Figure 2–7.** *Using Auto-Correction and suggested words.*

Your first inclination might be to tap the pop-up word, but that simply erases it from the screen. It is ultimately faster to keep typing or press the **Space** key when you see the correct word, as there will be more situations in which the word is either correct or will become correct as you keep typing—less finger travel in the long run.

After you learn to use the **Space** key, you will see that this pop-up guessing can be quite a time saver. After all, you were going to have to type a space at the end of the word anyways!

**Tip:** With Auto-Correction, you can save time by avoiding typing the apostrophe in many common contractions, such as "wont" and "cant." Auto-Correction will show you a little pop-up window with the contraction spelled correctly; all you need to do to select the correction is to press the **Space** KEY.

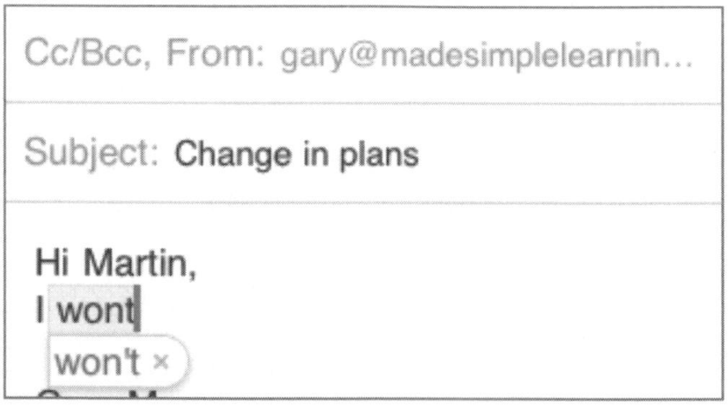

## Hearing Auto-Correction Words Out Loud

You can set your iPad to speak out the Auto-text and Auto-Correction words as they appear. This might be helpful to you to help selecting the correct word. To enable this type of speaking:

1. Tap the **Settings** icon.
2. Tap **General** in the left column.
3. Tap **Accessibility** near the bottom of the right column.
4. Set the switch next to **Speak Auto-text** to **On**.

After you enable this feature, whenever you are typing, you will hear the Auto Correction word that pops up. If you like the word you hear, then press the **Space** key to accept it, otherwise keep typing. It can save you some time from looking up from the keyboard.

# Accessibility Options

There are a number of useful features on the iPad to help with accessibility. The VoiceOver option will read to you from the screen. It will tell you what you tap on, what buttons are selected, and all the options. It will read entire screens of text as well. If you like to see things larger, you can also turn on the **Zoom** feature as described below.

# Getting Your iPad to Speak To You (VoiceOver)

One cool feature of the iPad is that you can turn on the VoiceOver feature so that the iPad will speak anything on the screen. You can even get it to read to you from any email, text document or even an iBook page.

To enable **VoiceOver**:

1. Tap the **Settings** icon.
2. Tap **General** in the left column.
3. Tap **Accessibility** near the bottom of the right column.
4. Tap **VoiceOver** in the left column.
5. Set the **VoiceOver** switch to **On**.

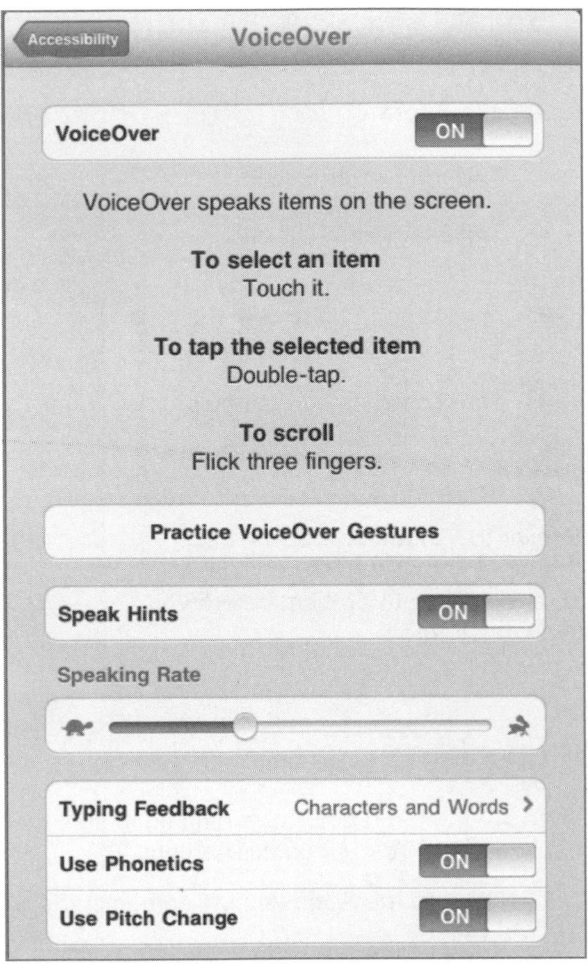


**Caution:** As shown on the screen to the right, the voice over gestures are different from the normal gestures. Tap the **Practice VoiceOver Gestures** button to get used to them.

Notice that you can adjust the **Speaking Rate** from slow to fast and have other adjustments such as **Typing Feedback**, **Use Phonetics** and **Use Pitch Change**. Give some of these a try to see which options work best for you.

When you type with VoiceOver, by default every character you type will be spoken. You can change this in the above settings screen to just words, just characters, or nothing.

To have an entire page read to you in the **iBooks** app, you need to simultaneously touch the bottom and top of the block of text on the screen. If you tap in the text with one finger, only a single line is read to you.

Tapping the top of a note in the **Notes** app will read the entire note to you.

## Using Zoom to Magnify the Entire Screen

You may want to turn on the Zoom feature if you find that the text, icons, buttons or anything on the screen is a little too hard to see. With the Zoom turned on, you can zoom the entire screen to almost twice the size. Everything is much easier to read.

> **NOTE:** You cannot use VoiceOver and Zoom at the same time, you need to choose one or the other.

To enable **Zoom**:

1. Tap the **Settings** icon.
2. Tap **General** in the left column.
3. Tap **Accessibility** near the bottom of the right column.
4. Tap **Zoom** in the right column.
5. Set the switch next to **Zoom** to **On**.

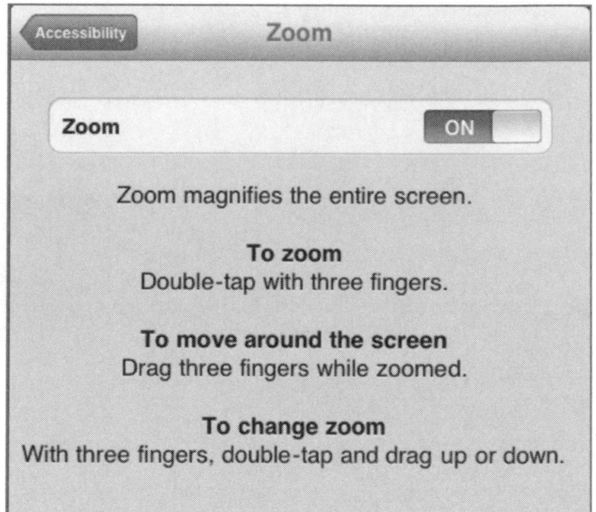


Similar to **VoiceOver**, **Zoom** uses the three fingered gestures. Make sure to take note of them before you leave the screen.

## White on Black

If the contrast and colors are difficult to see, then you might want to turn on the Whte on Black setting. To change this setting:

1. Get into the **Accessibility** screen in the **Settings** app as shown above.
2. Set the **White on Black** switch to On.

With this setting **On**, everything that was light on the screen becomes black, and everything that was dark or black becomes white.

## Triple-Click Home Button Options

You can set a triple-click of the **Home** button to do various things related to Accessibility.

1. Get into the **Accessibility** screen in the **Settings** app as shown above.
2. Tap **Triple-click the Home Button** near the bottom of the right column.
3. Choose from **Off**, **Toggle VoiceOver**, **Toggle White on Black**, or **Ask**.

# Magnifying Glass for Editing Text/Placing the Cursor

How many times have you been typing something and wanted to move the cursor precisely between two words, or between two letters?

This can be hard to do until you figure out the Magnifying Glass trick. What you do is this: Touch and hold your finger on the place where you want the cursor (see Figure 2–8). After a second or two, you will see the magnifying glass appear. Then, while you hold your finger on the screen, slide it around to position the cursor. When you let go, you will see the Copy/Paste pop-up menu, but you can ignore it.

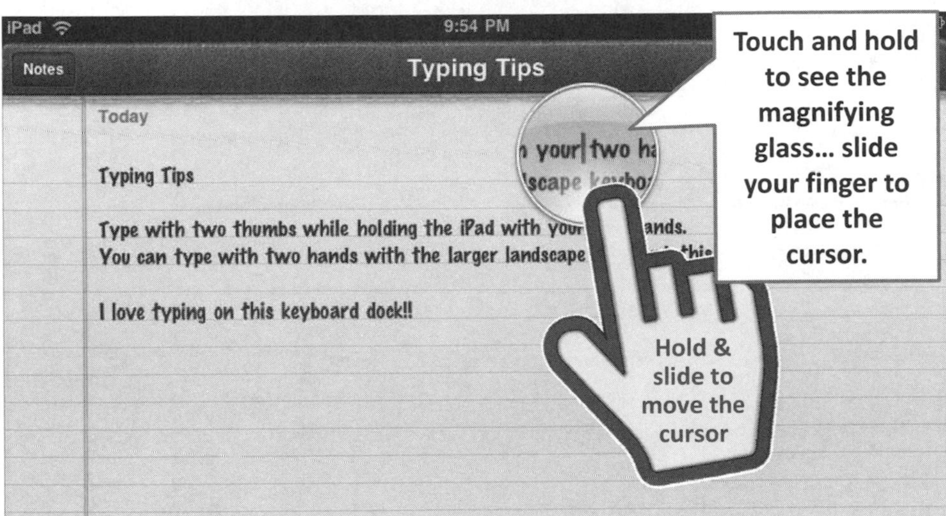


**Figure 2–8.** *Touch and hold the screen to see the magnifying glass and place the cursor.*

# Typing Numbers and Symbols

How do you type a number or a symbol using the on-screen keyboard on the iPad? When you are typing, tap the **.?123** key in the lower left corner to see numbers and common symbols such as $ ! ~ & = # . _ - +. If you need more symbols, from the number keyboard, tap the **#+=** key just above the **ABC** key in the lower left corner. See Figure 2–9.

> **TIP:** You even get an **Undo** key when you press the **.?123** key—a nice addition to any keyboard!

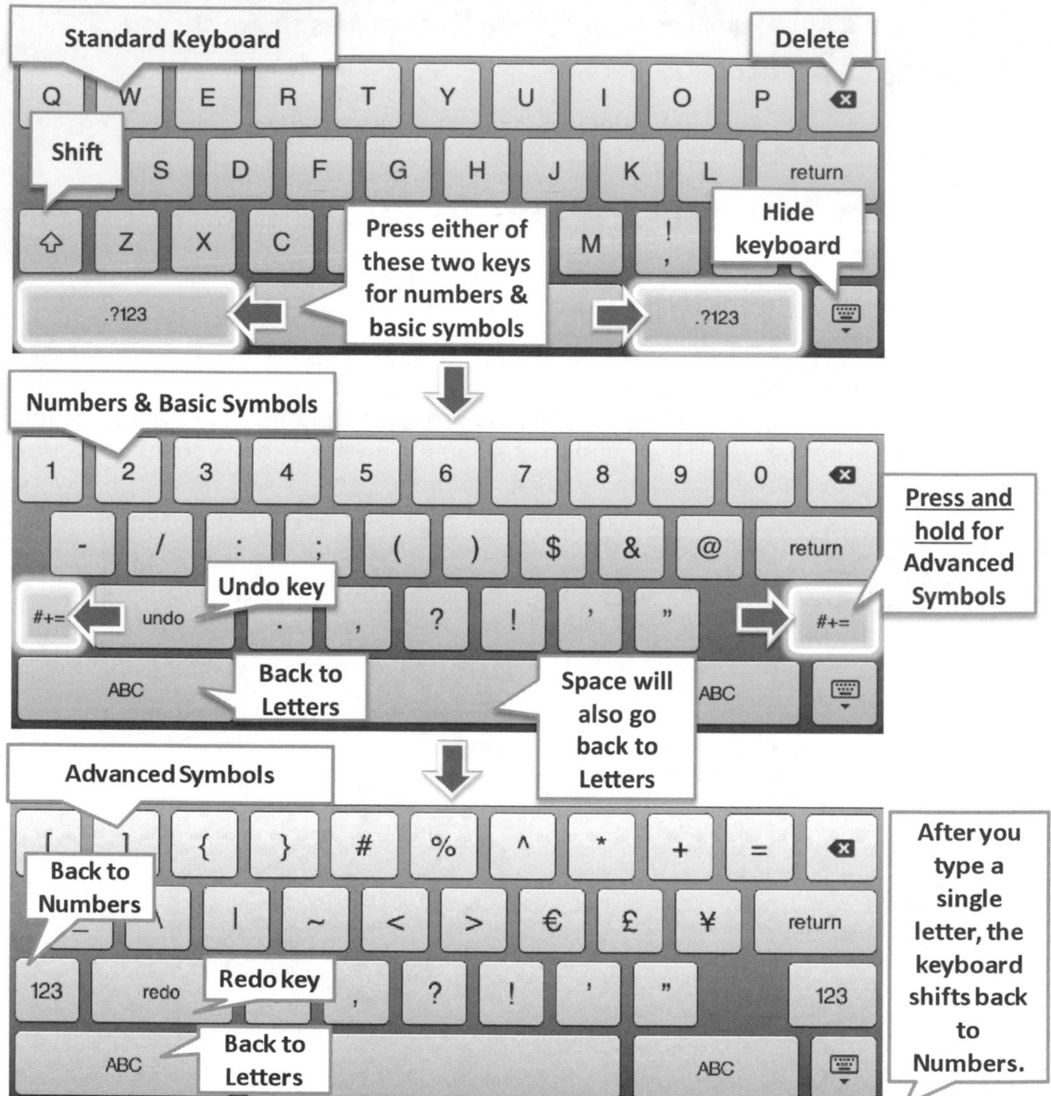


**Figure 2–9.** *Switching between Letters, Numbers, and Advanced Symbol keyboards.*

> **TIP:** Notice that the number and basic symbols keyboard will stay active until you either hit the **Space** key or tap the key for another keyboard, such as **ABC**.

# Touch and Slide Trick

*These tips are courtesy of Rene Ritchie from the iPhone/iPad Blog (*`www.tipb.com`*).*

## Typing Upper Case Letters

Normally to type uppercase letters, you would tap the **Shift** key then tap the letter.

The faster way to type single uppercase letters and symbols that require the **Shift** key is to touch the **Shift** key, keep your finger on the keyboard, , slide over to the key you want, and release.

For example, to type an uppercase "M," touch the right **Shift** key, then slide over to the "M" key and release.

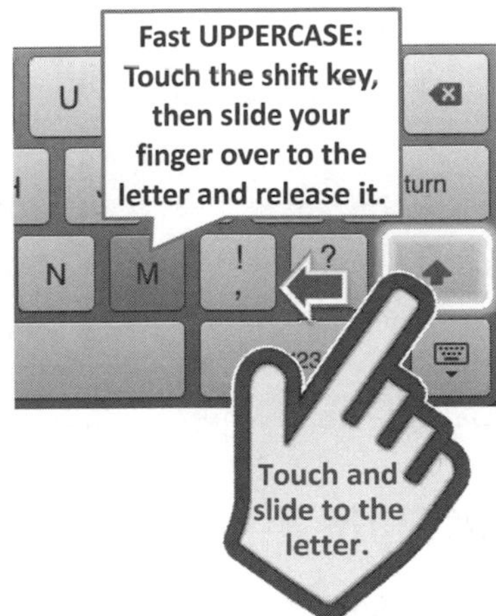
Fast UPPERCASE: Touch the shift key, then slide your finger over to the letter and release it.
U
N
M
!
?
turn
Touch and slide to the letter.

## Rapidly Typing a Single Number

If you have to type just a single number, then touch the **.?123** key and slide your finger up to the number. However, to type several numbers in a row, it's best to tap the **.?123** key, let go, and then tap each number.

## Typing Symbols that Require Shift

The same goes for the question mark and exclamation mark (which require you to press **Shift** on the Letter Keyboard.) Touch the **Shift** key then slide over and let go on the **?** key.

## Typing the Apostrophe

Press and hold the **Comma/Exclamation** key to see the apostrophe pop-up.

Since the apostrophe is highlighted in blue, simply let go of the key to type it.

> **TIP:** For most common contractions, your Auto-Correcting dictionary should automatically insert the apostrophe. For example, type "dont" then press the **Space** key to have the apostrophe inserted: "don't."

## Press and Hold Keyboard Shortcut for Typing Symbols and More

**What about symbols not shown on the keyboard?**

> **TIP:** You can type more symbols than are shown on the screen.

All you do is press and hold a letter, number, or symbol that is related to the symbol you want.

For example, if you wanted to type the EURO symbol (€), you would press and hold the **$** key until you saw the other options, slide up your finger to highlight, and then let go on the EURO symbol.

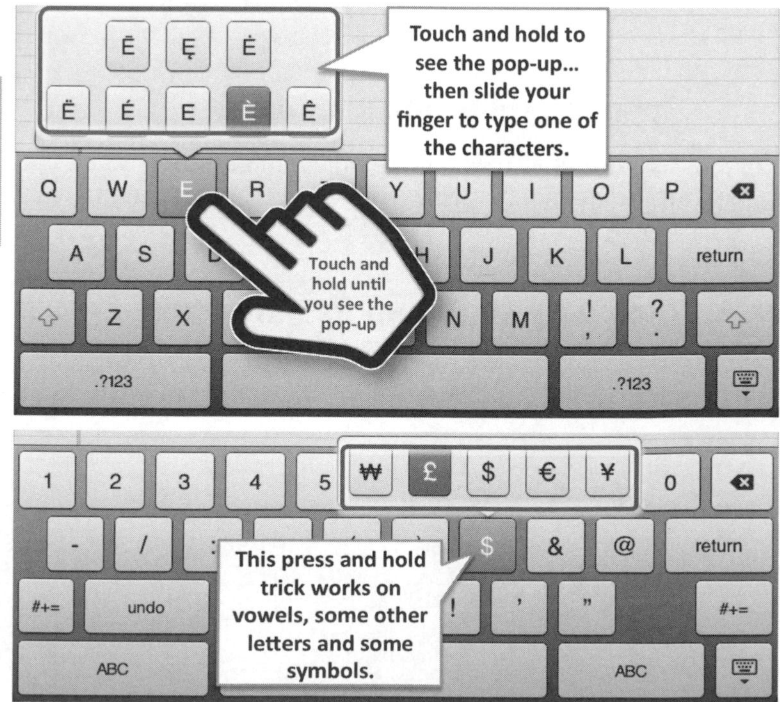

This tip also works with the **.com** key in the Safari web browser. You can get additional web site suffixes by pressing and holding this key.

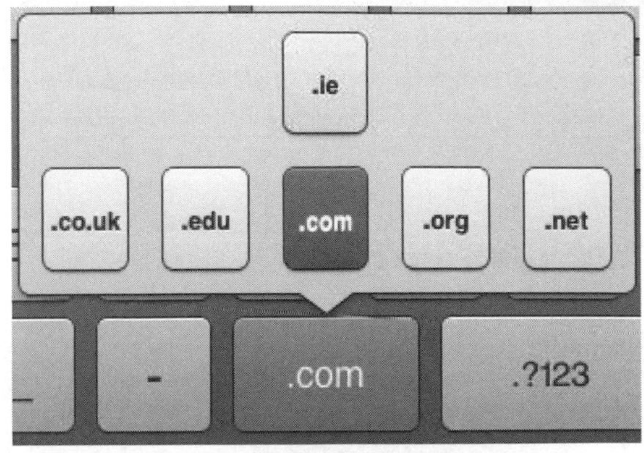


You see on the screen **.co.uk** plus **.ie,** which are not on the standard US keyboard. These are present because we have installed the English (UK) international keyboard. See earlier in this chapter for help with international keyboards.

**TIP:** There is a good bullet point character or the degree sign (depending on how you look at it) on the **Numbers** screen if you press and hold the **Zero** key (0). Also, press and hold the **?** and **!** keys to get their Spanish inverted cousins.

# Keyboard Options & Settings

There are a few Keyboard options to make typing on your iPad easier. The keyboard options are located in the **General** tab of your **Settings**.

1. Touch the **Settings** icon.
2. Touch **General** in the right column.
3. Touch **Keyboard** in the left column to see this screen.

## Auto-Correction ON / OFF

Using the built-in dictionary, **Auto-Correction** will automatically make changes in commonly misspelled words. For example, if you type in "wont," Auto-Correction will change it to "won't" on the fly. You need to make sure it is **ON** if you want this feature to work. (This is the default setting.)

**CAUTION:** As of publishing time, the Auto-Correction, Auto-Capitalization, and Double Space for Period shortcuts did not work with either the Wireless Keyboard or the Keyboard Dock. You just have to be more careful typing with the physical keyboard!

## Auto-Capitalization

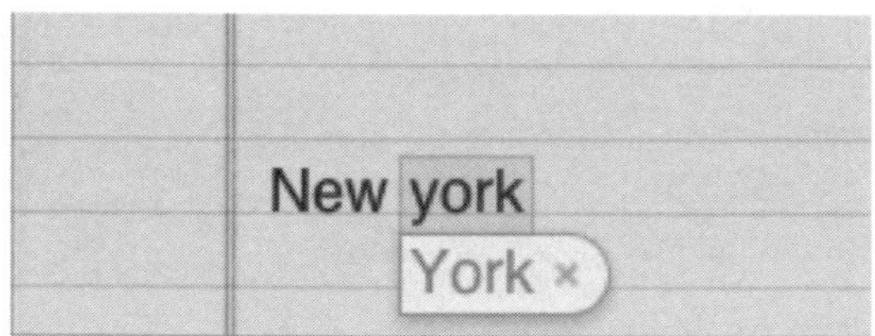


When you start a new sentence, words will automatically be capitalized if **Auto-Capitalization** is **ON**.

Also, common proper nouns will be correctly capitalized. For example, if you typed "New york," you would be prompted to change it to "New York"—again just pressing the **Space** key will select the correction. If you backspace over a capital letter, the iPad will assume the new letter you type should be capital as well.

This is also set to **ON** by default.

## Enable Caps Lock

Sometimes when you type, you may want to lock the caps by pressing and holding the **Cap** key—just like you do on a computer keyboard. Enabling **Caps Lock** will allow you to do this.

This is set to **OFF** by default.

## "." Shortcut

If you are an iPhone user or BlackBerry user, you might be familiar with the feature that will automatically put in a period at the end of the sentence when you double-tap the **Space** key. This is exactly the same feature that you can enable on the iPad. By default, this is also set to **ON**.

## Typing In Other Languages—International Keyboards

At publishing time, the iPad enables you to type in over a dozen different languages, including languages from Dutch to Spanish. Some of the Asian languages, such as Japanese and Chinese, offer two or three keyboards for different typing methods.

To enable various language keyboards, follow these steps:

1. Touch the **Settings** icon (refer to Figure 2–10).
2. Tap **General** in the left column.
3. Tap **Keyboard** near the bottom of the right column.
4. Tap **International Keyboards**.
5. Tap **Add New Keyboard** to add additional international keyboards.
6. Tap any keyboard/language listed to add that keyboard.
7. Now you will see the Keyboard listed on the available keyboards.
8. To adjust keyboard options, tap the listed Keyboard.
9. Tap **Edit** in the top right corner to change the keyboard order or delete a keyboard. To change the order, drag the left edge of the listed keyboard up or down. To delete a keyboard, tap the **red minus sign**, then tap **Delete**.

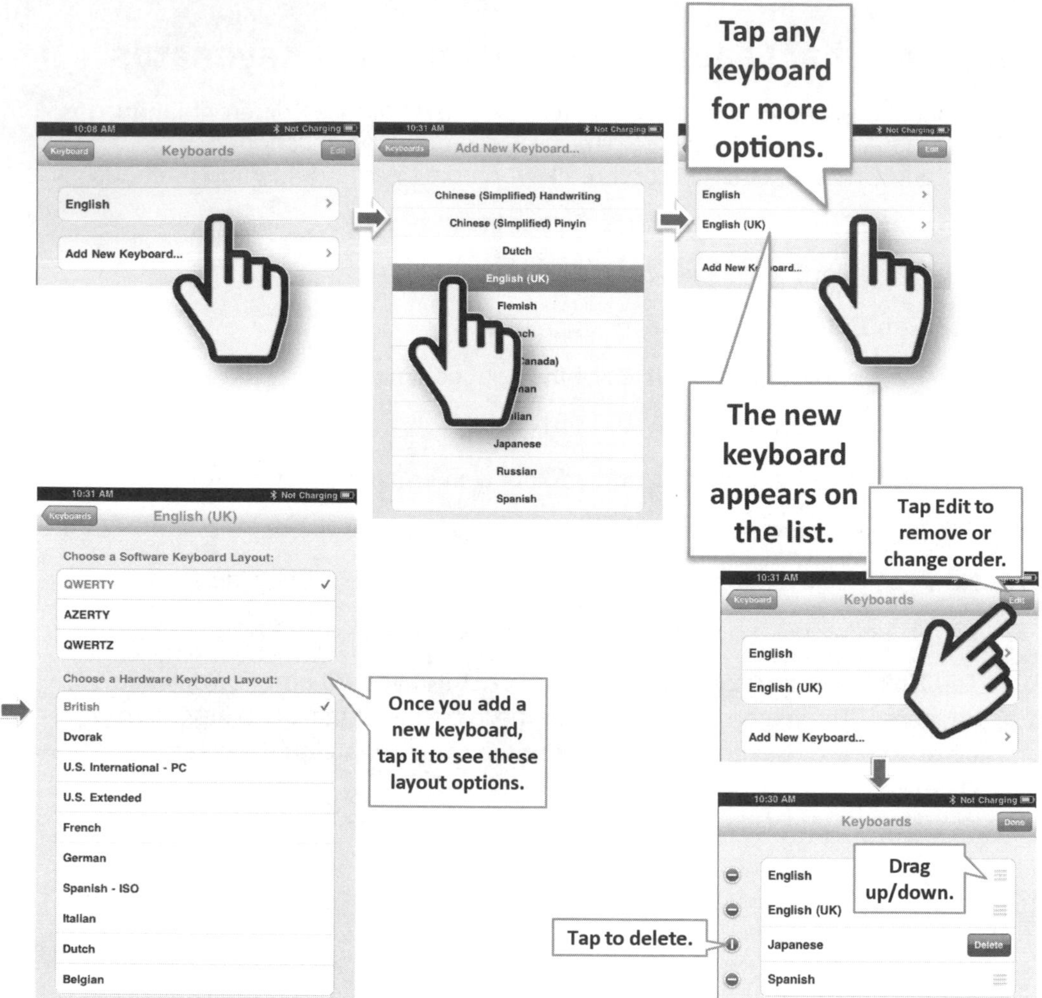


**Figure 2–10.** *Adding and customizing international keyboards.*

Once you have enabled a number of keyboards, tap the **Globe** key to cycle between all the languages (see Figure 2–11).

Japanese and some other languages provide several keyboard options to meet your typing preferences.

In some of the languages (such as Japanese, shown in Figure 2–11), you will see the letters typed change into characters. You will also see a row of other character combinations above the keyboard. When you see the combination you want, tap it.

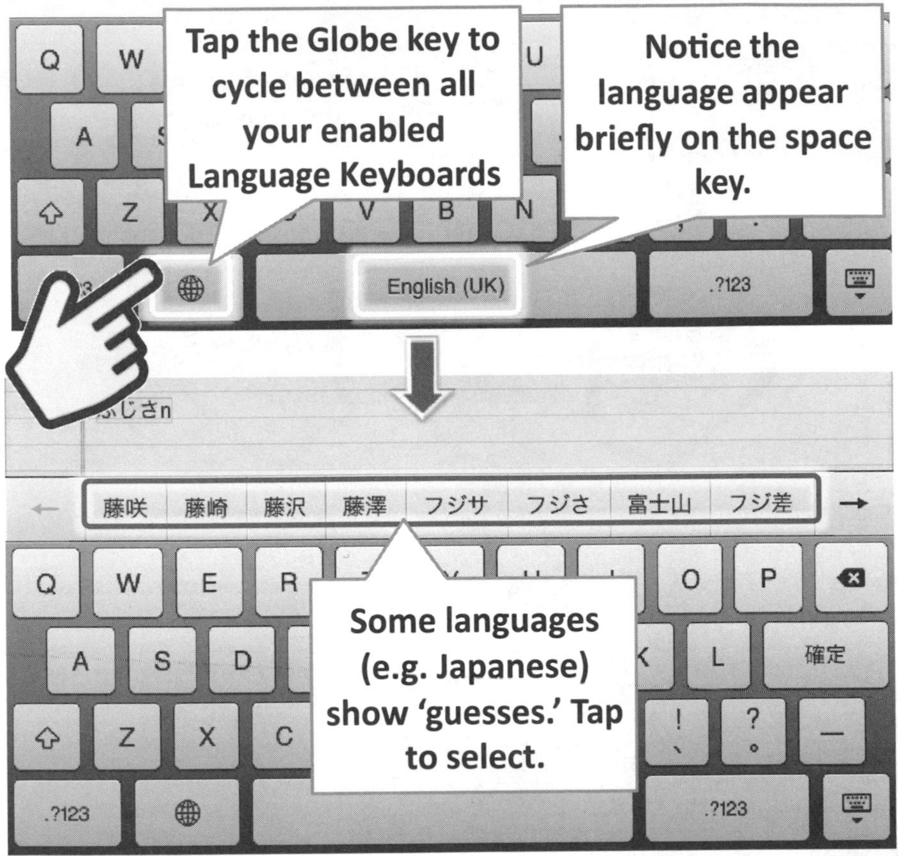


**Figure 2–11.** *Press the **Globe** key to cycle between International Keyboards.*

# Copy and Paste

Copy and Paste is very useful for taking text from your calendar and putting it in an e-mail or taking a note and placing it in an e-mail or in your Calendar—there are lots of ways to use for Copy and Paste. You can even copy text from your Safari web browser and paste it into a Note or a Mail message.

## Selecting Text with Double-Tap

If you are reading or typing text, you can double-tap to start selecting text for the copy. This works well in Mail, Messages, and Notes.

You will see a box with blue dots (handles) at opposite corners. Just drag the handles to select the text you wish to highlight and copy, as shown in Figure 2–12.

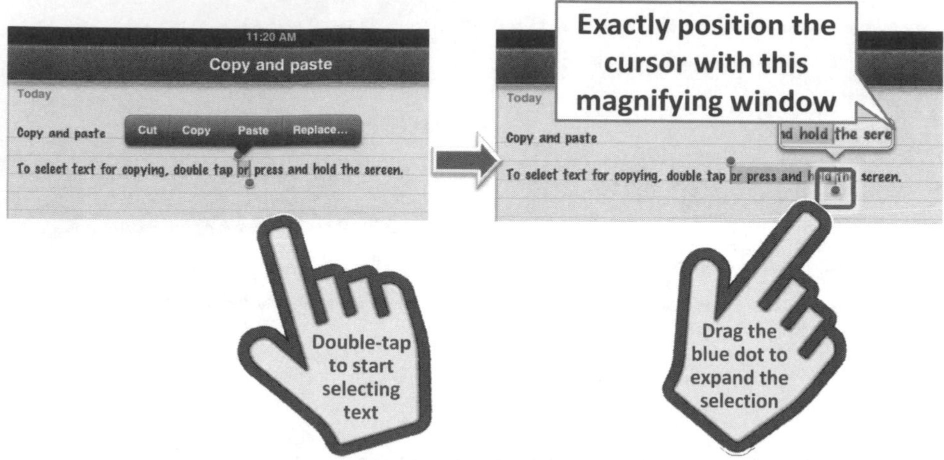


**Figure 2–12.** *Double-tap to start selecting text, then drag the blue dots to expand the selection.*

**TIP:** If you want to select all the text, double-tap the screen above or below the text. Then you should see a pop-up showing you Select or Select All. Tap **Select** to select a word. Tap **Select All** to highlight all the text.

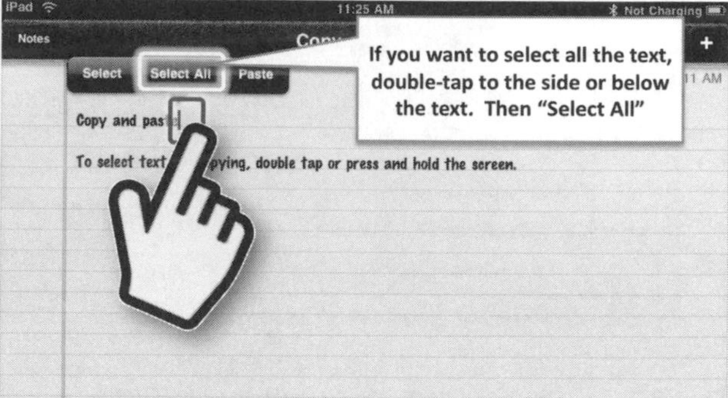


## Selecting Text with Two Finger Touch

The other way to select text requires that you touch the screen simultaneously with two fingers. This seems to work best if you are holding your iPad with one hand and use your thumb and forefinger from your other hand to touch the screen. What you want to do is touch the screen at the beginning and end of the text you want to select. Don’t worry if you cannot get the selection exactly on the first touch. After the first touch, use the blue handles to drag the beginning and end of the selection to the correct position, as shown in Figure 2–13.

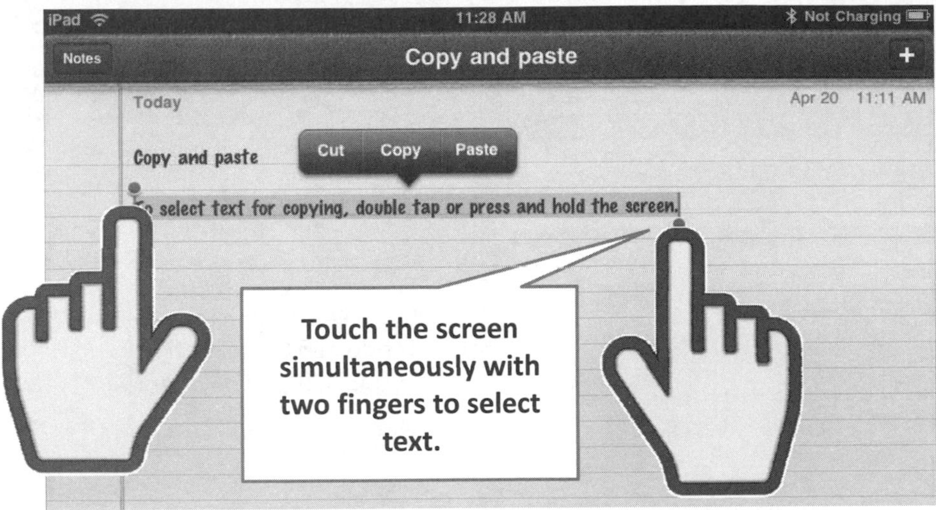


**Figure 2–13.** *Select text by touching the screen at the same time with two fingers.*

## Selecting Web Site or Other Non-Editable Text with Touch and Hold

In the Safari web browser and other places where you cannot edit the text, hold your finger on some text and the paragraph will become highlighted with handles at each of the corners.

Drag the handles if you want to select even more text.

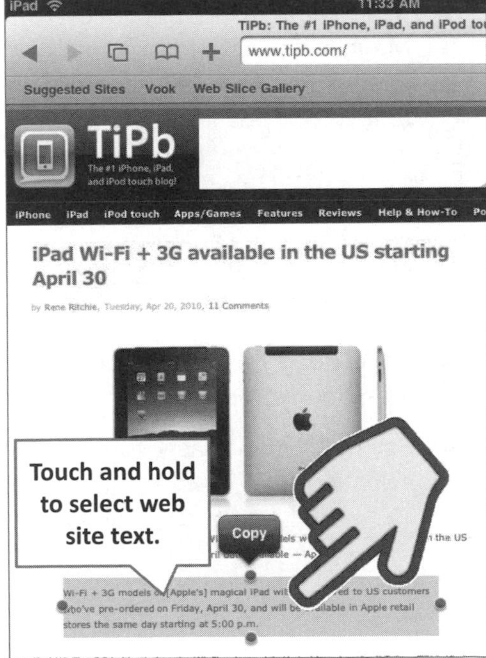


> **NOTE:** If you drag smaller than a paragraph, the selector will switch to fine-text mode and give you the blue handles on both ends of the selection to pick just the characters or words you want. If you drag your finger beyond a paragraph, you get the gross-text selector with which you can drag up or down to select whole reams of text and graphics.

## Cut or Copy the Text

Once you have the text that you wish to copy highlighted, just touch the **Copy** tab at the top of the screen. The tab will turn blue, indicating that the text is on the clipboard.

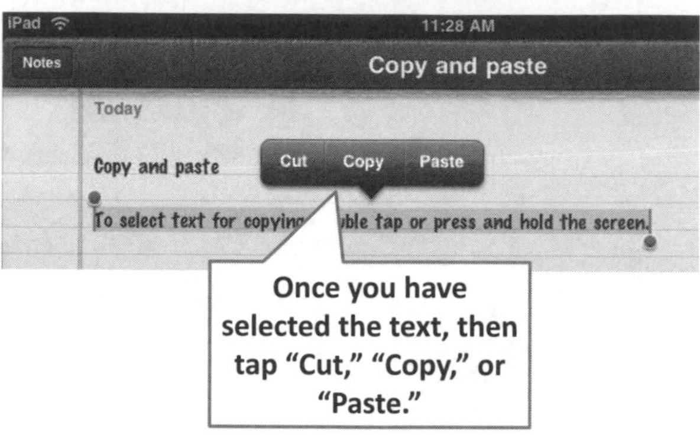


**NOTE:** If you have previously Cut or Copied text, then you will also see the Paste option, as shown.

## To Paste the Text

If you are pasting the text into the same Note or Mail message:

1. Use your finger to move the cursor to where you want to paste the text. Remember the Magnifying Glass trick (as we showed earlier in this chapter) to help you position the cursor.
2. Once you let go of the screen, you should see a pop-up asking you to **Select**, **Select All**, or **Paste**.
3. If you don't see this pop-up, then double-tap the screen.
4. Select **Paste** to paste your selection.

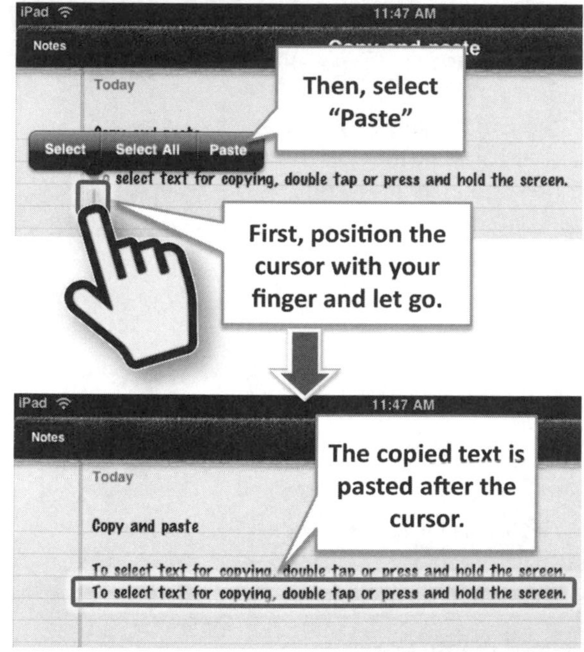

## To Paste Text or an Image Into Another Icon

To paste the text or image you have copied into another icon:

1. Press the **Home** button (refer to Figure 2–14 ).
2. Tap the icon into which you want to paste the text. In this case, lets tap **Mail**.
3. Tap the **Compose** icon to write a new e-mail.
4. Double-tap anywhere in the body of the message.
5. Tap **Paste**.

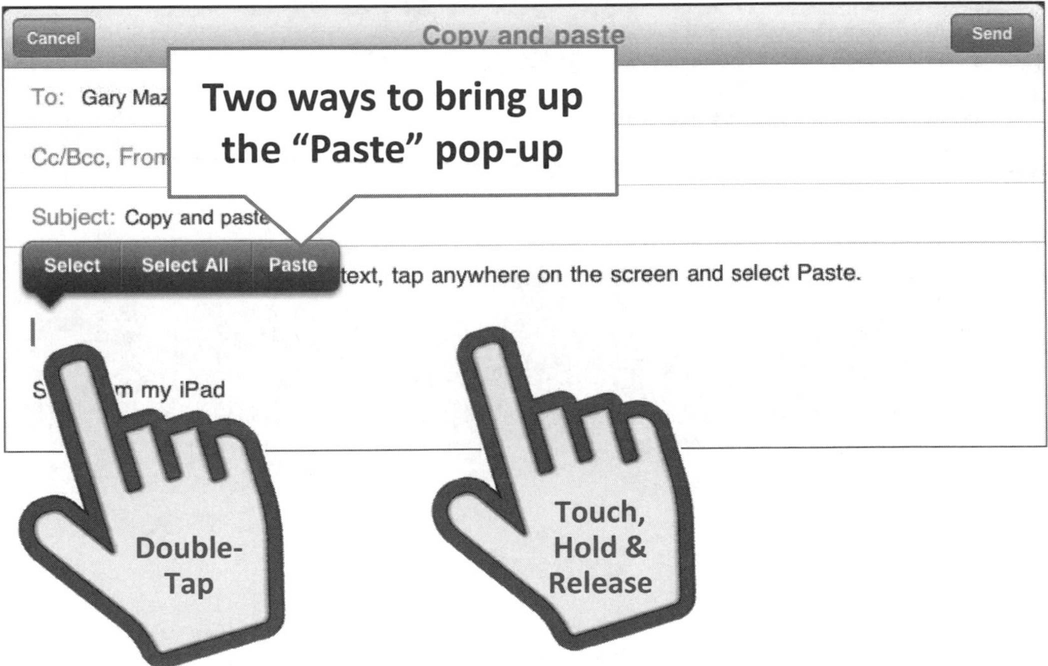


**Figure 2–14.** *Bring up the Paste command by either double-tapping or pressing, holding, and releasing.*

Move the cursor to the body of the text and either double-tap or touch, hold, and release your finger and you will see the Paste pop-up. Tap **Paste** and the text on the clipboard will be pasted right into the body of the e-mail.

## Shake to Undo Paste or Typing

One of the great new features in Copy and Paste is the ability to undo either typing or the Paste you just completed.

All you have to do is shake the iPad after the paste. A new pop-up appears giving you the option to undo what you have just done.

Tap **Undo Paste** and or **Undo Typing** to correct the mistake.

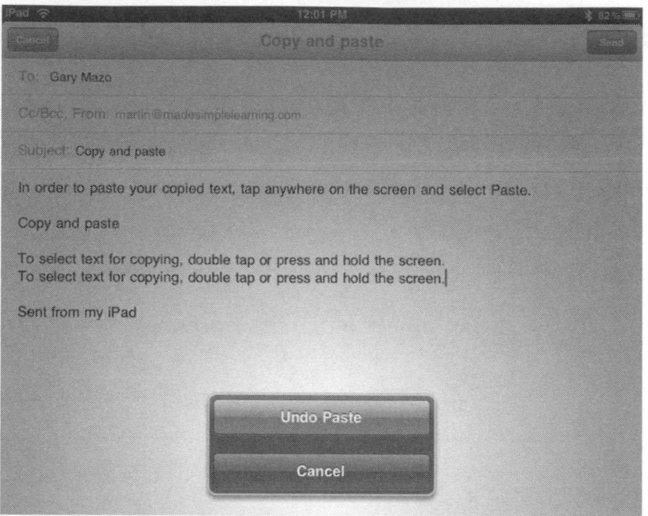


> **TIP:** There is an **Undo** button on the keyboard as well. Just press the **.?123** key and it is in the lower left corner.

> **TIP:** Delete Text by Selecting then Press Backspace
>
> If you ever want to delete a number of lines of text, a paragraph, or even all the text you just typed quickly with one or two taps, this tip is for you. Use the techniques above to select the text you want to delete. Then, simply press the **Delete** key in the lower left corner of the keyboard to delete all the selected text.

# Finding Things with Spotlight Search

A great feature on your iPad to find information is the **Spotlight Search**—Apple's proprietary search method for a global search through your iPad for a name, event, or subject.

The concept is simple; let's say you are looking for something related to Martin. You cannot remember if it was an e-mail, a Note, or a Calendar event, but you do know it was related to Martin.

This is the perfect time to use the **Spotlight Search** feature to find everything related to Martin on your iPad.

## Activating Spotlight Search

First, you need to get into the **Spotlight Search**, which resides to the left of the first page of the **Home** screen.

On the left side of the first circle (indicating the first page of your **Home** screen) is a very small magnifying glass.

Swipe to the right of this first page of icons to get to the **Spotlight Search** page.

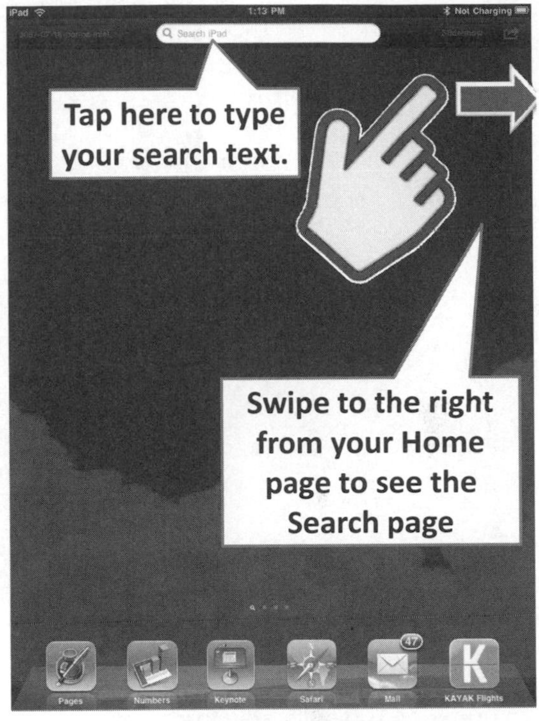
Tap here to type your search text.
Swipe to the right from your Home page to see the Search page
Pages
Numbers
Keynote
Safari
Mail
KAYAK Flights

> **TIP:** If you like to use Search a lot, then you can set it so that a double-click of your **Home** button will bring up Search. Start your **Settings** icon, tap **General** in the left column, then tap **Home** in the right column. Select Search under **Double-click the Home Button for:**

On the **Search** page, type in one or a few words for your search.

> **TIP:** If you are looking for a person, type their full name to more accurately find items from only that person (e.g., "Martin Trautschold"). This will eliminate any other Martins who might be in your iPad and make sure you find items only related to Martin Trautschold.

In the search result, you'll see all e-mails, appointments, meeting invitations, and contact information found. Tap one of the results in the list to view its contents.

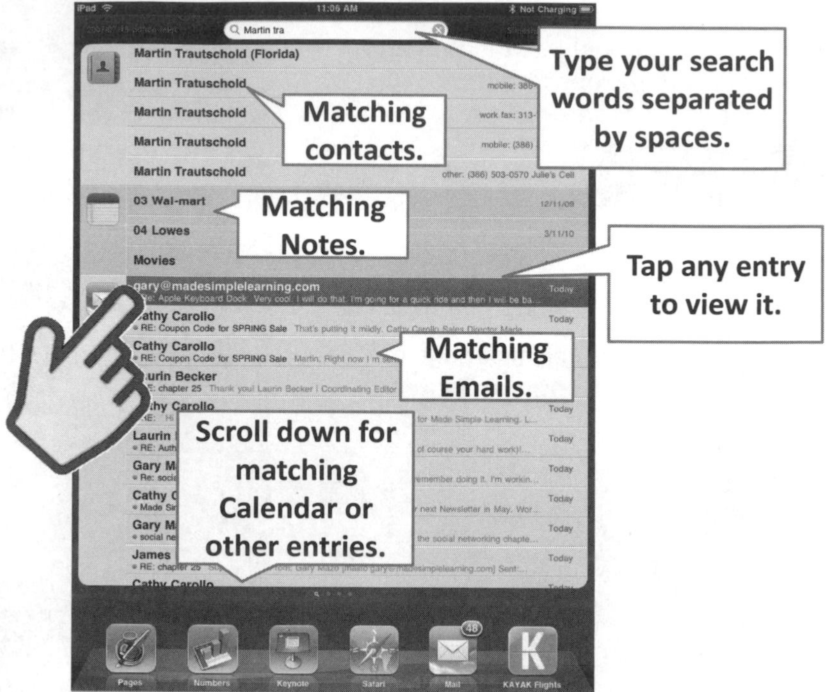


Your search results stay there until you clear them, so you can go back to **Spotlight Search** once again by swiping to the right from your **Home** screen.

To clear the search field, just touch the **X** in the search bar. To exit **Spotlight Search**, just press the **Home** key or swipe to the left.

Chapter 3

# Sync Your iPad with iTunes

In this chapter we will show you the steps to get set up to synchronize information between your iPad and your Windows or Mac computer. Besides syncing, iTunes can do so much more like organize your music, create playlists, buy songs, videos, and has Home Sharing and Genius features. To learn about these features, please check out Chapter 26, "Bonus iTunes User Guide."

Also in this chapter we will show you what to consider before you sync, how to setup the automatic sync of your personal information, and how to manually transfer information. With iTunes you can sync or transfer contacts, calendar, notes, apps, music, videos, documents, and picture libraries. iTunes also has the added benefit that it automatically will backup your iPad whenever you connect it to your computer. We even show you a few simple troubleshooting tips if things are not working quite right. Finally, we show you how to check for updates and install updated operating system software for your iPad.

> **TIP:** If you are new to iTunes, we strongly recommend you check out Chapter 26, "Bonus iTunes User Guide," to help you get the most out of iTunes.

## Before You Set Up Your iTunes Sync

There are a few things you need before you can start syncing using iTunes. We cover the prerequisites and answer a few common questions about the reasons to use iTunes. We also help you understand what happens if you own another Apple device, such as an iPhone or iPod, and start syncing with your iPad.

## Prerequisites Before You Sync

There are just a few things you need before you start syncing your iPad with iTunes.

1. Make sure you have version 9.1 or higher of iTunes installed on your computer. For how to install or update iTunes, see Chapter 26 "Bonus iTunes User Guide."
2. Create an iTunes account (Apple ID); see the "Create iTunes Account" section in Chapter 26, "iTunes Guide."
3. Get the white sync cable that came with your iPad. One end plugs into the bottom of your iPad near the **Home** button and the other plugs into the USB port on your computer.

## Can I Sync iTunes with Another iPhone, iPod touch, or iPod and My iPad?

**Yes!** As long as you are syncing to the same computer, you can sync many Apple devices (Apple says up to five, but we have heard of people syncing more) to the same iTunes account on a single computer.

> **CAUTION:** You cannot sync the same iPad, iPhone, or iPod to two different computers. When you attempt to do this, you will see a message similar to this: "Would you like to wipe this device (iPad, iPhone, iPod) and re-sync the new library?" If you say Yes, then all the music and videos on the device will be erased.

## There Are Other Sync Options (MobileMe and Exchange/Google)—Should I Use iTunes?

There are other ways to synchronize your personal information and e-mail, such as Exchange/Google and MobileMe, which we cover in Chapter 24: "Other Sync Methods." Keep in mind, however, that even if you choose to go with these other ways to sync, you will still need to use iTunes to

- Backup and restore your iPad
- Update the iPad operating system software
- Sync and manage your applications, also known as "apps"
- Sync your music library and playlists
- Sync movies, TV shows, podcasts, and iTunes U content

- Sync books
- Sync photos

## Considering Other Sync Options

Here we summarize your other synchronization options. What you choose to use for synchronization should be driven by where you currently store your e-mail, contacts, and calendar—your "Environment."

> **NOTE:** As you can see below, with some environments, you can wirelessly sync your contacts and calendars to your iPad.

**Table 3–1.** *Synchronization Options for Your Personal Information*

| Your Environment | Wireless Sync Using | Desktop Sync Using | Notes |
|---|---|---|---|
| Google for E-mail, Calendar, and Contacts | **Settings ➤ Mail,Contacts,Calendar ➤ Add Account ➤ Microsoft Exchange** | iTunes | This is free. |
| Google for E-mail (Do not want wireless sync with Google for Contacts and Calendar) | **Settings ➤ Mail,Contacts,Calendar ➤ Add Account ➤ Gmail** | iTunes required to sync Google Contacts and Calendar | This is free. |
| E-mail, Calendar and Contacts on Microsoft Exchange Server | **Settings ➤ Mail,Contacts,Calendar ➤ Add Account ➤ Microsoft Exchange** | iTunes | This is free. |
| E-mail, Calendar and Contacts in Yahoo! | E-mail only: **Settings ➤ Mail,Contacts,Calendar ➤ Add Account ➤ Yahoo!** | iTunes required to sync Yahoo! Contacts and Calendar | This is free. |
| E-mail, Calendar, and Contacts on various platforms. You are subscribed to MobileMe service. | **Settings ➤ Mail,Contacts,Calendar ➤ Add Account ➤ MobileMe** | MobileMe | This is free for 60 days, then US$99 for one user, US$149 for a family plan. ** *Pricing is valid as of publication time.* |

| Your Environment | Wireless Sync Using | Desktop Sync Using | Notes |
|---|---|---|---|
| E-mail, Calendar, and Contacts in AOL | E-mail only: **Settings ➤ Mail,Contacts,Calendar ➤ Add Account ➤ AOL** | iTunes required to sync AOL Contacts and Calendar | This is free. |
| LDAP (Lightweight Directory Access Protocol) Contacts | **Settings ➤ Mail,Contacts,Calendar ➤ Add Account ➤ Other ➤ Add LDAP Account** | Not available. | This is free. |
| CalDAV Calendar Account | **Settings ➤ Mail,Contacts,Calendar ➤ Add Account ➤ Other ➤ Add CalDAV Account** | Not available. | This is free. Must have access to CalDAV account in this format cal.server.com with a username and password. |
| Subscribed Calendar at your work | **Settings ➤ Mail,Contacts,Calendar ➤ Add Account ➤ Other ➤ Add Subscribed Calendar** | Not available. | This is free. Must have access to a subscribed calendar (web address, username and password). Access to server is in this format: myserver.com/cal.ics |

# Setup Your iTunes Sync

Now that you have thought about all the other options, you are ready to get started with setting up your iTunes sync. We show you all the steps to perform both automated syncs and manual transfers of information to your iPad using iTunes.

## The iPad Summary Screen (Manually Manage Music, Update, Restore, and More)

Once you connect your iPad to your computer, you can see important information, like your iPad's memory capacity in GB, installed software version, and serial number. You can also check for updates to the software version or restore data to your iPad. There are also several options that are available on this screen.

**iTunes Navigation Basics:**

Get a feel for the left nav bar. Click on various items in this left nav bar and notice that the main display window changes (see Figure 3–1).

The top nav bar inside the main window also changes based on what you have selected in the left nav bar.

For example, when you click on your iPad in the left nav bar, you will see tabs across the top of the main window that show information related to your device.

When you click on the iTunes store in the left nav bar, then you see tabs related to the store in the main window.

To see this screen:

1. Start up iTunes software on your computer.
2. Connect your iPad to your computer with the white USB cable supplied with the device. Plug one end into the bottom of the iPad near the **Home** button and plug the other end into a USB port on your computer.
3. If you have successfully connected your iPad, you should see your iPad listed under **DEVICES** in the left nav bar.
4. Click on your iPad in the left nav bar, then click on the **Summary** tab on the left edge of the main window (see Figure 3–1).
5. If you want to be able to drag-and-drop music and videos onto your iPad, you need to check the box next to "Manually manage music and videos."

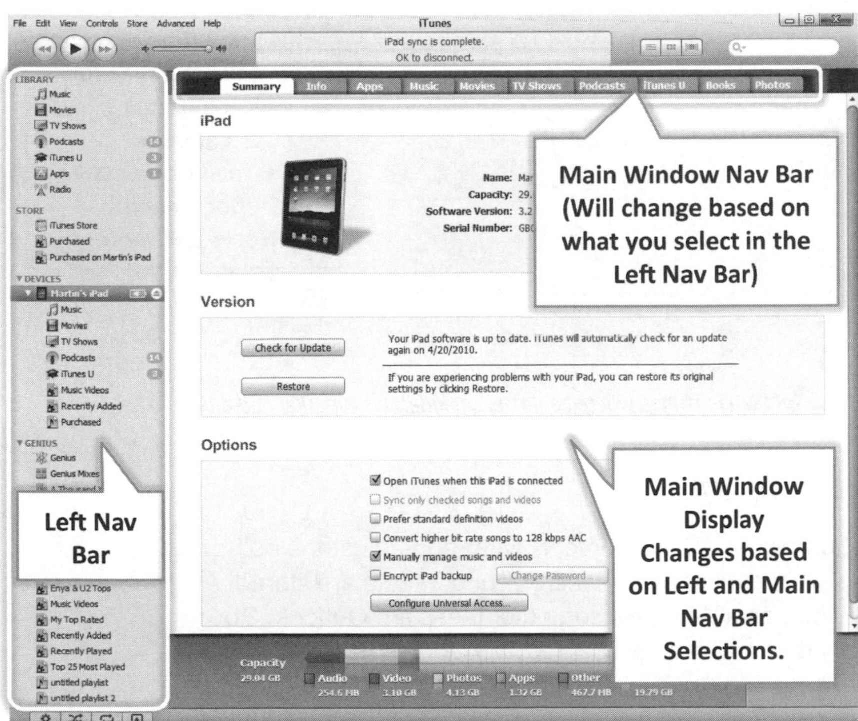


**Figure 3–1.** *The iPad summary screen in iTunes*

## Getting to the Sync Setup Screen (Info Tab)

To begin the setup of your contacts, calendar, e-mail and other syncs, follow these steps.

1. Start up iTunes software on your computer.
2. Connect your iPad to your computer with the white USB cable supplied with the device. Plug one end into the bottom of the iPad near the **Home** button and plug the other end into a USB port on your computer.
3. If you have successfully connected your iPad, you should see your iPad listed under **DEVICES** in the left nav bar.
4. Click the **Info** tab at the top to see the contacts (and other sync settings) in the main iTunes window, as shown in Figure 3–2.

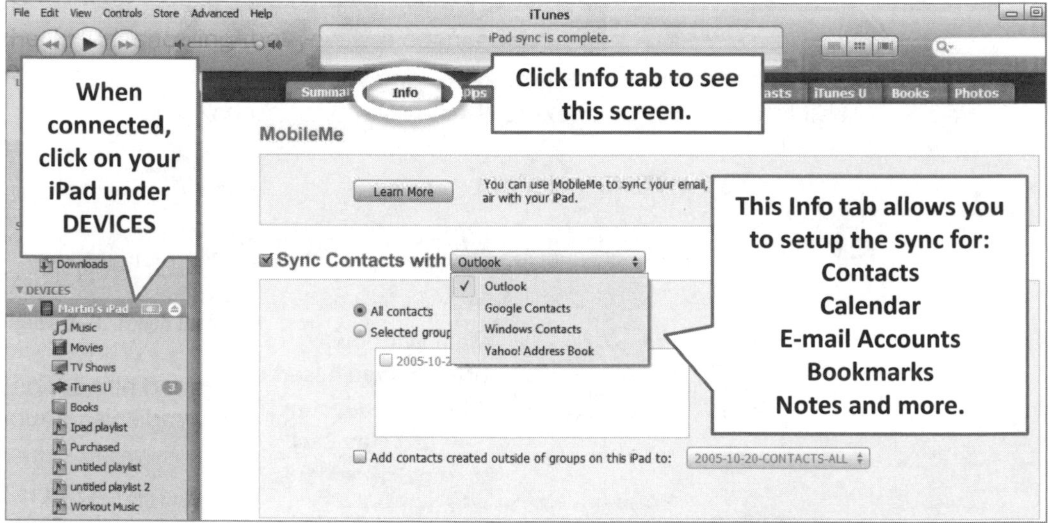


**Figure 3–2.** *Getting to the **Info** tab in iTunes where contacts, calendar, bookmarks, and more are set up*

## Contacts Sync Setup

1. Check the box next to "Sync Contacts with" and adjust the pull-down menu to the software or service where your contacts are stored. At publication time, on a Windows computer these are Outlook, Google Contacts, Windows Contacts, and Yahoo! Address Book. See Figure 3–3.

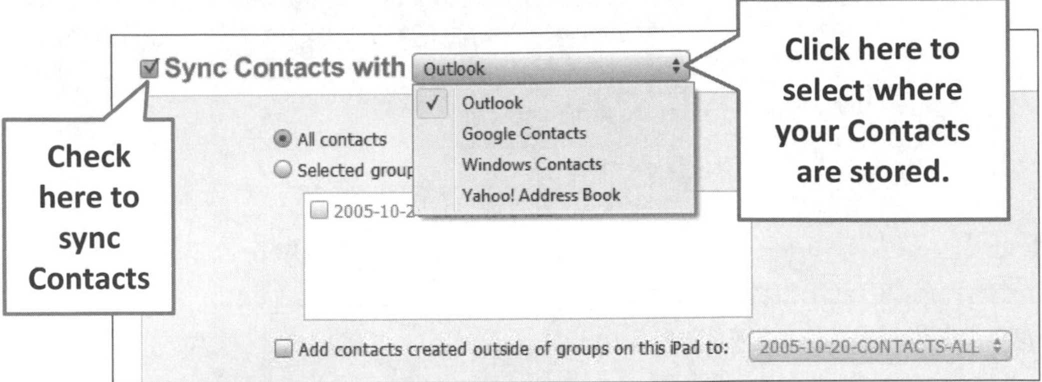


**Figure 3–3.** *Selecting software for syncing contacts (Windows)*

**CAUTION:** Whenever you switch between software or services in these sync settings screens (called the **Sync Provider**), they will affect every one of the mobile devices connected to your iTunes account. For example, if you sync contacts to your iPhone or iPod touch, these changes will also affect MobileMe. You will be changing the way contacts sync for any other devices connected to your iTunes account.

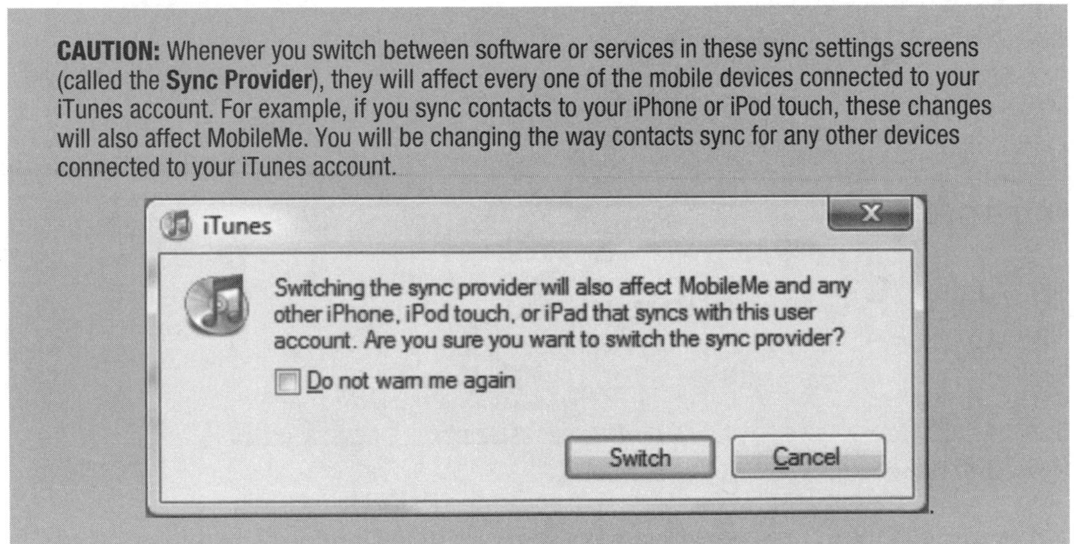


### Google Contacts Sync:

If you select Google Contacts, then you will be prompted to enter your Google ID and password, as shown in Figure 3–4.

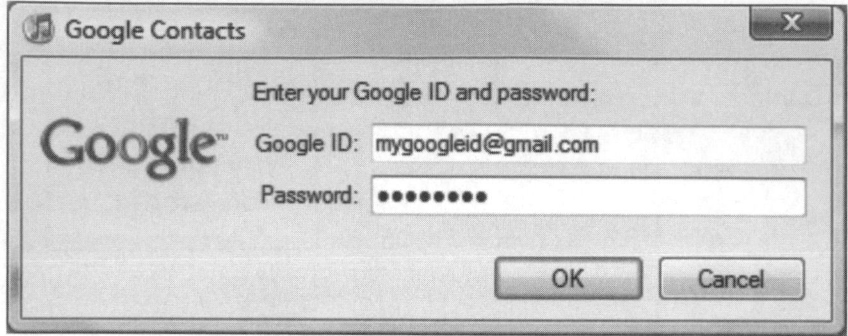


**Figure 3–4.** *Google Contacts sync login screen*

To change your Google ID or password, click the **Configure** button next to the "Sync Contacts with" at the top of this section.

**Yahoo! Address Book Sync:**

If you select Yahoo! Contacts, then you will be prompted to enter your Yahoo! ID and password, as shown in Figure 3–5.

**Figure 3–5.** *Yahoo! Address Book sync login screen*

To change your Yahoo! ID or password, click the **Configure** button next to the "Sync Contacts with" at the top of this section.

> **NOTE:** The options you see in this and other drop-down boxes in this **Info** tab will vary slightly depending on what software you have installed on your computer. For example, on a Mac, the contacts sync does not have a drop-down list; instead the other services, such as Google Contacts and Yahoo!, are shown as separate checkboxes (see Figure 3–6).

2. Select either of these options (Figure 3–6):

   a. **All Contacts** to sync all contacts in your address book (this is the default).

b. **Selected Groups** to sync contacts only within specific groups that you check off in the window below.

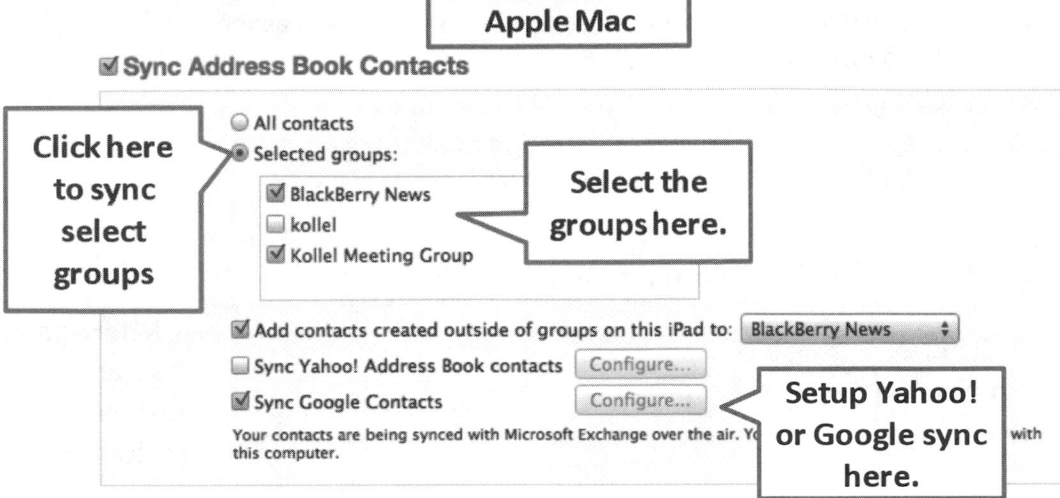


**Figure 3–6.** *Contacts sync groups setup (Apple Mac)*

**NOTE:** These contact groups cannot be created here—they must be created in the software application or service where your contacts are stored (e.g., Outlook, Google, Yahoo!, Entourage, etc.).

3. The last checkbox in Figure 3–6 allows you to specify a new group for any new contacts you add on your iPad that you do not explicitly assign to a group on the iPad.

4. To continue setting up your calendar, e-mail, and more, scroll down the page.

5. If you do not want to set anything else up for sync, then click the **Apply** button in the lower-right corner of the iTunes screen to start the sync.

**NOTE:** Depending on how many contacts you have to sync, the initial sync could take longer than 10 minutes, and may even require 30+ minutes. So you may want to plan to do this sync when you can let your iPad sit for 30 or more minutes (during lunch, after dinner, etc.).

## Calendar Sync Setup

1. Scroll down to see the calendar sync in the same **Info** tab as the contacts sync, as shown in Figure 3–7.
2. Check the box next to "Sync Calendars with" and adjust the pull-down menu to the software or service where your calendars are stored. This might be Outlook or something else on a Windows computer, and iCal on a Mac.

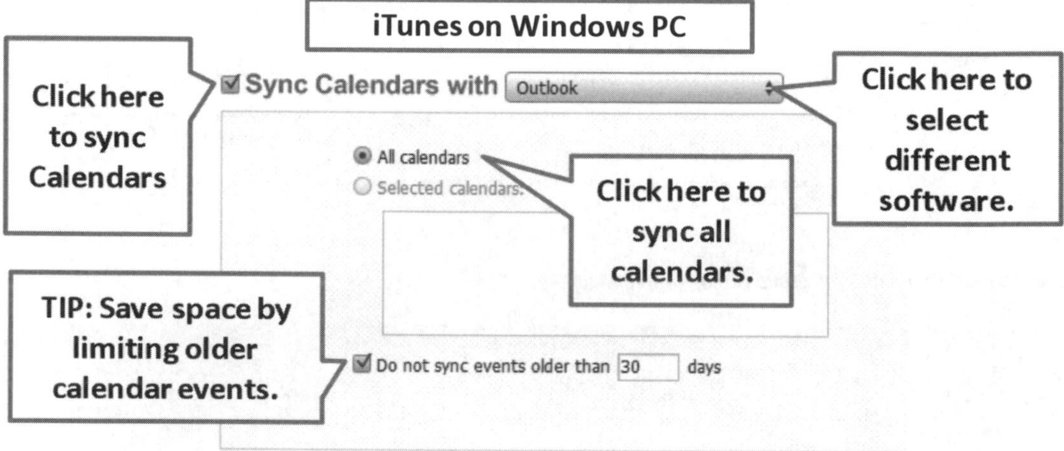


**Figure 3–7.** *Calendar sync setup (Windows PC)*

3. Select either of these options (Figure 3–8):
   a. **All Calendars** to sync all calendars (this is the default).
   b. **Selected Calendars** to sync only calendars that you have checked off in the window below.

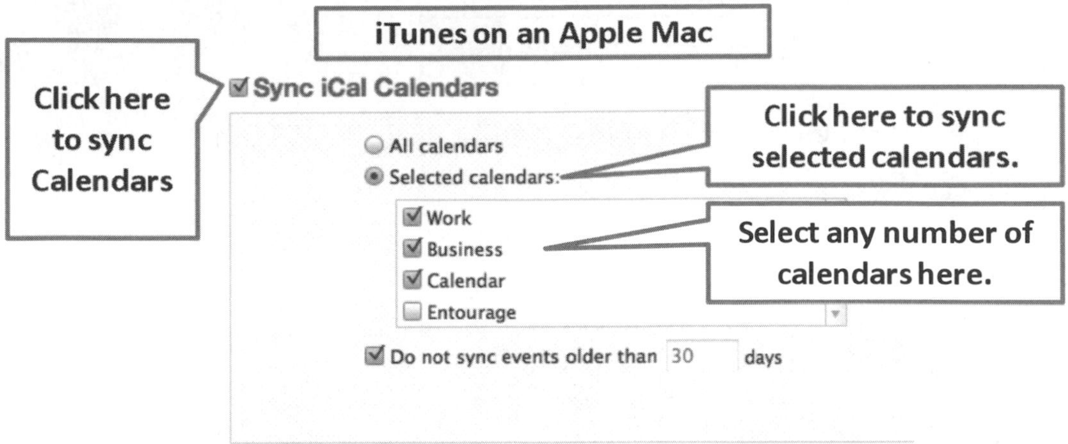


**Figure 3–8.** *Calendar sync setup (Apple Mac)*

4. If you want to save space and avoid clutter on your iPad, click the check box next to "Do not sync events older than 30 days." You can adjust the days up or down to fit your needs.
5. To continue setting up e-mail accounts, bookmarks and more, scroll down the page.
6. If you do not want to set anything else up for sync, then click the **Apply** button in the lower-right corner of the iTunes screen to start the sync.

> **NOTE:** For Mac users who use Microsoft Entourage, you will need to enable Entourage to sync with iCal. You do this by going into the **Preferences** settings in Entourage and then going to **Sync Services**, checking off the boxes for synchronizing with iCal and Address book (Figure 3–9).

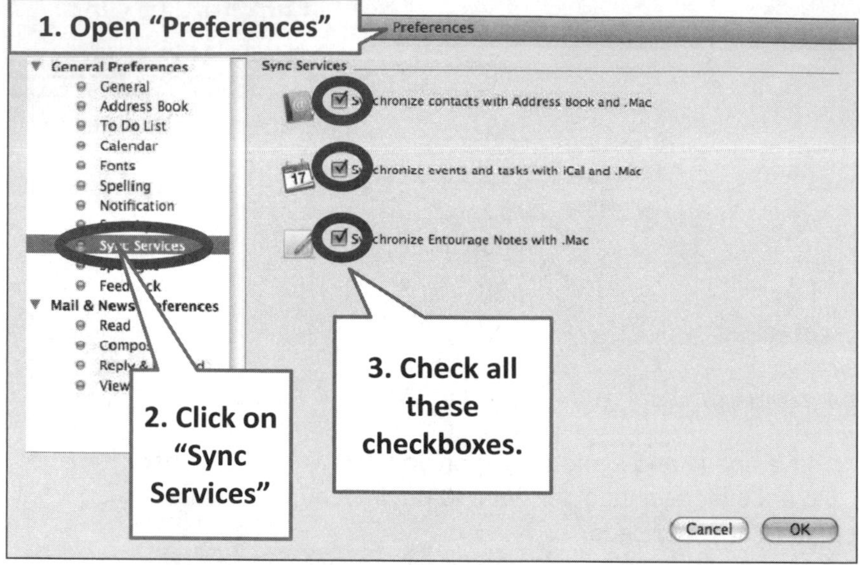


**Figure 3–9.** *Microsoft Entourage settings (Apple Mac)*

**NOTE:** As of the writing of this book, Entourage, unlike iCal, cannot handle multiple calendars.

## Sync E-mail Account Settings

It is important to keep in mind that the **Sync Mail Accounts** should really be called **Sync Mail Account Settings (without your password and or mail)**. What this means is that only the e-mail account settings are transferred to your iPad during the sync. It helps you by not having to type all the settings on the iPad itself.

**NOTE:** After syncing the e-mail account settings to your iPad, you will still have to enter your password for each e-mail account in the **Settings** icon > **Mail, Contacts, Calendars** for each e-mail account. You have to do this only one time on your iPad for each account.

1. Scroll down below the Calendar settings on the same **Info** tab in iTunes to see the Mail account settings.

2. Check the box next to "Sync Mail Accounts from" and adjust the pull-down menu to the software or service where your e-mail is stored (Figure 3–10). This might be Outlook on a Windows computer, or Entourage or iCal on a Mac.

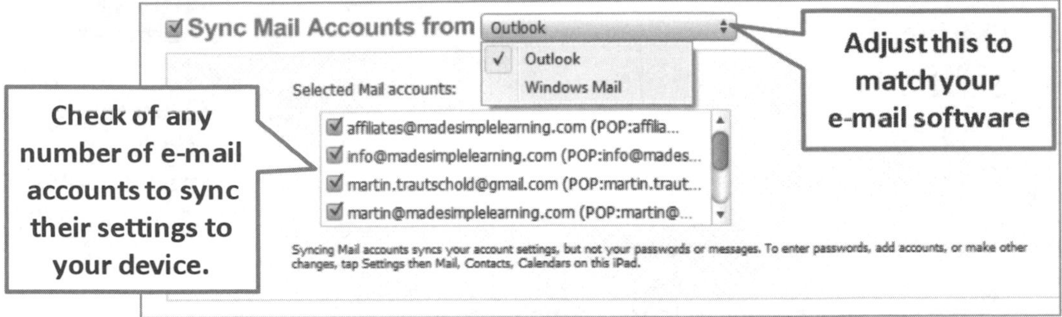


**Figure 3–10.** *E-mail accounts sync setup*

3. To continue setting up bookmarks, notes, and more, scroll down the page.

4. If you do not want to set anything else up for sync, then click the **Apply** button in the lower-right corner of the iTunes screen to start the sync.

## Sync Web Browser Bookmarks and Notes

One great feature of the iTunes sync is that you can sync the browser bookmarks from your computer to your iPad. This allows you to start browsing on your iPad with all your favorite sites immediately. You can also sync your notes from your computer to your iPad and keep them up-to-date in both places using iTunes.

> **NOTE:** As of publication time, only two web browsers are supported for iTunes sync: Microsoft Internet Explorer and Apple Safari. If you use Mozilla Firefox or Google Chrome, you could still sync your bookmarks, but you will have to install a free bookmark sync software (e.g., `www.xmarks.com`) to sync from Firefox or Chrome to Safari or Explorer. Then you can sync your browser bookmarks in a two-step process.

1. Scroll down below the e-mail settings on the same **Info** tab in iTunes to see the **Other** settings.

2. To sync your browser bookmarks, check the box next to "Sync bookmarks with" and adjust the pull-down menu to the web browser software you use (Figure 3–11). At this time, you can select only Internet Explorer or Safari.

3. To sync your notes, check the box next to "Sync notes with" and select the software or service where your notes are stored.

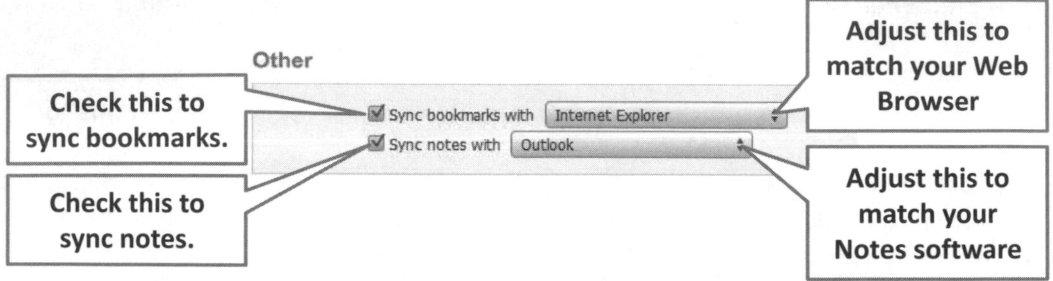


**Figure 3–11.** *Browser bookmarks and notes sync setup*

4. Click the **Apply** button in the lower-right corner of the iTunes screen to start the sync.

# Syncing Your iPad with iTunes

The syncing is normally automatic when you plug in your iPad to your computer's USB port. The only exception is if you have disabled the automatic sync.

## Keeping Track of the Sync

At the top of iTunes, inside the Status window, you will see what is happening with the sync. You may see "Syncing contacts with 'Martin's iPad'" or "Syncing calendars with 'Martin's iPad'." This allows you to see what is currently being synced.

## Handling Sync Conflicts

Sometimes, the iTunes sync will detect conflicts between the data in your computer and on your iPad, for example, the same contact entry with two different company names or the same calendar entry with two different notes. It is fairly straightforward to handle these conflicts.

1. In the Conflict Resolver window, click on the information that is correct. This turns the background a light blue. (The side not selected is white.) See Figure 3–12.

2. If there are any more conflicts, click the **Next** button until you finish resolving all conflicts.

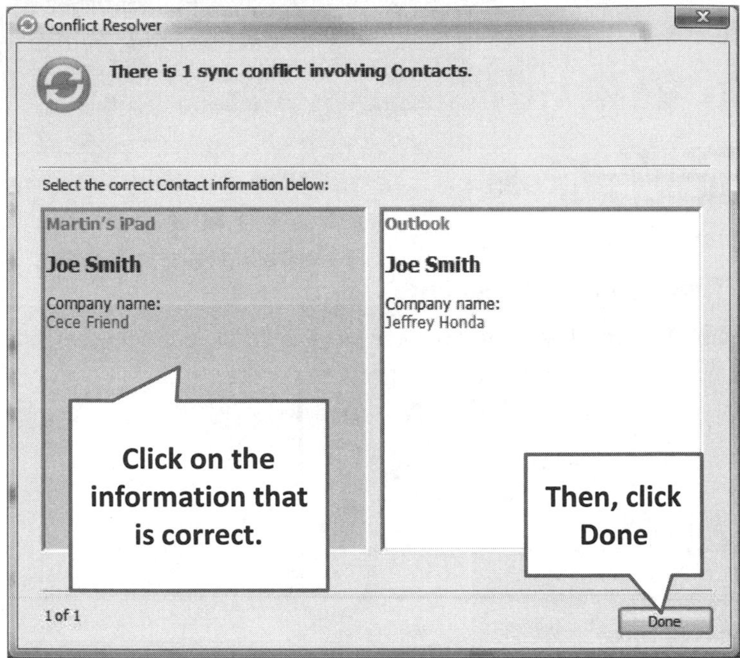


**Figure 3–12.** *iTunes Sync Conflict Resolver*

3. Click **Done** to close the window.

4. All your selections will be applied to the next sync with your iPad. You have the choice to **Sync Now** or **Sync Later** on the next screen (see Figure 3–13).

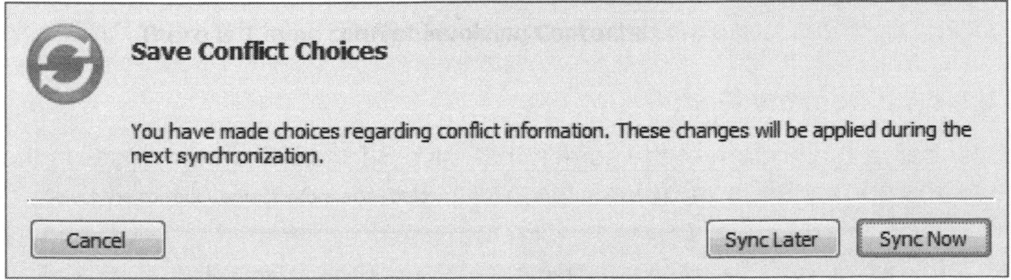


**Figure 3–13.** *iTunes Sync Conflict Resolver final screen*

**NOTE:** Conflicts that are found can cause the sync to stop in mid-process. Contacts are synced first, then the calendar. So if a contacts sync conflict is found, the calendar will not sync until the contacts conflict is resolved. Make sure to re-sync your iPad after you resolve conflicts to complete the sync.

## Cancelling the Sync in Progress

You can cancel the sync from iTunes or from your iPad.

**To cancel the sync from iTunes on your computer:**

Click the "X" inside the sync status window, as shown in Figure 3–14, to cancel the sync.

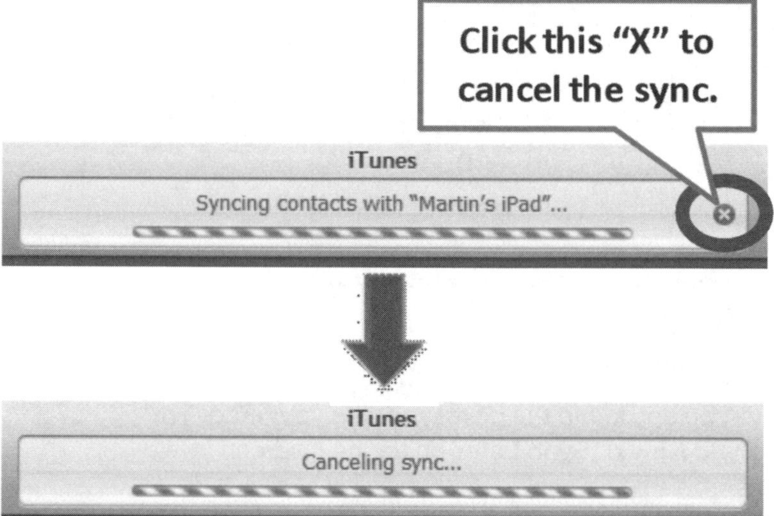


**Figure 3–14.** *Clicking the 'X' in the status window in iTunes to cancel the sync*

**To cancel the sync from the iPad:**

Slide the slider bar at the bottom of the screen that says **Slide to Cancel.** This is in the same place as the normal **Slide to Unlock** message.

## Why Might I Not Want to Use iTunes Automatic Sync?

There could be a few reasons to manually sync:

1. You don't want to fill up your iPad with too many music and video files.
2. The sync and backup process takes a long time, so you don't want it to happen every time you connect your iPad to your computer.

3. You plug your iPad into various computers to charge it up but don't want to be asked if you want to erase and re-sync your music every time.

**NOTE:** If you want to drag and drop music and videos, you need to make sure to check the box next to "Manually manage music and videos" in the **Summary** tab in iTunes.

## Manually Stopping the Auto Sync Before It Starts

There may be times you want to connect your iPad to your computer without the auto sync starting up. This could be because you don't have much time and want to quickly drag and drop a few new purchased songs to your iPad without syncing everything else.

To stop the normal auto-sync of your iPad, you can press several keys on your computer keyboard while connecting your iPad to your computer.

**On a Windows PC**:

Press and hold **Shift** + **Ctrl** while connecting your iPad to your computer.

**On a Mac**:

Press and hold **Command** + **Option** while connecting your iPad.

## Turning Off the Auto Sync Permanently

You can turn off the Auto Sync permanently in iTunes. You might want to do this if you prefer to have manual control over all the sync processes.

**CAUTION:** Turning off the Auto Sync also disables the automatic backup of your iPad every time you connect it to your computer. This setting would be best for a secondary computer, with which you might be charging your iPad but never want to sync it.

To turn off the Auto Sync in iTunes, follow these steps:

1. From the iTunes menu, select **Edit** and then **Preferences**.
2. Click on the **Devices** tab at the top.
3. Check the box next to "Prevent iPods, iPhones and iPads from syncing automatically" (see Figure 3–15).
4. Click the **OK** button to save your settings.

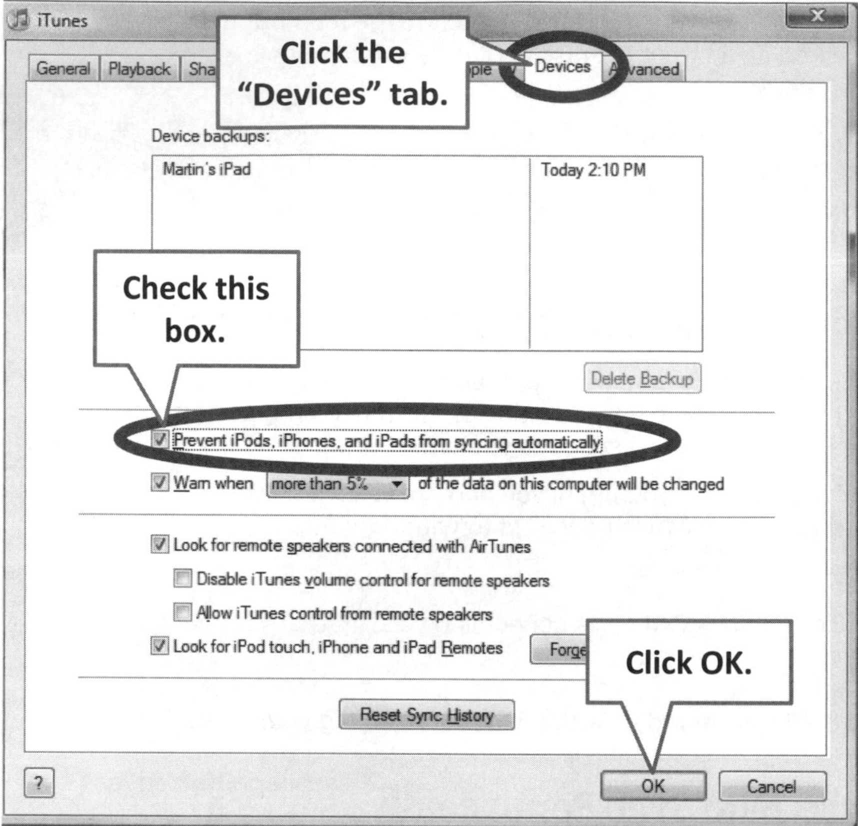


**Figure 3–15.** *Disabling auto-sync in iTunes*

# Getting a Clean Start with the Sync

Sometimes you will have issues with the sync and just need to get a fresh start. There are a few things you can do along these lines with iTunes: you can erase or reset the sync history so iTunes thinks it is syncing for the first time with your iPad, and you can force all information on the iPad to be replaced with information from your computer.

## Reset Sync History (Make iTunes Think It Is Syncing for the First Time)

To reset your sync history in iTunes follow these steps:

1. Select the **Edit** menu and then click on **Preferences** at the bottom.
2. Click the **Devices** tab at the top of the iTunes Preferences window.
3. Click the **Reset Sync History** button at the bottom, as shown in Figure 3–16.

4. You need to confirm your selection by hitting **Reset Sync History** in the pop-up window.

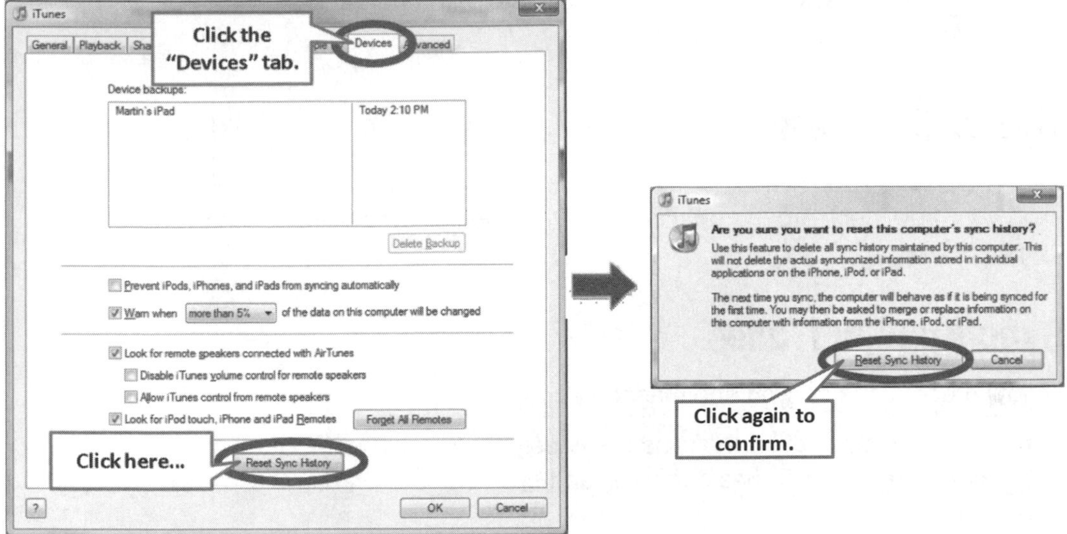


**Figure 3–16.** *Resetting sync history in iTunes (**Edit** > **Preferences** > **Devices** tab)*

## Replace All Information on the iPad (Next Sync Only)

Sometimes you need to get a fresh start with your iPad information. For whatever reason, you want to get rid of all the information on your iPad in one or all the synced apps and get a clean start. Follow these steps.

1. As you did to set up the sync previously, connect your iPad to your computer, start iTunes software, click on your **iPad** in the left nav bar, and click the **Info** tab on the top of the main window.
2. Scroll all the way down to the **Advanced** section (see Figure 3–17).
3. Check one, some, or all of the boxes as you desire.

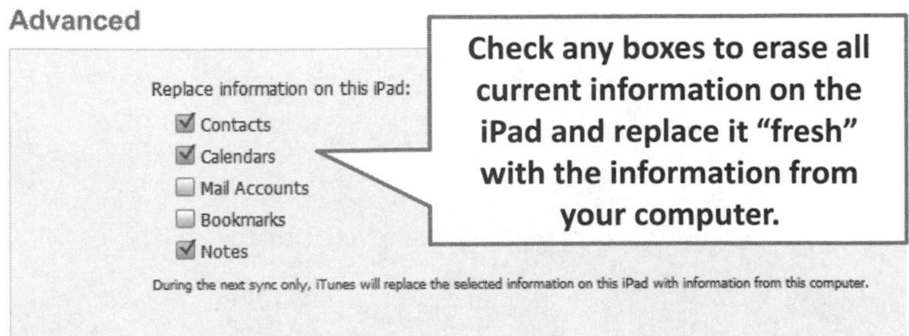


**Figure 3–17.** *Advanced area in the iTunes Info tab*

4. When you are ready, click the **Apply** button in the lower-right corner. The sync should happen immediately. All of the information for the apps you have checked will be erased from the iPad and replaced with the information from your computer.

# Apps: Sync and Manage Them

With iTunes, you can sync and manage your apps on your iPad. It is easy to drag and drop your app icons around on a particular **Home** screen page or even between pages on your iPad.

## Sync Apps in iTunes

Follow these steps to sync and manage apps:

1. As you did to set up the sync previously, connect your iPad to your computer, start iTunes software, and click on your **iPad** in the left nav bar.
2. Click the **Apps** tab on the top of the main window.
3. Click the checkbox next to "Sync Apps" in order to see all apps stored on your iPad and your **Home** screens, as shown in Figure 3–18.

> **NOTE:** To see what happens when you turn your iPad to horizontal mode while it is connected to iTunes, look at Figure 3–18, which shows the horizontal layout with the **Home** screens along the bottom.

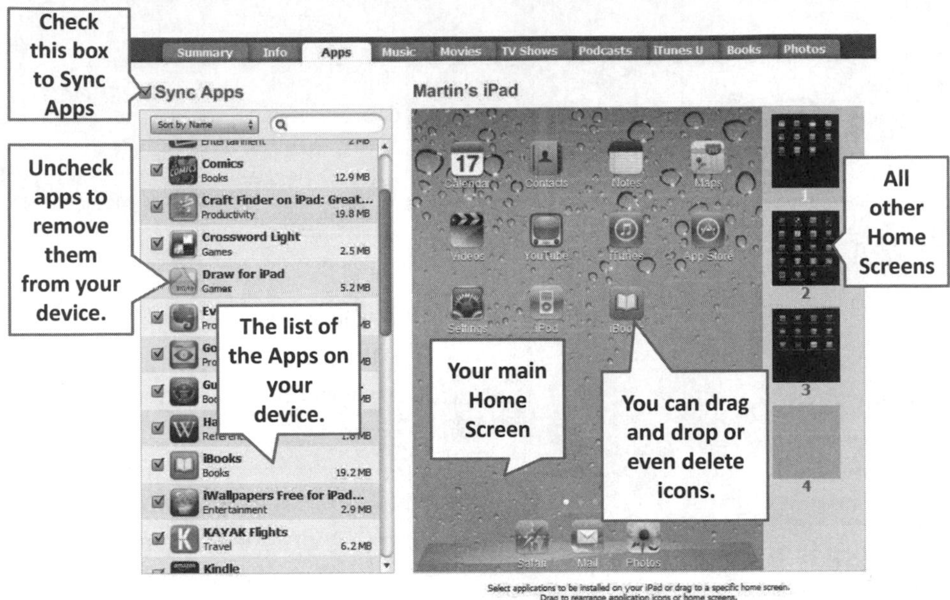


**Figure 3–18.** *Sync Apps screen in iTunes*

## Move Around or Delete Apps Using the Icons

It is very easy to move around and organize your apps in this screen in iTunes (see Figure 3–19).

**To move an icon within a screen**: Click on it and drag it around the screen.

**To move an icon between Home screen pages:** Click and drag it to the new page on the right column. Then the new page will expand in the main screen. Drop the icon in the main screen.

**To dock an app on the bottom dock:** Click and drag it down to drop it on the bottom dock. If there are already six icons on the bottom dock, then you need to drag one off to make room for the new icon. Only six icons maximum are allowed.

**To view another Home screen page:** Click on that page in the right column.

**To delete an app:** Click on it, and then click the little X in the upper left corner. Only apps you have installed can be deleted. You will not see an X on pre-installed apps like iTunes.

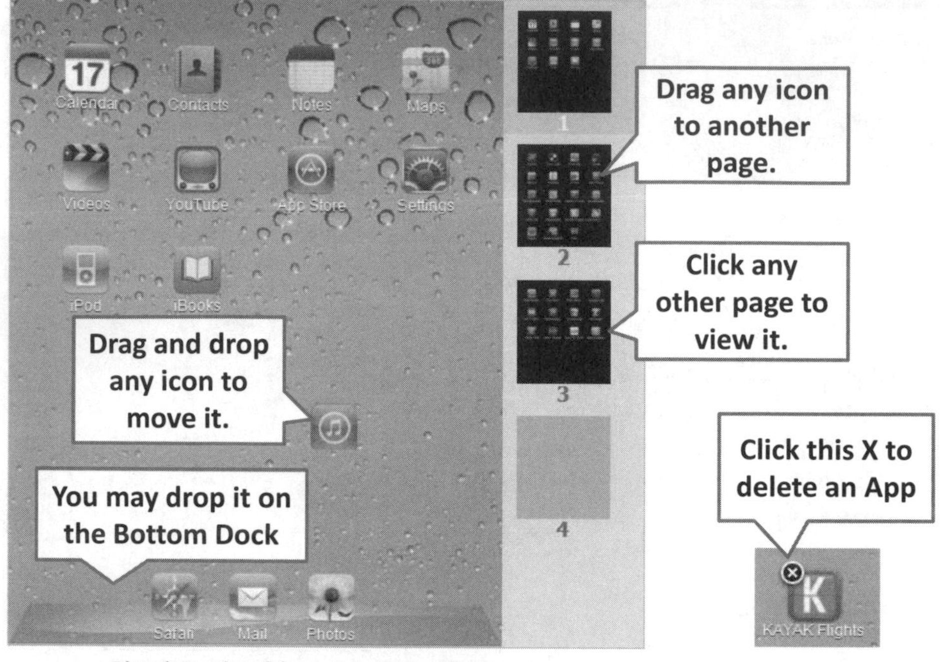


**Figure 3–19.** *Moving app icons or deleting apps using the icons on the Sync Apps screen in iTunes*

## Delete or Re-install Apps from the List of Icons

To delete an app, simply uncheck the box next to it and confirm your selection, as shown in Figure 3–20.

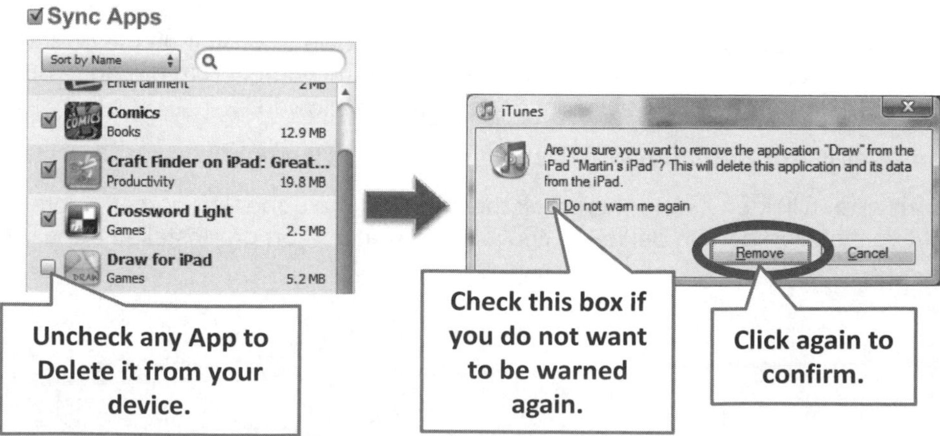


**Figure 3–20.** *Unchecking an app to delete it from your iPad*

**TIP:** Even if you delete an app from your iPad, if you have chosen to sync apps as shown, you can still re-install that app by re-checking the box next to it. The app will be re-loaded onto your iPad during the next sync.

# File Sharing (File Transfer) iPad with Computer

The other thing you can do in the **Apps** tab is transfer files between your computer and your iPad.

**TIP:** Some apps, such as GoodReader, come with wireless methods to transfer and share files. Check out the GoodReader section in Chapter 23 "New Media," for more information.

## Copying Files from Your Computer to Your iPad

To copy files from your computer to your iPad, follow these steps.

**NOTE:** To use iTunes for file sharing, you need to have at least one app installed on your iPad that can work with documents, spreadsheets, or presentation files. Examples of such apps are Pages, Numbers (Apple's spreadsheet), Keynote (presentation software), and GoodReader (multi-document reader).

1. As you did to set up the previous sync, connect your iPad to your computer, start iTunes software, and click on your **iPad** in the left nav bar.
2. Click the **Apps** tab on the top of the main window (see Figure 3–21).
3. Scroll down to the **File Sharing** section below the apps.

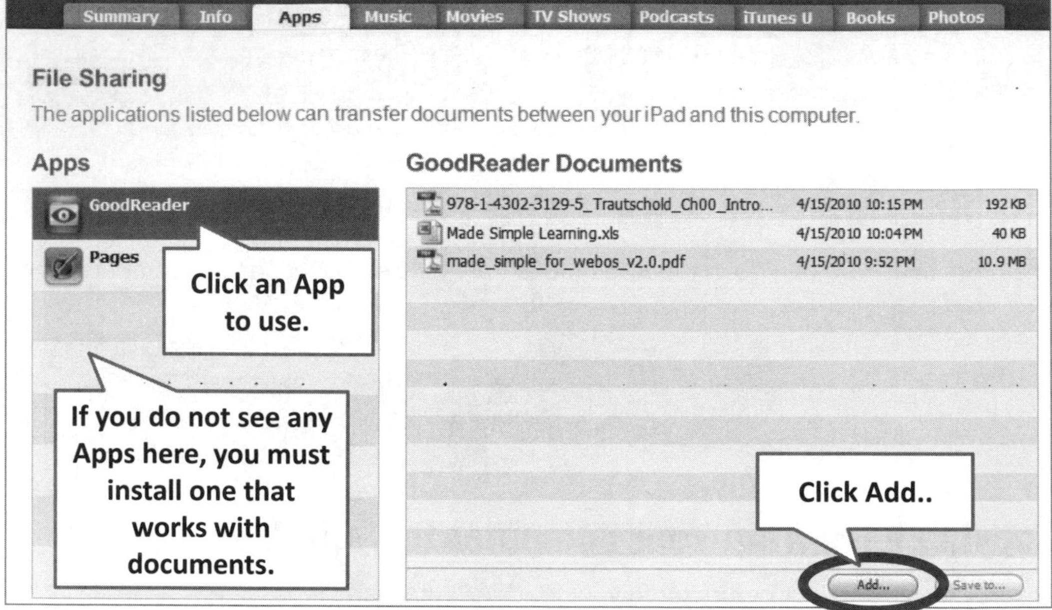


**Figure 3–21.** *Transferring files to your iPad*

4. Click on any app to use in the left column, and then click the **Add** button in the lower-right corner.

5. A window will pop up, asking you to select a file to transfer and click the **Open** button, as shown in Figure 3–22. The file will be transferred immediately to your iPad.

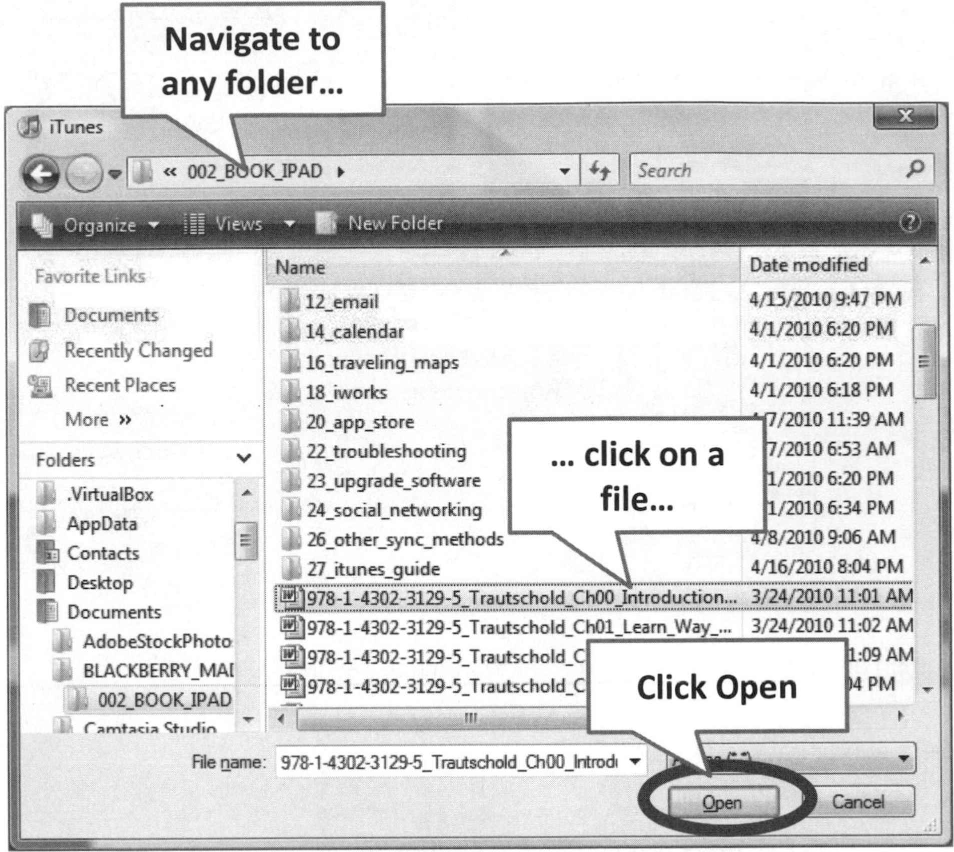


**Figure 3–22.** *Selecting a file to transfer to your iPad*

## Copying Files from Your iPad to Your Computer

To copy files from your iPad to your computer, follow these steps.

1. Connect your iPad to your computer, start iTunes software, and click on your **iPad** in the left nav bar.
2. Click the **Apps** tab on the top of the main window.
3. Scroll down to the **File Sharing** section below the apps (see Figure 3–23).

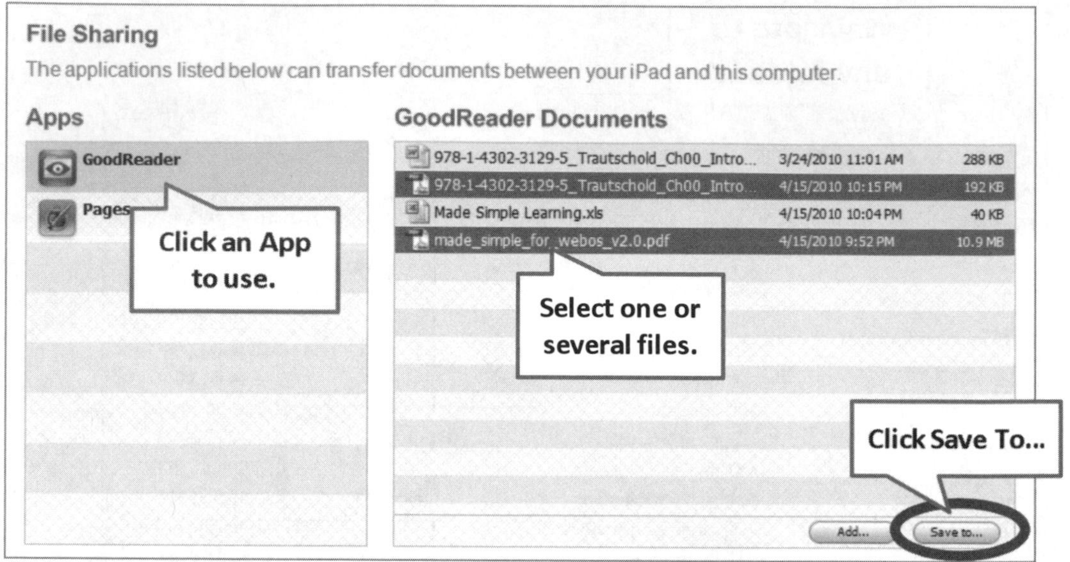


**Figure 3–23.** *Transferring files from your iPad*

4. Click on any app from which you want to transfer the files in the left column.
5. Select one or several files using any of these methods:
   a. Click on a single file.
   b. Hold the **Control** key (Windows) or **Option** key (Mac) and click on any number of files.
   c. Hold the **Shift** key and click on the top and bottom file in a list to select all files in that list.
6. After the file(s) are selected, click the **Save To** button in the lower-right corner.
7. A window will pop up asking you to select a folder on your computer to receive the files from your iPad. Locate and click on the folder, and then click the **Select Folder** button, as shown in Figure 3–24. The file(s) will be transferred immediately to your computer.

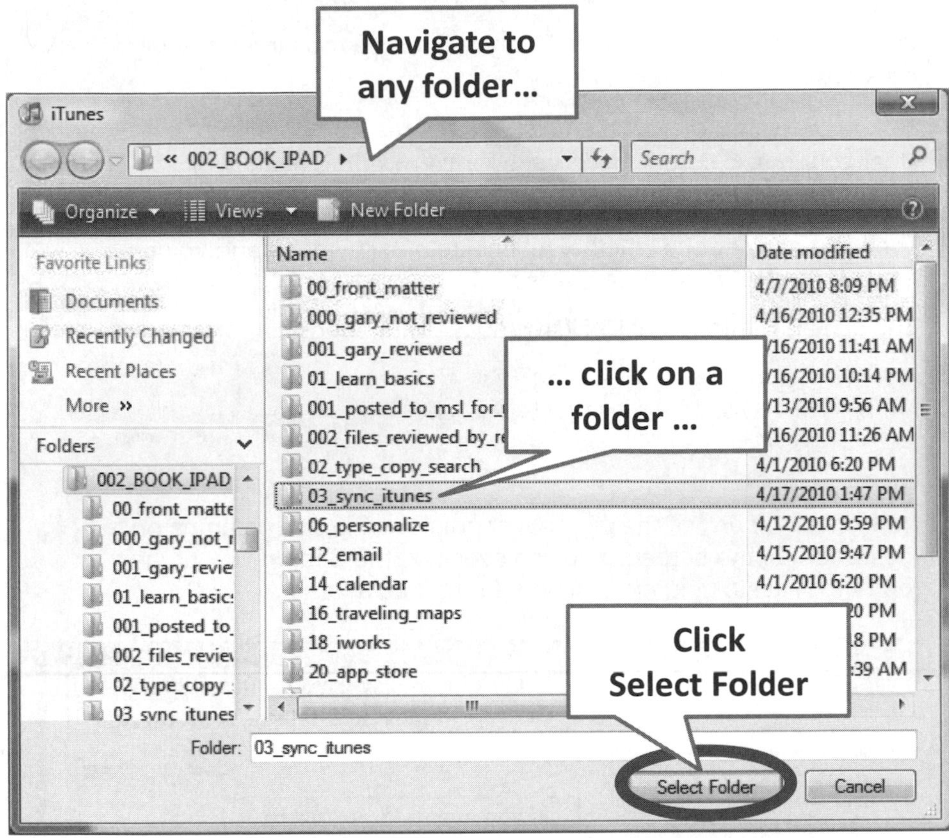


**Figure 3–24.** *Selecting a folder on your computer to receive files from your iPad*

# Music—Sync Automatically

When you click the **Music** tab, you can choose to sync your entire music library or selected items.

> **CAUTION:** If you have already manually transferred some music, music videos, or voice memos to your iPad, you will receive a warning message that all existing content on your iPad will be removed and replaced with the selected music library from your computer.

To sync music from your computer to your iPad, follow these steps.

1. Connect your iPad to your computer, start iTunes software, and click on your **iPad** in the left nav bar.
2. Click the **Music** tab on the top of the main window.

3. Check the box next to "Sync Music" (see Figure 3–25).
4. Only if you are sure that your music library will not be too large for your iPad, click next to "Entire music library."
5. Click next to "Selected playlists, artists, and genres," if you are unsure of whether your music library is too large, or you want to sync only specific playlists or artists.
   a. Then you can choose whether to include music videos and voice memos by checking those boxes.
   b. You can also automatically fill free space with songs.

**CAUTION:** We don't recommend checking this option because it will take up all the space in your iPad and leave no room for all those cool apps!

   c. Now check off any of the playlists or artists in the two columns on the bottom of the screen. You can even use the Search box at the top of the Artists column to search for particular artists.

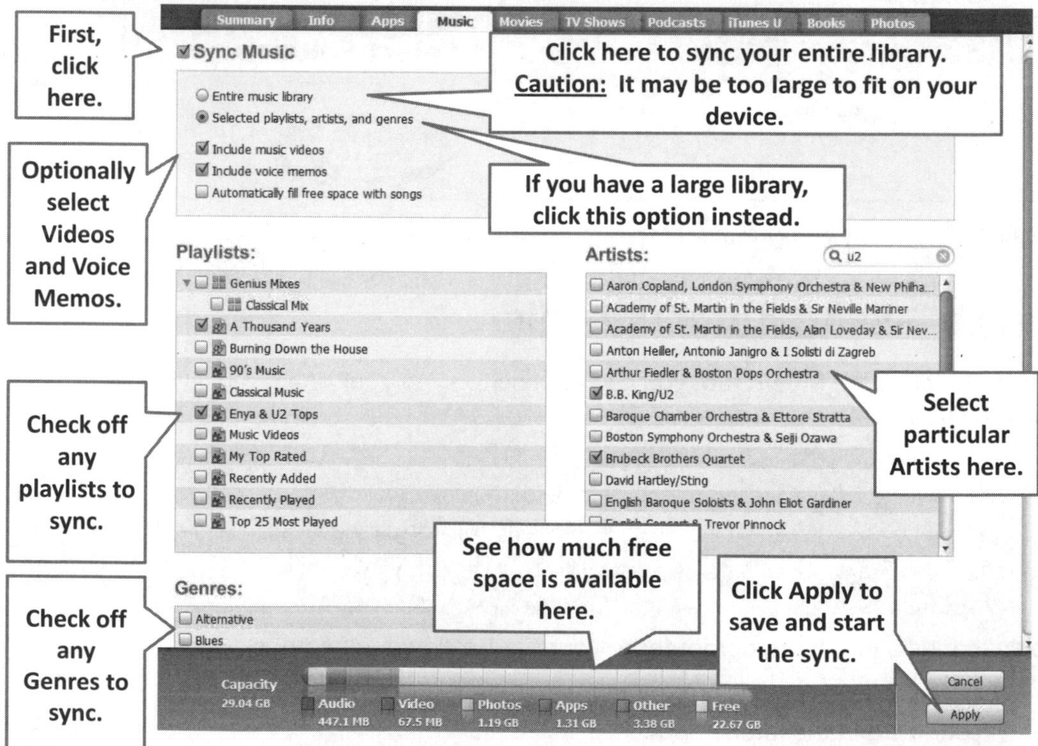


**Figure 3–25.** *Syncing music with your iPad*

6. When you are done with your selections, click the **Apply** button to start the music sync.

## Movies—Sync Automatically

When you click the **Movies** tab, you can choose to sync specific, recent, or unwatched movies, or all of them.

To sync movies from your computer to your iPad, follow these steps.

1. Connect your iPad to your computer, start iTunes software, and click on your **iPad** in the left nav bar.
2. Click the **Movies** tab on the top of the main window.
3. Check the box next to "Sync Movies" (see Figure 3–26).
4. If you would like to sync recent or unwatched movies, then check the box next to "Automatically include" and use the pull-down to select **All, 1 most recent, All unwatched, 5 most recent unwatched**, etc.

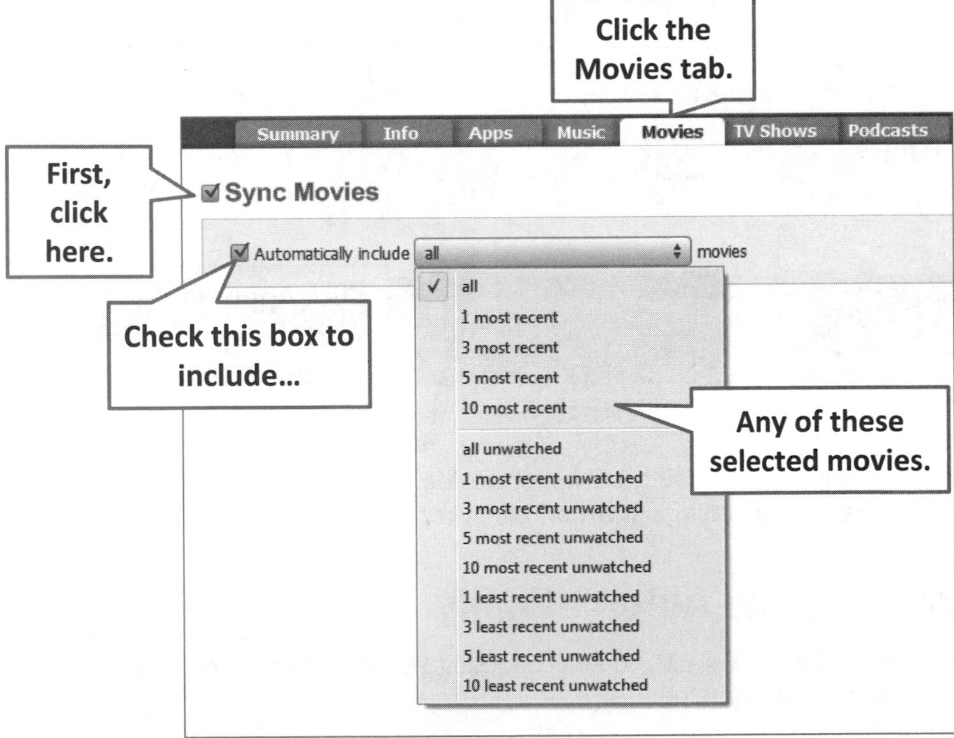


**Figure 3–26.** *Configuring movie sync to automatically include selections*

5. If you selected any item besides **All**, then you have the choice to sync specific movies or videos to your iPad. Simply check the boxes next to the movies you would like to include in the sync (see Figure 3–27).

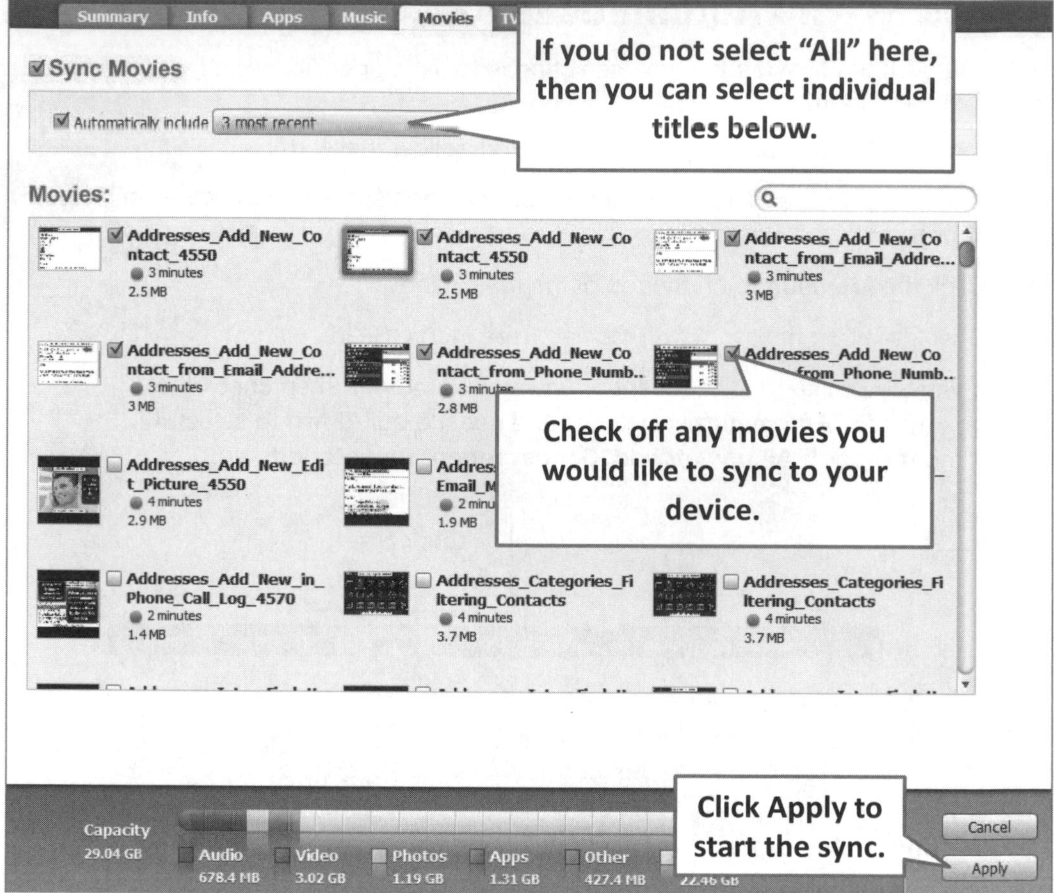


**Figure 3–27.** *Configuring movie sync to select individual movies in addition to the automatic selection*

6. When you are done choosing individual movies, then click the **Apply** button to save your settings and start the sync.

## TV Shows—Sync Automatically

When you click the **TV Shows** tab, you can choose to sync specific, recent, or unwatched TV shows, or all of them.

To sync TV shows from your computer to your iPad, follow these steps.

1. Connect your iPad to your computer, start iTunes software, and click on your **iPad** in the left nav bar.

2. Click the **TV Shows** tab on the top of the main window.
3. Check the box next to "Sync TV Shows" (see Figure 3–28).
4. If you would like to sync recent or unwatched TV shows, then check the box next to "Automatically include" and use the pull-down to select **All, 1 newest, All unwatched, 5 oldest unwatched**, **10 newest unwatched**, etc.

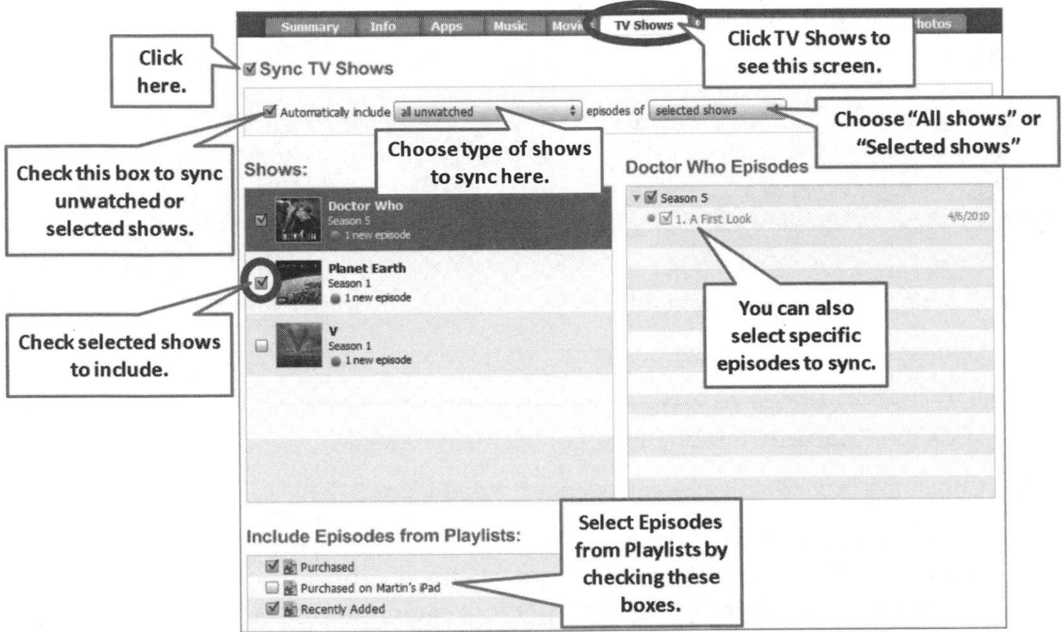


**Figure 3–28.** *Configuring TV show sync to automatically include selections*

5. Choose All Shows or Selected Shows next to "episodes of."
6. If you choose Selected Shows after "episodes of," then you can choose individual shows and even individual episodes in the two sections in the middle of the screen.
7. If you have playlists of TV shows, you can select those for inclusion by checking the boxes in the bottom section of the screen.
8. When you are done choosing individual TV shows, then click the **Apply** button to save your settings and start the sync.

## Podcasts—Sync Automatically

When you click the **Podcasts** tab, you can choose to sync specific, recent, or unplayed podcasts, or all of them.

> **TIP:** Podcasts are a series of audio or video shows that are usually regularly scheduled (e.g., daily, weekly, or monthly). Most are free to subscribe to in the iTunes store. When you subscribe and set up the auto sync as shown in this section, you will receive all your favorite podcasts on your iPad.
>
> Many of your favorite radio shows are recorded and broadcast as podcasts. We encourage you to check out the **Podcast** section of the iTunes store to see what might interest you. You will find podcasts on movie reviews, news shows, law school test reviews, game shows, old radio shows, educational content, and much more.

To sync podcasts from your computer to your iPad, follow these steps.

1. Connect your iPad to your computer, start iTunes software, and click on your **iPad** in the left nav bar.
2. Click the **Podcasts** tab on the top of the main window.
3. Check the box next to "Sync Podcasts" (see Figure 3–29).
4. If you would like to sync recent or unwatched TV shows, then check the box next to "Automatically include" and use the pull-down to select **All, 1 newest, All unplayed, 5 newest**, **10 most recent unplayed**, etc.

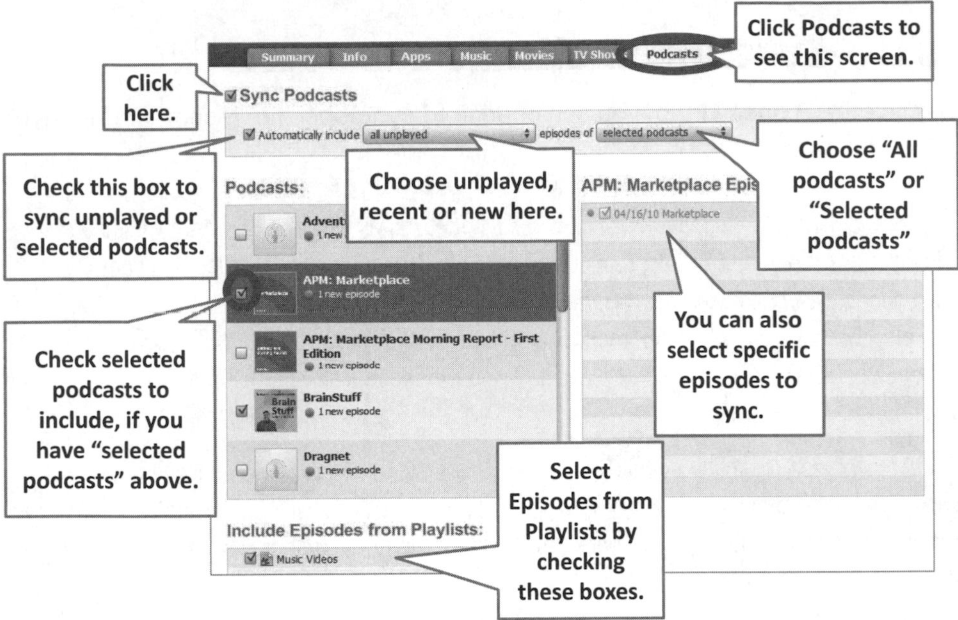


**Figure 3–29.** *Configuring podcast sync to automatically include selections*

5. Choose All Podcasts or Selected Podcasts next to "episodes of."
6. If you choose Selected Podcasts after "episodes of," then you can choose individual podcasts and even individual episodes in the two sections in the middle of the screen.
7. If you have playlists of podcasts, you can select those for inclusion by checking the boxes in the bottom section of the screen.
8. When you are done choosing individual podcasts, click the Apply button to save your settings and start the sync.

> **TIP:** After you sync these podcasts, you enjoy them in the **Podcasts** section of your iPod app on your device.

# iTunes U—Sync Automatically

When you click the **iTunes U** tab, you can choose to sync specific, recent, or un-played iTunes U content, or all content.

**TIP:** iTunes U podcasts are similar to audio or video podcasts, except that they are focused on educational content and are mostly produced by colleges and universities. iTunes U podcasts may be a series of audio or video shows that are done once or can be regularly scheduled (e.g., daily, weekly, or monthly). Most are free to subscribe to in the iTunes store. When you subscribe and set up the auto sync as shown in this section, you will receive all your favorite iTunes U podcasts on your iPad.

Check out the **iTunes U** section in the iTunes store. You may find your favorite college or university has shows to teach you Biology 101 or Astronomy 101. There is even a Stanford University course on how to develop iPhone apps! Say you want to brush up on your marketing skills—you can check out some marketing classes from top universities. Many of the top universities broadcast class lectures from famous professors in iTunes U. Go ahead and check it out—it is quite amazing what you will find!

To sync iTunes U content from your computer to your iPad, follow these steps.

1. Connect your iPad to your computer, start iTunes software, and click on your **iPad** in the left nav bar.
2. Click the **iTunes U** tab on the top of the main window.
3. Check the box next to "Sync Podcasts" (see Figure 3–30).
4. If you would like to sync recent or unplayed podcast, then check the box next to "Automatically include" and use the pull-down to select **All, 1 newest, All unplayed, 5 newest**, **10 most recent unplayed**, etc.

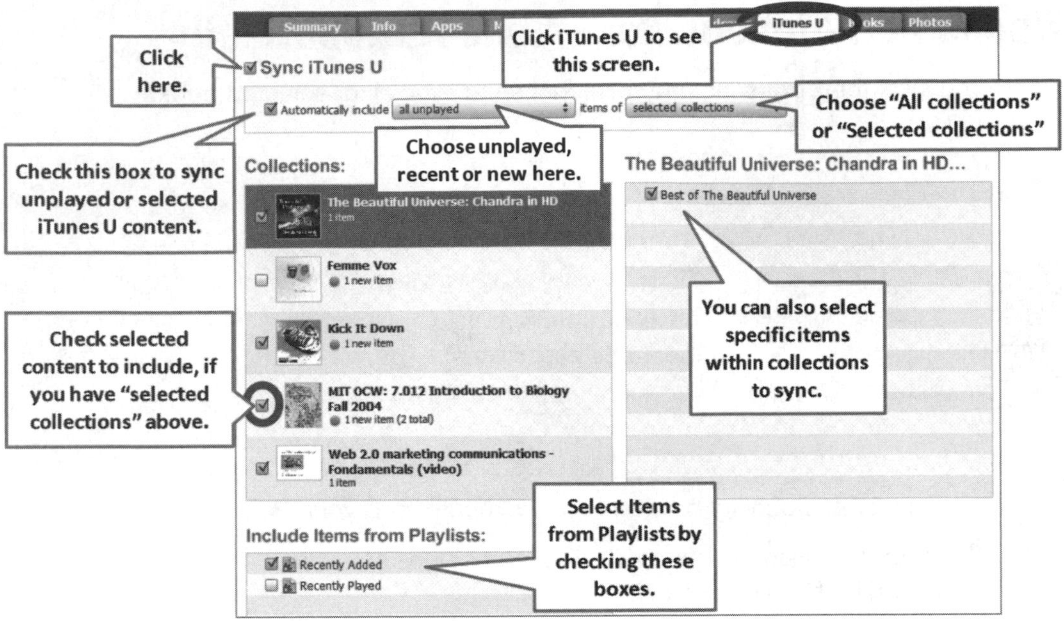


**Figure 3–30.** *Configuring podcast sync to automatically include selections*

5. Choose All Collections or Selected Collections next to "items of."
6. If you choose Selected Collections after "items of," then you can choose individual podcasts and even individual episodes in the two sections in the middle of the screen.
7. If you have playlists of podcasts, you can select those for inclusion by checking the boxes in the bottom section of the screen.
8. When you are done choosing individual items, then click the Apply button to save your settings and start the sync.

## Books and Audiobooks—Sync Automatically

When you click the **Books** tab, you can choose to sync all or selected books and audiobooks.

> **TIP:** Books are electronic versions of their paper cousins. These books are in a specific electronic format called "ePub." You buy them in the iBookstore on the iPad. You can also acquire books in the ePub format from other locations and sync them to your iPad using the steps described here. Books you acquire elsewhere must be unprotected or "DRM-Free" (Digital Rights Management free) in order to sync them to your iPad. You will read these books in the iBooks app or in other book reader apps on your iPad. Check out Chapter 8 "iBooks and E-Books" to learn more.

To sync books or audiobooks between your computer and your iPad, follow these steps.

1. Connect your iPad to your computer, start iTunes software, and click on your **iPad** in the left nav bar.
2. Click the **Books** tab on the top of the main window.
3. If you desire, check the box next to "Sync Books" and "Sync Audiobooks" (see Figure 3–31).
4. If you would like to sync all books, leave the default **All books** selection.
5. Otherwise, choose **Selected books** and make your choices by checking off specific books in the window.

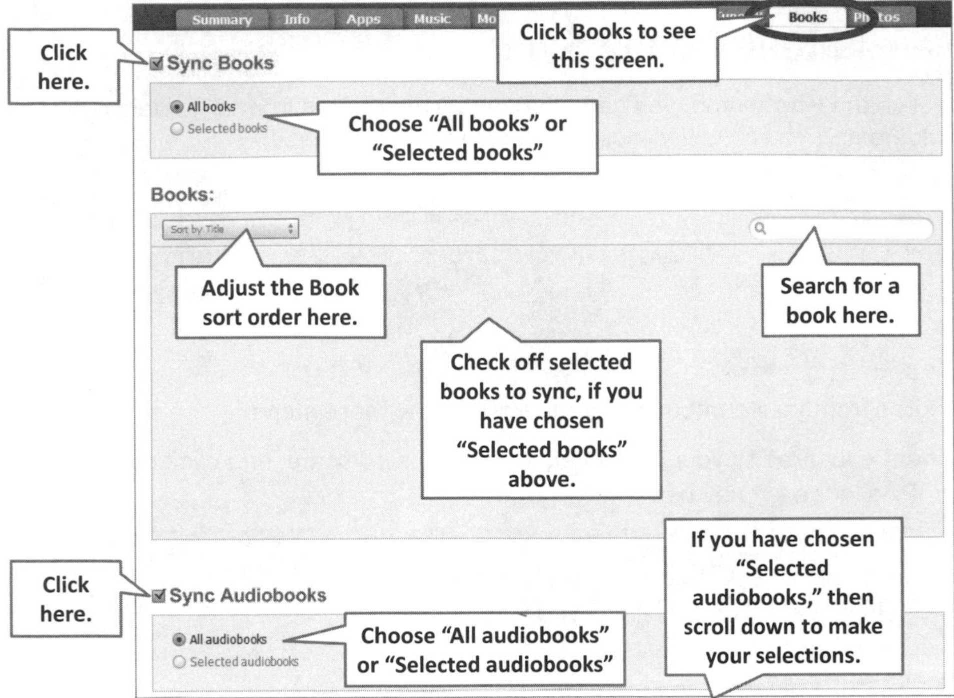


**Figure 3–31.** *Configuring books and audiobooks sync to automatically include selections*

6. If you would like to sync all audiobooks, leave the default **All audiobooks** selection.
7. Otherwise, choose **Selected audiobooks** and make your choices by checking off specific audio books in the window below this selection item.
8. When you are done choosing individual books and audiobooks, click the **Apply** button to save your settings and start the sync.

> **TIP:** After you sync these books, you can enjoy them in the iBooks app on your device. You can listen to audiobooks in the iPod app, where the **Audiobooks** tab is on the left side.

# Photos—Automatically Sync

When you click the **Photos** tab, you can choose to sync photos from all folders or selected folders and you can even include videos in those folders.

> **TIP:** You can create a beautiful electronic picture frame and share your photos on the beautiful iPad screen (see Chapter 15 "Working with Photos"). You can even use your photos to set the background wallpaper and screen lock wallpaper—see Chapter 6, "Personalize," for more information.

To sync photos from your computer to your iPad, follow these steps.

1. Connect your iPad to your computer, start iTunes software, and click on your **iPad** in the left nav bar.

> **TIP:** Mac users can also sync photos using iPhoto, including Events (time-based sync), Faces (person-based sync), and Places (location-based sync).

2. Click the **Photos** tab on the top of the main window.
3. If you desire, check the box next to "Sync Photos from."
4. Click the pull-down menu next to this item and select a folder from your computer where your photos are stored. If you want to grab all your photos, then you should go to the highest folder level possible (e.g., C: on your Windows computer or "/" on your Apple Mac). See Figure 3–32.

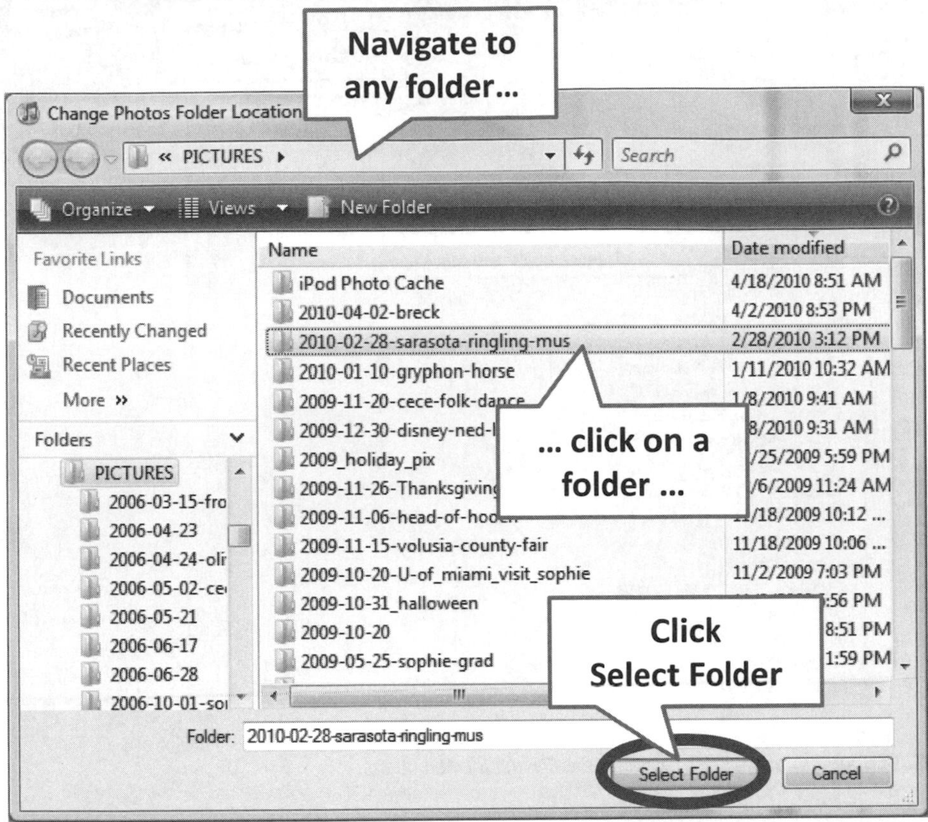


**Figure 3–32.** *Selecting a folder on your computer to sync your photos*

5. If you would like to sync all photos from the selected folder on your computer, select **All folders**, shown in Figure 3–33.

**CAUTION:** Because your photo library on your computer may be too large to fit on your iPad, you should be careful when checking **All folders**.

6. Otherwise, choose **Selected folders** and make your choices by checking off specific books in the window below.

7. You may also include videos that are in the folders by checking the box next to "Include videos."

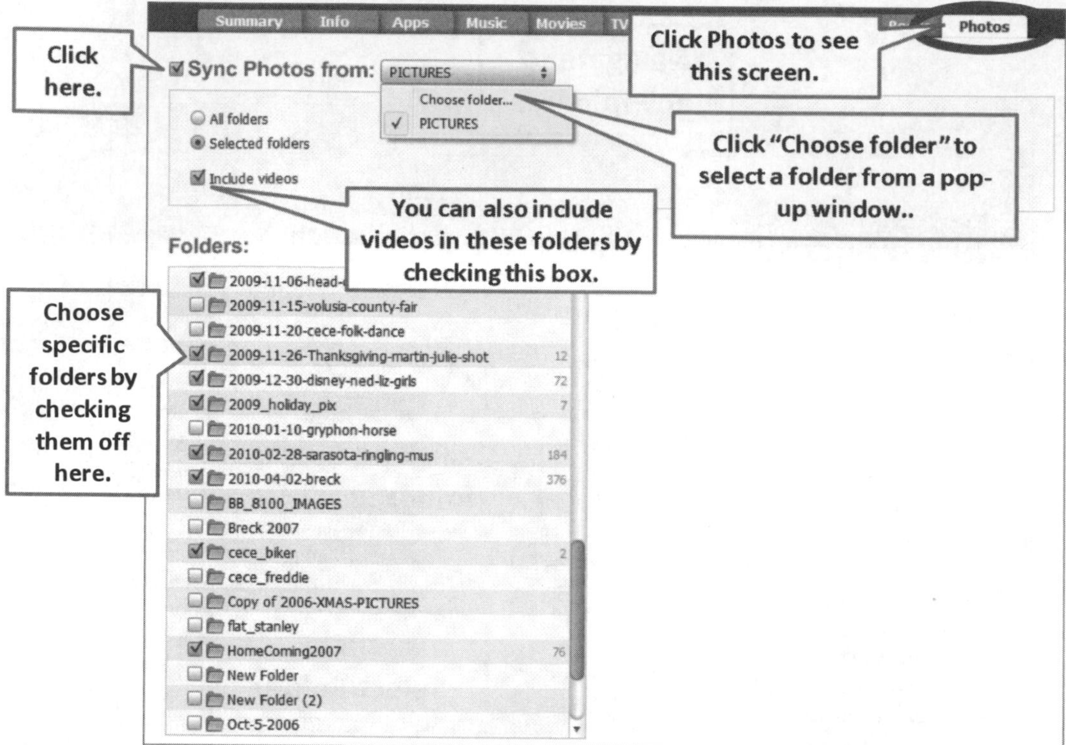


**Figure 3–33.** *Configuring photo sync to automatically include selections*

8. When you are done choosing your photos to sync, click the **Apply** button to save your settings and start the sync.
9. When the sync starts, you will set the status in the middle-top status window in iTunes.

# How You Know What Is New or Unplayed in iTunes

You may notice little numbers next to items in the left nav bar of iTunes. There are similar little blue numbers in the upper-right corner of items in the main window. These numbers show how many items are unplayed, unwatched, or, in the case of apps, require updates. See Figure 3–34.

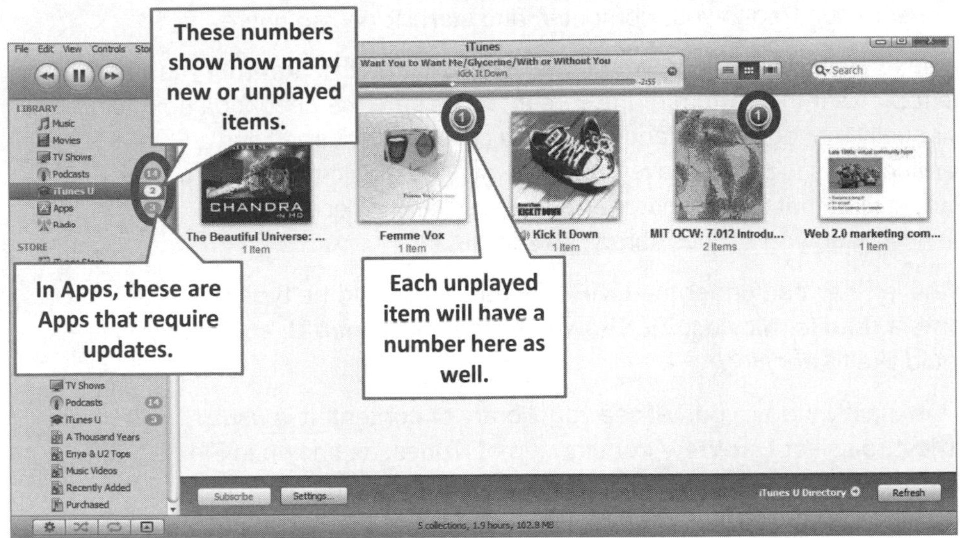


**Figure 3–34.** *Quickly Seeing Number of Unplayed Items.*

# Manually Transferring Music, Movies, Podcasts, and More on Your iPad (Drag-and-Drop Method)

The Auto Sync sections showed you how to automatically sync content to your iPad. In this section we show you how to manually transfer songs, videos, books, audiobooks, and more. The process is the same for each type of content, so we will show you how to do it for just one type of content, and then you will know how to do it for all types of content.

**TIP:** Use these same drag-and-drop techniques in order to add items to a playlist.

To manually transfer content from your computer to your iPad, follow these steps.

**NOTE:** If you have chosen to automatically sync content (e.g., music, movies, podcasts, etc.) then you will not be able to use this drag-and-drop method to copy items to your iPad. First you will have to check "Manually manage music and videos" in the **Summary** tab in iTunes before you try to drag and drop music or videos.

1. Connect your iPad to your computer, and start iTunes software.
2. In the left nav bar, click on your **iPad**. Then click on the **Summary** tab at the top. Near the bottom of the screen, make sure the checkbox next to "Manually manage music and videos" is checked. You may see a warning message if you have previously synced music or videos to your iPad, saying that all previously synced music and videos will be replaced with your iTunes library. This is OK.
3. In the left nav bar, under the **LIBRARY** heading, click the type of content (**Music**, **Movies, TV Shows, Podcasts, iTunes U**, etc.) that you would like to transfer.
4. In the main window you will see your library of content. It is usually easiest to select **List View** from the top of iTunes, as shown in Figure 3–35. This allows you to see all the content in a list and easily select a single item or group of items.

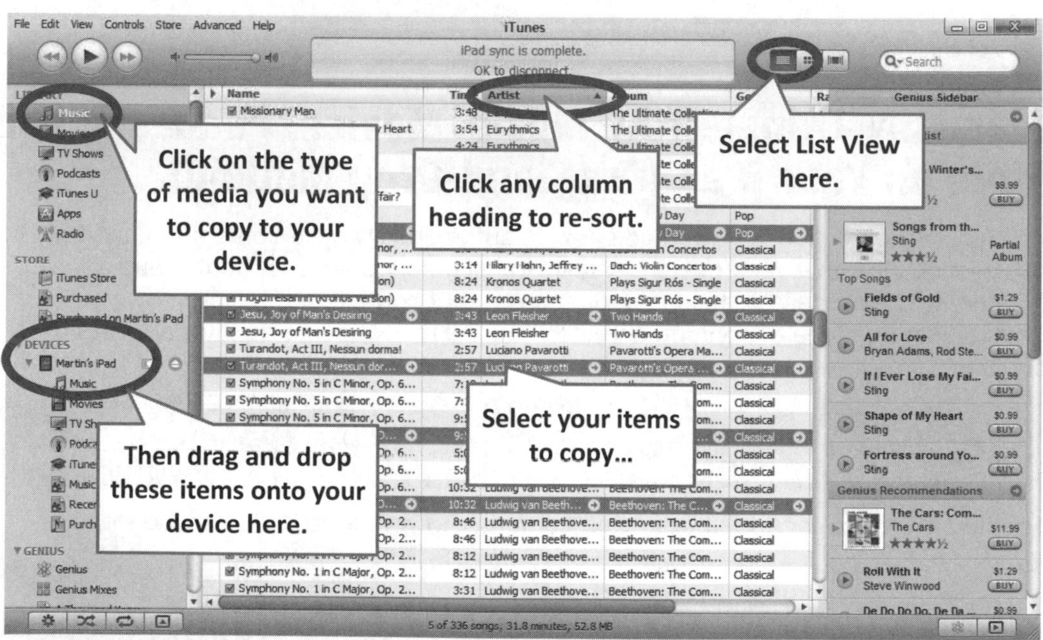


**Figure 3–35.** *Selecting media to drag and drop onto your device*

5. Start selecting content using any of these methods.

   a. To select an individual item, simply click on it to highlight it.

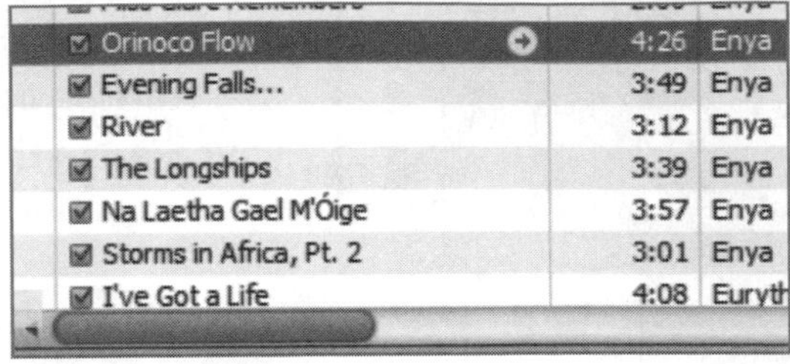


   b. To select items that are not in a continuous list, Windows users press and hold the Control key while clicking, and Mac users press and hold the Command key while clicking on items.

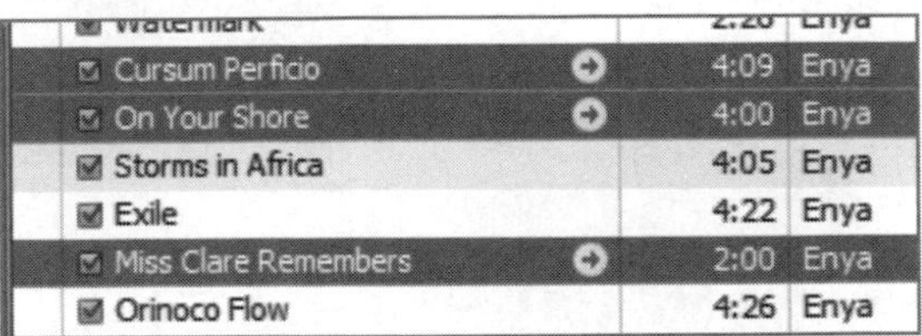


   c. To select items in a continuous list, press and hold the Shift key on your computer keyboard while clicking the top item, and then the bottom item in the list. All the items in between will be selected.

6. Then, to copy these items to your iPad, simply click and drag the selected item(s) over to your iPad and let go of the mouse button. All selected items will then be copied to your iPad. See Figure 3–36.

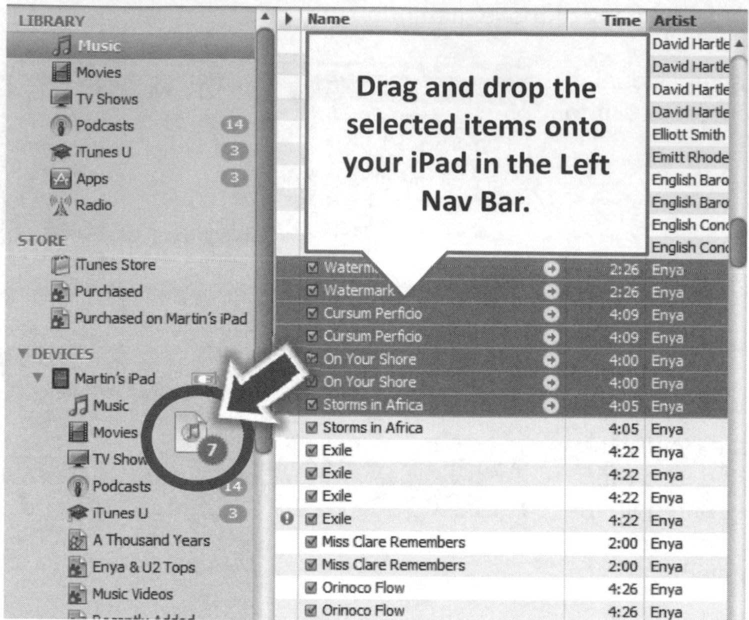
Drag and drop the selected items onto your iPad in the Left Nav Bar.

**Figure 3–36.** *Dragging and dropping selected items onto your device*

# Troubleshooting iTunes and the Sync

Sometimes iTunes does not behave exactly like you would expect it to, so here are a few simple troubleshooting tips.

## Check Out the Apple Knowledgebase for Helpful Articles

On your iPad or computer's web browser, go to this web page:

`http://www.apple.com/support/ipad/`

Then click on a topic in the left nav bar, as shown in Figure 3–37.

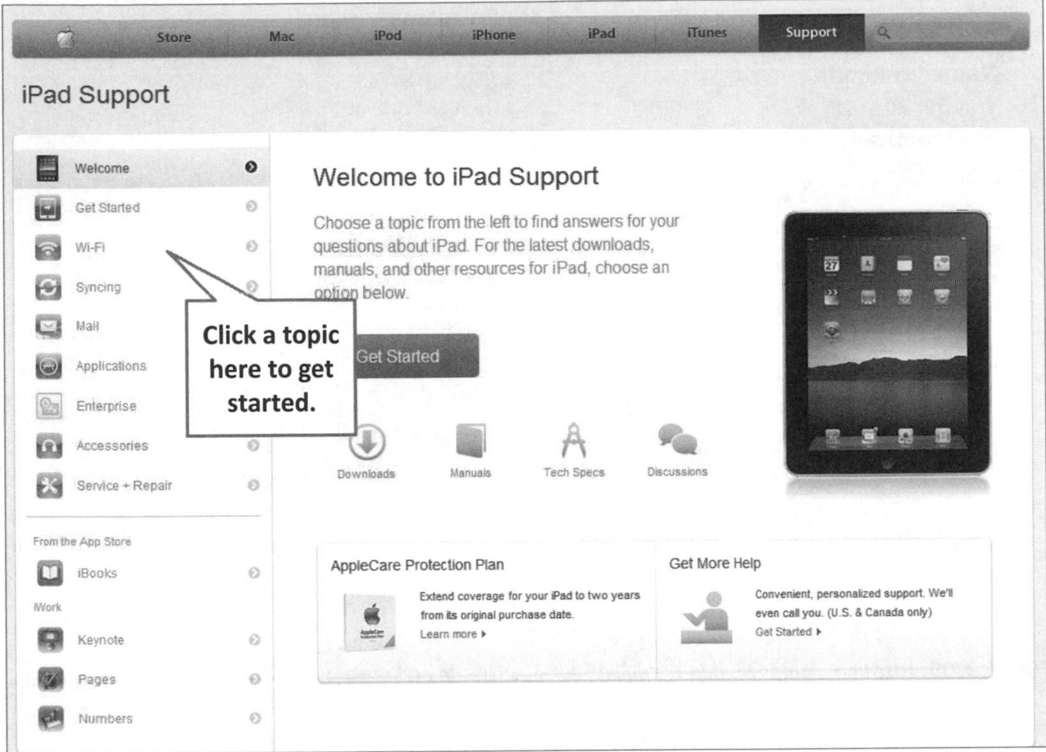


**Figure 3–37.** *Apple Knowlegebase web site for the iPad*

## iTunes Locked Up and Will Not Respond (Windows Computer)

1. Bring up the Windows Task Manager by simultaneously pressing **Ctrl** + **Alt** + **Del** keys on your keyboard. The Task Manager should look something like Figure 3–38.

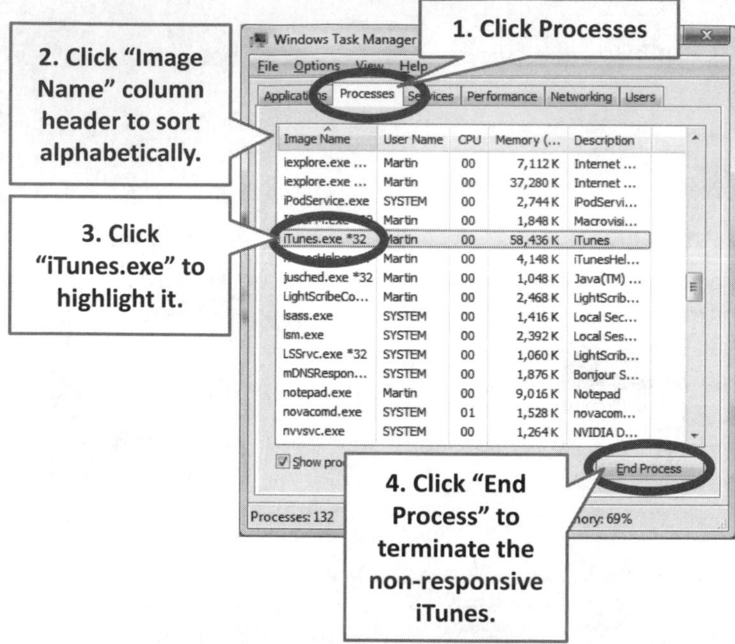


**Figure 3–38.** *Locating `iTunes.exe` in Windows Task Manager to end the process*

2. Then, to end the process, click **End Process** from the pop-up window asking "Do you want to end this process?" as shown in Figure 3–39.

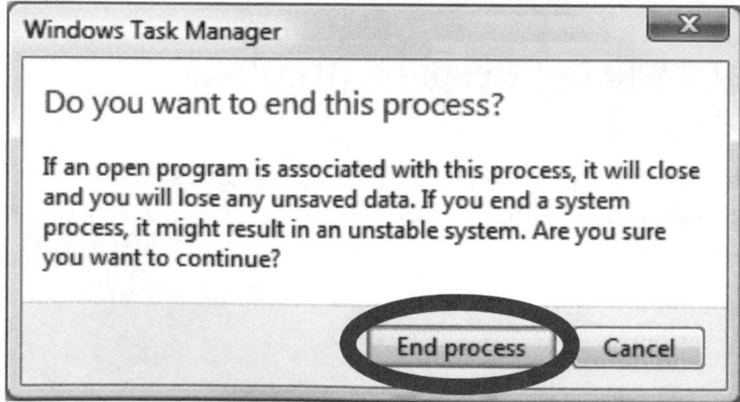


**Figure 3–39.** *Confirming to end process in Windows*

3. Now, iTunes should be forced to close.
4. Try restarting iTunes.
5. If iTunes will not start or it locks up, then reboot your computer and try it again.

# iTunes Locked Up and Will Not Respond (Mac Computer)

> **TIP:** Pressing **Command** + **Option** + **Escape** is the shortcut to bring up the Force Quit Applications window, shown in Figure 3–40.

1. Go up to the iTunes Menu at the top and click.
2. Click on **Quit iTunes.**
3. If that doesn't work, go to any other program and click on the small "Apple" in the upper left-hand corner.
4. Click on **Force Quit** and the list of running programs will be displayed.
5. Highlight iTunes and click on the **Force Quit** button.
6. If this does not help, then try rebooting or restarting your Mac.

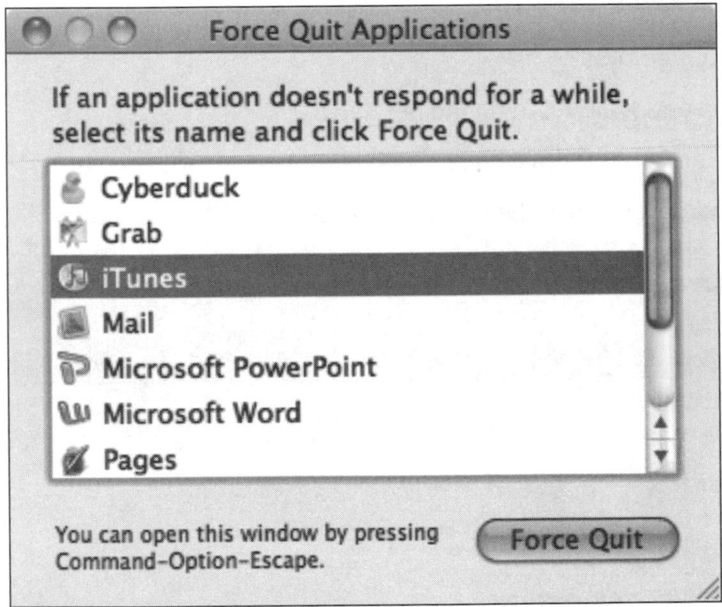


***Figure 3–40.*** *Force Quit Applications window on Mac computers*

# Update Your iPad Operating System

You can check for updated software and install updated operating system (OS) software using iTunes.

> **NOTE:** Do this update when you won't mind being without your iPad for 30 minutes or more. Updating your iPad OS could take quite a while, depending on how much information you have stored on your computer (since it has to be backed up and then restored after the OS update), the speed of your computer's Internet connection (to download the latest iPad OS), and the overall speed of your computer.

Normally your iTunes will automatically check for updates on a set schedule, about every two weeks. You can see from Figure 3–41 that this iTunes will check for updated software on 5/5/2010.

1. Start iTunes software.
2. Connect your iPad to your computer.
3. Click on your **iPad** listed under DEVICES in the left nav bar.
4. Click on the **Summary** tab in the top nav bar.
5. Click the **Check for Update** button in the center of the screen in the **Version** section.

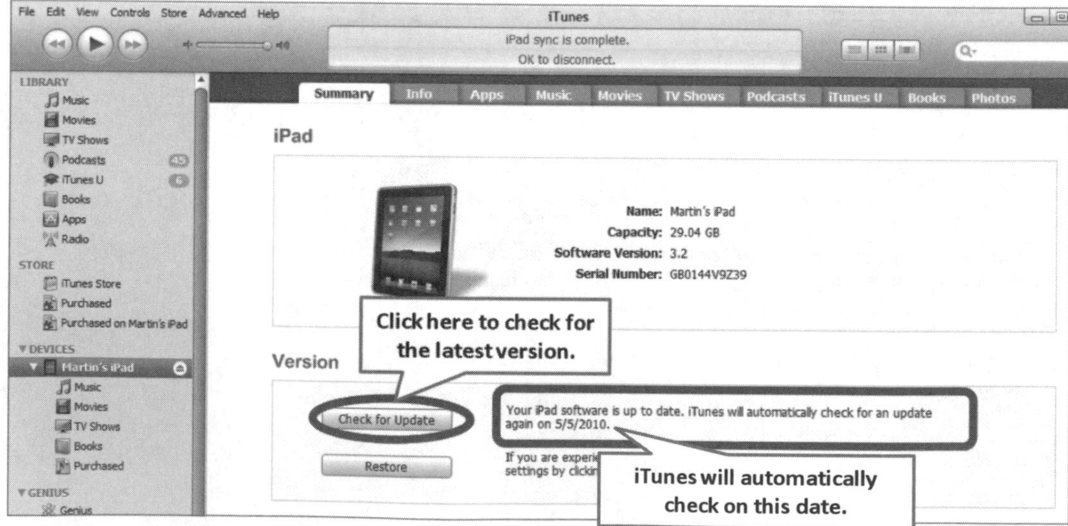


*Figure 3–41. Checking for updated software*

6. If you have the latest version, you will see a pop-up window saying something like "This version of the iPad software (3.2) is the current version." Click **OK** to close the window.
7. If you do not have the latest version, then a window will tell you a new version is available and ask if you would like to update. Click **Yes** or **Update**.
8. Then iTunes will download the latest iPad OS from Apple. This might take a while if you have a slower Internet connection on your computer.
9. Next iTunes will backup your iPad, which might take a while if your iPad is full with data.
10. Now the new OS will be installed and your iPad erased.
11. Finally, you are presented with the screen shown in Figure 3–42.
    a. Choose Set Up as a New iPad if you want to erase all data.
    b. Choose Restore from a backup and make sure you select the correct backup file (usually the most recent one).

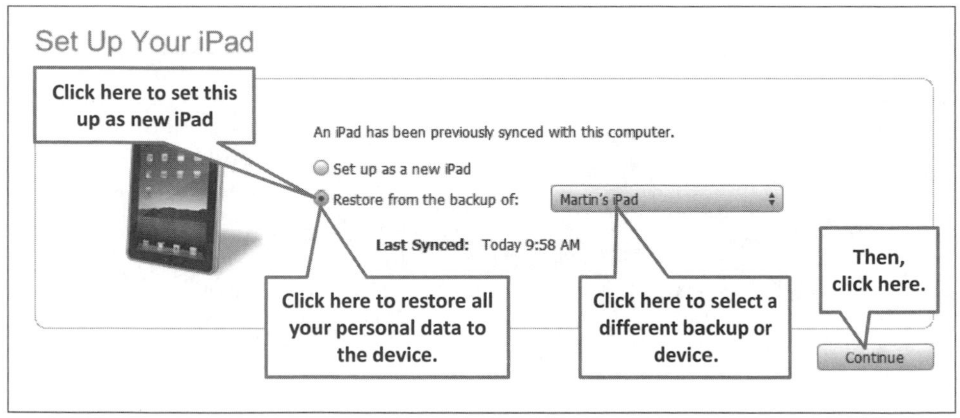


**Figure 3–42.** *Setting up your iPad as a new device or restoring from a backup file*

12. Now your iPad will be restored or set up as you selected.
13. Your iPad OS update is complete.

Chapter 4

# Wi-Fi and 3G Connections

We live in a connected world. Wireless Internet (Wi-Fi) access has become the rule, not the exception—chances are you're already using Wi-Fi at your home or office. Now you can use it to connect your iPad. And if your iPad has a 3G radio, you can also connect to the Internet anywhere you have cellular data coverage—a much wider area than Wi-Fi networks.

In this chapter we'll talk about the differences between the two types of connections for your iPad: Wi-Fi (wireless local area network) and 3G (cellular service—the wide area data network used by your mobile phone). We'll show you all the ways to get connected or disconnected from these two types of networks. There may be times you want to disable or turn off your 3G connection and only use Wi-Fi to save money in data connection charges.

The beauty of the iPad is that it has wireless Internet access built in. Once you connect your iPad to a wireless (Wi-Fi or 3G) network, you can be sending e-mail and surfing the Web in minutes. And once you discover all the great apps and books available, you'll never want to be disconnected again.

**NOTE:** Your iPad may not have a 3G connection. Some iPads come with only the Wi-Fi connection and do not have the ability to connect to a 3G cellular network.

How do you know which iPad you have? A 3G-enabled iPad will have a black plastic strip along the top edge which shows more prominently along the back side of the iPad to aid in data reception.

## What Can I Do When I'm Connected to a Wi-Fi or 3G Network?

Following are some of the things you can do when connected . . .

- Access and download apps (programs) from the App Store.
- Access and download music, videos, podcasts, and more from iTunes on your iPad.
- Browse the Web using Safari.
- Send and receive e-mail messages.
- Use social networking sites that require an Internet connection, like Facebook, Twitter, etc.
- Use your iPad as a phone with the Skype app (See Chapter 22: Social Networking).
- Play games that use a live Internet connection.
- Anything else that requires an Internet connection.

# Wi-Fi Connections

Every iPad comes with Wi-Fi capability built in. If you have a 3G model (you can tell it's 3G because there is a black plastic strip along the top edge), then you have both 3G and Wi-Fi. So let's take a look at getting connected to the Wi-Fi network. Things to consider about Wi-Fi connections are:

- No additional cost for network access and data downloads (if you are using your iPad in your home, office, or a free Wi-Fi hotspot).
- Wi-Fi tends to be faster than a Cellular Data 3G connection.
- More and more places, including airplanes, provide Wi-Fi access, but you may have to pay a one-time or monthly service fee.

## Setting Up Your Wi-Fi Connection

To setup your Wi-Fi connection, follow these steps:

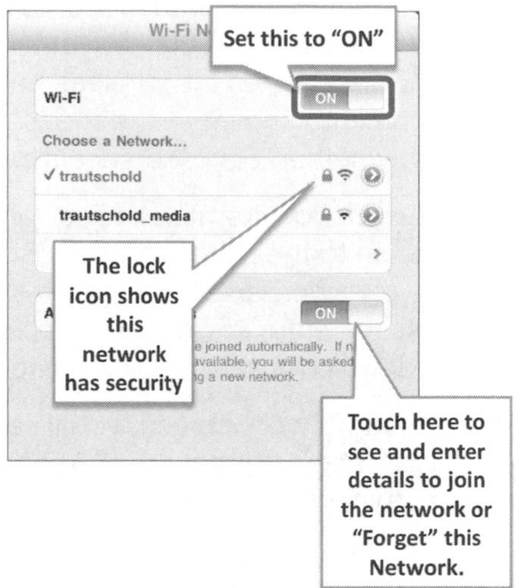


1. Tap the **Settings** icon
2. Tap **Wi-Fi** in the left column to see the screen shown at the right.
3. Make sure the **Wi-Fi** switch is set to **On**. Tap it if it is **Off**.
4. Once Wi-Fi is **ON**, the iPad will automatically start looking for wireless networks.
5. The list of accessible networks is shown below the **Choose a Network...** option. You can see in this screenshot that we have two networks available.

To connect to any network listed, just touch it. If the network is unsecure (does not require a password), you will be connected automatically.

**NOTE:** Some places, like coffee shops, use a web-based login instead of a username/password screen. In those cases, when you click on the network (or try to use Safari), iPad will slide up a browser screen and you'll see the web page along with login options.

# Secure Wi-Fi Networks—Entering a Password

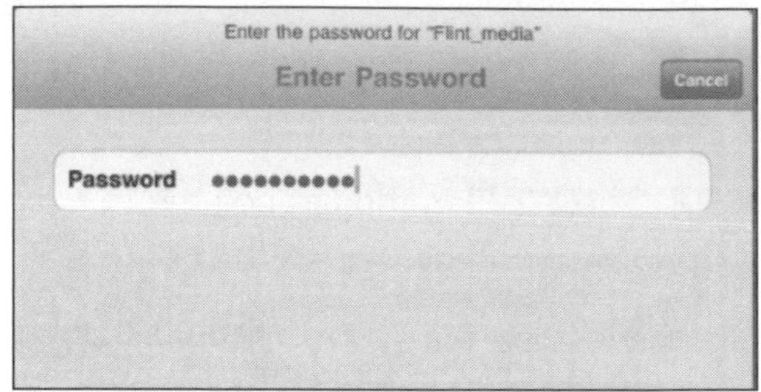


Some Wi-Fi networks require a password to log in. This is set when the network administrator creates the wireless network. You will have to know the exact password, including whether it is case-sensitive.

If the network does require a password, you will be taken to the password-entry screen. Type the password exactly as given to you and press the enter key on the on-screen keyboard (which is now labeled as **Join**).

On the next network screen: you'll see a checkmark showing that your are connected to the network.

**TIP:** You can paste into the password dialog, so for longer, random passwords, you can transfer them to your iPad (in an email message) and just copy and paste them. Just remember to delete the e-mail immediately after to keep things secure.

## Switching to a Different Wi-Fi Network

At times you may want to change your active Wi-Fi network. This might occur if you are in a hotel, apartment or other place where the network selected by the iPad is not the strongest network, or you want to use a secure network instead of an unsecure one.

To switch from the currently selected Wi-Fi network, tap the **Settings** icon, touch **Wi-Fi** in the left column, then touch the name of the Wi-Fi network you want to join. If that network requires a password, you'll need to enter it to join. (See Figure 4–1.)

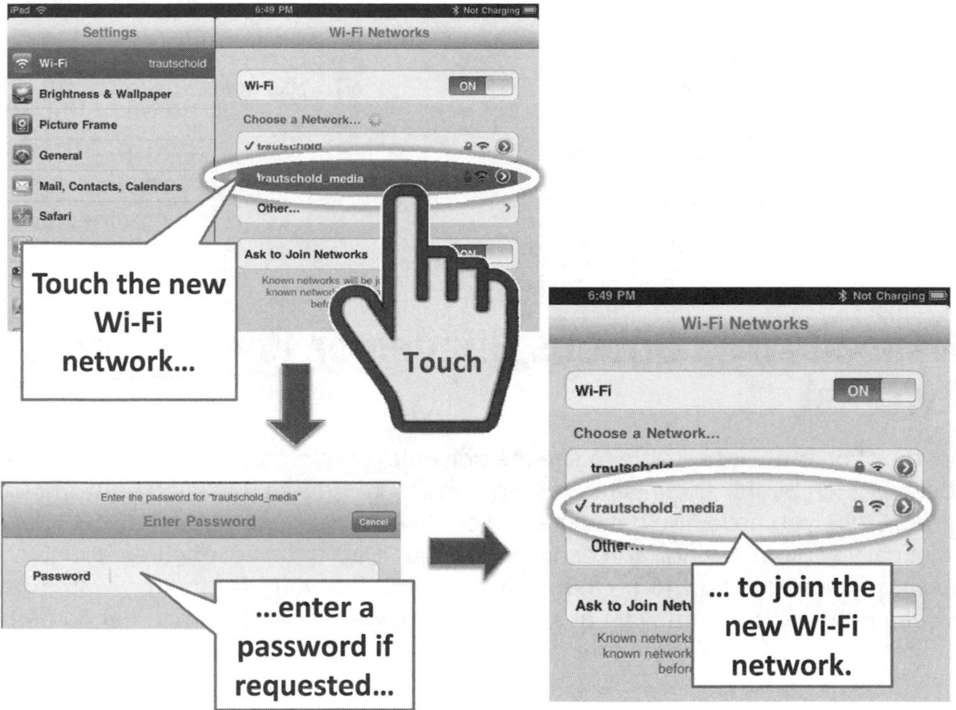


**Figure 4–1.** *Switching to a different Wi-Fi network*

Once you type the correct password (or if you touched an open network), your iPad will join that network.

## Verifying Your Wi-Fi Connection

To verify that you are connected to a Wi-Fi network, look for the network name with the checkmark next to it.

When you go back to the **Settings** screen, you should now see the name of your Wi-Fi network with a checkmark next to it in the list under Choose a Network.

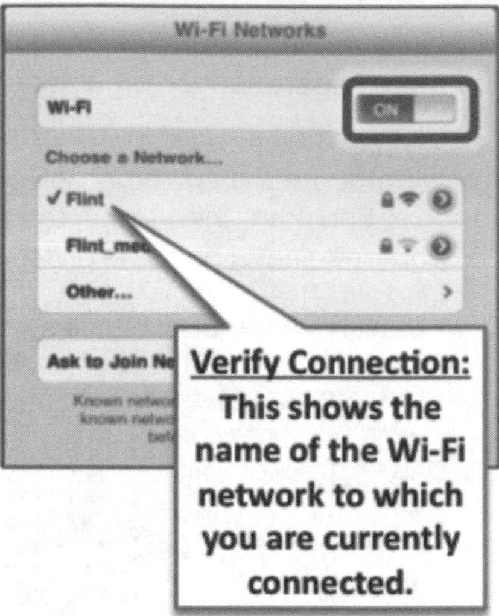


## Advanced Wi-Fi Options (Hidden or Undiscoverable Networks)

Sometimes you may not be able to see the network you want to join because the name has been hidden by the administrator. Below you learn how to join such networks on you iPad. Once you have, the next time you come in contact with that network it will join automatically without asking. You can also tell your iPad to ask every time it joins a network; we show you how to do that below as well. Sometimes you may want to erase or forget a network. Say you were at a one-time convention and want to get rid of the associated network, you'll learn that here, too.

## Why Can't I See the Wi-Fi Network I want to Join?

Sometimes, for security reasons, people don't make their networks discoverable and you have to manually enter the name and security options to connect.

As you can see in Figure 4–2, your list of available networks includes **Other**…. Touch the **Other** tab, and you can manually enter in the name of a network you would like to join.

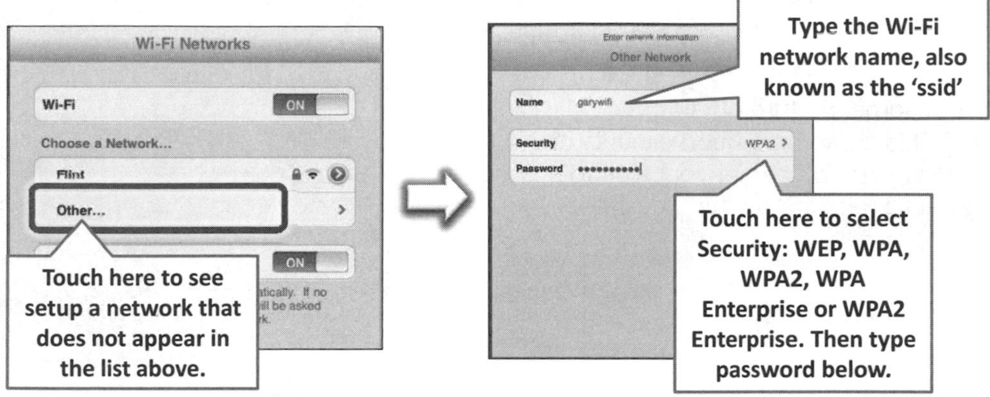


**Figure 4–2.** *You can manually enter the name of a Wi-Fi network.*

Type in the Wi-Fi network name and then touch the **Security** tab and choose which type of security is being used on that network. If you are unsure, you'll need to find out from the network administrator.

When you have the information you need, enter it along with the proper password and this new network will be saved to your network list for future access.

## Reconnecting to Previously Joined Wi-Fi Networks

The nice thing about the iPad is that when you return to an area with a Wi-Fi network you previously joined (whether it was an open or a secure, password-protected, network) your iPad will automatically join the network without asking you again. However, you can turn off this automatic-joining feature as described below.

## Ask to Join Networks

By default, this switch is set to **On** and you will join known or visible Wi-Fi networks automatically. If networks are available that are not known to you, you will be asked before being connected.

If the switch is set to **Off**, you will be automatically connected only to known networks and you'll have to follow the procedure we described for manually joining unknown networks.

Why might someone turn off automatically joining a network? This could be a good security measure if, for example, you don't want your kids to be able to join a wireless network on the iPad without your knowledge.

## Forget (or Erase) a Network

If you find that you no longer want to connect to a network on your list, you can "forget" it—i.e., take it off your list of networks. Just touch the small blue arrow next to that network. The screen that follows shows the network details of that particular connection.

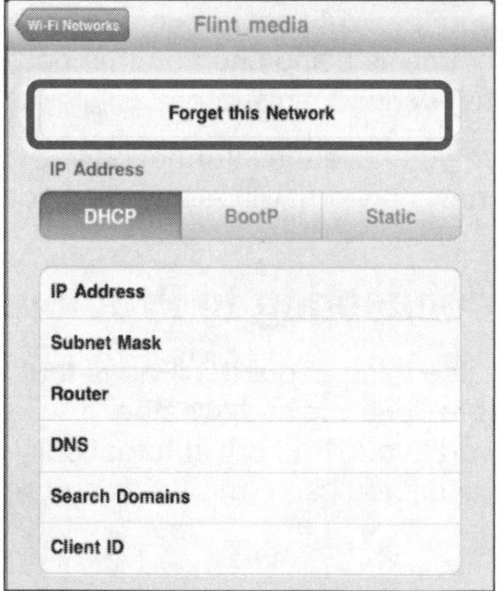

Touch **Forget this Network** at the top of the screen. You will be prompted with a warning. Just touch **Forget Network** and the network will no longer show up on your list.

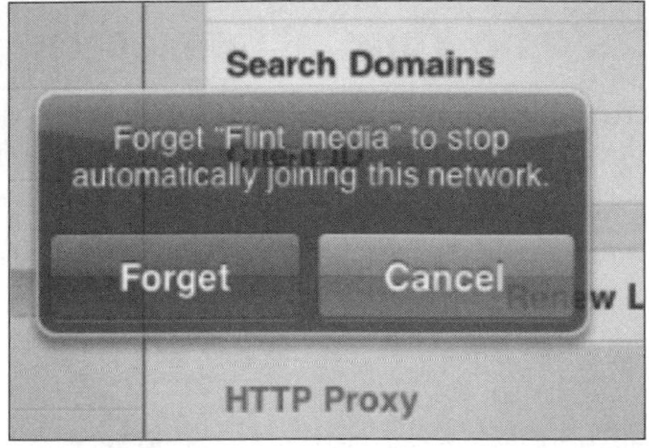


## 3G Cellular Data Connection

If you have a 3G iPad, you will also be able to connect to the cellular data network – the same network you connect to with an iPhone or other mobile phone. Things to consider about Cellular Data Connections:

- Wider availability than a Wi-Fi connection—you can connect to 3G in a car or away from a city, whereas Wi-Fi is not typically be available in these locations.
- Extra monthly service fees for access to the Cellular Data network.
- In the US, AT&T charges about $15 for 250MB per month and about $30 for unlimited data.

**NOTE:** Orange UK, Vodafone UK, O2, and Rogers Canada will all be announcing pricing in late May when the iPad ships internationally.

## Setting Up Your 3G Connection

Before you can connect to the 3G cellular network, you have to purchase a cellular data plan from your wireless carrier. For the iPad in the US, this is currently AT&T.

**TIP:** You might be able to save yourself some money with cellular data plan charges by doing the following:

- Always use Wi-Fi when possible
- Start with the lower cost cellular data plan ($14.99 for 250MB)
- Monitor your cellular data usage throughout the month to make sure you are not going to exceed the lower cost data plan.

You may find that you can live with the lower cost plan if you use Wi-Fi for most of your data needs.

To do this:

1. Tap the **Settings** icon on your iPad.
2. Tap **Cellular Data** in the left column.
3. Set the switch next to **Cellular Data** to **On**. (See Figure. 4–3.)
4. The first time you do this, you will see a pop-up window asking you to setup your account.
   a. Enter your personal information, username and password that is specific to this new Cellular Data plan. This account is not connected your email account, cell phone plan or any other account so you could enter the same information or make it different.

**NOTE:** As of publishing time, the wireless carrier in the US (AT&T) only offered recurring billing plans. What this means is that you set up the plan once, and you are billed every month until you cancel the plan.

   b. Scroll down to see the rest of the screen and select your data plan by tapping the screen.
   c. Enter your credit card information.
5. Tap the **Next** button.

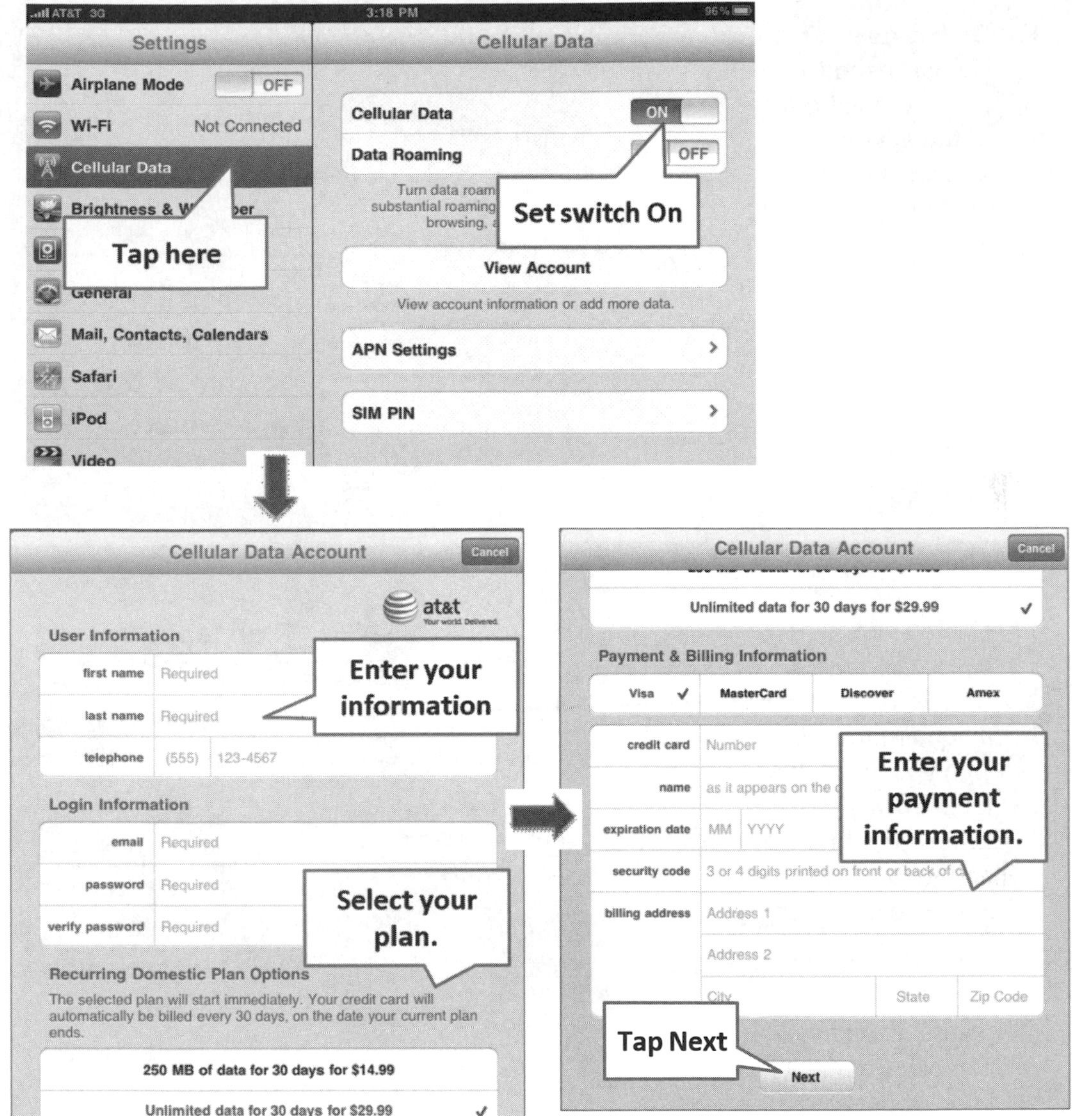


**Figure 4–3.** *Buying a cellular data plan*

6. On this next screen, you will need to swipe to the bottom of the agreement and tap **Agree** to continue. (Assuming you agree.)

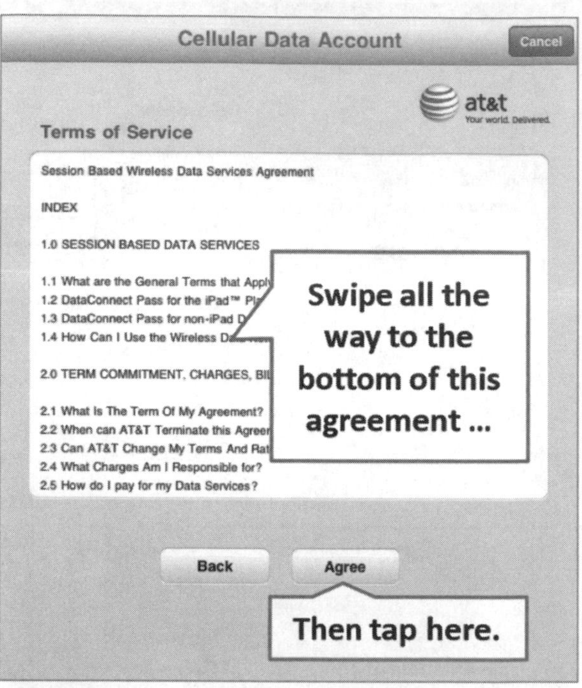


7. If you are traveling with your iPad, then tap **Add International Data** and follow the steps in the next section.

8. If you do not want to add the international plan at this time (you can always add it later), then tap **Submit** to finish.

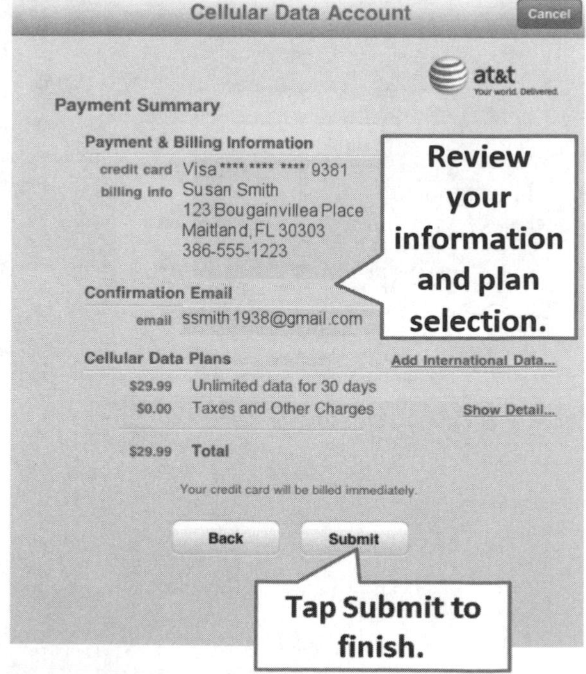

9. After taping **Submit**, you will see a window similar to this one. Tap **Ok** to close the window.

Cellular Data Account

at&t
Your world. Delivered.

AT&T is updating your iPad account.
It may take a few minutes to process the update.
You will be notified when this is complete.

OK

10. Finally, when your new cellular data plan is setup, you will see a pop-up message similar to this one.

## Adding an International Data Plan

If you plan on taking a trip, you may want to add an International Data plan to your iPad. It is easy to do by following these steps:

1. Tap the **Settings** icon.
2. Tap **Cellular Data** in the left column.
3. Tap **View Account** in the right column.
4. Login to the account by entering your Cellular Data username and password you used when you created this account.
5. Tap **Add International Plan** (see Figure 4–4).
6. On the International Data Plan window
    a. Select your One-Time International Plan.
    b. Adjust your plan Start Date to match your travel needs.

c. Tap the View Full List of Countries link at the bottom to verify the plan will support the countries you need.

d. Finally, tap **Done**.

e. You may need to confirm your selection on the following screen.

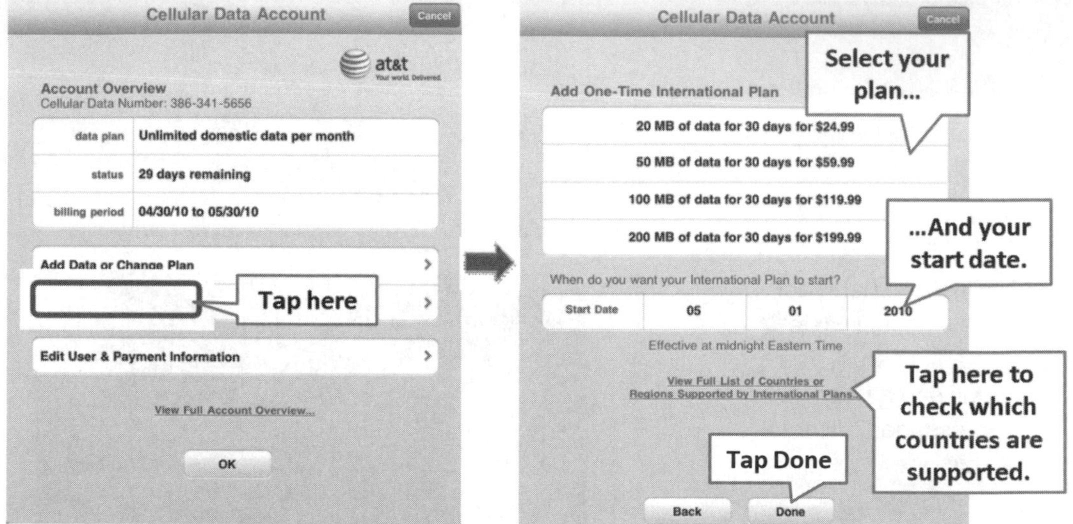


**Figure 4–4.** *Buying an International Cellular Data Plan*

## Monitoring Your Cellular Data Usage and Changing Your Plan

If you purchase the limited use data plan (the $15 plan for 250MB/month), you will want to check periodically to see how much data you are using on a daily basis.

To do this, follow these steps:

1. Tap the **Settings** icon.
2. Tap **Cellular Data** in the left column.
3. Tap **View Account** in the right column.
4. Login to the account by entering your Cellular Data username and password you used when you created this account. (See Figure 4–2 above).
5. Look at your **data plan**, **status** and **billing period** listed in the **Account Overview** section at the top. You will only see actual data usage in megabytes (MB) if you have selected a plan that limits the amount of data you have purchased (e.g. 250 MB).

6. If you want to change you plan or add data, then tap **Add Data or Change Plan** and follow the steps to adjust your plan.

**NOTE:** The iPad will notify you when you have 20%, 10%, and 0 left on your 250MB plan and you'll have the option of renewing that plan for another $14.99 or upgrading to the $30 unlimited plan.

**INTERNATIONAL TRAVEL—HOW TO AVOID LARGE CELLULAR (3G) DATA ROAMING BILLS (FOR 3G IPAD MODELS ONLY)**

We've heard of people who traveled to another country being surprised with $300 or $400 monthly roaming charges after their trip. You can avoid these by taking a few easy steps before and during your trip.

**TIP:** Try to use your Wi-Fi connection at free Wi-Fi networks overseas to keep your Cellular data roaming charges to a minimum.

1. Sign up for a one-time International Data plan as shown above in the "Adding An International Data Plan" section. In most cases, activating the international data plan allows you to save some money over the standard data roaming charges.
2. Learn about any Data Roaming Charges. Check with your cellular data supplier about any data roaming charges. You can try searching on your phone company's web site, but usually you'll have to call the help desk and specifically ask what the iPad data roaming charges are for the country or countries you'll be visiting. If you plan to use e-mail, mapping, web browsing, or any other data services, you should specifically ask about whether any of these services are charged separately.
3. Explore buying and using a foreign SIM Card (MicroSIM format).

Your iPad cellular data supplier may not offer special deals on international data roaming plans or may have rates that are unreasonably high. In such cases, you can insert a SIM card that you'll purchase in the foreign country.

**CAUTION:** The iPad uses a MicroSIM and almost all other phones use a MiniSIM. This may make it hard to find an international carrier with a SIM card that will fit.

Often, inserting a SIM card for the country you're in will eliminate or greatly reduce data roaming charges. However, do carefully check the cost of data on that foreign SIM card. Using a foreign SIM card may save you hundreds of dollars, but it's best to do some Web research or try to talk to someone who recently traveled to the same country to make sure.

# Airplane Mode – Turn Off 3G and Wi-Fi

Often when you are flying on an airplane, the flight crew will ask you to turn off all portable electronic devices for takeoff and landing. Then, when you get to altitude, they say "all approved electronic devices" can be turned back on.

You can turn off the iPad by pressing and holding the power button on the top right edge, then **Slide to Power Off** with your finger.

If you have a 3G/Cellular Data iPad, then you can turn on **Airplane Mode** in the **Settings** icon as follows:

1. Tap the **Settings** icon.
2. Set the switch next to **Airplane Mode** in the top of the left column to **On**.

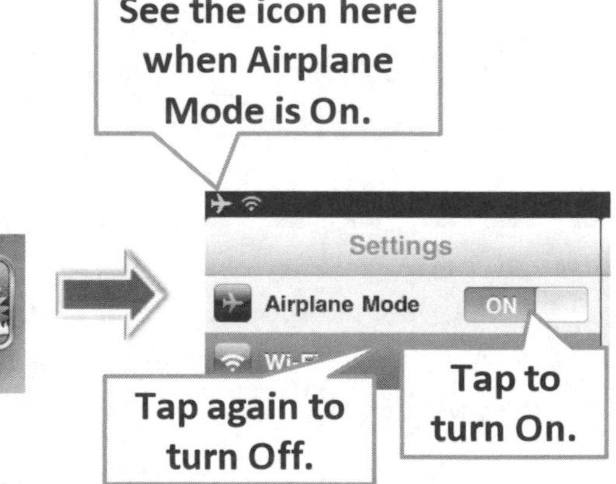

See the icon here when Airplane Mode is On.
Settings
Settings
Airplane Mode
ON
Tap again to turn Off.
Tap to turn On.

**TIP:** Some airlines do have in-flight Wi-Fi networks, so in this case you will want to leave your Wi-Fi turned **On**.

You can turn **Off** or **On** your Wi-Fi connection by following these steps (Figure 4–5):

1. Tap the **Settings** icon.
2. Tap **Wi-Fi** in the top of the left column.
3. Set the switch next to **Wi-Fi** in the top of the right column to **Off**.

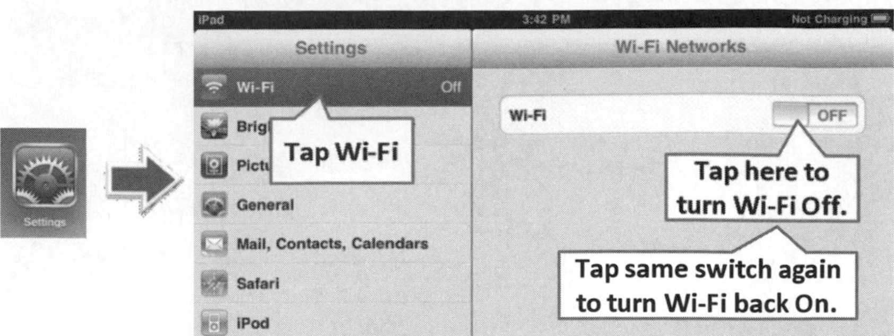


**Figure 4–5.** *How to Turn Wi-Fi Off or On.*

Chapter 5

# Moving, Docking, and Deleting Icons

iPads are very customizable. In this chapter we will show you how to move icons around and put your favorite icons just where you want them. You've got up to eleven pages of icons to work with, and you can adjust the look and feel of those pages so it suits your tastes.

Like a Mac computer or an iPhone, the iPad has a **Bottom Dock** where you can put the icons for your favorite apps. iPads come with four standard icons in the **Bottom Dock**, but you can replace these or add to them to have up to six icons always available at the bottom of your screen.

**TIP:** You can also move or delete icons using iTunes on your computer. Check out our **Bonus iTunes User Guide** in Chapter 26 for more information.

# Moving Icons to the Bottom Dock—Docking Them

When you turn your iPad on, you'll notice the four icons locked to the bottom dock: **Safari**, **Mail**, **Photos**, and **iPod**.

Suppose you decide you want to change one or more of these for apps you use more often. Fortunately, moving icons to and from the bottom dock is easy.

If you prefer, you can keep the standard four and add two more for a total of six icons in the **Bottom Dock** for easy access.

Keep up to 6 icons that you want to see all the time. These icons will always remain visible even when you slide the other icon screens left/ right.
Bottom Dock

## Starting the Move

Press the **Home** button to get to your **Home Screen**. Now, touch and hold any icon on the **Home Screen** for a couple of seconds. You'll notice that all the icons start to shake.

Just try moving a couple of icons around at first. You'll see that when you move an icon down, the other icons in the row move to make space for it.

Once you have the feel for how the icons move, you are ready to replace one of the **Bottom Dock** icons. While the icons are shaking, take the icon you wish to replace from the **Bottom Dock** and move it up to the main screen.

> **NOTE:** You can have up to six icons in the **Bottom Dock**, so if you already have six there, you will have to remove one to replace it with a new one.

Suppose you want to replace the standard **iPod** icon with your **App Store** icon. The first thing to do is just hold the **iPod** icon and move it up a row—out of the **Bottom Dock**, as shown in Figure 5–1.

To stop the icons shaking, tap your **Home** button.

**Figure 5–1.** *Swapping icons in the Bottom Dock*

Next, locate your **App Store** icon and move it down to the **Bottom Dock**. As you'll see, the icon becomes sort of transparent until you actually set it into place.

When you are sure that you have the icons just where you want them, simply press the **Home** button once and the icons lock into place... Now, you have the **App Store** icon in the Bottom Dock where you want it.

# Moving Icons to a Different Icon Page

iPads can hold 20 icons on a page (not including the dock) and you can find these pages by swiping (right to left) on your **Home Screen**. With all the cool apps available, it is not uncommon to have five, six, or even more pages of icons. You can have up to eleven pages filled with icons if you feel adventurous!

> **NOTE:** You can also swipe from left to right on any screen except the **Home Screen**. On the **Home Screen**, swiping left to right takes you to **Spotlight Search**; see Chapter 2 for more information.

You may have an icon you rarely use on your first page and you want to move it way off to the last page. Or you may want to move an icon you often use from the last of the icons pages to the first page. Both are very easy to do; it's very much like moving icons to the **Bottom Dock**, as discussed above.

1. Touch and hold any icon to initiate the moving process.
2. Touch and hold the icon you wish to move. As shown in Figure 5–2, let's say we want to move the **MLB at Bat** icon to the first page. (Baseball season is here and I need to follow the Red Sox!)

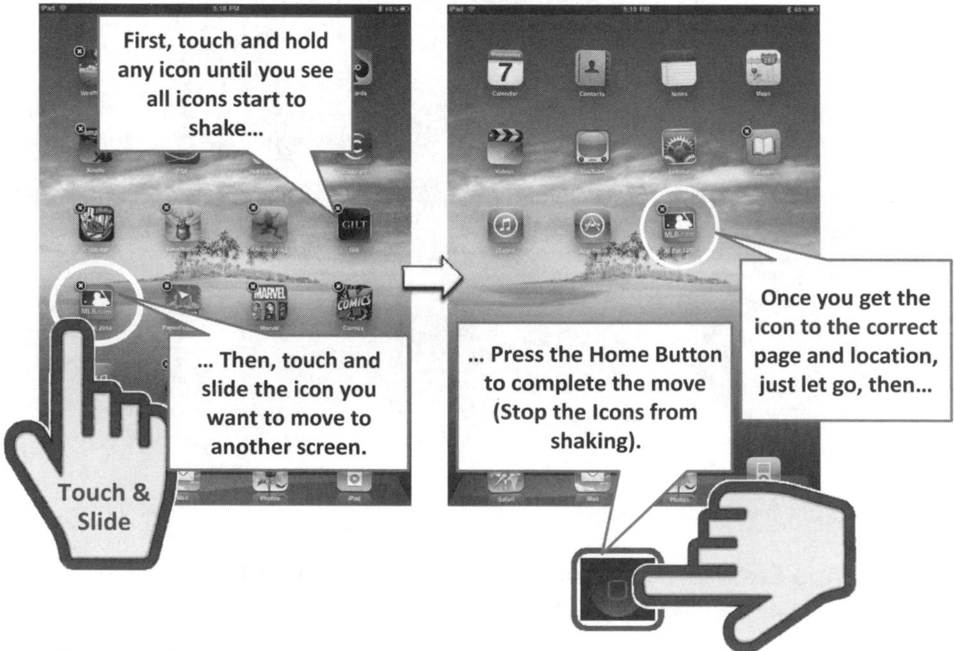


**Figure 5–2.** *Moving icons from one page to another*

3. Now drag and drop the icon onto another page. To do this, you touch and hold the **MLB at Bat** icon and drag it to the left. You will see all of my pages of icons move by. When you get to the first page, you just release the icon and it is now placed at the very beginning.
4. Press the **Home Key** to complete the move and stop the icons from shaking.

## Deleting Icons

Be careful—it is as easy to delete an icon as it is to move it, but when you delete an icon on the iPad, you are actually deleting the program it represents. This means you won't be able to use the program again without reinstalling or downloading it.

Depending on your Application Sync settings in iTunes, the program may still reside in your Applications folder in iTunes. In that case, you would be able to easily reinstall the deleted app if you wanted to by checking that application in the list of apps to sync in iTunes.

As Figure 5–3 shows, the deleting process is similar to the moving process. Touch and hold any icon to initiate deleting. Just as before, touching and holding makes the icons shake and allows you to move or delete them.

> **NOTE:** You may only delete programs you have downloaded to your iPad; the preinstalled icons and their associated programs can't be deleted. You can tell which programs can be deleted because the icons contain a small black x in the upper left corner.

Just tap the **x** on the icon you'd like to delete. You will be prompted to either **Delete** or **Cancel** the delete request. If you select **Delete**, the icon and its related app are removed from your iPad.

**Figure 5–3.** *Deleting an icon—and its associated program*

## Resetting All Your Icon Locations (Factory Defaults)

Occasionally, you might want to go back to the original, factory default icon settings. This might be the case when you've moved too many new icons to your first page and want to see all the basic icons again.

To do this, touch the **Settings** icon. Then touch **General** in the left column and, finally, scroll all the way to the bottom to touch **Reset** in the right column.

**NOTE:** Built-in apps will get sorted back into the order they were in when Apple shipped the iPad.

On the **Reset** screen, touch **Reset Home Screen Layout** near the bottom. Now all your icons will be returned to the original settings.

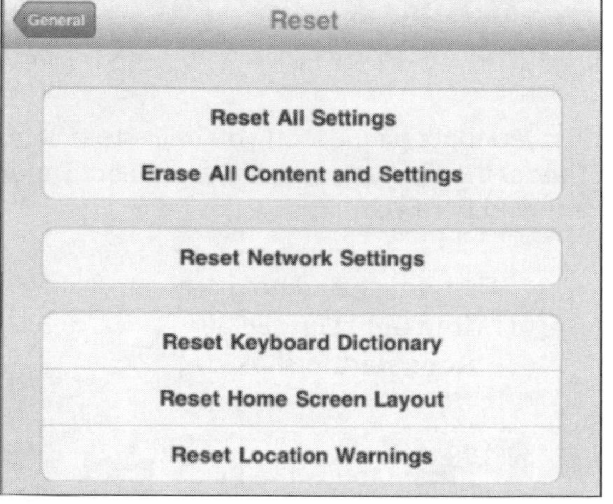


**CAUTION:** Be careful you don't touch one of the other **Reset** options, as you can inadvertently erase your entire iPad if you touch the wrong button. If you do, you'll have to restore data from your iTunes backup.

Chapter 6

# Personalize & Secure Your iPad

In this chapter you will learn some great ways to personalize your iPad—and how to protect your iPad with passcode security. You can download some great free wallpaper and change the wallpaper for your **Lock** and **Home** screens. You can personalize the sounds your iPad makes by adjusting whether you hear a sound when you receive or send e-mail, lock the iPad, type using the keyboard or are alerted before an event on your calendar. You can also customize the **Picture Frame** settings (This is the app that shows your pictures when the device is locked). You can vary times, transitions, and even select which albums of pictures are shown. Many aspects of the iPad can be fine-tuned to meet your needs and tastes—to give your iPad a more personal look and feel.

## Changing your Lock Screen and Home Screen Wallpapers

There are actually two screens you can personalize on your iPad by changing the wallpaper.

The first is the **Lock Screen**, which appears when you first turn on your iPad, or wake it up. The wallpaper for this screen image is shown behind the **Slide to Unlock** slider bar.

The next one is the **Home Screen.** The wallpaper for this is shown behind the icons.

You can use the wallpaper pictures that come with the iPad or you can use your own images.

**TIP:** You may want the wallpaper for your **Lock Screen** to be less personal than your **Home Screen** wallpaper. For example, you might choose to put a generic landscape image on your **Lock Screen** and a picture of a loved one on your **Home Screen**.

There are a couple of ways to change the wallpaper on the iPad. The first way is very straightforward.

## Changing Wallpaper from your Settings

Touch the **Settings** icon, then touch the **Brightness & Wallpaper** tab in the left-hand column. The settings for brightness and wallpaper will appear in the right-hand column.

To begin selecting wallpaper, touch the images of your currently selected wallpaper under **Wallpaper** on the right side of the screen, as shown in Figure 6–1.

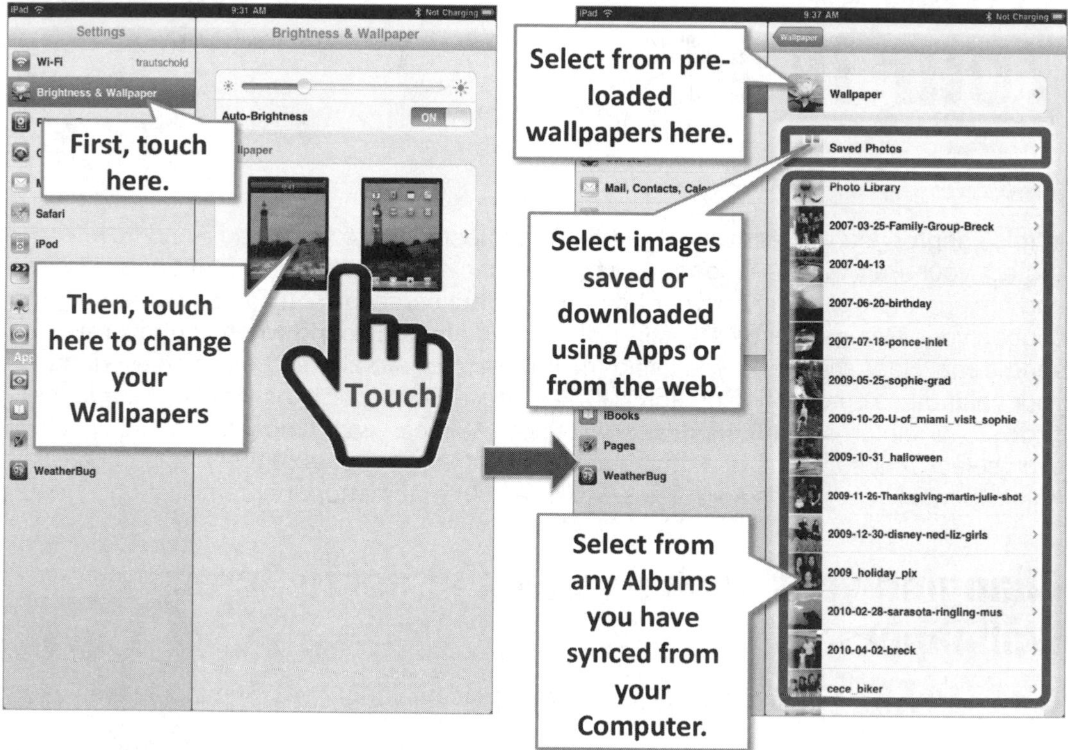


**Figure 6–1.** *Changing wallpaper starting from the Settings icon*

On the right side of the screen (Figure 6–1, right image), you'll see some albums or image folders. You have some choices:

- Tap the **Wallpaper** tab at the top to see all the preloaded wallpaper pictures for the iPad.
- Tap the **Saved Photos** album, which contains any images you've saved from the Web, from screenshots (which you take by pressing and hold the **Home** button and **Power/Sleep** key) or even from wallpaper apps.

Tap any of the albums displayed below **Saved Photos**. These additional albums will be visible only if you have synced photos from iTunes.

Once you tap any of the albums, you'll see all the images within that album, as in Figure 6–2.

Tap any of the images in the album to see it on the full screen.

When previewing the image on the full screen, you can:

- Zoom in or out by pinching your fingers open or closed.
- Tap the **Cancel** button to return to the album if you don't like the image.
- Tap the **Set Lock Screen** button to set the image only for your **Lock Screen**.
- Tap the **Set Home Screen** button to set the image only for your **Home Screen**.
- Tap the **Set Both** button to set the image for both your **Lock** and **Home Screens**.

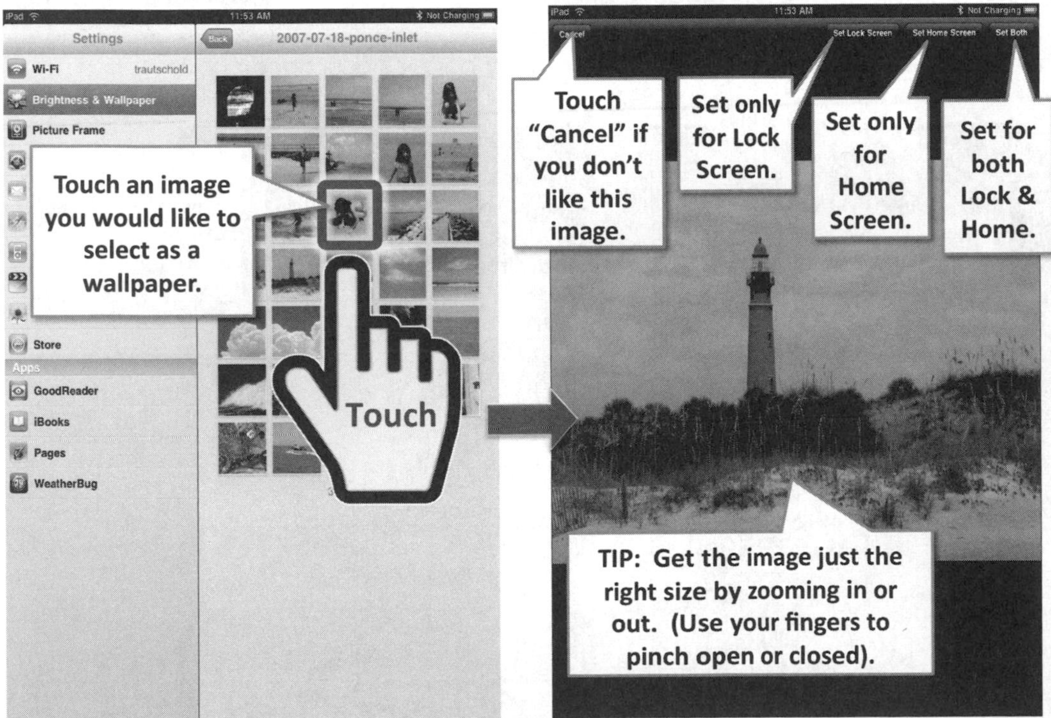


**Figure 6–2.** *Select a picture from an album to change your wallpaper.*

## Change Wallpaper from any Picture

The second way to change your wallpaper is to view any picture in your **Photos** collection and select it as your wallpaper.

Tap the **Photos** icon to get started. To learn more about working with photos, check out Chapter 15, "Photos."

Touch the photo album you want to look through to find your wallpaper.

When you find a photo you want to use, touch it and it will open on your screen.

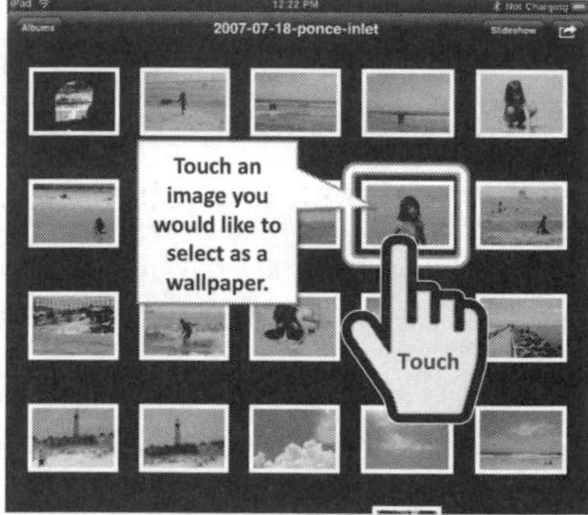


After you preview the image, as in Figure 6–3, tap the **Set as** icon on the top right corner of the screen and select **Use As Wallpaper**. Zoom in or out as you desire and then set as either your **Lock** or **Home Screen** or both, as described above.

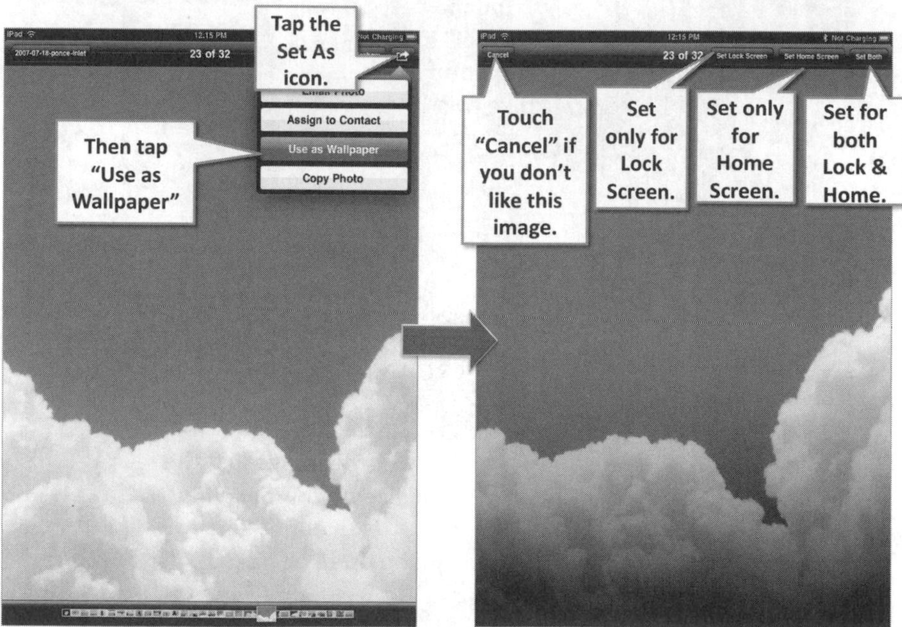


**Figure 6–3.** *Start from the Photos icon to use an existing photo or image as wallpaper.*

If you decide you'd rather use a different picture, choose **Cancel** and pick a different one.

# Download Great Wallpaper from Free Apps

Go to the **App Store** and do a search for **Backgrounds**. (See Chapter 20, "App Store" for help.) You'll find a number of free and low-cost apps designed specifically for your iPad. In this section we highlight one called **Backgrounds HD,** which has hundreds of beautiful background images you can download for free to your iPad.

> **NOTE:** With **Backgrounds HD,** as with most wallpaper apps, you will need a live Internet connection—either Wi-Fi or 3G. Because image files tend to be quite large, you should probably stick with Wi-Fi unless you have an unlimited monthly data plan for your 3G cellular data network.

## Downloading the Wallpaper from the Free App

After you download and install **Backgrounds HD**, tap the program's icon to start it up.

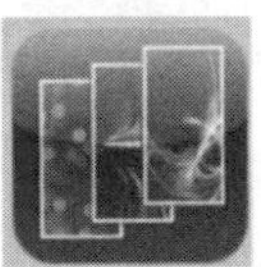

The app has a number of backgrounds to choose from. You can search for a particular background by tapping the **Search Backgrounds** window in the upper left corner, as shown in Figure 6–4. You can also choose to view **Popular** or **Recent** backgrounds using the buttons on the top.

Finally, if you would like to view all backgrounds in a particular category or by a certain artist, you can select those categories in the top right portion of the main screen. Some of the categories at publishing time were **Funny**, **Artsy**, **Quotes**, **Love**, **Nature**, **Flowers** and **Animals**.

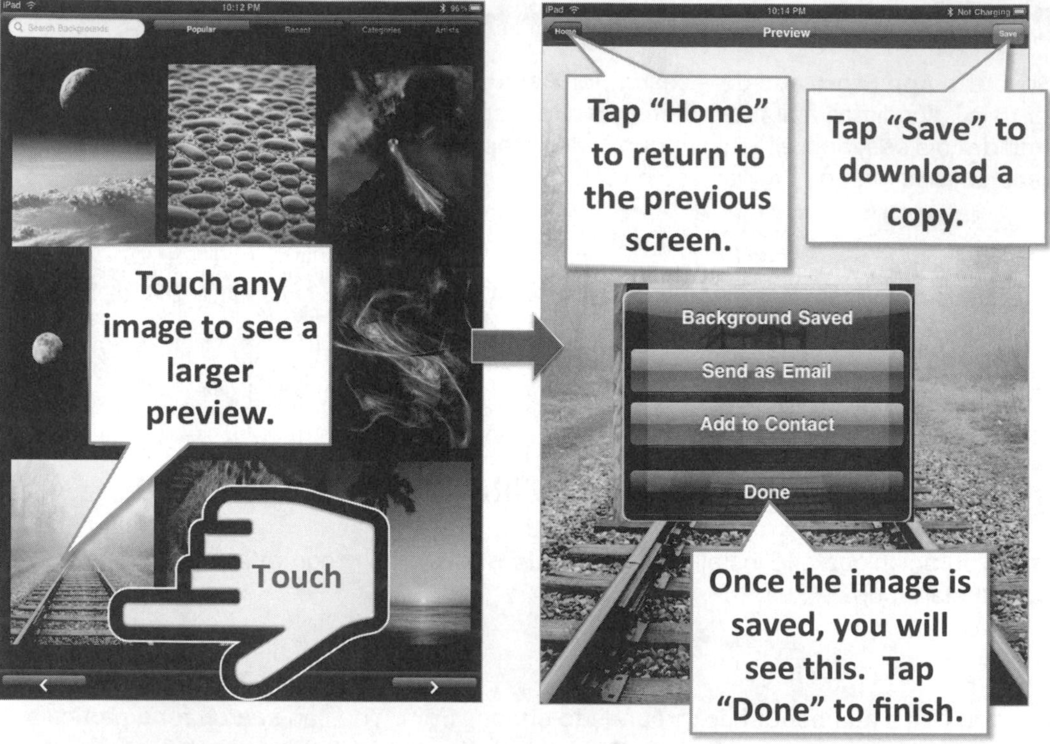


**Figure 6–4.** *Previewing free wallpaper from the* ***Backgrounds HD*** *app*

After touching any wallpaper to bring it to a full-screen preview, click the **Save** button in the upper right corner to save a copy into your **Saved Photos** album and then click the **Done** button.

If you don't like the image, click the **Home** button in the upper left corner to get back to the thumbnail images.

## Selecting the Downloaded Wallpaper

Once you've chosen a wallpaper image and saved to your iPad, you'll need to select it using the steps described earlier in this chapter that show how to change wallpaper using the **Settings** icon.

Be aware that the downloaded wallpaper will be in the **Saved Photos** album. After you tap **Saved Photos** to open it, you'll need to flick all the way to the bottom to see your recent entries.

# Adjusting Sounds on your iPad

You can fine-tune your iPad so that it does or does not make sounds when you receive new mail, send mail, the caledar alarm rings, the keyboard clicks or the when it is locked. To adjust sounds, follow these steps:

1. Tap your **Settings** icon.
2. Tap **General** in the left column.
3. Tap **Sounds** in the right column.
4. Tap any of the switches to turn **On** or **Off** the sound when the event occurs.

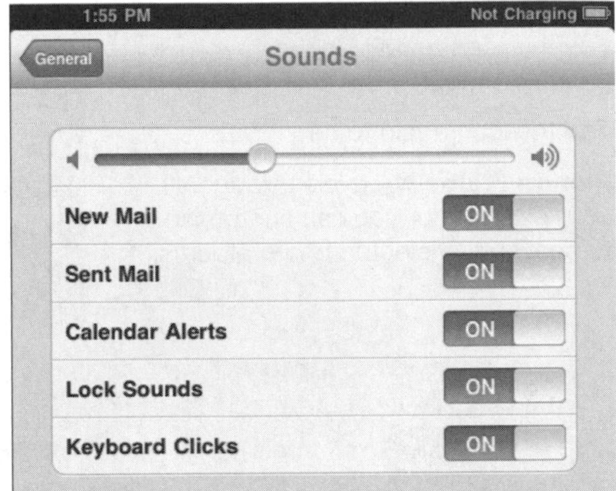


**TIP:** On a related note to sounds, you can lock the maximum volume playable from the iPod app. Go into Settings > iPod > Volume Limit > Lock Volume Limit. We show you how to do this in Chapter 7: "Music."

# Personalize Your Picture Frame

**Picture Frame** is the app that lets you display a slideshow of photos on your locked iPad (see Figure 6–5). We'll describe the many ways you can customize the display.

## Starting or Stopping the Picture Frame App

You may have noticed the little icon next to the **slide to unlock** slider bar when your iPad is locked. This is the **Picture Frame** icon.

Tap this icon to turn your iPad into an electronic Picture Frame.
slide to unlock

Tap this icon to turn on the electronic picture frame.

Tap the icon again to turn it off.

**Picture Frame** will cycle through all your pictures, or you can customize it to show only selected photo albums.

**CAUTION:** If you have private pictures stored on your iPad, it could get quite embarrassing if **Picture Frame** accidentally displays these photos while in locked mode. This section shows you how to restrict the albums that are used for the slideshow.

**NOTE:** You can disable **Picture Frame** by setting a passcode security lock on your iPad. We show you how later in this chapter on page 182.

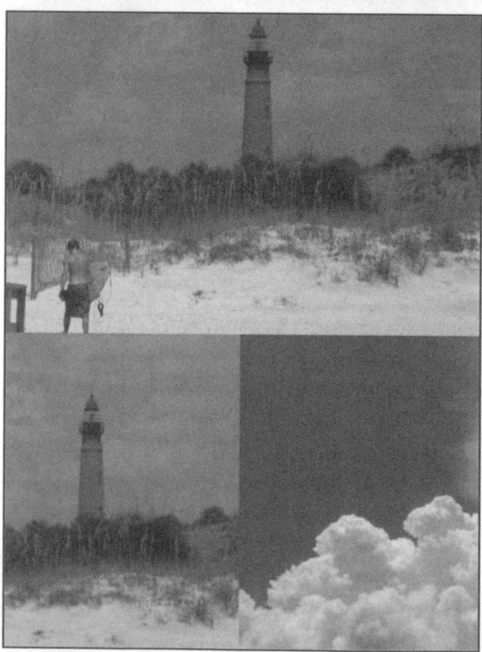

**Figure 6–5.** ***Picture Frame*** *can present a slideshow when your device is locked.*

## Customizing Your Picture Frame

Depending on the types of pictures you have stored on your iPad, you will almost certainly want to set up your **Picture Frame** to display just the albums or photos you want. To do this:

1. Tap the **Settings** icon.
2. Tap **Picture Frame** in the left column.
3. Now, you can adjust various settings for the picture frame: (Figure 6–6).
4. If you want to show only one picture on the screen at a time, select **Dissolve**. If you want three to four images at once, select **Origami**. **Origami** will show 2-4 images on the screen and them have them fold over on eachother sort of like you are folding paper.
5. **Zoom in on Faces** is selectable only if you've chosen the **Dissolve** transition. This is a neat feature that will zoom in on **any face**s detect**ed in the indivi**dual photos,
6. Set **Shuffle** to **ON** if you want **Picture Frame** to **randomly** go through the selected photos.
7. If you want all your photos to be included in the slideshow (the default setting), select **All Photos**.
8. People often want to keep some photos private. To do so, select **Albums**, then tap or check the albums to include. (The check indicates that an album will be included.)

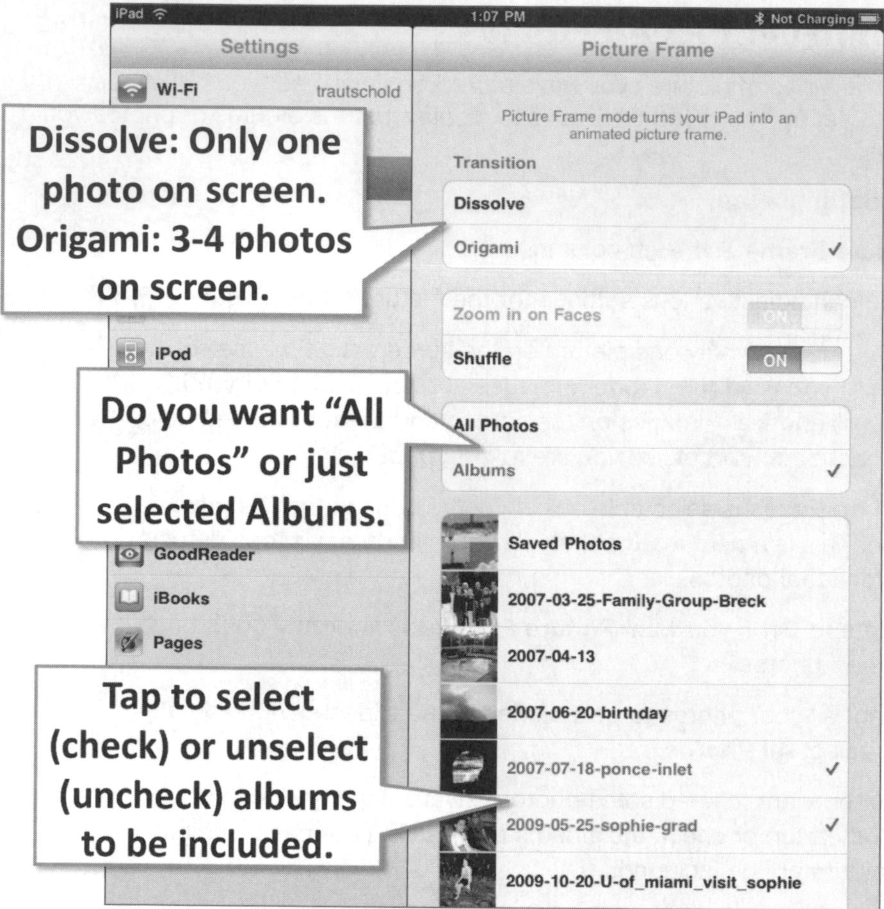


**Figure 6–6.** *Choosing how to customize* ***Picture Frame***

**TIP:** To really control what Picture Frame displays, set up an album on your computer with only the images you are happy to have everyone see when the device is locked. Then sync that album to your iPad using iTunes. For help with this, check out Chapter 3 "Sync with iTunes."

## Keyboard Options

You can fine-tune your keyboard by selecting various languages and changing settings like **Auto-Correction** and **Auto-Capitalization**. See Chapter 2, "Typing Tips, Copy/Paste, & Search" for keyboard options and how to use the various features.

# How to Secure Your iPad with a Passcode

Your iPad can hold a great deal of valuable information. This is especially true if you save information like the Social Security numbers and birth dates of your family members. It is a good idea to make sure that anyone who picks up your iPad can't access all that information. Also, if your children are like ours, they'll probably pick up your cool iPad and start surfing the Web or playing a game. You might want to enable some security restrictions to keep them safe.

## Setting a Passcode to Lock Your iPad

Touch the **Settings** icon and then the **General** tab in the left column. Now scroll down and tap on the **Passcode Lock** item.

Here you have the option of setting a four-digit passcode that prevents unauthorized access to your iPad and your information. If the wrong passcode is entered, however, even you won't be able to access your information, so it is a good idea to use a code you'll easily remember or to write it down somewhere secure. (See Figure 6–7.)

Use the keyboard to enter a four-digit code. You will then be prompted to enter your code once more.

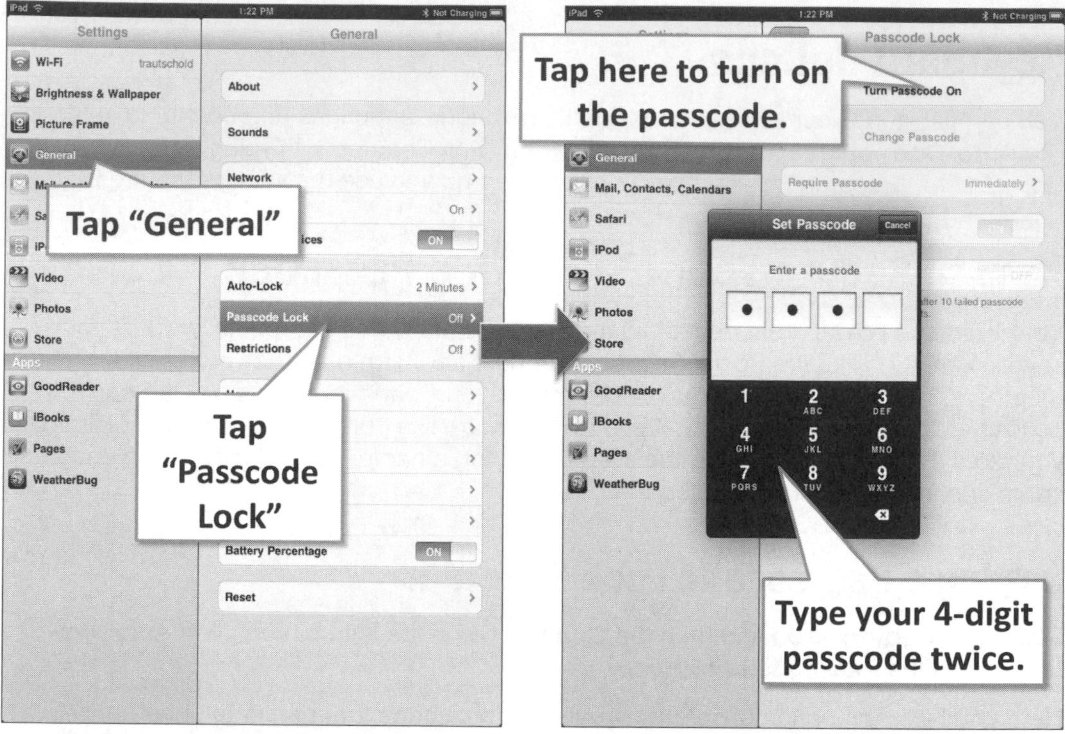


**Figure 6–7.** *Enabling security by setting a passcode*

## Passcode Options: Change Time-Out, Disable Picture Frame, Erase All Data after 10 Attempts

Once you have set your passcode, you will be presented with a few options:

**Turn Passcode Off**
**Change Passcode**
**Require Passcode** (Immediately, 1 min., 5 min., 15 min., 1 hour, 4 hours)

1:29 PM Not Charging
General
Passcode Lock
Turn Passcode Off
Change Passcode
Require Passcode After 1 min.
Picture Frame OFF
Erase Data ON
Erase all data on this iPad after 10 failed passcode attempts.

**NOTE:** Setting a shorter time for **Require Passcode** is more secure. Setting the time as **Immediately**, the default, is most secure. However, using a setting of one minute may save you the headache of retyping your passcode if you accidentally lock your iPad.

Picture Frame (default is **ON**); set to **OFF** to prevent the pictures from being seen in locked mode.

**Erase Data** (default is **OFF;** if this is set to **ON,** all data will be erased after ten unsuccessful attempts to enter the passcode.

**CAUTION:** You may want to set **Erase Data** to **OFF** if you have young children who like to bang away at the security to unlock the keyboard when it comes out of sleep mode and is locked. Otherwise, you may end up with your iPad being erased frequently.

## Setting Restrictions

You might decide you don't want your kids listening to explicit lyrics in music on your iPad. You may also not want them to visit YouTube and watch content you find objectionable. Setting these restrictions is quite easy on your iPad.

Once again, Touch the **General** tab under **Settings** and tap **Restrictions**.

You will see a large button that says **Enable Restrictions**.

When you touch this, you'll be prompted to enter a **Restrictions Passcode**—just pick a four-digit code you will remember.

**NOTE:** This a separate passcode from your main iPad passcode, you could set it to be the same to remember it easily, however that could be problematic if you let your family know the main passcode, but do not want them adjusting the restrictions.You will need to enter this passcode to turn off restrictions later.

Notice that you can adjust whether to allow certain apps at all: **Safari**, **YouTube**, **iTunes**, **Installing Apps** or **Location**.

**OFF = RESTRICTED**

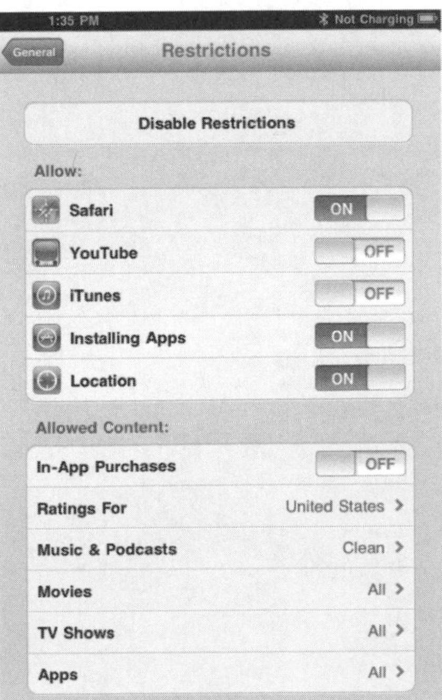

You might think that **ON** means something is restricted, but it is the opposite. In order to disable or restrict something, you need to touch the slider next to it and change it to **OFF**. If you look at the word **Allow:** above all the tabs, then it makes sense.

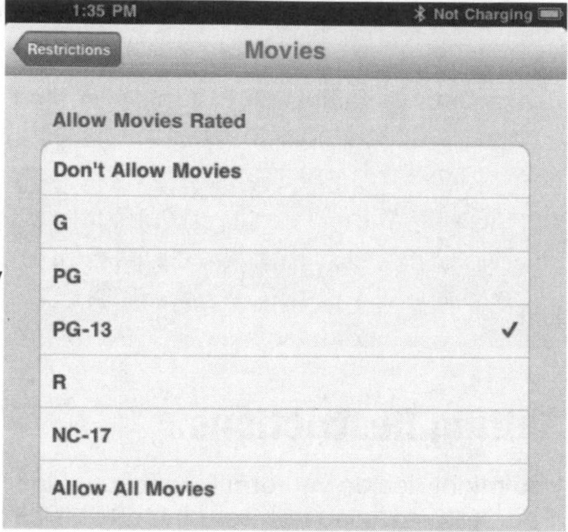


As you can see, you can restrict access to lyrics for **Music & Podcasts** to what is **Clean**.

You can also restrict which ratings for **Movies**, **TV Shows** and **Apps** to allow to be played on this iPad.

In the example in the image to the right, only movies with ratings up to PG-13 can be played. Movies with ratings of R and NC-17 can't be played.

Chapter 7

# Playing Music

In this chapter we show you how to turn your iPad into a great music player. Since it comes from Apple, which popularized electronic music players, you can bet the iPad has some great capabilities. We will show you how to play and organize the music you buy from iTunes or sync from your computer and how to view playlists in many ways and quickly find songs. We will also show you how to use the Genius feature to have the iPad locate and group similar songs in your library—it's sort of like a radio station that plays only music you like.

**TIP:** Learn how to buy music right on your iPad in Chapter 19, "iTunes on the iPad. Find out how to buy music using iTunes on your computer or load your music CDs onto iTunes so you can sync them with your iPad in the "iTunes Guide" in Part 4.

We will also show you how to stream free music using a free app called Pandora. With Pandora, you can select from a number of Internet radio stations or create your own by typing in your favorite artist's name.

## Your iPad as a Music Player

Your iPad is probably one of the best music players on the market today. The generous screen size really allows you to interact with your music, playlists, cover art and the organization of your music library. You can even connect your iPad via Bluetooth to your home or car stereo so you can listen to beautiful stereo sound from your iPad!

**TIP:** Check out Chapter 10: "Bluetooth" to learn how to hook up your iPad to your Bluetooth stereo speakers or car stereo.

Whether you use the built in iPod Music app or an Internet radio app like Pandora, you will find that you have unprecedented control over your music on the iPad.

# The iPod App

Most music is handled through the **iPod** app—the icon is on the **Home Screen**. This icon is usually in the **Bottom Dock** of icons—the last one on the right.

Touch the **iPod** icon and, as Figure 7–1 shows, you'll see five soft keys across the bottom:

- **Songs:** - See an alphabetical list of songs (also searchable)
- **Artists:** - See an alphabetical list of artists (searchable like your Address Book)
- **Albums:** See an alphabetical list of albums (also searchable).
- **Genres:** See your music organized by musical genres.
- **Composers:** See an alphabetical listing of musical composers.

**NOTE:** The **Composers** soft key is dynamic. It only shows up if it's applicable to the currently selected playlist, but it's always there in the **Music** app.

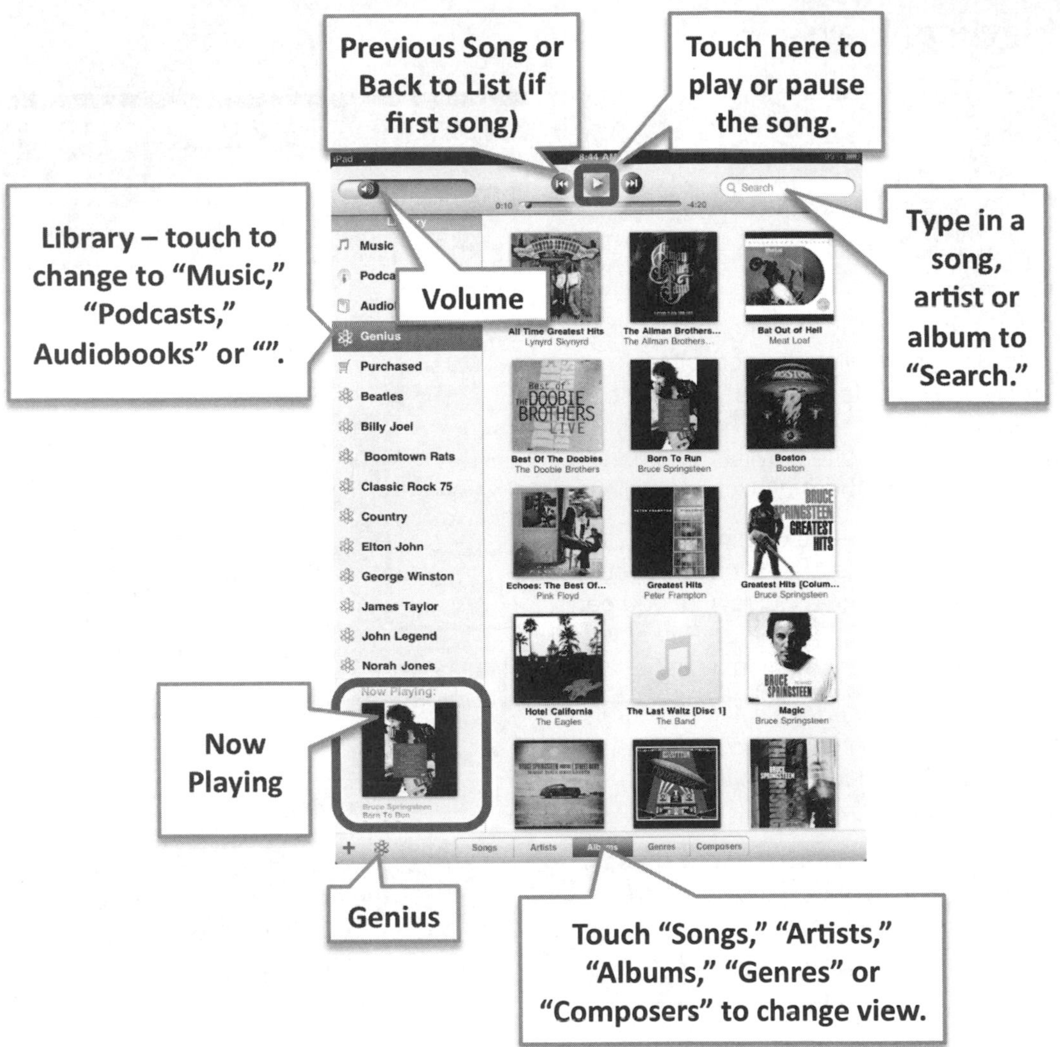


**Figure 7–1.** *iPod* ***Home Screen*** *layout*

> **TIP:** You can turn the iPad sideways if it is easier to hold. Everything functions exactly the same on this screen regardless of the orientation of the screen.

## Playlists View

**Note**: A playlist is a list of music you create and can be made up of any genre, artist, year of recording, or collection of songs that interest you.

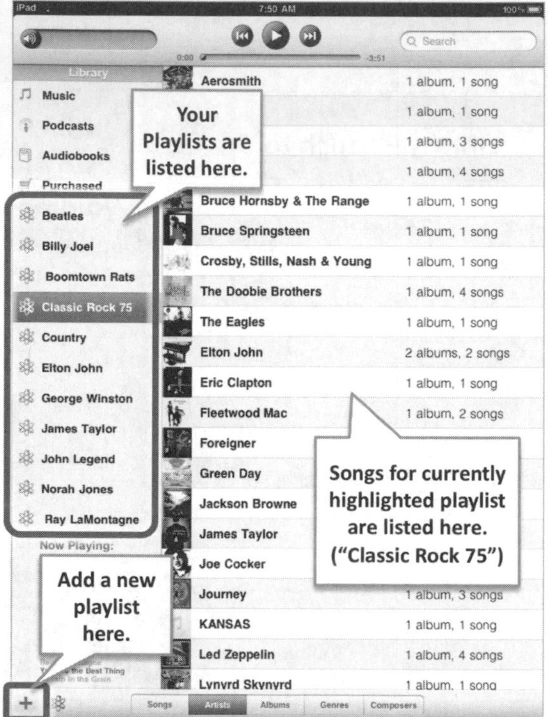


Many people group together music of a particular genre, like classical or rock. Others may create playlists with fast beat music and call it "workout," or "running music." You can use playlists to organize your music just about any way you please.

Playlists are created either in iTunes on your computer and then synced to your iPad (see the "iTunes Guide"), or you can create a playlist right on your iPad as we describe in the next section.

Once you've synced a playlist to your iPad or created one on your iPad, it shows up on the left-hand side of the iPod screen, under **Library**.

In this example, we touched our **Classic Rock 75** playlist and all the songs from that playlist are listed.

To go to a different playlist, we just touch a different playlist along the left hand side.

**NOTE:** You can edit the contents of some of your playlists on your iPad. However, Genius playlists that are created on your computer or iPad can't be edited on the iPad itself.

## Creating Playlists on the iPad

The iPad lets you create unique playlists on the device that can be edited and even synced with your computer. Let's say you want a new selection of music in your iPad playlist. Just create the playlist as we show you below and add songs. Whenever you want, you can remove those songs and add new ones—it couldn't be easier!

To create a new playlist on the iPad, touch the **plus sign** in the lower left corner.

Give your playlist a unique name (we'll just call this one "iPad playlist") and then touch **Save**.

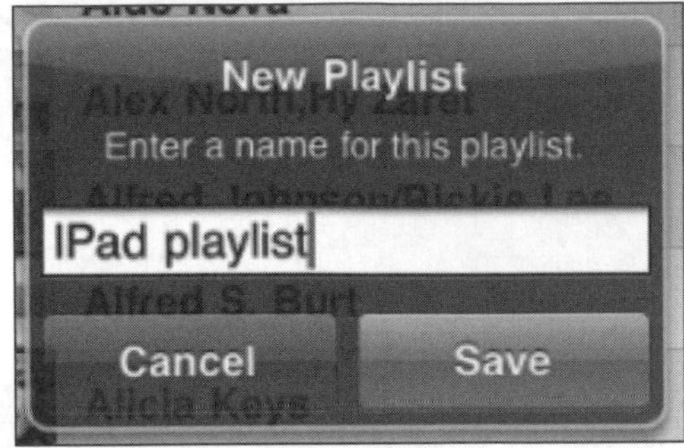


The iPad then displays the **Add Songs** screen. Touch anywhere in the song name for any song you want to add to the new playlist.

You know a song is selected and will be added to the play list when it turns gray.

> **NOTE:** Don't get frustrated trying to remove or deselect a song you tapped by mistake. You can't remove or deselect songs on this screen; you have to click **Done**, then remove them on the next screen. (We show you below.)

Select **Done** at the top right and the playlist contents will be displayed.

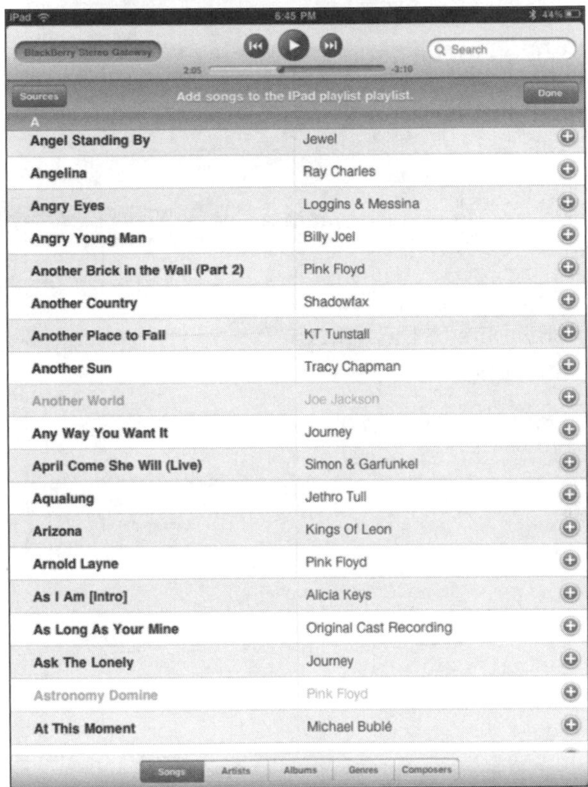

If you tapped a song or two by mistake or changed your mind, after you click **Done** you can remove songs on the next screen.

To delete a song:

1. Tap the red circle to the left of the song name.
2. Tap the **Delete** button to the right of the song.

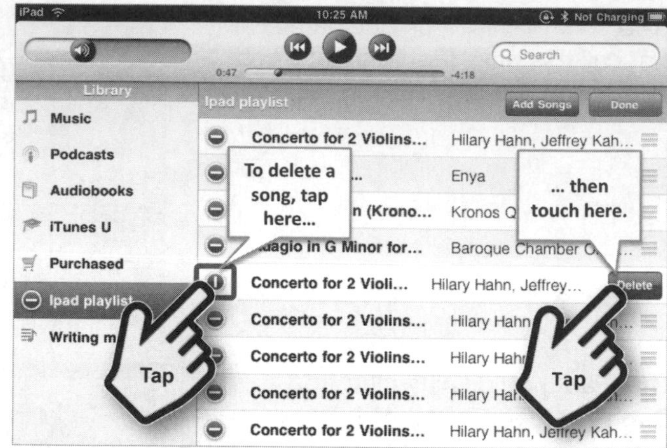


To move a song up or down in a playlist:

1. Touch and hold the three gray bars to the right of the song.
2. Drag the song up or down and then let go.

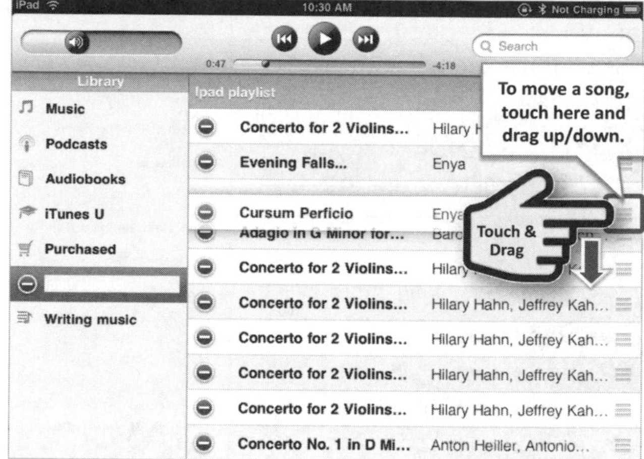

When you are sure you are done, just touch **Done** in the upper right corner and your playlist will be set.

To change the playlist later, touch the **Edit** button and follow the steps above.

iPad playlist Edit

| | |
|---|---|
| **Across The Universe** | The Beatles |
| **All I Can Do Is Write About It** | Lynyrd Skynyrd |
| **All I Really Want To Do** | Bob Dylan |
| **All the Way Home** | Bruce Springsteen |
| **All the Wild Horses** | Ray LaMontagne |
| **Almost** | Tracy Chapman |
| **Another World** | Joe Jackson |
| **Astronomy Domine** | Pink Floyd |

## Searching for Music

Almost every view from your iPod app (**Playlists**, **Artists**, **Videos**, **Songs**, etc.) has a search window in the upper right corner, as shown in Figure 7–2. Tap once in that search window and type a few letters of the name of an artist, playlist, video, or song to instantly see a list of all matching items. This is the best way to quickly find something to listen to or watch on your iPad.

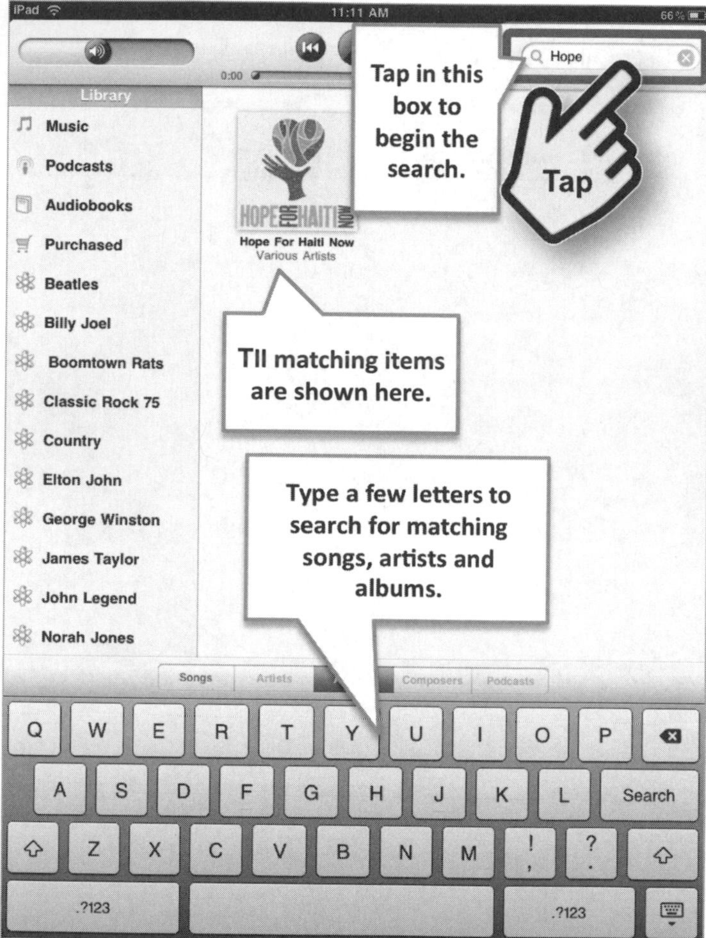


**Figure 7–2.** *Searching for music*

# Changing the View in the iPod App

The **iPod** app is very flexible when it comes to ways of displaying and categorizing your music. Sometimes, you might want to look at your songs listed by the artist.. Other times, you might want to see a particular album or song. The iPad lets you easily change the view to help manage and play just the music you want at a given moment.

## Artists View

Artists

The **Artists** view lists all the artists on your iPad, or, if you are in a playlist and select **Artists**, it will list the artists in that playlist.

Flick through the list to move to the first letter of the artist's name you are looking for.

When you find the artist's name, touch that name and all the songs by that artist will be listed, with a picture of the album art to the left.

| Artist | |
|---|---|
| Aerosmith | 1 album, 1 song |
| America | 1 album, 1 song |
| Billy Joel | 1 album, 3 songs |
| Boston | 1 album, 4 songs |
| Bruce Hornsby & The Range | 1 album, 1 song |
| Bruce Springsteen | 1 album, 1 song |
| Crosby, Stills, Nash & Young | 1 album, 1 song |
| The Doobie Brothers | 1 album, 4 songs |
| The Eagles | 1 album, 1 song |
| Elton John | 2 albums, 2 songs |
| Eric Clapton | 1 album, 1 song |
| Fleetwood Mac | 1 album, 2 songs |
| Foreigner | 2 albums, 3 songs |
| Green Day | 1 album, 1 song |
| Jackson Browne | 2 albums, 2 songs |
| James Taylor | 1 album, 1 song |
| Joe Cocker | 1 album, 1 song |
| Journey | 1 album, 3 songs |
| KANSAS | 1 album, 1 song |
| Led Zeppelin | 1 album, 4 songs |
| Lynyrd Skynyrd | 1 album, 1 song |

Artists Albums Genres Composers

**TIP:** Use the same navigation and search features as you do with your **Contacts** app (the address book).

## Songs View

Touching the **Songs** tab shows you a list of every song on your iPad.

If you know the exact name of the song, flick through the list or touch the first letter of the song in the alphabetical list to the right.

## Albums View

The music on your iPad is also organized by albums, which you'll see when you touch the **Albums** tab at the bottom.

Again, you can scroll through the album covers or touch the first letter of the album name in the alphabetical list and then make your selection.

Once you choose an album, all the songs on that album will be listed.

To close the pop-up window with the list of songs, simply tap anywhere outside that window.

## Genres

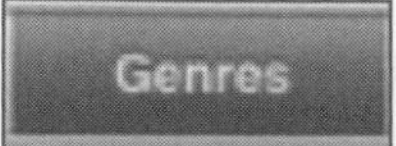


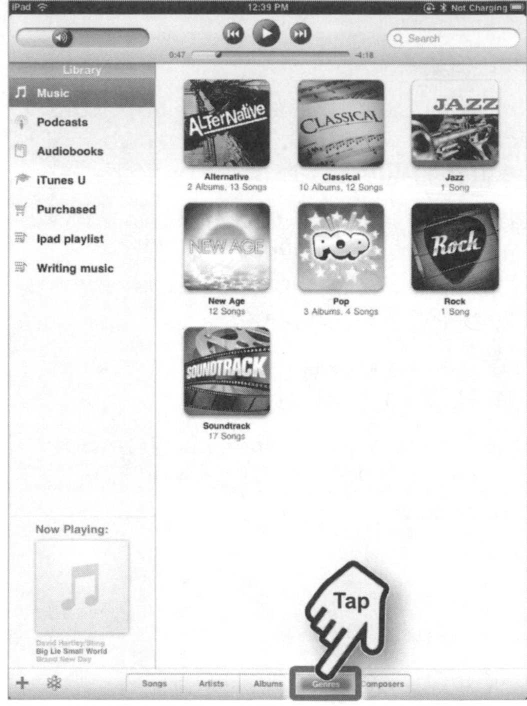


The **Genres** tab arranges your music into music types. This can be an easier way to find your music and to have more of a "themed" listening experience.

At times, you may want to hear a rock or jazz mix; you could select those particular genres and start playing some or all the songs.

In this image, we touched **Rock**, and the iPad popped up a little window showing us how many albums and songs we have in that particular genre.

Rock
17 Albums, 24 Songs
272 Songs, 1235 Mins.

| | | |
|---|---|---|
| ► | Born To Run | 4:30 |
| 2. | Behind Blue Eyes | 3:42 |
| 3. | Melissa | 3:56 |
| 4. | Life In The Fast Lane | 4:46 |
| 5. | Rock and Roll | 3:40 |
| 6. | Paradise By The Dashboard Light | 8:28 |
| 7. | Up On Cripple Creek | 5:31 |
| 8. | The Rising | 4:50 |

## Composers

As with the other views, touching the **Composers** tab at the bottom lists your music in a specific way.

Sometimes you forget the title of the song but you know the composer. Browsing the **Composers** on your iPad can help you find just what you are looking for.

Similar to other views, the **Composer** view tells you how many albums and songs are by each composer.

| | |
|---|---|
| Allen Collins | 1 album, 1 song |
| Bruce Springsteen | 3 albums, 3 songs |
| David Gilmour, Roger Waters,... | 1 album, 1 song |
| don henley/glenn frey/joe walsh | 1 album, 1 song |
| don henley/glenn frey/john da... | 1 album, 1 song |
| Eric Clapton, Jim Gordon | 1 album, 1 song |
| Freddie Mercury | 1 album, 1 song |
| Graham Nash | 1 album, 2 songs |
| Gregg Allman & Stephen Alai... | 1 album, 1 song |
| James Robert Robinson 1943-... | 1 album, 2 songs |
| Jim Steinman | 1 album, 2 songs |
| Johnston, Tom | 1 album, 1 song |
| Pete Townshend | 1 album, 1 song |
| Simmons, Patrick | 1 album, 1 song |
| Tom Scholz | 1 album, 1 song |

## Viewing Songs in an Album

When you're in **Albums** view, just touch an album cover and the cover will flip, showing you the songs on that album (see Figure 7–3).

> **TIP**: When you start playing an album, the album cover may expand to fill the screen. Tap the screen once to bring up (or hide) the controls at the top and bottom. You can use these controls to manage the song and screen as we describe below.

To see the songs on an album that is playing, tap the **List** button and the album cover and the cover will turn over, revealing all the songs on that album. The song that is playing will have a small blue arrow next to it.

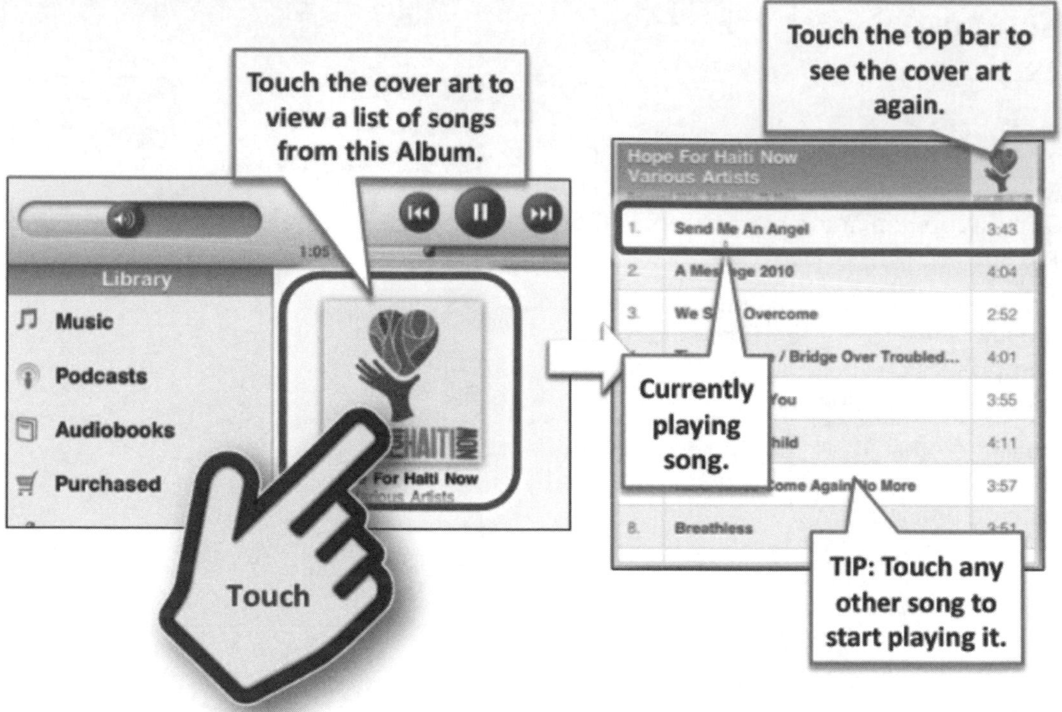


**Figure 7–3.** *Touch the album cover to see the songs on it.*

Tap the title bar above the list of songs and the album cover will return to its place in your music library.

**NOTE:** This only works when you are in **Album** view. If you touch an album cover in **Artists** view, the song associated with that album cover will start to play.

## Playing Your Music

Now that you know how to find your music, it is time to play it! Find a song or browse to a playlist using any of the methods listed above. Simply tap the song name and it will begin to play.

This screen shows a picture of the album from which the song originates, and the name of the song at the top.

Along the top of the screen you'll find the **Volume** slider bar, and the **Previous Song**, **Play/Pause**, and **Next Song** buttons.

If you want to see other songs on the album, just double-tap the album cover and the screen will flip to show the other songs on that album.

To just view a list of songs in the album, touch the **List** button in the lower right hand corner.

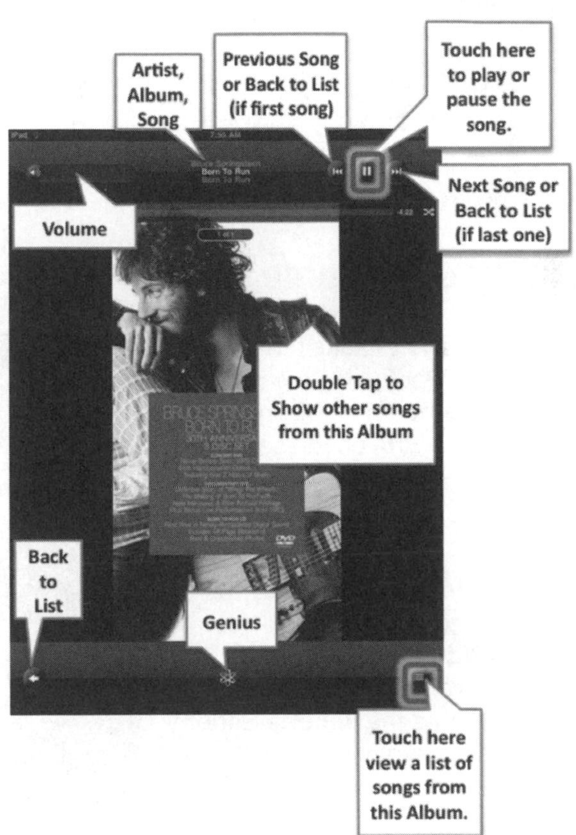


## Pausing and Playing

Tap the pause symbol (if your song is playing) or the play arrow (if the music is paused) to play or resume your song.

## To Play the Previous or Next Song

If you are in a playlist, touching the **Next** arrow (to the right of the **Play/Pause** button) will advance you to the next song in the list. If you are searching through your music by album, touching **Next** will advance to the next song on the album. Touching the **Previous** button will do the reverse.

> **NOTE:** If you're at the beginning of a song, **Previous** will take you to the previous song. If the son is already playing, **Previous** will go to the beginning of the current song (and a second tap would go to the previous song).

## Adjusting the Volume

There are two ways to adjust the volume on your iPad: using the external **Volume** buttons or using the **Volume Slider** control on the screen.

The external **Volume** buttons are on the upper right side of the device. Press the **Volume Up** key (the top button) or the **Volume Down** key to raise or lower the volume. You'll see the **Volume Slider** control move as you adjust the volume. You can also just touch and hold the **Volume Slider** key and adjust the volume up or down.

> **TIP:** To quickly mute the sound, press and hold the **Volume Down** key for about 2 seconds.

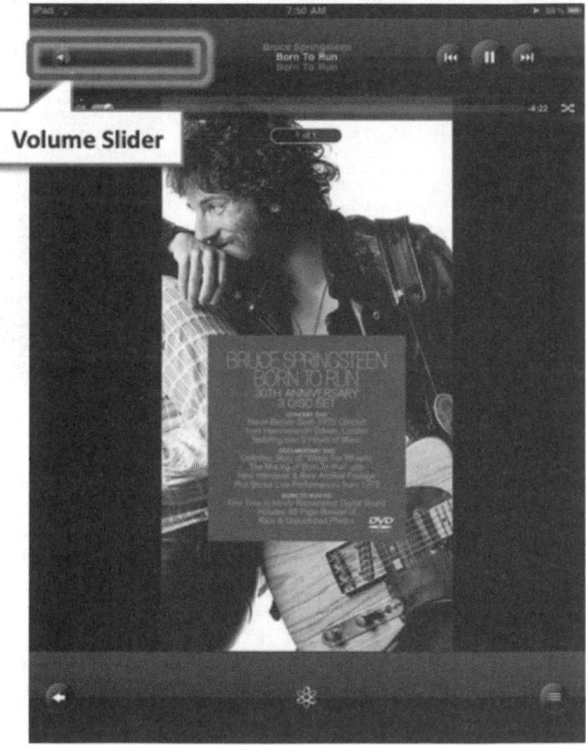

## Double-Click the Home Button for iPod Controls

You can play your music while you are doing other things on your iPad, like reading and responding to e-mail, playing a game, browsing the Web. Sometimes, you might want to bring up your iPod controls quickly. Usually, a quick double-tap to the **Home** button on the bottom will bring up the "now playing" **iPod** controls in the middle of the screen, as shown in Figure 7–4.

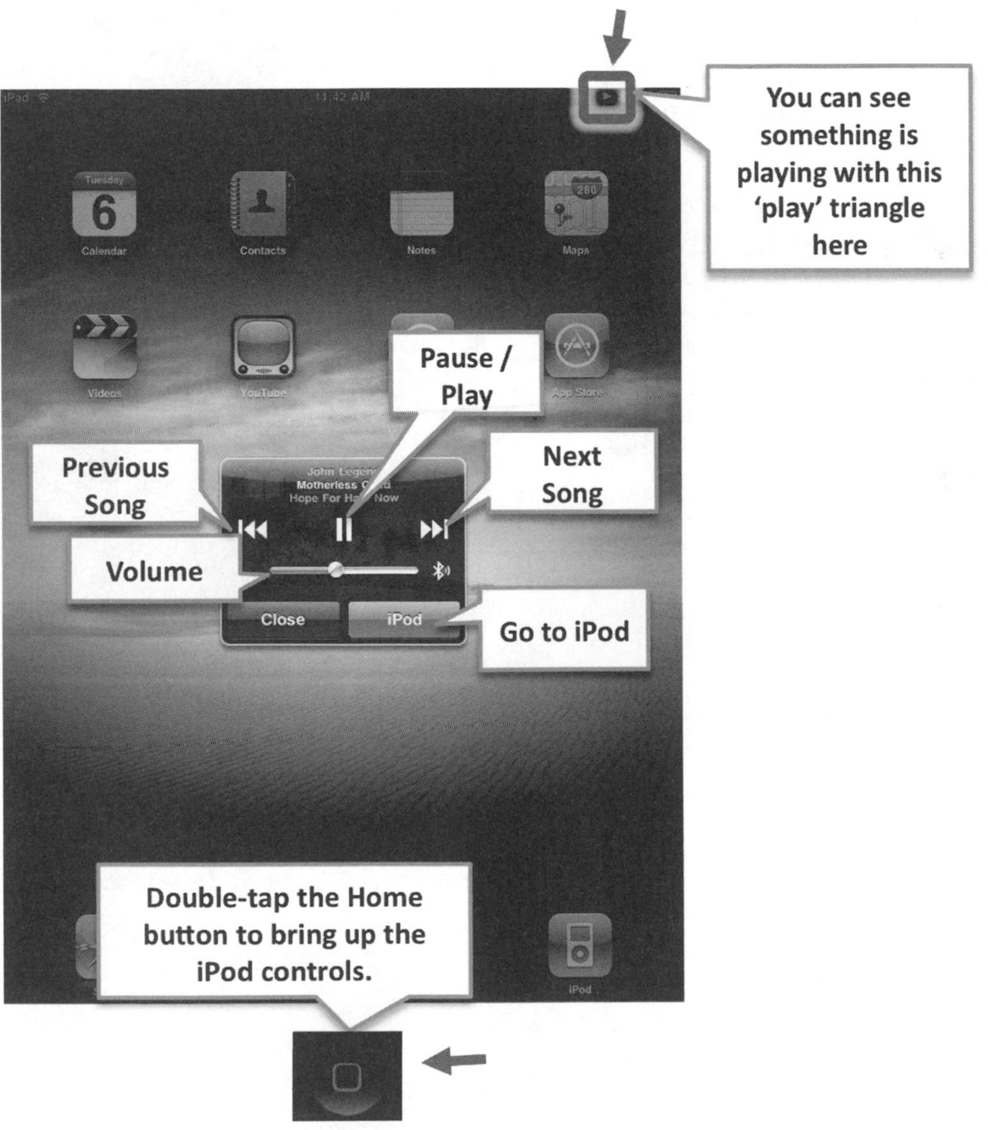


**Figure 7–4.** *Double-tap the* ***Home*** *button to bring up the* ***iPod*** *music controls.*

If double-tapping the **Home** button does not bring up the **iPod** music controls, or you want to disable this feature, you need to go into the **Settings** app.

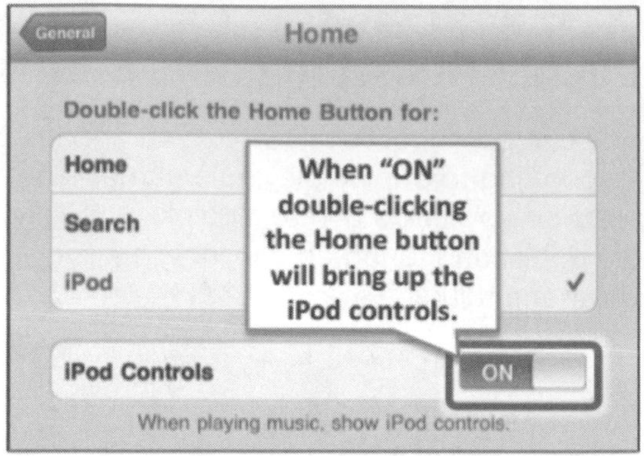


In **Settings**, tap **General** in the left column, then scroll down and tap on **Home**. Make sure the **iPod Controls** near the bottom are **ON** or **OFF** to meet your needs.

When you set the **iPod Controls OFF,** double-clicking the **Home** button will not bring them up.

## Repeating, Shuffling, Moving around in a Song

In play mode, you can activate additional controls by simply tapping the screen anywhere on the album cover. You'll then see an additional slider (the scrubber bar) at the top, along with the symbols for **Repeat**, **Shuffle,** and **Genius**.

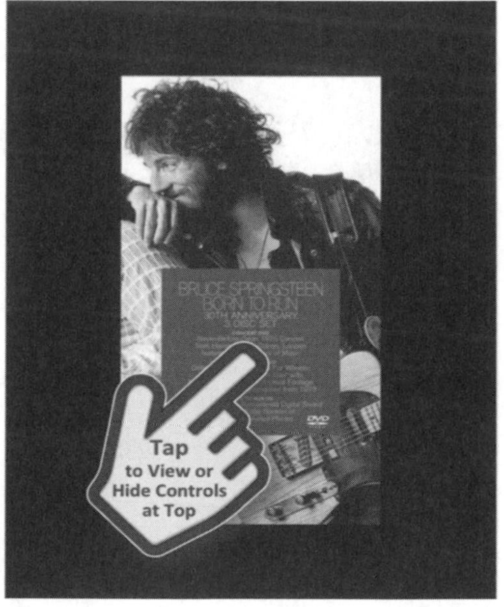

## Moving to Another Part of a Song

Slide the scrubber bar to the right and you'll see the elapsed time of the song (displayed to the far right) change accordingly. If you are looking for a specific section of the song, drag the slider and then let go and listen to see if you are in the right place.

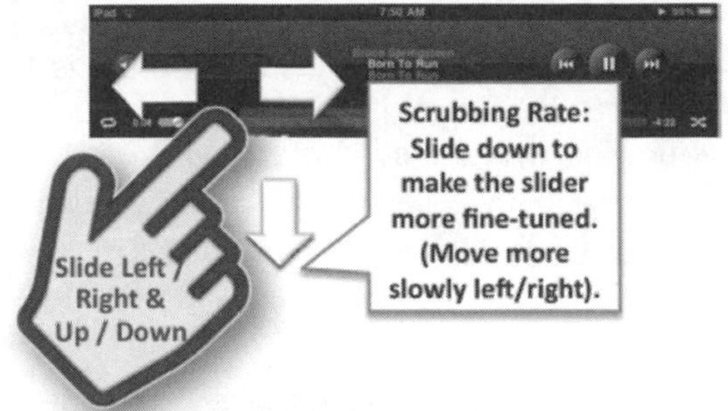


**TIP:** To make the slider move more slowly (i.e., to fine-tune it), drag your finger down the screen. This is called the scrubbing rate.

## Repeat One Song and Repeat All Songs in Playlist or Album

To repeat the song you are listening to, touch the **Repeat** symbol at the left of the top controls twice until you see it turn blue with a 1 on it.

To repeat all songs in the playlist, song list, or album, touch the **Repeat** icon until it turns blue (and does not have a 1 on it).

To turn off the **Repeat** feature, press the icon until it turns white again.

## Shuffle

If you are listening to a playlist or album or any other category or list of music, you might decide you don't want to listen to the songs in order. Touching the **Shuffle** symbol rearranges the music to play in random order. You know **Shuffle** is turned on when the icon is blue and off when it is white.

# Genius

Apple has a new feature for iTunes called **Genius Playlists**. If the Genius feature is activated in iTunes, it will show up here on your iPad with the symbol shown.

**NOTE:** You must enable **Genius Playlists** using iTunes on your computer. Check out our "iTunes Guide" chapter to learn how.

What the Genius feature does is create a playlist by associating similar songs with the one you're listening to. Unline a random "shuffle" of music, Genius will scour your music library and then create a new playlist of 25, 50, or 100 songs (you set the Genius features in iTunes on your computer).

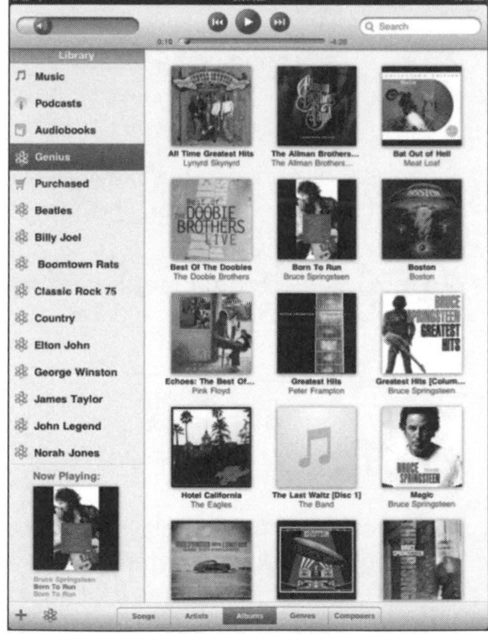


Genius is a great way to mix up your music and keep it fresh—playing the type of music you like but also finding some buried songs that may not be part of your established playlists.

**TIP:** To create permanent Genius playlists, just create them in iTunes on your computer and sync them to your iPad. The Genius playlists you sync from iTunes can't be edited or changed on the iPad itself, but you can save, refresh or delete Genius playlists created on the iPad.

## Now Playing

Sometimes you're having so much fun exploring your options for playlists or albums that you get deeply buried in a menu and then find yourself just wanting to get back to the song you're listening to. Fortunately, this is always very easy to do because at the bottom left of most of the music screens will be a **Now Playing** icon to touch.

**TIP:** To get back to the small album cover view in the bottom left-hand corner, tap the screen to bring up the controls, then press the left arrow in the lower left corner to get back to the previous view.

## Viewing Other Songs on the Album

You may decide you want to listen to another song from the same album rather than going to the next song in the playlist or genre list.

In the lower right corner of the **Now Playing** screen you'll see a small button with three lines on it. (If you don't see any controls, tap the screen once to bring them up.)

Tap that button and the view switches to a small image of the album cover. The screen now displays all the songs on that album.

Touch another song on the list and that song will begin to play.

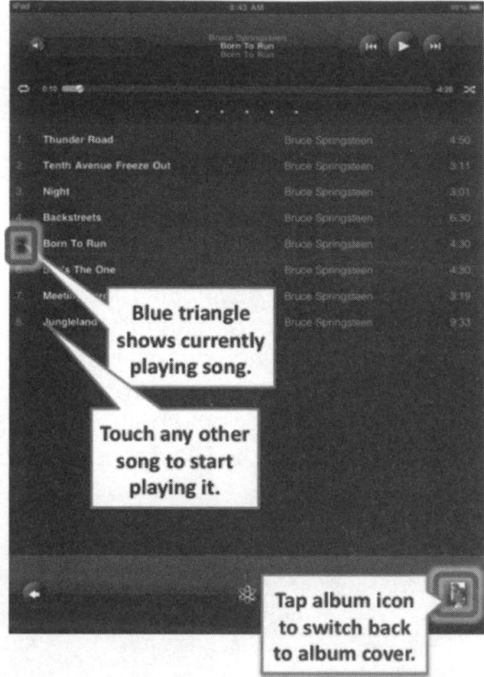


> **NOTE:** If you were in the middle of a playlist or a Genius Playlist and you start listening to another song from an album, you will not be taken back to that playlist. You'll need to either go back to your playlist library or tap **Genius** to make a new **Genius** Playlist.

## Adjusting Music Settings

There are several settings you can adjust to tweak your music-playing to your tastes. You'll find these in the **Settings** menu. Just touch the **Settings** icon on your **Home Screen**.

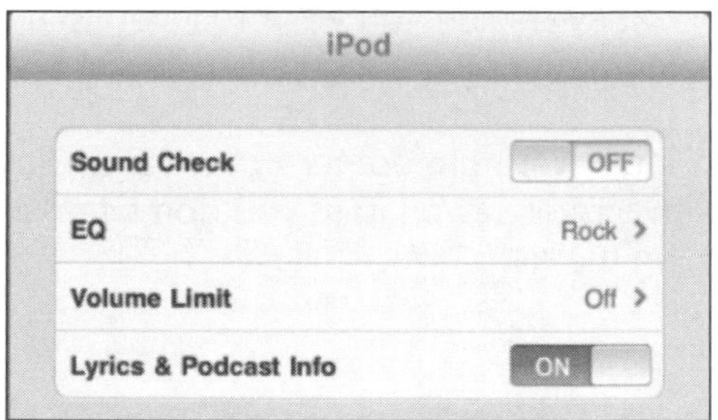


In the middle of the **Settings** screen, touch the **iPod** tab to bring you to the **iPod** music settings screen. There are four settings you can adjust on this screen; **Sound Check**, **EQ**, **Volume Limit**, and **Lyrics & Podcast Info**.

## Using Sound Check (Auto Volume Adjust)

**TIP:** Because songs are recorded at different volumes, sometimes during playback a particular song might sound quite loud compared to another. **Sound Check** can eliminate this. If **Sound Check** is set to **ON**, all your songs will play back at roughly the same volume.

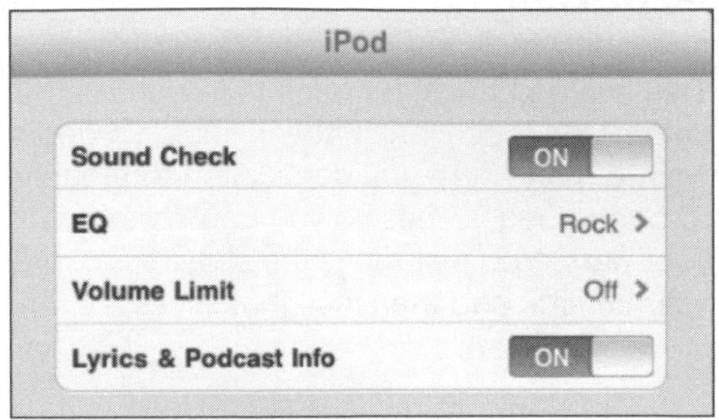


## EQ (Sound Equalizer Setting)

Sound equalization is very personal and subjective. Some people like more bass in their music, some like more treble, and some like more of an exaggerated mid-range. Whatever your music tastes, there is an **EQ** setting for you.

**NOTE:** Using the **EQ** setting can diminish battery capacity somewhat.

Just touch the **EQ** tab and then select either the type of music you most often listen to or a specific option to boost treble or bass. Experiment, have fun, and find the setting that's perfect for you.

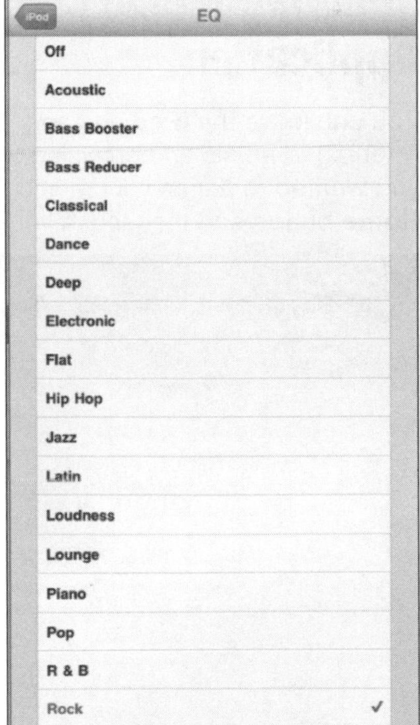

## Volume Limit (Safely Listen to Music at Reasonable Volumes)

This is a great way for parents to control the volume on their kids' iPads. It is also a good way to make sure you don't listen too loudly through headphones so you don't damage your ears. You just move the slider to a volume limit and then lock that limit.

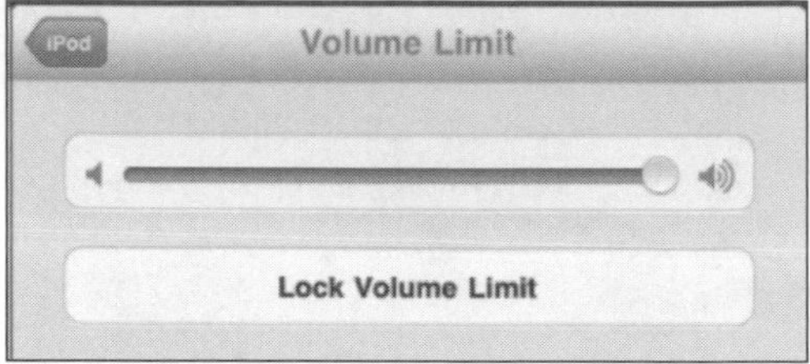


To lock the volume limit, touch the **Lock Volume Limit** button and enter a 4-digit passcode. You will be prompted to put your passcode in once more and the volume limit will then be locked.

# Showing Music Controls When in Another Application

You can leave the **iPod** app and your music will continue to play. Let's say you were listening to music and browsing the Web or checking your e-mail at the same time. If you wanted to adjust your music, your first inclination would probably be to press the **Home** button and then touch your **iPod** icon.

> **NOTE:** For this to work, you need adjust the settings of the **Home** button as we described earlier in this chapter on page 201.

The easiest way to see the music controls while in another program is to double-click the **Home** button. This brings up just the music controls for you to adjust and you don't even have to leave the other program.

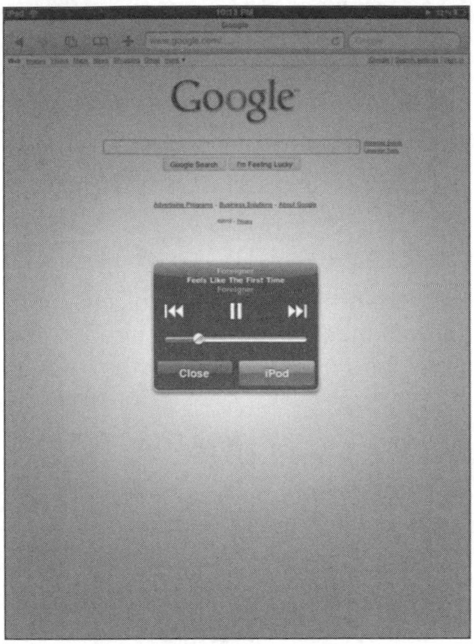


## Showing Music Controls When Your iPad is Locked

This even works if your iPad is locked. Just double-click the **Home** button and the controls for adjusting the music show up on the top locked screen. There is no reason to unlock the screen and then go to the Music program to find the controls.

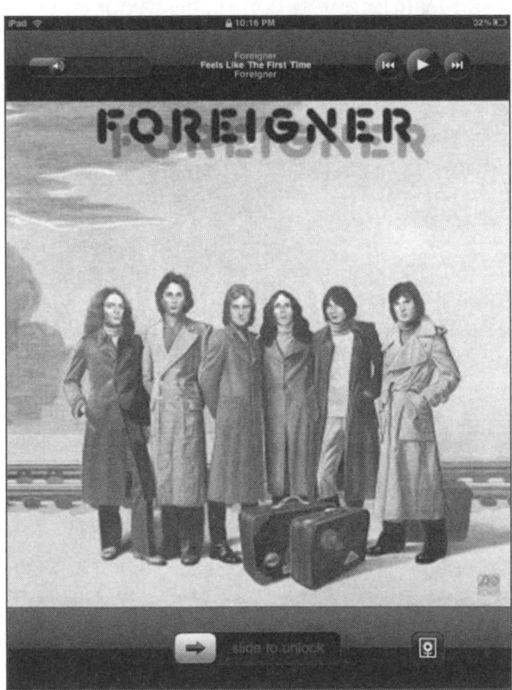


Notice in the image to the right that the screen is still locked—yet the music controls are now visible along the top. You can pause, skip, go to a previous song or adjust the volume without actually unlocking the iPad.

# Listening to Free Internet Radio (Pandora)

While your iPad gives you unprecedented control over your personal music library, there may be times when you want to just "mix it up" and listen to some other music.

**TIP:** A basic Pandora account is free and can save you considerable money compared with buying lots of new songs from iTunes.

Pandora grew out of the Music Genome Project. This was a huge undertaking. A large team of musical analysts looked at just about every song ever recorded and then developed a complex algorithm of attributes to associate with each song.

**NOTE:** Pandora may have some competition by the time you read this book. Right now there's one other competitor called Slacker Personal Radio, but there will probably be more. If you want to find more options, try searching the App Store for "iPad Internet Radio." Please also note that Pandora is a US-only application and Slacker available is only in the US and Canada. Hopefully, more options will begin to pop up for international users.

## Getting Started with Pandora

With Pandora you can design your own unique radio stations built around artists you like. Best of all, it is completely free!

Start by downloading the Pandora app from the App Store. Just go to the App Store and search for Pandora.

Now just touch the Pandora icon to start.

The first time you start Pandora, you'll be asked to either create an account or to sign in if you already have an account. Just fill in the appropriate information—an email address and a password are required—and you can start designing your own music listening experience.

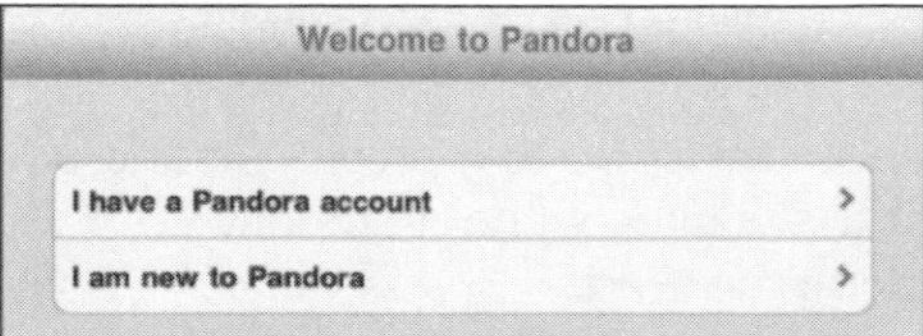

Pandora is also available for your Windows or Mac computer and for most smartphone platforms. If you already have a Pandora account, all you have to do is sign in.

## Pandora's Main Screen

Your stations are listed along the left-hand side. Just touch one of your stations and it will begin to play. Usually, the first song will be from the actual artist chosen and the next songs will be from similar artists.

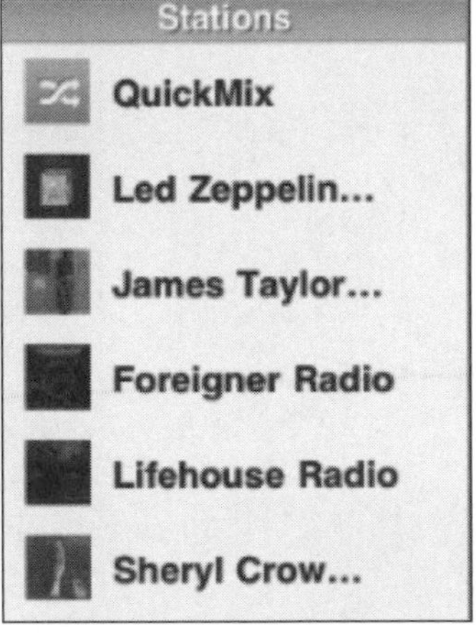

The large screen of the iPad lets you see lots of information.

There will be a small album cover in the **Now Playing** window in the lower left corner—very much like the **Now Playing** album cover in the iPod music app.

In the middle of the page you'll see a nice bio of the artist, which changes with each new song.

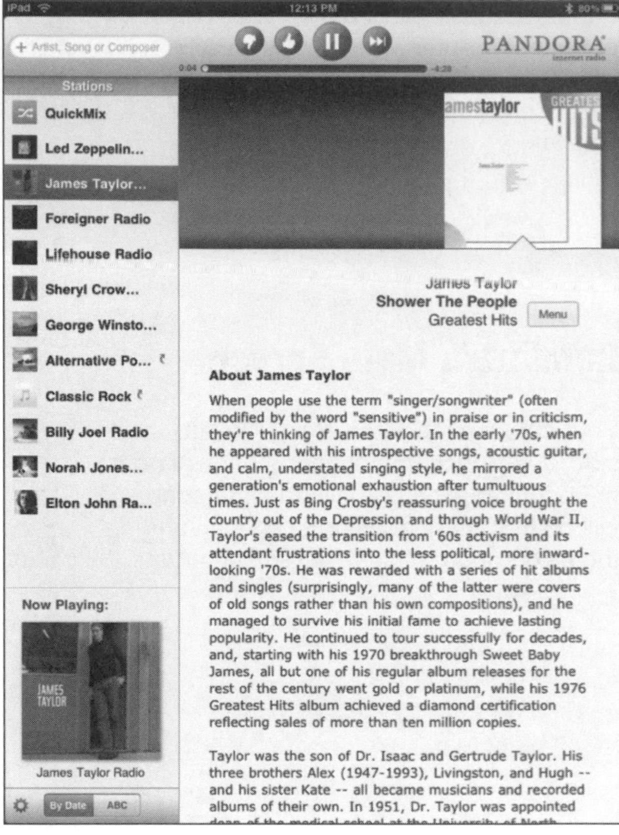


## Thumbs Up or Thumbs Down in Pandora

If you like a particular song, touch the thumbs-up icon and you'll hear more from that particular artist.

Conversely, if you don't like an artist on this station, touch the thumbs-down icon and you won't hear that artist again.

You can also pause the song and come back later, or skip to the next selection in your station.

**NOTE:** With a free Pandora account, you are limited with the number of skips per hour you can make. You also will occasionally hear advertising. To get rid of these restrictions, upgrade to a paid "Pandora One" account as we show you below.

## Pandora's Menu

Above the bio to the right is a **Menu** button. Touch this and you can bookmark the artist or song, or go to iTunes to buy music from this artist.

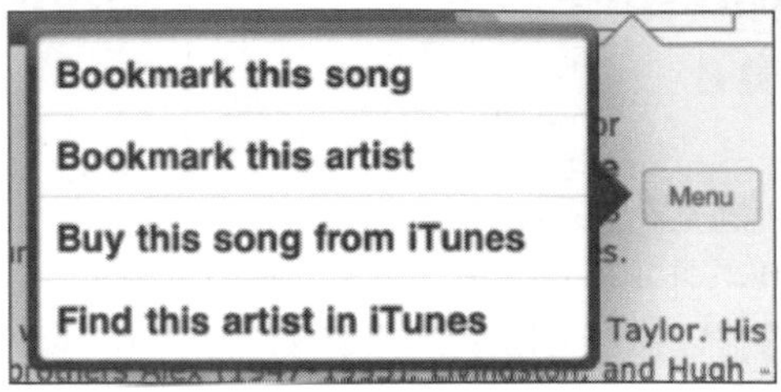


## Creating a New Station in Pandora

Creating a new station couldn't be easier.

Just touch the search window where you see **Artist, Song or Composer** in the upper left corner and type in the name of an artist, song, or composer.

When you find what you are looking for, touch the selection and Pandora will immediately start to build a station around your choice.

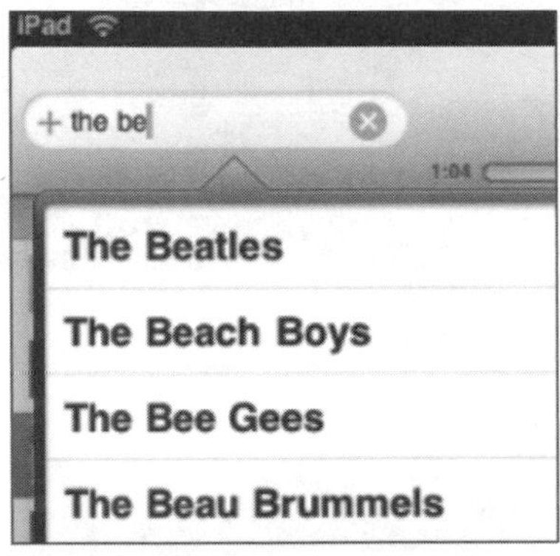


You'll then see the new station listed with your other stations.

You can build up to 100 stations in Pandora.

> **TIP:** You can organize your stations by pressing the **By Date** or **ABC** buttons in the bottom left corner of the screen.

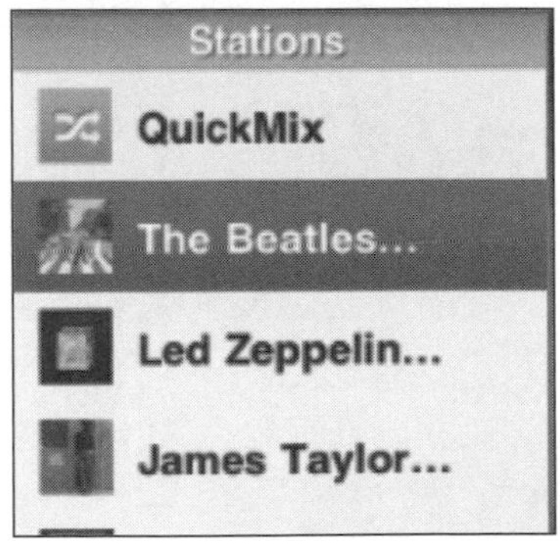

## Adjusting Pandora's Settings—Your Account, Upgrade and More

You can sign out of your Pandora account, adjust the audio quality, and even upgrade to Pandora One (which removes advertising) by tapping the settings icon in the lower left corner of the screen. (See Figure 7–5.)

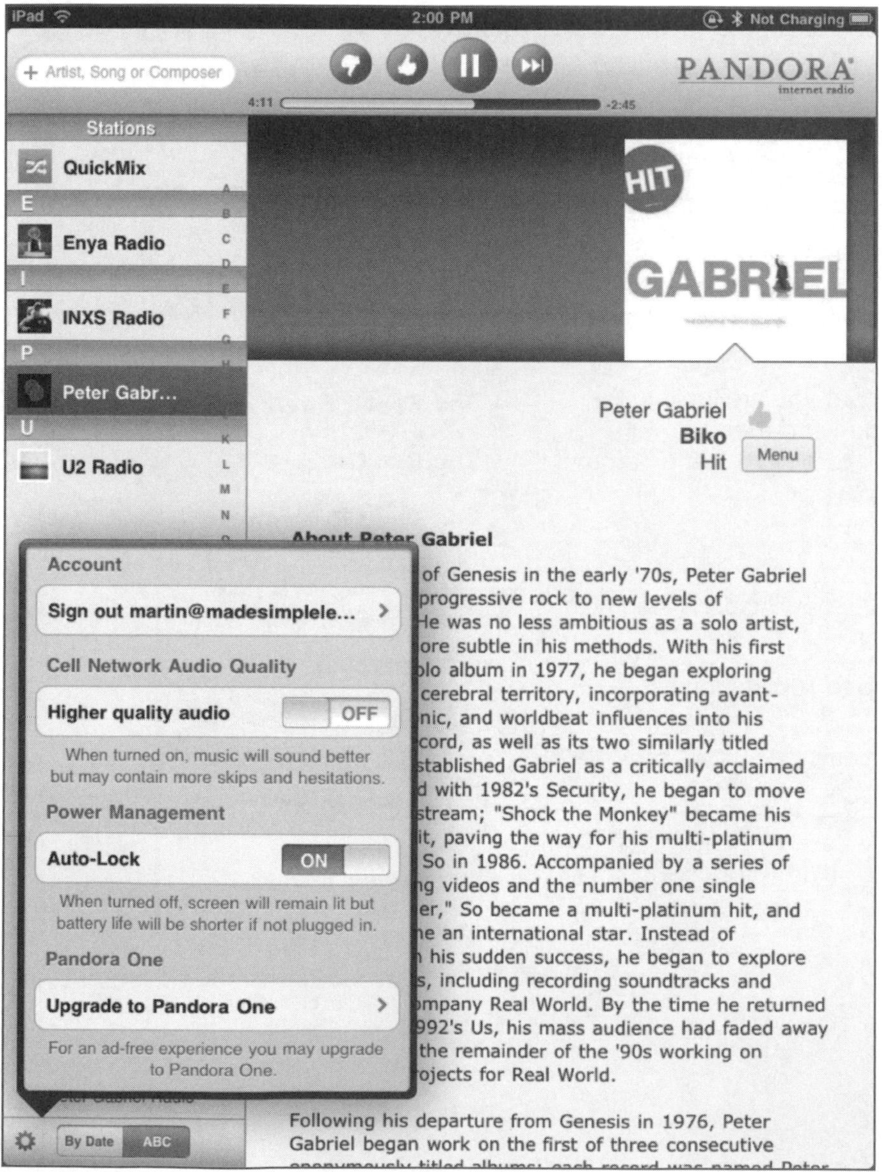


**Figure 7–5.** *Setting options in Pandora*

To sign out, tap your account name.

To adjust the sound quality, move the switch under **Cell Network Audio Quality** either **ON** or **OFF**. When you are on a cellular network, setting this off is probably better, otherwise you may hear more skips and pauses in the playback.

> **NOTE:** This only applies to the iPad + 3G models.

When you are on a strong Wi-Fi connection, you can set this to **ON** for better quality. See our "Wi-Fi and 3G Connections" chapter to learn more about the various connections.

To save your battery life, you should set the **Auto-Lock** to **ON**, which is the default. If you want the force the screen to stay lit, then switch this to **OFF**.

To remove all advertising, tap the **Upgrade to Pandora One** button. A web browser window will open and you'll be take to Pandora's web site to enter your credit card information. As of publishing time, the annual account cost is $36.00, but that may be different by the time you read this book.

Chapter 8

# iBooks and E-Books

Ever since the iPad was announced, one of the features touted has been its ability as an E-Book reader. In this chapter we will show you that what emerged was an unparalleled book-reading experience. We will cover iBooks, how to buy and download books, and how to find some great free classic books. We will show you other EBook reading options using the third-party Kindle and Kobo (formerly Shortcovers) readers on your iPad.

The iPad uses Apple's proprietary E-Book reader, iBooks. In this chapter, we will show you how to download the iBooks app, how to shop for books in the iBooks store, and how to take advantage of all the iBooks features

With iBooks, you can interact with a book like never before. Pages turn like a real book, you can adjust font sizes, look up words in the built-in dictionary, and search through your text.

In the App store, you can also find apps for Amazon's Kindle reader and the Kobo reader. Both the Kindle reader and the Kobo reader offer a great reading experience on the iPad.

## Download iBooks

The very first time you open the App store on your iPad, you will be prompted to download the free iBooks app. Select **Download** and iBooks will be downloaded and installed on the iPad.

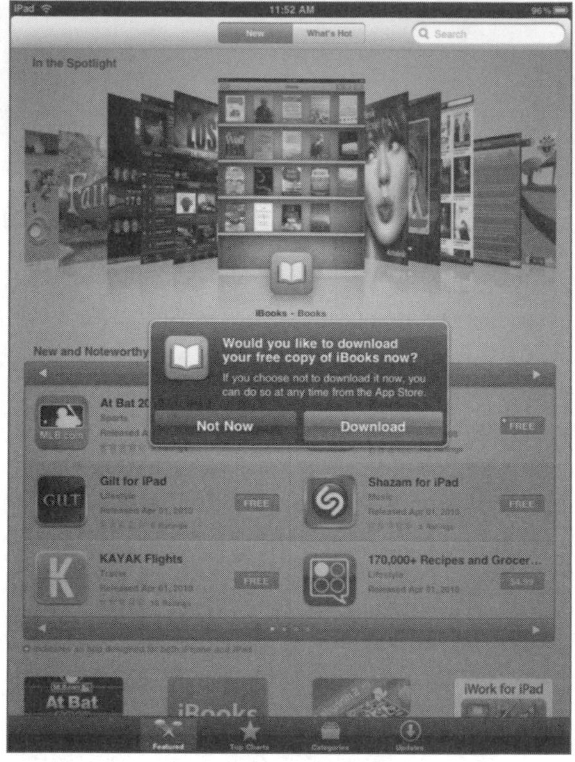


## The iBooks Store

Before you can start enjoying your reading experience, you need to load up your iBooks library with titles. Fortunately, many books can be found for free in the iBooks store, including the complete Gutenberg Collection of classics and public domain titles.

Just touch the **Store** button in the upper left-hand corner of your bookshelf, and you will be taken to the iBooks store.

The iBooks store is arranged much like the App store. There is a **Categories** button in the top left, next to the **Library** button. Touch this to see all the available categories from which you can choose your books.

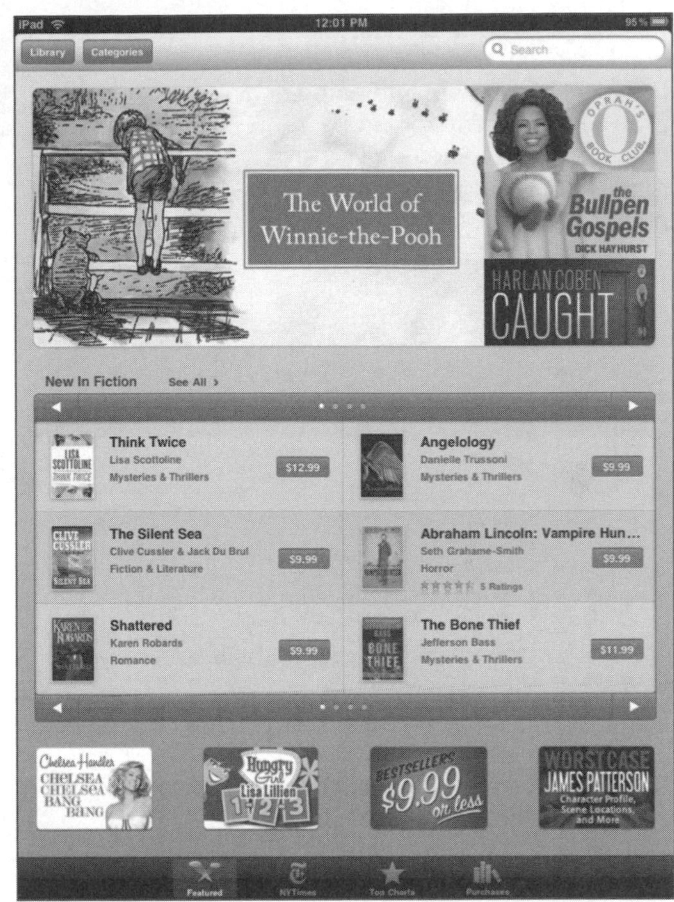


Featured books are highlighted on the front page of the store, with **New** and **Featured** titles displayed for browsing.

At the bottom of the store are four soft keys: **Featured**, **NYTimes**, **Top Charts**, and **Purchases**. Touch the **NYTimes** button

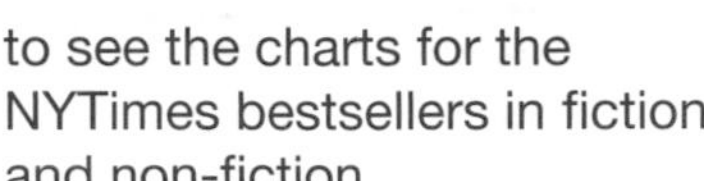

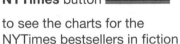

to see the charts for the NYTimes bestsellers in fiction and non-fiction.

Touch the **Top Charts** button to see all the bestselling and top free books in the store.

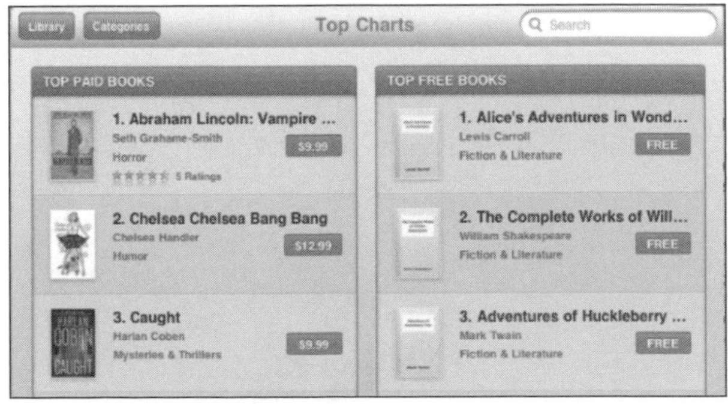


Touch the **Purchases** button to see all the books you have purchased or downloaded for your library.

Purchasing a book is much like purchasing an app. Touch the book title in which you are interested and browse the description and customer reviews. When you are ready to purchase the title, touch the price button.

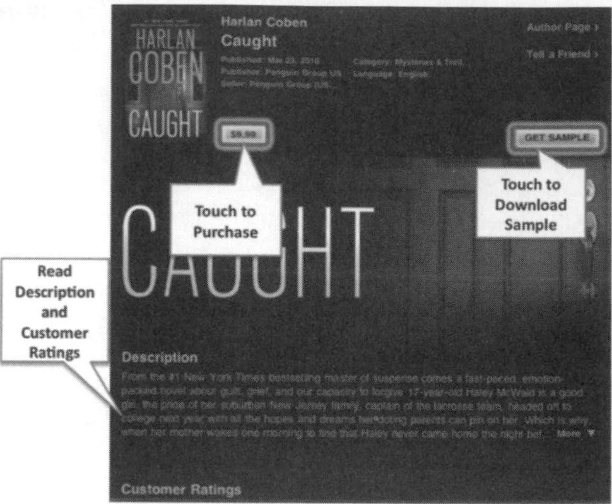


**NOTE:** Many titles have a sample download. This is a great idea if you are not sure that you want to purchase the book. Just download a sample, and you can always purchase the full book from within the sample.

Once you decide to download a sample or purchase a title, the view shifts to your bookshelf and you can see the book being deposited onto your bookshelf. Your book is now available for reading.

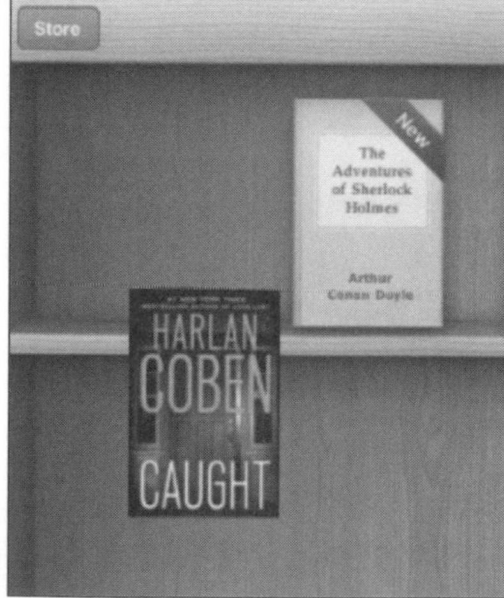

## Using the Search Window

Just like iTunes and the App store, iBooks gives you a search window in which you can type virtually any phrase. You can search for an author, title, or series. Just touch the search window and the on-screen keyboard pops up. Type in an author, title, series, or genre of book.

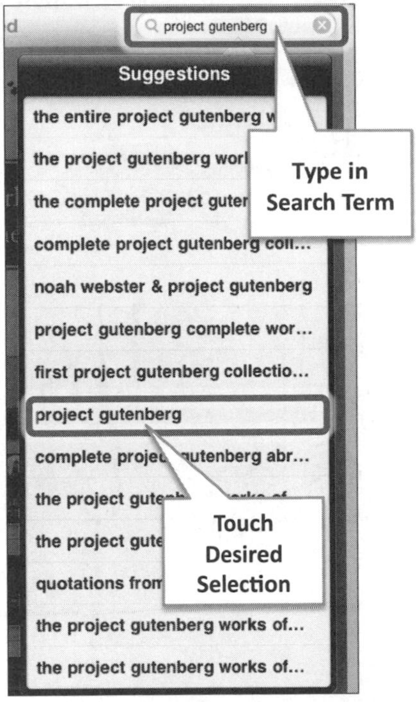


**TIP:** To search for lots of free books, do a search for "Gutenberg Project" to see thousands of free public domain titles.

You will see suggestions pop up that match your search; just touch the appropriate suggestion to go to that title.

## Reading iBooks

Touch any title in your bookshelf to open it for reading. The book will open to the very first page, which is often the title page or other "front matter" in the book.

In the upper left-hand corner, next to the **Library** button, is a **Table of Contents** button, as you can see in Figure 8–1. To jump to the table of contents, either touch the **Table of Contents** button or simply turn the pages to advance to the table of contents.

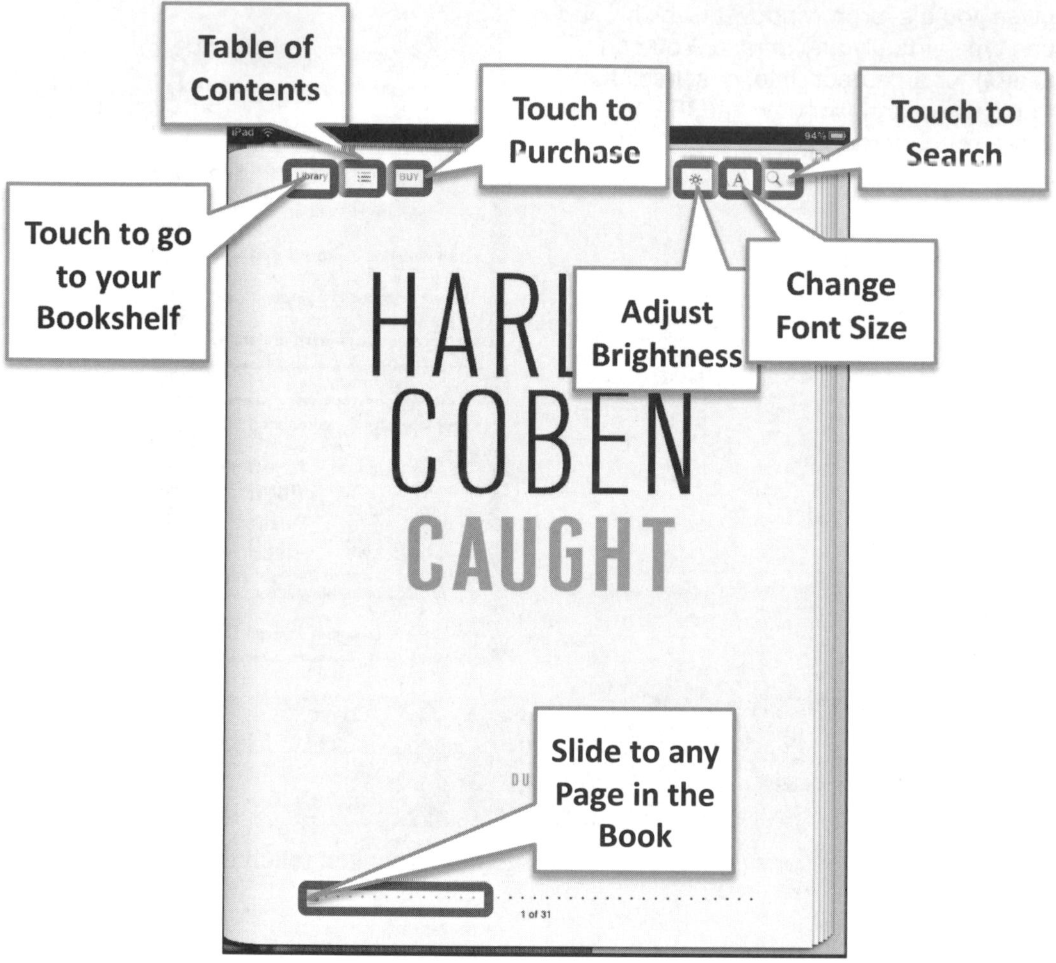


**Figure 8–1.** *iBooks page layout*

Pages can be turned in one of three ways: You can either touch the right-hand side of the page to turn to the next page, or slowly touch and hold the screen on the right-hand edge of the page, and, while continuing to touch the screen, gently and slowly move your finger to the left.

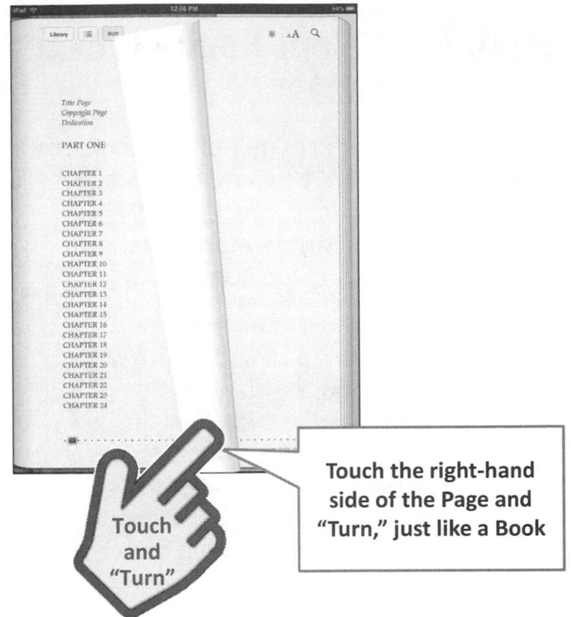
Touch the right-hand side of the Page and "Turn," just like a Book
Touch and "Turn"

**TIP:** If you move your finger very slowly you can actually see the words on the backside of the page as you "turn" it—a very cool visual effect.

The last way to turn pages is to use the slider at the bottom of the page. As you slowly slide from left to right you will see the page number on top of the slider. Release the slider and you can advance to that particular page number.

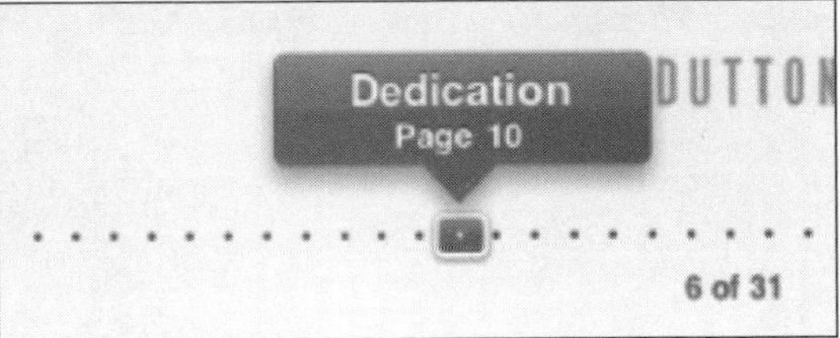
Dedication
Page 10
6 of 31

## Customizing Your Reading Experience: Brightness, Fonts, and Font Sizes

In the upper right-hand corner of the book, there are three icons available to help make your reading experience that much more immersive (see Figure 8–2).

Touch the **Brightness** icon and you can adjust the brightness of the book.

If you are reading in bed in a very dark room, you might want to slide it all the way down to the left. If you are out in the sunlight, you may need to slide it all the way up to the right. However, remember that the screen brightness is one of the things that consumes battery power more than most other features, so turn it back down when you don't need it so bright anymore.

**NOTE:** This adjusts the brightness only within iBooks. To adjust the global brightness of the iPad, use the control in the Settings app. (Go to the Settings icon > Brightness & Wallpaper.)

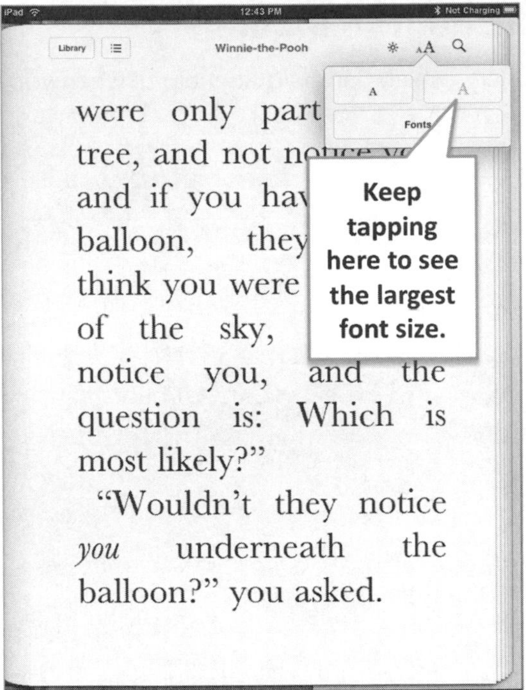


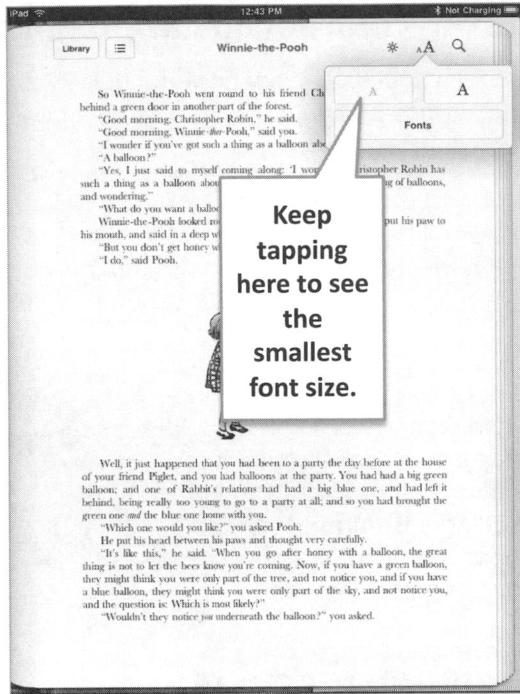


**Figure 8–2.** *iBooks adjusting font sizes*

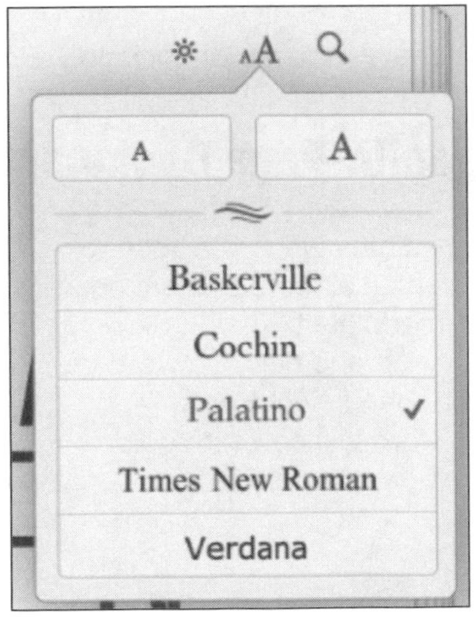


The next icon is the **Font Size and Type** adjustment.

**To Increase the Font Size:**

Tap the large "A" multiple times.

**To Decrease the Font Size:**

Tap the small "A" multiple times.

There are five available font styles. (There may well be more fonts when you read this book.)

Have fun and try out some of the various fonts. The default selection is the Palatino font, but all of the fonts look great, and the larger font size can make a difference for some. The goal is to make this as comfortable and as enjoyable a reading experience as possible.

## Grow Your Vocabulary Using the Built-in Dictionary

iBooks contains a very powerful built-in dictionary, which can be quite helpful when you run across a word that is new or unfamiliar.

> **TIP:** Using the built-in dictionary is an easy and fantastic way to build your vocabulary as you read. Instead of thumbing through a dog-eared dictionary to find the word, you will see the definition instantly appear in the pop-up window!

Accessing the dictionary could not be easier. Just touch and hold on any word in the book. A pop-up will appear with the options of using the **Dictionary**, setting a **Bookmark**, or using **Search** to find other occurrences of this particular word.

Touch **Dictionary**, and a pronunciation and definition of the word will be displayed.

## Setting an In-Page Bookmark

There may be times when you wish to highlight a particular word and set an in-text bookmark. Just like you did previously, touch and hold the word in question and then select **Bookmark**. The chosen word will now turn color and be set as a bookmark.

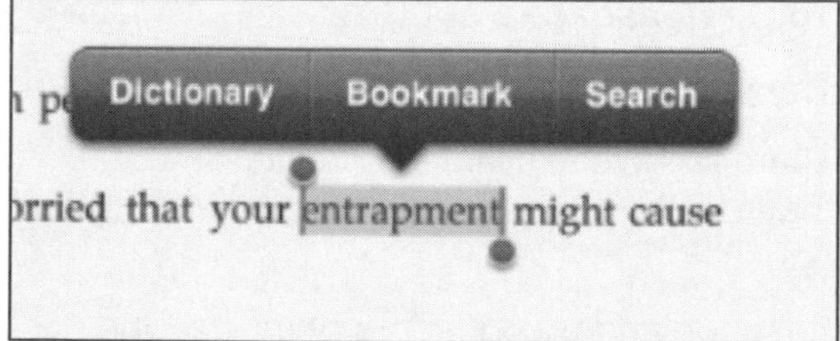

Touch the bookmarked word and a new set of options is available. You can either unbookmark the word or change the color of the bookmark.

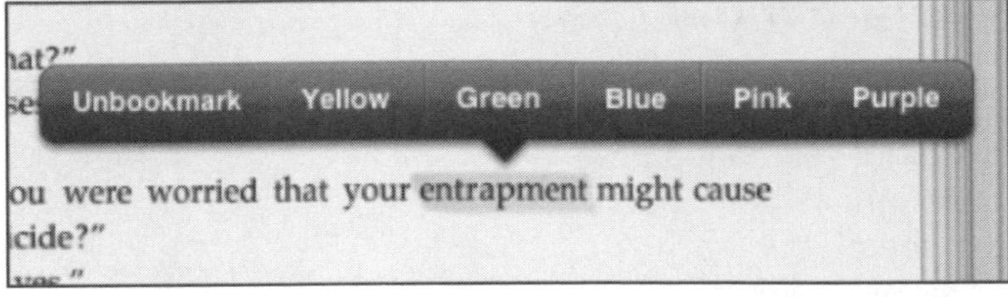


To view your bookmarks, just touch the **Table of Contents** icon at the top left of the screen (next to the **Library** icon) and then touch **Bookmarks**. Touch on the bookmark highlighted and you will jump to that section in the book.

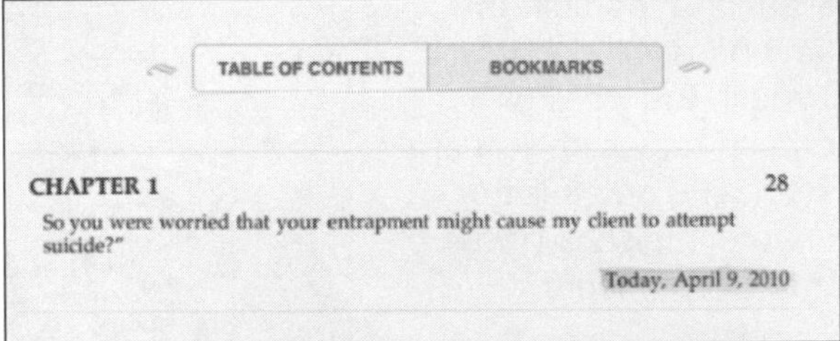


**TIP:** You do not need to set a bookmark every time you leave iBooks. iBooks will automatically remember where you left off in your book. Even if you jump to another book, when you return to the book you were just reading, you will return to exactly where you left off.

## Using Search

iBooks contains a powerful search feature built right in. Just touch the search bar (as in other programs on the iPad) and the built-in keyboard will pop up. Type in the word or phrase for which you are searching and a list of chapters is shown where that word occurs.

Just touch the selection desired and you will jump to that section in the book. You also have the option of jumping right to Google or Wikipedia by touching the appropriate buttons at the bottom of the search window.

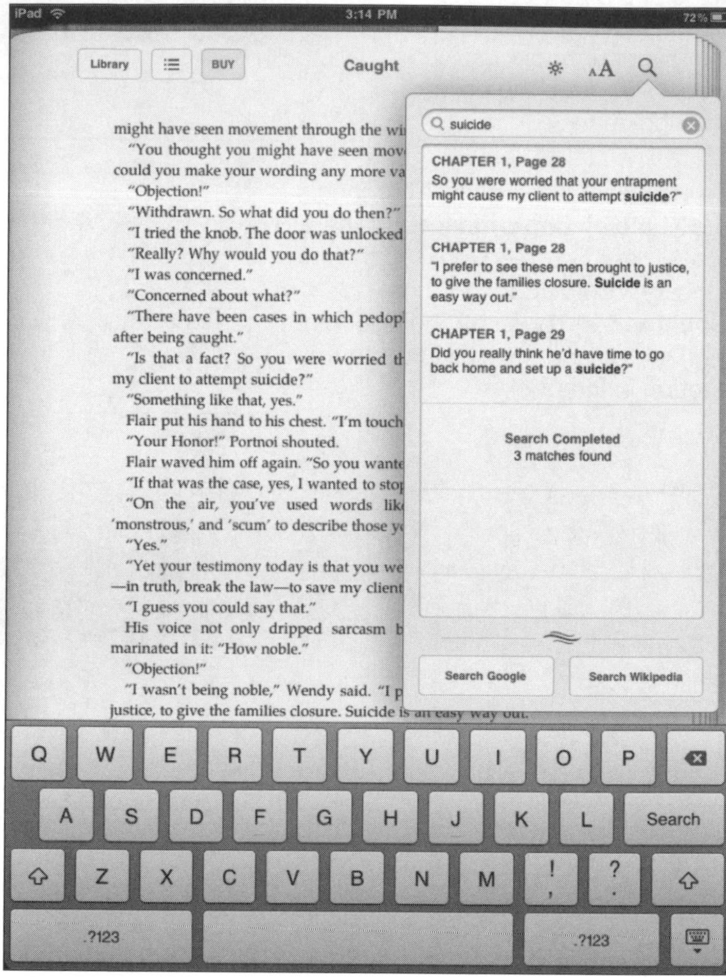


**NOTE:** Using the Wikipedia or Google search will take you out of iBooks and launch Safari.

## Deleting Books

Deleting books from your iBooks library is very similar to deleting applications from the iPad.

In the "Library" view, just touch **Edit** in the top right-hand corner.

Once you touch the **Edit** button, you will notice a small black "x" in the upper left-hand corner of each book.

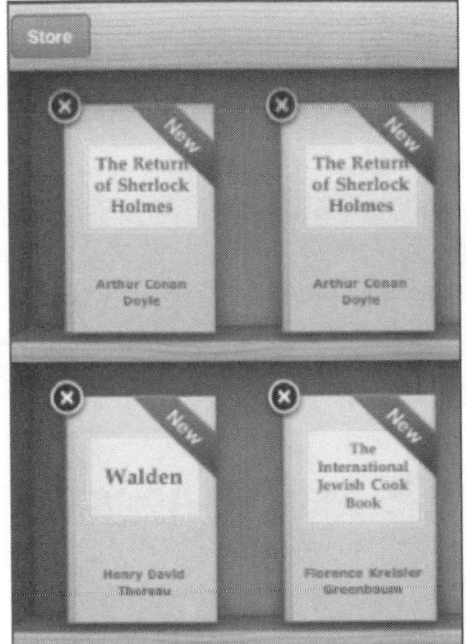


Just touch the "x" and you will be prompted to **Delete** the book. Once you touch **Delete**, the book will disappear from the shelf.

## Other E-Book Readers: Kindle and Kobo

iBooks, as we have shared, offers an unparalleled E-Book reading experience. There are, however, other E-Book reader apps available for the iPad that are worth checking out.

Many users already have a Kindle and have invested in their Kindle library. Others use Kobo E-Reader software (formerly Shortcovers) and have invested in a library of books for that platform.

Fortunately, both E-Book platforms have apps in the iPad App store. When either program is downloaded and installed, you can sign in and read your complete library on your iPad.

**NOTE:** No matter which of these other E-Readers you choose, you can always just "sign in," see your complete library, and pick up just where you left off in your last book—even if you started reading on a different device.

## Download E-Reader Apps

Go to the App store and then touch **Categories** and from there, touch **Books**. There you will find the Kindle app and the Kobo app. Both are free apps, so just touch the **Free** button and the downloads will initiate.

**TIP:** It is usually faster to just "search" by the name of the app if you know which one you are looking for.

Once the E-Reader software is installed, just touch the icon to start the app.

## Kindle Reader

Amazon's Kindle reader is the world's most popular E-Reader. Millions of people have Kindle books, so the Kindle app allows you to read your Kindle books on your iPad.

**TIP:** If you use a Kindle device, don't worry about signing in from your iPad. You can have several devices tied to your single account. You will be able to enjoy all the books you purchased for your Kindle right on the Kindle app on the iPad.

Just touch the Kindle app and either sign in to your Kindle account or create a new account with a user name and password.

Once you sign in, you will see your Kindle books on the home page. You can either touch a book to start reading, or touch the **Shopping Cart** to start shopping in the Kindle store.

**NOTE:** Touching the Shopping Cart will start up your Safari browser. From there you can purchase Kindle books. Once you are done, you will need to exit Safari and start up the Kindle app once again.

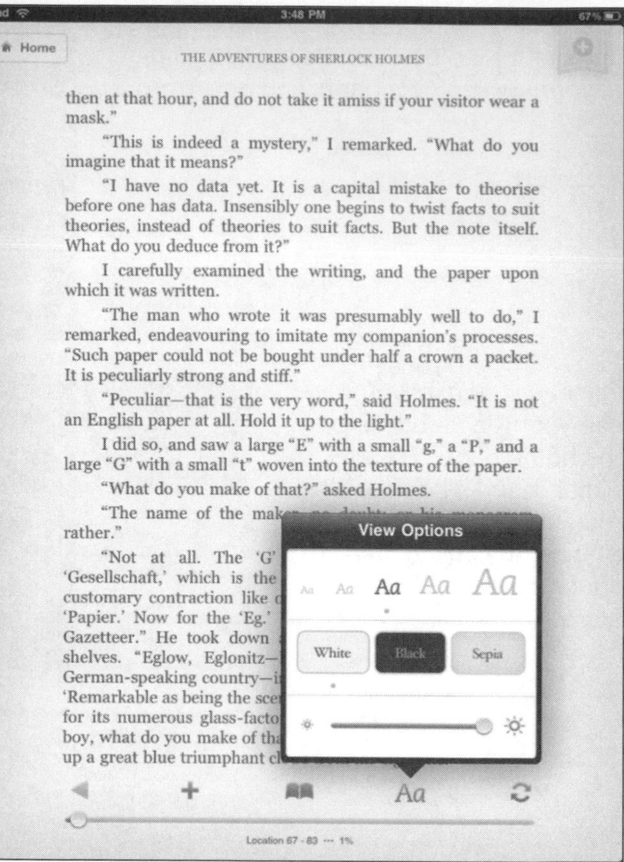


To read a Kindle book, touch on the book cover. The options for reading can be found along the bottom row of icons.

You can add a bookmark by touching the plus (**+**) button. Once the bookmark is set, the plus (**+**) turns to a minus (**-**).

You can go to the cover, table of contents, or beginning of the book (or specify any location in the book) by touching the button.

The font, as well as the color of the page, can be adjusted. One very interesting feature is the ability to change the page to "**Black**," which is great when reading at night.

To advance pages, either swipe from right to left, or touch the right-hand side of the page. To go back a page, just swipe from left to right or touch the left-hand side of the page.

Tap the screen and a slider appears at the bottom, which you can move to advance to any page in the book.

## Kobo Reader

Like the Kindle Reader, the Kobo Reader asks you first to sign in to your existing Kobo Books account. All of your existing Kobo Books will then be available for reading.

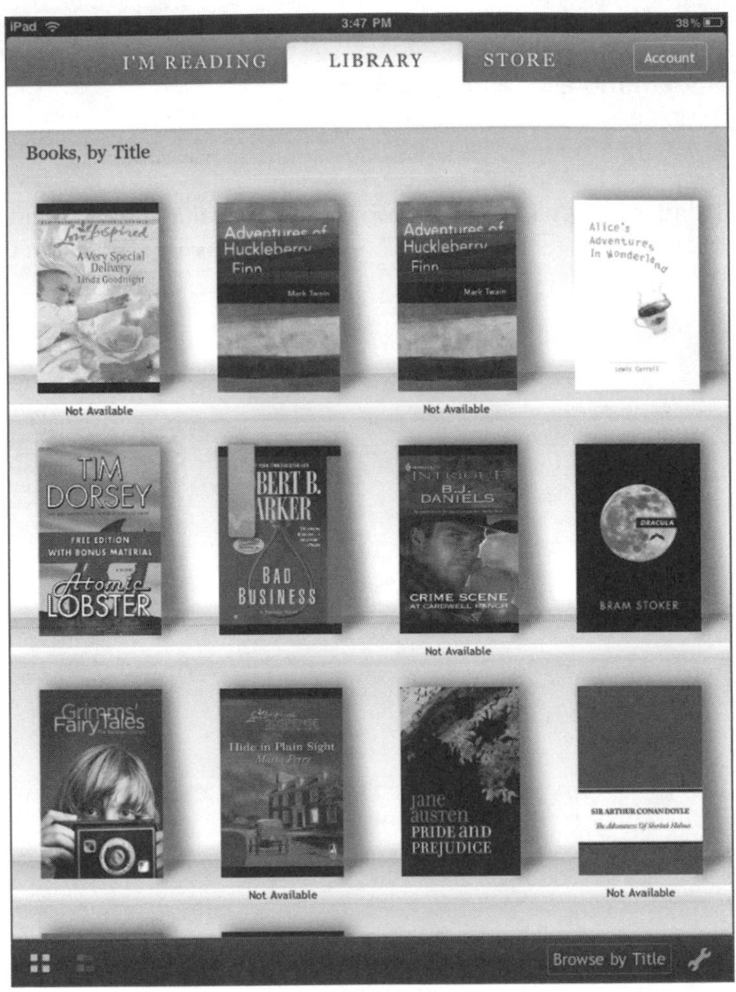


Kobo uses a "bookshelf" approach, similar to iBooks. Tap the book cover for whichever book you wish to open.

Or, touch the **I'm Reading** tab to pick up with what you were reading last. You can also directly go to the Kobo store to purchase books by touching the **Store** tab.

Along the top of the Kobo Reader are three buttons: **Table of Contents**, **Overview**, and **Bookmarks**.

Just touch any button to advance to the particular feature desired.

Along the bottom are four icons: **Font**, **Brightness**, **Add Bookmark**, and **Display Settings**. Touch any of the buttons to make adjustments to your viewing.

To advance pages in the Kobo Reader, touch the right-hand side of the page. To go back a page, just touch the left-hand side of the page. You can also use the slider at the bottom to advance through the pages.

Chapter 9

# Viewing Videos, TV Shows, & More

The iPad is an amazing "media consumption" device. Nowhere is this more apparent than in the various video-viewing applications available.

In this chapter we will show you how you can watch movies, TV shows, podcasts and music videos on your iPad. You can buy or download for free from the iTunes store or iTunes University. You can also link your iPad to your Netflix account (and most likely other video rental services soon), allowing you to watch streaming TV shows and movies.

With your iPad you can also watch YouTube videos and videos from the web on your Safari browser and through various apps like the **ABC** app from the App store.

> **NOTE:** As of publishing, Netflix and ABC are U.S.-only apps. We hope similar apps will make their way to the international market.

## Your iPad as a Video Player

The iPad is not only a capable music player; it is a fantastic portable video playing system. The widescreen, fast processor, and great operating system make watching anything from music videos to TV shows and full-length motion pictures a real joy. The size of the iPad is perfect for sitting back in a chair or watching on an airplane. It is also great for the kids in the back seat of long car trips. The ten-hour battery life means you can even go on a coast-to-coast flight and not run out of power! You can buy a "power inverter" for your car to keep the iPad charged even longer. (See the "Charging Your iPad and Battery Tips" section in Chapter 1.)

# Loading Videos onto Your iPad

You can load videos on your iPad just like your music, through iTunes from your computer or right from the iTunes icon on your iPad.

If you purchase or rent videos and TV shows from iTunes on your computer, then you will manually or automatically sync them to your iPad.

# Watching Videos on the iPad

Click on your **Videos** icon, which is usually on the first page of icons on your **Home** screen.

> **NOTE:** You can also watch videos from the **YouTube** icon, the **Safari** icon and other video-related apps you load from the App store.

## Video Categories

Along the top of the **Videos** screen are several category buttons: **Movies, TV Shows, Podcasts**, and **Music Videos.**

The default view is the **Movies** view, so if you have movies loaded on the iPad, they will be visible.

You may see more or fewer categories depending on the types of videos you have loaded on your iPad. If you have only **Movies** and **iTunes U** videos, then you would see only those two category buttons. Just touch any of the other categories to show the corresponding videos in each category.

# Playing a Movie

Movies

Just touch the movie you wish to watch and it will begin to play (see Figure 9–1). Most videos take advantage of the relatively large screen–real estate of the iPad and they play in widescreen or landscape mode. Just turn your iPad to watch.

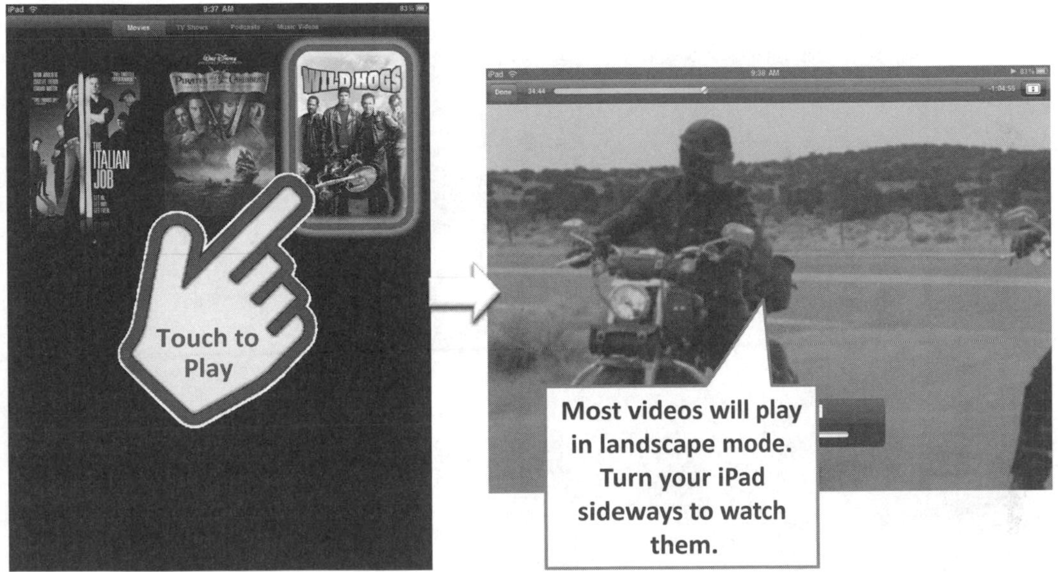
WILD HOGS
THE ITALIAN JOB
Touch to Play
Most videos will play in landscape mode. Turn your iPad sideways to watch them.

**Figure 9–1**. *Playing a video*

When the video first starts, there are no menus, no controls, and nothing on the screen except for the video.

## To Pause or Access Controls

Touch anywhere on the screen and the control bars and options will become visible (see Figure 9–2). Most are very similar to those in the Music player. Tap the **Pause** button and the video will pause.

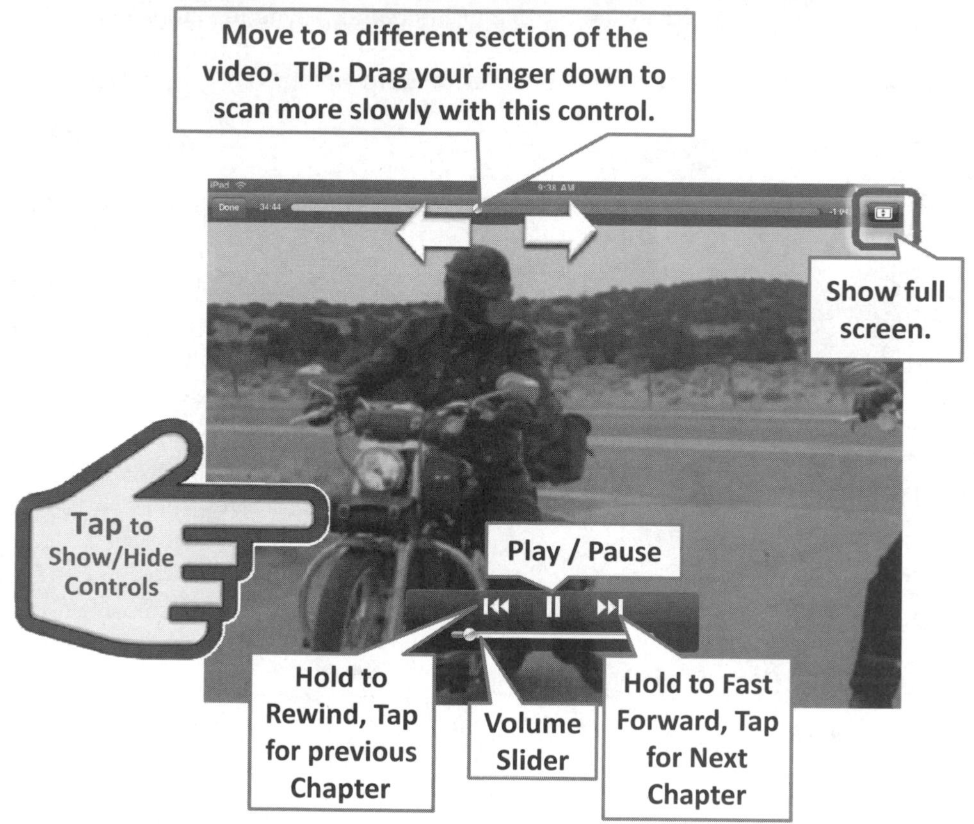


**Figure 9–2.** *Video controls*

## Fast-Forward or Rewind the Video

On either side of the **Play/Pause** button are typical **Fast-Forward** and **Rewind** buttons. To jump to the next chapter-specific part of the video, just touch and hold the **Fast-Forward** button (to the right of **Play/Pause**. When you get to the desired spot, release the button and the video will begin playing normally.

To rewind to the beginning on the video, tap the **Rewind** button. To rewind to a specific part or location, touch and hold like you did while you were fast-forwarding the video.

**NOTE:** If this is a full-length movie with several chapters, tapping either **Reverse** or **Fast-Forward** will move either back or ahead one chapter.

## Using the Time Slider Bar

At the top of the video screen is a slider that shows you the elapsed time of the video. If you know exactly (or approximately) which point in the video you wish to watch, just hold and drag the slide to that location. Some people find this to be a little more exact than holding down the **Fast-Forward** or **Rewind** Buttons.

**TIP:** Drag your finger down to move the slide more slowly. In other words, start by touching the slider control, then drag your finger down the screen—notice that the further down the screen your finger is, the slower the slider moves left or right. The screen may say "Scrubbing"—this just means to lower the sensitivity of how fast the slider moves.

## Changing the Size of the Video (Widescreen vs. Full Screen)

Most of your videos will play in widescreen format. However, if you have a video that was not converted for your iPad or is not optimized for the screen resolution, you can touch the expand button, which is to the right of the upper Status bar.

You will notice that there are two arrows. If you are in full-screen mode, the arrows are pointing in towards each other. If you are in widescreen mode, the arrows are pointing outwards.

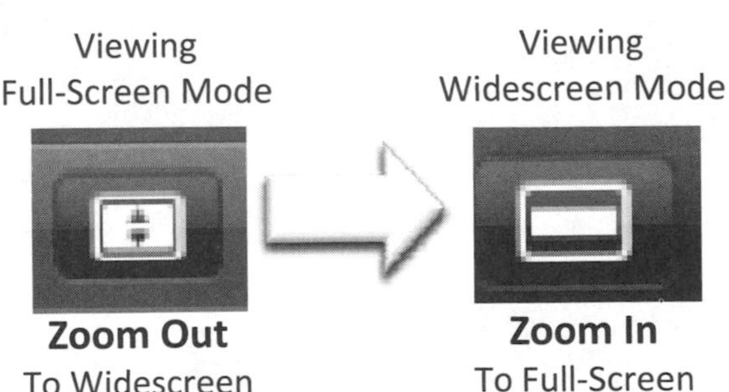


In a widescreen movie that is not taking up the full screen of the iPad, touching this button will zoom in a bit. Touching it again will zoom out.

**NOTE:** You can also simply "double-tap" the screen to zoom in and fill the screen as well. Be aware that, just like on your widescreen TV, when you try to force a non-widescreen video into widescreen mode, sometimes you will lose part of the picture.

## Using the Chapters Feature

Most full-length movies purchased from the iTunes store, and some that are converted for the iPad, will give you a Chapters feature—very much like you were watching a DVD on your home TV.

Just bring up the controls for the video by tapping the screen, and then select **Done**.

This will bring you back to the main page for the movie.

Touch the **Chapters** button in the upper right corner, and then scroll through to and touch the chapter you wish to watch.

## Viewing the Chapters

You can scroll through or flick through quickly to locate the scene or chapter that you wish to watch.

You will also notice that to the far right of each chapter is the exact time (relative to the start of the movie) that the chapter begins.

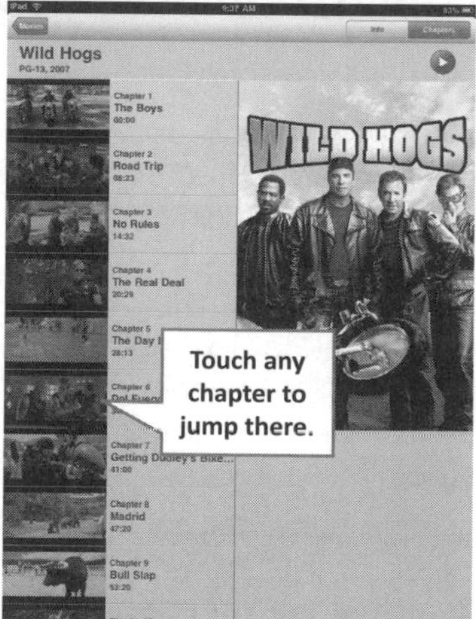


In addition to the chapter menu, mentioned previously, you can also quickly advance to the previous or next chapter in a movie by tapping the **Rewind** or **Fast-Forward** buttons. One tap moves you one chapter in either direction.

> **NOTE:** The Chapters feature usually works only with movies that are purchased from the iTunes store. Movies that are converted and loaded on usually will not have chapters.

# Watching a TV Show

The iPad is great for watching your favorite TV shows. You can purchase TV shows from the iTunes store, and you can download sample shows from some iPad apps, like the **ABC** app.

Just touch the **TV Shows** tab at the top to see the shows you have downloaded on your iPad. Scroll through your available shows and touch **Play**. The video controls work just like the controls when you watch a movie.

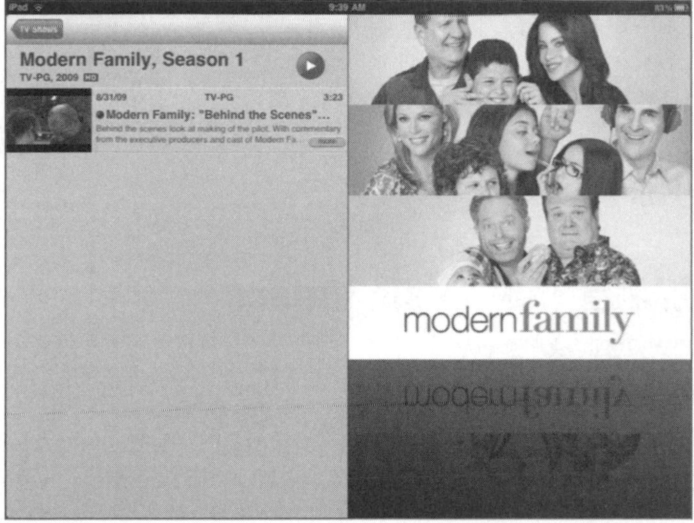


# Watching Podcasts

Podcasts

We normally think of podcasts as being audio-only broadcasts that can be downloaded through iTunes. Video podcasts are now quite prevalent and can be found on any number of sites, including many public broadcasting websites and on iTunes U, a listing of university podcasts and information found within iTunes.

iTunes U Story from Gary Mazo:

"Recently, I was browsing the **iTunes U** section inside the iTunes app on the iPad with my son, who was just accepted to CalTech. We were wondering about the housing situation and, lo and behold, we found a video podcast showing a tour of the CalTech dorms. We downloaded it and the podcast went right into the podcast directory for future viewing. We were able to do a complete virtual tour of the housing without flying out there from the East Coast."

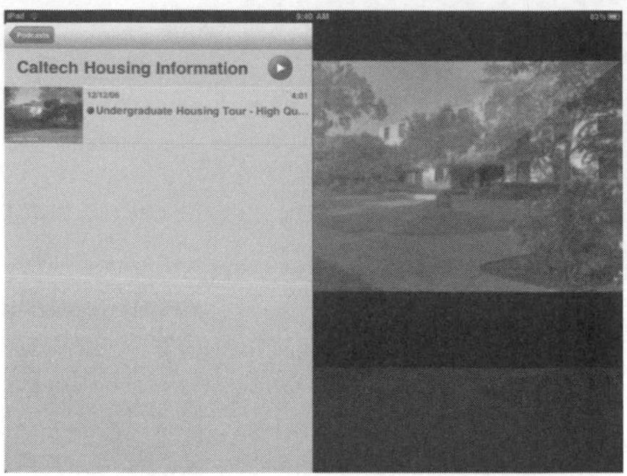


# Watching Music Videos

Music Videos

Music videos are available for your iPad from a number of sources. Often, if you buy a "Deluxe" album from iTunes, it might include a music video or two. Music videos can also be purchased from the iTunes store, and many record companies and recording artists make them available for free on their websites.

Music videos will automatically get sorted into the **Music Videos** section of your **Videos** app.

Touch the **Music Videos** tab and start playing the video. The controls work just as they do in all other video applications.

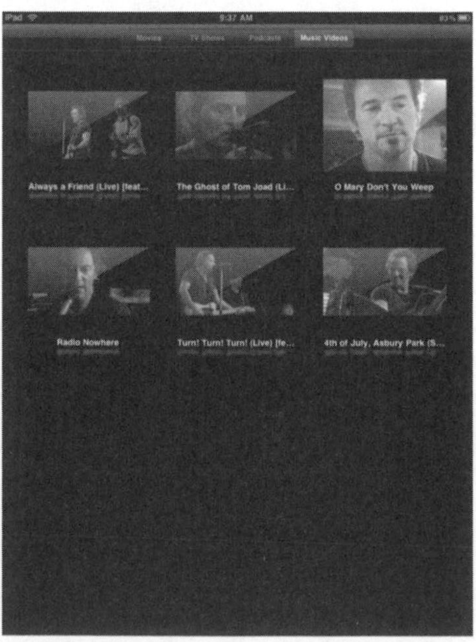

# Video Options

As in your music player, there are a few options that you can adjust for the video player. These options are accessed through the **Settings** icon from your **Home** screen.

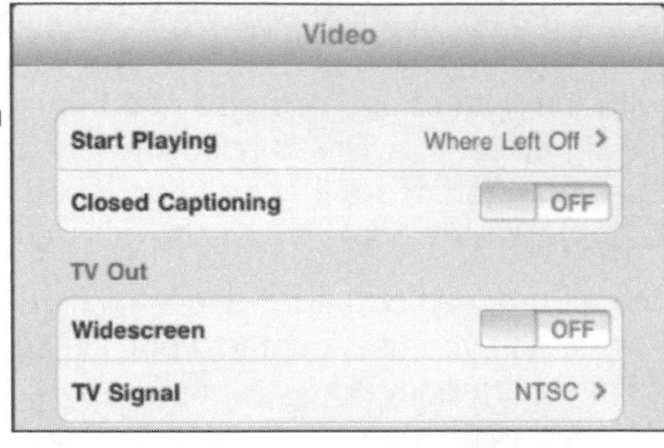


Touch the **Settings** icon and then scroll down to touch **iPad** and then to the **Video** options.

## Start Playing Option

Sometimes, you will have to stop watching a particular video. This option lets you decide what to do the next time you want to watch. Your options are to either watch the video from the beginning or from where you left off. Just select the option that you desire and that will be the action from now on.

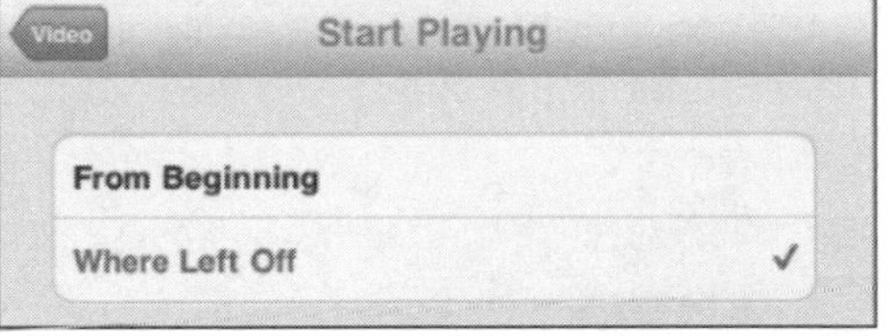


## Closed Captioned

If your video has closed captioned capabilities, when this switch is turned to **On**, closed captioning will be shown on your screen.

## TV-Out: Widescreen

There are many third party gadgets out there that allow you to watch the video from your iPad on some external source, either a TV or computer screen, or even an array of video glasses that simulate watching on a very large screen monitor. Most of these require that your TV widescreen setting be set to **On**. By default, it is set to **Off**.

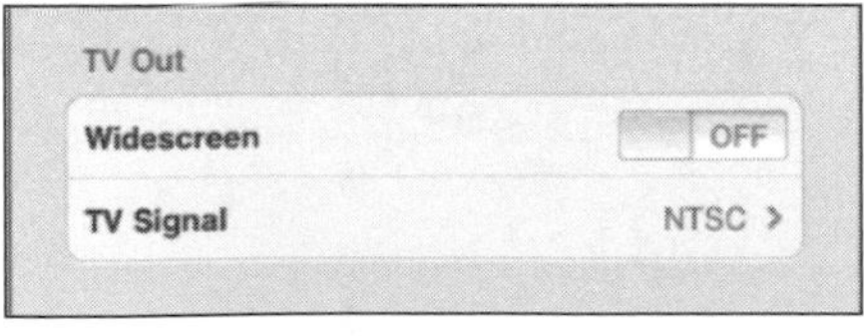


**TIP:** You can purchase a VGA adapter to plug your iPad into a VGA computer monitor to watch movies. See our the "Accessories" section of our Quick Start Guide for more information.

## TV Signal

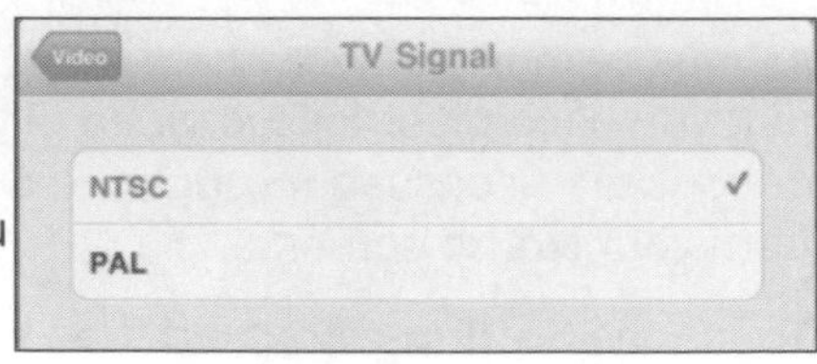


There are some advanced ways of taking content from your iPad and playing them on your TV or DVR with the right cable. You also need to have the right TV signal setting. This is typically changed only if you use your iPad in another country. If you live in the U.S., your TV works with the NTSC standard.

Most European countries use PAL. If you are not sure which you use, contact your TV, cable, or satellite company.

# Deleting Videos

To delete a video (to save space on your iPad) just choose the category from which you wish to delete the video—as you did at the start of this chapter (see Figure 9–3).

**NOTE:** If you're syncing videos from iTunes, make sure to uncheck it there as well, or iTunes just might sync it right back to the iPad on the next sync!

Just touch and hold on a particular video you wish to delete. Just like deleting an app, a small black "x" will appear in the top left-hand corner. Touch the "x" and you will be prompted to delete the video.

Touch the **Delete** button and the video will be deleted from your system.

**NOTE:** This deletes the video only from your iPad—a copy will still remain in your video library in iTunes if you want to once again load it back onto your iPad. However, if you delete a rented movie from the iPad, it will be deleted permanently!

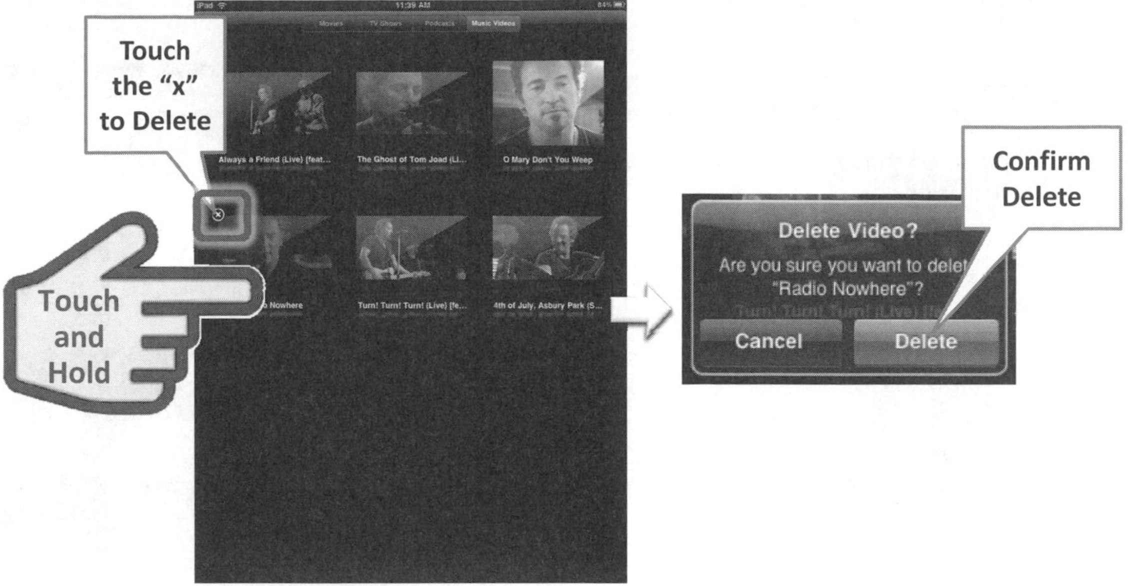


**Figure 9–3.** *Delete video*

# YouTube on your iPad

Watching YouTube videos is certainly one of the most popular things for people to do on their computers these days. YouTube is as close to you as your iPad.

Right on your **Home** screen is a **YouTube** icon. Just touch the **YouTube** icon and you will be taken to the YouTube app.

## Searching for Videos

When you first start YouTube, you usually see the **Featured** videos on YouTube that day.

Just scroll through the video choices as you do in other apps.

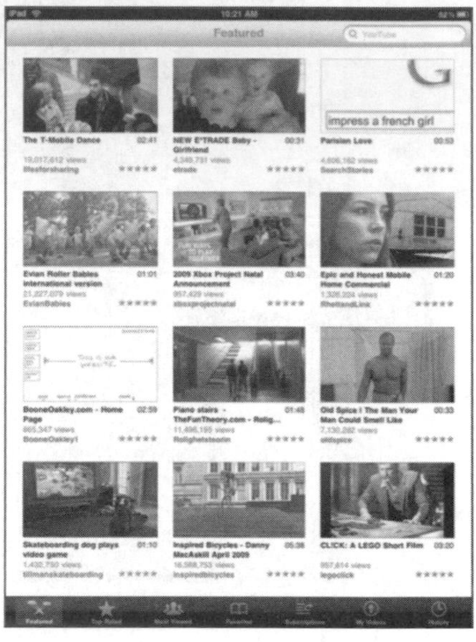

## Using the Bottom Icons

Along the bottom of the YouTube app are seven icons; **Featured**, **Top Rated**, **Most Viewed**, **Favorites**, **Subscriptions, My videos,** and **History**. Each is fairly self-explanatory.

To see the videos that YouTube is featuring that day, just touch the **Featured** icon. To see those videos that are most-viewed online, just touch the **Most Viewed** icon.

After you watch a particular video, you will have the option to set it as a favorite on **YouTube** for easy retrieval later on. If you have set bookmarks, they will appear when you touch the **Favorite** icon.

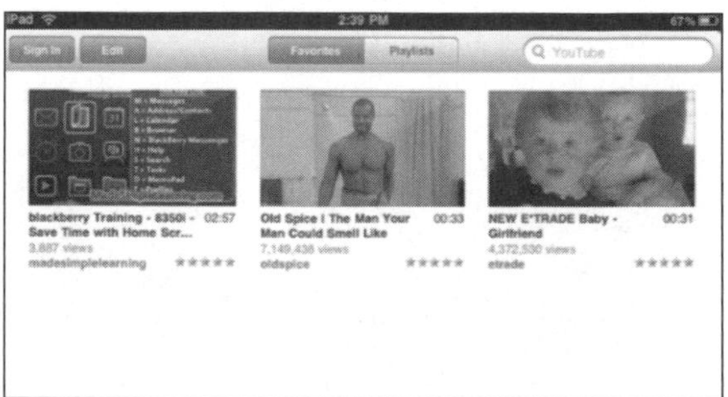

You can search the huge library of YouTube videos. Touch the search box as in previous apps, and the keyboard will pop up. Type in a phrase, topic, or even the name of a video.

In this example, I am looking for the newest Made Simple Learning video tutorial—so I just type in "Made Simple Learning" and I see the list of videos to watch.

When I find the video I want to watch, I can touch on it to see more information. I can even rate the video by touching on the video during playback and selecting a rating.

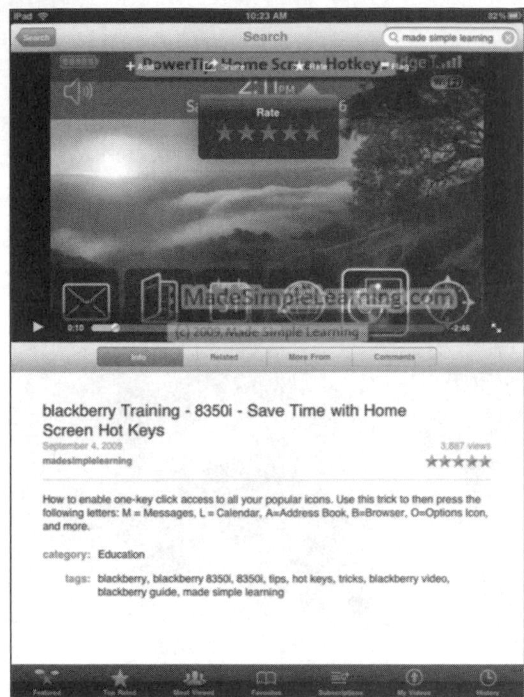

## Playing Videos

Once you have made your choice, touch the video you want to watch. Your iPad will begin playing the YouTube video in portrait or landscape mode (see Figure 9–4).

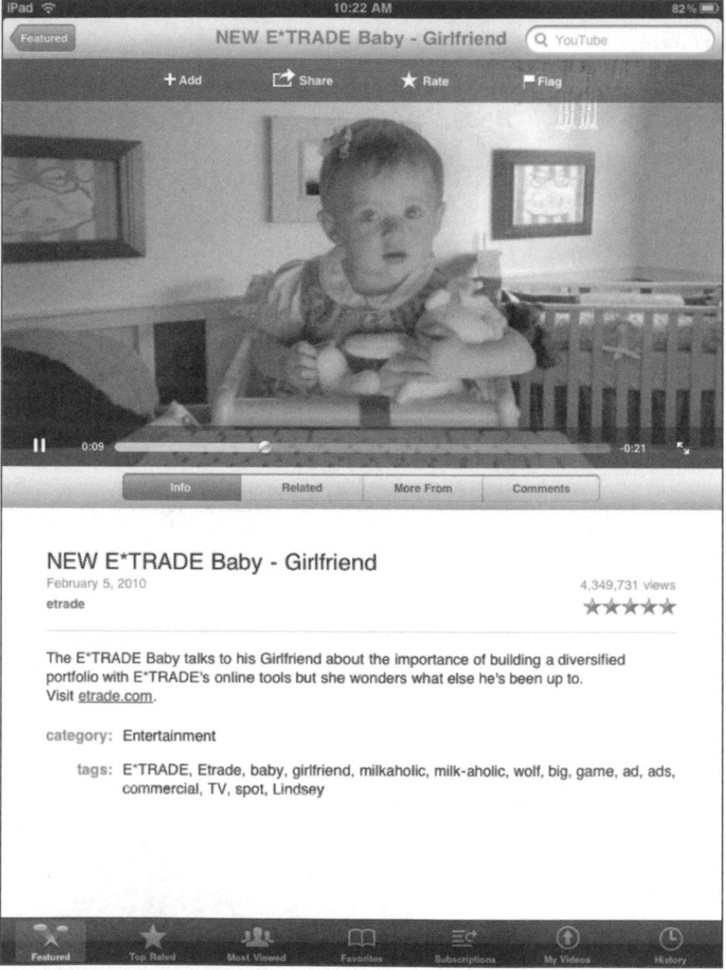


**Figure 9–4.** *Video playing in portrait mode*

## Video Controls

Once the video begins to play, the on-screen controls disappear, so you see only the video. To stop, pause, or activate any other options while the video is playing, just tap the screen (see Figure 9–5).

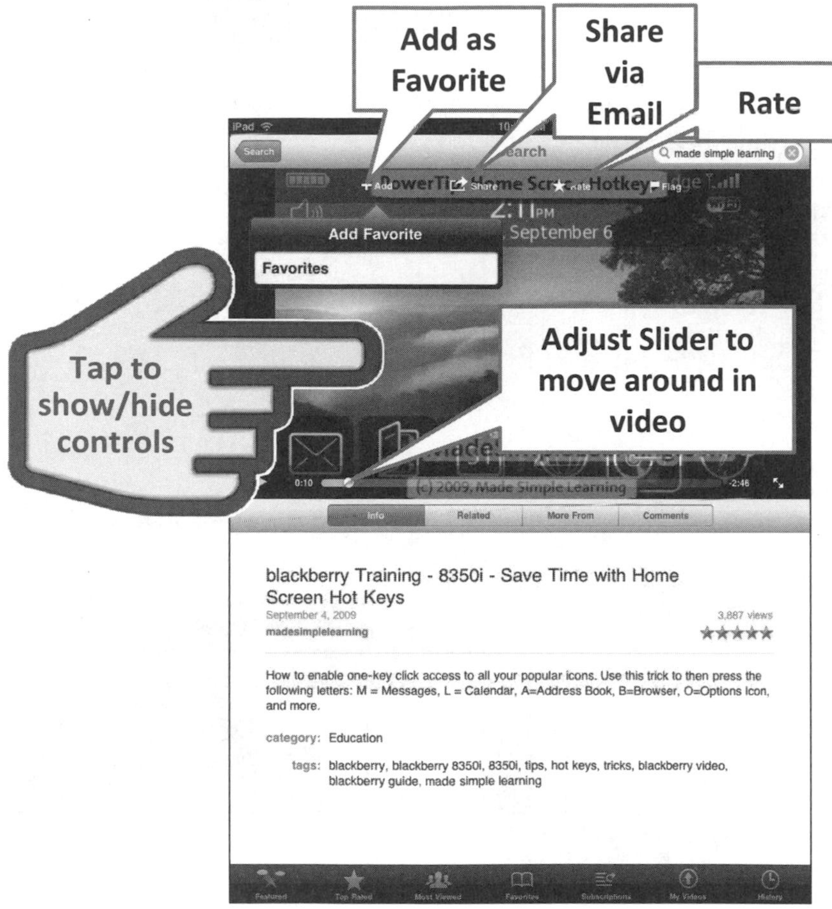


**Figure 9–5.** *Options within YouTube*

The on-screen options are very similar to watching any other video. Along the bottom is the slider, showing your place in the video. To move to another part in the video, just drag the slider.

To fast-forward through the video (in landscape mode,) just touch and hold the **Fast-Forward** arrow. To quickly move in reverse, just touch and hold the **Reverse** arrow. To advance to the next video in the

YouTube list, just tap the **Fast-Forward/Next** arrow. To watch the previous video in the list, just tap the **Reverse/Back** arrow.

To set a favorite, touch the **Favorite** icon.

To email the video, just touch the **Share** icon and your email will start with the link to the video in the body of the email. Type the recipient as we showed you in Chapter 15 when you sent a picture via email.

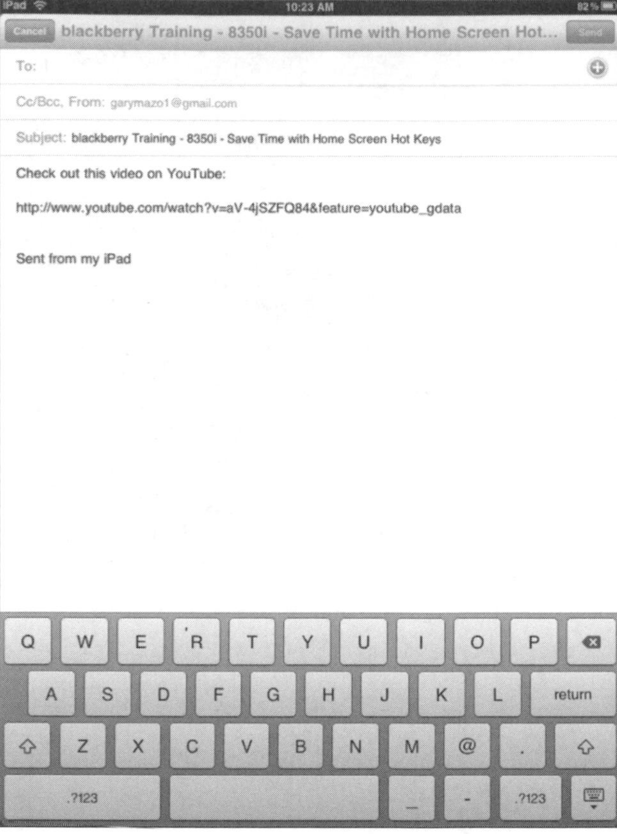

## Checking and Clearing your History

Touch the **History** icon 

in the lower right-hand corner of the page. Your recently viewed videos appear.

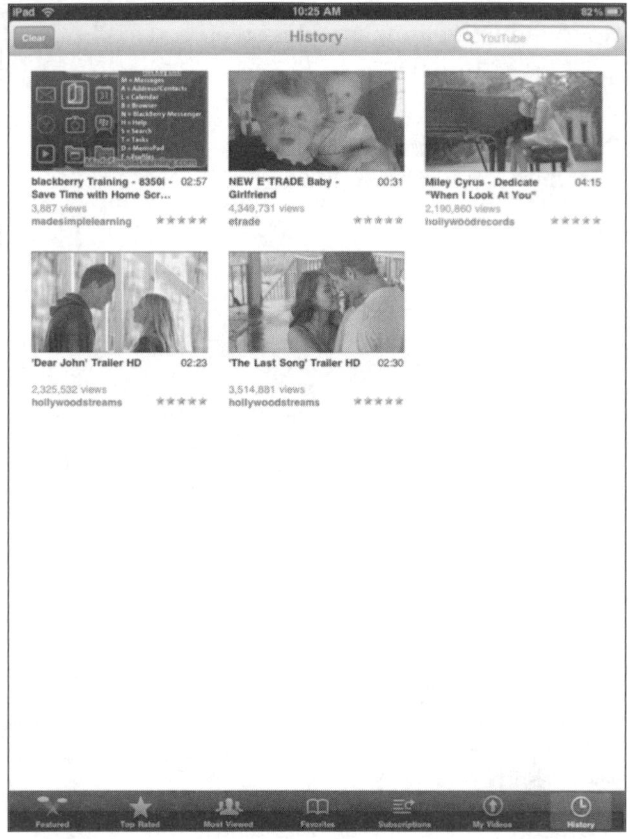


If you want to clear your history, just touch the **Clear** button in the upper left corner.

To watch a video from your history, just touch it and it will start to play.

## Netflix on the iPad

In recent years, Netflix has grown to become a leading source of video rentals for consumers. Most recently, Netflix added video “streaming” of content delivered wirelessly to computers and other set-top boxes for your TV.

Now, Netflix is available to iPad users through the Netflix app in the App store.

Go to the App store, as we showed you in our **App Store** chapter, and search for the Netflix app.

Choose the **Download** button (the app is free) and you are on your way.

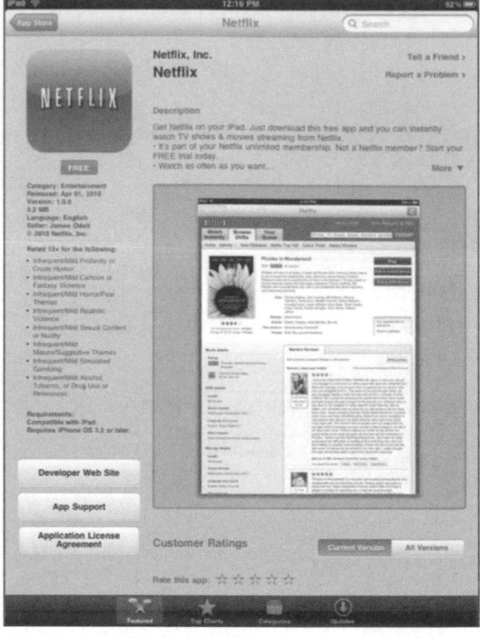


You need an active Netflix account, so either create one when you start up the app or just sign into your Netflix account if you already have one.

The beauty of the Netflix app is that you can add DVDs to your queue and have them sent out to you, and you can also watch TV shows and movies instantly—streaming them right to the iPad.

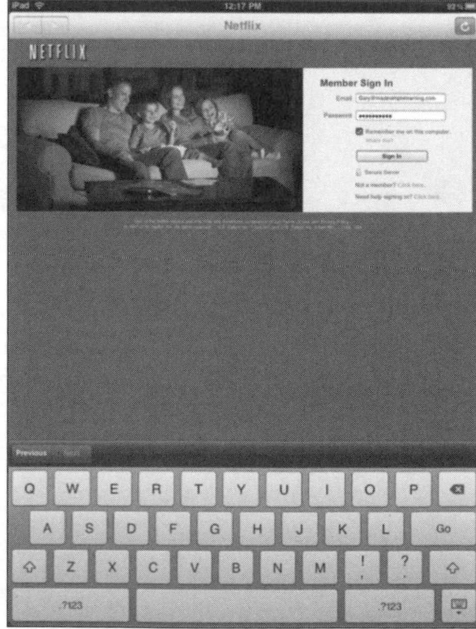

Navigating Netflix is very easy and just like using Netflix on your computer. You have a top bar with tabs for **Watch Movies Instantly**, **Watch TV Shows Instantly**, **Browse DVDs**, and **Your Queue.**

When you make your selection, you will see what you have recently watched (so you can resume watching), as well as video categories based on the preferences you selected when you established your Netflix account.

Each row of videos slides right to left to show you more options. If you don't find what you are looking for, just touch the search window and type in the name of a movie, actor, director, or genre.

Once you find the movie or TV show you want to watch, touch **Play Now** and the movie will begin to stream to your iPad. The video controls are exactly like those in all the other video-playing apps for the iPad.

> **CAUTION:** Netflix uses a great deal of data, so make sure you have a strong Wi-Fi signal if you are streaming over Wi-Fi or, if you are using 3G cellular data, make sure you have an adequate data plan.

# Watching Other TV Shows

At the time of publication, since the iPad was so new, there were limited options for watching other network shows and movies. This should change quickly, and, by the time you read this, more TV shows will be available, with more added every month.

One of the best options at launch time was the **ABC** app, available for free download in the App store.

Once the app is downloaded, your favorite TV shows are available for streaming. ABC streams their most popular shows, with several full episodes available. This app also uses large amounts of data, so make sure you have a good Wi-Fi connection or an unlimited 3G plan before you stream TV shows.

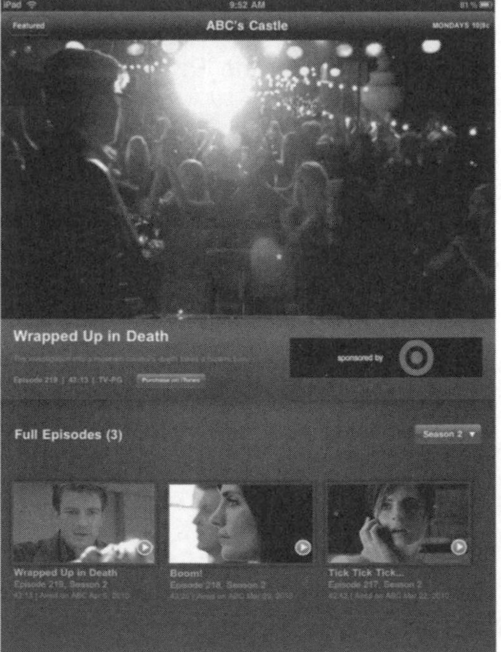

Chapter 10

# Bluetooth on the iPad

In this chapter we will show you how to pair your iPad with any Bluetooth device, whether it be another computer, stereo speakers, or a wireless keyboard accessory. iPad users are surprised to find out that the iPad actually ships with Bluetooth 2.0 Stereo Technology. Thanks to the technology known as A2DP, you can stream your music to a capable Bluetooth stereo.

**NOTE:** You must have a capable third-party Bluetooth adapter or Bluetooth stereo to stream your music via Bluetooth technology. Also, there is no AVRCP profile support, so many music controls on a Bluetooth device (like Play, Pause, or Skip) won't work quite yet.

Think of Bluetooth as a short-range, wireless technology that allows your iPad to connect to various peripheral devices without wires. Popular devices are headsets, computers, and vehicle sound systems.

Bluetooth is believed to be named after a Danish Viking and king, Harald Blåtand, whose name has been translated as *Bluetooth*. King Blåtand lived in the tenth century and is famous for uniting Denmark and Norway. Similarly, Bluetooth technology unites computers and telecom. His name, according to legend, is from his very dark hair, which was unusual for Vikings. Blåtand means dark complexion. There does exist a more popular story that the king loved to eat blueberries, so much so that his teeth became stained with the color blue.

Sources:

- `http://cp.literature.agilent.com/litweb/pdf/5980-3032EN.pdf`
- `http://www.cs.utk.edu/~dasgupta/bluetooth/history.htm`
- `http://www.britannica.com/eb/topic-254809/Harald-I`

# Understanding Bluetooth

Bluetooth allows your iPad to communicate with things wirelessly. Bluetooth is a small radio that transmits from each device. Before you can use a peripheral with the iPad, you have to "pair" it with that device to connect it to the peripheral. Many Bluetooth devices can be used up to 30 feet away from the iPad.

## Bluetooth Devices that Work with the iPad

Among other things, the iPad works with Bluetooth headphones, Bluetooth stereo systems and adapters, Bluetooth car stereo systems, and Bluetooth wireless keyboards. The iPad supports A2DP, which is known as Stereo Bluetooth.

# Pairing with a Bluetooth Device

Your primary uses for Bluetooth might be with Bluetooth headphones, Bluetooth stereo adapters, or a Bluetooth keyboard. Any Bluetooth headphones should work well with your iPad. To start using any Bluetooth device, you need to first pair (connect) it with your iPad.

## Turn On Bluetooth

The first step to using Bluetooth is to turn the Bluetooth radio **On**.

Tap your **Settings** icon.

Then, touch the **General** tab in the left column.

You will see the **Bluetooth** tab in the right-hand column.

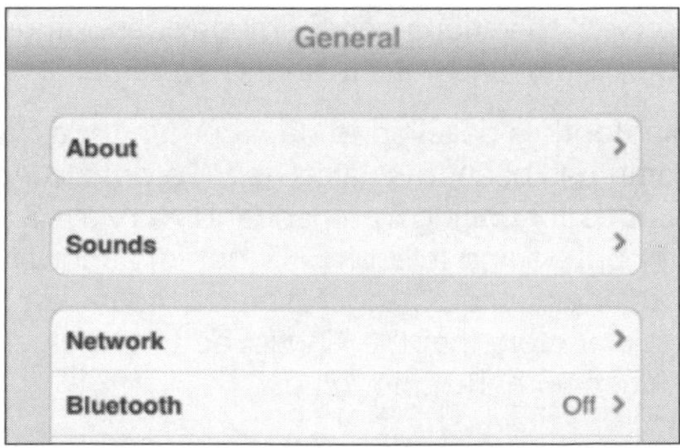

By default, Bluetooth is initially **Off** on the iPad. Tap the switch to move it to the **On** position.

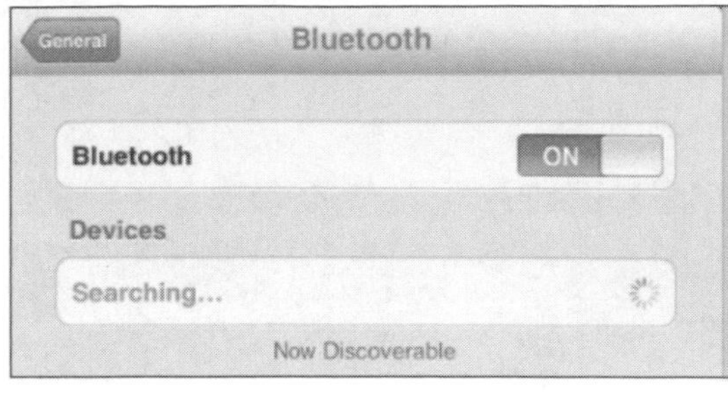


> **TIP:** Bluetooth is an added drain on your battery. If you don't plan on using Bluetooth for a period of time, think about turning the switch back to **OFF**.

## Pairing with Headphones or any Bluetooth Device

As soon as you turn Bluetooth **On**, the iPad will begin to search for any nearby Bluetooth device—like a Bluetooth headset or keyboard (see Figure 10–1). For the iPad to find your Bluetooth device, you need to put that device into "pairing mode." Read the instructions carefully that came with your headset—usually there is a combination of buttons to push to achieve this.

> **TIP:** Some headsets require you to press and hold a button for five seconds until you see a series of flashing blue or red/blue lights. Some accessories, such as the Apple wireless Bluetooth keyboard, automatically start up in pairing mode.

Once the iPad detects the Bluetooth device, it will attempt to automatically pair with it. If pairing takes place automatically, there is nothing more for you to do.

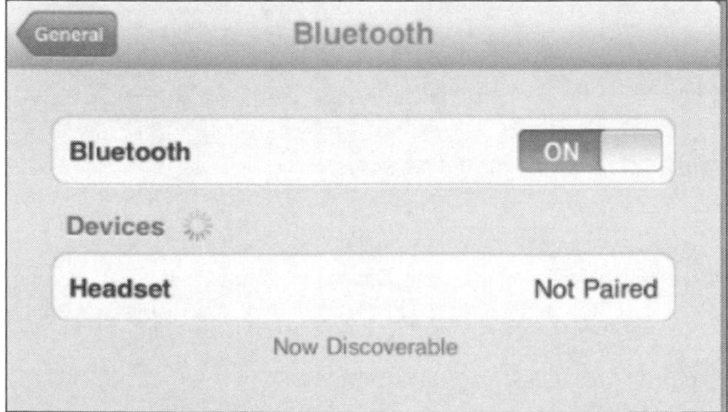


**Figure 10–1.** *Bluetooth device discovered but not yet paired*

If the image in Figure 10–2 stays unchanged, then tap the device (e.g., Apple wireless keyboard) to bring up a pop-up window that asks for a pairing ID.

**NOTE:** In the case of a Bluetooth device, such as a keyboard, you maybe asked to enter a randomly-generated series of numbers (passkey) on the keyboard itself. See Figure 10–2.

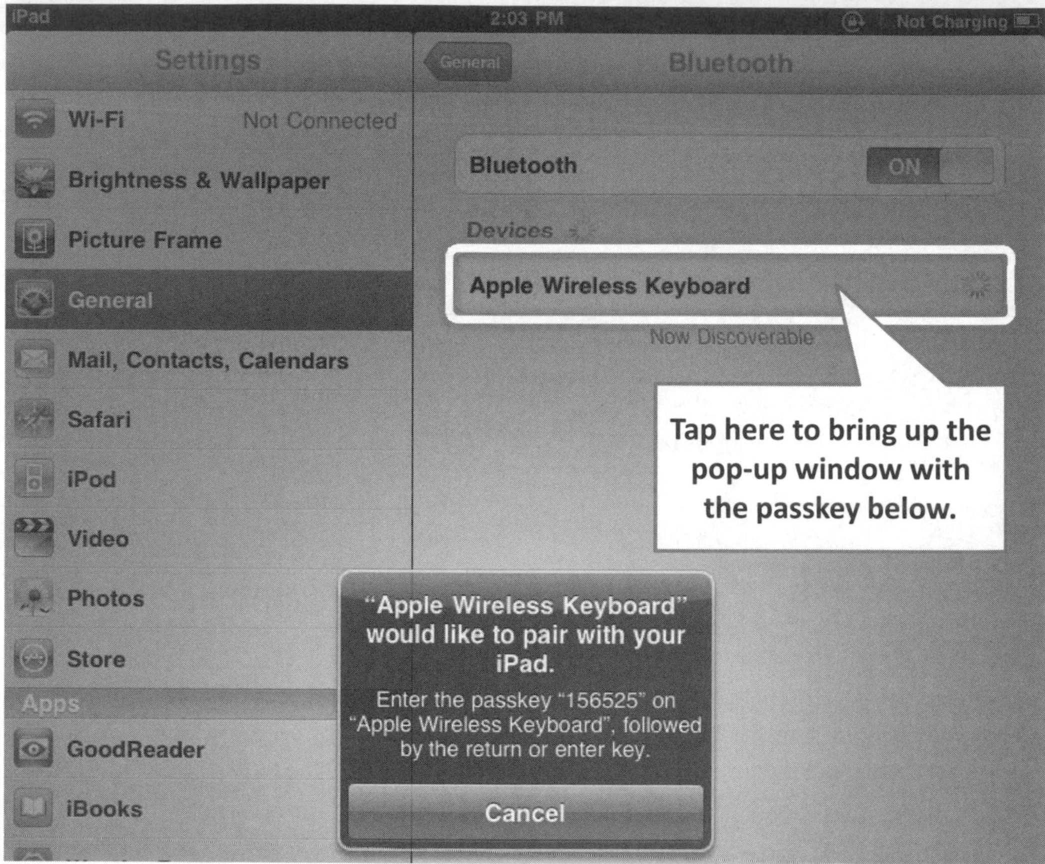


**Figure 10–2.** *To pair a Bluetooth keyboard, touch the listed device for the passkey.*

If the iPad asks for a PIN or pass code to be entered, the keyboard will be displayed, and you will enter the four-digit pass code supplied by the headset manufacturer. Most devices use 0000 or 1234, which is why the iPad can try to automatically pair with most devices. Check your headset documentation to learn the correct pass code or PIN for your device.

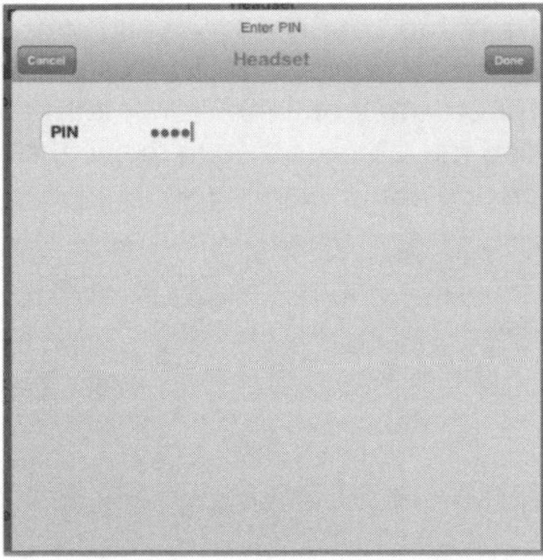


# Bluetooth Stereo (A2DP)

One of the great features of today's advanced Bluetooth technology is the ability to stream your music without wires via Bluetooth. The fancy name for this technology is A2DP, but it is simply known as Stereo Bluetooth.

## Connect to a Stereo Bluetooth Device

The first step to using Stereo Bluetooth is to connect to a capable Stereo Bluetooth device. This can be a car stereo with this technology built in, or a pair of Bluetooth headphones or speakers.

Put the Bluetooth device into pairing mode as per the manufacturer's instructions, and then go to the Bluetooth setting page from the **Settings** icon, as we showed you earlier in the chapter.

Once connected, you will see the new Stereo Bluetooth device listed under your Bluetooth devices. Sometimes it will simply be listed as "Headset." Just touch the device and you will see the name of the actual device next to the **Bluetooth** tab in the next screen, as shown here.

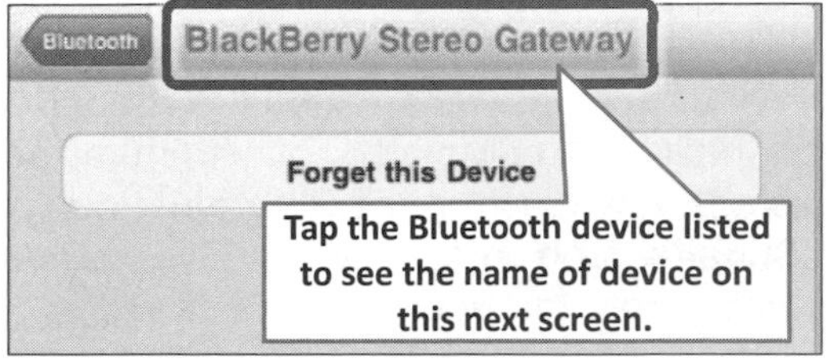

Next, tap your **iPod** icon and start up any song, playlist, podcast, or video music library. You will now notice a small **Bluetooth** icon in the lower left-hand corner of the screen. Tap the **Bluetooth** icon to see the available Bluetooth devices for streaming your music (see Figure 10–3).

> **NOTE**: If you are in the **Now Playing** view, the **Bluetooth** icon will be down at the bottom, towards the right-hand side.

**Figure 10–3.** *Select Bluetooth device*

In the previous screens, we selected the **BlackBerry Stereo Gateway** by tapping it. Now, your music will now start to play from the selected Bluetooth device. You can verify this again by touching the **Bluetooth** icon on the screen once more. You should see the **Speaker** icon next to the new Stereo Bluetooth device and you should hear your music coming from that sound source as well.

# Disconnect or Forget a Bluetooth Device

Sometimes, you might want to disconnect a Bluetooth device from your iPad.

It is easy to get this done. Get into the Bluetooth settings as you did earlier in this chapter. Touch the device you want to disconnect in order to bring up the next screen, then tap the **Forget this Device** button and confirm your choice.

> **NOTE:** Bluetooth has a range of only about 30 feet, so if you are not nearby or not using a Bluetooth device, turn off **Bluetooth**. You can always turn it back on when you are actually going to be using it.

This will delete the Bluetooth profile from the iPad. (See Figure 10–4.)

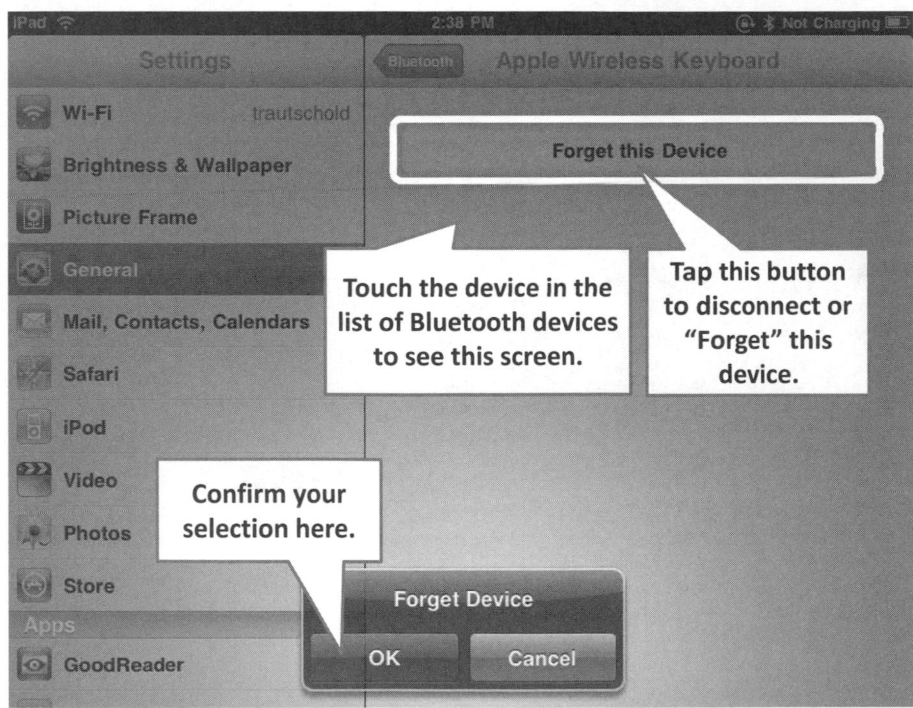


**Figure 10–4.** *Forget or disconnect a Bluetooth device.*

Chapter 11

# Surf the Web with Safari

Now we'll take you through one of the most fun things to do on your iPad: surfing the web. You may have heard web surfing on the iPad is a more intimate experience than ever before—we agree! We'll show you how to touch, zoom around, and interact with the Web like never before with Safari on your iPad. You'll learn how to set and use bookmarks, quickly find things with the search engine, open and switch between multiple browser windows and even easily copy text and graphics from web pages.

## Web Browsing on the iPad

You can browse the web to your heart's content via Wi-Fi or with your iPad's 3G connection (on Wi-Fi + 3G models.) The iPad has what many feel is the most capable mobile browsing experience available today. Web pages look very much like web pages on your computer. With the iPad's ability to zoom in, you don't even have to worry about the smaller screen size inhibiting your web browsing experience. In short, web browsing is a much more personal experience on the iPad.

You can browse in portrait or landscape mode, whichever you prefer. You can also quickly zoom into a video by double-tapping it or pinching open on it, which is natural to you because those are the motions to zoom in text and graphics.

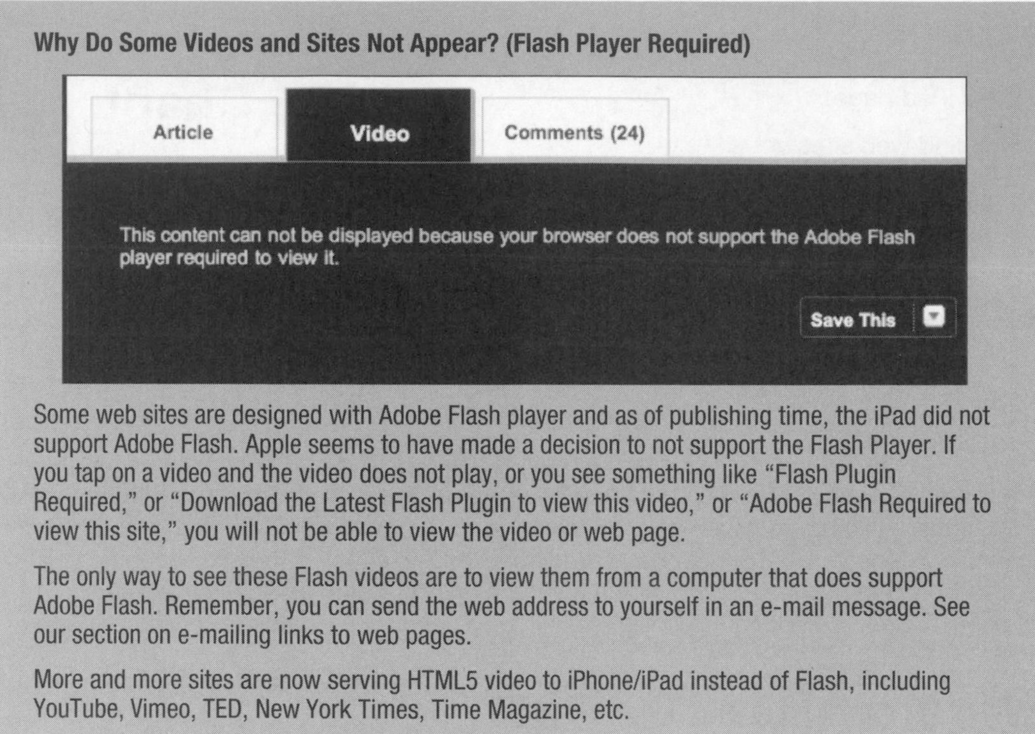


**Why Do Some Videos and Sites Not Appear? (Flash Player Required)**

Some web sites are designed with Adobe Flash player and as of publishing time, the iPad did not support Adobe Flash. Apple seems to have made a decision to not support the Flash Player. If you tap on a video and the video does not play, or you see something like "Flash Plugin Required," or "Download the Latest Flash Plugin to view this video," or "Adobe Flash Required to view this site," you will not be able to view the video or web page.

The only way to see these Flash videos are to view them from a computer that does support Adobe Flash. Remember, you can send the web address to yourself in an e-mail message. See our section on e-mailing links to web pages.

More and more sites are now serving HTML5 video to iPhone/iPad instead of Flash, including YouTube, Vimeo, TED, New York Times, Time Magazine, etc.

## An Internet Connection Is Required

You do need a live Internet connection on your iPad, either Wi-Fi or 3G (cellular data), in order to browse the web. Check out the Connectivity section in Chapter 4 on Wi-Fi and 3G to learn more.

## Launching the Web Browser

You should find the Safari (web browser) icon on your **Home Screen**. Usually, the **Safari** icon is in the lower left of the **Bottom Dock**.

Touch the **Safari** icon and you will be taken to the browser's home page. Most likely, this will be Apple's iPad page.,

As you find web sites you like, you can set bookmarks to easily jump to the web sites you like. We will show you how to do that later in this chapter.

## Layout of Safari Web Browser Screen

Figure 11–1 shows how a web page looks in Safari, and the different actions you can take in the browser.

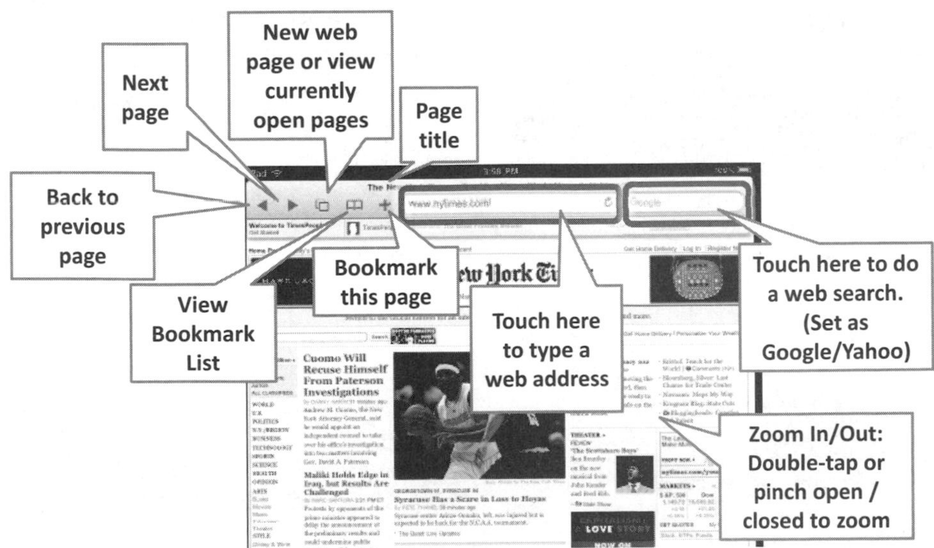


**Figure 11–1.** *Safari web browser page layout*

As you look at your screen, notice that the **Address Bar** is in the upper left side of the screen. This displays the current web address. To the right is the **Search** window. By default, this is set to Google search, but you can change that if you want.

At the top of the screen are 5 icons; **Back**, **Forward**, **Add Bookmark, Bookmarks** and **Pages view**.

## Typing a Web Address

The first thing you'll want to learn is how to get to your favorite web pages. It's just like on your computer—you type in the web address (URL) into the browser. To start, tap the **Address Bar** at the top of the browser as shown in Figure 11–2. You'll then see the keyboard appear and the window for the browser expand. Start typing and press the **Go** key to go to that page.

> **TIP:** Remember to use the colon, forward slash, underscore, dot, and .com keys at the bottom to save time.

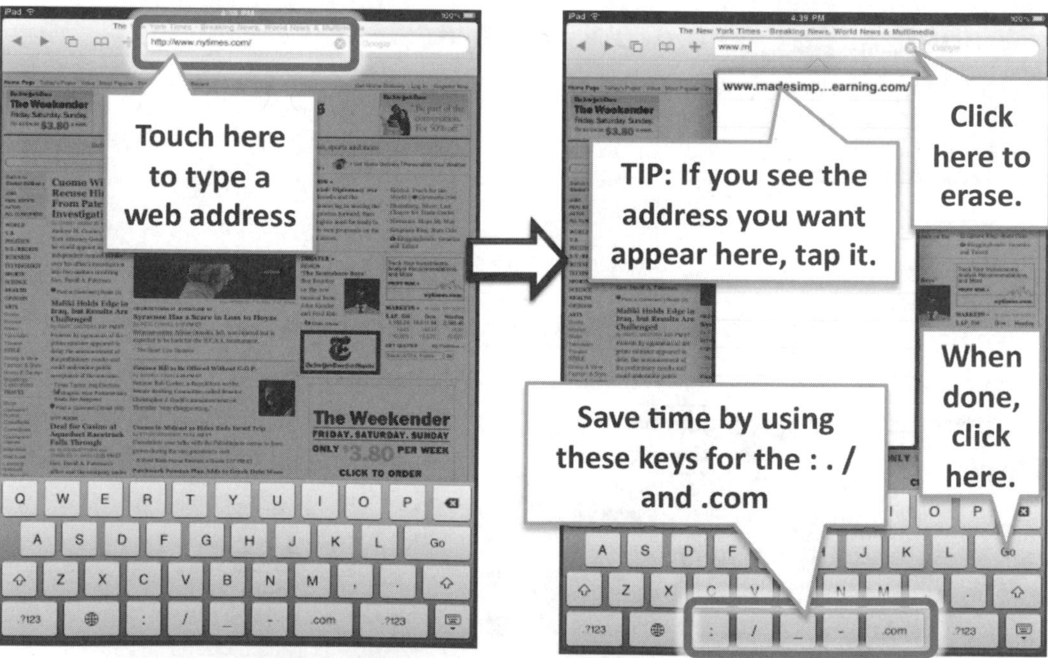


**Figure 11–2.** *Typing in a web address*

> **TIP:** Press and hold the .com key to see all the options: .org, .edu, .net, .de, etc.

# Moving Backward or Forward Through Open Web Pages

Now that you know how to enter web addresses, you'll probably be jumping to various web sites. The **Forward** and **Back** arrows make it very easy to go to recently visited pages in either direction, as Figure 11–3 shows. If the **Back** arrow is grayed out, the section below about using the **Open Pages** button can help.

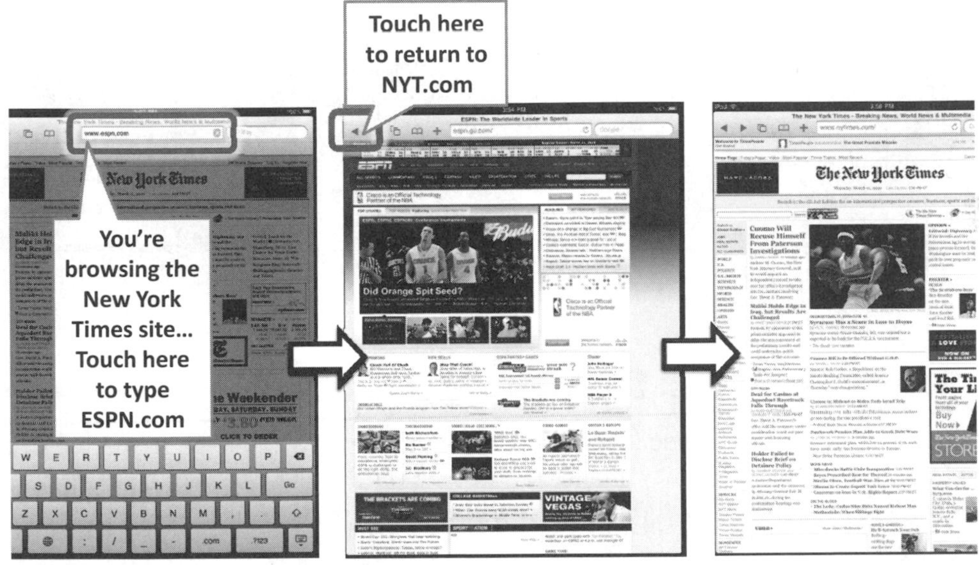


**Figure 11–3.** *Returning to a previously viewed web page*

Let's say you were looking at the news on the New York Times web site, then you jumped to ESPN to check sports scores. To go back to the New York Times page, just hit the **Back** arrow. To return to the ESPN site again, touch the **Forward** arrow.

# Moving Between Web Pages when the Back Button Doesn't Work

Sometimes when you click a link, the web page you were viewing moves to the background and a new window pops up with new content (another web page, a video, etc.). In such cases, the **Back** arrow in the new browser window does nothing!

Instead, you have to tap the **Open Pages** icon (just to the right of the arrows) to see a list of open web pages and then tap the one you want. In the example shown in Figure 11–4, we touched a link that opened a new browser window. The only way to get back to the old one was to tap the **Open Pages** icon and select the desired page.

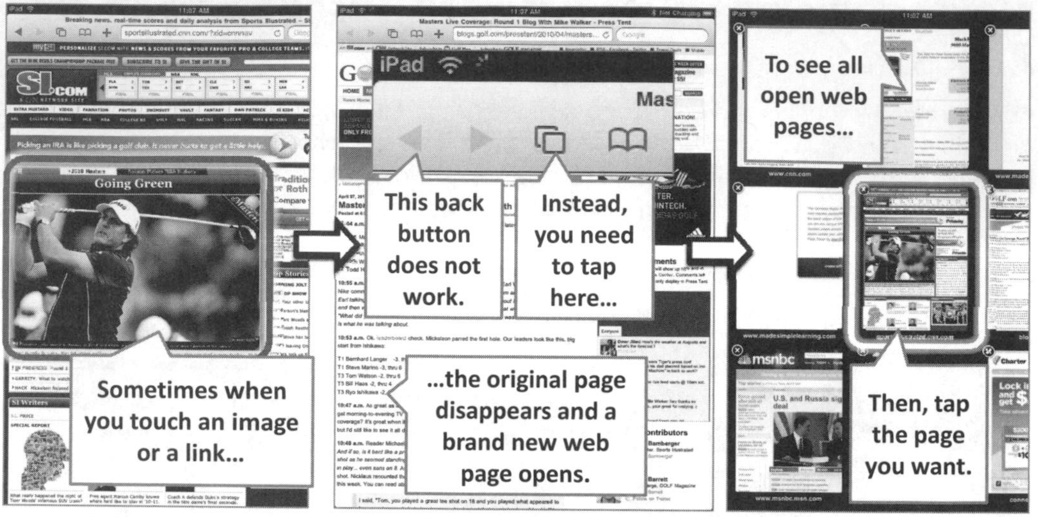


**Figure 11–4.** *Jumping between open web pages when the **Back** button doesn't work*

## Jumping to the Top of the Web Page

Sometimes web pages can be quite long, which can make scrolling back to the top of the page a bit laborious. One easy trick is to just tap on the black title bar of the web page and you'll automatically jump to the top of the page, as shown in Figure 11–5.

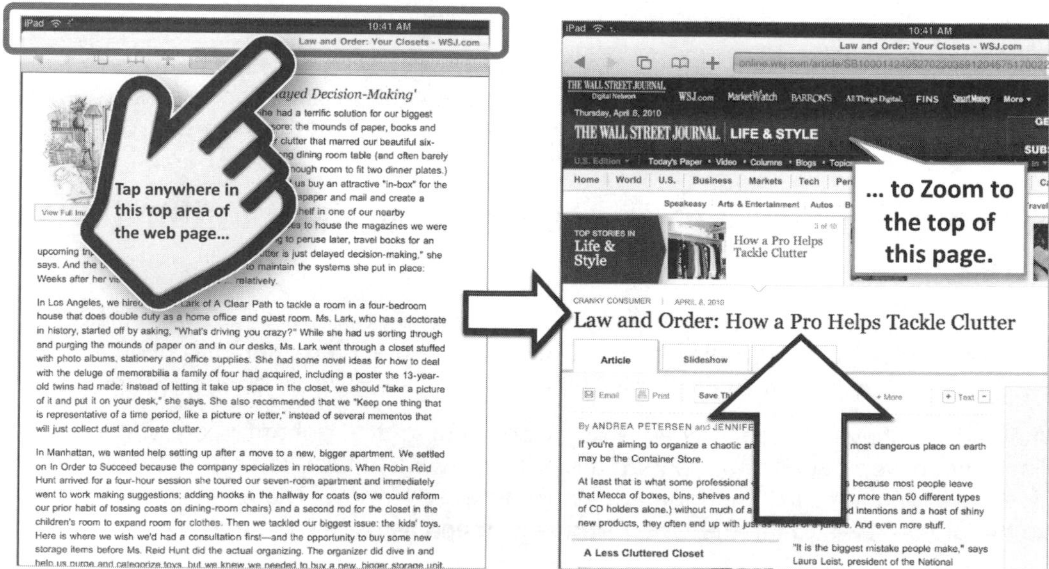


**Figure 11–5.** *Jump quickly to the top of a web page by tapping at the top*

## E-mail a Web Page

Sometimes while browsing you find a page so compelling you just have to send it to a friend. Touch the **plus sign** (+) next to the **Address Bar** and select **Mail Link to this Page** (see Figure 11–6). This creates an e-mail message with the link that you can send.

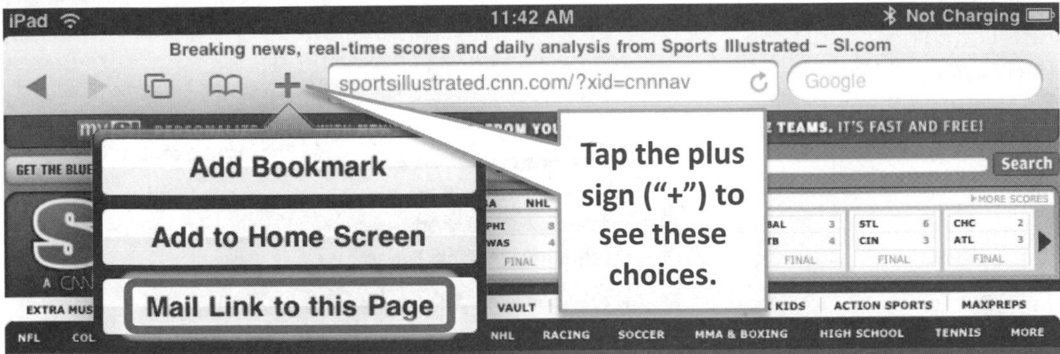


**Figure 11–6.** *E-mail a link to a web page*

## How to Print a Web Page

The iPad (as of publishing time) did not have a built-in **Print** command. You have a few options, but none of them are simple.

*Option 1:* E-mail yourself or a colleague the web page link and print it from that printer. If you are traveling and staying at a hotel with a business center, you may be able to send it to someone at the business center or front desk to print the page.

*Option 2:* Buy a network printing app from the App Store that allows you to print to a networked printer. Of course, this only works if you have access to a networked printer. It's usually best if you do this from your home or office network and can get help setting up, as it can be quite challenging.

## Adding Bookmarks

Just like on your home computer, you can set bookmarks on your iPad. To add a new bookmark, simply touch the plus sign (+) at the top of the web screen.

After touching **+** you'll see three options. Choose **Add Bookmark** to add a new bookmark.

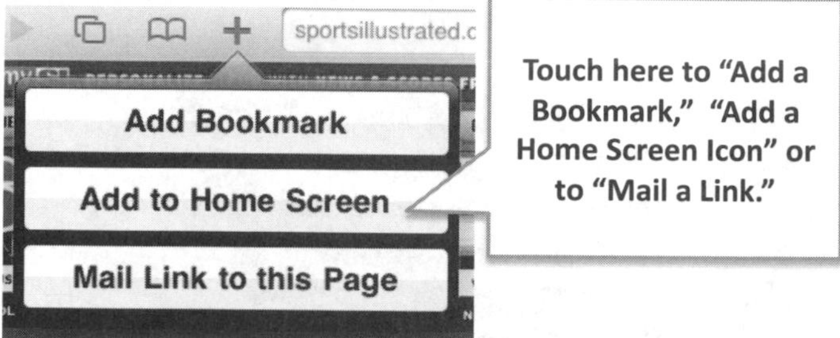
sportsillustrated.c
Add Bookmark
Add to Home Screen
Mail Link to this Page
Touch here to "Add a Bookmark," "Add a Home Screen Icon" or to "Mail a Link."

After adding the new bookmark, you can edit its name (the web address is shown underneath the editing window). You can also choose the folder where you'd like the bookmark to appear. By default, it will go in your **Bookmarks** folder, but you can place it in any folder available to you, such as News, Popular, or Bookmarks menu.

Press **Save** to save your changes.

Save

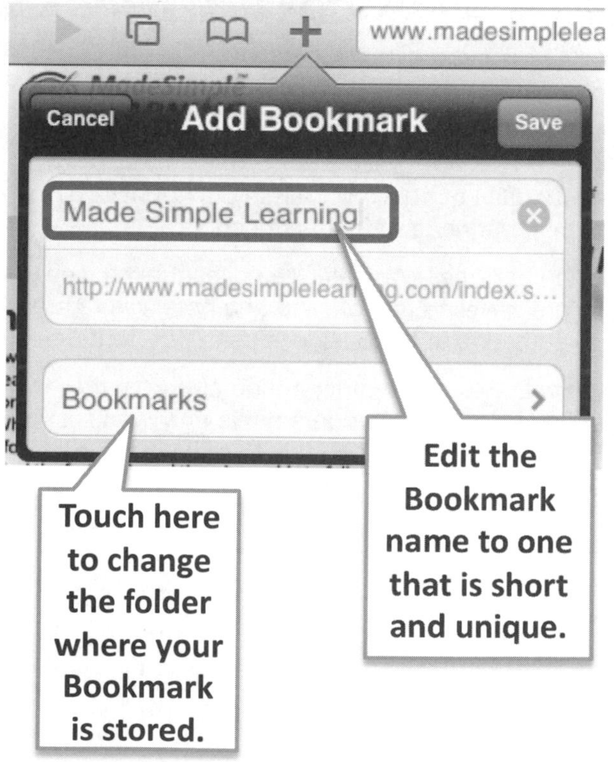
www.madesimplelea
Cancel
Add Bookmark
Save
Made Simple Learning
http://www.madesimplelea g.com/index.s...
Bookmarks
Touch here to change the folder where your Bookmark is stored.
Edit the Bookmark name to one that is short and unique.

## Using Your Bookmarks

Once bookmarks are set, simply touch the **Bookmarks** icon from any web page to see them.

When you touch the **Bookmarks** icon, you'll find tabs for your **History**, **Bookmarks Bar,** and **Bookmarks Menu.** Under that you'll see preinstalled bookmarks for your iPad.

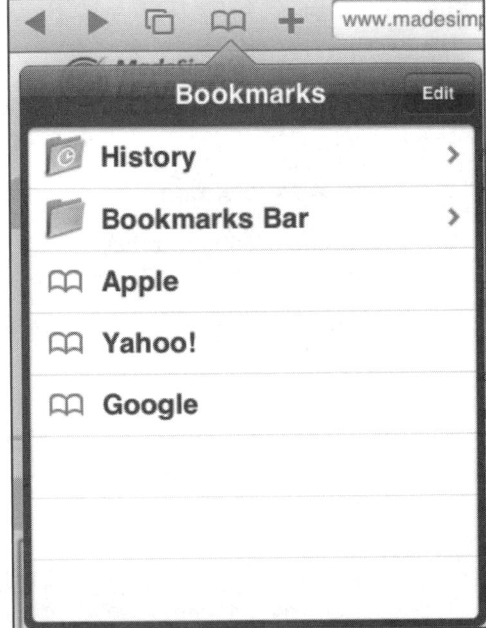


Bookmarks you add will, by default, go into your **Bookmarks Bar** unless you specify another spot.

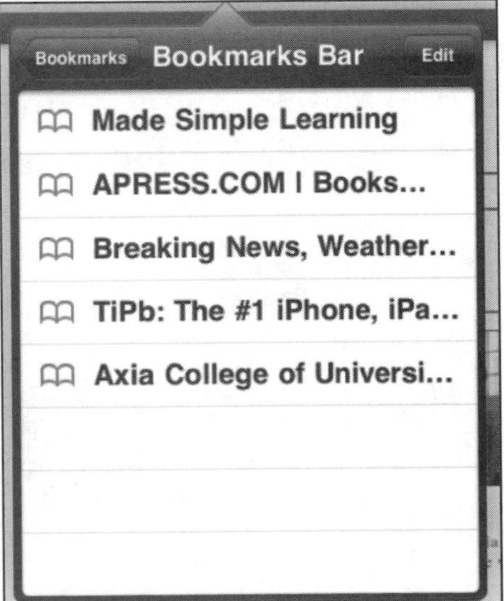


**TIP:** When you are creating your bookmarks, adjust the folder where the bookmark is stored by tapping the Folder name under the name of the Bookmark.

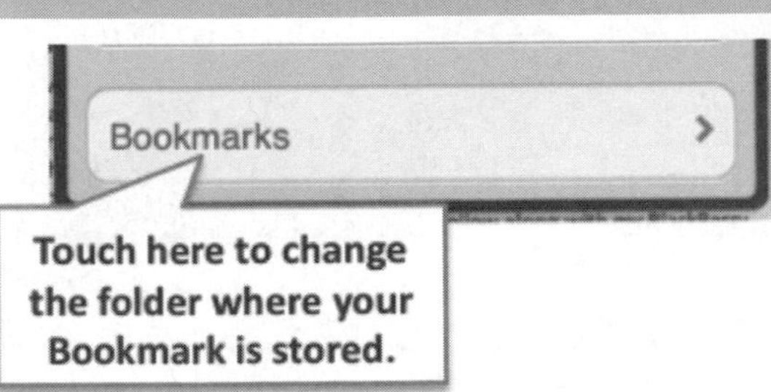

Bookmarks
Touch here to change the folder where your Bookmark is stored.

# Add a Web Page Icon to Your Home Screen

If you love a web site or page, it's very easy to add it as an icon to your **Home Screen**. That way, you can instantly access the web page without going through the **Safari** > **Bookmarks** > select bookmark process. You'll save lots of steps by putting the icon on your **Home Screen** (see Figure 11–7). This is especially good for quickly launching web apps, like Gmail or Buzz from Google, or web app games.

Here's how to add the icon:

1. Touch the **plus sign** (+) next to the address bar in the top of the browser.
2. Touch **Add to Home Screen**.
3. Adjust the name; you may want to put in the name of the site, but keep it short because there's not much room below the icons.
4. Tap the **Add** button in the upper right corner.

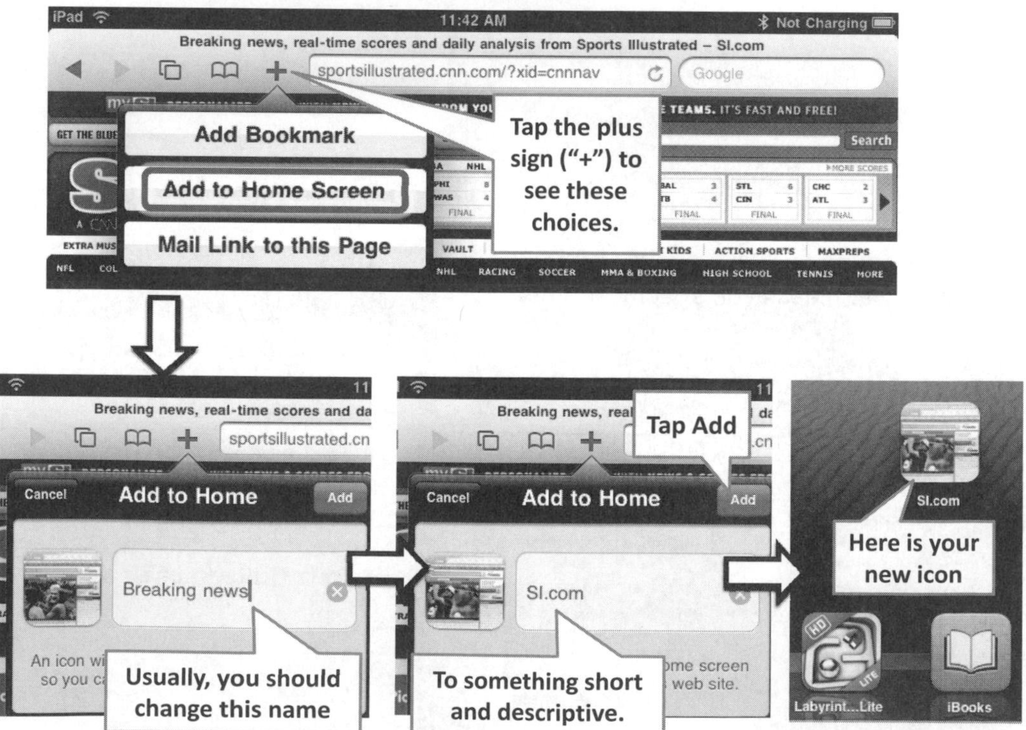


**Figure 11–7.** *How to add an icon for a web page to your Home Screen*

## Browsing from Web History

A very useful tool on your iPad is the ability to browse the web from your **History**, just as you would on a computer.

Touch the **Bookmarks** icon and you'll see a tab marked **History**.

Touch the **History** tab and your recent web travels will be listed. If you haven't cleared your history lately, you may see one tab that says **Earlier Today** and another for other dates with stored history.

Just touch the name of a web site listed, and Safari will load that page in the browser window.

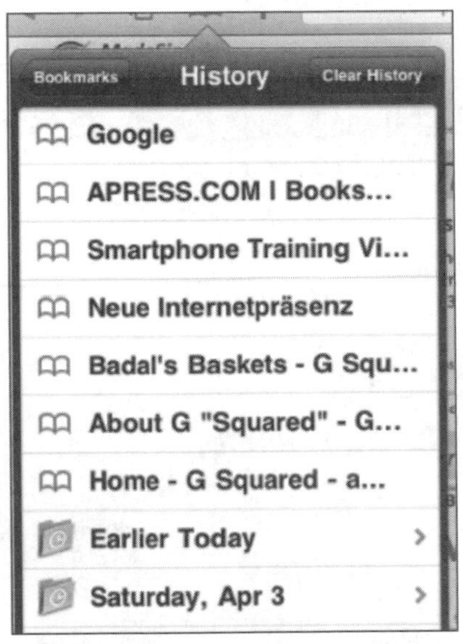


To remove all the sites in your **History**, touch the **Clear History** button in the upper right, then the red **Clear History** button.

## Adding Folders, Editing and Deleting Bookmarks

It is very easy to accumulate quite a collection of bookmarks since it's so easy to set them up. You may find you no longer need a particular bookmark, or you may want to organize them by adding new folders.

To manage your bookmarks, tap the **Edit** button at the bottom left corner of your Bookmarks menu.

You will notice that a red **minus sign** (-) appears to the left, and each bookmark turns into a tab that can be touched (see Figure 11–8).

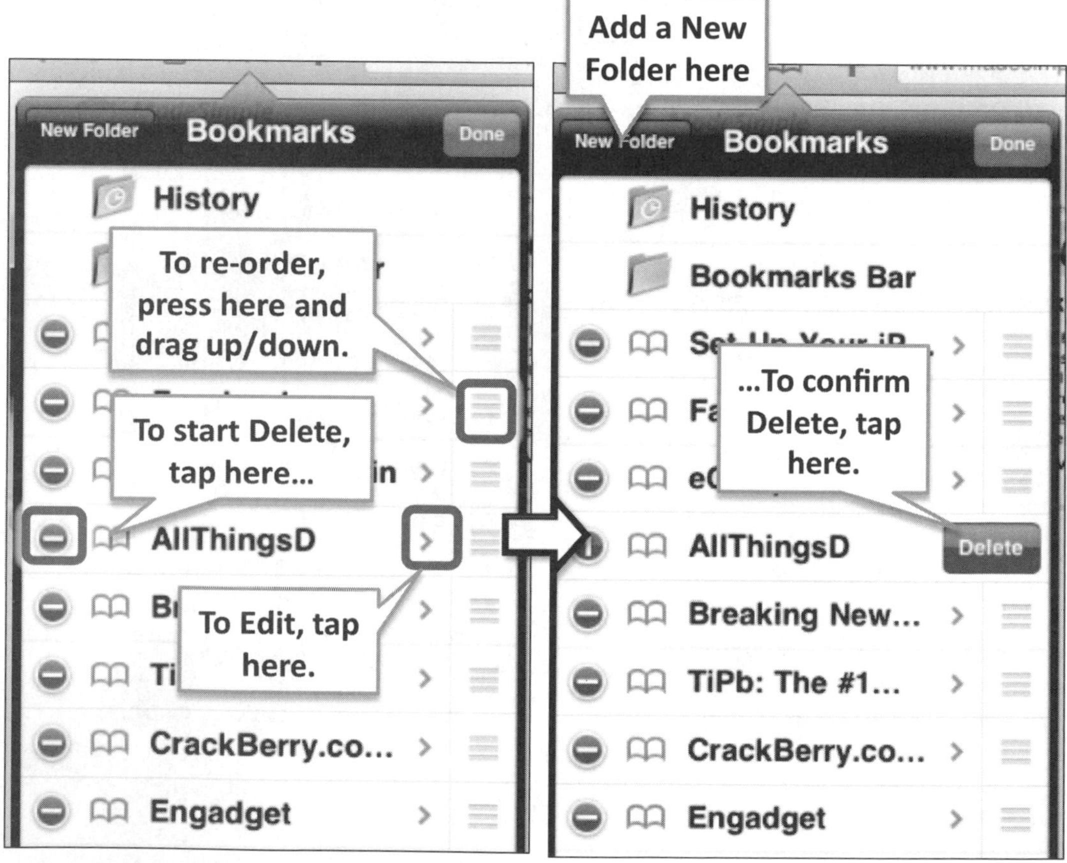


**Figure 11–8.** *Reorder and delete bookmarks*

To delete the bookmark, just touch the red **minus sign** and you'll see the **Delete** button pop up. Touch **Delete**, confirm the delete and the bookmark will disappear from your menu.

To reorder bookmarks, just touch the icon at the right edge of each bookmark and drag up or down as you like.

To add a new folder, touch the **New Folder** button in the upper left corner. Type the name of the folder, select the location (folder) in which to place your new folder, and click **Done**

## Using the New Pages Button

On our home computers, many of us have come to rely on tabbed browsing— it allows us to have more than one web page open at a time so we can quickly move from one to another. The iPad has a similar feature you can access by touching the **New Page** icon at the top left of the of the web status bar. (This is the same icon you used to move through open pages earlier in this chapter.)

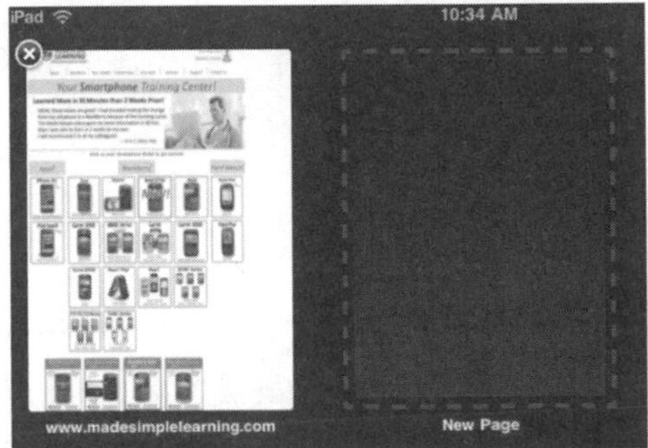


When you first touch this button, the web page you are currently viewing becomes small and moves to the left side of the screen.

Touch the **New Page** button and the browser will load a blank page, ready for you to input a new web address.

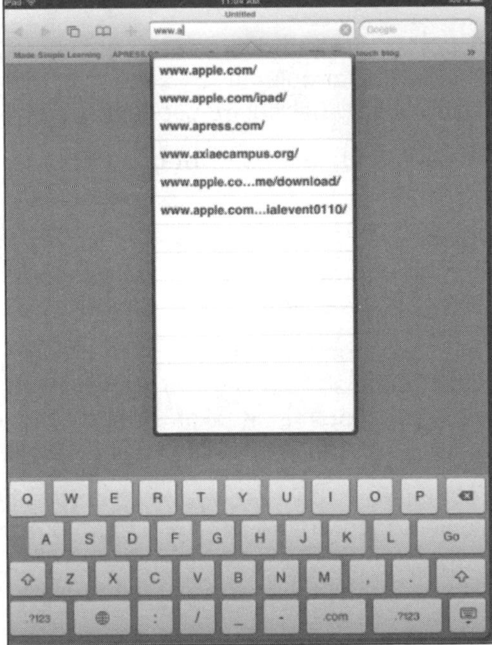


Now, just add a web address by touching the **Address Bar**, which brings up the keyboard. Type in the web address you want. Notice that there's no space bar on this keyboard—just touch the period (.) for the dot, or the .com button to fill out the address if the site has "com" at the end of the name.

Now when you touch the **New Page** icon, you can just touch the page you wish to view and it will load into the screen. As you did before, you can also touch the **New Page** button to load yet another new page into the browser window.

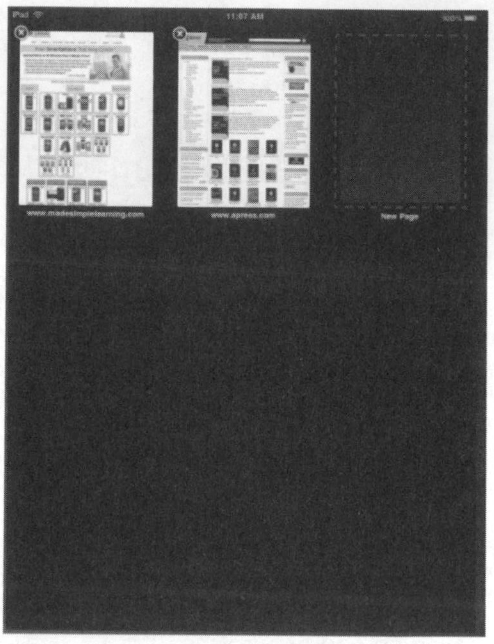


## Zooming In and Out in Web Pages

Zooming in and out of web pages is very easy on the iPad. There are two primary ways of zooming—double-tapping and pinching.

*Double-tapping:* If you tap twice on a column of a web page, the page will zoom in on that particular column. This lets you home in on exactly the right place on the web page, which is very helpful for pages that aren't formatted for a mobile screen.

To zoom out, just double-tap once more. See graphically how this looks in the Quick Start Guide.

*Pinching:* This technique lets you zoom in on a particular section of a page. It takes a little bit of practice, but will soon become second nature. Take a look in the Quick Start Guide to see graphically how it looks.

Use your thumb and forefinger and place them close together at the section of the web page you wish to zoom into. Slowly pinch out, separating your fingers. You will see the web page zoom in. It takes a couple of seconds for the web page to focus, but it will zoom in and be very clear in a short while.

To zoom out to where you were before, just start with your fingers apart and move them slowly together; the page will zoom out to its original size.

# Activating Links from Web Pages

When you're surfing the Web, often you'll come across a link that will take you to another web site. Because Safari is a full-function browser, you can just touch the link and you will jump to a new page.

If you want to return to the previous page, just press the **Back** arrow as shown earlier.

# Adjusting Browser Settings

As with other settings we've adjusted so far, the settings for Safari are found in the **Settings** app.

To access this app, touch the **Settings** icon and then touch **Safari**.

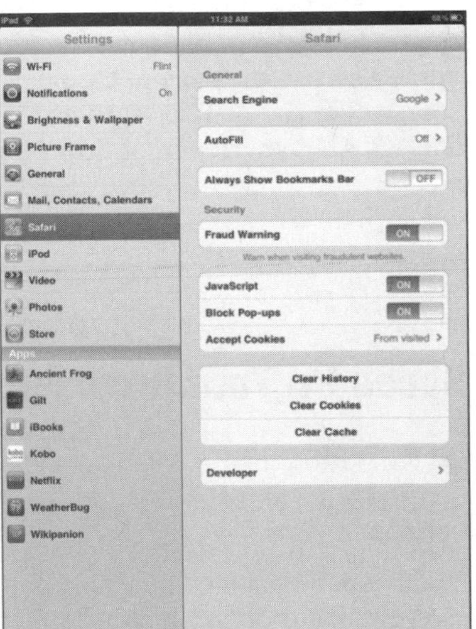


## Changing the Search Engine

By default, the search engine for the Safari browser is **Google**. To change this to **Yahoo**, just touch the **Search Engine** tab and then choose **Yahoo**.

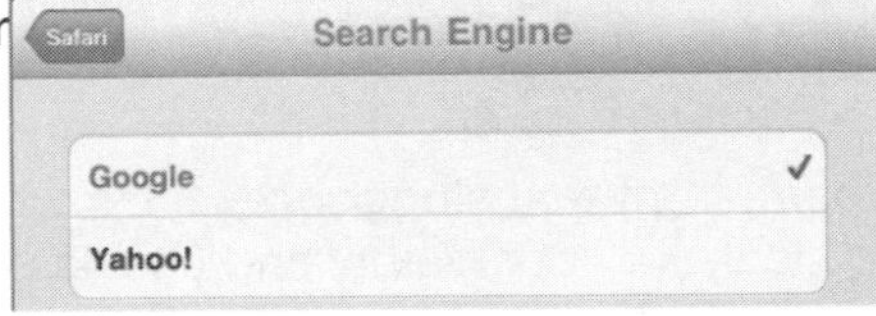

## Adjusting Security Options

Under the **Security** heading, **JavaScript**, and **Block Pop-ups** should, by default, be set to **ON**. You can modify either of these by just sliding the switch to **OFF**.

**NOTE:** Many popular sites like Facebook require JavaScript to be ON.

You'll also see the **Accept Cookies** tab here, which you can adjust to accept cookies **Always**, **Never,** or **From visited**.

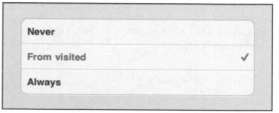


## Speed Up Your Browser: Clear History and Cookies

On the bottom of the Safari settings screen, you can see the **Clear History** and **Clear Cookies** buttons.

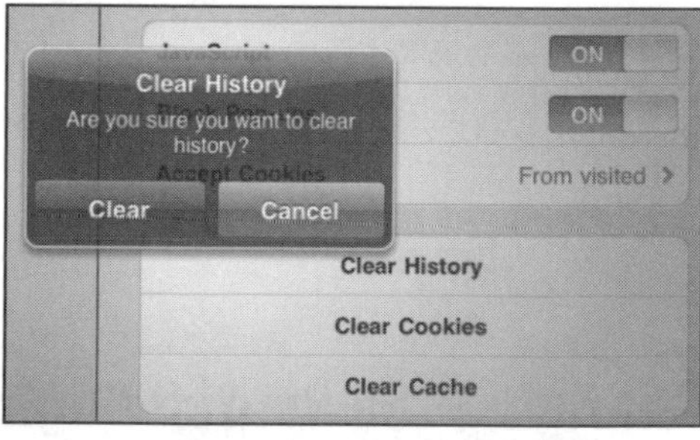


If you notice your web browsing getting sluggish, it's probably a good time to clear out both your **History** and **Cookies**.

**TIP:** It is also a good privacy measure as it prevents others from seeing where you've been browsing.

To preempt that sluggishness, it's a good idea to clear out your history and cookies on a fairly regular basis.

## AutoFill Name, Password, E-mail, Address, and More

**AutoFill** is a convenient way to have the browser automatically fill out web page forms that ask for your name, address, phone number, or even username and password.

To enable **AutoFill**, touch the **AutoFill** tab in the Safari **Settings**. To use AutoFill to input your contact information, move the slider next to Use Contact Info to the On position.

To have **AutoFill** fill in names and passwords, move the slider next to **Names and Passwords** to **On**.

To set the correct **Contact Info**, touch the **My Info** tab and your contact list will be displayed. Just choose your own contact information as shown in Figure 11–9.

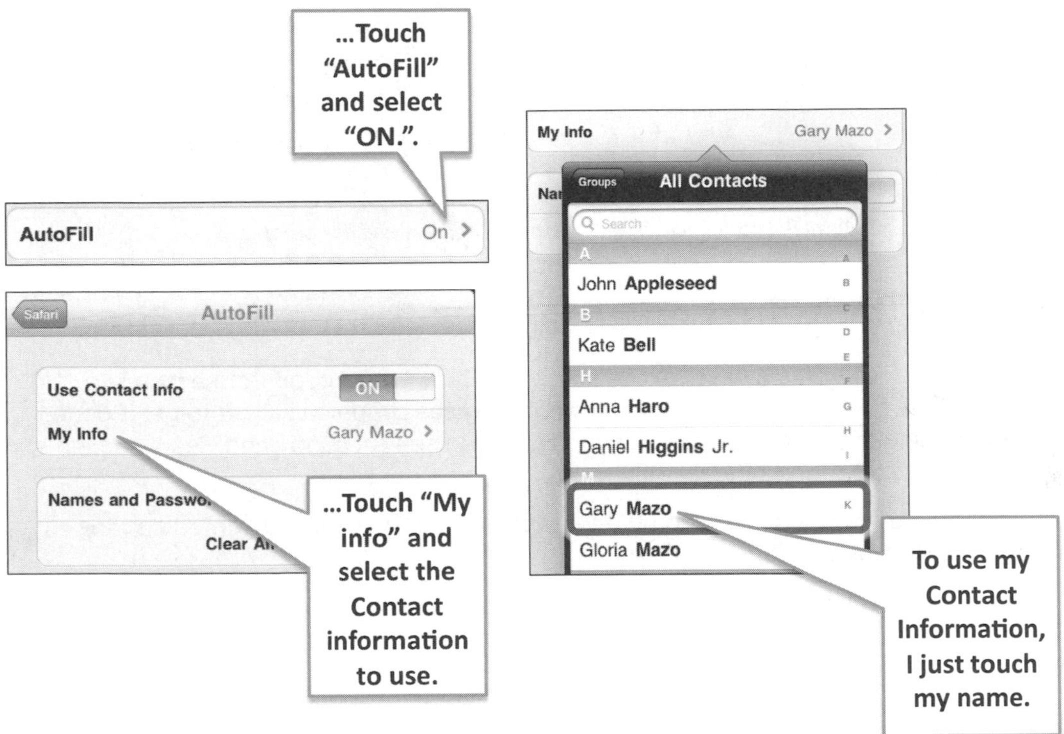


**Figure 11–9.** *Setting up **My Info** in **AutoFill**.*

Once **AutoFill** is enabled, just go to any web page that has a field to fill out. As soon as you touch the field, the keyboard will come up at the bottom of the screen. At the top of the keyboard, you will see a small button that says **AutoFill**. Touch it and the web form should be filled out automatically (Figure 11–10).

> **CAUTION:** Having your name and password entered automatically means that anyone who picks up your iPad will be able to access your personal sites and information.

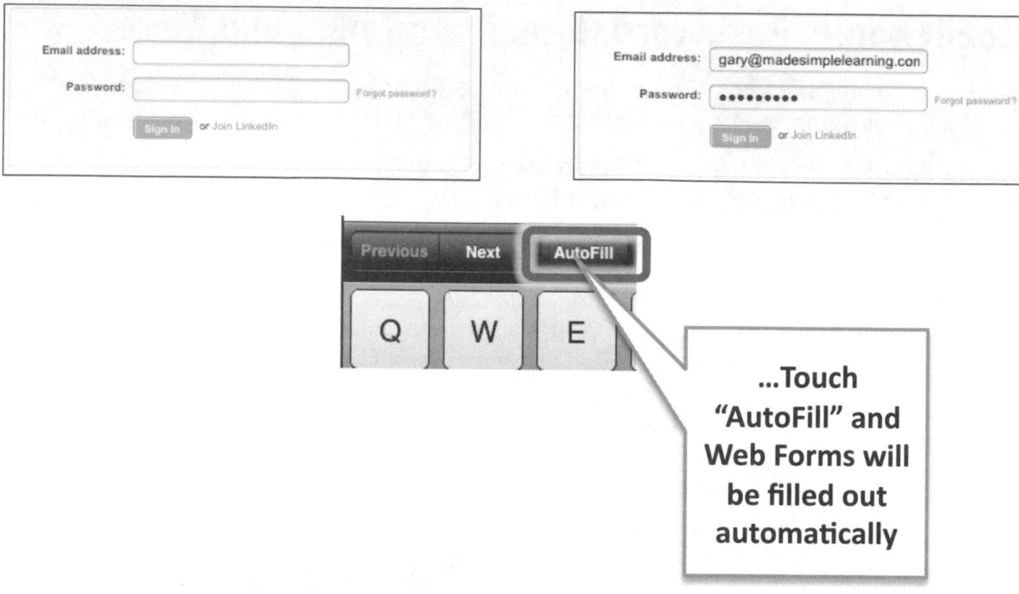


**Figure 11–10.** *Using **AutoFill** to automatically enter an e-mail address and password*

# Save or Copy Text and Graphics from a Web Site

From time to time you may see text or a graphic you want to copy from a web site. We tell you briefly how to do this in this section, but to see graphically how to get it done, including using the **Cut** and **Paste** functions, please see the Copy and Paste section in Chapter 2. Here's a quick look:

To copy a single word, touch and hold the word until you see it highlighted and the **Copy** button appears. Then tap **Copy.**

To copy a few words or entire paragraph, touch and hold a word until it is highlighted. Then drag the blue dots left or right to select more text. You can flick up or down to select an entire paragraph. Then tap **Copy**.

> **TIP:** Selecting a single word puts it in word selection mode where you can drag to increase or decrease the number of words selected. If you go past a single paragraph, it will typically switch to element selection mode where instead of corners you get edges that you can drag out to select multiple paragraphs, images, etc.

To **Save** or **Copy** a graphic, touch and hold the picture or image until you see the pop-up asking if you would like to **Save** or **Copy** the image.

# Using Browsing History to Save Time and Find Sites

The advantage of keeping your frequently visited sites in history is that you can load them from the **History** tab when you go into the browser menu (see Figure 11–11). Also, sometimes you want to go back to a certain site, but you can't remember the name; checking your history will show you the exact site you wish to visit.

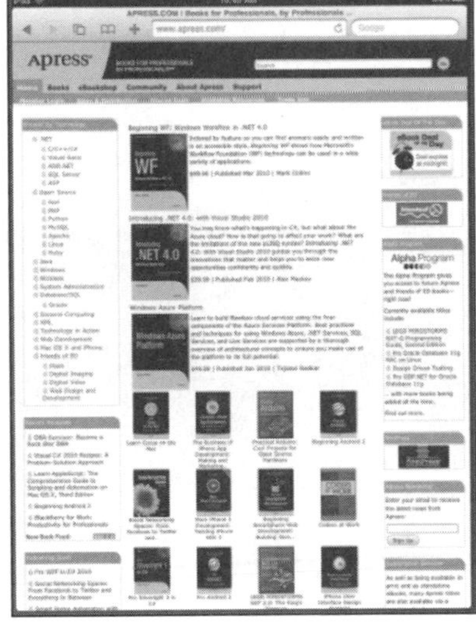


**Figure 11–11.** *Using Browser History*

Chapter 12

# E-mail

In this chapter, we will help you explore the world of e-mail on your iPad. You will learn how to set up multiple e-mail accounts, check out all the various reading options, open attachments, and clean up your **Inbox**.

And for cases when e-mail is not working quite right, you will learn some good troubleshooting tips to help you get back up and running.

## Getting Started with E-mail

Setting up e-mail on your iPad is fairly simple. You can sync e-mail account settings from iTunes (see Chapter 3's, "Sync E-mail Account Settings" section), or you can set up e-mail accounts directly on your iPad. You do need a network connection to get e-mail up and running.

## A Network Connection Is Required

Mobile e-mail is certainly all the rage today. You can view, read, and compose replies to e-mails already synced to your iPad without a network connection; however, you will need to have network connectivity (either Wi-Fi or 3G/cellular) to send and/or receive e-mail from your iPad. Check out Chapter 4: "Wi-Fi and 3G Connectivity" to learn more. Also check out the "Reading the Top Connectivity Status Icons" section in the Quick Start Guide in Part 1.

**TIP:** If you are taking a trip, simply download all your e-mail before you get on the airplane; this lets you read, reply, and compose your messages. All e-mails will be sent once you land and re-establish your connection to the Internet.

## Setting up E-mail on the iPad

You have two options to set up your e-mail accounts on the iPad.

1. Use iTunes to sync e-mail account settings.
2. Set up your e-mail accounts directly on the iPad.

If you have a number of e-mail accounts that you access from an e-mail program on your computer (e.g., **Microsoft Outlook**, **Entourage**, and so on), then it is easiest to use iTunes to sync your accounts. See the "Sync E-mail Account Settings" section in Chapter 3 for help.

If you only have a few accounts, or you do not use an e-mail program on your computer that iTunes can sync with, then you will need to set up your e-mail accounts directly on the iPad.

## Entering Passwords for E-mail Accounts Synced from iTunes

In the "Sync E-mail Account Settings" section of Chapter 3, we showed you how to sync your e-mail account settings to your iPad. After this sync completes, all of your e-mail accounts should be visible on your iPad in the **Settings** icon. All you will need to do is enter the password for each account.

To enter your password for each synced e-mail account, follow these steps (see Figure 12–1).

1. Touch the **Settings** icon.
2. Touch the **Mail, Contacts and Calendars** option in the left column.
3. Under **Accounts** in the right column, you should see all your synced e-mail accounts listed.
4. Tap any listed e-mail account, type its password, and click **Done**.
5. Repeat for all listed e-mail accounts.

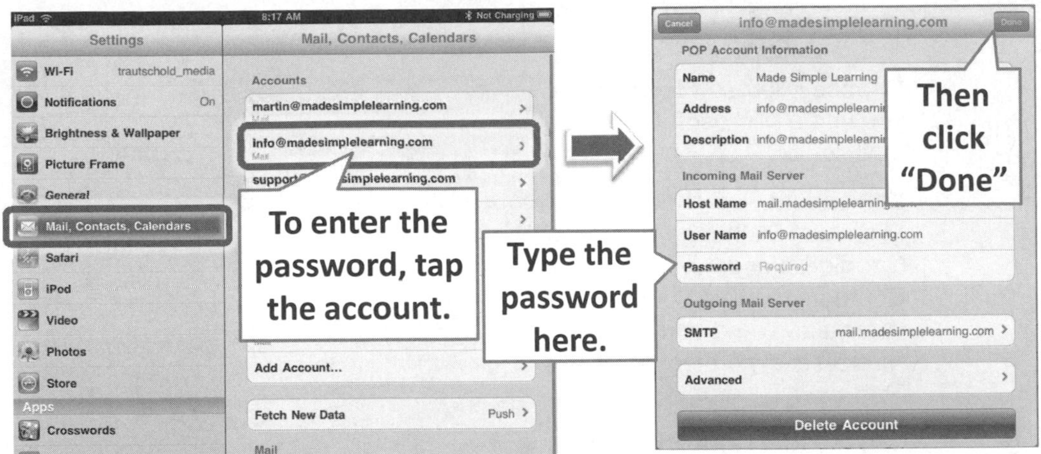


**Figure 12–1.** *Entering passwords for each e-mail account synced from iTunes*

# Set up Your E-mail Accounts on the iPad

To add a new e-mail account on your iPad, follow these steps:

1. Touch the **Settings** icon.
2. Touch the **Mail, Contacts and Calendars** option in the left column.
3. Tap **Add Account** below your e-mail accounts.

   If you have no accounts set up, you will only see the **Add Account** option.

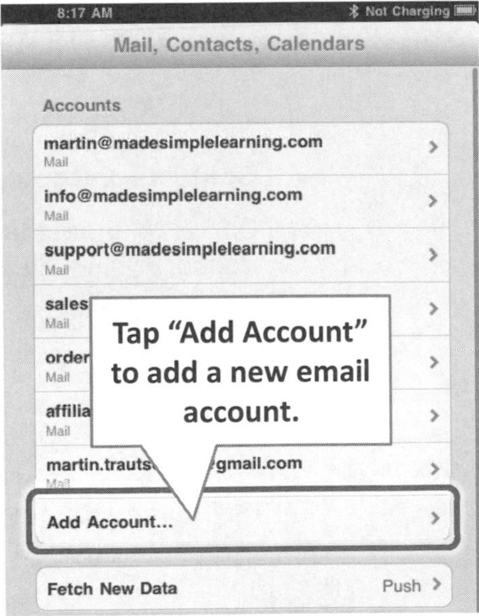


**TIP:** To edit any e-mail account, just touch that account.

4. Choose which type of e-mail account to add on this next screen.
   - Choose Microsoft Exchange if you use a Microsoft Exchange e-mail server.
   - You should also choose Microsoft Exchange if you use Google Calendar, and Google Contacts to store your personal information, and you want to wirelessly sync them to your iPad.
   - Choose MobileMe if you use this service.

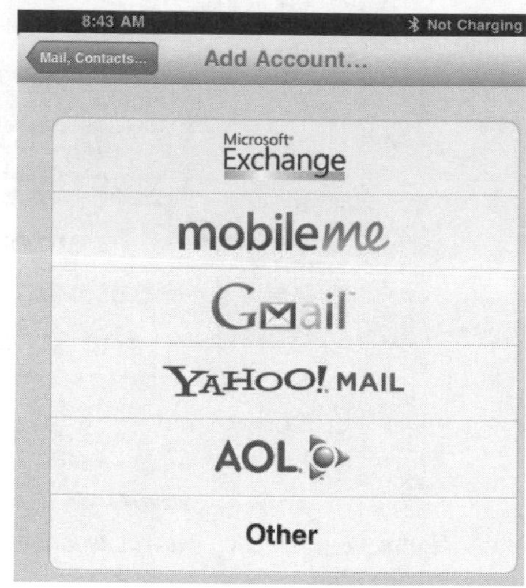


**NOTE:** We will show you how to set up both **Google/Microsoft Exchange** and **MobileMe** in Chapter 24.

   - Choose **Gmail** if you use Google for only your e-mail, but you do *not* (or do *not* want to) wirelessly sync e-mail with your **Google Contacts** or **Google Calendar**.
   - Choose **Yahoo! Mail** if you use Yahoo!
   - Choose **AOL** if you use AOL.
   - Choose **Other** if none of the above apply, and you want to sync a standard POP or IMAP e-mail account. Then choose **Add Mail Account** from the next screen.

5. Type your name as you would like others to see it when they receive mail from you into the **Name** field. Then, add the appropriate information into the **Address**, **Password**, and a **Description** fields.

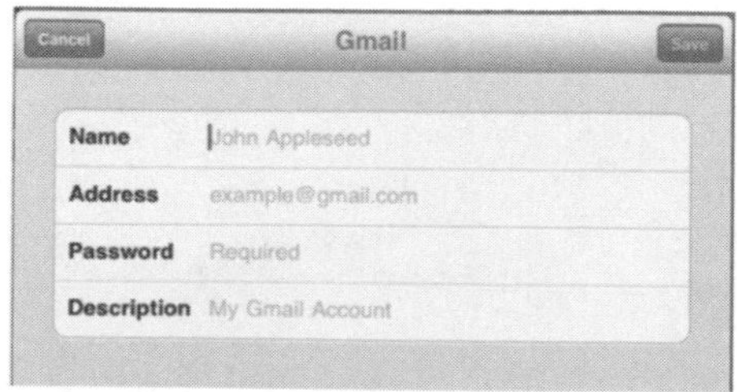


6. Tap the **Save** or **Next** button in the

upper right corner.

## Specifying Incoming and Outgoing Servers

Sometimes, the iPad will not be able to automatically set up your e-mail account. In these cases, you will need to manually enter a few more settings for your e-mail account.

> **TIP:** You may be able to find the settings for your e-mail provider by doing a web search for your e-mail provider's name and "e-mail settings." For example, if you use **hotmail.com**, then you might search for "POP or IMAP e-mail settings for **hotmail.com**." If you cannot find these settings, then contact your e-mail provider for assistance.

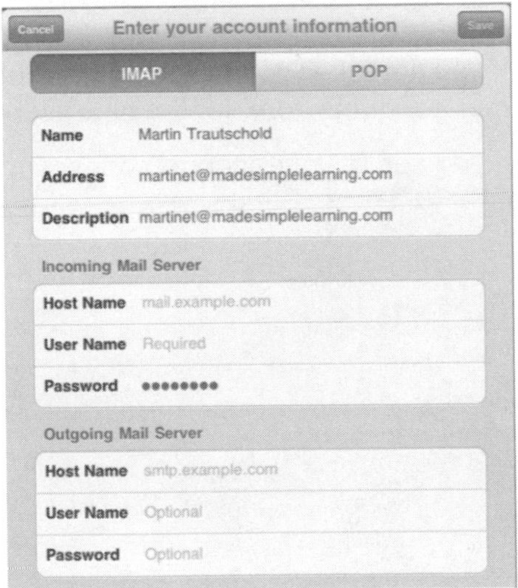


If the iPad is unable to log in to your server given just your e-mail address and password, then you see a screen similar to this one.

Under **Incoming Mail Server**, type the appropriate information into the **Host Name**, **User Name**, and **Password** fields. Usually, your incoming mail server is something like **mail.nameofyourisp.com**.

Type in **Outgoing Mail Server** information, which usually looks like either **smtp.nameofyourisp.com** or **mail.nameofyourisp.com**.

You can try to leave the **Name** and **Password** fields blank – if that doesn't work, you can always go back and change them.

You may be asked if you want to use SSL (secure socket layer) – a type of outgoing mail security that may be required by your e-mail provider. If you don't know whether you need it or not, just check the mail settings with your e-mail provider.

**CAUTION:** The authors recommend that you use SSL security whenever possible. If you do not use SSL, then your login credentials, messages, and any private information is sent in plain text (unencrypted), leaving it open to snoopers.

## Verifying that Your Account Is Set Up

Once all the information is put in, the iPad will attempt to configure your e-mail account. You may get an error message – in which case you need to review the information you input.

If you are taken to the screen that shows all your e-mail accounts, look for the new account name.

If you see it, your account was set up correctly.

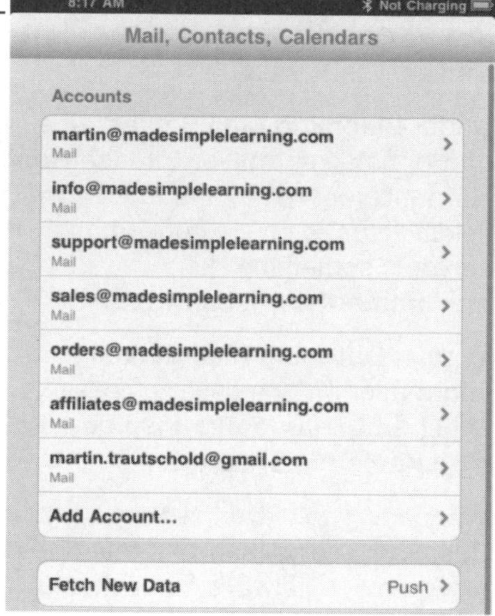

## Fixing the Cannot Get Mail Error

If you try to enter the **Mail** icon, you receive an error that says "Cannot Get Mail – No password provided for (your account)." If this happens, then review this chapter's "Enter Passwords for E-mail Accounts Synced from iTunes" section.

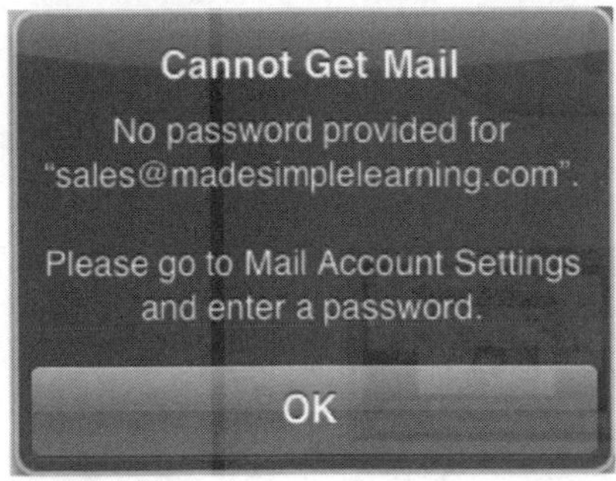


# Navigating Around Your Mail

Now that you have set up your e-mail accounts on your iPad, you are ready to learn how to navigate through your e-mail.

## The Two Views of E-mail

You will enjoy two views of your e-mail on the iPad: **Portrait** (vertical) and **Landscape** (horizontal). The **Portrait** view gives you a full screen view of each e-mail message and allows you to focus on the message. The **Landscape** view shows you your **Inbox** on the left side and your e-mail on the right side (see Figure 12–2).

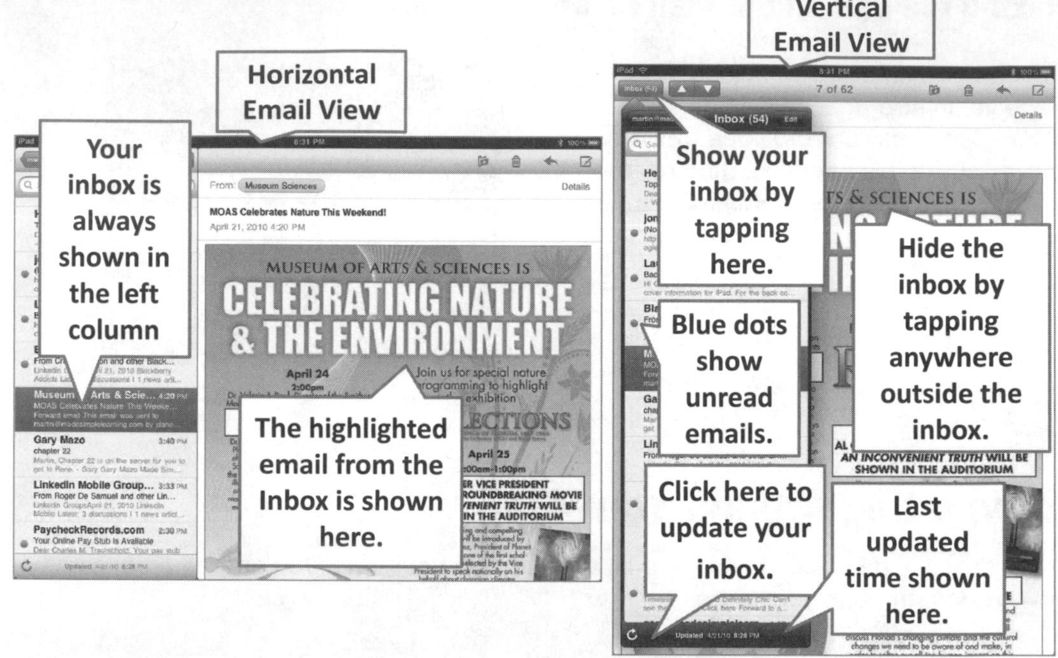


**Figure 12–2.** *Two views of e-mail on your iPad*

> **TIP:** If you are setting your iPad down on the desk or holding it in your lap, then you may want to use the **Lock** switch to lock your view in either vertical or horizontal mode, so it does not keep flipping around. The **Lock** switch is located just above the volume keys on the upper portion of the right edge of your iPad. See the "Screen Rotation Lock" section of Chapter 1 for help.

## Moving Between Your Mail Folders and Accounts

If you have more than one e-mail account on your iPad, you will want to know how to switch between the various accounts.

To move between your accounts, follow these steps (see Figure 12–3).

1. If you are in **Portrait** mode, tap the **Inbox** button in the top left of the screen. If you are in **Landscape** mode, then you can skip to Step 2 below.
2. Tap your **E-mail address** button next to the word **Inbox** at the top.
3. Tap the **Accounts** button in the same place.
4. Now you will see all your e-mail accounts; tap any **E-mail account** box to view it.

5. Now you will see all folders synced to your iPad from that e-mail account. Tap any folder (such as the **Inbox** folder) to view its contents.

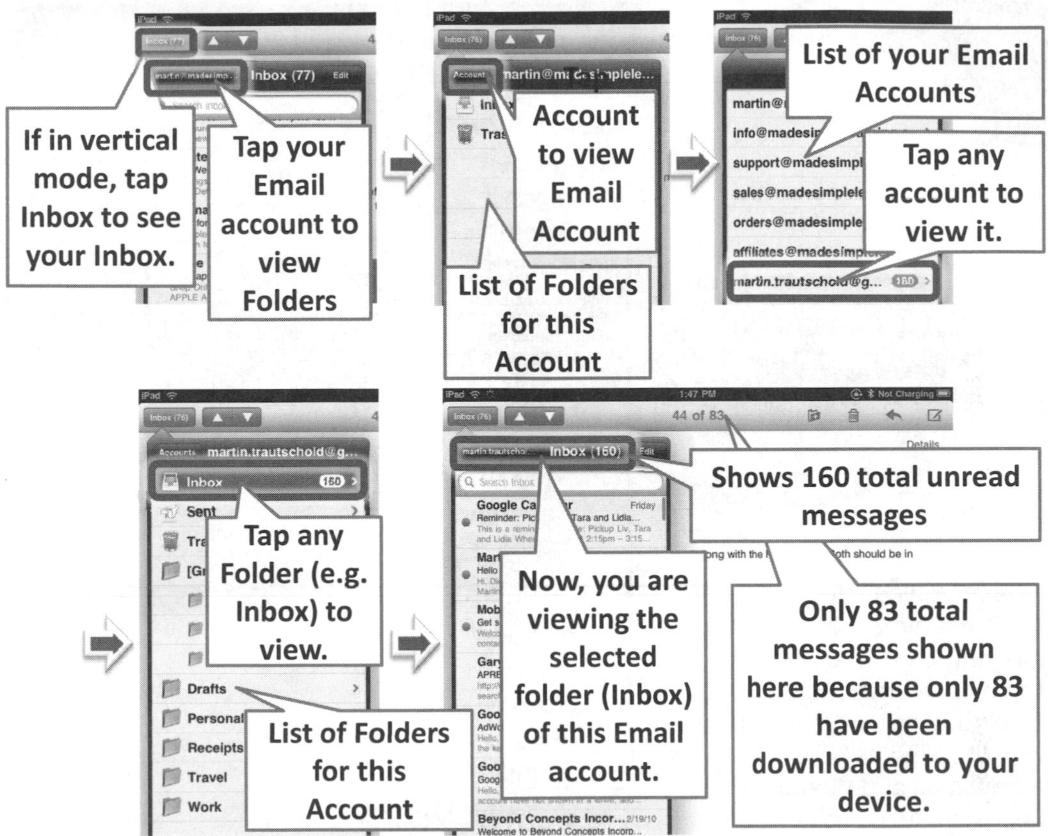


**Figure 12–3.** *Switching between e-mail accounts and e-mail folders on your iPad*

# Compose and Send E-mail

To launch the e-mail program, just touch the **Mail** icon on your **Home** screen.

**TIP:** If you left the **Mail** icon while viewing a particular e-mail, list of folders, or an account, then you will be returned directly to that same place.

If you are going into your e-mail for the first time, you may see an empty **Inbox**. Hit the **Refresh** button in the lower left corner of the window to pull in the latest e-mail. The iPad will begin to check for new mail and then display the number of new messages for each account.

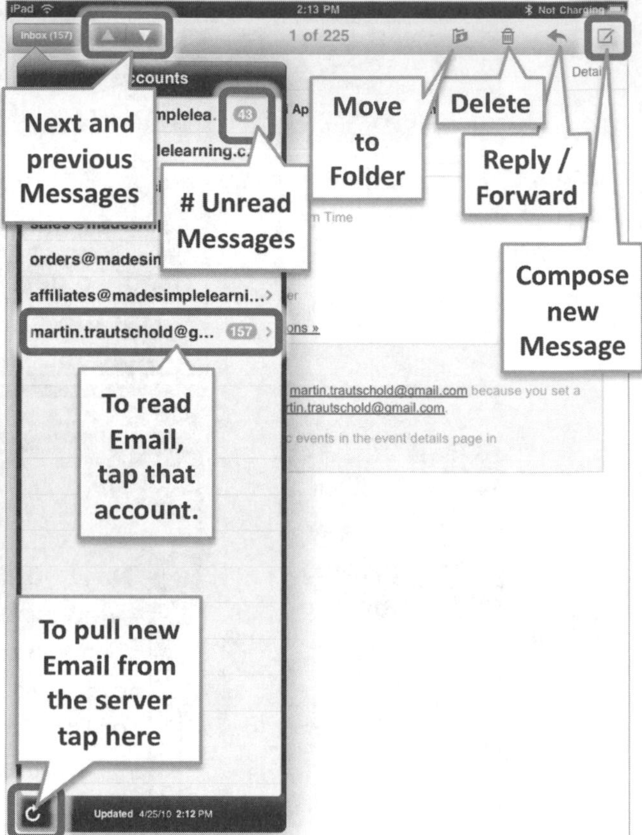

## Composing a New E-mail Message

When you start the **Mail** program, your first screen should be your **Accounts** screen. At the bottom right-hand corner of the screen, you will see the **Compose** icon. Just touch the **Compose** icon to get started creating a new message.

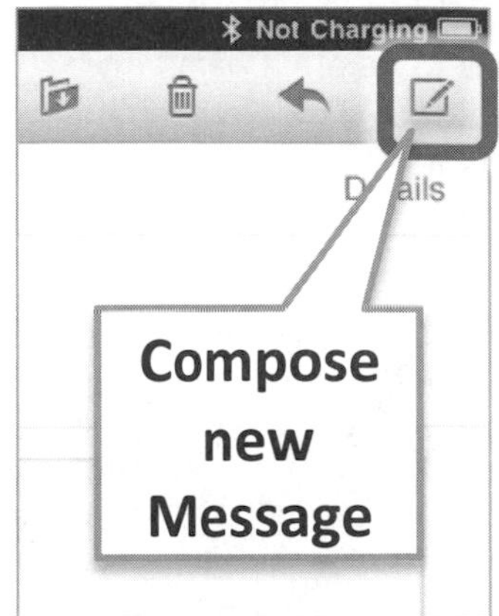


## Addressing Your Message - Choose the Recipients

You have a few options for selecting recipients, depending on whether or not the person is in your **Contact List** on your iPad.

**Option 1** – Type an e-mail address; notice the **@** and **.** keys on the bottom, which help your typing.

**Option 2** – Type a few letters of someone's first name; hit the space key, and then type a few letters of that person's last name. The person's name should appear on the list; tap to select that person's name.

**Option 3** – Hit the **+** sign to view your entire **Contact List** and search or select a name from it.

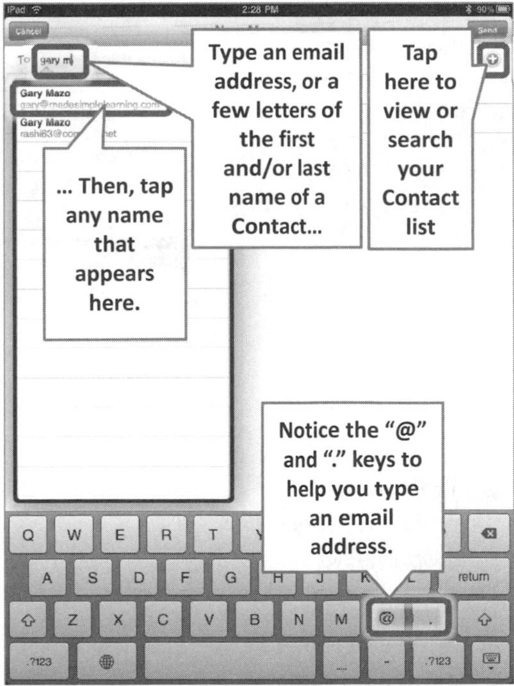

## DELETING A RECIPIENT

If you need to delete a name from the recipient list (**To:**, **Cc:**, or **Bcc:**), tap the name and hit the **Backspace** key.

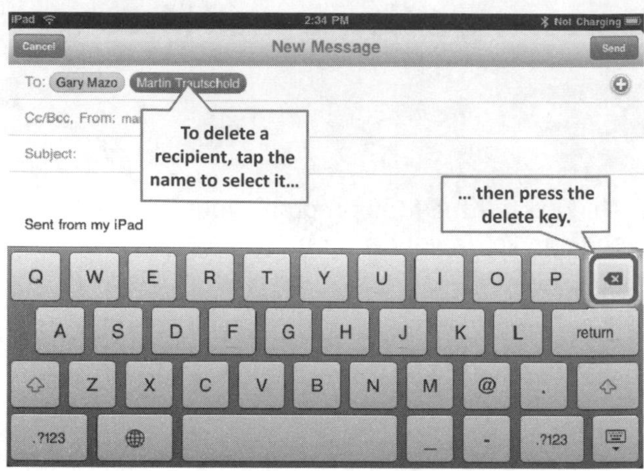


**TIP:** If you want to delete the last recipient you typed (and the cursor is sitting next to that name), hit the **Delete** key once to highlight the name and hit it a second time to delete it.

# Changing the E-mail Account to Send from

If you have more than one e-mail account set up, the iPad will use whichever account is set as the default account. (This is set in **Settings** > **Mail, Contacts, Calendars** > **Default Account**.)

Follow these steps to change the e-mail account you send from.

1. Tap an e-mail's **From:** field to highlight it.
2. Tap the **From:** field again to see a list of your accounts.
3. Tap the new e-mail account to see it listed in the e-mail's **From:** field.

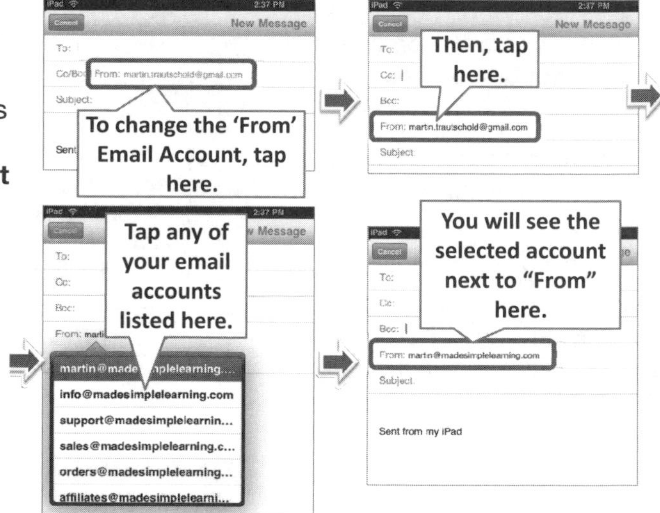

## Typing a Subject

Now you need to enter a subject for your e-mail.

1. Touch the **Subject:** line and enter text for the **Subject:** field of the e-mail.
2. Press the **Return** key or tap the **Body** section of the e-mail to move the cursor to the **Body** section.

## Typing Your Message

Now that the cursor is in your body of the e-mail (under the subject line), you can start typing your e-mail message.

### E-MAIL SIGNATURES

If you have set up an e-mail signature for the account you are using, it will be displayed at the bottom of the **Body** field of the e-mail message. See the "Changing Your E-mail Signature" later in this chapter to learn how to change your e-mail signature.

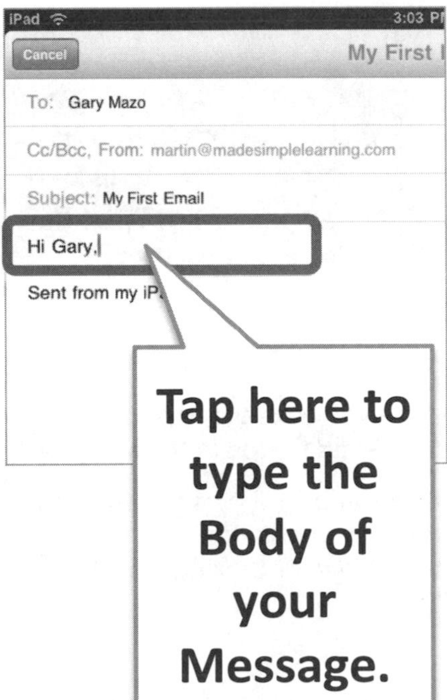

## Keyboard Options

While you are typing, remember you have two keyboard options – the smaller **Portrait** (vertical) keyboard and the larger **Landscape** (horizontal) keyboard (see Figure 12–4).

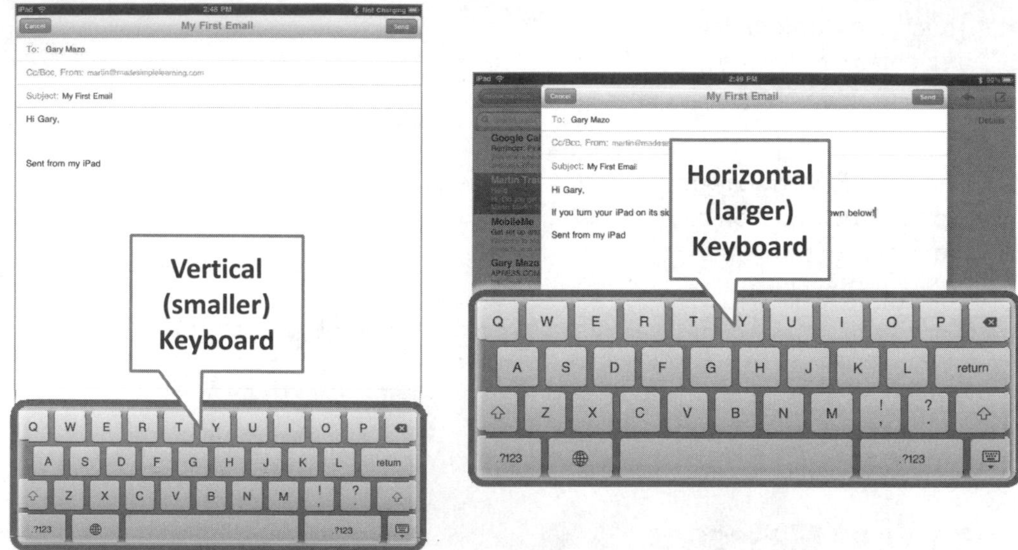


**Figure 12–4.** *You have two built-in keyboards: the smaller vertical keyboard and the larger horizontal one.*

**TIP:** It is much easier to type with your hands when the keyboard is larger. Once you get the hang of typing on the larger keyboard with two hands, you will find that it is much faster than typing with one finger. See Chapter 2's "Typing, Copy/Paste, and Search" section for more typing tips.

## Send Your E-mail

Once you have typed your message and proofread the text, tap the blue **Send** button in the top right-hand corner.

Your e-mail will be sent, and you should hear the iPad's **Sent** sound, which confirms that your e-mail was sent (unless you have disabled this sound in your **Settings** icon).

## Saving a Message As a Draft and Sending It Later

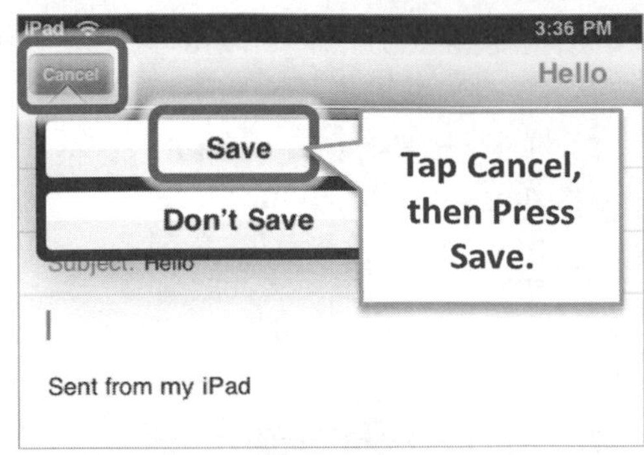


If you are not ready to send your message, but want to save it as a draft message to send later, follow these steps:

1. Compose your message, as described earlier.
2. Press the **Cancel** button in the upper right corner.
3. Select **Save** from the **Cancel** drop down list to save this as a draft.

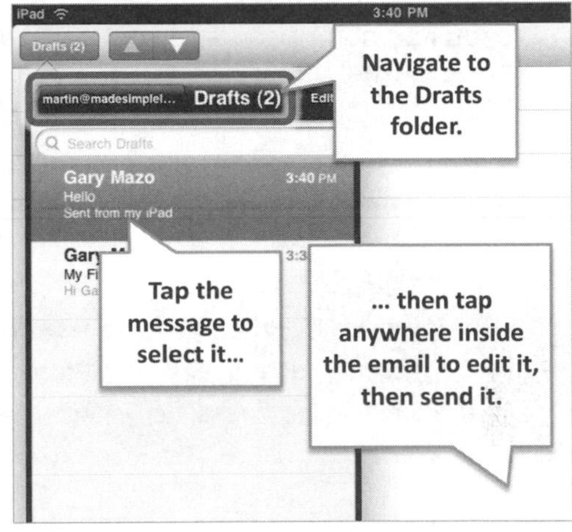


Later, when you want to locate and send your draft message, follow these steps:

1. Open the **Drafts** folder in the e-mail account from which you composed this message See the "Moving Between Your Mail Folders and Accounts" section in this chapter for help getting into the **Drafts** folder.
2. Tap the e-mail message in the **Drafts** folder to open it.
3. Tap anywhere in the message to edit it.
4. Press the **Send** button.

## Checking Sent Messages

Follow these steps to confirm that the e-mail was sent correctly:

You want the Sent Folder
iPad
Sent
martin@madesimplele...
Sent
Edit
Search Sent
Gary Mazo
2:54 PM
My First Email
Your most recent sent emails will be listed at the top.
Tap here to update the list.
Updated 4/25/10 2:58 PM

1. Tap the **E-mail account name** button in the upper left corner to see the mail folders for the account you just used to send your message.
2. Tap the **Sent** folder.
3. Verify that that the top e-mail you see in the list is the one you just composed and sent.

**NOTE:** You will only see the **Sent** and **Trash** folders if you have actually sent or deleted e-mail from that account on the iPad. If your e-mail account is an IMAP account, you will see many folders other than those described in this chapter.

## Reading and Replying to Mail

In order to read your e-mail, follow these steps:

1. Navigate to the **Inbox** for the e-mail account you want to view using the steps described earlier in this chapter.
2. To read any message, just touch it from your **Inbox**.
3. New, unread messages are shown with a small blue dot to the left of the message.
4. Flick your finger up or down in the **Inbox** to scroll through your messages.
5. When you are reading a message, swipe up or down to scroll through it.

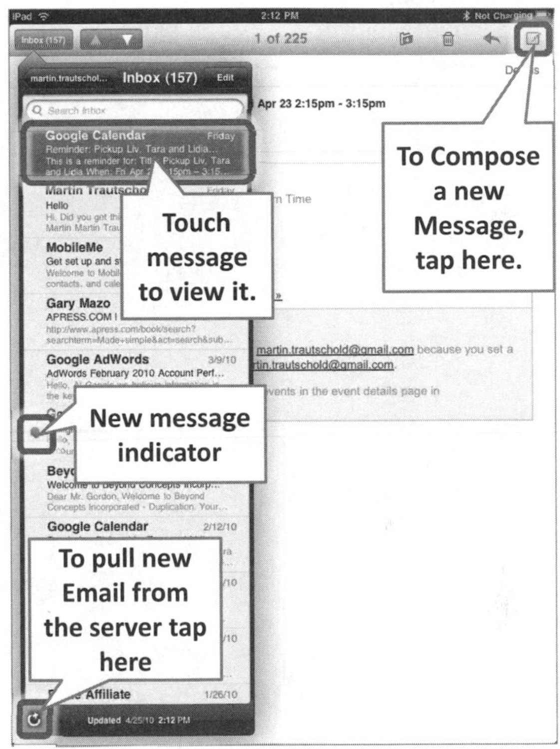


## Zooming In or Out

As when browsing the Web, you can zoom in to see your e-mail in larger text. You can also double-tap, just as you do on the Web; and you can also **Pinch** to zoom in or out (see the "Zooming" section in our Quick Started Guide in Part 1 of this book.)

## E-mail Attachments

Some e-mail attachments are opened automatically by the iPad, so you don't even notice that they were attachments. Examples include Adobe PDF files and some types of image, video, and audio files. You may also receive documents such as Apple **Pages**,

**Numbers**, **Keynote**, Microsoft **Word**, **Excel**, and **PowerPoint** files as attachments. You will need to open these.

## Knowing When You Have an Attachment

Any e-mail with an attachment will have a little **Paperclip** icon next to the sender's name, as shown to the right. When you see that icon, you know you have an attachment.

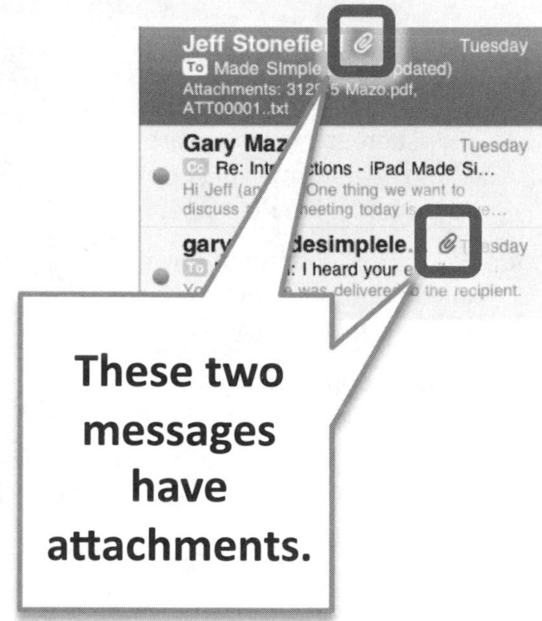
These two messages have attachments.

## Receiving an Auto-open Attachment

Now say you received a one-page **Adobe PDF** file or an image. (Multi-page **PDF** files require that you tap to open them.) Once you open the mail message with this kind of attachment, you will see it directly below the message (see Figure 12–5).

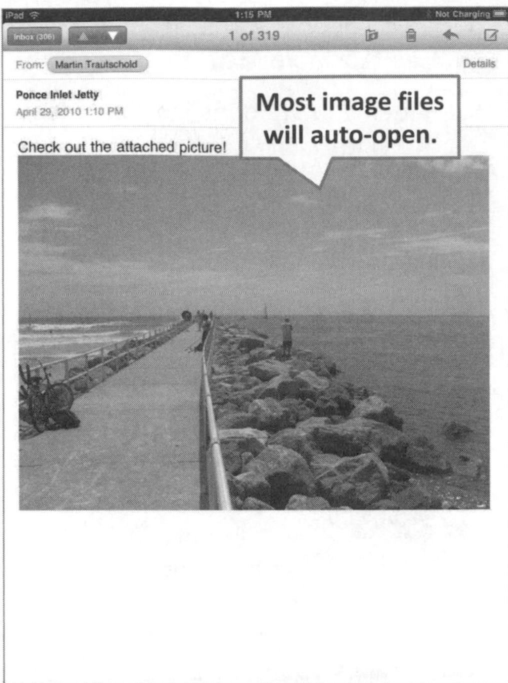


**Figure 12–5.** *Some attachments will automatically open under the e-mail message.*

> **TIP:** If you want to save or copy an auto-opened attachment, simply press and hold it until you see the pop-up window. At this point, you can select **Copy** or **Save Image**. When you save an image, it will be placed in your **Photos** app in the **Saved Photos** album.

## Opening E-mail Attachments

Instead of immediately opening in the body of the email as we just described, other types of attachments, such as spreadsheets, word processing documents, and presentation files, will need to be manually opened..

### Tap for Quick Look Mode

To open in a **Quick Look** mode, follow the steps below:

1. Open the message with an attachment (see Figure 12–6).
2. Quickly tap the attachment to instantly open it in **Quick Look** mode.
3. You can navigate around the document. Remember you can zoom in or out and swipe up or down.

4. If you open a spreadsheet with multiple tabs or spreadsheets, you will see tabs across the top. Touch another tab to open that spreadsheet.

5. When you are done looking at the attachment, tap the document once to bring up the controls, and then tap **Done** in the upper left corner.

6. If you would like to look at the opened document in another app (such as **Numbers**) so you can edit it, then tap the **Open In** button in the upper right corner.

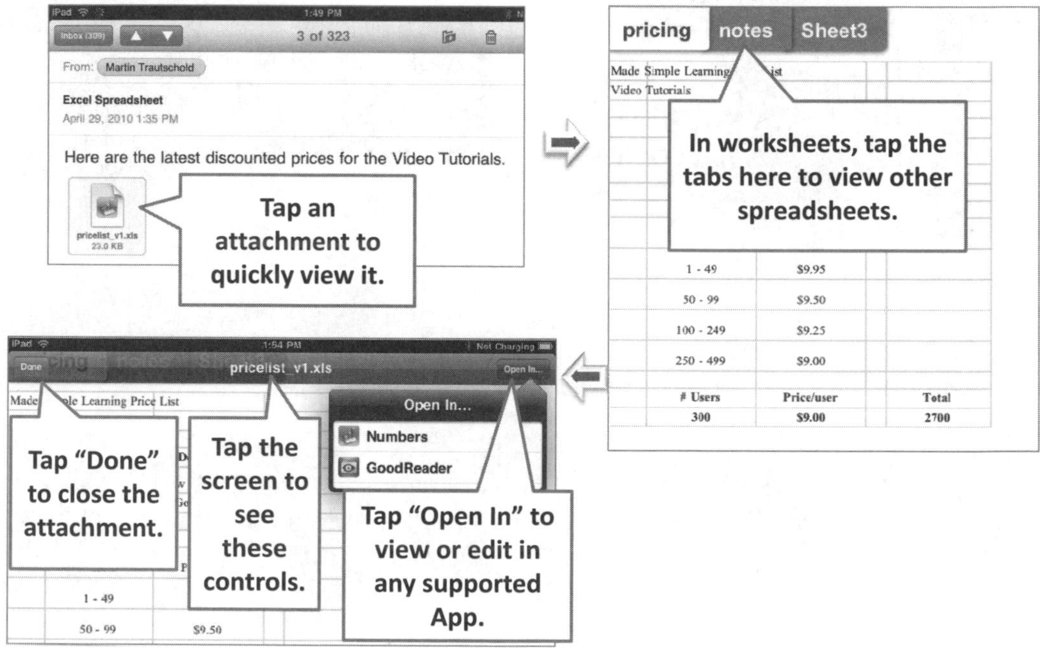


**Figure 12–6.** *Quickly viewing attachments by tapping them*

## Opening and Editing Docs in Other Apps

If you want to open the attachment in another application such as **GoodReader**, **Pages**, **Numbers**, or **Keynote**, then follow these steps.

1. Open the e-mail message.

2. Press and hold the attachment until you see the pop-up window.

3. Select the **Open In** option.

4. Select the application you would like to use from the list (Figure 12–7 shows us choosing **Pages**).

5. Finally, you can edit the document, save it, and e-mail it back to the sender.

> **TIP:** We show you exactly how to edit, save, and send documents with the **Pages**, **Numbers**, and **Keynote** apps in Chapter 18's "iWork: Productivity on Your iPad" section.

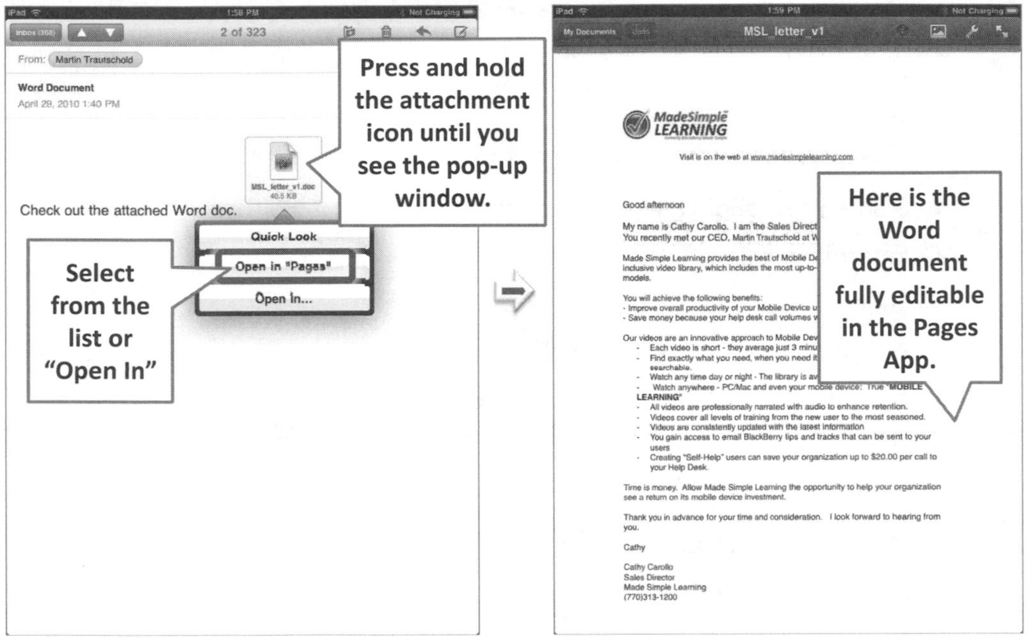


**Figure 12–7.** *Opening attachments in other apps*

# Cannot Open E-mail Attachments

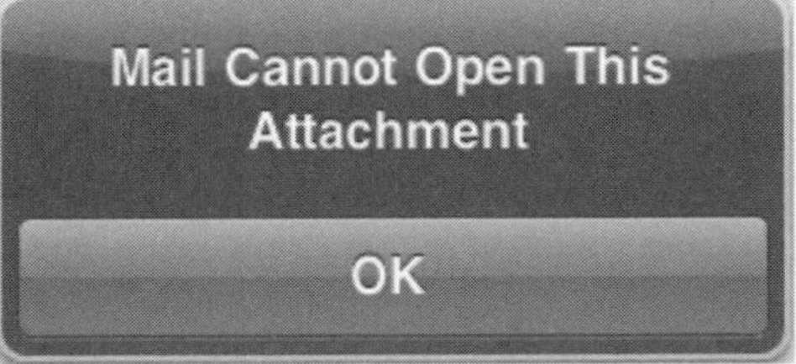


When you try to open an attachment, you may get an error message similar to the one shown to the right. In this example, we tried to click an attachment of the type **winmail.dat**, which failed.

The **Mail** app on the iPad can handle many types of attachments that come via e-mail – but not all. The attachments supported on the iPad are:

- **.doc** and **.docx** (**Microsoft Word** documents)

- **.htm** and **.html** (web pages)
- **.key** (a **Keynote** presentation document)
- **.numbers** (an **Apple Numbers** spreadsheet document)
- **.pages** (an **Apple Pages** document)
- **.pdf** (an **Adobe Reader** file)
- **.ppt** and **.pptx** (**Microsoft PowerPoint** presentation documents)
- **.txt** (a text file)
- **.vcf** (a contact file)
- **.xls** and **.xlsx** (Microsoft Excel spreadsheet documents)
- **.mp3** and **.mov** (audio and video formats)
- Audio formats supported:
    - HE-AAC (V1)
    - AAC (16 to 320 Kbps)
    - Protected AAC (from iTunes Store)
    - MP3 (16 to 320 Kbps)
    - MP3 VBR
    - Audible (formats 2, 3, and 4)
    - Apple Lossless
    - AIFF
    - WAV
- Video formats supported:
    - H.264 video up to 720p at 30 frames per second
    - Main Profile level 3.1 with AAC-LC audio up to 160 Kbps, 48kHz
    - Stereo audio in **.m4v**, **.mp4**, and **.mov** file formats
    - MPEG-4 video, up to 2.5 Mbps, 640 by 480 pixels, and at 30 frames per second
    - Simple Profile with AAC-LC audio up to 160 Kbps, 48kHz, stereo audio in **.m4v**, **.mp4**, and **.mov** file formats
    - Motion JPEG (M-JPEG) up to 35 Mbps, 1280 by 720 pixels, 30 frames per second, and audio in ulaw
    - PCM stereo audio in **.avi** file format

In any case, you should make sure your attachment is not in some other unsupported format type.

## Reply, Forward or Delete a Message

At the bottom of your e-mail-reading pane is a toolbar.

From this toolbar, you can move the message to a different mailbox or folder; delete it; or reply, reply all, or forward it.

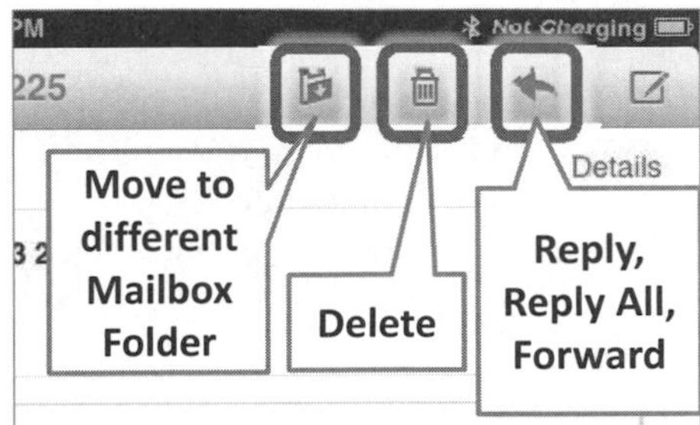


Touch the small arrow to see these option buttons appear: **Reply**, **Reply All**, and **Forward**.

> **NOTE:** The **Reply All** button appears only if there was more than one recipient for the e-mail message.

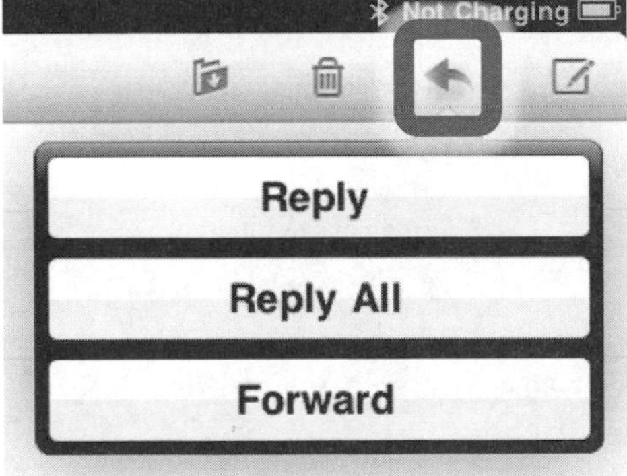

## Replying to an E-mail

Most likely, the **Reply** command is the one you will use most often.

1. Touch the **Reply** button.

   You will see that the original sender is now listed as the recipient in the **To:** line of the e-mail. The subject will automatically state: "Re: *(Original subject line)*."

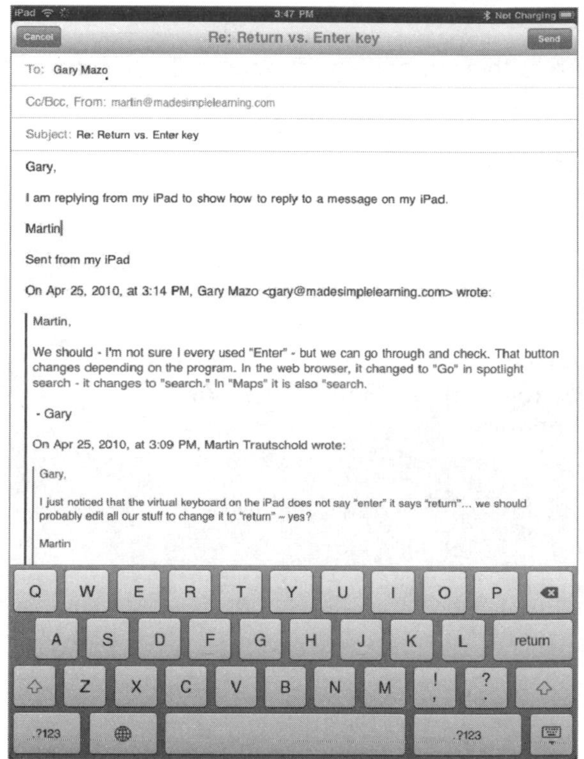


2. Type your response.
3. When you are done, just touch the blue **Send** button at the top right-hand corner of the screen.

> **NOTE:** You may see various colors of text on the screen in an e-mail. Each color will correspond to a different message and different author.

## Using Reply All

Using the **Reply All** option is just like using the **Reply** function, except that all of the original recipients of the e-mail and the original sender are placed in the address lines. The original sender will be in the **To:** line, and the other recipients of the original e-mail will be listed on the **Cc:** line. You will only see the **Reply All** option if more than one person received the original e-mail.

## Using the Forward Button

Sometimes, you get an e-mail that you want to send to someone else. The **Forward** command will let you do that (see the "E-mail Attachments" section in this chapter for more about working with attachments.)

**NOTE:** You need to forward attachments to send them to others. If you want to send someone any attachments from an e-mail you receive, you must choose the **Forward** option. (Note that choosing the **Reply** and **Reply All** options will not include the original e-mail attachment(s) in your outgoing message.)

When you do touch the **Forward** button, you may be prompted to address whether you want to include attachments (if there were any) from the original message.

At this point, you follow the same steps described previously to type your message, add addressees, and send it.

# Cleaning up Your Inbox

As you get more and more comfortable with your iPad as an e-mail device, you will increasingly find yourself using the **Mail** program. It will eventually become necessary to occasionally do some e-mail housecleaning. You can delete or move e-mail messages easily on your iPad.

## Deleting a Single Message

To delete a single message from your **Inbox**, follow these steps.

4. Swipe right or left on a message in the **Inbox** to bring up the **Delete** button.
5. Tap **Delete** to remove the message.

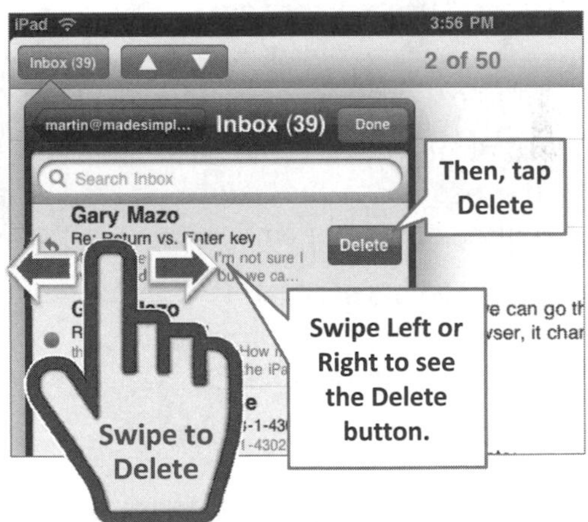

## Deleting or Moving Several Messages from Any Folder

Deleting several messages is very easy on the iPad. Follow these steps to do so.

1. View any mail folder on your iPad.
2. Tap the **Edit** button.

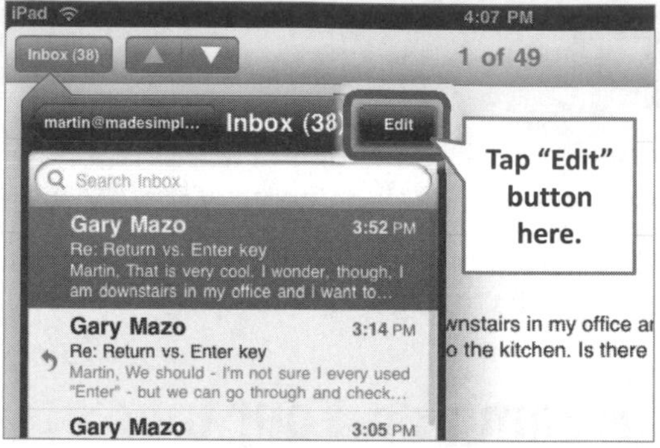


3. Select one or more messages by tapping them. You will see a red check mark for each selected message.
4. Once the messages are selected, you can delete or move them.
5. To delete the selected messages, tap the **Delete** button at the bottom.
6. To move the selected messages, tap the **Move** button and select the folder to which you want the messages moved.

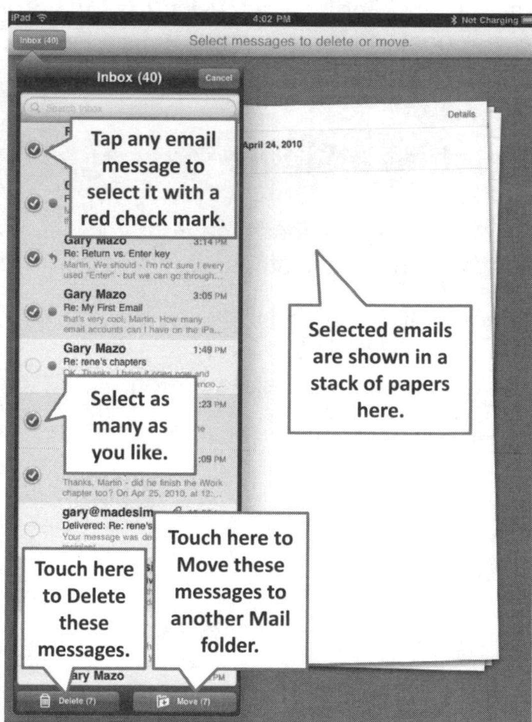


**CAUTION:** You do not get another prompt before a file is deleted, so be sure that you do want to delete the messages before choosing that option. While the message will be deleted on your device, a copy will still remain on the server.

## Deleting from the Message Screen

Another way to delete messages can be found in the **Message** screen. Follow these steps to do so.

1. Open any message to read it.
2. Tap the **Trash Can** icon in the top left portion of the screen.

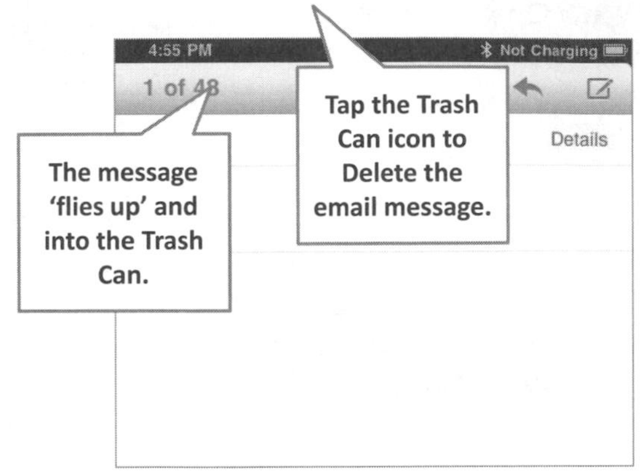
4:55 PM
Not Charging
1 of 48
Details
Tap the Trash Can icon to Delete the email message.
The message 'flies up' and into the Trash Can.

You will see the e-mail shrink and fly into the **Trash Can**, so it can be deleted.

**TIP:** You can set your iPad to ask you before deleting e-mail if you go into your **Settings** icon; tap **Mail, Contacts, Calendars**; and set the switch next to **Ask Before Deleting** to **Yes**.

You can organize your mail by moving it into other folders. E-mail messages can be moved out of your **Inbox** for storage or for reading at another time.

**NOTE:** In order to create folders in addition to the default **Inbox** and **Trash** folders, you need to set them up in your main e-mail account and sync them to your iPad. We will show you how to do this in this chapter's" "Fine Tune Your E-mail Settings" section.

## Moving an E-mail to a Folder While Viewing It

Sometimes, you may want to organize your e-mail for easy retrieval later. For example, you might receive an e-mail about an upcoming trip and want to move it to the **Travel** folder. Sometimes you receive e-mails that require attention later, in which case you can move them to the **Requires Attention** folder. This can help you remember to work on it later.

To move an e-mail message, follow these steps.

1. Open the e-mail message.
2. Tap the **Move** icon in the upper right corner.
3. Choose a new folder and the message will be moved out of the **Inbox**.

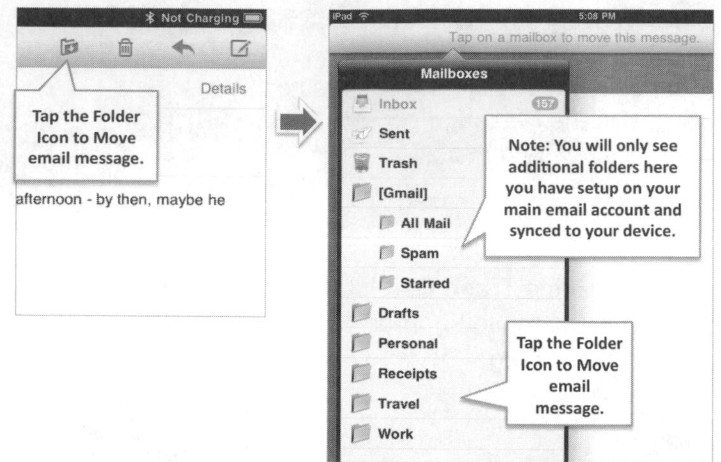


## Copy and Paste from an E-mail

Here are a few tips to select text or pictures and copy them from an e-mail message:

- Double-tap text to select a word, then drag the blue handles up or down to adjust the selection. Next, select **Cut** or **Copy**.

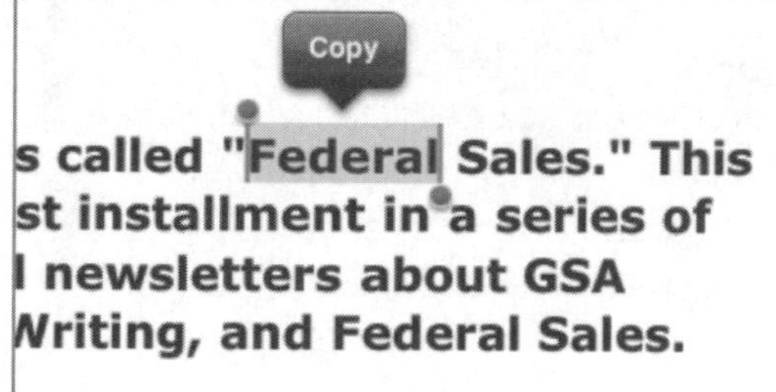


- Press and hold text, then choose **Select** or **Select All**.

- Press and hold an image, then select **Save Image** or **Copy**.

For a more complete description, please check out the "Copy and Paste" section in Chapter 2.

# Searching for E-mail Messages

The iPad has some good search functionality to help you find your e-mails. You can search your **Inbox** by the **From:**, **To:**, **Subject**, or **All** fields. This helps you filter your **Inbox**, so you can find exactly what you are searching for.

## Activating E-mail Search

Get to the **Inbox** of the account you wish to search. If you scroll up to the top, you will now see the familiar **Search** bar at the top of your **Inbox** (see Figure 12–8).

If your e-mail account supports the feature, you can also search the server for e-mail messages. At the time of writing, a few of the supported types of searchable e-mail accounts include **Exchange**, **MobileMe**, and **Gmail IMAP**. Follow these steps to search through your e-mail on a server.

1. Touch the **Search** bar to see a new menu of soft keys under the **Search** bar.
2. Type the text you wish to search for.
3. Touch one of the soft keys under the search window:
    a. **From** – Searches only the sender's e-mail addresses
    b. **To** – Searches only the recipients' e-mail addresses
    c. **Subject** – Searches only message **Subject** fields
    d. **All** – Searches every part of the message

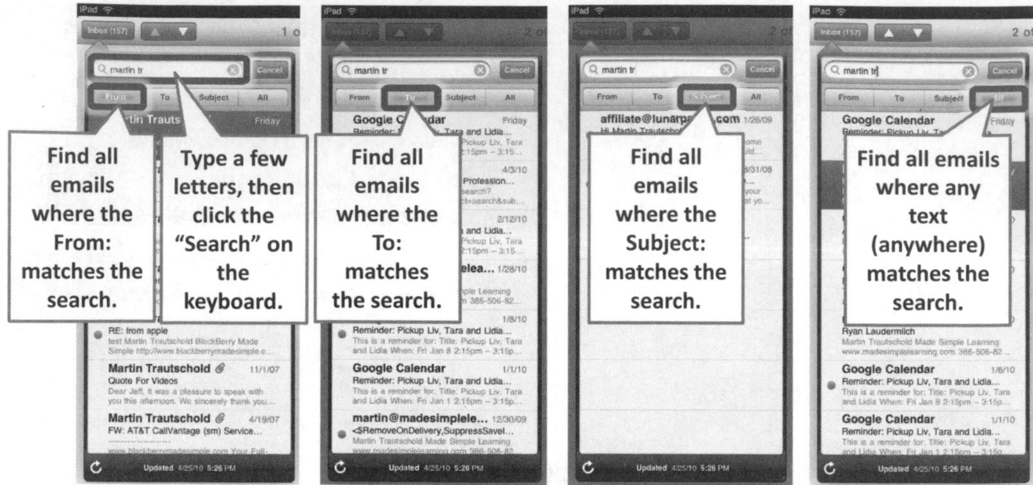


**Figure 12–8.** *Searching for e-mail using the From, To, Subject, or all text fields*

For example, assume I want to search my **Inbox** for an e-mail I received from Martin. I would type Martin's name in the **Search** box and then touch **From**. My **Inbox** would then be filtered to show only the e-mails from Martin.

> **NOTE:** If you have multiple e-mail accounts, you will not be able to search all of your inboxes at the same time – you can only search one inbox at a time. For a more global search, just use the **Spotlight Search** feature shown in the "Finding Things with Spotlight Search" section of Chapter 2.

# Fine Tune Your E-mail Settings

You can fine tune your e-mail accounts on your iPad with the myriad options available in the **Settings** app.

Follow these steps to change these settings:

1. Tap the **Settings** icon.
2. Tap **Mail, Contacts, Calendars** in the left column.

The sections that follow explain the adjustments you can make.

## Adjusting Your Mail Settings

Under the **Accounts** section, you can see all the e-mail settings listed under **Mail**. The **Default** settings may work well for you; but if you need to adjust any of these, you can follow these steps.

**Show** – This is how many e-mails are pulled from the server. Adjust anywhere from 25 – 200 messages (the default is 50 recent messages).

**Preview** – This is how many lines of text in addition to the **Subject** are shown in the **Inbox** preview. You can adjust this value from **None** to 5 lines (the default is 2 lines).

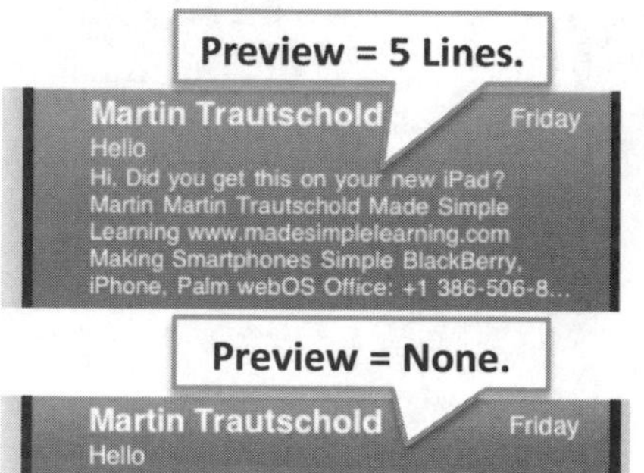


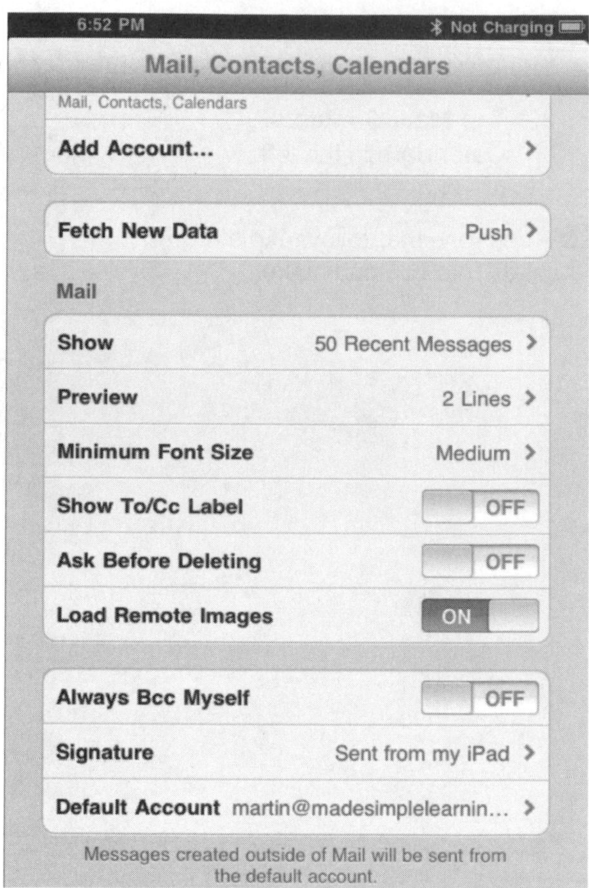


**Minimum Font Size** – This is the default font size shown when opening an e-mail the first time. It is also smallest font size that you are allowed to zoom out to when viewing an e-mail. Your options are **Small**, **Medium**, **Large**, **Extra Large**, and **Giant** (the default is **Medium**).

**Show To/Cc Label** – With this option **ON**, you will see a small **To** or **Cc** label in your **Inbox** before the subject; this label shows which field your address was placed in (the default is **OFF**).

**Ask Before Deleting** – Turn this option **ON** to be asked every time you try to delete a message (the default is **OFF**).

**Load Remote Images** – This option allows your iPad to load all the graphics (remote images) that are placed in some e-mail messages. (the default is **ON**).

**Always Bcc Myself** – This option sends a blind carbon copy (Bcc) of every e-mail you send from your iPad to your e-mail account (the default is **OFF**).

## Changing Your E-mail Signature

By default, e-mails you send will say "Sent from my iPad" – unless you change the **Signature** line of the e-mail.

Tap the **Signature** tab and type in the new e-mail signature you want at the bottom of e-mails sent from the iPad.

When you are done editing the **Signature** field, tap the **Mail, Contacts...** button in the upper left-hand corner, and you will be returned to the **Mail** settings screen.

## Changing Your Default Mail Account (Sent From)

If you have multiple e-mail accounts set up on your iPad, you should set one of them – usually, the one you use most – as your **Default Account**. When you simply select the **Compose** from the **E-mail** screen, the default account is always chosen. Follow these steps to change the e-mail account you send from by default.

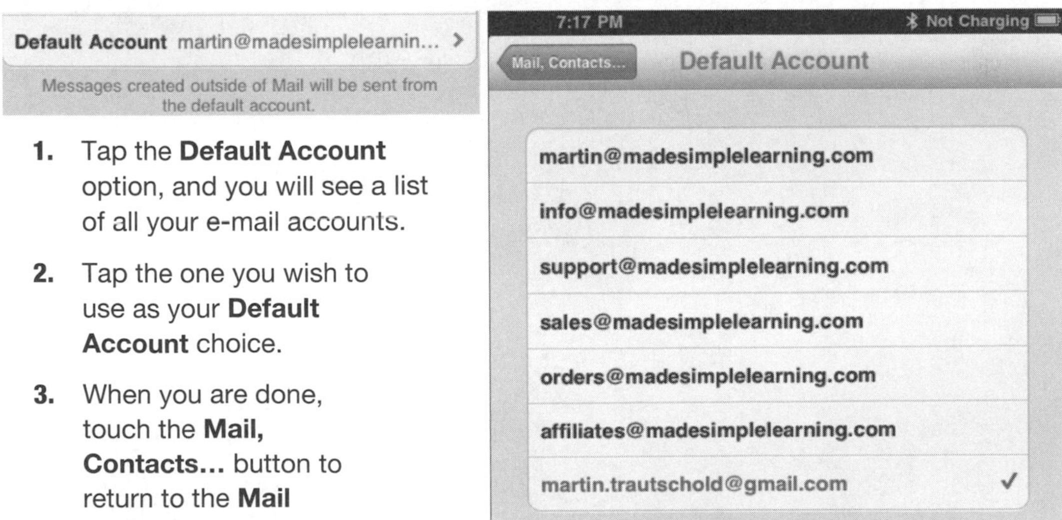


1. Tap the **Default Account** option, and you will see a list of all your e-mail accounts.
2. Tap the one you wish to use as your **Default Account** choice.
3. When you are done, touch the **Mail, Contacts...** button to return to the **Mail** settings menu.

## Toggling Sounds for Receiving and Sending E-mail

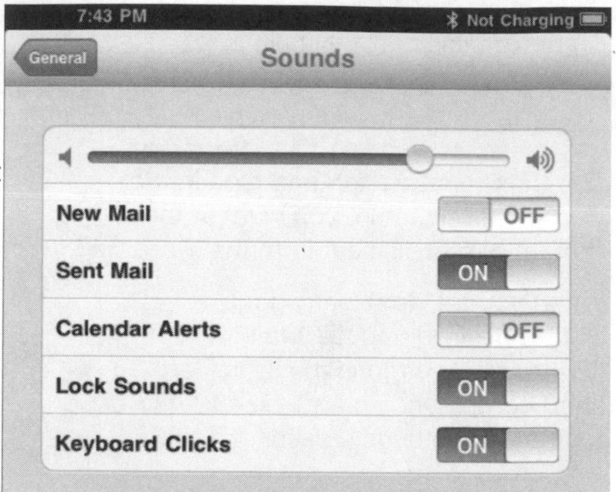


You may notice a little sound effect every time you send or receive e-mail. What you hear is the default setting on your iPad.

If you would like to disable this or adjust it, you do so in the **Settings** icon.

1. Tap your **Settings** icon.
2. Tap **General** in the left column.
3. Tap **Sounds** in the right column.
4. You will see various switches to turn on or off sound effects. Tap **New Mail** and **Sent Mail** to adjust the **ON** or **OFF** options.

> **Note**: At the time of writing, the user is not able to change the sounds associated with these functions. Adjustable sounds and tones may be added in future software updates.

## Advanced E-mail Options

To get to the **Advanced** options for each e-mail account, follow these steps:

1. Touch the **Settings** icon.
2. Touch **Mail, Contacts, Calendars** in the left column.
3. Touch an e-mail address listed under **Accounts** in the right column.
4. At the bottom of the mail settings pop-up window, tap the **Advanced** button to bring up the **Advanced** dialog.

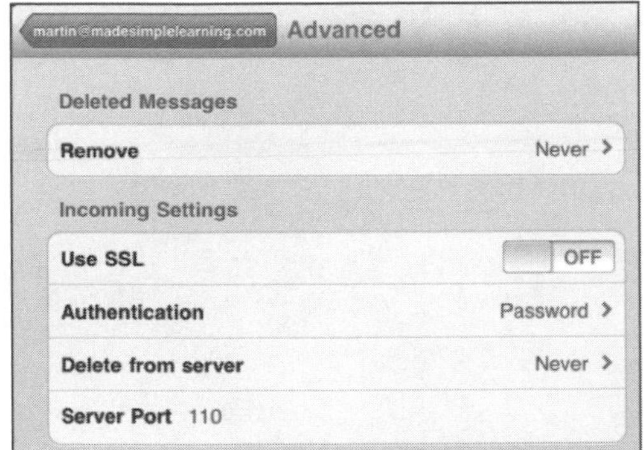


## Remove E-mail Messages from iPad After Deletion

You can select how frequently you want e-mail removed completely from your iPad once it is deleted.

Touch the **Remove** tab and select the option that is best for you – the default setting is **After one week**.

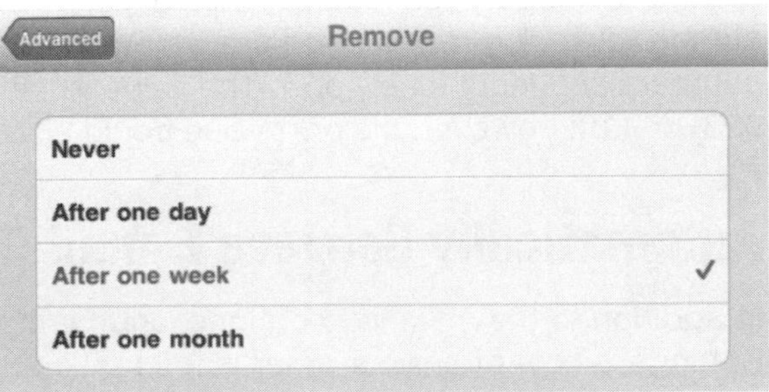

## USE SSL/Authentication

These features were discussed previously, but this option supplies another location to access these features for a particular account.

## Delete from Server

You can configure your iPad to handle the deletion of messages from your e-mail server. Usually, this setting is left at **Never**, and this function is handled on your main computer. If you use your iPad as your main e-mail device, you might want to handle that feature from here. Follow these steps to remove deleted e-mails on the server from your iPad.

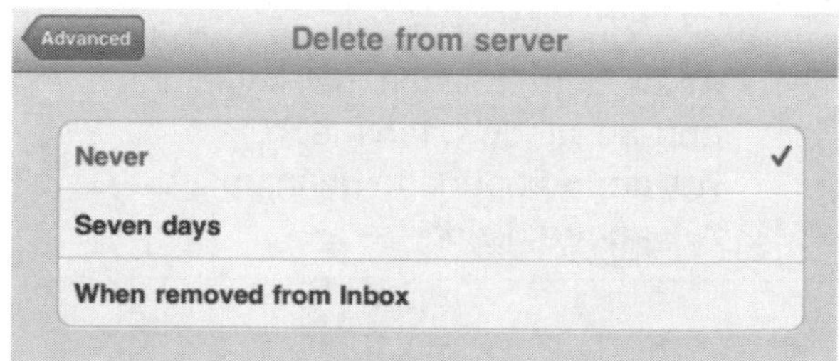


1. Touch the **Delete from Server** tab to select the feature that best suits your needs: **Never**, **Seven Days**, or **When removed from Inbox**.
2. The default setting is **Never**. If you want to choose **Seven Days**, that option should give you enough time to check e-mail on your computer as well as your iPad, and then decide what to keep and what to get rid of.

## Changing the Incoming Server Port

As you did with the **Outgoing Server Port** earlier, you can change the **Incoming Server Port** if you are having trouble receiving e-mail. It is very rare that your troubles will be related to the port you receive mail on – so it is rare that you would need to change this number. If your e-mail service provider gives you a different number, just touch the numbers and input a new port. The value for an **Incoming Server Port** is usually 995, 993, or 110; however, the port value could also be another number.

# Automatically Retrieve E-mail (Fetch New Data)

In addition to the Advanced options, another option you can configure in the E-Mail Settings is how often your email is fetched or pulled to your iPad. By default, your iPad automatically receives mail or other contact or calendar updates when they are "pushed" from the server.

You can adjust this setting by taking the following steps.

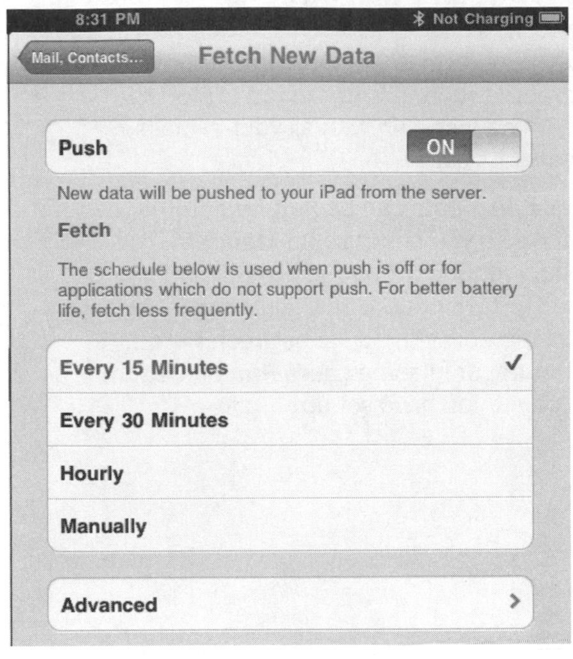


3. Touch the **Settings** icon.
4. Touch **Mail, Contacts, Calendars** in the left column.
5. Touch **Fetch New Data** under the e-mail accounts in the right column.
6. Set **Push** to **ON** (default) to automatically have the server push data.
7. Adjust the timing schedule to pull data from the server. This is how frequently applications should pull new data from the server.

**NOTE:** If you set this option to **Every 15 Minutes**, you will receive more frequent updates, but sacrifice battery life compared to a setting of **Hourly**.

Having automatic retrieval is very handy if you just want to turn on your iPad and see that you have messages – otherwise, you need to remember to check.

### Advanced Push options

At the bottom of the **Fetch New Data** screen, touch the **Advanced** button to see a new screen with all your e-mail accounts listed.

Most accounts can be **Fetched** on the schedule you set or set to **Manual**, which requires you to retrieve data using the **Update** button. This screen gives you the ability to adjust between **Fetch**, **Manual**, or in some cases **Push** for each account you have set up.

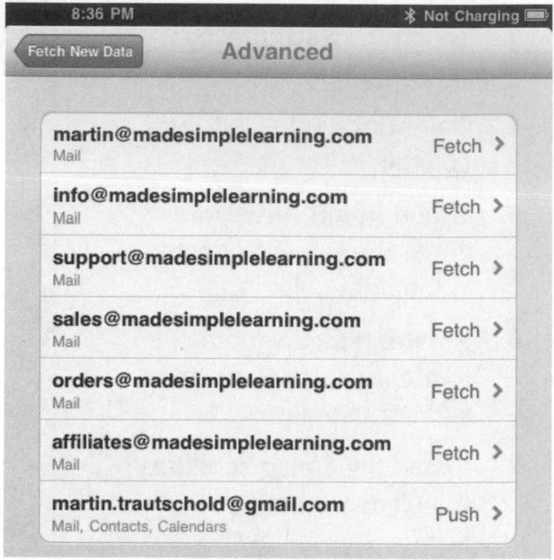


## Troubleshooting E-mail Problems

Usually, your e-mail works flawlessly on your iPad. Sometimes, whether it is a server issue, a network connectivity issue, or an e-mail service provider requirement; e-mail may not work as flawless as you would hope.

More often than not, there is a simple setting that needs to be adjusted or a password that needs to be re-entered.

If you try out some of the troubleshooting tips that follow and your e-mail is still not working, then your e-mail server may just be down temporarily. Check with your e-mail service provider to make sure your mail server is up and running; you might also check whether your provider has made any recent changes that would affect your settings.

**TIP:** If these tips that follow do not solve the problem, please check out Chapter 25 for more troubleshooting tips and resources.

## E-mail Isn't Being Received or Sent

If you can't send or receive e-mail, your first step should be to verify you are connected to the Internet. Look for Wi-Fi or 3G connectivity in the upper left corner of your **Home** screen (see the "How Do I Know When I'm Connected?" section of "Quick Start Guide" for details.

Sometimes, you need to adjust the outgoing port for e-mail to be sent properly. Do so by following these steps.

1. Tap **Settings**.
2. Touch **Mail, Contacts and Calendars** in the left column.
3. Touch your e-mail account that is having trouble sending messages under **Accounts** in the right column.
4. Touch **SMTP** and verify that your outgoing mail server is set correctly; also check that it is set to On.
5. Touch **Outgoing Mail Server** at the top and verify all the settings, such as Host Name, User Name, Password, SSL, Authentication, and Server Port. You might also try 587, 995, or 110 for the Server Port value; sometimes that helps.
6. Click **Done** and the e-mail account name in the upper left corner to return to the E-mail settings screen for this account.
7. Scroll down to the bottom and touch **Advanced**.
8. You can also try a different port setting for the server port on this screen, such as 587, 995, or 110. If those values don't work, contact your e-mail service provider to get a different port number and verify your settings.

## Verify your Mail Account Settings

To verify your account settings, follow these steps.

1. Tap the **Settings** icon.
2. Tap **Mail, Contacts, Calendars** in the left column.
3. If you received an error message from a particular e-mail account, touch that that account.

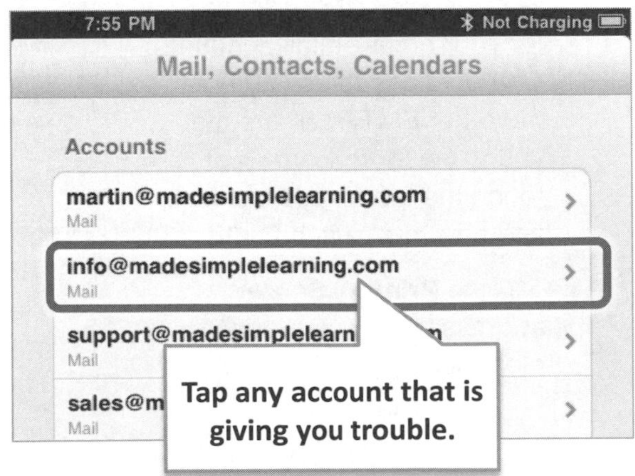

4. Verify that the **Account** is set to **ON**.
5. Verify that your e-mail **Address** is correct in the **POP Account Information** section.
6. Verify that the information in the **Host Name**, **User Name**, and **Password** fields is correct.
7. If you received an error message while trying to send an e-mail, the issue will be most likely in the **SMTP** settings in your **Outgoing Mail Server** area.
8. Tap **SMTP** to adjust more settings.

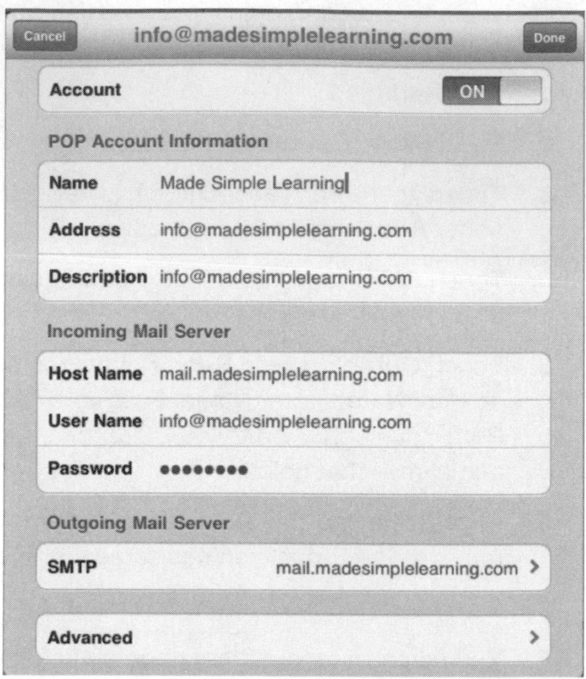


9. Touch the **Primary Server** tab and make sure that it is set to **On**.
10. Underneath the **Primary Server** tab, you will see other SMTP servers that are used for your other e-mail accounts. One option is to use one of the other SMTP servers that you know is working – just touch the tab for that server and turn that switch to **On**.
11. Tap the **Primary Server** address to view and adjust more settings.

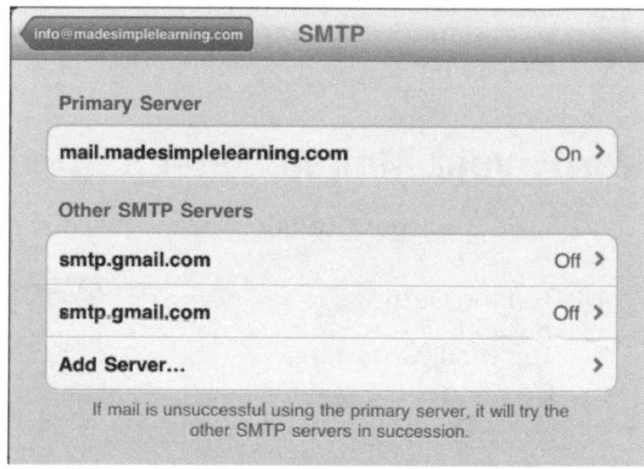

12. Verify that the **Primary Server** is **ON**.

13. Contact your e-mail service provider to verify other settings, such as **Host Name**, **User Name**, **Password**, **SSL**, **Authentication**, and **Server Port**. We will share more details and some tips about these settings in the sections that follow.

14. Tap the **Done** button when finished and then tap the button with your email account listed in the upper left corner to return to previous screens. Or, you can tap the **Home** button to exit to your Home Screen.

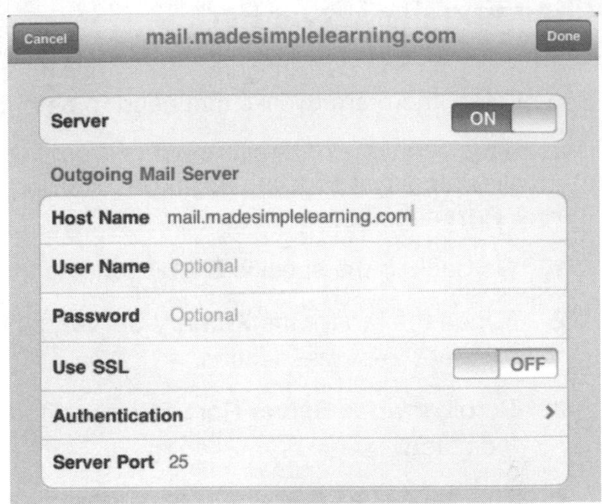


## Using SSL

Some SMTP servers require the use of Secure Socket Layer ("SSL") security. If you are having trouble sending e-mail and the **Use SSL** switch is set to **OFF**, try setting it to **ON** and see if that helps.

## Changing the Method of Authentication

Under the SSL switch is an **Authentication** tab – usually, **Password** is the correct setting. We don't recommend that you change this setting unless you have specific directions from your e-mail service provider to make a change.

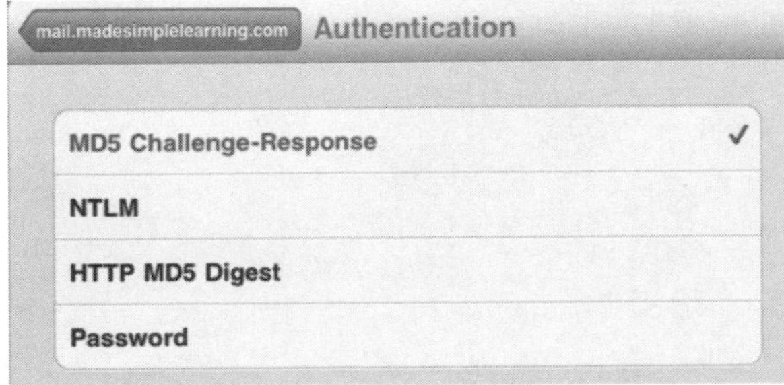

## Changing the Server Port

Most often, when you configure your e-mail account, the server port is set for you. Sometimes, there are tweaks that need to be made that are specific to your ISP.

If you have been given specific settings from your ISP, you can change the server port to try to alleviate any errors you might be receiving. Follow these steps to change the **Server Port** settings.

1. Go back to the specific **SMTP** settings for your account.
2. Touch the tab for the **Primary Server**, as you did in the "Verify Mail Account Settings" section.
3. Scroll down to **Server Port** and touch the screen on the number indicated.
4. This causes a keyboard to pop up where you can input a new port number (the one given you by your ISP.) Most often, the number provided by your ISP will be 995, 993, 587, or 110; however, if you're given a different number, just input it.
5. When you are done, touch the **SMTP** tab in the upper left-hand corner to return to the previous screen.

Chapter 13

# Working with Contacts

Your iPad gives you immediate access to all your important information. Just like your computer or your smartphone, your iPad can store thousands of contacts for easy retrieval. In this chapter we'll show you how to add new contacts (including from an e-mail address), customize your contacts by adding new fields, organize your contacts with groups, quickly search or scroll through contacts, and even show a contact's location with the iPad **Maps** app. We will also show you how to customize your Contacts view so it is sorted and displayed just the way you like it. Finally, you will learn a few troubleshooting tips that will save you some time when you run into difficulties.

The beauty of the iPad is how it integrates all of the apps so you can e-mail and map your contacts right from the contact entry.

## Loading Your Contacts onto the iPad

In Chapter 3: "Sync Your iPad with iTunes", we show you how to load your contacts onto the iPad using iTunes on your Mac or Windows computer. You can also use the Google Sync or MobileMe services described in the Chapter 26: "Other Sync Methods."

> **TIP:** You can add new contact entries from e-mail messages you receive. Learn how in Chapter 12.

## When Is Your Contact List Most Useful?

The Contacts app is most useful when two things are true:

1. You have many names and addresses in it.
2. You can easily find what you need.

## Two Simple Rules to Improve Your Contact List

We have a couple of basic rules to help make your Contact list on your iPad more useful.

**Rule 1: Add anything and everything to your Contacts.**

> You never know when you might need that obscure restaurant name, or that plumber's number, etc.

**Rule 2: As you add entries, make sure you think about how to find them in the future (First, Last, Company).**

> We have many tips and tricks in this chapter to help you enter names so that they can be instantly located when you need them.

**TIP:** Here' a good way to find restaurants: Whenever you enter a restaurant into your contacts list, make sure to put the word "restaurant" into the company name field, even if it's not part of the name. Then when you type the letters "rest," you should instantly find all your restaurants!

## Adding a New Contact Right on Your iPad

You can always add your contacts right on your iPad. This is handy when you're away from your computer—but have your iPad—and need to add someone to your Contacts. It's very easy to do. Here's how.

## Start the Contacts App

From your **Home Screen**, touch the **Contacts** icon and you'll see the **All Contacts** list, as shown in Figure 13–1. Tap the **+** in the lower right corner to add a new contact.

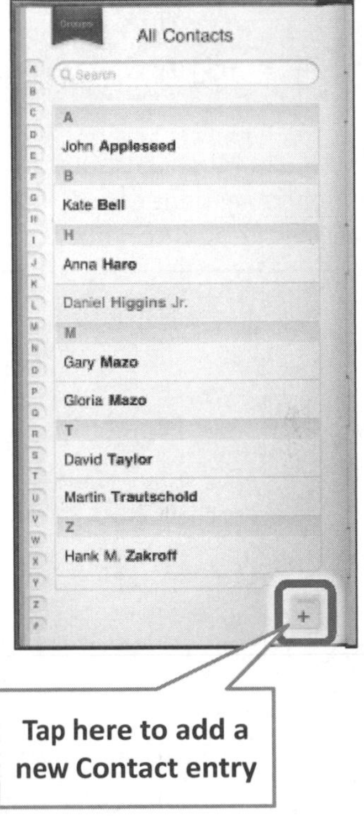


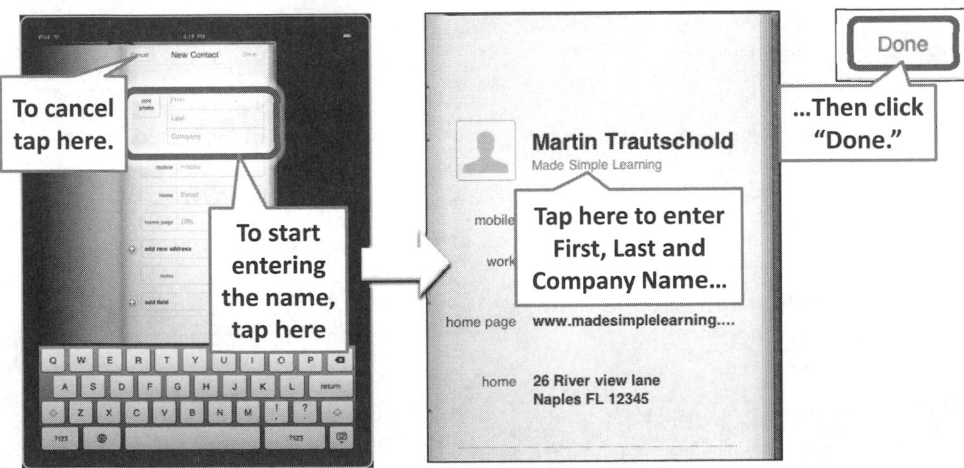


**Figure 13–1.** *Entering a contact name*

Touch the **First Last** button and enter the new contact's first and last name. You can also add a company name.

**TIP:** Keep in mind that the Contacts search feature uses First, Last, and Company names. When you add or edit contacts, adding a special word to the Company name can help you find a particular contact later. For example, adding the words "Cece friend" to the Company field can help you find all of Cece's friends quickly using the search feature.

Under the **First Last** button are five more buttons, as shown in Figure 13–2. Each is activated by either touching the green + to the left of the button (when available) or just touching the button itself.

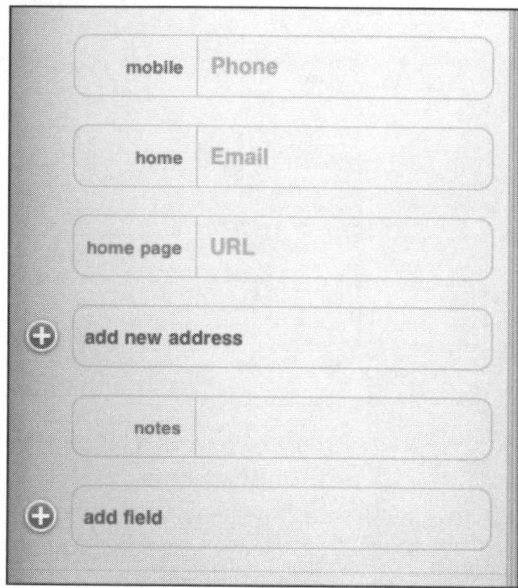


**Figure 13–2.** *Available contact fields*

# Adding a New Phone Number

Touch the **Phone** button and use the number keyboard to input the phone number.

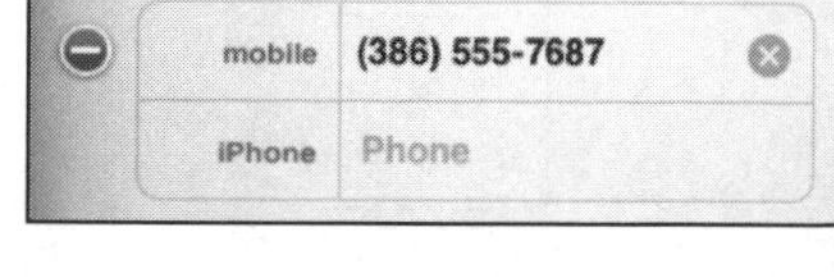


**TIP:** Don't worry about parentheses, dashes or dots, the iPad will put the number into the correct format. Just type the digits of the area code and number. If you know the country code, it's a good idea to put that in as well.

Next, choose which type of phone number this is—mobile, home, work, or other type. There are nine fields you can choose from, and there's also a **Custom** field if you find none of the built-in fields apply.

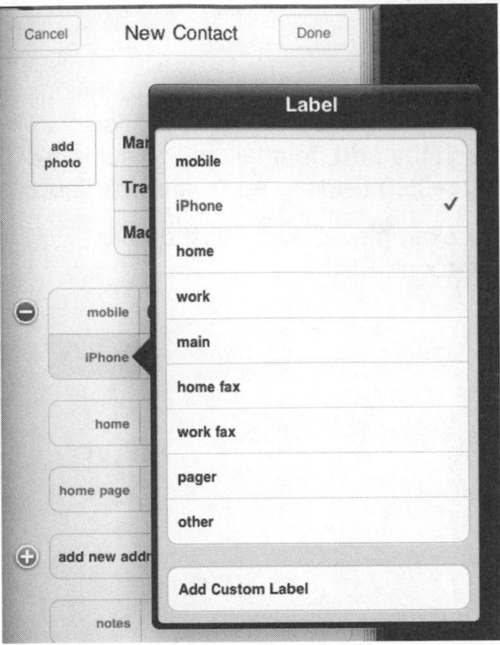


**TIP:** Sometimes you need to add a pause to a phone number, for example when the phone number is for someone at an organization where you have to dial the main number and then an extension. This is easy to do on the iPad. You just add a comma between the main number and the extension like this: 386-555-1234 , 19323. When you dial this number, say from your iPhone, the phone would dial the main number, pause for 2 seconds, then dial the extension. If you need more of a pause, simply add more commas.

## Adding an E-mail Address and Web Site

Touch the **Email** tab and enter the e-mail address for your contact. You can also touch the tab to the left of the e-mail address and select whether this is a home, work, or other e-mail address.

Under the **Email** field you'll also find a h**ome page** field in which you can enter the address of your contact's web site.

The iPad gives you the option to include only the fields that are relevant for a particular contact. Just touch the **add field** tab and select any of the suggested fields to add to that particular contact.

For example, to add a **Birthday** field to this contact, just touch **Birthday**.

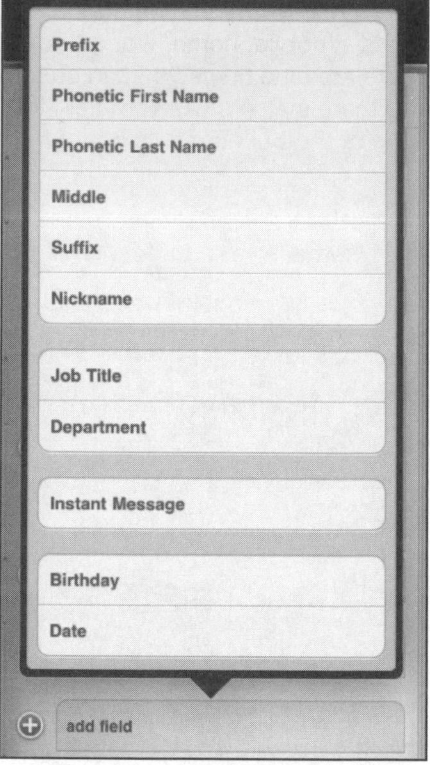


When you touch **Birthday**, you're presented with a wheel.. You can turn the wheel to the corresponding date to add the birthday to the contact information.

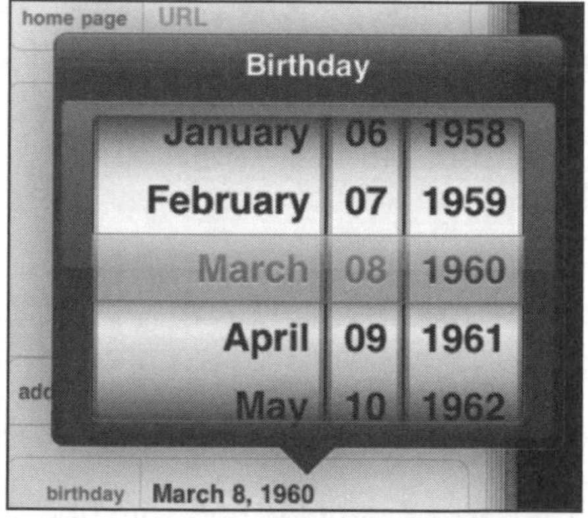


**TIP:** Suppose you met someone at the bus stop—someone you wanted to remember. Of course you should enter your new friend's first and last name (if you know it), but also enter the words "bus stop" in the Company name field. Then when you type the letters "bus" or "stop," you should instantly find everyone you met at the bus stop, even if you can't remember their names!

## Adding the Address

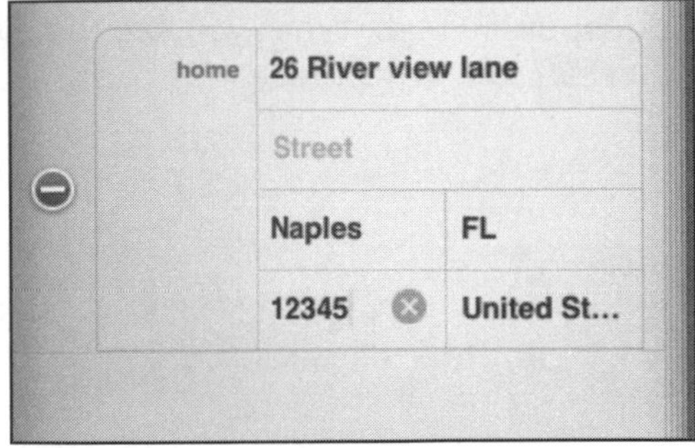


Below the **home** field are the fields for adding the address. Input the **Street**, **City**, **State** and **Zip Code**. You can also specify the **Country** and whether this is a home or work address.

When you are done, just touch the **Done** button in the upper right corner of the **New Contact** form.

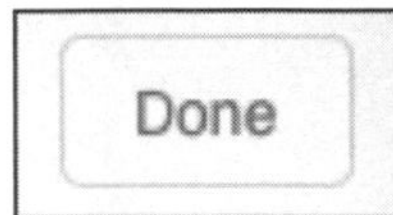


## Adding a Photo to Contacts

From the **New Contact** screen we've been working in, just touch the **Add Photo** button next to the **First Last** tab.

If you are changing a photo, when you are in "edit contact" mode, you'll see **edit** at the bottom of the existing photo.

After you touch the **add photo** button, you'll see that you can choose an existing photo. If there's a photo already in place, you can edit or delete it as well.

To choose an existing photo, select the Photo Album where the picture is located and touch the corresponding tab. When you see the picture you want to use, just touch it.

You'll notice that the top and bottom of the photo become grayed out and that you can manipulate the picture by moving it, pinching to zoom in or out, and then arranging it in the picture window.

Once the picture is sitting where you want it, just touch the **Use** button in the upper right corner and that picture will be set for the contact.

**TIP:** If you just moved into a new neighborhood, it can be quite daunting to remember everyone's name. A good practice to follow is to add the word "neighbor" into the **Company** name field for every neighbor you meet. Then, to instantly call up all your neighbors, simply type the letters "neigh" to find everyone you've met!

## Searching Your Contacts

Let's say you need to find a specific phone number or e-mail address. Just touch your **Contacts** icon as we did above and you'll see a search box at the top of your **All Contacts** list, as in Figure 13–3.

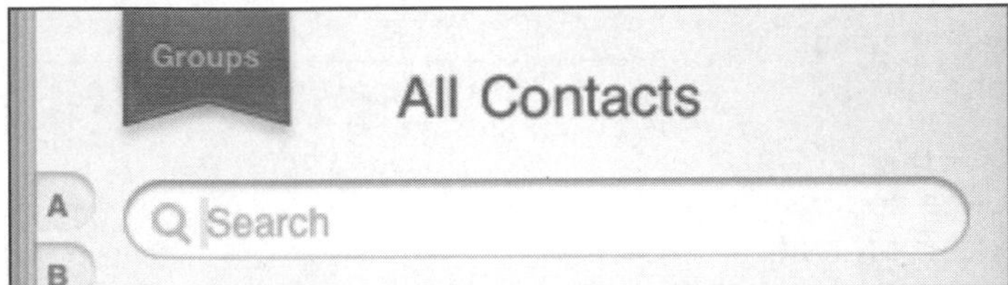


**Figure 13–3.** *The contacts search box*

Enter the first few letters of any of these three searchable fields:

- First Name
- Last Name
- Company Name

The iPad begins to filter immediately and displays only those contacts that match the letters typed.

**TIP:** To further narrow the search, hit the space key and type a few more letters.

When you see the correct name, just touch it and that individual's contact information will appear.

## Quickly Jump to a Letter by Tapping and Sliding on the Alphabet

If you hold your finger on the alphabet on the left edge of the screen and drag it up or down, you can jump to that letter.

## Search by Flicking

If you don't want to manually input letters, you can just move your finger and flick from the bottom up and you'll see your Contacts move quickly on the screen. Just continue to flick or scroll until you see the name you want. Tap the name and the contact information will appear.

## Search Using Groups

If you have your contacts sorted by groups on your PC or Mac and you sync your iPad with the computer, those groups will be synced to your iPad. Just touch the **Groups** tab at the top left of the **All Contacts** window and select which group you'd like to search within.

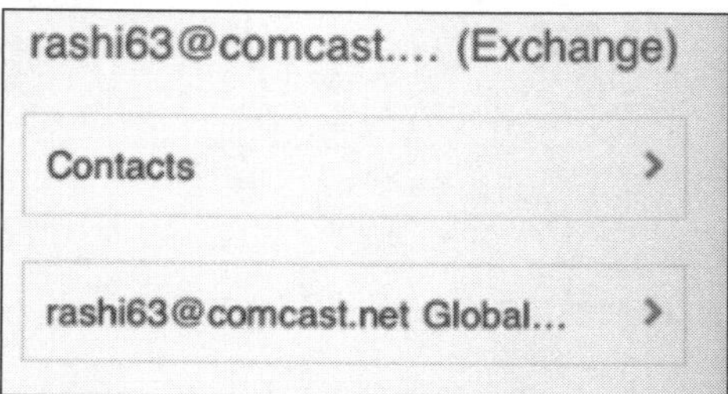


This example shows two groups—one is from a Microsoft Exchange account (i.e., a company e-mail account), and one from regular contacts.

If you have an Exchange ActiveSync account and your company has enabled it, your Exchange Global Address List shows up here, under Groups, as well. You can search to find anyone in your company there.

> **NOTE:** You can't create groups on the iPad, they must be created on your computer and synced to your iPad.

## Adding Contacts from E-mails

Often you'll receive an e-mail and realize that the contact is not in your address book. Adding a new contact from an e-mail is easy.

Open the e-mail from the contact you'd like to add to your contacts list. Then, in the e-mail's **From** field, just touch the name of the **Sender** next to the **From:** tag.

If the **Sender** is not in your address book, you'll be taken to a screen that lets you choose whether to add that e-mail address to an existing contact or to create a new one.

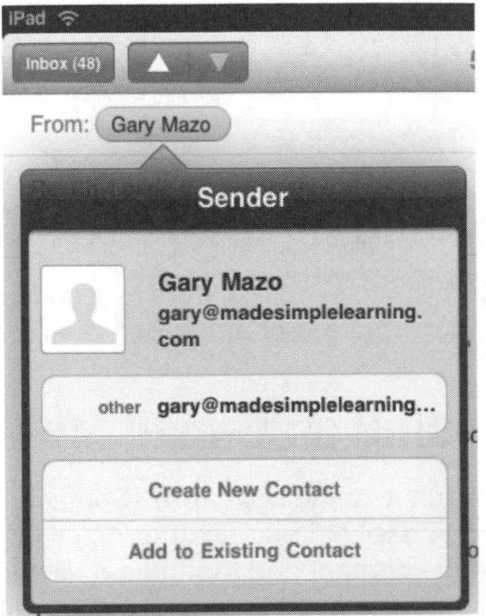


If you select **Create a New Contact**, you'll be taken to the same **New Contact** screen we saw earlier (Figure 13–1).

But suppose this is someone's personal e-mail address and you already have an entry for that person with the work e-mail. In that case, you would select **Add to Existing Contact** and choose the correct person. Then you'd give this e-mail address a tag, personal in this case.

> **TIP:** Learning the names of parents of your school-age children can be fairly challenging. In the **First** field, however, you can add not just your child's friend's name but the parent's names as well (e.g., **First: Samantha (Mom: Susan Dad: Ron)**. Then in the **Company** field, add in the name of your child and "school friend" (e.g., **Cece school friend**) Now, just typing your child's name in your **All Contacts** list's search box, you'll instantly find every person you ever met at your child's school. Now you can say "Hello Susan, great to see you again!" without missing a beat. *Try your best to covertly look up the name.*

## Sending a Picture to a Contact

If you want to send a picture to a contact, you will need to do that from the Photos app (See our "Photos" chapter (See Chapter 15: "Working With Photos").

## Sending an E-mail Message from Contacts

Since many of the core apps (Contacts, Mail, and Messages) are fully integrated, one app can easily trigger another. So, if you want to send an e-mail to one of your contacts, open the contact and tap the e-mail address. The Mail app will launch and you can compose and send an e-mail message to this person.

Start your **Contacts** by touching the **Contacts** icon. Either search or flick through your contacts until you find the contact you need.

email **martin@madesimplelearni...**

In the contact information, touch the e-mail address of the contact you'd like to use.

You'll see that the **Mail** program launches automatically with the contact's name in the To: field of the e-mail. Type and send the message.

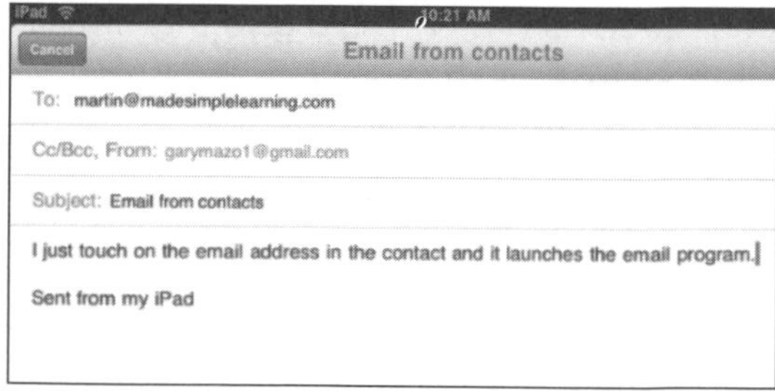

## Showing Your Contacts Addresses on the Map

One of the great things about the iPad is its integration with Google Maps. This is very evident in the Contacts app. Let's say you want to map the home or work address of any contact in your address book. In the old days (pre-iPad), you'd have to use Google or MapQuest or some other program and laboriously retype or copy and paste the address information. Very time-consuming—but you don't have to do this on the iPad.

Simply open the contact as you did earlier. This time, touch the address at the bottom of the contact information.

home **150 Flint Street**
**Marstons Mills MA 02648**

Your **Maps** app (which is powered by Google Maps) immediately loads and drops a push-pin at the exact location of the contact. The contact name will appear in above the push-pin.

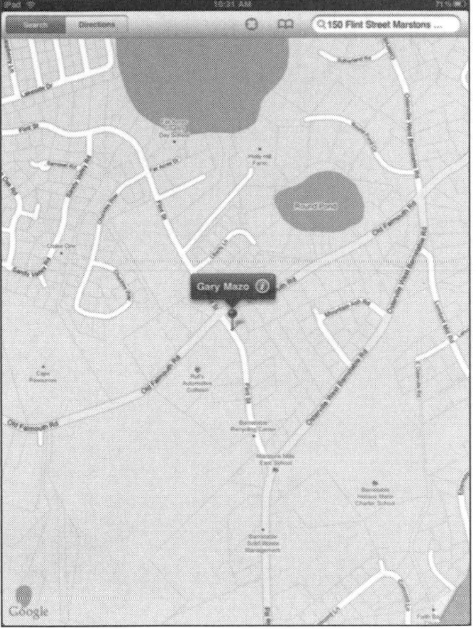

Touch the tab on the top of the push-pin to get to the info screen.

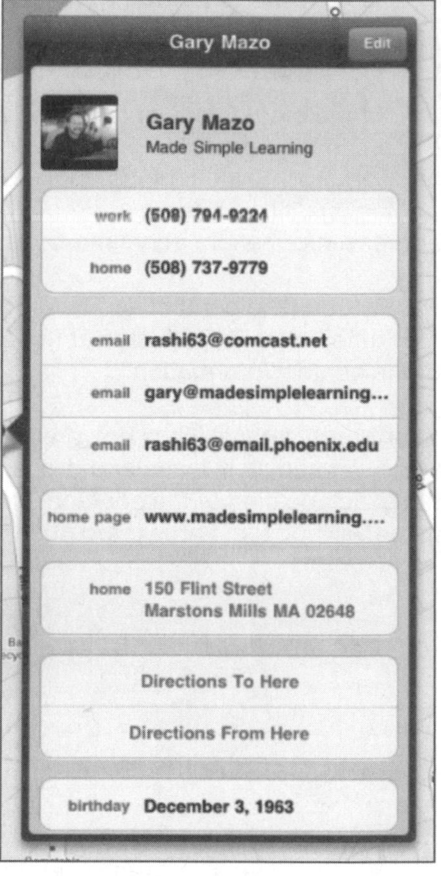


Now you can select **Directions To Here** or **Directions From Here**.

Then type the correct start or end address and touch the Route button in the lower right corner. If you decide you don't want the directions, just tap the Clear button in the top left.

What if you had just typed the address in your Maps app, not clicked from your contact list? In that case, you might want to touch **Add to Contacts** to add this address.

**TIP:** To return to your contact information, tap the **Home** button and then tap **Contacts**.

## Changing your Contact Sort Order and Display Order

Like other settings, the Contacts options are accessible via the **Settings** icon.

Touch the **Settings** icon and scroll down to **Mail, Contacts, Calendars** and touch the tab.

Scroll down and you'll see **Contacts**, with two options underneath. To change the sort order, touch the **Sort Order** tab and select whether you want your contacts sorted first by first name or last name.

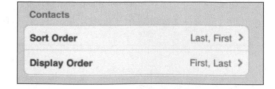

You may want to change how your contacts are displayed. Here's where you get it done; you can choose **First, Last** or **Last, First**. Tap the **Display Order** tab and choose whether you want your contact displayed in first-name or last-name order. Tap the **Mail, Contacts...** button in the upper left corner to save your settings changes.

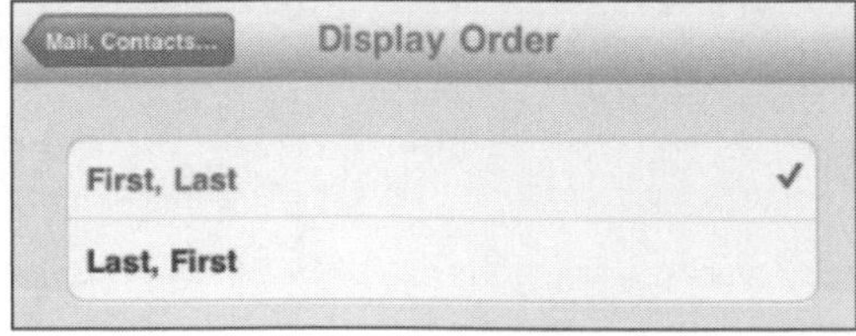


## Searching for Global Address List (GAL) Contacts

Open your Contacts app as you normally would and touch the **Groups** button in the top left corner. Look for the group that has **Global** next to it in your Group list and touch it. This gives you access to your Global Address List if you are connected to your organization's server.

# Contact Troubleshooting

Sometimes, your Contacts app might not work the way you expect. If you don't see all your contacts, review the steps in the Chapter 3: "Sync Your iPad with iTunes" or Chapter 24: "Other Sync Methods" on how to sync with your address book application. Make sure you have selected **All Groups** in the settings in iTunes.

**TIP:** If you are syncing with another contact application, such as **Contacts** in Gmail, make sure you select the option closest to **All Contacts** rather than a subset like a particular group.

## When Global Address List Contacts Don't Show up (For Microsoft Exchange Users)

First, make sure you are connected to a Wi-Fi or 3G cellular data network.

Next, check your Exchange settings and verify you have the correct server and login information. To do so, tap the **Settings** button, then scroll to and touch **Mail, Contacts and Calendar**. Find your Exchange account on the list and touch it to look at the settings. You may need to contact technical support at your organization to make sure your Exchange settings are correct.

Chapter 14

# Your Calendar

The iPad makes the old calendar that used to hang on the fridge obsolete. In this chapter, we will show you how to utilize the **Calendar** app of the iPad to its full potential. We will show you how to schedule appointments, how to manage multiple calendars, how to change views on your calendar and even how to deal with meeting invitations.

**NOTE:** Most of this chapter we talk about syncing your iPad calendar with another calendar because it is nice to have your calendar accessible on your iPad and other places. If you choose, you can also use your iPad in a 'stand alone' mode, where you do not sync to any other calendar. In this case all the steps we describe of adding events, viewing and managing events all apply equally to you. It is critical, however, that you use the iTunes automatic backup feature to save a copy of your calendar just in case something happens to your iPad.

## Manage Your Busy Life on Your iPad

The **Calendar** app is a powerful and easy to use application that helps you manage your appointments, keep track of what you have to do, set reminder alarms, and even create and respong to meeting invitations (for Exchange users).

## Today's Day and Date Shown on Calendar Icon

The **Calendar** icon is usually right on your iPad **Home** screen. You will quickly notice that your **Calendar** icon changes to show today's date and day of the week. The icon to the right shows that it is a Monday and the 19th of the month.

**TIP:** If you use your iPad's **Calendar** app often, you might want to think about pinning or moving it to the **Bottom** dock – you learned how to do this in the section on docking icons in Chapter 5.

## Syncing or Sharing Your Calendar(s) with Your iPad

If you maintain a calendar on your computer or on a web site such as **Google Calendar**, you can synchronize or share that calendar with your iPad either using iTunes and your sync cable or by setting up a wireless synchronization (see Chapters 3 and 24 for more information on syncing).

After you set up the calendar sync, all of your computer calendar appointments will be synced with your iPad calendar automatically, based on your sync settings (see Figure 14–1).

If you use iTunes to sync with your calendar (e.g., **Microsoft Outlook**, **Entourage**, or Apple's **iCal**), your appointments will be transferred or synced every time you connect your iPad to your computer.

If you use another method to sync (e.g., **Mobile Me**, **Exchange**, or similar), this sync is wireless and automatic, and it will most likely happen without you having to do anything after the initial setup process.

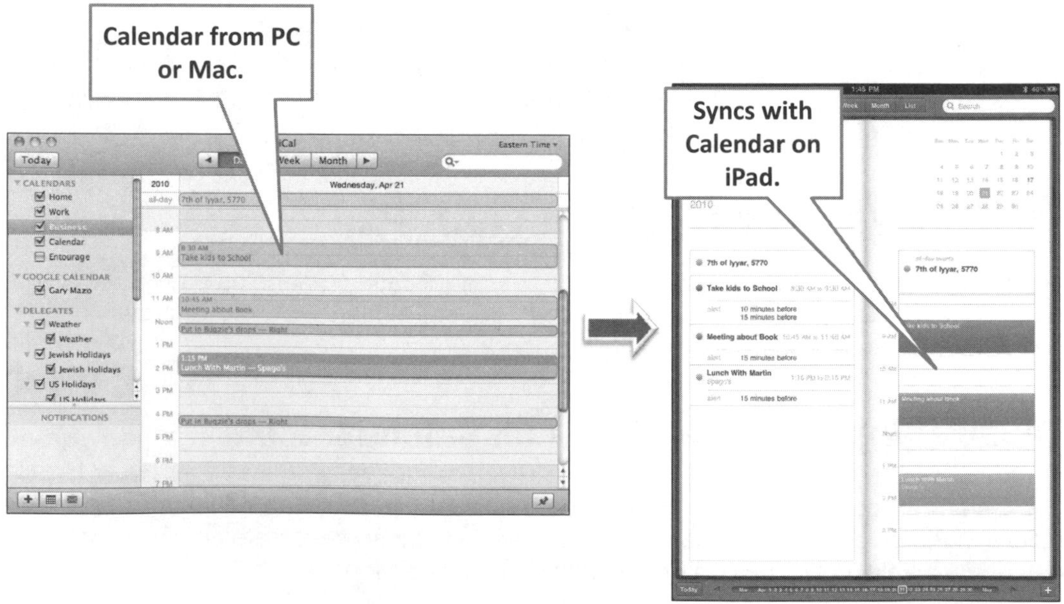


***Figure 14–1.*** *Syncing PC or Mac Calendar to iPad*

## Viewing Your Schedule and Getting Around

The default view for the Calendar is your **Day** view. It will show you at a glance any upcoming appointments for your day. Appointments are shown in your calendar (see Figure 14–2). If you happen to have several different calendars that you have set up on your computer, such as **Work** and **Home**, then you will see these as separate colors on your iPad's calendar.

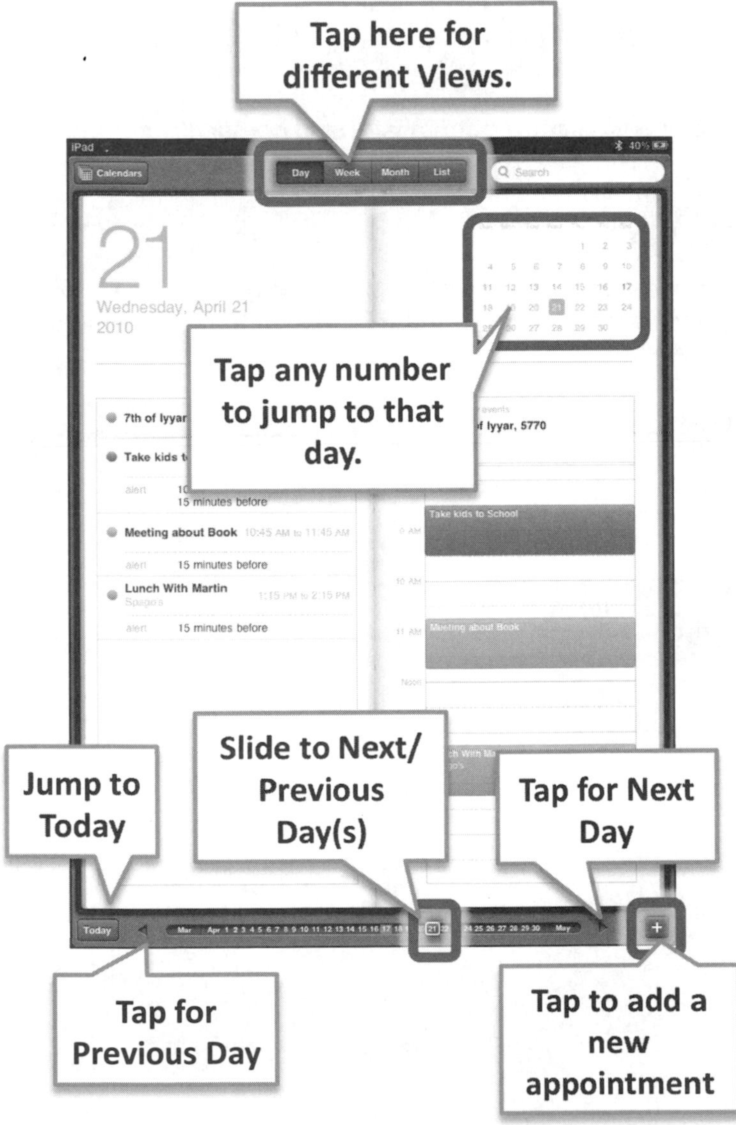


**Figure 14–2.** *The Calendar Day View Layout*

You can manipulate the calendar in various ways:

**Move a day at a time** – If you tap the triangles next to the **Slider** at the bottom, you move forward or backward a day.

**Change views** – Use the **Day**, **Week**, **Month**, and **List** buttons at the top to change the view.

> **TIP:** Drag the slider at the bottom by moving left or right to advance quickly through days.

**Jump to today** – Use the Today button at the bottom left-hand corner.

## The Calendar's Four Views

Your iPad's **Calendar** app comes with four views: **Day**, **Week**, **Month**, and **List**. You can switch views by tapping the name of the view at the bottom of the screen. Here's a quick overview of the four views.

**Day view** – When you start the **Calendar** app, the default view is usually the **Day** view. This allows you to quickly see everything you have scheduled for the day. At the top of the **Calendar** app are buttons to change the view.

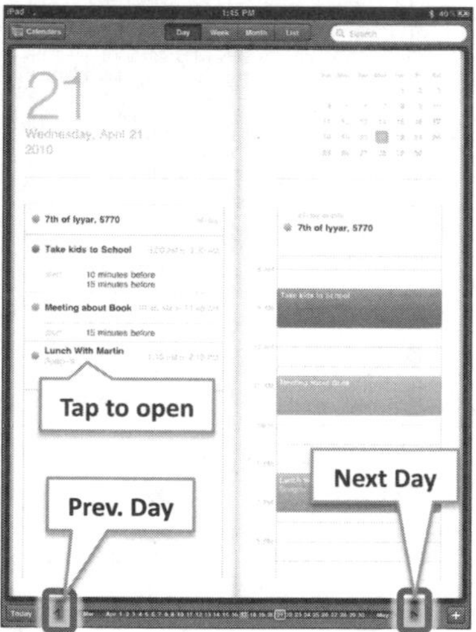

**List view or Agenda view** – Touch the **List** view button at the top, and you can see a list of your appointments along the left-hand side.

Depending on how much you have scheduled, you could see the next day or even the next week's worth of scheduled events.

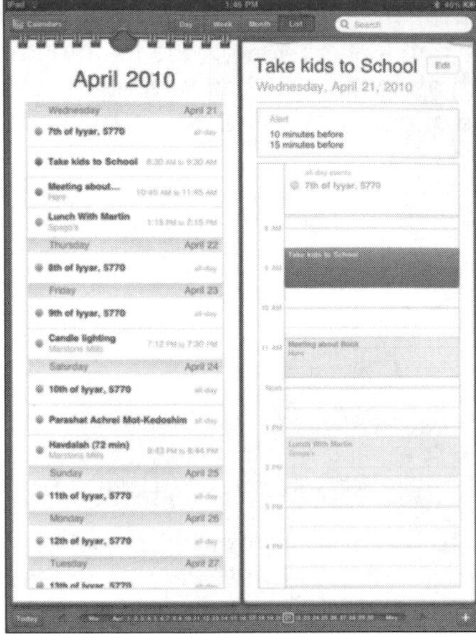


**Week view** – Touch the **Week** view button at the top, and you can see all your appointments for the week.

Similarly, tap any appointment to see details about that appointment.

Once you see the details, you can tap the **Edit** button to change them.

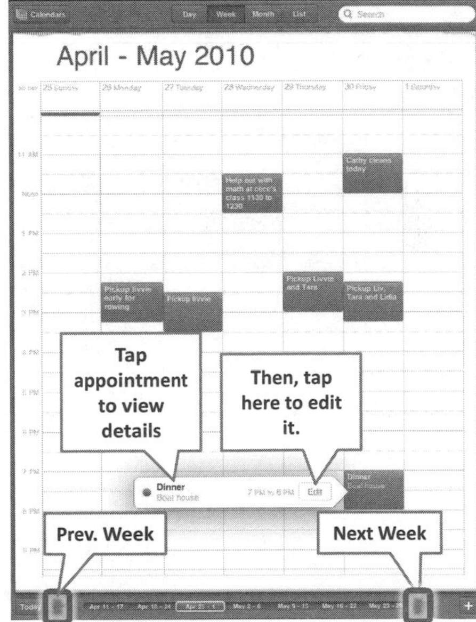

**Month view** – Touch the **Month** view and you can see a layout of the full month. Days with appointments have a small dot in them. The current day will show up highlighted in blue.

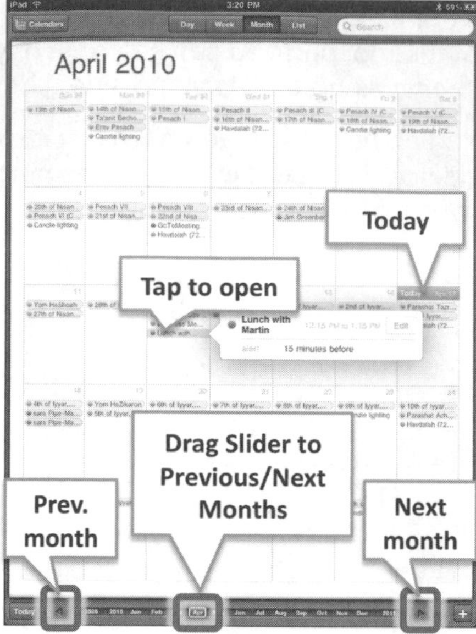


> **Tip**: Double-tap on any day to jump to the **Day** view for that date. To return to **Today** view, just touch the **Today** tab at the bottom left.
>
> Today

**Go to the next month** – Tap the triangle to the right of the **Month** slider at the bottom.

**Go to the previous month** – Tap the triangle to the left of the **Month** slider.

To advance days in **Day** view, just touch the arrows to either side of the **Date** slider at the bottom.

> **NOTE:** While you can scroll in the **Calendar** app, you cannot swipe through your days, which runs counter to what you might expect.

## Working with Several Calendars

Your iPad's **Calendar** app can track various calendars. The number of calendars you see depends on how you set up your synchronization using iTunes or other sync methods. In the example that follows, we have categorized personal appointments in our **Home** calendar and categorized work appointments in a separate **Work** calendar.

In the appointments in our **Calendar** app, we have our **Home** calendar appointments showing up in red and our **Work** appointments in orange or green.

When you set up your **Sync** settings, you were able to specify which calendars you wanted to sync with your iPad. You can customize your calendar further by following these instructions.

**Changing the colors** – You will need to change the color of the calendar in the program on your computer that is synced to your iPad; this will change the colors on your iPad.

**Adding a new calendar** – It's a two-step process to add a new calendar to sync with your iPad.

1. Set up that new calendar on your computer's **Calendar** program.
2. Adjust your Sync settings to make sure this new calendar syncs to your iPad.

**Viewing only one calendar** – To view just one calendar at a time, tap the **Calendars** button at the top and select only the calendar you wish to see.

# Adding New Calendar Appointments/Events

You can easily add new appointments right on your iPad, and they will be synced (or shared with) your computer the next time the sync takes place.

## Adding a New Appointment

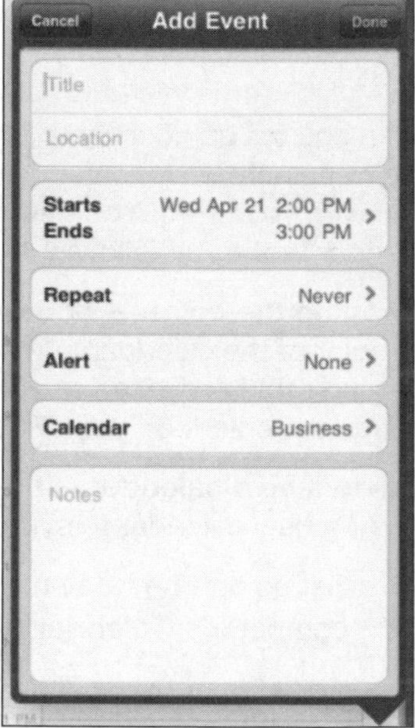


Your instinct will most likely be to try to touch the screen at a particular time to set an appointment; unfortunately, this is not how setting appointments work.

To add a new calendar event from any **Calendar** view, follow these steps.

1. First, tap the + icon at the bottom right corner of the screen. The **Add Event** screen will now show.

2. Next, touch the box marked **Title** and **Location**.

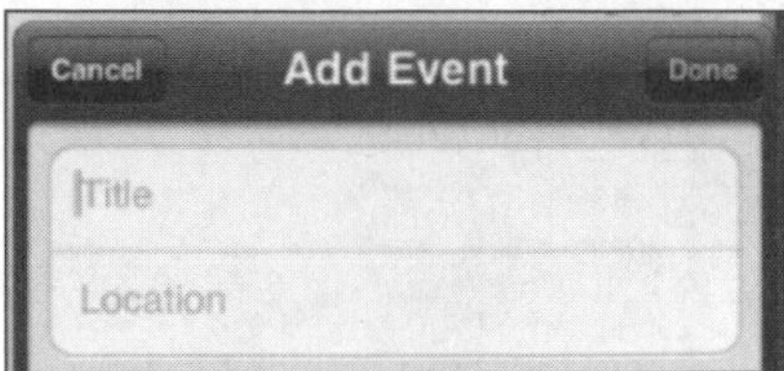


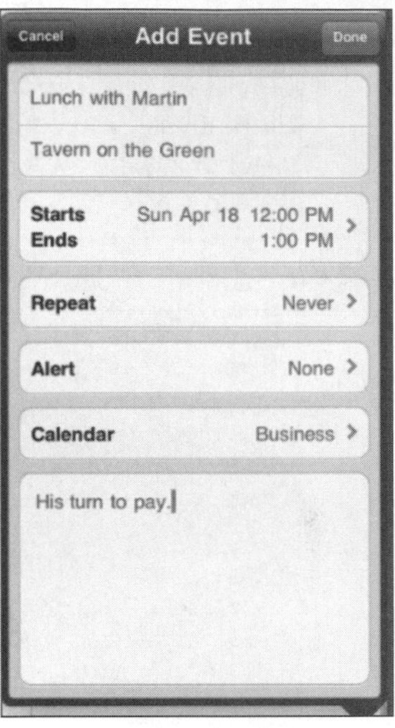


3. Type in a title for the event and the location (optional). You might type "Meet with Martin" as the title and input the location as "Office."
4. Or, you might choose to type "Lunch with Martin" and then choose a very expensive restaurant in New York City.
5. Touch the blue **Done** button in the upper right corner to return to the **Add Event** screen.

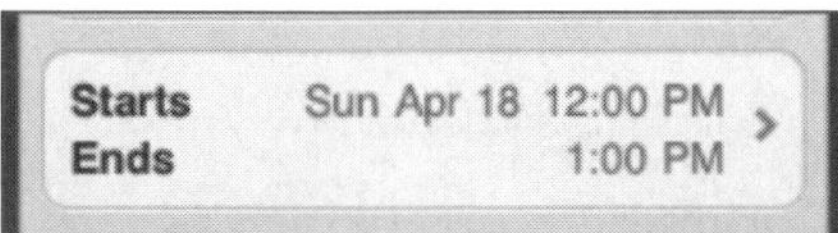


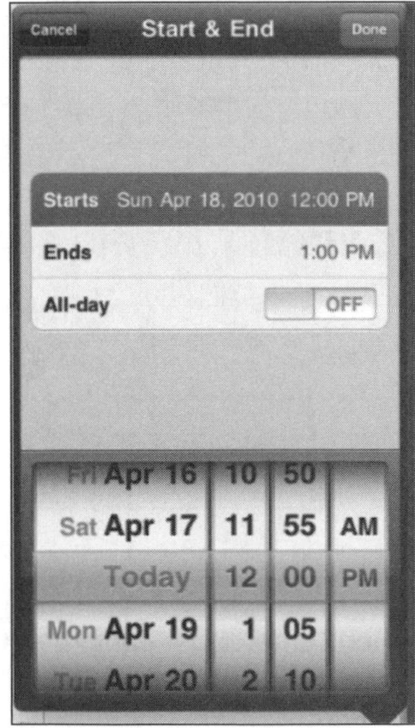


6. Touch the **Starts** or **Ends** tab to adjust the event timing. To change the start time, touch the **Starts** field to highlight it in blue. Then, move the rotating dials at the bottom to reflect the correct date and start time of the appointment.

7. To change the end time, touch the **Ends** field and use the rotating dials.

   Alternatively, you can set an all-day event by touching the switch next to **All-day** to set it to **ON**.

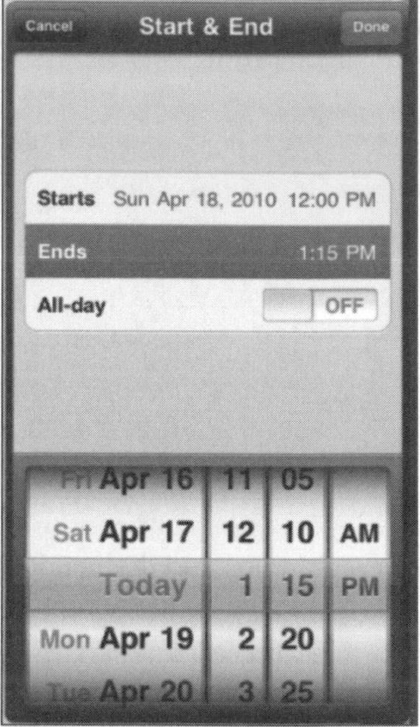

NOTE: You will see a tab labeled **Invitees** before the **Repeat** tab only if you sync to an Exchange calendar. We show you how to use this Invitees tab to invite people to calendar events in Chapter 24: "Other Sync Methods."

## Recurring Events and Alerts (Alarms)

Some of your appointments happen every day, week, or month at the same time. If the appointment you are scheduling is a repeating or recurring appointment, just touch the **Repeat** tab and then select the correct option from the list.

Touch **Done** to get back to the main **Event** screen.

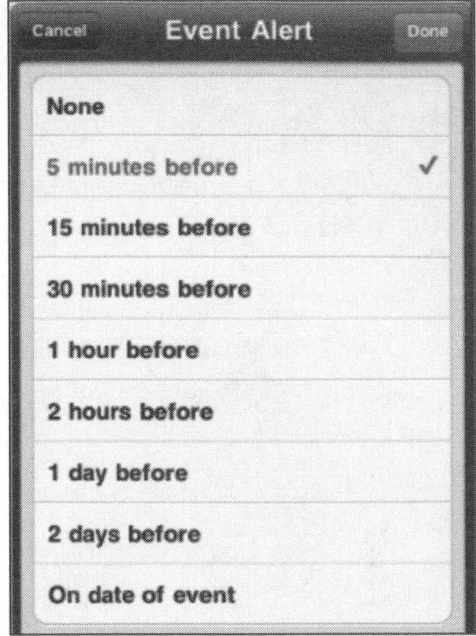


An audible reminder of an upcoming appointment – an *alert* – can help keep you from forgetting an important event. Follow these steps to create an alert.

1. Touch the **Alert** tab and then select the option for a reminder alarm. You can have no alarm at all or set a time anytime from five minutes before the event all the way to two days before – whatever works best for you.
2. Touch **Done** to get back to the main **Event** screen.
3. After you add an alert, you are given the option to add a second (optional) alert.

This can be really useful if you need a second reminder to ensure you do not miss the event.

For example, if you need to pick up your kids at the bus stop, you might want one alert 15 minutes ahead of time, then a final alert 5 minutes ahead of time, so you can be absolutely certain that you don't miss the pickup.

**TIP:** Another good example of two alerts occurs when you have to take your child out of school for a doctor or dentist appointment.

Set the first alert for the night before to write a note to the school and give it to your child.

Set the second alert for 45 minutes prior to the time, so you can leave enough time to pick up your child and get her to the appointment.

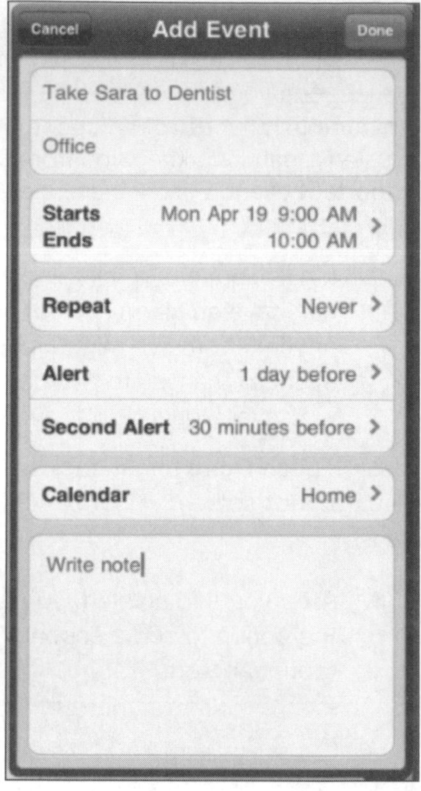


## Choosing Which Calendar to Use

If you use more than one calendar in **Outlook**, **Entourage**, **iCal** or some other program and you sync your iPad with that program, you will have various calendars available to you.

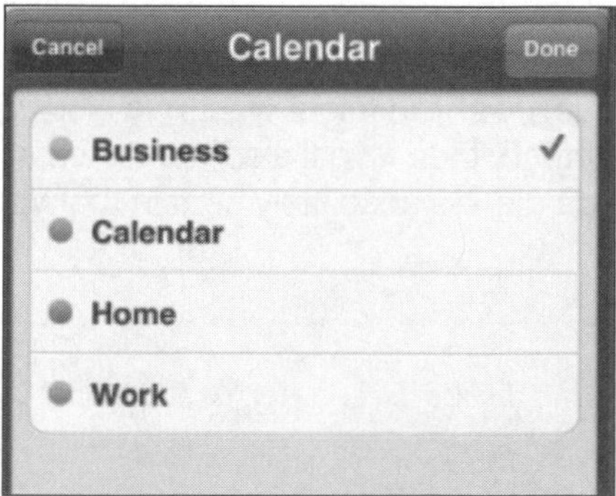


**NOTE:** If you create an event and choose an **Exchange** calendar, you'll have an option to invite other users to the event

Touch the **Calendar** button in the upper left corner to see all your calendars.

Tap the calendar you want to use for this particular event. Usually, the calendar selected is the last one you selected for the previous event you scheduled on your iPad.

## Switching an Event to a Different Calendar

You will notice that when you edit the calendar event on your iPad, you will not have the option to switch calendars.

If you wish to change the scheduled calendar on your iPad, you will need to delete the original event and schedule a new event on the preferred calendar.

**TIP:** To delete the calendar event, tap the event, and then select the **Edit** button. Swipe to the bottom of the **Edit** screen and select **Delete Event**. Next, you will need to confirm that you want to delete the event.

## Adding Notes to Calendar Events

If you want to add some notes to this calendar event, tap Notes and type a few notes.

**TIP:** If this is a meeting somewhere new, you could type or copy/paste some driving directions.

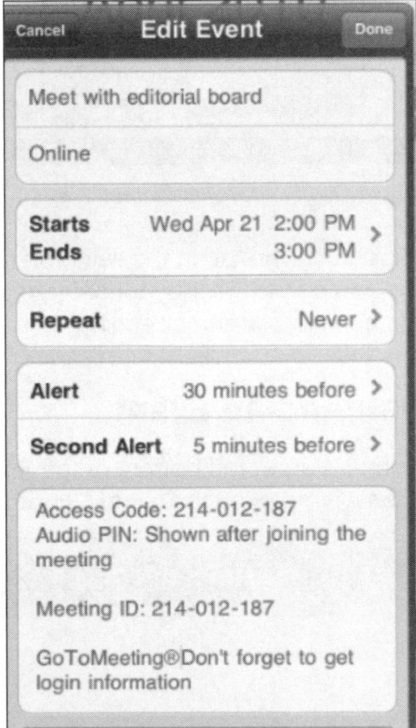

## Editing Appointments

Sometimes, the details of an appointment may change and need to be adjusted (see Figure 14–3). Fortunately, this is an easy task on your iPad.

First, locate the appointment that needs to change and touch it. In the upper right-hand corner, you will see the **Edit** button. Touch **Edit**, and you will return to the **Edit Event** screen showing the appointment details.

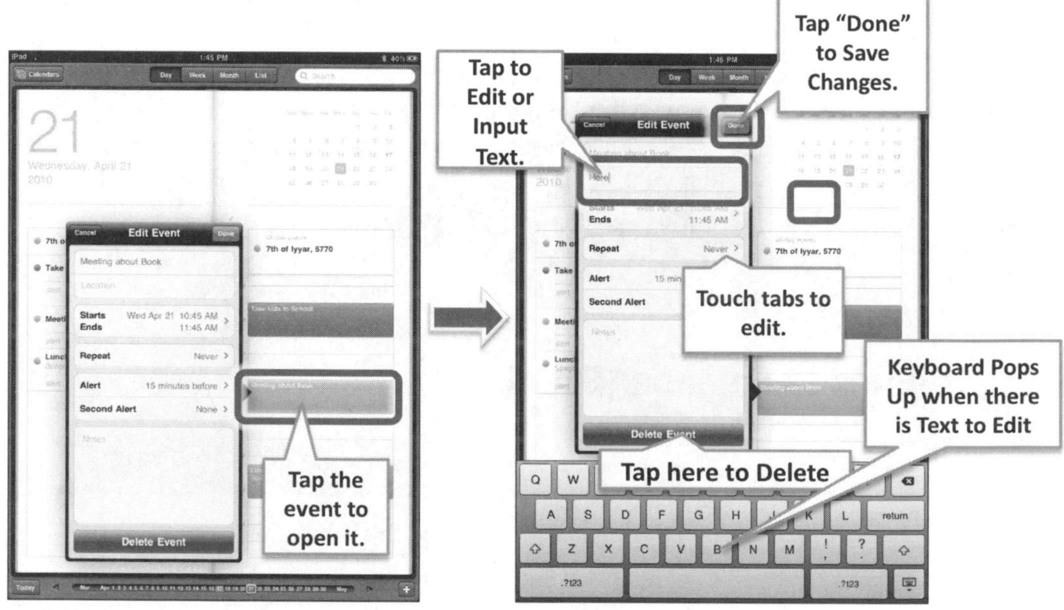


**Figure 14–3.** *Edit an Appointment.*

Just touch the tab in the field you need to adjust. For example, you can change the time of this appointment by touching the **Starts** or **Ends** tab, and then adjusting the time for the event's starting or ending time.

## Deleting an Event

Notice that, at the bottom of the **Edit** screen, you also have the option to delete this event. Simply touch **Delete Event** at the bottom of the screen to do so.

# Meeting Invitations

For those who use Microsoft Exchange, Microsoft Outlook or Entourage regularly, meeting invitations become a way of life. You receive a meeting invitation in your e-mail, you accept the invitation, and then the appointment gets automatically placed in your calendar.

On your iPad, you will see that invitations you Accept get put right into your calendar.

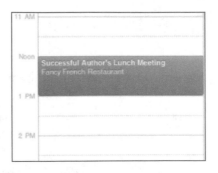

> **NOTE:** If you use an Exchange calendar or Google calendar, you can invite people and reply to meeting invitations on your iPad. See the "Working with the Google or Exchange Calendar" section of Chapter 24 "Other Sync Methods" to learn more.

If you touch the meeting invitation in your calendar, you can see all the details that you need: the dial in number, the meeting ID, and any other details that might be included in the invitation.

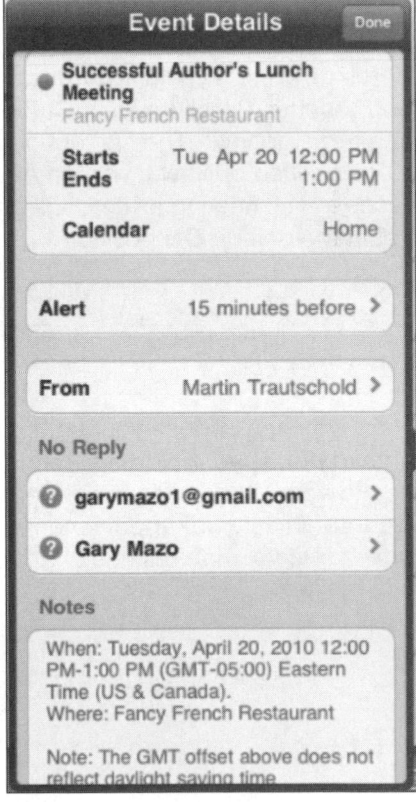

**NOTE:** As of writing, you can accept meeting invitations on your iPad from your Exchange account, and you can create them as long as you choose the **Exchange** calendar. Invitations will also transfer automatically from **Entourage**, **iCal**, or **Outlook** if you have **iTunes** set to sync with those programs.

## Calendar Options

There are just a few options to adjust in your **Calendar** app; you can find these in the **Settings** app. Just touch **Settings** from your **Home** screen.

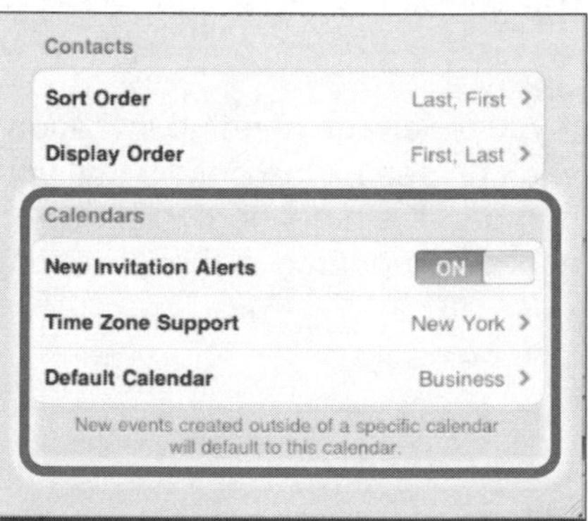


Scroll down to the **Mail, Contacts, Calendars** tab and touch it. Scroll down to **Calendars**, and you will see three options. The first option is a simple switch to be notified of New Invitation Alerts – if you receive any meeting invites, it is good to keep this set in the default **ON** position.

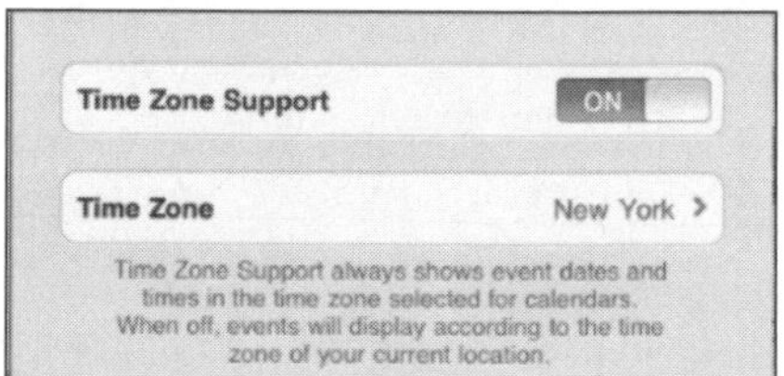

Next, you can choose your time zone. This setting should reflect your **Home** settings from when you set up your iPad. If you are traveling, however, and want to adjust your appointments for a different time zone, you can change this to any other city you would like.

## Changing the Default Calendar

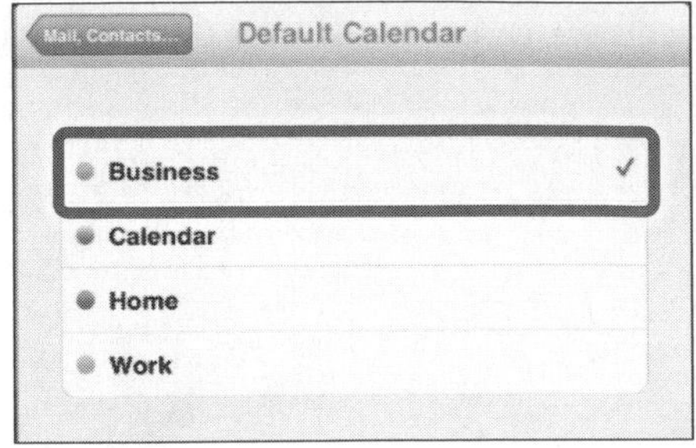


We mentioned earlier that you can have multiple calendars displayed on your iPad. This option allows you to choose which calendar will be your **Default** calendar.

That means that when you go to schedule every new appointment, this calendar will be selected by default.

If you wish to use a different calendar – say, your **Work** calendar – you can change that when you actually set the appointment, as shown earlier in this chapter.

Chapter 15

# Working with Photos

Viewing and sharing your pictures on the iPad is truly a joy, due in large part to the beautiful high-resolution screen and the way it instantly flips the pictures around so others can view them. In this chapter, we discuss the many ways to get pictures onto your iPad. We also show you how you to use the touch screen to navigate through your pictures, and how to zoom in and out and manipulate your photos.

**TIP:** Did you know you can take a picture of the entire screen of your iPad by pressing two keys simultaneously? This is great to show someone a cool app or to prove that you got the high score on Tetris!

How to get it done: Press both the **Home** button and the **Power/Sleep** button on the top right edge. If you have done this correctly, the screen should flash and you'll hear a camera sound. The screen capture you have taken will be in your **Saved Photos** album in the **Photos** app.

## How to Get Photos onto Your iPad

You have many options for loading photos onto your device:

*Sync using iTunes:* Probably the simplest way is to use iTunes to sync photos from your computer. We describe this in detail in Chapter 3: "Sync Your iPad with iTunes."

*Receive as e-mail attachments:* While this is not useful for large numbers of pictures, it works well for one or a few photos. Check out Chapter 12: "Email on your iPad" for more details about how to save attachments. (Once saved, these images show up in the **Saved Photos** album.)

*Save images from the Web:* Sometimes you'll see a great image on a web site. Press and hold it to see the pop-up menu and then select **Save Image**. (Like other saved images, these end up in the **Saved Photos** album.)

*Download images from within an app:* A good example of this is the **Wallpaper** app shown in Chapter 6: "Personalize & Secure your iPad."

*Sync with iPhoto (for Mac users):* If you use a Mac computer, your iPad will most likely sync automatically with iPhoto.

Here are a few steps to get **iPhoto** sync up and running:

1. Connect your iPad and start **iTunes**.
2. Go to the **Photo** tab along the top row of **Sync Options**.
3. Choose the **Albums**, **Events**, **Faces**, or **Places** you want to keep in sync with the iPad.

*Drag and drop (for Windows users):* Once you connect your iPad to your Windows computer, it will appear in Windows Explorer as a **Portable Device**, as shown in Figure 15–1. Here are the steps to follow to drag and drop photos between your iPad and computer.

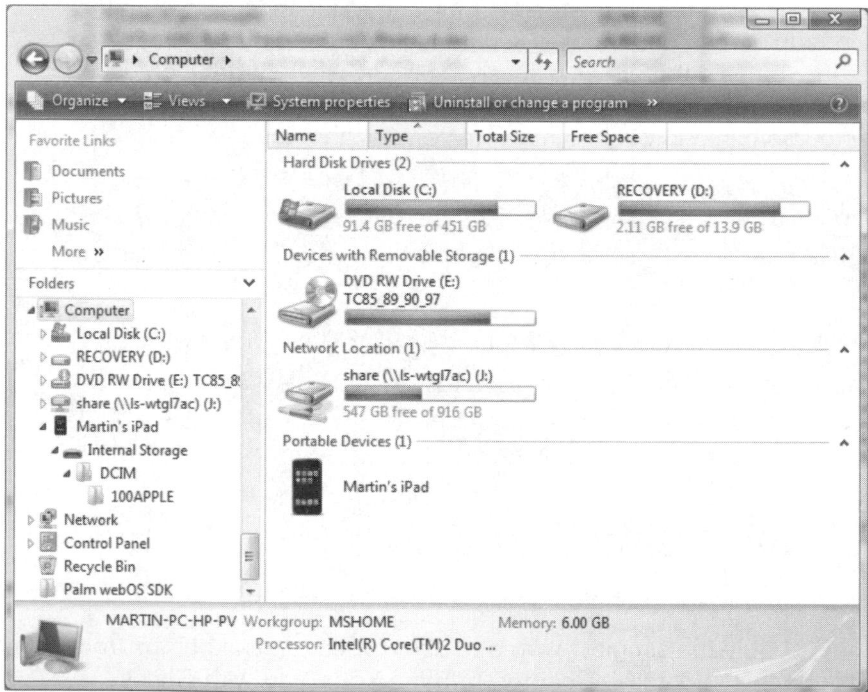


**Figure 15–1.** *Windows Explorer showing the iPad as a Portable Device (connected with USB Cable)*

1. Double-click on the iPad image under **Portable Devices** to open it.
2. Double-click on **Internal Storage** to open it.
3. Double-click on **DCIM** to open it.
4. Double-click on **100APPLE** to open it.
5. You will see all the images in the **Saved Photos** album on your iPad.

6. To copy images to your iPad: Select, then drag and drop images from your computer into this folder to put them on your iPad.
7. To copy images from your iPad, select and drag and drop images out of this folder onto your computer.

**TIP:** Here's how to select multiple images in Windows:

Draw a box around the images, or click on one image and then press Ctrl+A to select them all.
Hold down the Ctrl key and click on individual pictures to select them.
Right-click on one of the selected pictures and choose **Cut** (to move) or **Copy** (to copy) all of the selected images.
To paste the images, press and click on any other disk or folder, such as **My Documents** and navigate to where you want to move or copy the files. Then right-click again and select **Paste.**

## Using Your iPad as an Electronic Picture Frame

We show you how to use your iPad as an electronic picture frame when it is in Locked mode, and how to disable this feature, in our Chapter 6: "Personalize & Secure your iPad".

# Viewing Your Photos

Now that your photos are on your iPad, you have a few very cool ways to look through them and show them to others.

## Launch from the Photos Icon

If you like using your **Photos** icon, you might want to place it in your **Bottom Dock** for easy access if it's not already there (see Chapter 5).

To get started with photos, touch the **Photos** Icon.

The first screen shows your **Photo Albums**, which were created when you set up your iPad and synced with iTunes. In Chapter 3, we showed you how to choose which photos to sync with your iPad. As you make changes to the library on your computer, they will be automatically updated on your iPad.

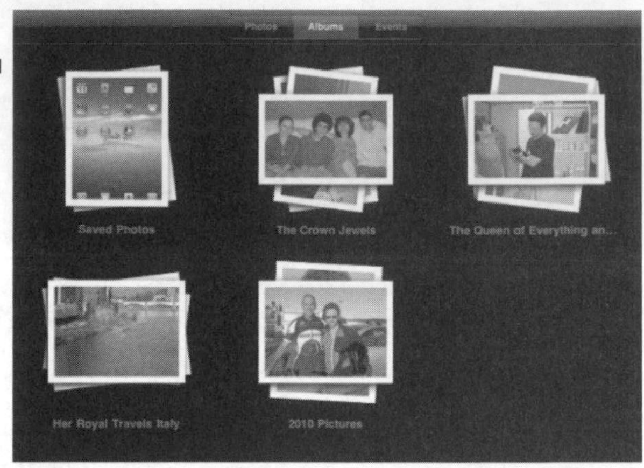


## Choose a Library

From the **Photo Albums** page, touch one of the library buttons to show the photos in that album. We touched the **Photo** library and immediately the screen changed to show us thumbnails of the pictures in this library.

Tap and drag your finger up and down to view all the pictures. You can flick up or down to quickly move throughout the album.

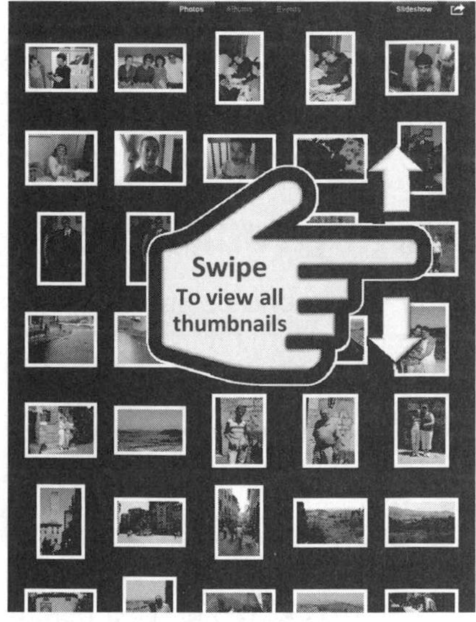

## Preview an Album by Pinching Open

When you're trying to locate a particular image, one of the cool things you can do on your iPad is to preview a particular album by pinching it open.

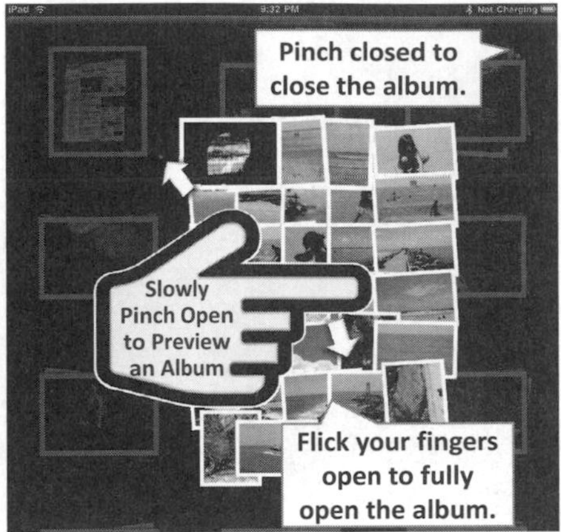
Pinch closed to close the album.
Slowly Pinch Open to Preview an Album
Flick your fingers open to fully open the album.

Place two fingers on the album and slowly "pinch open" your fingers. Notice that all the images spread out across the screen.

If you see the photo you want, continue pinching open to fully open the album. End your pinch with a flick to open the album.

If you don't see the image you want, simply close your fingers again to close the album and then try another one.

**TIP:** You can close an album that is fully open by "pinching closed" across the entire screen of thumbnails.

# Working with Individual Pictures

Once you locate the picture you want to view, just tap on it. The picture then loads into the screen.

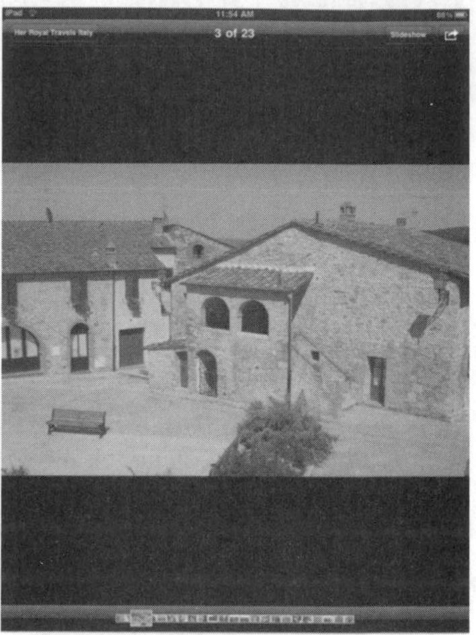


**NOTE:** Usually, your pictures will not take up the full screen on your iPad especially if they were shot in landscape mode.

**TIP:** The picture to the right was shot in landscape mode, so to see it in a full screen you'll have to turn your iPad on its side or just double-tap it to fill the screen.

## Move Between Pictures

The swipe gesture is used to move from one picture to the next. Just swipe your finger left or right across the screen, and you can move through your pictures.

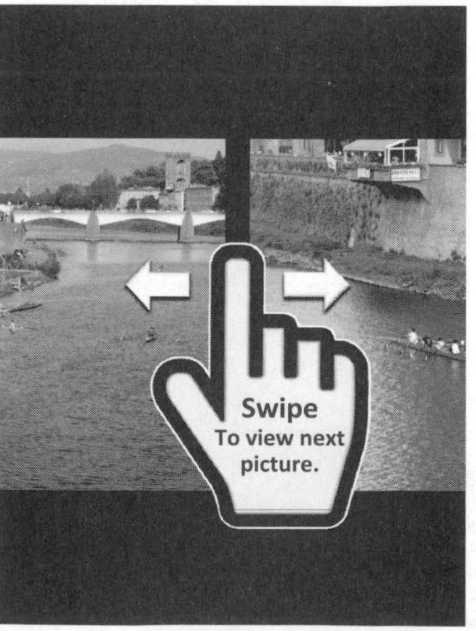


**TIP:** Drag your finger slowly to move more gradually through that the picture library.

When you reach the end of an album, just tap the screen once and you'll see a tab in the upper left corner that has the name of the photo album. Touch that tab and you'll return to the thumbnail

Her Royal Travels Italy

page of that particular album. You can also pinch to return to the thumbnail page.

To get back to your main photo album page, just touch the button that says **Albums** in the top left corner.

## Use the Thumbnail Bar to Move Between Pictures

Instead of swiping left and right to move between your pictures, you can bring up the soft-key controls on the screen. To do this, simply tap the screen once. Tap it again to make the soft keys disappear.

Along the very bottom of the screen, you'll see a small thumbnail bar over which you can gently slide your finger (Figure 15–2). You can quickly slide through the whole album using this bar. You can also just tap on a thumbnail to see that particular picture.

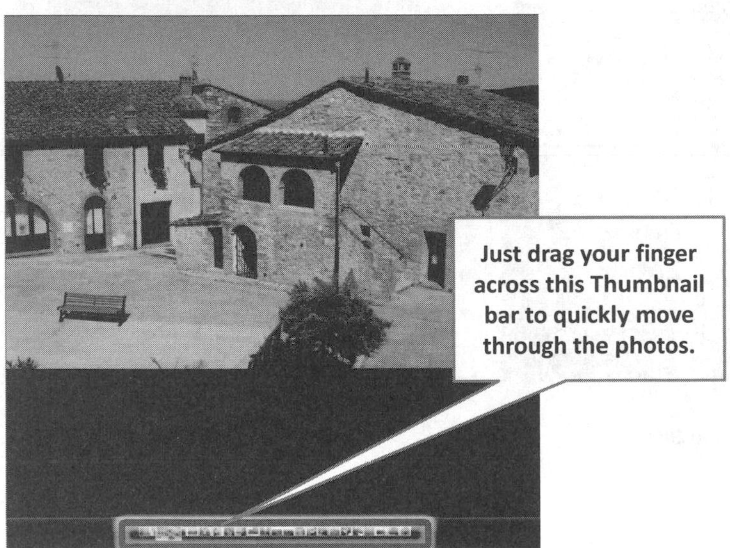

Just drag your finger across this Thumbnail bar to quickly move through the photos.

**Figure 15–2.** *Use the thumbnail bar to advance through pictures*

# Zooming in and Out of Pictures

As described in the "Quick Start Guide" section of the book, there are two ways to zoom in and out of pictures on your iPad: double-tapping and pinching.

## Double-Tapping

As the name describes, this is a quick double-tap on the screen to zoom in on the picture as shown in Figure 15–3. You will be zoomed in to the spot where you double-tap. To zoom out, just double-tap once more.

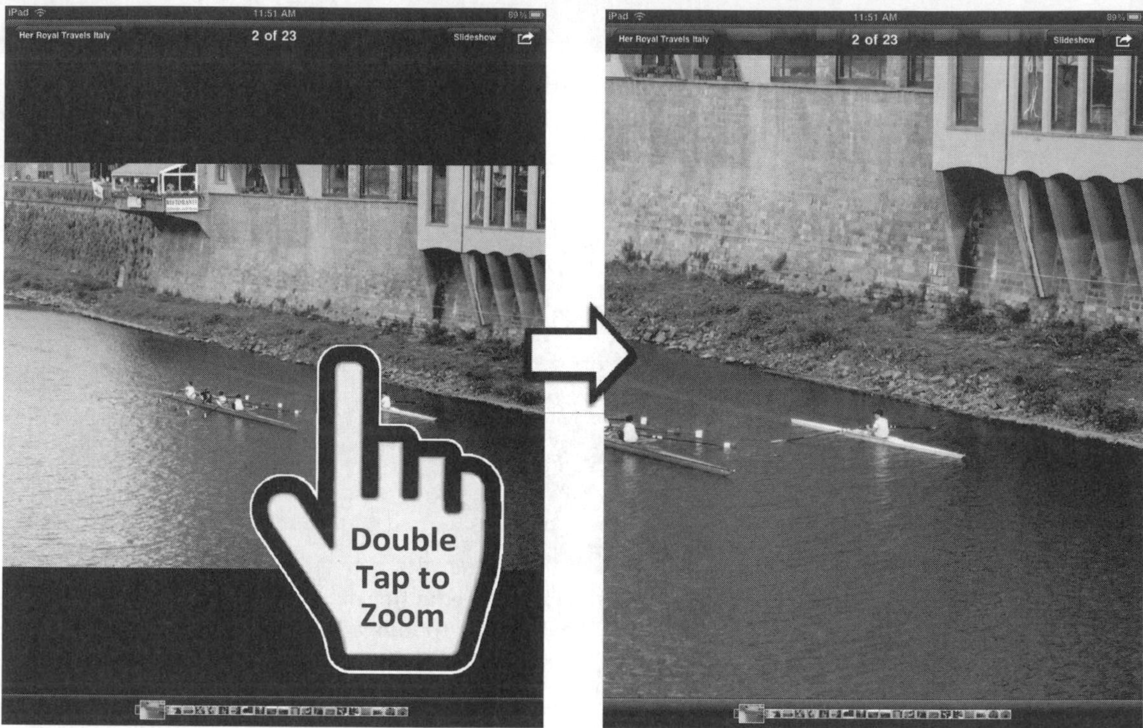


**Figure 15–3.** *Double-tap to a picture to zoom*

## Pinching

Also described in the "Quick Start Guide" section of this book, pinching is a much more precise form of zoom. While double-tapping only zooms in or out to one set level, pinching really allows you to zoom in or out just a little bit or quite a lot.

To pinch, hold your thumb and forefinger close together and then slowly (while touching the screen) separate them, making the picture larger. To zoom in, start with your thumb and forefinger apart and move them together.

> **NOTE:** Once you have activated the zoom using either method, you will not be able to easily swipe through your pictures until you return the picture back to its standard size.

# Viewing a Slideshow

You can view the pictures in your photo album as a slide show if you'd like. Just tap the screen once to bring up the on-screen soft keys. In the upper right corner is a **Slideshow** button—just touch once to start the slide show. You can start the slide show from either the **Photo Library** screen of from any picture you are viewing.

**Slideshow Options** let you adjust the how long each picture remains on the screen, as well as choose music, transitions and other settings as shown in Figure 15–4. To end the slide show, just tap the screen.

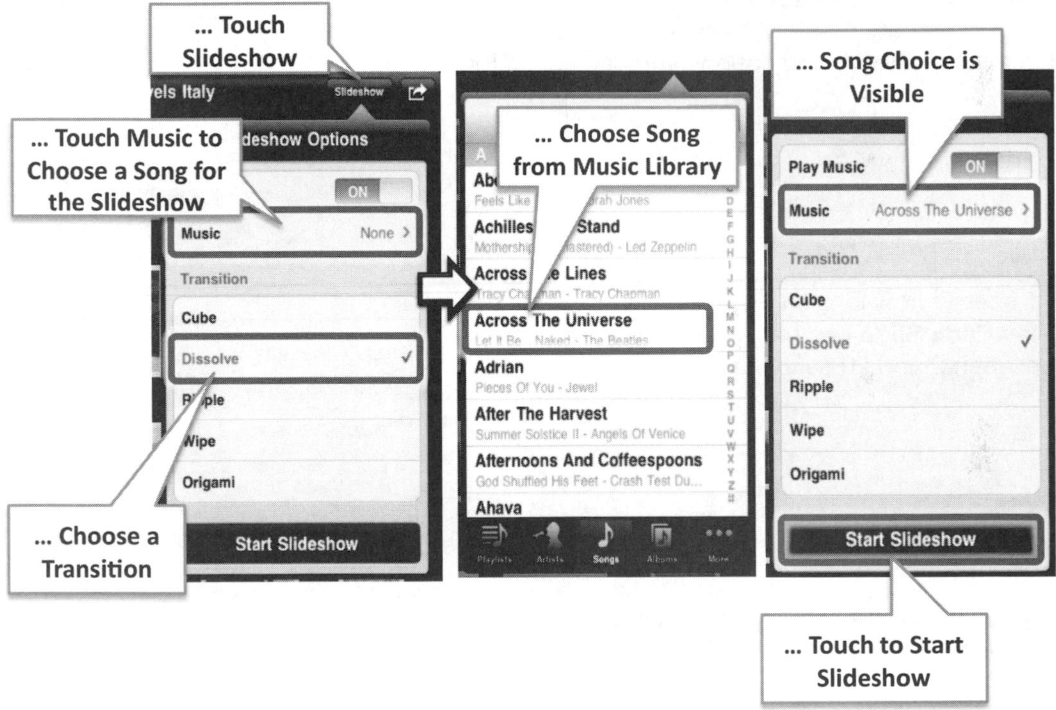


**Figure 15–4.** *Configuring your slide show*

## Adjusting Slideshow Options

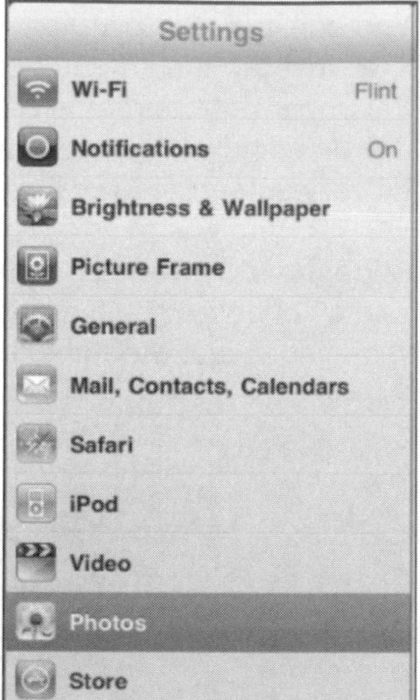


To configure a slideshow, you will need to change your settings. To do so, touch the **Settings** icon on the **Home Screen**.

Scroll down to the **Photos** tab and touch the screen. You will then see the various options you can use, including four options you can adjust for slideshows.

To specify how long to play each slide, touch the **Play Each Slide For** tab. You can choose a range between 2 and 20 seconds.

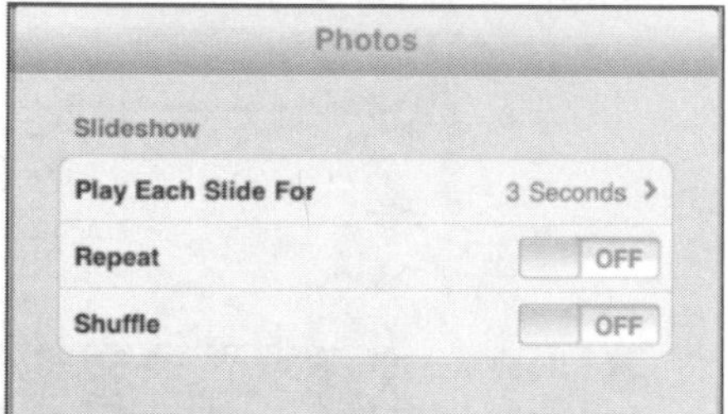


If you want pictures to repeat in a slideshow, just move the **Repeat** switch to **ON**.

If you want the pictures to move in an order different from the way they are listed, just choose **Shuffle** and, just like the Shuffle command on the music player, the pictures will play in a random order.

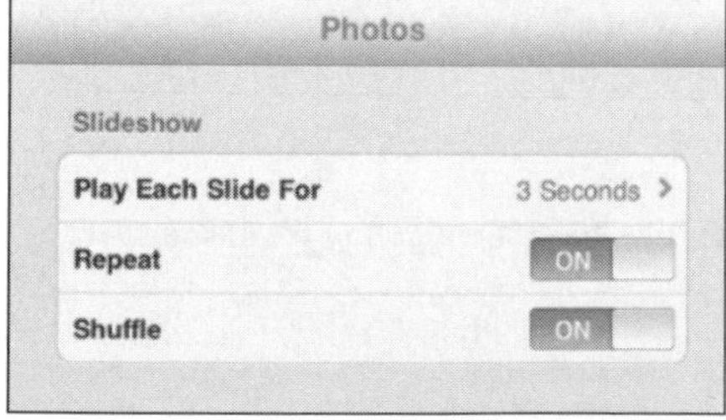

# Using a Picture as Your iPad Wallpaper

We show you how to select and use a picture as your iPad wallpaper (and more wallpaper options) in Chapter 6: "Personalize & Secure your iPad".

> **NOTE:** You can have different pictures for your **Home Screen** and **Lock Screen** or use the same picture for both.

# E-mailing a Picture

As long as you have an active Internet connection (Wi-Fi or 3G; see our Wi-Fi and 3G Connections chapter), you can send any picture in your photo collection via e-mail. Tap the **Share** button on the top right edge of the black bar on the top of your screen. If you don't see the black bar, tap the screen once. (Figure 15-5).

Choose the **Email Photo** option and the Mail app will automatically launch (Figure 15–5).

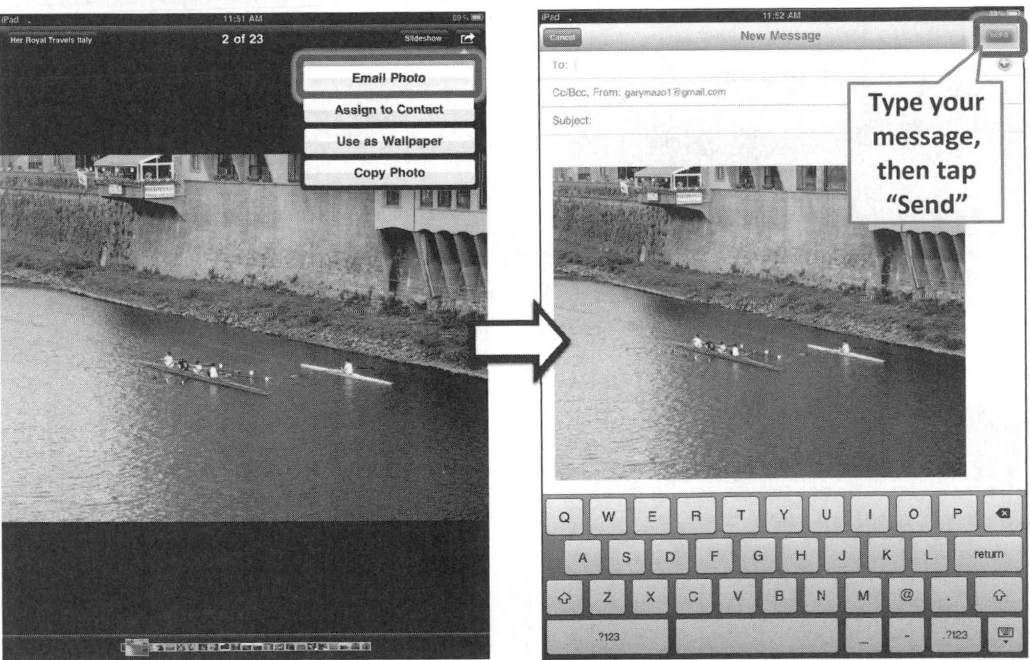


**Figure 15–5.** *Emailing a photo*

Touch the **To** field as you did in the "Email on your iPad" chapter and select the contact to receive the picture. Tap the blue **+** button to add a contact.

Type in a subject and a message and then touch **Send** in the upper right corner—that's all there is to it.

# E-mail, Copy, or Delete Several Pictures At Once

If you have several pictures you want to e-mail, copy, or delete at the same time, you can do it from the thumbnail view, as shown in Figure 15–6.

> **NOTE:** The **copy** function allows you to copy and paste multiple pictures into an e-mail or other app. **Share** renames the image to photo.png; **copy-and-paste** leaves it with the DCIM folder file name.png. **Share** also reduces the pixel size of large photos while **copy** retains the original pixel size.
>
> At publishing time, you could only **share** or **e-mail** a maximum of five pictures. This may change with future software. You can, however, copy more than five pictures.

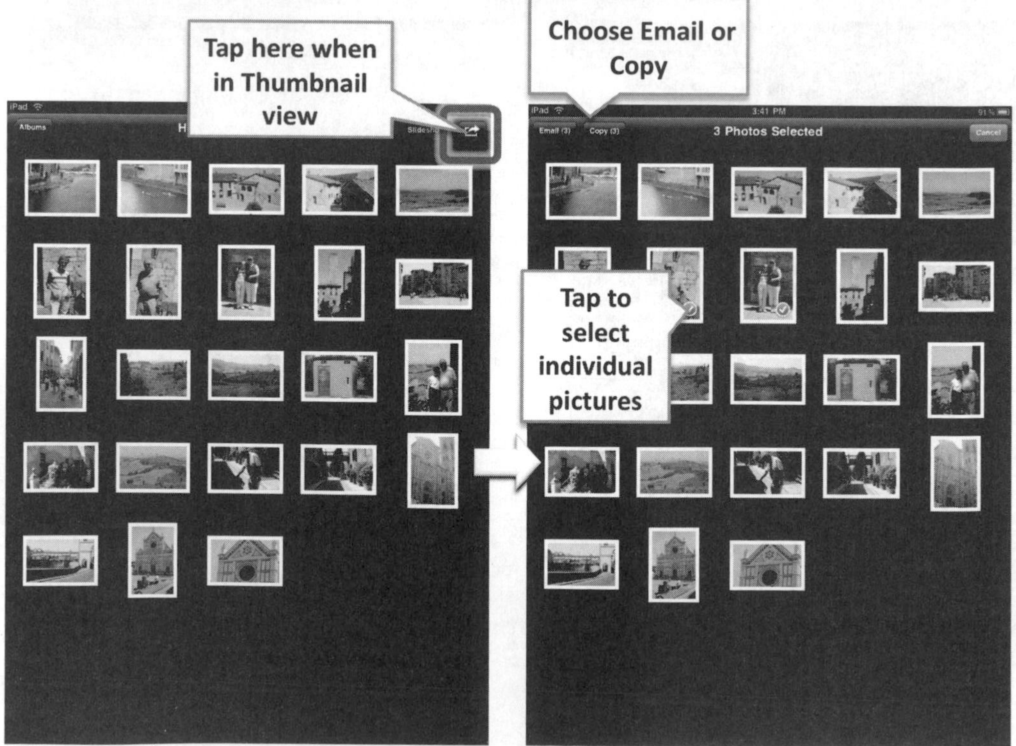


**Figure 15–6.** *Selecting multiple images to e-mail*

## Assign a Picture to a Contact

In Chapter 13, we talked about adding a picture when editing a contact. You can also find a picture you like and assign it to a contact. First, find the photo you want to use.

As we did with wallpaper, and e-mailing a photo, tap the **Options** button—the one furthest to the right of the upper row of soft keys. If you don't see the icons, tap the screen once.

When you touch the **Options** button, you'll see a drop-down of choices: **Email Photo**, **Assign to Contact**, **Use as Wallpaper** and **Copy Photo**.

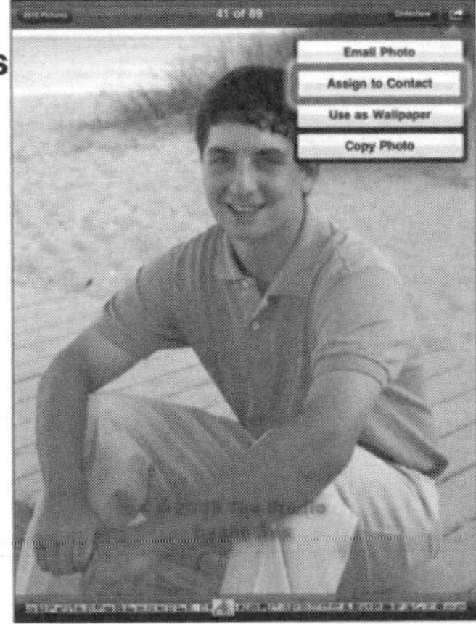


Touch the **Assign to Contact** button.

You will see your Contacts on the screen. You can either perform a search using the search bar at the top or just scroll through your contacts.

Once you find the contact to which you would like to add the picture, touch the name.

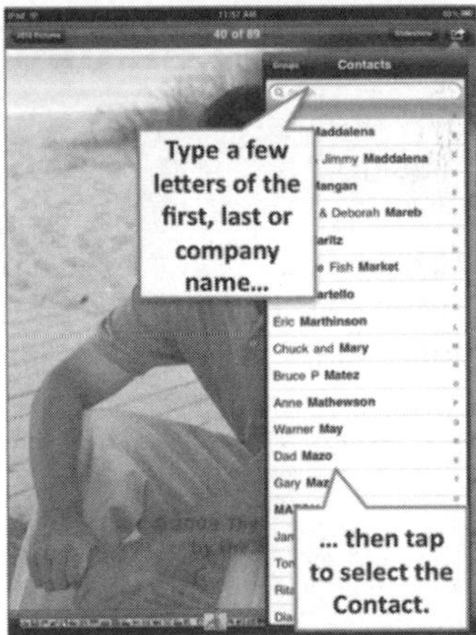

You will then see the **Move and Scale** screen. Tap and drag the picture to move it; use pinch to zoom in or out.

When you have it just as you want, touch the **Use** button to assign the picture to that contact.

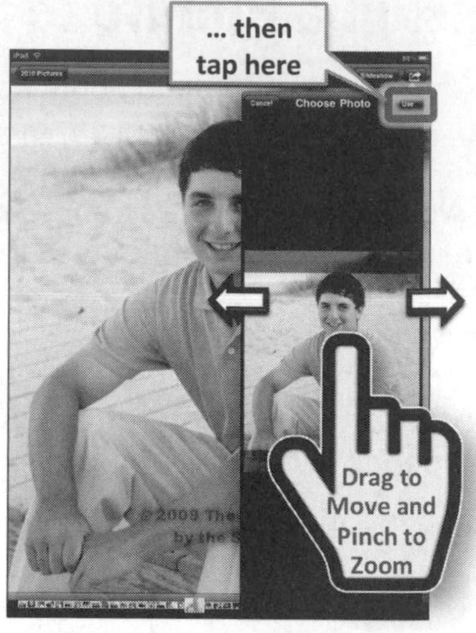


**NOTE:** You will return to your **Photo Library**, not to the contact. If you want to check that the picture did get set to your contact, exit the **Photo** app, start the **Contact** app, and then search for that contact.

## Deleting a Picture

Why are there some pictures you can't delete from your iPad (the **Trash Can** icon is missing)?

You'll notice that the **Trash Can** icon is not visible for any photo that is synced from iTunes. You can only delete such pictures from your computer library. Then, the next time you sync your iPad, they will be deleted.

When you are looking through pictures in your **Saved Photos** (which is not synced with iTunes, but is comprised of pictures you save from an e-mail or download from the Web), you'll see the **Trash Can** icon in the bottom icon bar. This **Trash Can** icon does not appear when you are viewing pictures from your **Photos Library** or other synced albums.

If you don't see the bottom row of icons, tap the photo once to activate them. Then tap the **Trash Can** icon. You will be prompted with the option to delete the picture.

Touch **Delete Photo** and the picture will be deleted from your iPad.

## Downloading Pictures from Web Sites

We have shown you how you can transfer pictures from your computer to your iPad and save them from e-mails. You can also download and save pictures right from the Web onto your iPad.

> **CAUTION:** We strongly encourage you to respect image copyright laws as you download and save images from the Web. Unless the web site indicates an image is free, you should check with the web site owner before downloading and saving any pictures.

## Find a Picture to Download

The iPad makes it easy to copy and save images from web sites. This can be handy when you are looking for a new image to use as wallpaper on your iPad.

First, tap the **Safari** web browser icon and type a search for iPad wallpaper to locate a few sites that might have some interesting possibilities. (See our Chapter 11: "Surfing the Web with Safari" for help.)

Once you find a picture you want to download and save, tap, and hold it to bring up a new menu of options that includes **Save Image** (among others), as shown in Figure 15–7. Choose this option to save the picture in your Saved Photos album.

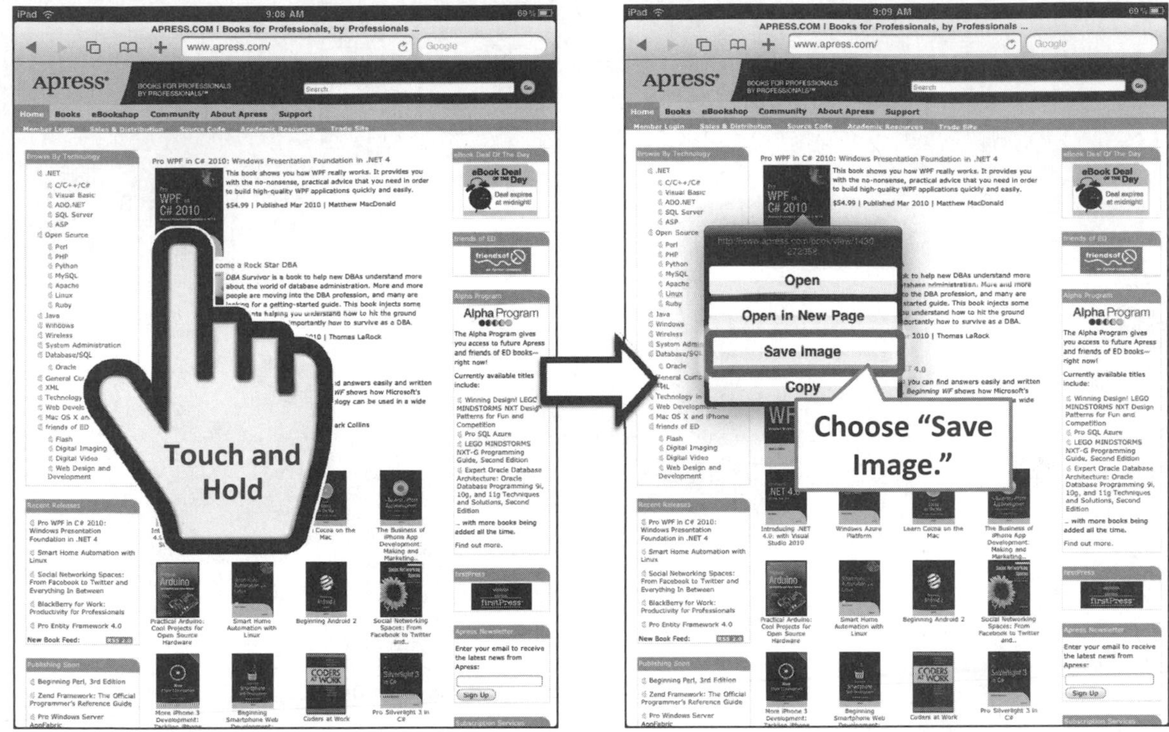


**Figure 15–7.** *Saving an image from a web site.*

Now touch your **Photo** icon and you should see the picture in the **Saved Photos** album.

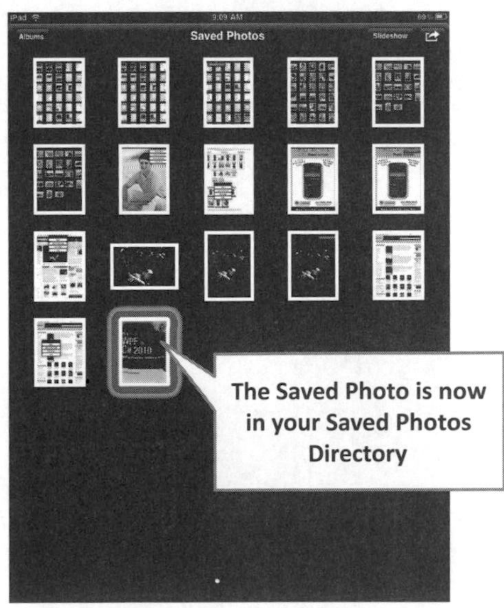

Chapter 16

# Maps

Mapping on your iPad, whether you have a 3G+Wi-Fi or a Wi-Fi-only model, is pretty amazing. As we explore the power of the Maps app in this chapter, you'll see how to find your location on the map—even if you're just using Wi-Fi. You'll learn how to change views between classic, satellite, hybrid, and terrain. You'll also see how, if you need to find out the best route, you can check out the traffic and construction view using Maps. If you want to find the closest pizza restaurant, golf course, or hotel to your destination, that's easy, too. And you can use Google's Street View right from your iPad to help you get to your destination. It is easy to add an address you have mapped to your contacts. There's also a digital compass feature that can be quite handy and is fun to play with.

## Getting Started with Maps

The beauty of the iPad is that the programs are designed to work with one another. You've already seen how your Contacts are linked to the **Maps** app.

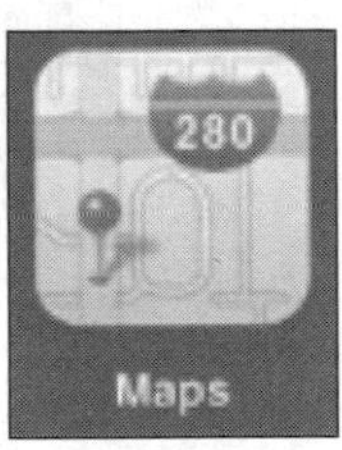


The **Maps** app is powered by Google Maps—the leader in mobile mapping technology. With **Maps** you can locate your position, get directions, search for things nearby, see traffic, and much more.

Simply touch the **Maps** icon to get started.

## Determining Your Location (the Blue Dot)

When you start the **Maps** program, you can have it start at your current location.

1. Tap the small circle at the center of the upper navigation bar.

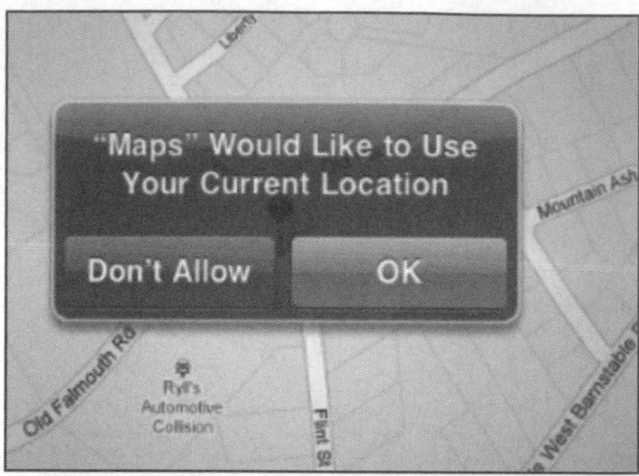


2. Maps will ask to use your current location—touch **OK** or **Don't Allow.**

   We suggest choosing **OK**, which makes it much easier to find directions from or to your current location.

**NOTE:** Even if you only have the Wi-Fi-equipped iPad, it will still be able to find your approximate location. The Wi-Fi iPad uses Skyhook router-based locations. This is usually accurate, but if someone moved to a new state with an old router, the iPad might think you are still in that old location.

## Various Map Views

The default view for **Maps** is **Classic,** a basic map with a generic background and streets shown with their names. **Maps** can also show you a **Satellite** view, or a combination of **Satellite** and **Classic** called **Hybrid**. There's also the new **Terrain** view, which looks like a relief map. Finally, another view called **List** view appears only when you perform a search that generates a list of turn-by-turn directions. You can switch among all the views using the steps below.

## Changing Your Map Views

To change from one map view to another:

1. Touch the turned-up edge of the map in the lower right corner.
2. The corner of the map turns up to reveal buttons for views, traffic, pin, and more. (See Figure 16–1.)
3. Tap the view you'd like to switch to:
   - **Classic**—a regular map with street names (Figure 16–2).
   - **Satellite**—a satellite picture with no street names (Figure 16–1).
   - **Hybrid**—a combination of satellite and classic, i.e., a satellite view with street names (Figure 16–2).
   - **Terrain**—a relief map showing the terrain such as mountains. (Figure 16–3.)

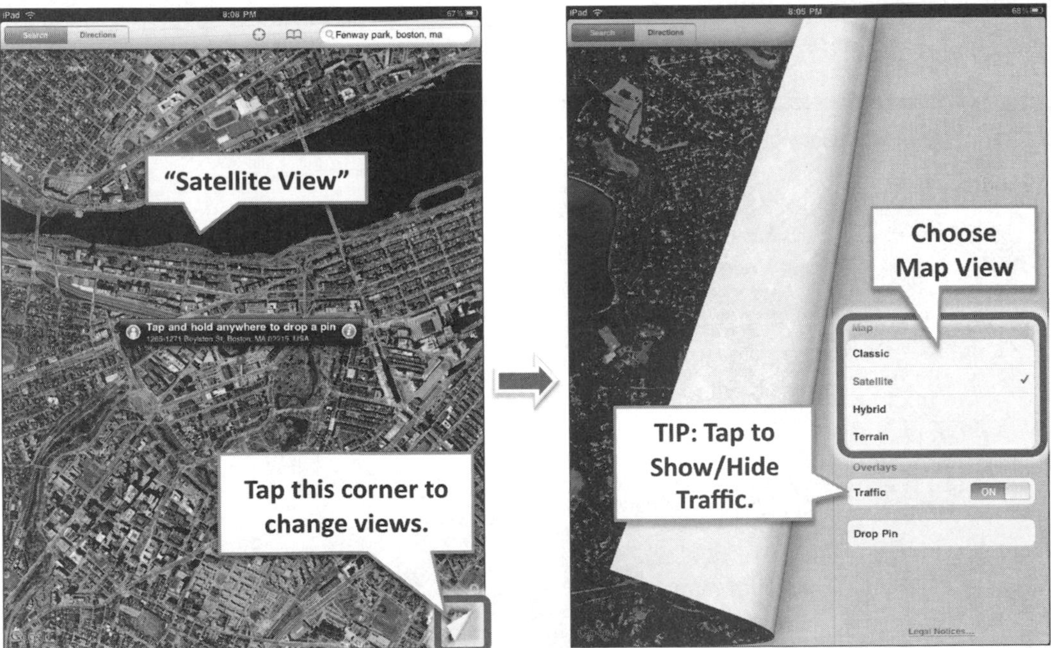


**Figure 16–1.** *Satellite view and how to change to another map view*

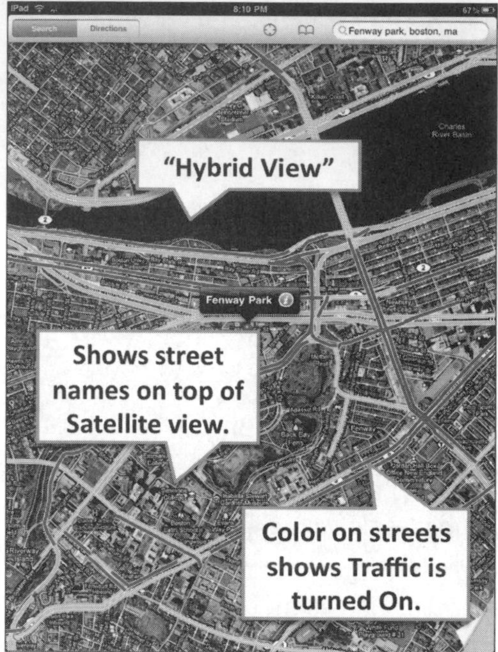


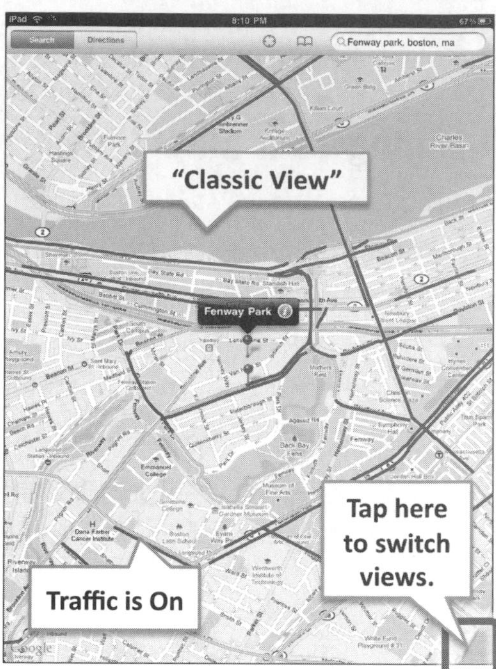


**Figure 16–2.** *Hybrid and classic views with traffic enabled*

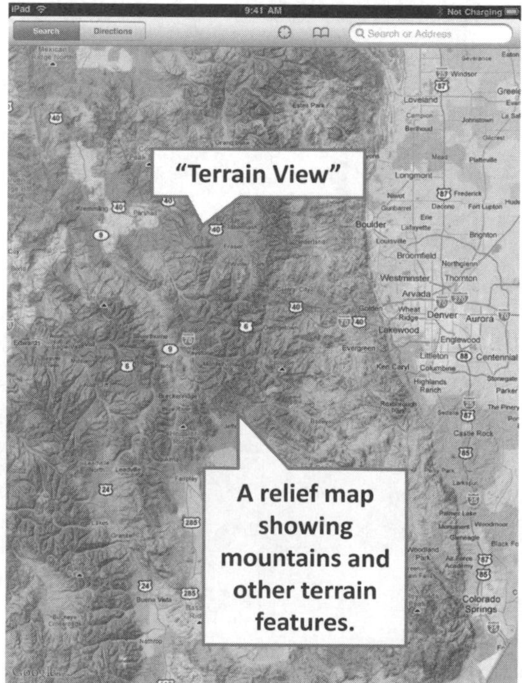


**Figure 16–3.** *Terrain view—a relief map of the Rocky Mountains west of Denver, Colorado*

As noted, **List** view is only available when your search produces multiple results (like "pizza 32174") or you've asked for directions, as shown in Figure 16–4.

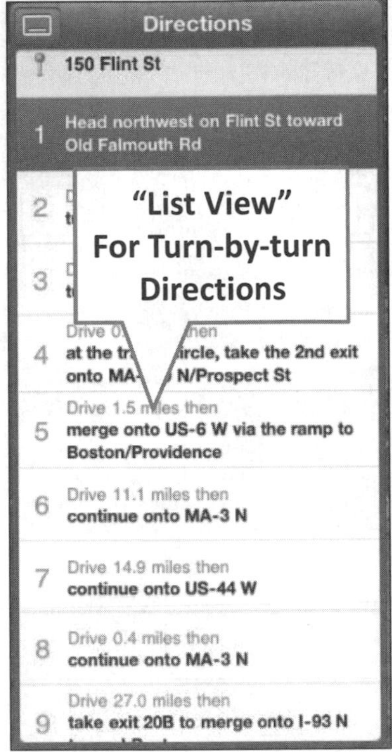


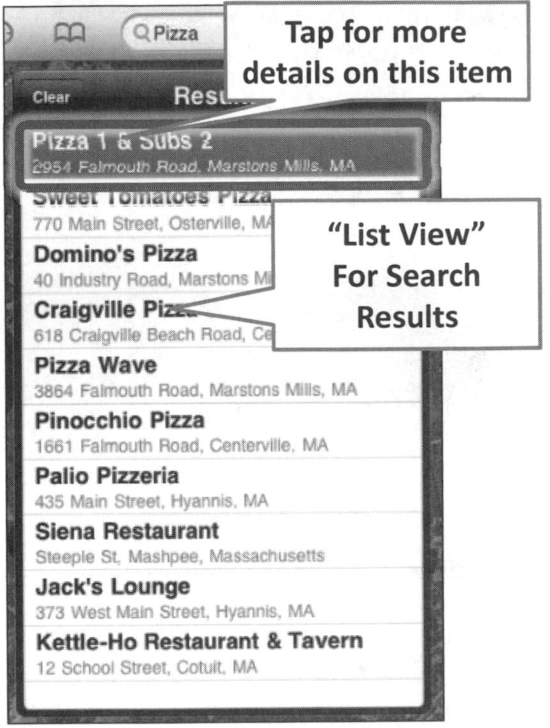


**Figure 16–4.** *List views for directions and search results*

## Checking Traffic

Your Maps program can not only tell you how to get somewhere, it can check traffic along the way. This feature is supported only in the US for now.

1. Tap the lower right corner of the map to see the options.
2. Turn **Traffic** to **ON**.

**TIP:** You can also "turn" the page like a book to get to this view. The animation is just like using the iBooks app.

On a highway, if there is a traffic situation, you usually see yellow lights instead of green, and sometimes, the yellow might be flashing to alert you to traffic delays.

You may even see construction worker icons to indicate construction zones.

**Maps** uses color on major streets and highways to indicate the speed that traffic is moving:

Green = 50 MPH or more

Yellow = 25 – 50 MPH

Red = Less than 25 MPH

Gray (or no color) = No traffic data is currently available

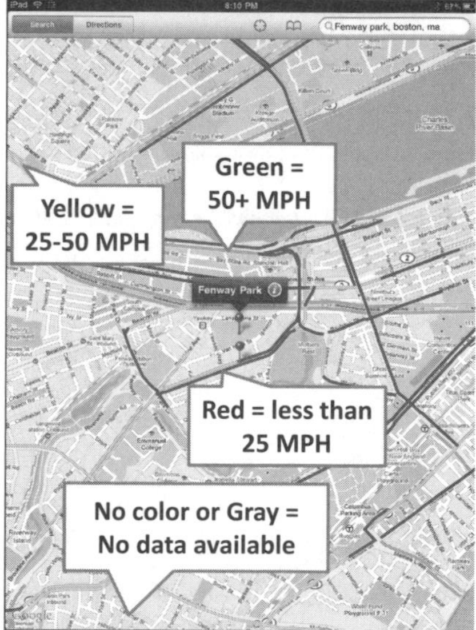

## Search for Anything

Because Maps is tied to Google Maps, you can search for and find just about anything: a specific address, type of business, a city, or other point of interest, as shown in Figure 16–5.

1. Touch the **Search** bar in the top right corner of the screen.

2. Type in your address, point of interest, or town and state you would like to map on your iPad.

### Google Maps Search Tips

Enter just about anything in the search:

- First Name, Last Name, or Company Name (to match your Contacts)
- 123 Main Street, City (some or all of a street address)
- Orlando Airport (find an airport)
- Plumber, painter, roofer (any part of a business name or trade)
- Golf courses + city (find local golf courses)
- Movies + city or ZIP/postal code (find local movie theaters)
- Pizza 32174 (search for local pizza restaurants in ZIP Code 32174)
- 95014 (ZIP Code for Apple Computer headquarters in California, USA)
- Apress Publishing

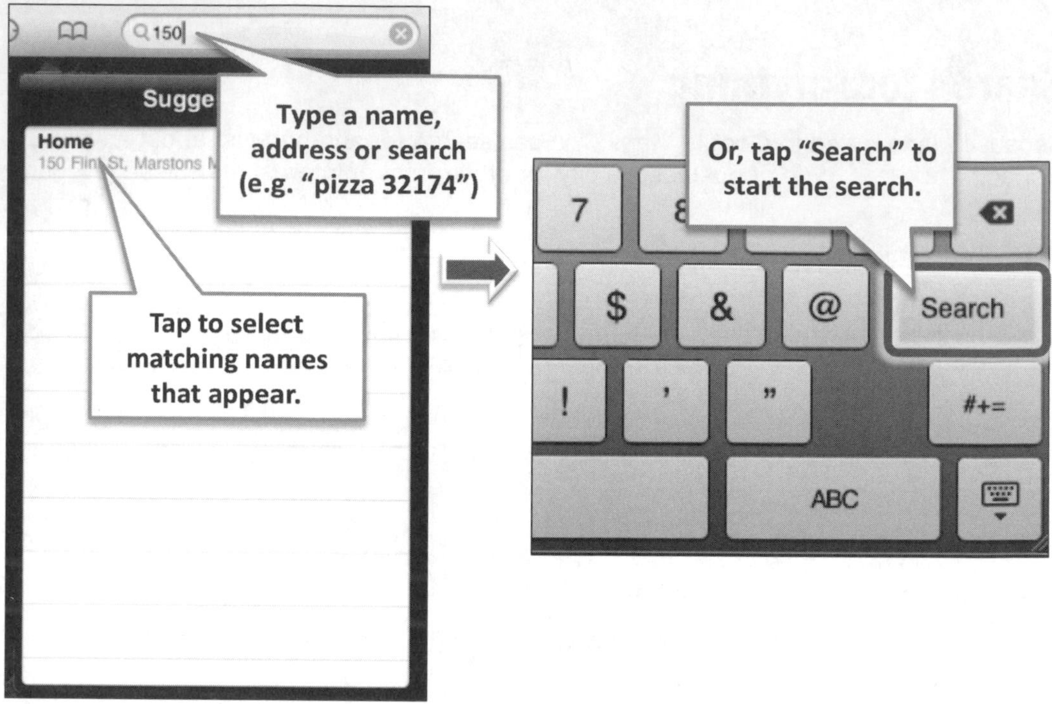


**Figure 16–5.** *Searching in the Maps app*

To use numbers, tap the **123** key on the keyboard. For letters, touch the **ABC** to switch back to a letter keyboard,

# Mapping Options

Now that your address is on the **Maps** screen, there are a number of options available to you.

1. Touch the blue **Information** icon next to the address to see some of these.
2. If you have mapped one of your contacts, you'll see the contact details as shown in Figure16–6. You can also get directions, share a location, or add as a bookmark.

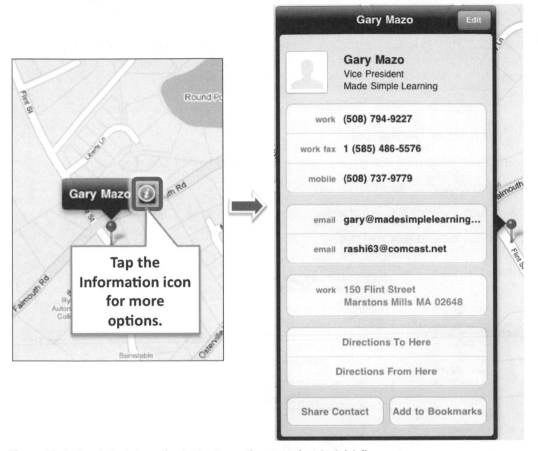

**Figure 16–6.** *Touch the information button to see the mapped contact details.*

1. If you have mapped an address or point of interest, you'll see a different screen when you tap the information button. You'll find a small street view image and buttons to get **Directions**, **Add to Contacts**, **Share Location,** or **Add to Bookmarks,** as shown to the right.

## Working with Bookmarks

Bookmarks work in **Maps** very much as they do in the Safari web browser app. A bookmark simply sets a record of places you've visited or mapped and want to remember in the future. It is always easier to look at a bookmark than have to do a new search.

### Adding a New Bookmark

Bookmarking a location is a great way to make it easy to find that place again.

1. Map a location as shown in Figure 16–7.
2. Touch the blue **information** icon next to the address.
3. Touch **Add to Bookmarks**.

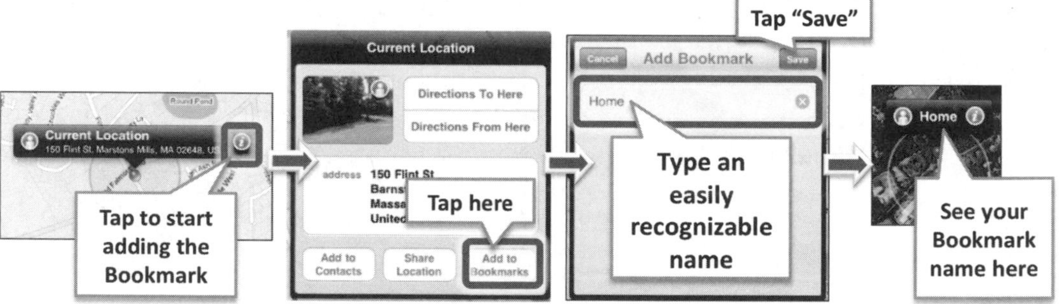


**Figure 16–7.** *Adding a bookmark.*

4. Edit the bookmark name to make is short and recognizable—in this case, we edit the address to simply say **Home**.
5. When you are done, just touch **Save** in the top right corner.

**TIP:** You can search for bookmark names just as you search for names in your Contacts.

## Accessing and Editing Your Bookmarks

To view your bookmarks, follow these steps:

1. Tap the **Bookmarks** icon next to the search window in the top row.
2. Tap any bookmark to immediately jump to it.
3. Tap the **Edit** button at the top of the bookmarks to edit or delete bookmarks.
    a. To reorder the bookmarks, touch and drag the right edge of each bookmark up or down.
    b. To edit the name of a bookmark, touch it and retype the name. After editing the name, touch the **Bookmarks** button in the top left to get back to your list of bookmarks.
    c. To delete a bookmark, swipe to the left or right on the bookmark and tap the **Delete** button.
4. Tap the **Done** button when you are finished editing your bookmarks.

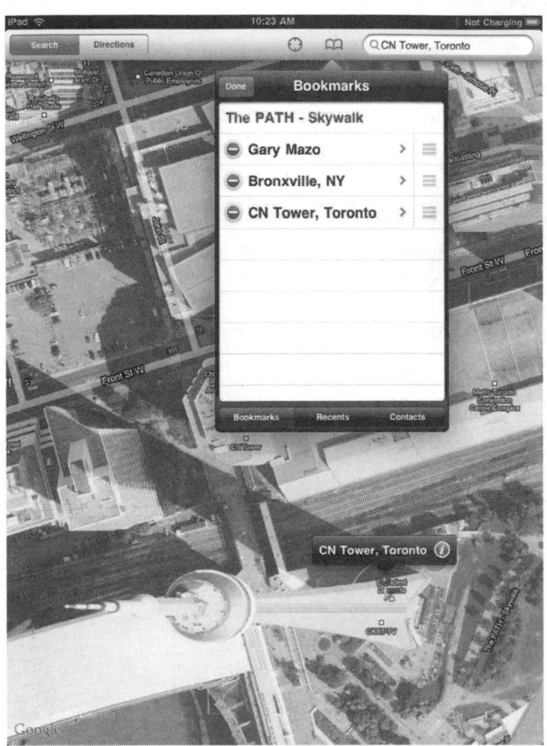


## Add a Mapped Location to Contacts

It is easy to add a location you mapped to your contact list.

1. Map an address.
2. Tap the **information** button.

3. Tap Add to Contacts. 

4. Tap either **Create a New Contact** or **Add to Existing Contact**.

5. If you choose **Add to Existing Contact**, you then scroll through or search your contacts and select a name. The address will automatically be added to that contact.

## Searching for Things (Stores, Restaurants, Hotels, Movies, Anything) Around Your Location

1. Map a location on the map or use the blue dot for your current location.

2. Tap the search window. Let's say we want to search for the closest pizza restaurants, so we type **pizza**.

All local pizza restaurants will be mapped.

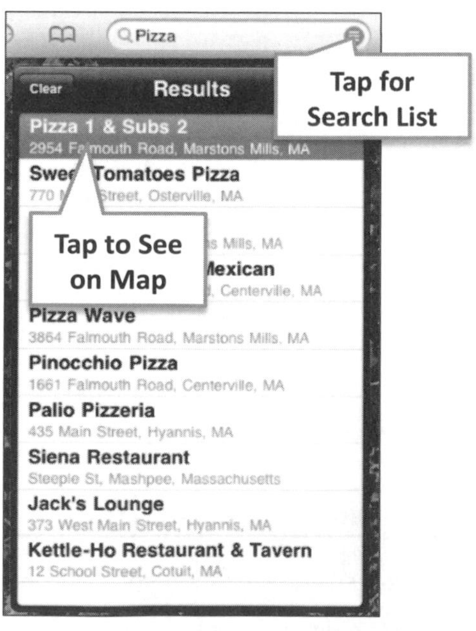


3. Notice that each mapped location may have a **street view** icon on the left and the **information** icon on the right.

4. If you want to zoom in or out, you can pinch the screen open or closed, or you can double-tap the screen.

5. Just as with any mapped location, when you touch the blue **information** icon, you can see all the details, even the pizza restaurant's phone number, address, and web site.

6. If you want directions to the restaurant, just touch **Directions to Here** and a route is instantly calculated.

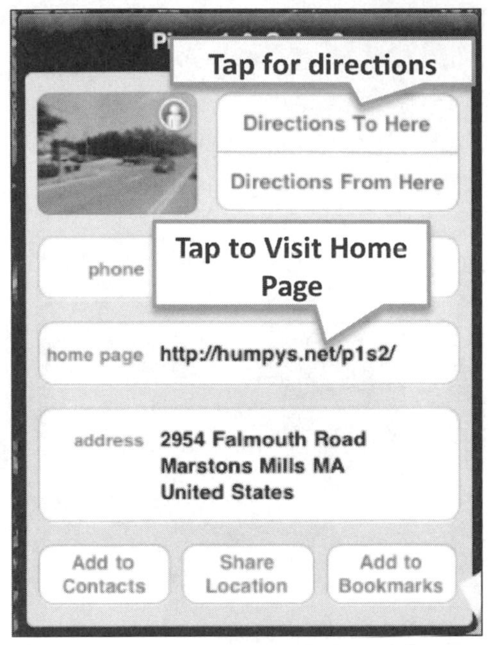


**NOTE:** If you touch the **Home Page** link you will exit **Maps** and **Safari** will start up. You will then need to restart **Maps** again when you're done.

## Zooming In and Out

You can zoom in and out in the familiar way by double-tapping and pinching. To zoom in by double-tapping, just double-tap on the screen as you would on a web page or picture.

## Dropping a Pin

Let's say you're looking at the map and you find something you'd like to set either as a bookmark or as a destination.

In this example, we are zooming in and looking around greater Boston. We stumble upon Fenway Park and decide it would be great to add it to our bookmarks, so we drop a pin on it as shown in Figure 16–8.

1. Map a location or move the map to a location where you'd like to drop the pin.

2. Tap the lower right corner of the map. 

3. Tap **Drop Pin**.

4. Now, drag the pin around the map by touching and holding it. We move it right onto Fenway Park.

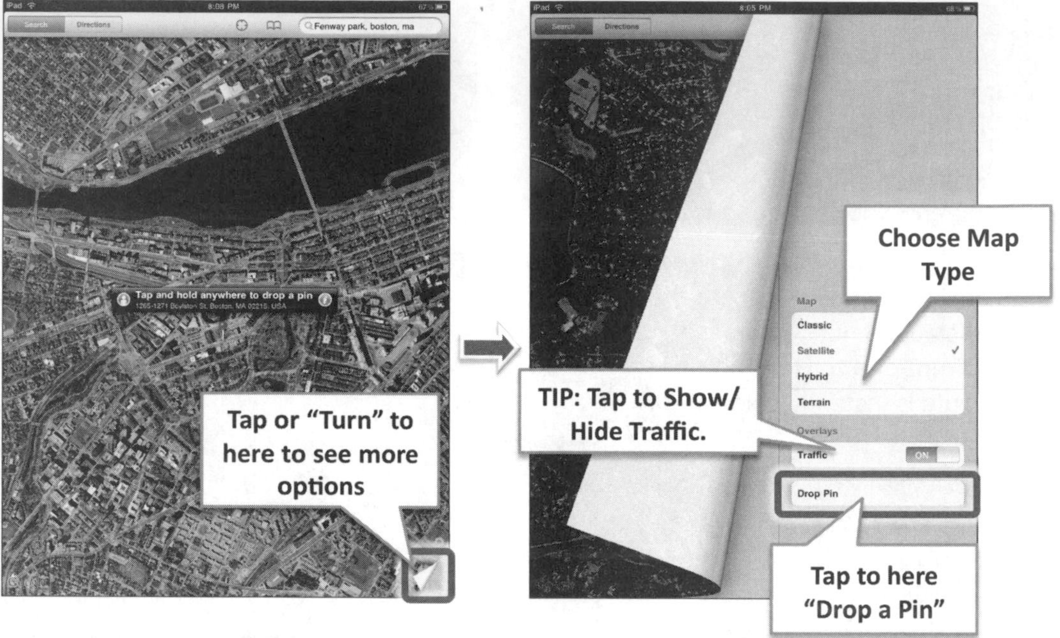


**Figure 16–8.** *How to drop a pin*

> **TIP:** How can you find the street address of any location on the map?
>
> When you **Drop a Pin**, Google Maps will show you the actual street address. This is very handy if you find a location by looking at **satellite**, **hybrid** or **terrain** view, but need to get the actual street address.
>
> Dropping a pin is also a great way to keep track of where you parked—very helpful in an unfamiliar location (especially with the iPad 3G.).

## Using Street View

**Google Street View** (Figure 16–9) is really fun in **Maps** on the iPad. Google has been hard at work photographing just about every address across the United States and elsewhere. The pictures are then fed into their database and that's what shows up when you want to see a picture of your destination or waypoint.

> **NOTE:** Google Street View is not international yet, but should be at some point in the not-too-distant future.

If there is a street view available, you will see a small icon to the left of the address or bookmark on the map—a small orange icon of a person.

In this example, Gary wants to check the **street view** of his wife Gloria's store on Cape Cod.

1. In this case, to map the address, we tapped on the work address under Gloria's name on our Contacts list. We could have mapped it by typing an address in the search window, by searching for a type of business, or by touching the address in the **Contacts** app.
2. To the left of Gloria's name is the street view icon.
3. We tap the icon to immediately shift to a street view of the address.
4. What is very cool is that we can navigate around the screen in a 360-degree rotation by swiping left, right, or even up or down, looking at the places next to and across the street from our destination.

To return to the map, we just touch the lower right corner of the screen.

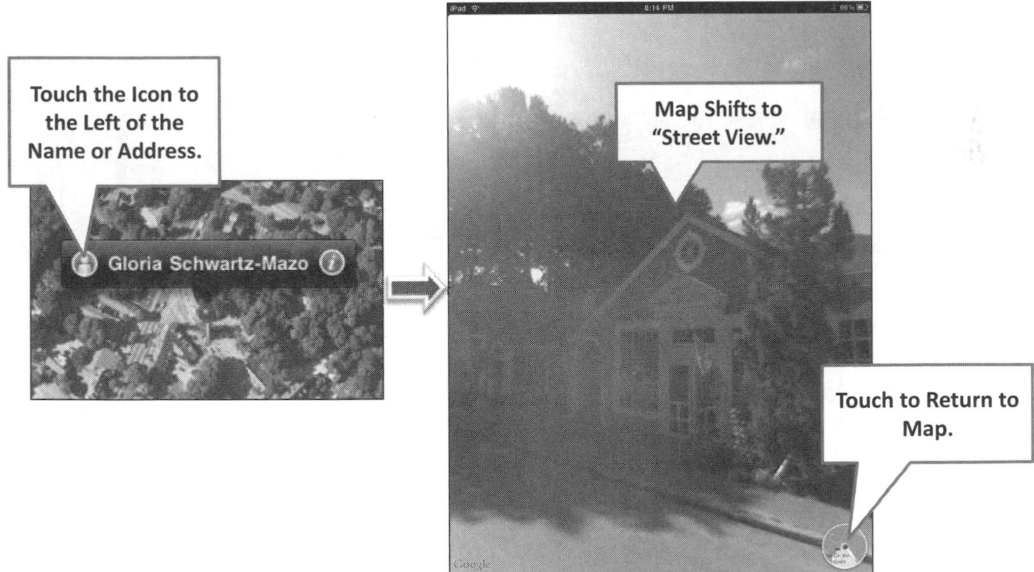


**Figure 16–9.** *Using Google Street View*

# Getting Directions

One of the most useful functions of the Maps program is that you can easily find directions to or from any location. Let's say we want to use our current location and get directions from Gloria's store to Fenway Park in Boston.

## Tap the Current Location Button First

To find directions to or from your current location, you don't have to waste time typing your current address—just locate yourself by tapping the current location button in the center of the top information bar. You may need to repeat it a few times until you see the blue dot on the screen.

Now you can do one of two things:

- Tap the **Directions** button at the left end of the top information bar, or
- Touch the blue **i** as we did above and then select **Directions from Here** (see Figure 16–10). You will notice that your recent searches appear. Choose one, if appropriate or type in a new location in the search bar.

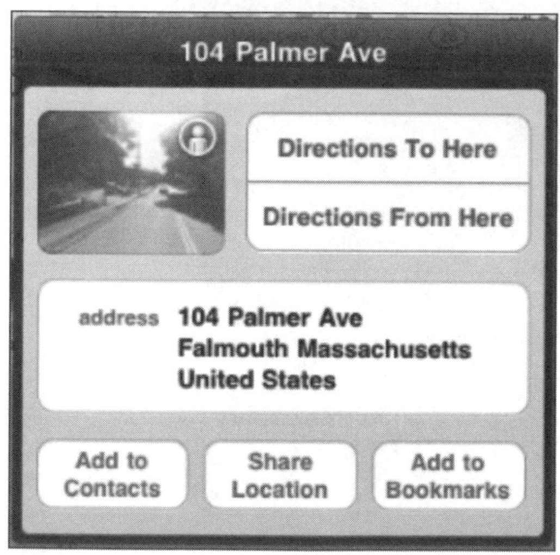


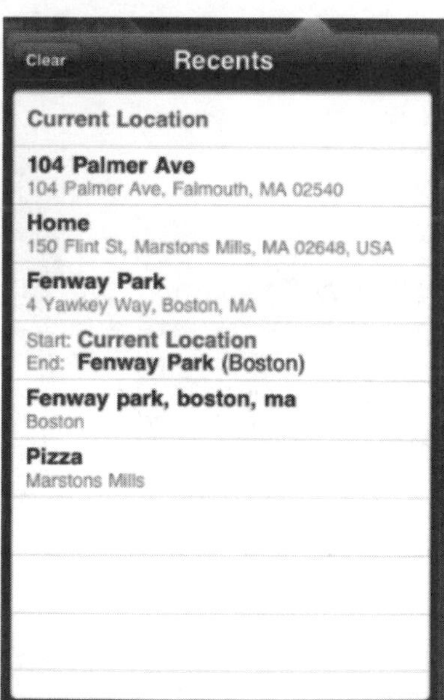


**Figure 16–10.** *Choose* ***Directions From Here*** *and then* ***Recents****.*

## Choose Start or End location

1. Touch the blue **information** icon above the pin.
2. Tap **Directions From Here**.
3. We could tap **Bookmarks**, **Recents,** or **Contacts** to find our destination.
4. In this case, we tap **Bookmarks**.
5. Tap **Fenway Park**.

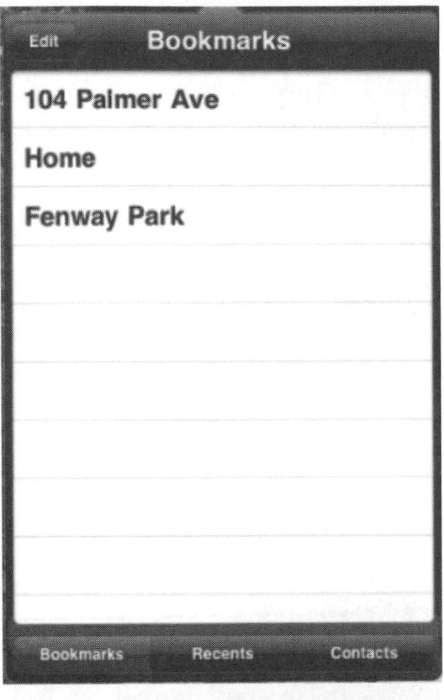


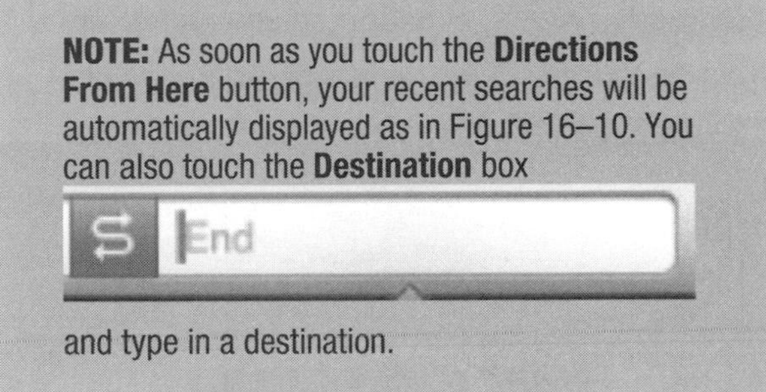

**NOTE:** As soon as you touch the **Directions From Here** button, your recent searches will be automatically displayed as in Figure 16–10. You can also touch the **Destination** box



and type in a destination.

6. After we select Fenway Park from Bookmarks, the routing screen takes us to an overview screen.
7. A green pushpin is dropped at the start location and a red one is dropped at the end location—in this case, Fenway Park.

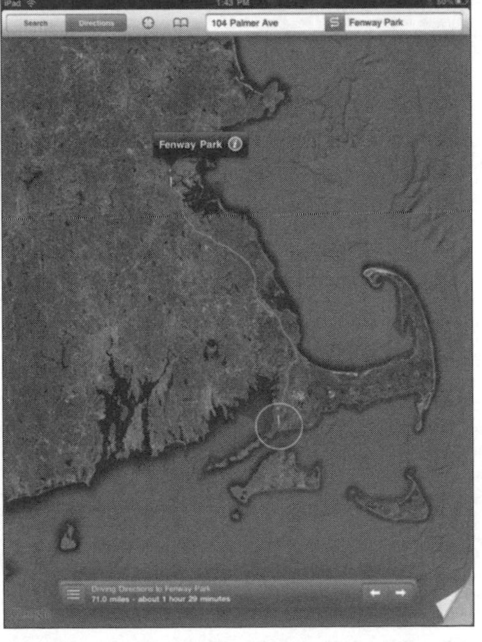

# Looking at the Route

Before you start the trip, you will see a **Start** button in the lower right corner of the screen. Tap the **Start** button and the routing directions begin. The Start button changes to Arrow buttons that allow you to move between the steps in the trip.

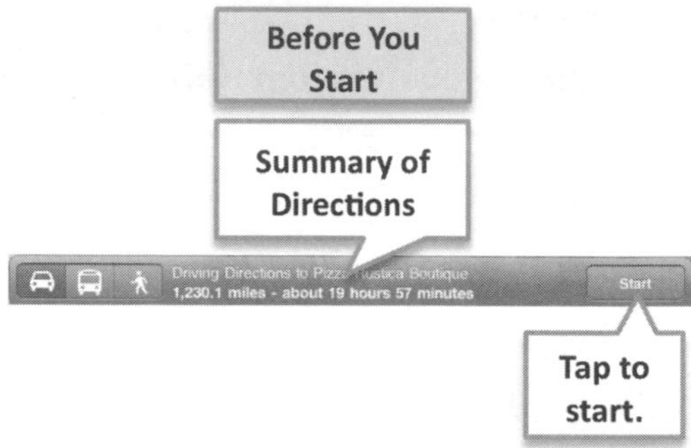


As Figure 16–11 shows, you can look at the route as either a path on the map or as a list.

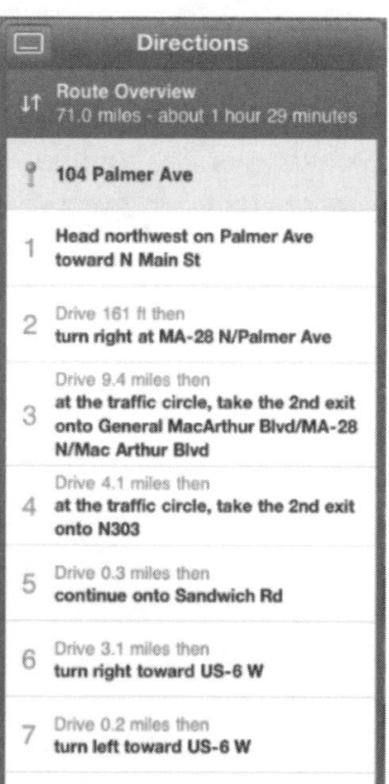


**Figure 16–11.** *Two ways of viewing directions*

You can move the screen with your finger to look at the route, or just touch the arrows at the bottom to show the route in step-by-step snapshots.

You can also touch the **List** button, which will shows detailed step-by-step directions.

## Switching between Driving, Transit, and Walking Directions

Before you start your directions, you can choose whether you are driving, using public transportation, or walking by tapping the icons on the left side of the blue bar at the bottom of the directions screen, as shown in Figure 16–12.

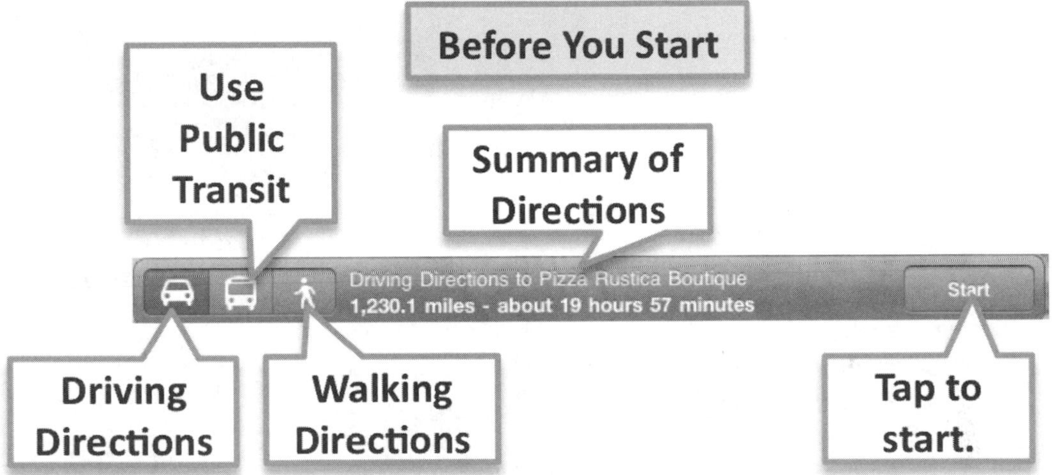


**Figure 16–12.** *Choosing your mode of transportation*

## Reversing the Route

To reverse the route, touch the **Reverse** button, which is at the top between the **Start** and **End** fields. This can be useful if you're not great about reversing directions on your own or if your route uses lots of one-way streets.

# Maps Options

Currently, the only setting that affects your Maps app is **Location Services,** which is critical for determining your current location.

1. Touch the **Settings** icon.
2. Tap the **General** tab in the left column.
3. Now find the **Location Services** switch about halfway down. Move this switch to the **ON** position so that **Maps** can approximate your location.

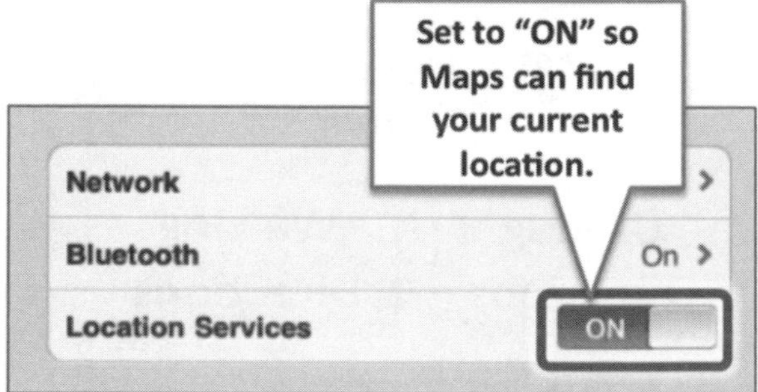


> **NOTE:** Keeping the **Location Services** switch **ON** will reduce battery life by a small amount. If you never use Maps or care about your location, set it to **OFF** to save your battery life.

# Using the Digital Compass

The iPad has a very cool **digital compass** feature built in. This can be helpful when you need to literally get your bearings and figure out which way is north.

## Calibrating and Using the Digital Compass

Before you can use the digital compass, you need to calibrate it. You should only need to calibrate the compass the first time you use it.

1. Start **Maps** as you normally would.
2. Tap the current location button twice—it changes from [icon] to [icon].
3. You'll see a small digital compass appear on the screen, as shown in Figure 16–13.
4. The first time you use digital compass, the calibration symbol appears on the screen [icon] .
5. Move your iPad in a "figure 8" pattern as shown on the screen.

> **NOTE:** The iPad may ask you to move away from any source of interference while you go through the calibration process.

6. Hold your iPad level to the ground. If you calibrated it successfully, the compass will rotate and point north.

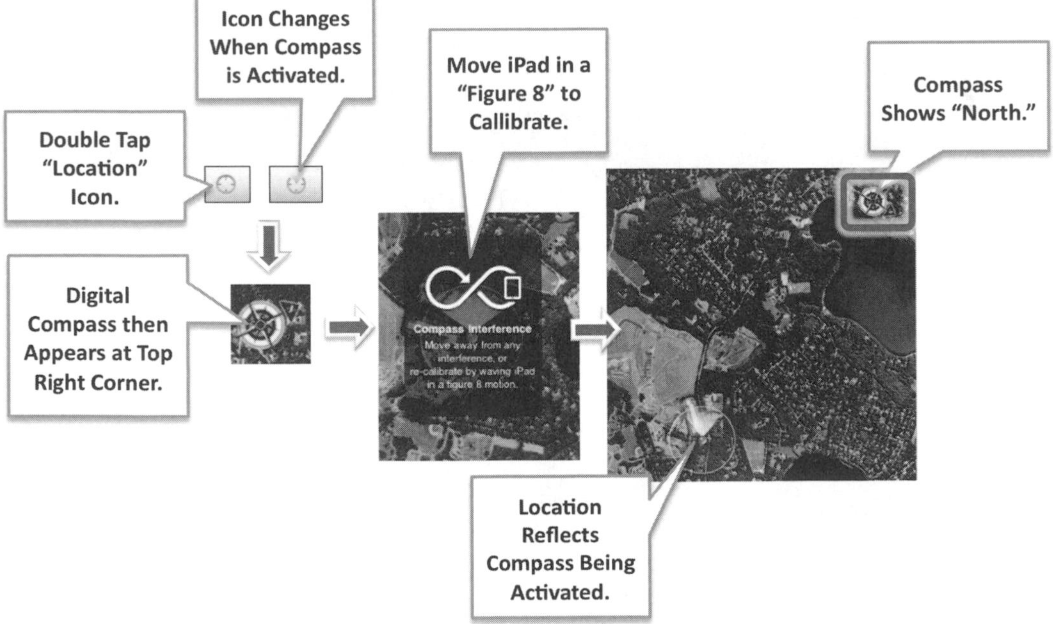


**Figure 16–13.** *Using the digital compass*

Chapter 17

# Eliminate Your Paper Notes

In this chapter, we will give you an overview of the **Notes** app, which you can use to write notes, make grocery lists, and make lists of movies you'd like to watch or books you'd like to read. We will show you how to organize and even email notes to yourself or others. Ideally, we hope that Notes will become so easy on the iPad that you can eventually get rid of most, if not all, of your paper sticky notes!

## Exploring Notes Apps

In addition to the built-in **Notes** app, there are a number of free or low-cost note applications you can obtain from the App Store. We will show you how to use one of these note apps called **Evernote** later in this chapter. This app is quite powerful and allows you to sync notes wirelessly with a web site, store and organize voice notes, add pictures and other mixed media to your notes.

**TIP:** The **Notes** app that comes with the iPad is pretty basic and utilitarian. If you need a more robust notes application that you can sort, categorize, import items into (PDF, Word, and so on), have folders, search, and more; you should check out the App Store on your iPad. Do a search for "notes," and you will find at least a dozen notes-related apps ranging from $0.99 and up.

## The Notes App

If you are like many people, your desk is filled with little yellow sticky notes – notes to do everything imaginable. Even with our computers, we still tend to leave these little notes as reminders. One of the great things about the iPad is that you can write your notes on familiar yellow notepaper, and then keep them neatly organized and sorted. You can even email them to yourself or someone else to make sure that the information is not forgotten.

The **Notes** app on the iPad gives you a convenient place to keep your notes and simple "to do" lists. You can also keep simple lists, such as a grocery list, or a list for other stores, such as a hardware or pet store. If you have your iPad with you, you can add items to these lists as soon as they occur to you, and they can be accessed and edited at any time.

## Getting Started with Notes

Like all other applications, simply tap the **Notes** icon to start it.

After starting the **Notes** app, you see what looks like a typical yellow note pad.

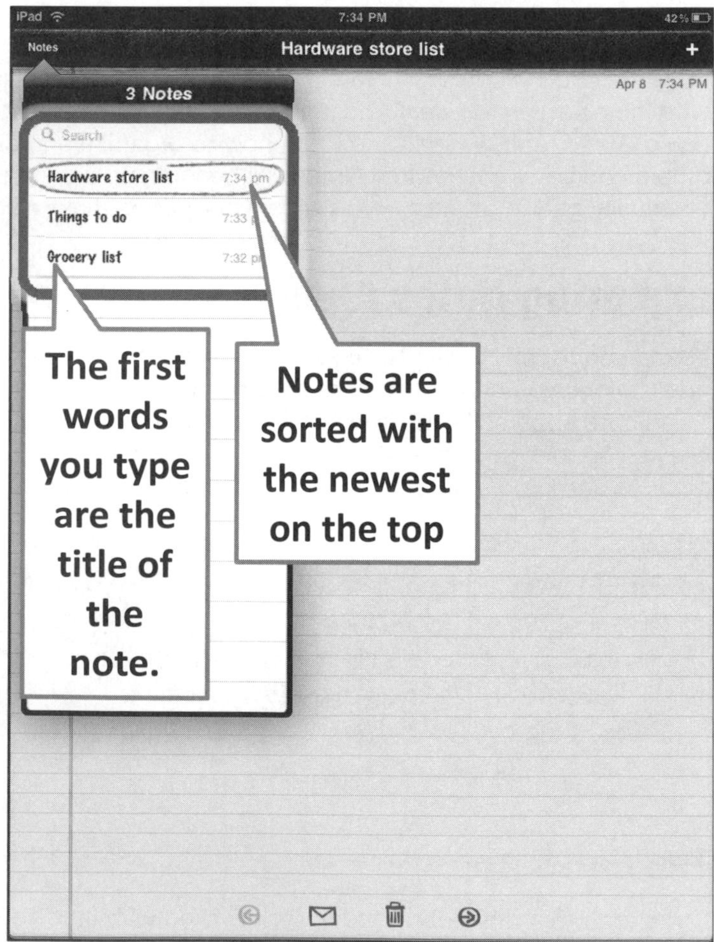

## How Are My Notes Sorted?

You see that all notes are listed in reverse chronological order, with the most recently edited notes at the top and the oldest at the bottom.

The date that is shown is the last time and date that the particular note was edited, not when it was first created. So you will notice the order of your notes moving around on the screen.

This sorting can be a good thing because your most recent (or frequently edited) notes will be right at the top.

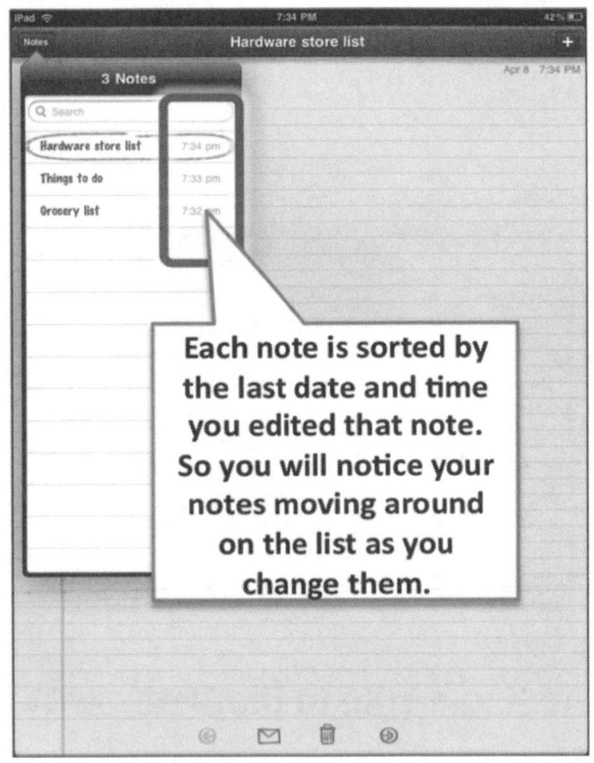


> **TIP:** If you want a nice app to keep track of your To-Do lists, you should check out the **Things for iPad** is a very nice task and To-Do app. It is currently US $9.99 in the App Store.

## Adding a New Note

To start a new Note touch the + sign  in the upper right-hand corner.

The notepad is blank, and the keyboard pops up for you to begin typing. You can hide the keyboard if you wish by tapping the **Hide Keyboard** key in the bottom right-hand corner.

> **TIP:** You can tilt your iPad on its side to see the larger keyboard.

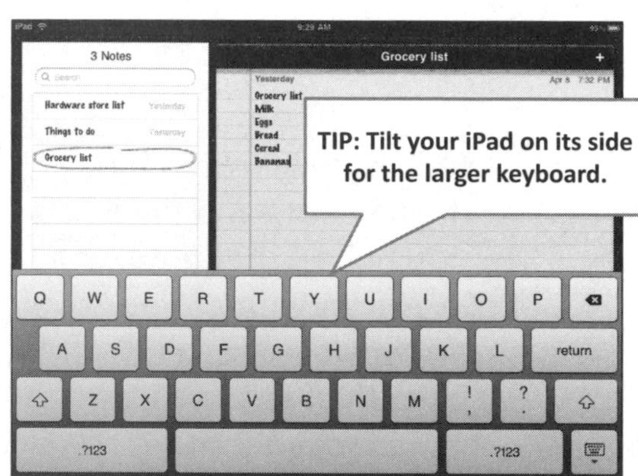

## Adding a Title to the Note

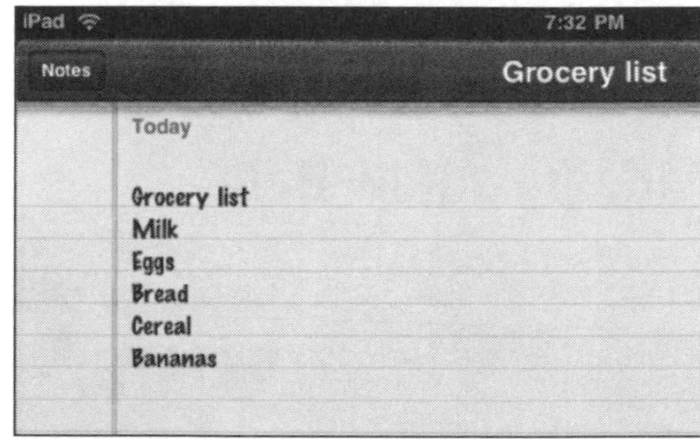


The first few words you type before you hit the **Return** key will become the title of the Note. So think about what you want as the title and type that first. In the image shown, "**Grocery list**" becomes the title of the note.

Put a new item on each line, and tap the Return key to go to the next line.

When you are done, touch the **Notes**

button in the top left-hand corner to return to the main **Notes** screen.

## Viewing or Editing Your Notes

Your **Notes** appear in the list as tabs to touch. Touch the name of the note you wish to view or edit (see Figure 17–1). The contents of the note are then displayed.

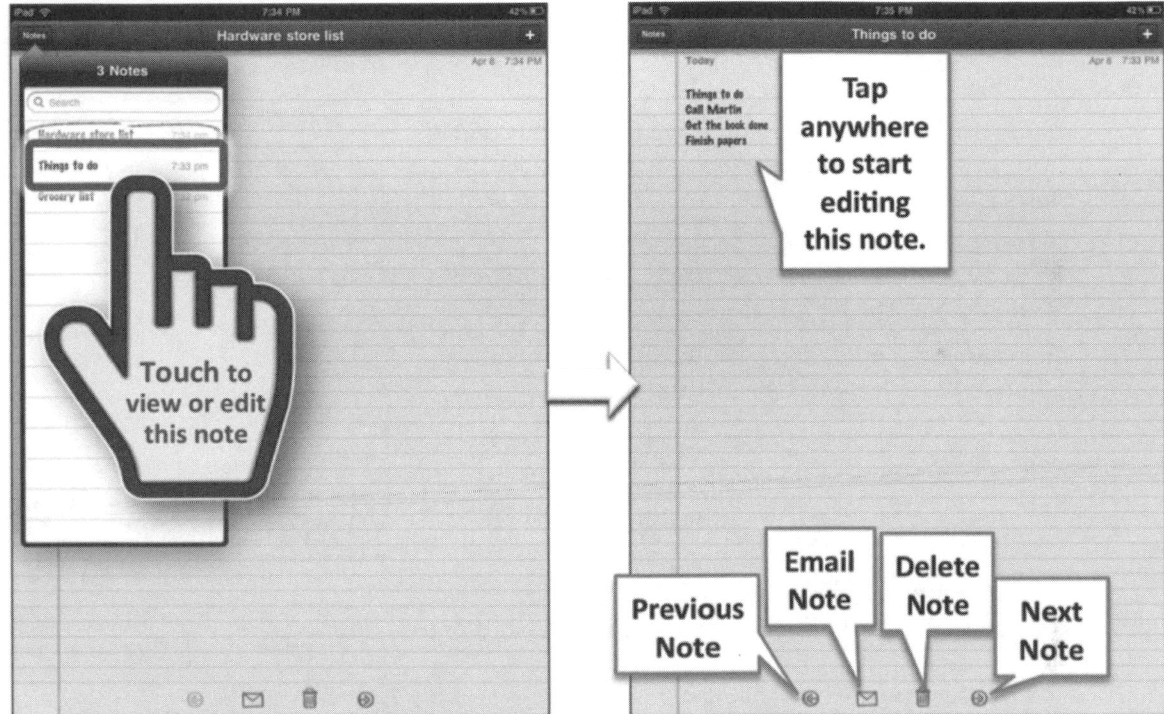


**Figure 17–1.** *Editing, emailing, or deleting your notes*

You can scroll in **Notes** as you do in any program. You will notice the date and time the note was last edited appear in the upper right-hand corner (see Figure 17–1).

When you are done reading the note, just touch the **Notes** button in the top left-hand corner to return to the main **Notes** screen.

To advance through multiple notes, just touch the arrows at the bottom of the screen.

Touch the forward arrow. The page turns, and you can see the next note. To go back, just hit the Back arrow.

## Editing Your Notes

You can easily edit or change the contents of a note. For example, you might keep a "Things to Do" note and quickly edit it when you think of something else to add to the list (or when your family reminds you to get something from the store!).

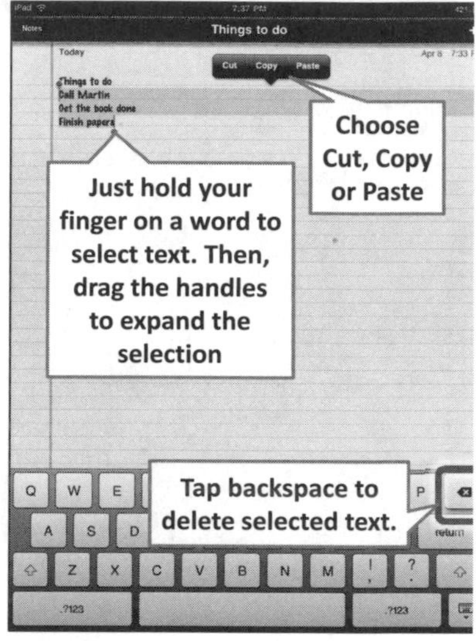


Touch the "Things to Do" note, and then touch the screen anywhere; the cursor moves to that spot for editing.

If you double-tap on a word, the blue handles used in "Copy and Paste" appear. Just drag the handles to select text.

If you touch and hold your finger on a word, a magnifying glass appears, so you can find the exact spot you are looking for.

Release your finger, and the "Select" menu appears. Choose **Select**, **Select All**, or **Paste**.

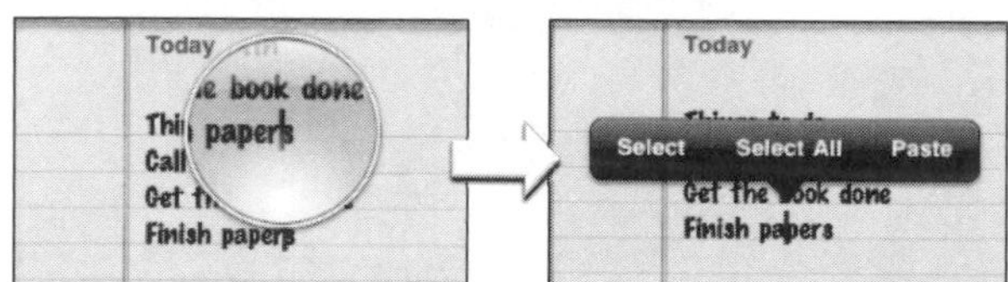


You can also use the **Delete** key to delete a word or a line.

> **TIP:** Using the copy handles is the best way to select a large amount of text; it is faster and more precise.

When done editing, touch the **Notes** button.

## Deleting Notes

To delete a note, tap it to open it from the main Notes screen and then touch the **Trash can** icon at the bottom.

The iPad prompts you to **Delete Note** or just **Cancel**.

## Emailing a Note

One of the notes app's convenient features is the ability to email a note (see Figure 17–2). Let's say we wrote a grocery note and wanted to email it to our spouse. From the text of the note, touch the **Envelope** icon at the bottom of the screen.

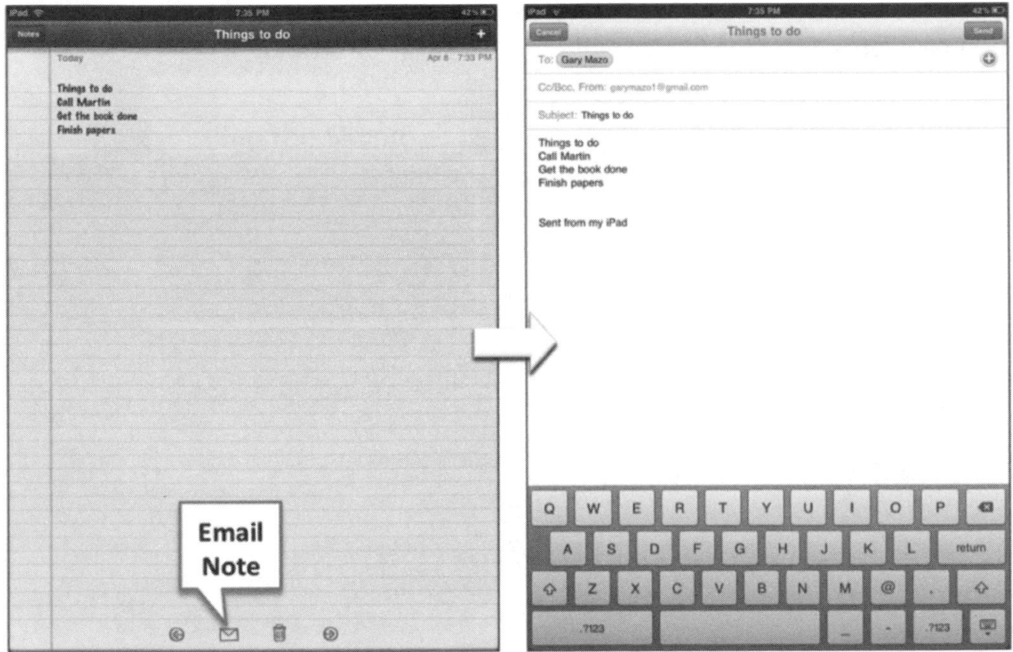


**Figure 17–2.** *Emailing a note*

Now we see the **Compose New Mail** screen with the subject as the title of the note and the body of the message as the contents of the note. Address and send the note as we would any other email. Touch the **To** line of the email, touch the +  sign, and find the contact we wish to use.

Once I have all the information we need in the email, we just touch **Send** to send our note on its way.

> **TIP:** Instead of hitting the **Shift** key to get a quotation mark, you can just hold down the comma for a second, and a quote pops up. Hitting space twice automatically inserts a period. Holding down a character gives you accent/variant options. Tapping the numbers toggle puts you in numbers entry mode and leaves you there. Sliding from the number toggle to the character you want and then letting go inserts the character. It also automatically switches you back to alphabet mode.

## Another Note App: Evernote

A visit to the App Store will show you several Note Taking Apps designed for the iPad. Prices range from free to about US $20.00.

A good free alternative to the built-in **Notes** app is called **Evernote**. **Evernote** is great because, when you enter a note in **Evernote**, you can "auto synchronize" it with your Mac, iPhone, BlackBerry, or PC. All text is searchable, and you can even "geo-locate" (have your iPad track your location and tie it to a particular note) using **Evernote**.

> **TIP:** You can even record voice notes with **Evernote**.

## Getting Started with Evernote

Start by going to the App Store and downloading **Evernote**.

Once **Evernote** is downloaded and installed, you need to touch the **Evernote** icon to start the application.

The first time you use **Evernote**, you will be prompted to sign up for a free account. Type in your email address and set a password, and you are ready to start.

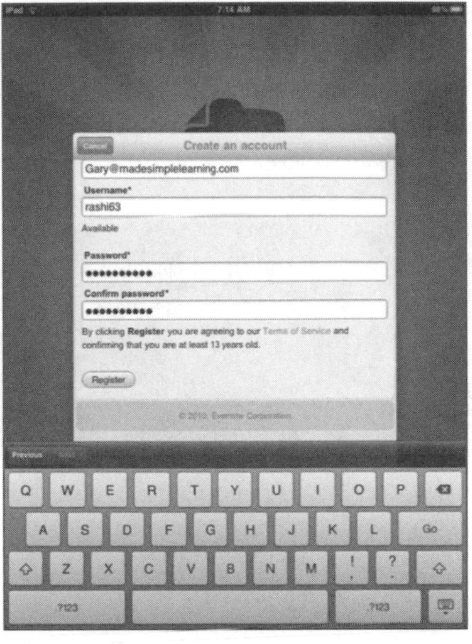


## Adding and Tagging Notes

The home screen shows you your notes. To add a new note, just touch the **New note** button in the lower left-hand corner and type your note.

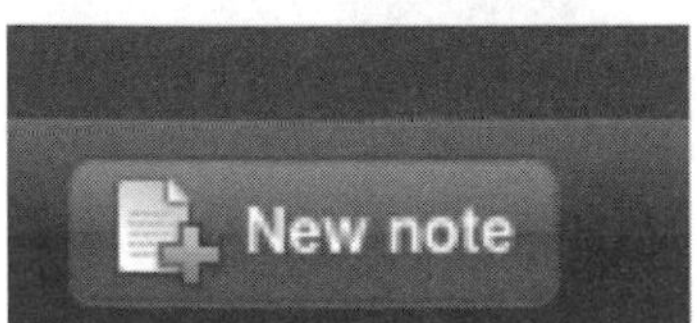


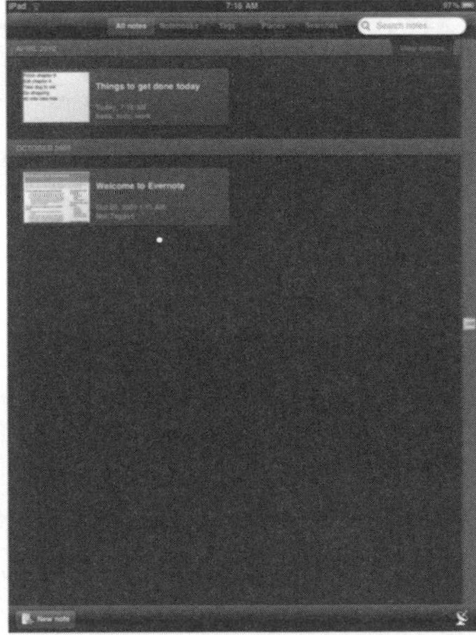

Give your note a unique title and then add some tags to the note. These tags are used to help organize your notes, and they can be useful when searching through your notes. For example, I have set tags, such as "book," "todo," and "work." If I add those tags to appropriate notes, my notes can be sorted by those individual tags.

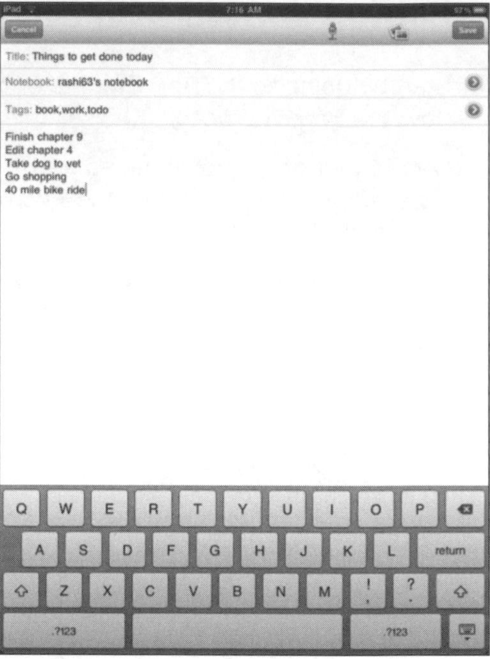

Once you type a few tags separated by commas, these are added to a pull-down list, so they are easier to select in the future. This also helps you avoid mis-typing any of your tags (see Figure 17–3).

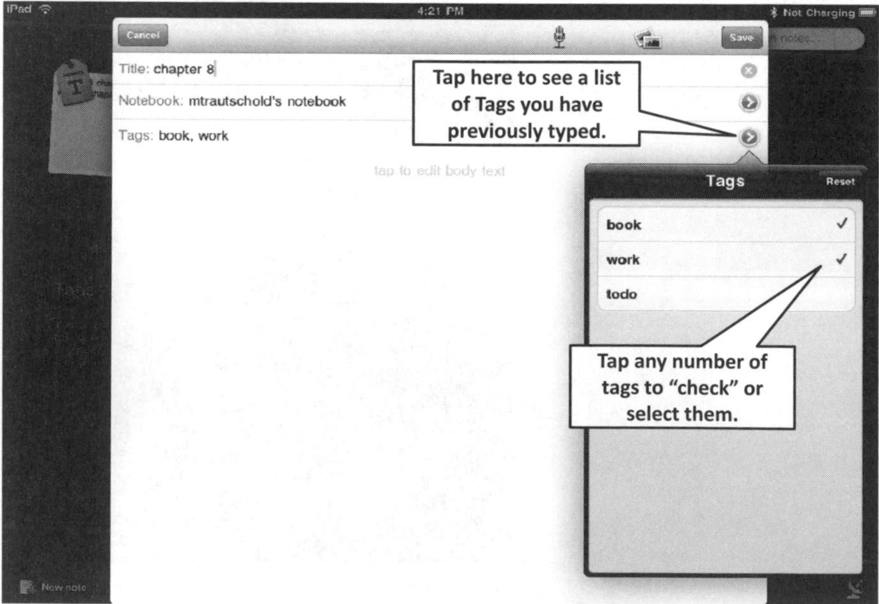


**Figure 17–3.** *Tagging a note in Evernote*

## Adding a Voice Recording to Your Evernote

By tapping the **Microphone** icon in the upper bar when you are adding or editing a note, you can record your voice (or anything else around you) to add to your current note.

## Adding a Picture from Your Library to Your Evernote

You can easily add any picture from your Photo library to a note in **Evernote** by touching the **Photos** icon in the top of the **Edit Note** window (next to the **Save** button (see Figure 17–4). **Evernote** will even identify the text in the picture and make that text searchable.

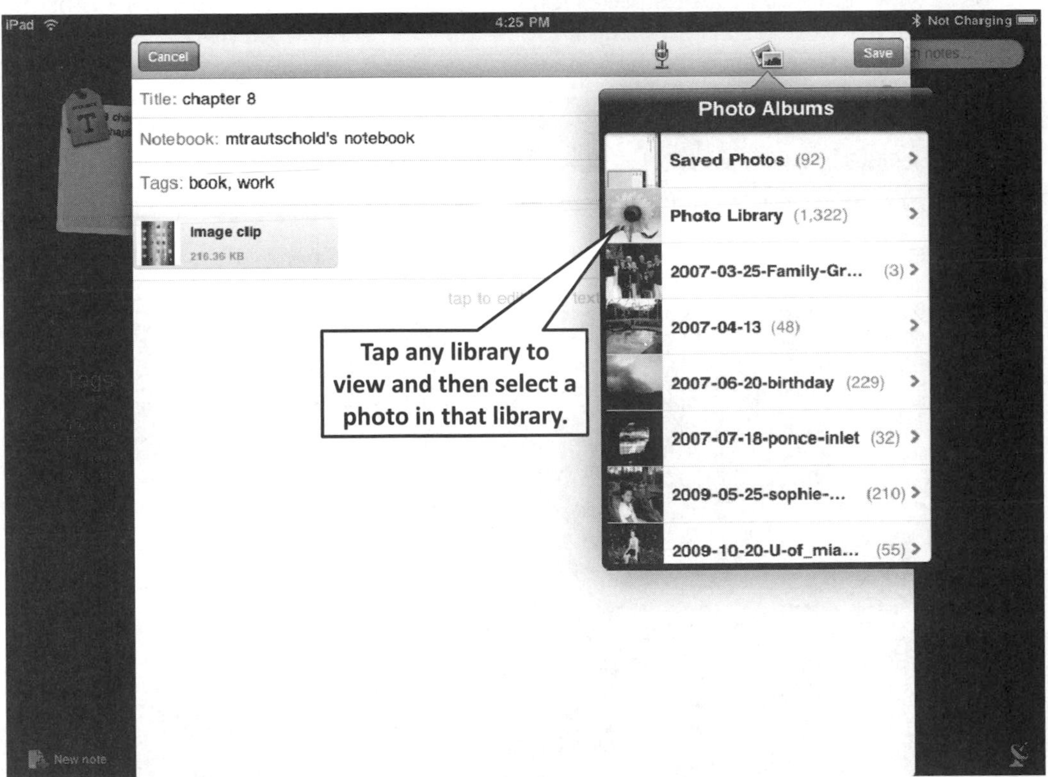


**Figure 17–4.** *Adding a photo from your library to a note in Evernote*

## Emailing or Editing a Note in Evernote

You can also email your notes by touching the **Envelope** icon at the bottom of the screen, just as you can in the **Notes** app.

To edit a note, just touch the **Pencil** icon at the bottom of the screen. This brings up the editing screen.

## Various Views of Evernotes

You have various options for customizing the ways you view your notes in **Evernote**. Select any of the views listed across the top of the main screen: **All notes**, **Notebooks**, **Tags**, **Places**, or **Searches**.

Touch **All notes** to view all your notes. See Fig 17–7 in the Viewing Options section.

Touch **Notebooks** to see all your notebooks (see Figure 17–5).

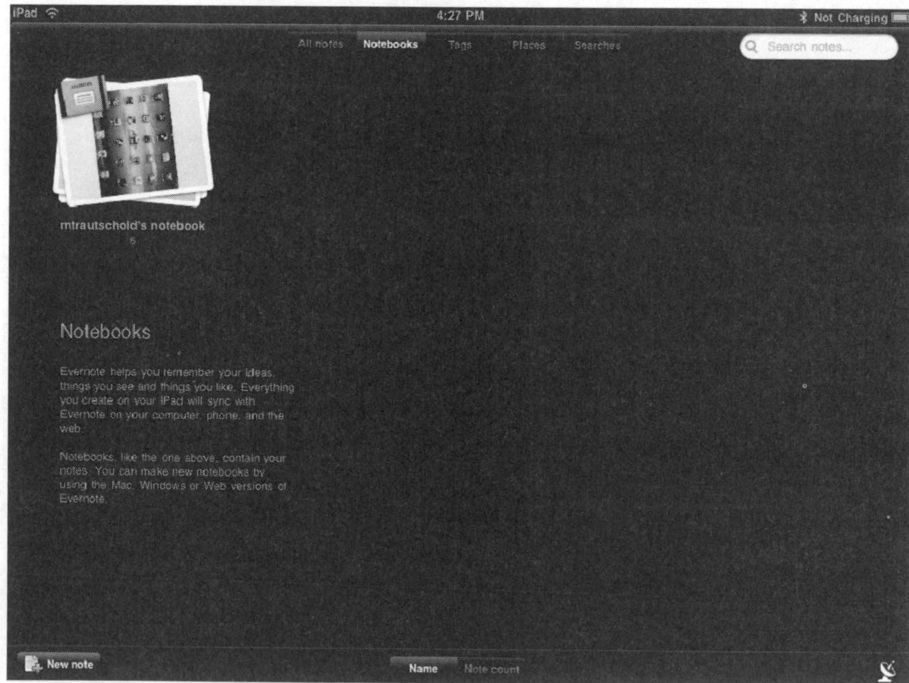


**Figure 17–5.** *The Evernote Notebooks view*

## The Evernote Places View

One cool Evernote view: You can have Evernote tag your notes by the place where you took your note. For example, if you traveled to another state, province, or country, Evernote would track that you took notes in that particular region.

> **NOTE:** At publishing time, the Wi-Fi only iPad did not seem to track location of notes. This may be fixed by the time you read this book.

Figure 17–6 shows a note taken in California, USA.

**Figure 17–6.** *The Evernote Places view*

## Evernote Viewing Options

You have various options to customize your views of your notes in **Evernote**. Tap the **View options** tab under the search box in the upper right-hand corner to customize your current view. In Figure 17–7, we have customized by selecting **Title** for **Sort By** and **Thumbnails** for **View by**.

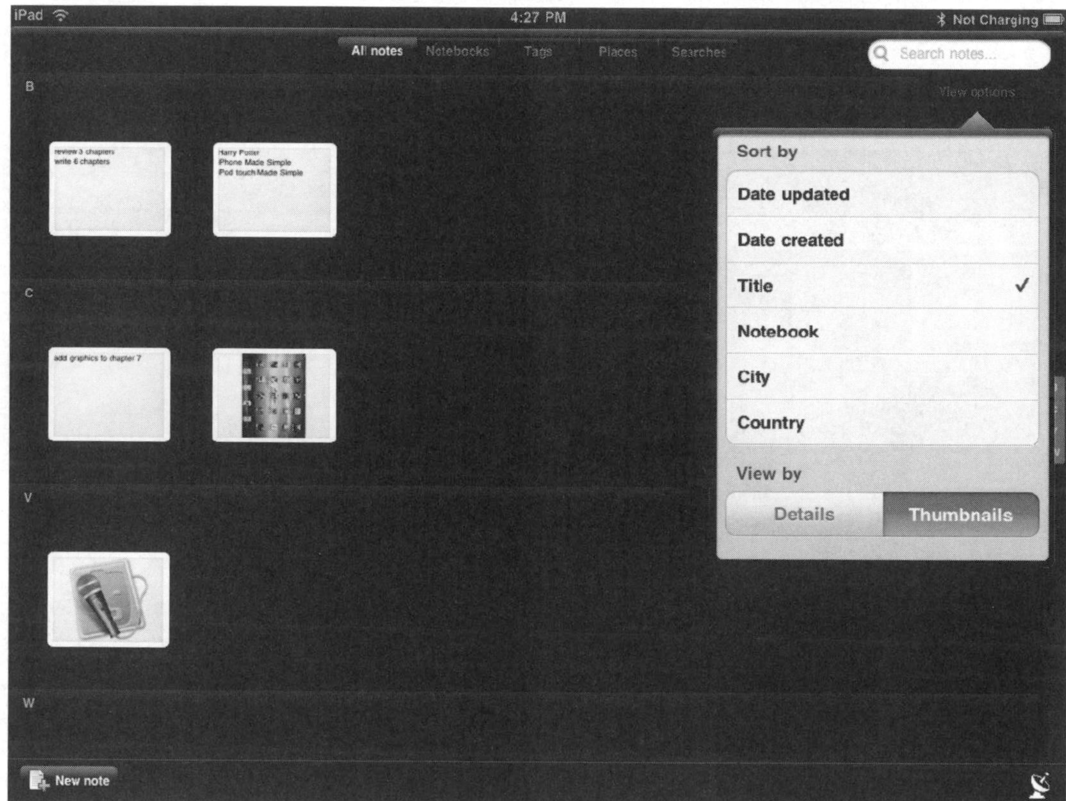


**Figure 17–7.** *Evernote All Notes view with the viewing options shown*

## Evernote Synchronization and Settings

To synchronize your notes with the **Evernote** server for retrieval on your Mac, PC, or other Evernote-connected device (such as a BlackBerry or iPhone), you would touch the **Radar Dish** icon in the lower-right portion of the screen to make the **Synchronization and Settings** screen appear.

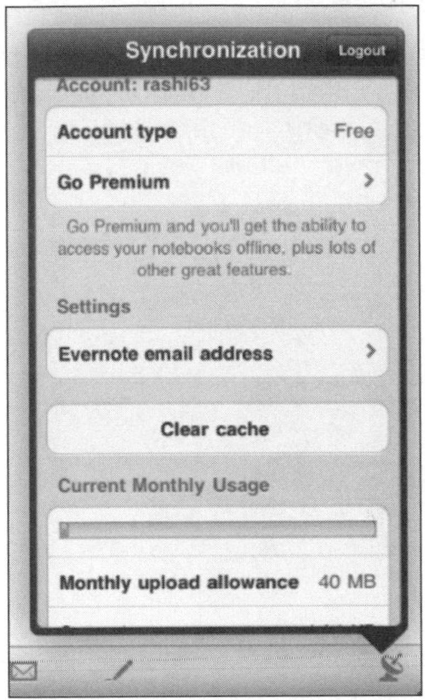


If you scroll down the **Synchronization** screen, you can check out your total usage of your Free (or paid) account.

The Free account gives you 40 MB of data, which is more than 100,000 text notes. Tap the **Approximate notes remaining** option to get a feel for how many picture or voice notes this might include.

If you are running out of space, then you might want to Upgrade by touching **Go Premium** option in the top of the Synchronization window.

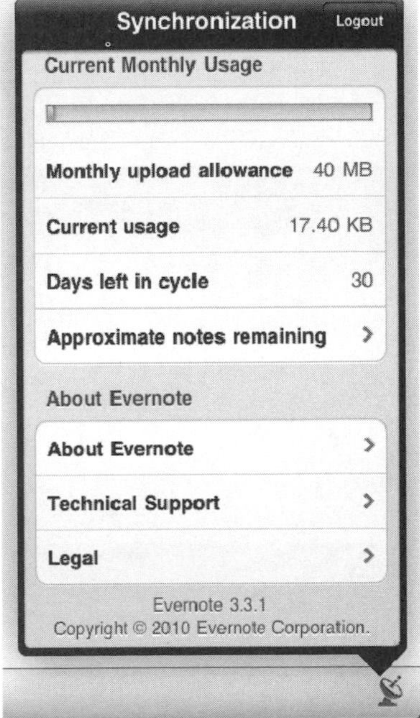

## Viewing or Updating Evernotes on Your Computer or Other Mobile Device

One of the cool things about **Evernote** is that it wirelessly synchronizes or shares notes with your account on the **Evernote** server. You can then log in to your account from your PC, Mac, iPhone, or BlackBerry to check out or update your notes. This is a great feature if you have multiple devices, and you would like to stay up-to-date or add notes from any of them.

Chapter 18

# iWork: Productivity on Your iPad

You already know that your iPad is great at "consuming" content. It is your music player, your video player, and your gaming console, and it brings you news, weather, sports, and more. The iPad isn't just for fun and games, though.

With the addition of iWork (**Pages**, **Keynote**, and **Numbers**) your iPad can also "create" content—not just "consume" it. **Pages** is just like Microsoft Word and can produce word processing documents that are Word compatible.

**Numbers** is like Excel and **Keynote** is like PowerPoint. Each has wonderfully creative tools built in and each can produce professional Microsoft Office–compatible documents that you can then email, upload to an online account, or present on your iPad.

In this chapter, we will show you how to download, create, and share documents for all three of the iWork programs.

# Downloading iWork

iWork is comprised of three parts, **Pages**, **Keynote**, and **Numbers**—each of which need to be downloaded from the App store.

You may find the three iWork apps in the **Top Paid** or **Top Grossing** apps in the **Top Charts** section of the App store.

You can also search for **Pages**, and then from the **Pages** download page, get to **Keynote** and **Numbers** by looking in the **More iPad Apps by Apple, Inc.** section in the lower-left corner.

The other way to find iWork is to tap the **Categories** button at the bottom of the App store and then touch the **Productivity** link.

# Creating Documents with iWork Pages Word Processor

**Pages** is Apple's word processing program. If you use a Mac, you will be familiar with the layout and functionality of the **Pages** program. While not meant to be a full substitute for a desktop word processor, **Pages** is quite capable and can allow you to edit and create very professional-looking documents.

With **Pages** you can not only create documents, you can also then send them via email or upload them to an online account for easy viewing, sharing, and printing.

## Using Pages for the First Time

When you first start **Pages**, you will see that there is one sample document entitled “Getting Started.” This is a great tutorial for many of the features found within **Pages**. We recommend going through this document and reading about the various styles, objects, and toolbars associated with **Pages**.

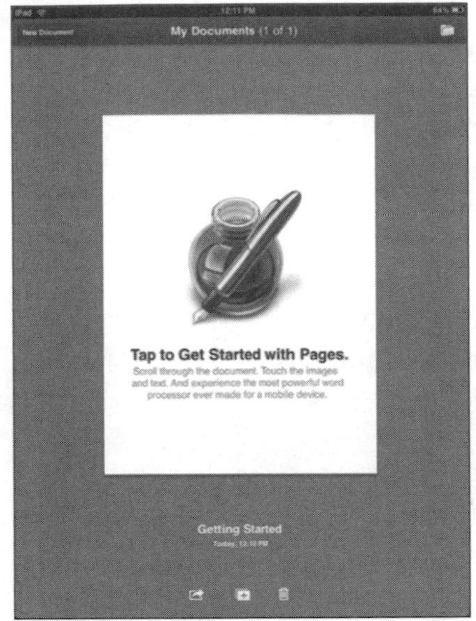


To start a new document, touch the **New Document** button at the bottom. When you touch the **New Document** button, you have the option of either starting a new document from scratch or duplicating the document that is showing.

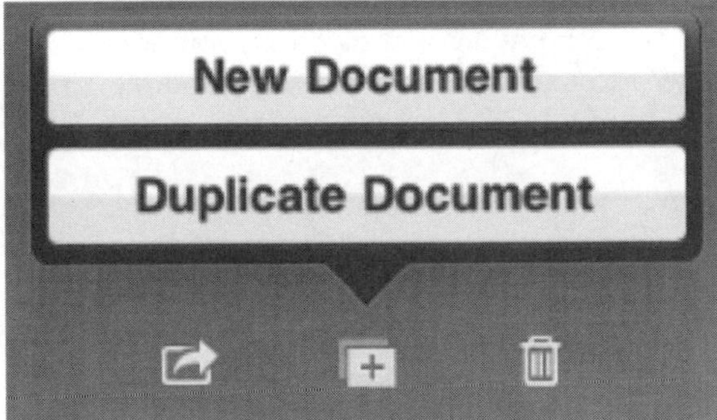


**TIP:** If you want to use an existing document as a template, it is useful to choose Duplicate Document. Otherwise, choose New Document to start a new project.

# Choose a Template

When you choose **New Document**, you have 16 available templates from which to choose. The templates are general, like **Poster, Proposal,** or **Term Paper**. You can choose to start with a template (which might make the formatting easier) or simply choose **Blank** (at the top left) to start with a blank page (see Figure 18-1).

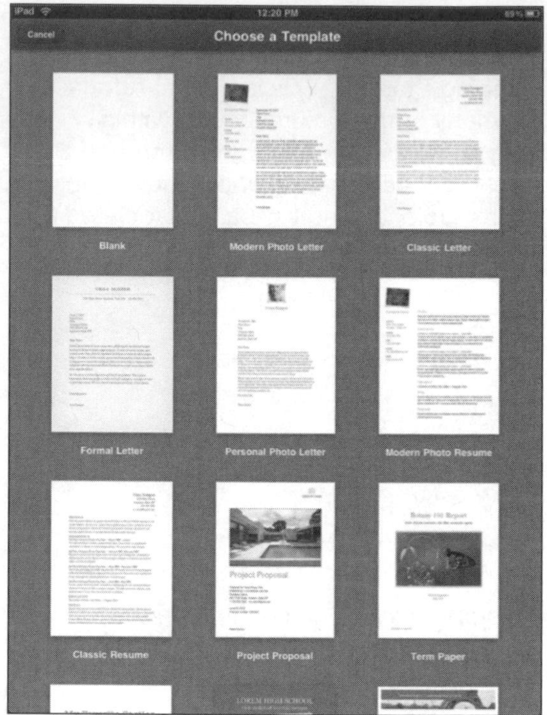


Everything within the template can be changed or adjusted, so don't be afraid to experiment.

> **NOTE:** Templates are very helpful for things like resumes and letters, documents that require a certain format and presentation.

Once you make your selection, you are ready to start writing and editing to turn the template into the perfect document.

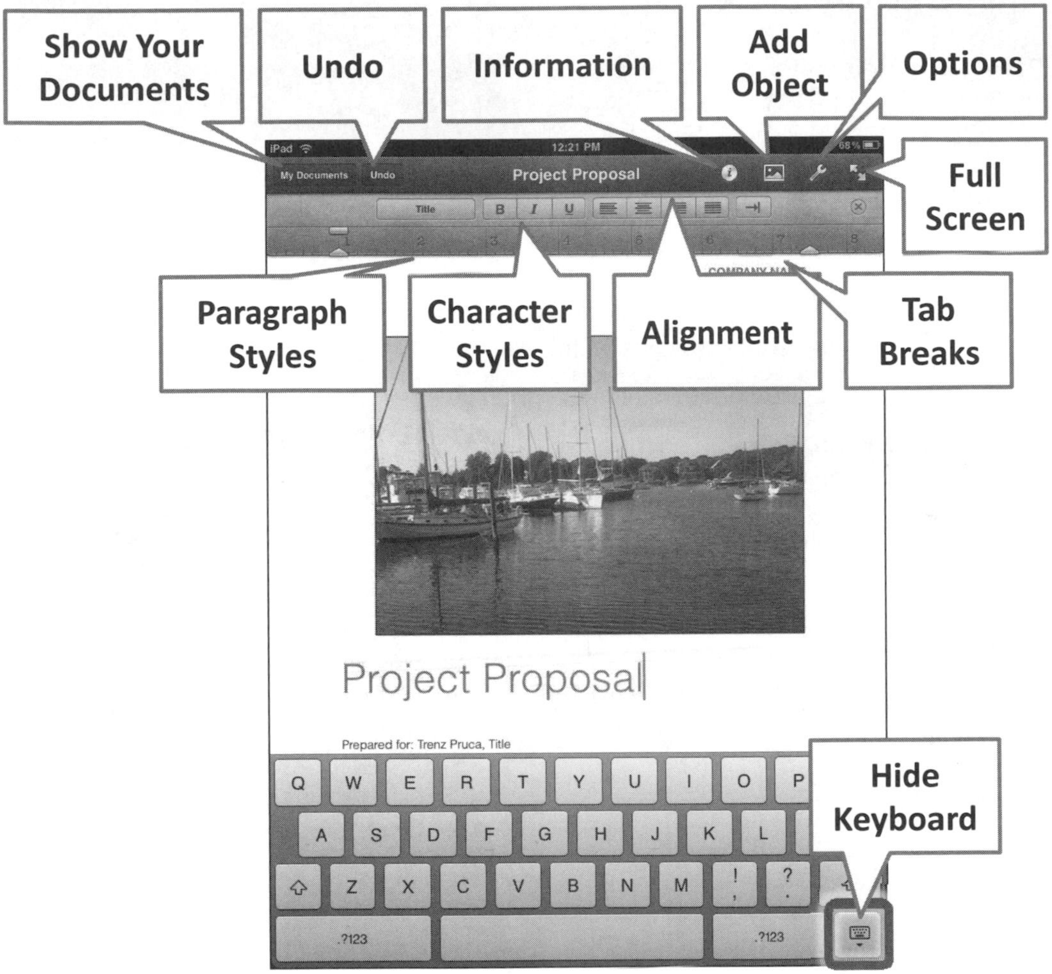

**Figure 18-1.** *Page layout in* ***Pages***

## Working With Tools and Styles

Like any fully-functioning word processor, **Pages** gives the user many options for adding various styles to the document. The built-in toolbars give you easy access to customizing virtually every aspect of your document.

There are four specific buttons on the toolbar in the upper right-hand corner that will prove to be quite useful in your writing; **Information**, **Picture/Object, Tools**, and **Styles**.

## Information Button

The **Information** button sits to the left of the four toolbar buttons.

This button is where you turn to:

- Set a particular style, such as Heading, Subheading, or Caption
- Change the font, font size, or color
- Change the settings for lists with bullets and numbers
- Change the alignment/justification and line spacing

To change Heading, Subheading, or other style, just touch the **Style** button after you touch the **Information** button. Scroll through the list to choose the appropriate style and then touch it. A check mark will then appear next to the style you have chosen.

You can also add **Bold**, *Italics*, Underline, or ~~Strikethrough~~ by touching the appropriate button.

## Selecting Text to Apply a Style or Cut/Copy

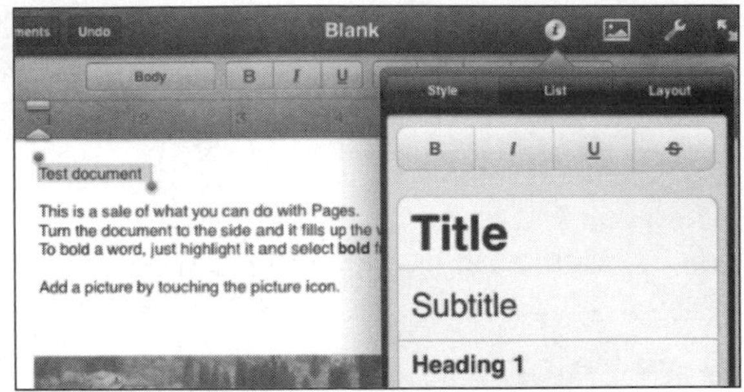


The style you select can be applied to the next text you type or it can be applied to selected text already in the document.

To select text you have typed:

1. Double-tap to select a word.
2. Triple-tap to select a paragraph.

To select text in a **Pages** template:

1. Press and hold a word to select it.
2. Double-tap to select a paragraph.

Once the text is selected, choose the style to apply to the text you have selected by using the tool bar or the **(i) Info** button, as shown.

## Picture/Object Button

Next to the **Information** button you will find the **Picture/Object** button. Touch this button to insert media, tables, charts, or shapes into the document.

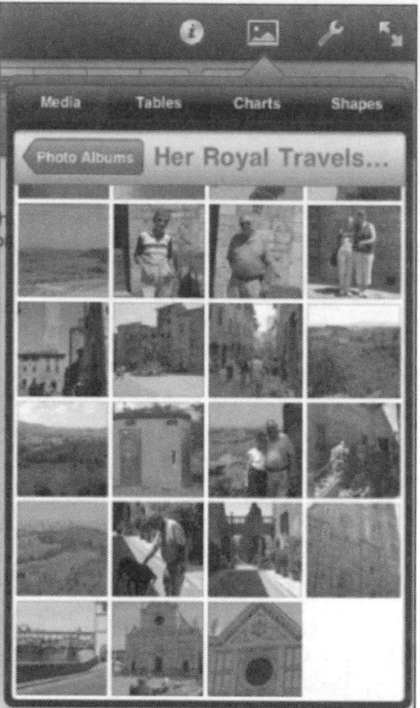


When you first touch this button, you will see the **Media** tab highlighted and all your photo albums visible.

To choose a photo, navigate through the available albums and select the corresponding photo to use.

To add a table to the document, touch the **Table** tab and choose from the various table formats shown.

**NOTE:** There are six screens of tables to look through. Swipe from right to left to advance through the screens.

To insert a chart:

1. Touch the **Chart** tab and swipe through the screens.
2. Tap the chart you want to insert.

To edit the data behind the chart (see Figure 18-2):

1. Double-tap the chart so that it flips around, showing you a data table.
2. Type the data needed to create the chart.
3. Press **Done** in the upper right corner when finished to see the updated chart.

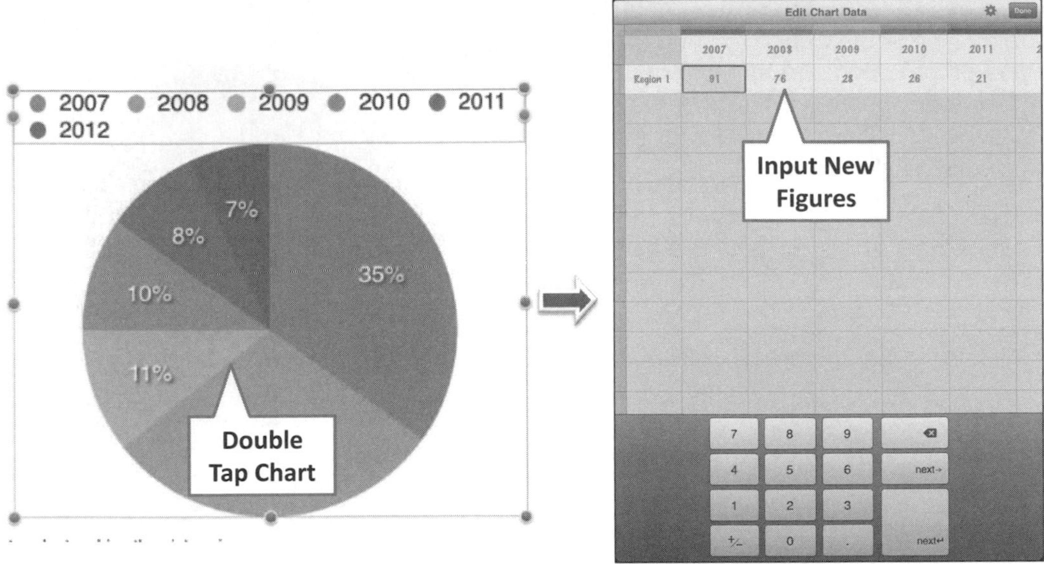


**Figure 18-2.** *How to customize charts in* ***Pages***

To insert a shape:

1. Touch the **Shape** tab and swipe through the screens.
2. Tap the shape you want to insert.

To move or resize the shape:

1. Press and hold the shape to drag it around the page.
2. Touch the two corners and pinch open or closed to make it smaller or larger.
3. Put two fingers inside the shape and spin it around to rotate the shape.

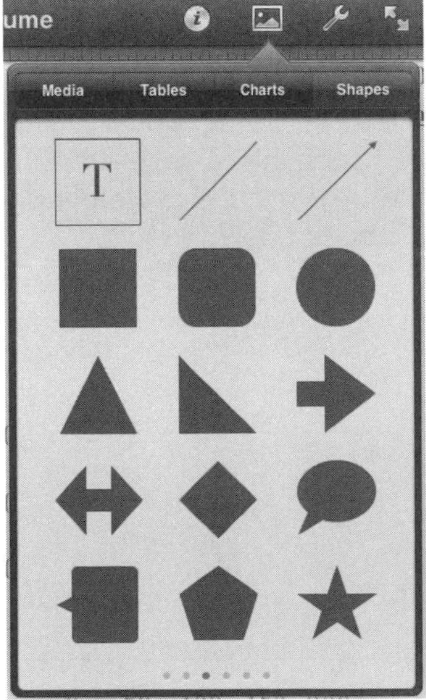

To move or resize the picture, chart, or object, simply tap once to bring up the blue dots. Touch and hold the object and move it anywhere you wish on the page. You will notice that text will move around the object as you move it.

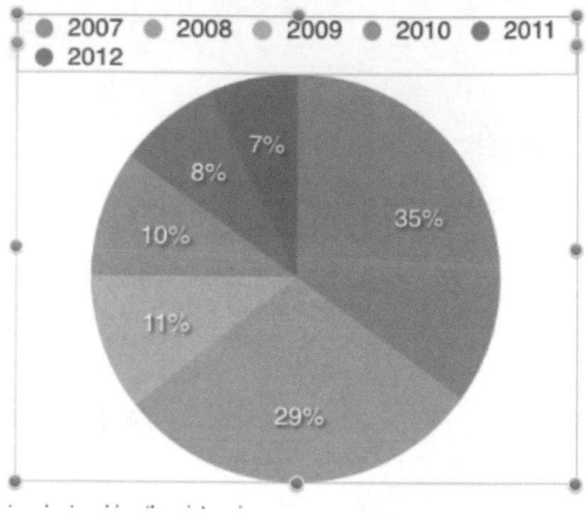


> **TIP:** To change or adjust the text wrapping, simply touch the Information button while the picture or object is highlighted and choose Arrange. Touch the Wrap button and choose a style for the word wrap.

## Tools Button

Next to the **Pictures/Objects** button is the **Tools** button. Touch this to access the **Document Setup**, **Find**, **Go to Help**, **Edge Guides**, and **Check Spelling** tools.

Touch the **Document Setup** tool and you will see what looks like a blueprint. To add or edit a header or footer, touch the **Tap to Edit Header/Footer** buttons.

To adjust the margins, just drag the triangles in from the sides or from the top and bottom of the page.

When you are done with your adjustments, simply touch the **Done** button

in the upper left-hand corner.

To hide all tool bars and just focus on a blank screen for writing, touch the **Full Screen** icon in the upper right-hand corner. To enable the tool bar once again, just tap on the screen.

## Style Buttons and Ruler

The **Style** buttons and Ruler are visible only when you are in a field with editable text. Simply touch the screen anywhere text can be input or edited and you will see the ruler at the top (see Figure 18-3).

**NOTE:** If you turn your iPad to landscape orientation, the menus and style bar disappear. To get the menus and style bar back, turn your iPad back to portrait orientation.

At both edges of the ruler, there are sliding guides for tabs and indentations. Simply slide to adjust the margins and tabs for your document.

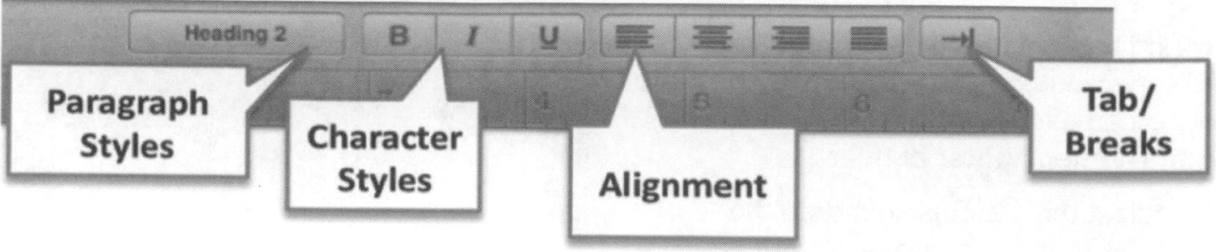


**Figure 18-3.** ***Style*** *buttons*

On top of the ruler, you will find many of the same buttons that we saw when we touched the **Information** button. You can adjust the paragraph styles, the character styles, align or justify text, and set tabs, page breaks, and column breaks by touching the appropriate button.

> **TIP:** It is always easier to apply styles when you have first selected a word by double-tapping—then choose a style to apply.

## Navigator

Navigator is a very cool tool built into **Pages**.

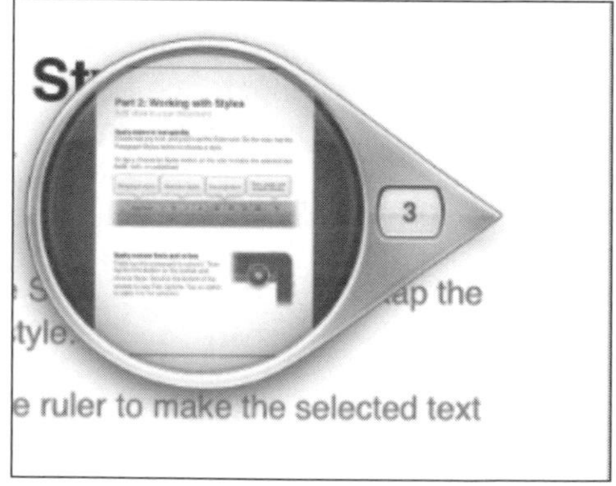

1. Hold your finger along the right-hand edge of the page and slowly drag down or up.
2. A small magnifying glass appears with a little "snapshot" of the pages in the document.
3. Each little bit you move downwards shows the next page.
4. When you find the page you wish to read or edit, remove your finger from the screen and you will jump to that page.

# Numbers Spreadsheet

**Numbers** is a powerful spreadsheet program, much like **Numbers** for the Mac or Microsoft Excel for Windows.

**Numbers** allows you to create, edit, and read complex spreadsheets, input and calculate formulas, and set up multiple worksheets (displayed across the top of each file as file folder tabs known as "sheet tabs") within a spreadsheet.

# Using Numbers for the First Time

Just like with **Pages**, **Numbers** comes with a "Getting Started" file to help you with some of the various features of the program. It is a very good idea to thumb through this guide before you start creating your own spreadsheets.

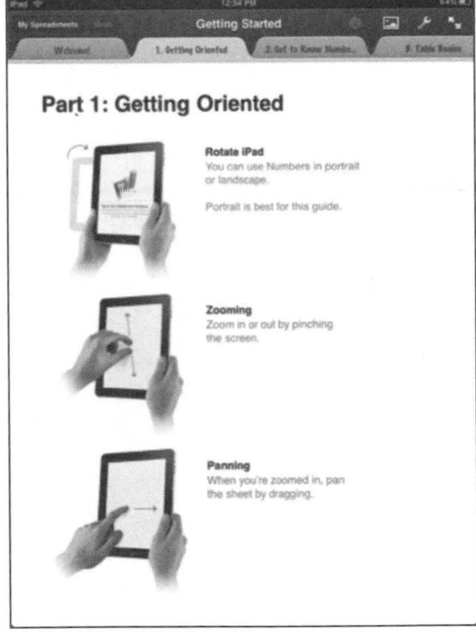

## Choosing a Template

As with **Pages**, the **New Document** button gives you the option of starting a new spreadsheet or using a duplicate spreadsheet.

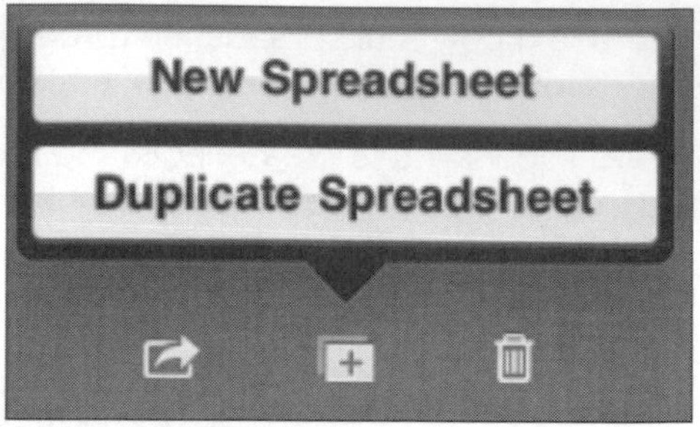


**NOTE**: To use Duplicate Spreadsheet, you need to have the spreadsheet you wish to "duplicate" in the main window.

1. Touch the **New Document** button and you will be asked to choose a template.
2. Choose **Blank** to start from scratch or choose one of the templates provided to get started.

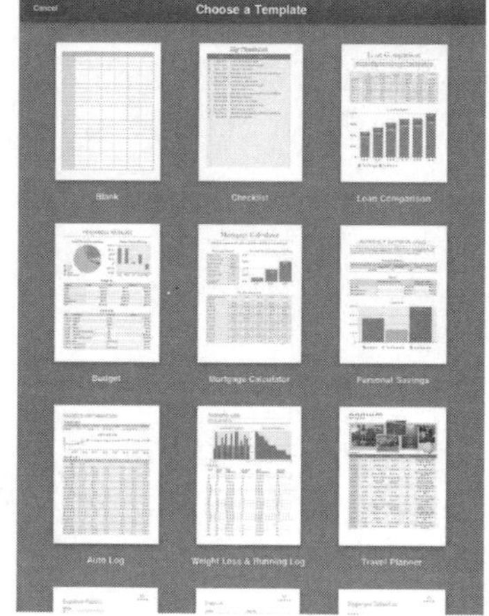


In the following example, we chose the **Budget** template to work with.

## Using the Toolbar in Numbers

In the upper right-hand corner, just like in **Pages**, you will find the **Numbers** toolbar. The icons are identical to those in **Pages**, but the functions are a bit different (see Figure 18-4).

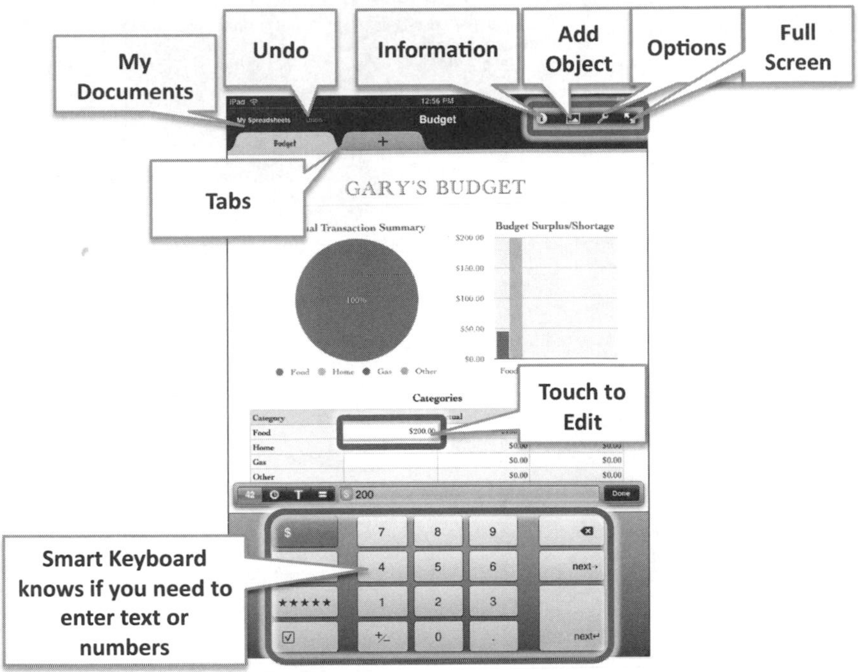


**Figure 18-4.** *Page layout in* ***Numbers***

## Information Button

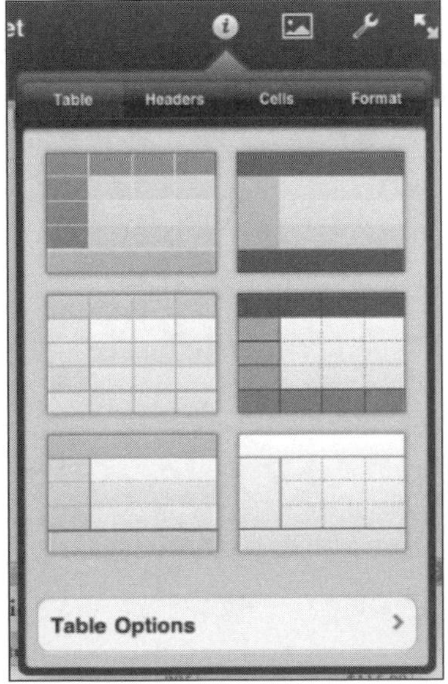


The **Information** button looks identical and sits in the same place as it does in **Pages**. In order to use the **Information** button, you need to have text, a chart, graph, or object highlighted. Simply touch anywhere to activate the **Information** button.

Touch a chart and the chart options are displayed. Touch a table and the table options are displayed.

In this example, we touched a chart and then touched the **Information** button. We touched **Chart Options** and can now choose everything from text size to font to the type of chart. The options are truly staggering.

Take some time to walk through the "Getting Started" guide to see all the options available.

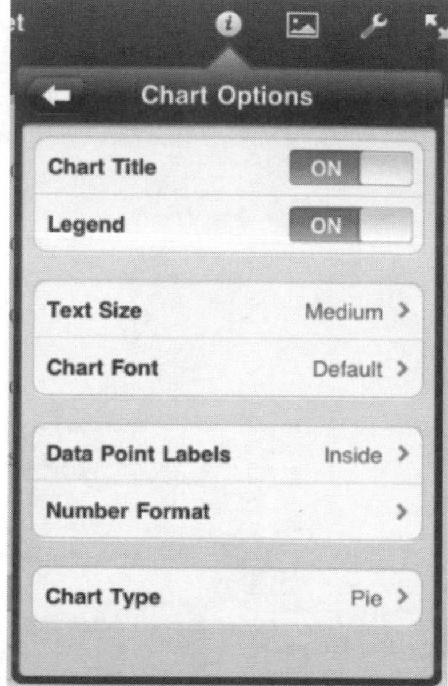


**TIP:** We could write a full book on each of these programs. Take some time to just touch icons and options to see for yourself how things change as you make individual selections. Have fun—this is very powerful and creative software to work and play with!

## Picture/Object Button

Next to the **Information** button you will find the **Picture/Object** button. Touch this button to insert media, tables, charts, or shapes into the document. This button functions exactly the same as it does in **Pages**.

## Tools Button

Next to the **Pictures/Objects** button is the **Tools** button. Touch this to access the **Find**, **Go to Help**, **Edge Guides**, and **Check Spelling** tools.

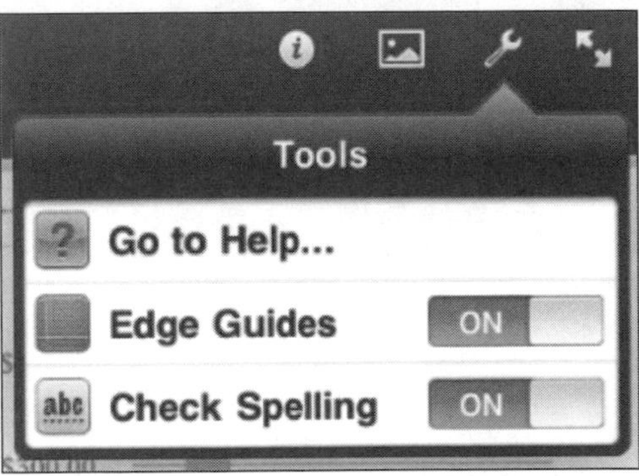

Use the **Find** button to search for any word or phrase in the document—just like **Pages**.

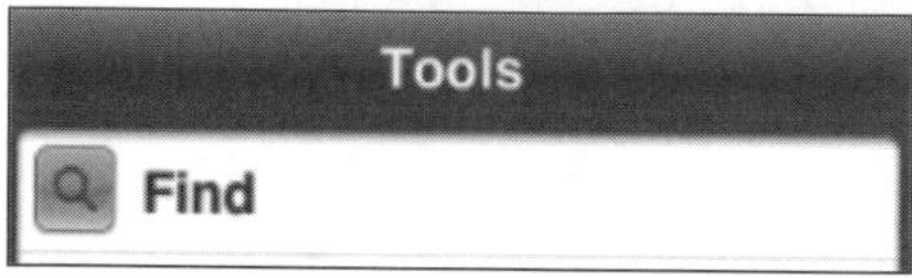


When the word is located, the text will be highlighted in yellow. Just touch to edit.

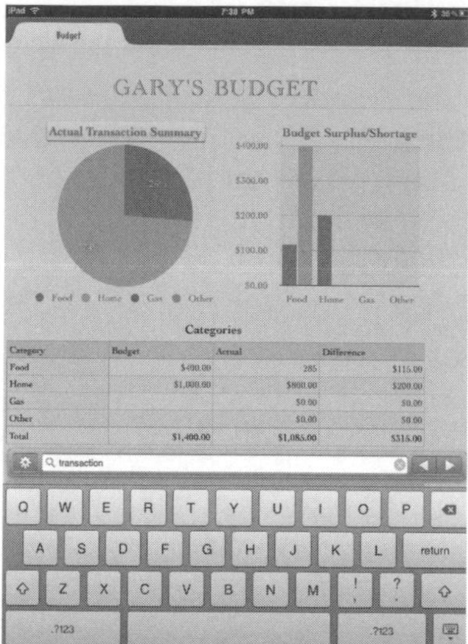


Use **Go to Help** to jump to the Apple web site for support with iWork.

> **NOTE:** Remember that the iPad does NOT multi-task. That means that if you use Go to Help and jump to the web browser, you will exit **Numbers**, **Pages**, or **Keynote** and then you will need to re-enter the program once you leave the browser. Multi-tasking will be available in some programs in version 4.0 of the iPad operating system, due to arrive this fall.

The **Edge Guides** and **Check Spelling** toggles are exactly the same as in **Pages**.

## Editing Cells, Charts, and Graphs

This is a very powerful spreadsheet program. Just like a traditional spreadsheet program on your computer, you can edit each cell, input formulas, and customize charts and graphs.

## Working with Charts and Graphs

The first time working with **Numbers**, we suggest you open one of the templates. In this example we are using the **Budget** template. Notice the pie chart, which is based on four criteria.

1. Double-tap the chart to select it, then the cells used to create the chart are highlighted.
2. Double-tap an individual cell and the formula calculator pops up.

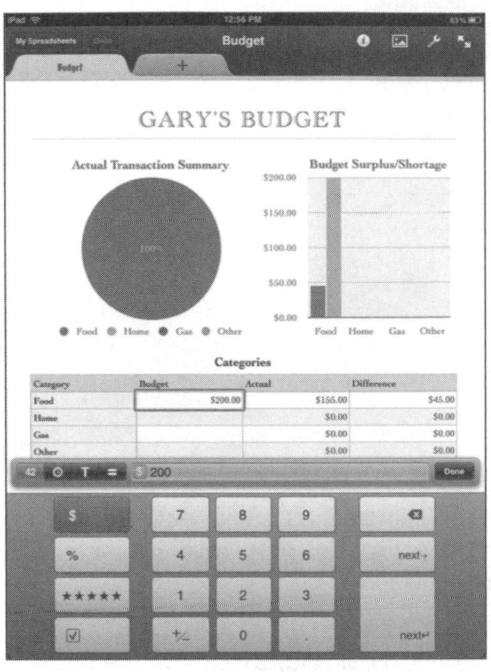


**Numbers** senses what type of field you are trying to enter. In the **Budget** template, **Numbers** knows we need to enter dollar amounts. Simply type in a new amount and press the **Done** button, and the changes will be reflected in the chart above.

When you touch a box that is looking for text, the text input keyboard will pop up. All these changes will then be reflected in the chart. You can see how using a template can make things go quickly and easily for you.

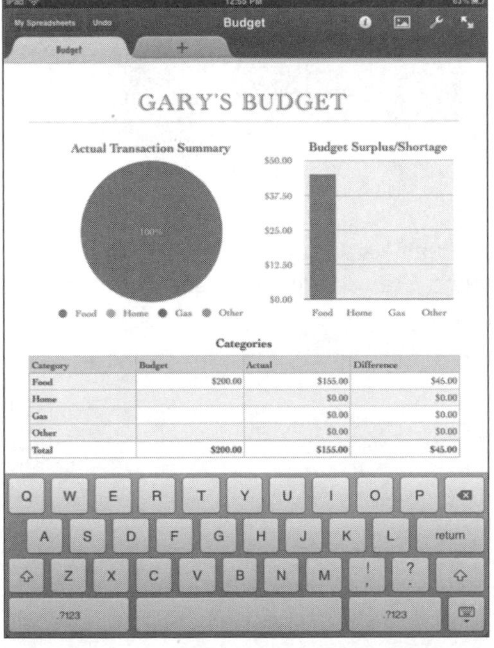

## Working with Tables

If you have spent any time at all working with spreadsheets, you know that tables are a mainstay of spreadsheet construction.

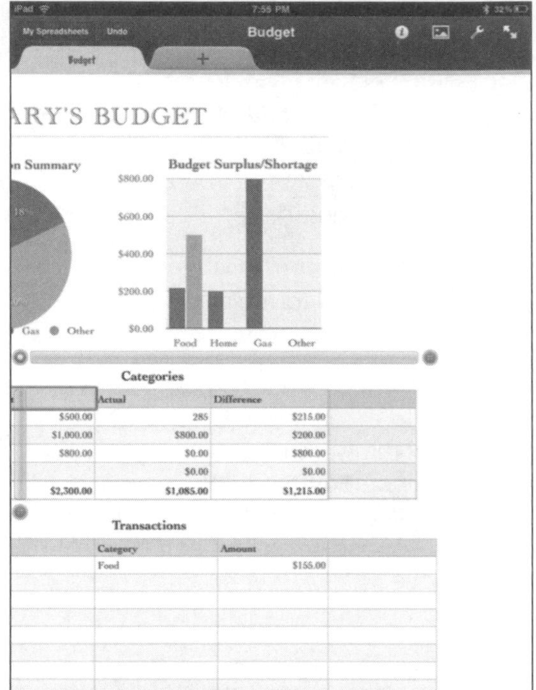


In the **Budget** template, I have touched and highlighted a table.

If you hold and drag the column handle, you can add a column to the table.

The row handle will add or remove rows when you move it up or down.

To move the table entirely, just touch and hold the top bar and re-position the table where you desire.

> **TIP:** It is easy to make mistakes when using **Numbers**. If something doesn't look right, just touch the Undo button to undo the last edit or addition. Touch Undo a couple of times to keep "undoing" things you might not have wanted to do.

There really is so much more to do with **Numbers**—we again encourage you to read the "Getting Started" guide to see additional features!

# Keynote Presentations

**Keynote** is the third jewel in the triple crown of iWork. **Keynote** is comparable to **Keynote** on your Mac or Microsoft PowerPoint on your PC. Like **Pages** and **Numbers**, **Keynote** is a very powerful and capable piece of presentation software. We won't be able to cover every aspect of this software, but we can get you started and working with presentations using **Keynote**.

## Using Keynote for the First Time

Just like **Pages** and **Numbers**, **Keynote** comes with a "Getting Started" file to help you with some of the various features of the program. It is a very good idea to thumb through this guide before you start creating your own spreadsheets.

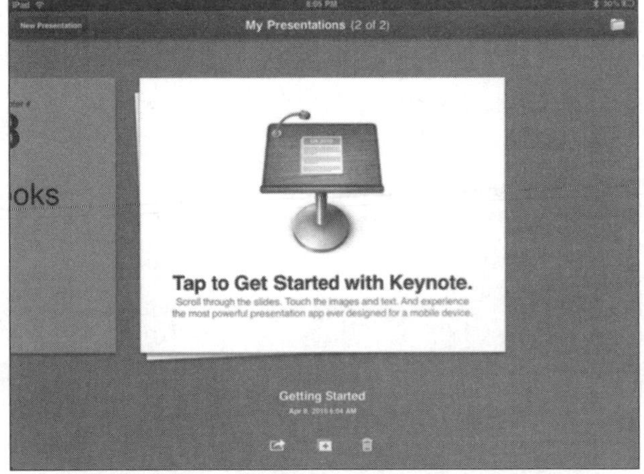


**NOTE:** Unlike **Pages** and **Numbers**, **Keynote** works only in landscape mode since this is presentation software.

## Choosing a Template

As with **Pages**, the **New Presentation** button gives you the option of starting a new presentation or using a duplicate presentation.

**NOTE:** You need to have the presentation you wish to "duplicate" visible in the main window.

Touch the **New Presentation** button and you will be asked to choose a template.

You can select from several blank presentations ("White," "Black," or "Gradient") to start from scratch or choose one of the templates or themes provided to get started.

In the following example, we chose the **Parchment** template to work with.

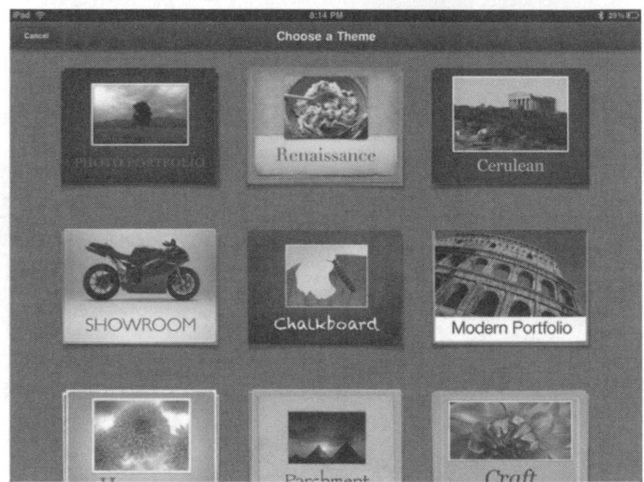


## Using the Toolbar in Keynote

In the upper right-hand corner, just like in **Pages** and **Numbers**, you will find the **Keynote** toolbar. The icons are similar to those in **Pages** and **Numbers**, but the functions are a bit different, as shown in Figure 18-5.

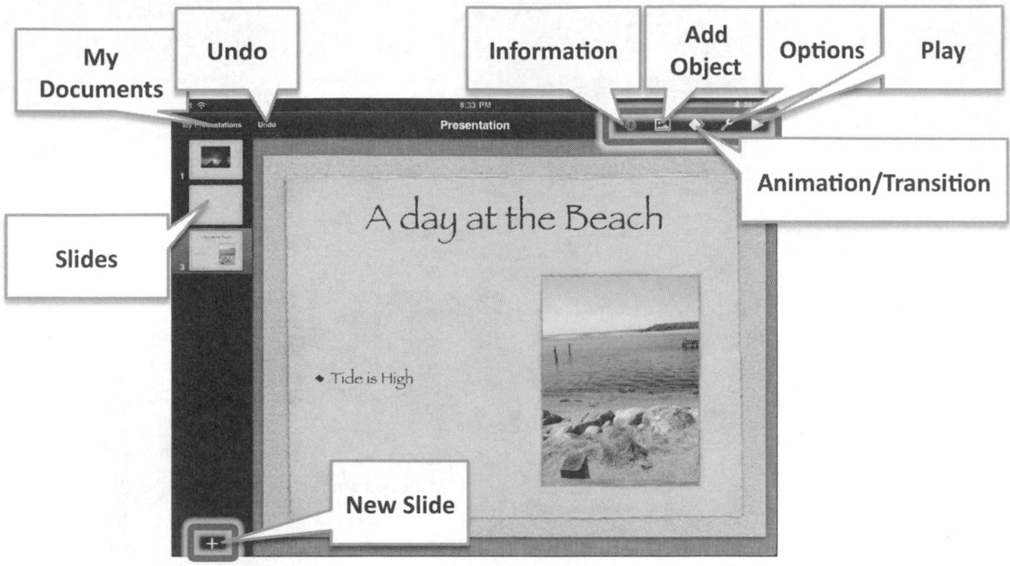


**Figure 18-5.** *Page layout in **Keynote***

## Information Button

The **Information** button looks identical and sits in the same place as it does in **Pages**. In order to use the **Information** button, you need to have a text box, picture, graph, or object highlighted. Simply touch anywhere to activate the object and then tap the **Information** button.

Touch a text box and the text options are displayed. Touch a picture and the picture options are displayed.

In this example, we touched a text box and then touched the **Information** button.

We touched **Text Options** and can now choose everything from text size to font to the style of text.

The options are truly staggering. Take some time to walk through the "Getting Started" guide to see all the options available.

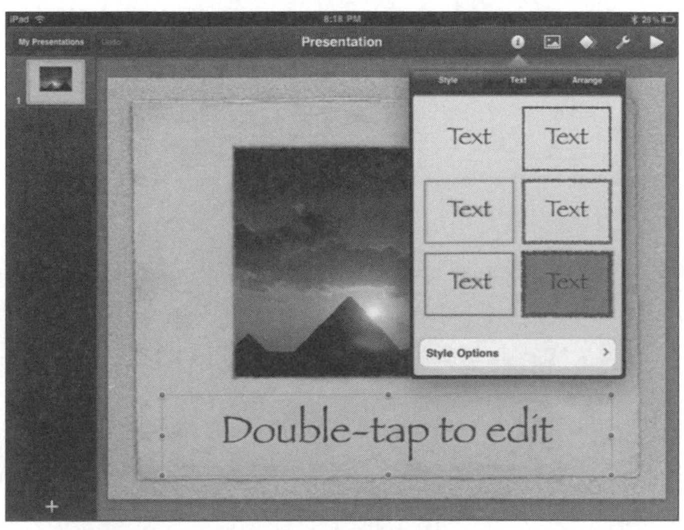

**TIP:** We could write a full book on each of these apps. Take some time to just touch icons and options to see for yourself how things change as you make individual selections. Have fun—this is very powerful and creative software to work and play with!

## Picture/Object Button

Next to the **Information** button you will find the **Picture/Object** button. Touch this button to insert media, tables, charts, or shapes into the document. This button functions exactly the same as it does in **Pages** and **Numbers**.

**TIP:** In all three programs, pictures can be rotated just by touching and holding two fingers on the picture and rotating your fingers—very cool!

## Tools Button

Next to the **Pictures/Objects** button is the **Tools** button. Touch this to access the **Find**, **Go to Help**, **Edge Guides, Slide Numbers**, and **Check Spelling** tools.

Use the **Find** button to search for any word or phrase in the document—just like **Pages** and **Numbers.** When the word is located, the text will be highlighted in yellow. Just touch to edit.

Use **Go to Help** to jump to the Apple web site for support with iWork.

> **NOTE**: Remember that presently the iPad does not multi-task. That means that if you use Go to Help and jump to the web browser, you will exit **Numbers**, **Pages**, or **Keynote**, and then you will need to re-enter the program once you leave the browser.

The **Edge Guides**, **Slide Numbers**, and **Check Spelling** toggles are exactly the same as in **Pages**.

## Add a Slide

1. To add a slide, touch the button in the lower left-hand corner.
2. Choose the style of slide you wish to add.
3. Double-tap to edit the text and use the tool buttons to add images or objects as you did before.

## Animation Button

1. In **Keynote**, you can customize the transition animation from one slide to the next.

2. Touch the **Animation** button to see an **Animation** tab next to each slide in the presentation.

> **NOTE:** You can also add magic moves, which duplicates the slide and then lets you change aspects and animates those changes.

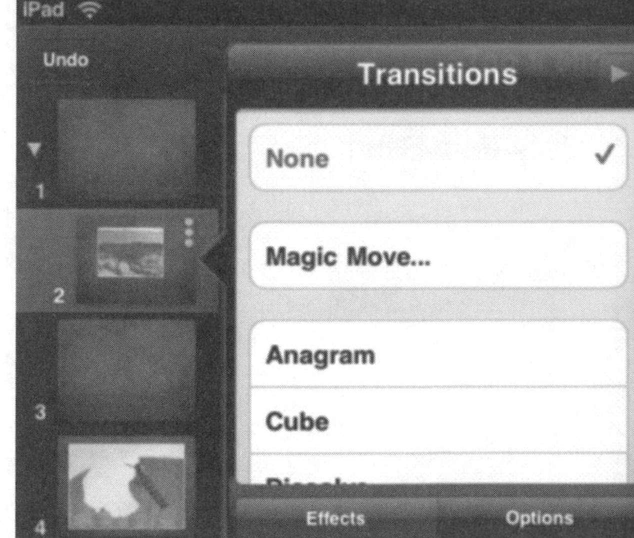


3. Touch the tab to see the **Transitions** menu.
4. Choose an effect and then tap the **Options** button at the bottom to adjust the timing of the transition and whether it occurs when tapping the screen or after the previous transition.
5. Tap **Done** in the upper-right corner when you are finished working with transitions.

## Play Button

To play the slideshow, just touch the **Play** button in the top right-hand corner. Based on the transition settings you set, the presentation will begin to play.

## Sharing your Work

The Share function in iWork is the same in each of the three programs. Touch the **Share** button and three options are presented to you: **Send via Mail**, **Share via iWork.com**, or **Export**.

### Send via Mail

Sending a document, spreadsheet, or presentation via email is very easy with iWork. Make sure the document, spreadsheet, or presentation is in the main window with the Share commands underneath.

Choose **Send via Mail** and your Mail app will load with the file shown as an attachment. Add a recipient as we showed you in Chapter 12, type in your message, and then just touch **Send**.

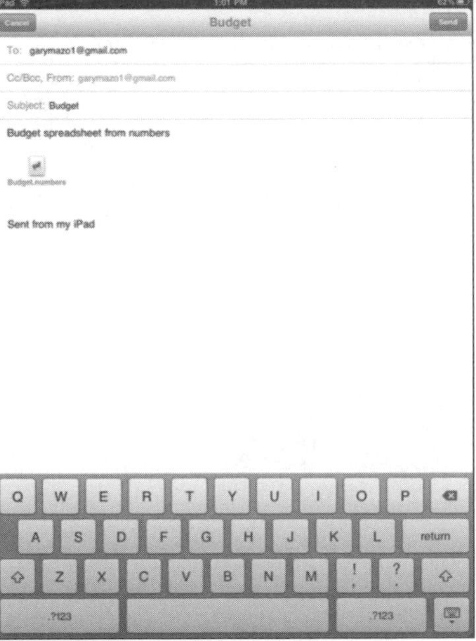

## Share via iWork

When you touch **Share via iWork.com**, a window pops up asking you to input your Apple ID or your MobileMe ID and password. Input the correct information and your file is now stored online for easy retrieval from any computer. This is a great way to share and collaborate on work.

Once you try to use iWork.com for the first time, you will be asked to send a verification email.

Check the verification email and follow the instructions to begin sharing your work online.

Login to iwork.com, sign in with your Apple ID and password, and your "Shared Documents" will now be available.

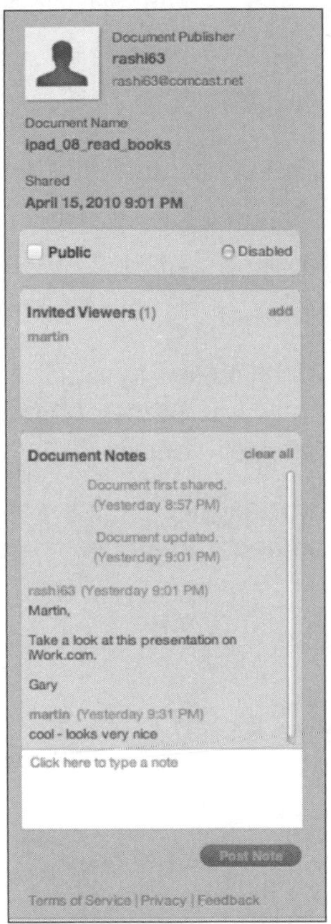


**TIP:** This is a great way to collaborate on work and also to send something from your iPad that might be too large to email to someone to view and print.

## Printing a File

At publishing time, the iPad does not offer a native "Print" command. So you have a few options.

Option 1: You can email the document to yourself, a colleague, or other person and print it from a computer.

Option 2: You could acquire a printing app from the App store. One of the well-reviewed apps out there at publishing time is **PrintCentral for iPad** (US$9.99), which allows you to print to a networked printer or a printer connected to your PC or Mac.

## Faxing a File via E-Fax Service

This is a great trick if you are away from your home or office and want to get a quick print-out or send a quick fax.

**NOTE:** In order to do this, you have to first sign up for an electronic fax service such as `www.efax.com` so you can send faxes as email attachments.

Once you have your e-fax account, then you can send the document to a fax machine as an email attachment:

1. Choose the **Share** > **Send via Email** in any of the iWork apps.
2. Choose **PDF format**.
3. Address the email message with the fax number in the format required by your e-fax service. Some of the services have the following format: (fax number)@faxsend.com or `3865551212@faxsend.com`
4. Then, once the email is sent, it is converted to a fax by your fax service and sent to the appropriate fax machine.

## Export a File

1. Choose **Share** > **Export** in any of the iWork apps.
2. Choose the file type in which you would like the document to be transferred to the computer.
3. Transfers are handled through iTunes the next time you connect the iPad to the computer. The usual formats are the default for the particular application. You also have a PDF option for export.

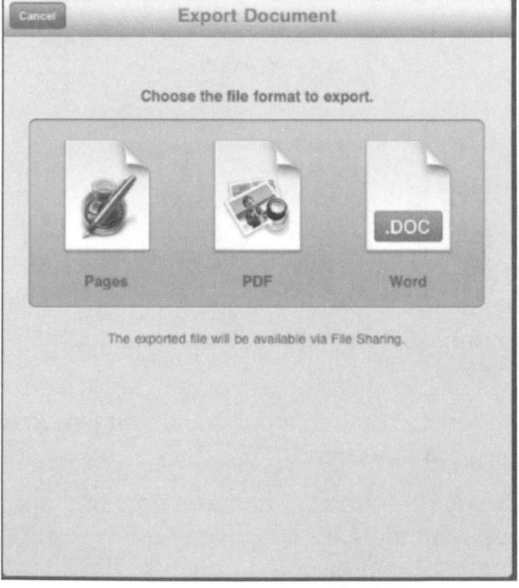


**NOTE: Pages** can export to Word for Mac and PC, but **Keynote** and **Numbers** cannot yet export to their Microsoft PC equivalents (PowerPoint and Excel). You can always choose to export to a PDF file from any of the iWork programs.

In the next section we will cover how to then "import" these documents into your iPad using file sharing.

## File Sharing

File sharing is the ability to take a document that you create in iWork and "share" it via iTunes. File sharing takes place in iTunes through the **Apps** tab at the top of the screen. Click on **Apps** and scroll down to the **File Sharing** section at the bottom of the screen.

> **TIP:** We also show you how to use file sharing in the "File Sharing" section of Chapter 3: "Sync with iTunes."

Each program that is installed on your iPad and capable of file sharing is shown at the bottom.

1. Click on the app from which you have shared the file (in this case **Keynote**).
2. Then all the documents that you have shared on my iPad are shown.

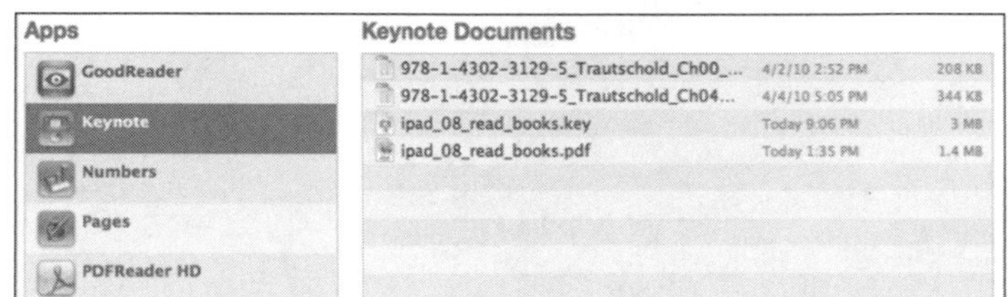


3. Highlight the document to save and then touch the **Save To** button in the lower right-hand corner.

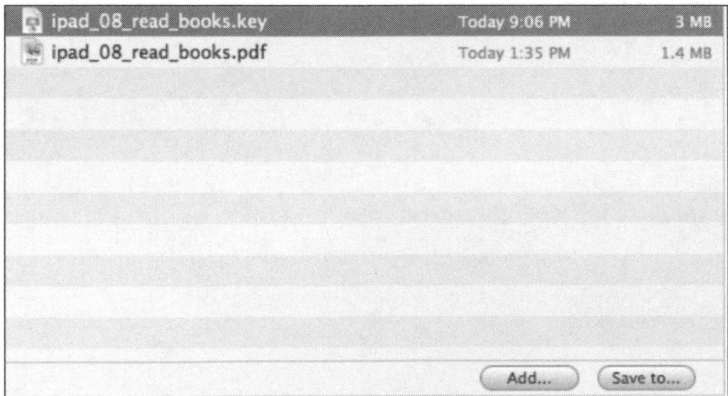

4. From there, you simply navigate to the folder in which you want to save the document.

5. Now, the file is on your computer for easy viewing, editing, and printing.

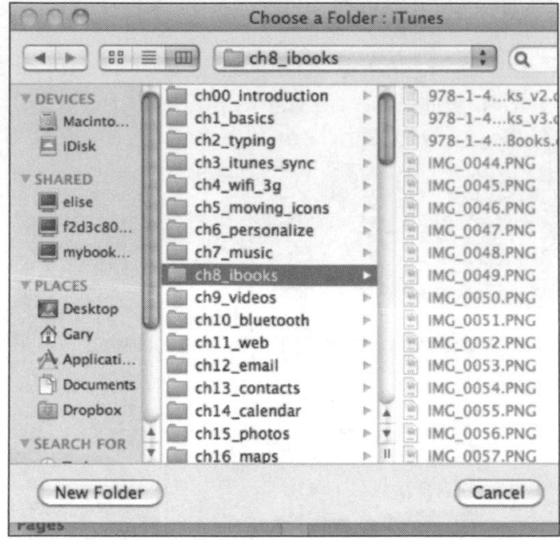

Chapter 19

# iTunes on Your iPad

In this chapter, you will learn how to locate, buy, and download media using the **iTunes** app right on your iPad. With iTunes, you will be able to download music, movies, TV shows, podcasts, audiobooks, and free educational content from leading universities with iTunes U. You will also learn how to redeem iTunes gift cards.

Some of us still remember going to the record store when that new single or album came out. It was an exciting feeling, browsing through all the vinyl albums, then tapes and CDs, and looking at all the music we wanted.

Those days are pretty much long gone with the iPad. All the music, movies, TV shows, and more are available right from the iPad itself.

iTunes is a music, video, TV, podcast, and more store – virtually every type of media you can consume on your iPad is available for purchase or rent (and often for free) right from the iTunes store.

## Getting Started with iTunes on the iPad

Earlier in this book, we showed you how to get your music from iTunes on your computer into your iPad (see chapter 3). You can also learn more about using iTunes on your computer in Chapter 26. One of the great things about iTunes is that it is very easy to buy or obtain music, videos, podcasts, and audiobooks, and then use them in minutes right on your iPad.

The iPad allows you to access iTunes (the mobile version) right on your device. After you purchase or request free items, they will be downloaded to your **iPod** app or **Videos** app on the iPad. They will also be automatically transferred to your iTunes library on your computer the next time you perform a sync, so you can also enjoy the same content on your computer.

## A Network Connection Is Required

You do need an active Internet connection (either Wi-Fi or 3G/cellular) in order to access the iTunes store. Check out Chapter 4 to learn more about network connectivity.

## Starting iTunes

When you first received your iPad, **iTunes** was one of the icons on the first **Home** screen page. Touch the **iTunes** icon, and you will be taken to the mobile iTunes Store.

**NOTE:** The **iTunes** app changes frequently. Since the **iTunes** app is really a web site, it is likely to change somewhat between the time we wrote this book and when you are looking at it on your iPad. Some of the screen images or buttons may look slightly different than the ones shown in this book.

## Navigating iTunes

iTunes uses icons similar to other programs on the iPad, so getting around is quite easy. There are three buttons at the top and seven icons or soft keys at the bottom to help you. Look at Figure 19–1 to see the soft keys and features. Scrolling is just like scrolling in any other program; move your finger up or down to look at the selections available.

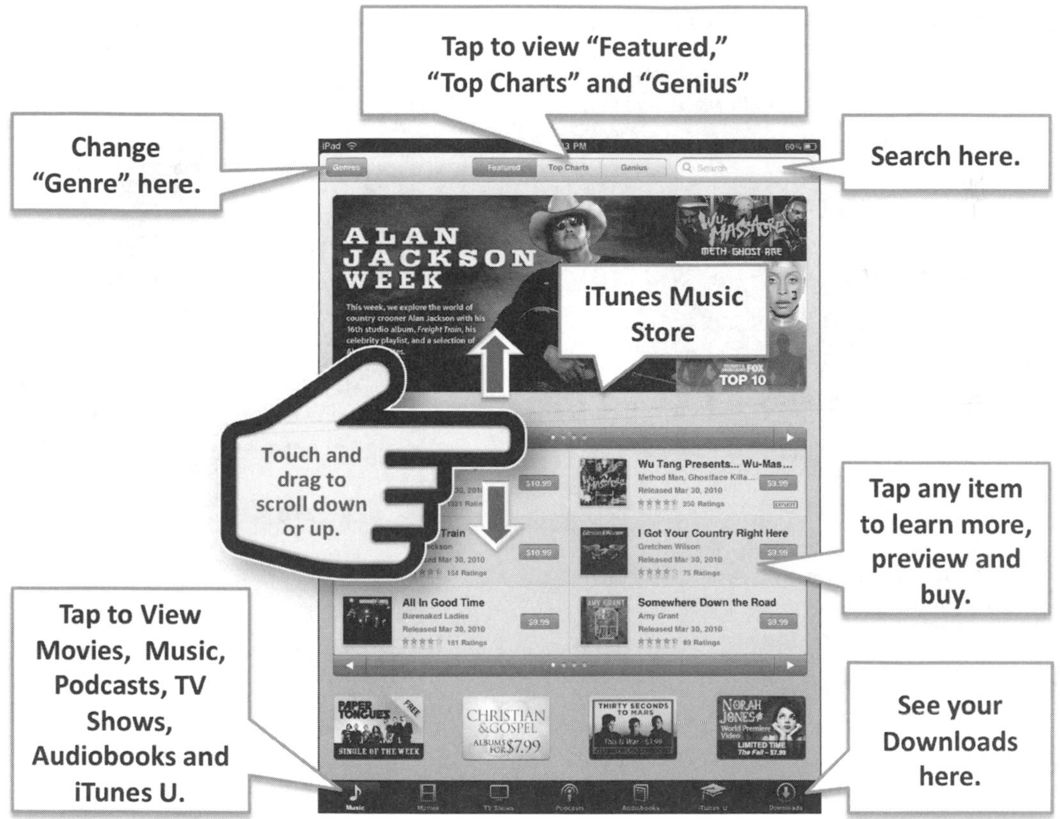


**Figure 19–1.** *The iTunes layout*

# Finding Music with Featured, Top Charts, and Genius

Along the top of the iTunes music store screen are three buttons: **Featured**, **Top Charts**, and **Genius**. By default, you are shown the **Featured** selections when you start iTunes.

## Top Charts –the Popular Stuff

If you like to see what is popular in a particular category, you will want to browse the **Top Charts** category. Tap **Top Charts** at the top, and then tap a category or genre to see what is popular for that category.

> **CAUTION:** These songs or videos are selling well, but that doesn't mean that they will appeal to you. Always give the item a preview and check out the reviews before you pay for it.

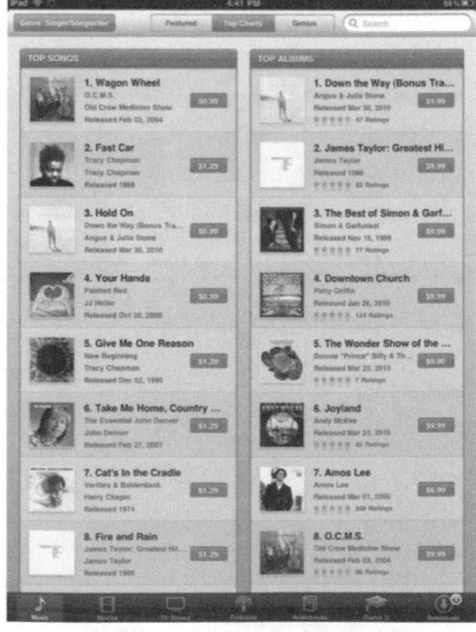

Tap the **Genre** button in the upper left corner to select a particular genre. For example, if you touch **Singer Songwriter**, you will see the top ten songs or albums in that category only.

The initial view shows you the **Top Songs** on the left and **Top Albums** on the right.

You simply scroll as you would in any other program on the iPad.

## Genres – Types of Music

Touch the **Genres** button to browse music based on a genre. This is particularly helpful if you have a favorite type of music and would like to browse just that category.

There is quite an extensive list of genres to browse; just scroll down the list as you would in any other iPad program.

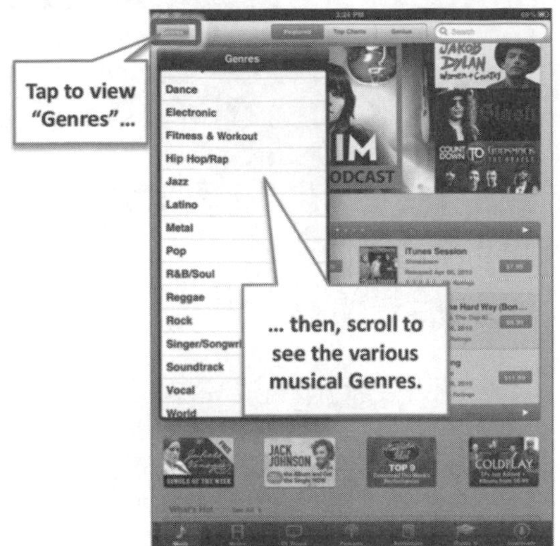


Go ahead and browse through the music until you see something that you would like to preview or buy.

## Browsing for Videos (Movies)

Touch the **Movies** or **TV Shows** buttons on the bottom to browse all the video-related items (see Figure 19–2).

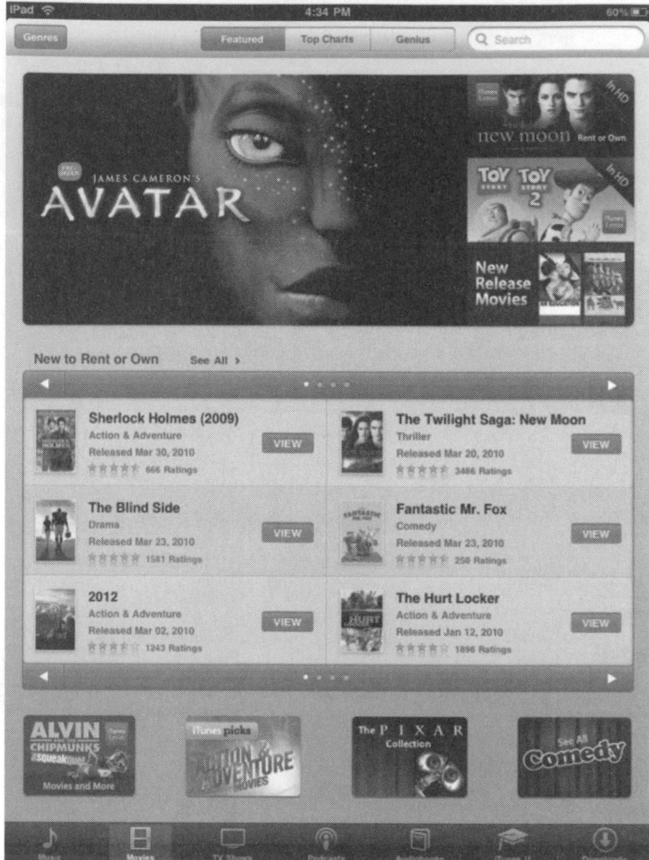


**Figure 19–2.** *Browsing the Movie category in iTunes on your iPad.*

You can also use your finger to scroll all the way to the bottom of the page to check out the links there, including these links in particular:

- **New to Own**
- **New to Rent**
- **All HD Movies**

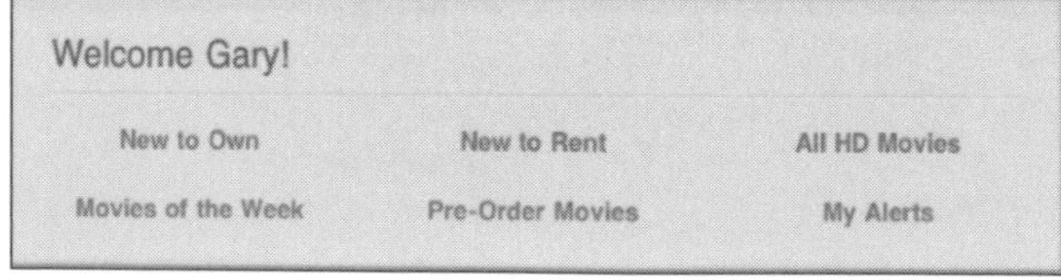

Tap on any movie or video to see more details or preview the selection. You have the option to rent or buy some movies and TV shows.

**Rentals** – Some movies are available for rent for a set number of days.

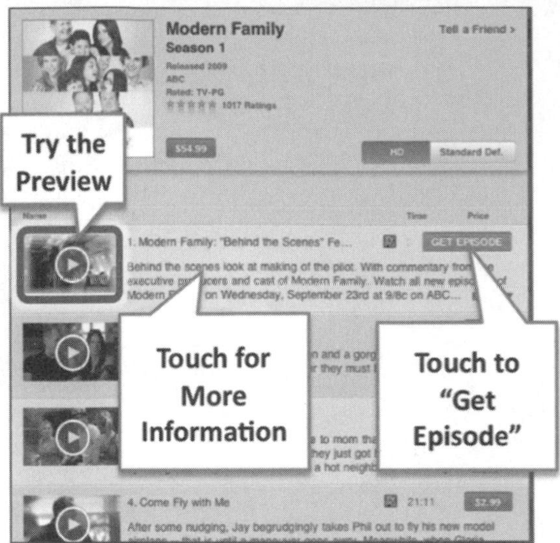


> **NOTE:** Rental period in the US is 24 hours and rental period in Canada is 48 hours. Other countries may vary slightly.

**Buy** – This allows you to purchase and own the movie or TV show forever.

## Finding TV Shows

When you're done checking out the movies, tap the **TV Shows** button at the top to see what is available from your favorite shows (see Figure 19–3).

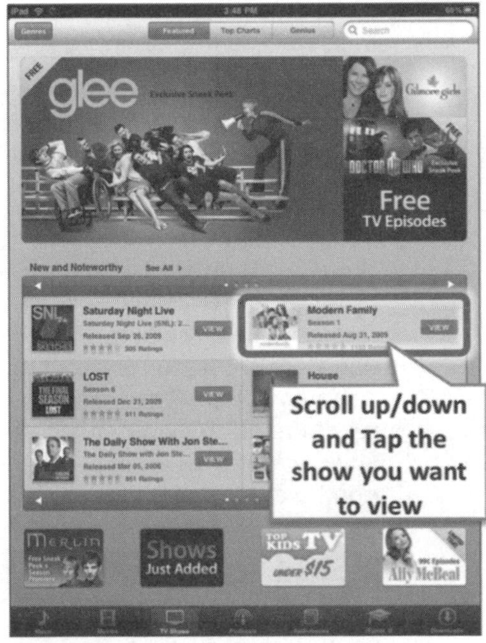


When you tap on a TV series, you will see the individual episodes available. Tap any episode to check out the 30-second preview. See Chapter 9 for more on watching videos. When you're finished with the preview, tap the **Done** button.

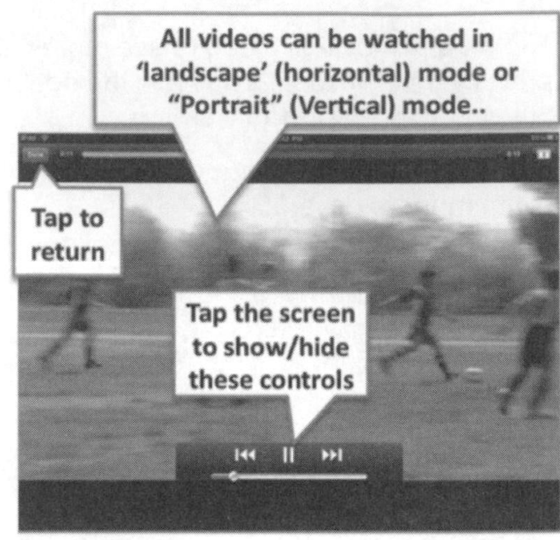


**Figure 19–3.** *Buying and watching a TV show*

When you are ready to buy, you can choose to buy an individual episode or the entire TV series. Many, but not all TV Series, allow you to purchase individual episodes.

Maybe you want to get your fix of *Modern Family* and see the pilot episode that you missed. You can do this quickly and easily on your iPad.

> **NOTE:** There is also a **Free TV Episode** category, where you can get samples and bonus content.

## Audiobooks in iTunes

Audiobooks are a great way to enjoy books without having to read them. Some of the narrators are so fun to listen to, it is almost like watching a movie. For example, the narrator of the Harry Potter series can do dozens of truly amazing voices. We recommend that you try out an audiobook on your iPad; audiobooks are especially great when you are on an airplane and want to escape from the rest of the passengers, but don't want to have the light on.

> **TIP:** If you're a big audiobook listener, getting an **Audible.com** subscription can get you the same content at cheaper prices.

If you are an audiobook aficionado, be sure to check out the audiobooks in iTunes.

You can use the top three buttons to browse the audiobooks in iTunes:

- **Featured**
- **Top Charts**
- **Categories**

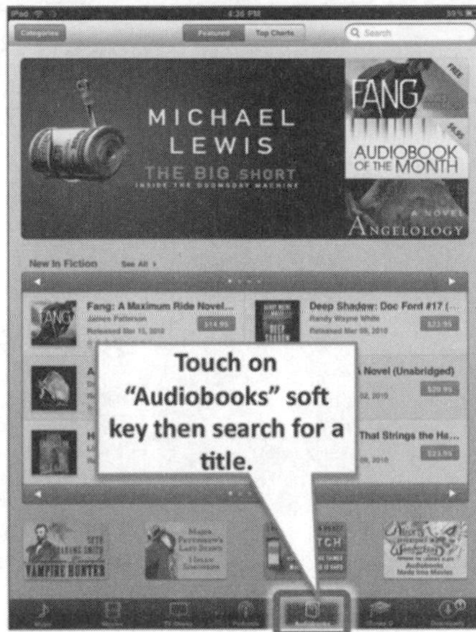


## iTunes U – Great Educational Content

If you like educational content, then check out **iTunes U**. You will be able to browse whether your university, college, or school has its own section.

One good example we discovered in just a few minutes of browsing around was a panel discussion with three Nobel Prize winning economists moderated by Paul Solmon (Economic correspondent for the PBS News Hour). You can find the podcast in **iTunes U** ➤ **Universities & Colleges** ➤ **Boston University** ➤ **BUNIVERSE - Business** ➤ **Audio** Like much of the content in **iTunes U**, it was free!

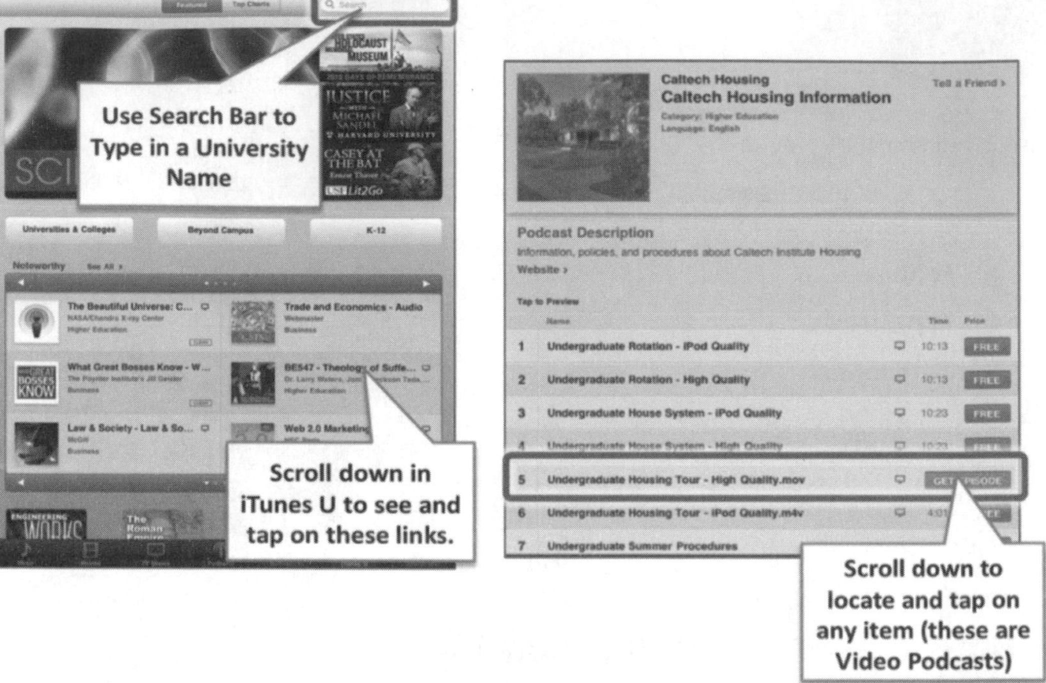


**Figure 19–4.** *You can earch for a particular university, then browse iTunes U by that university.*

If you are in a location with a good wireless signal, you can tap the title of the audio or video item, and then listen to or watch it streaming (see Figure 19–5). If your signal gets interrupted, however, you will lose your place in the video. There are many advantages to actually downloading the file (if possible) for later viewing, not least of which is that you get more control of the video-watching experience.

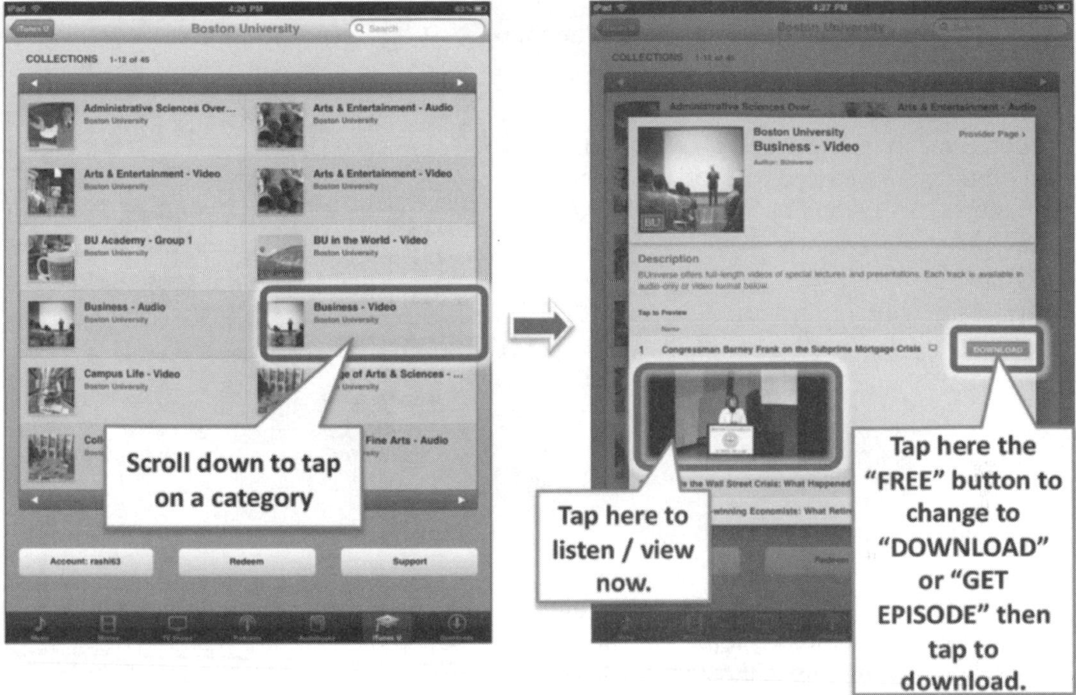


**Figure 19–5.** *View or download content*

## Download for Offline Viewing

If you know you are going to be out of wireless coverage for a while, such as on an airplane or in the subway, you will want to download the content for later, offline viewing or listening. Tap the **Free** button to change it to a **Download** button, and then tap it again. You can then monitor the download progress (some larger videos may take 10 minutes or more to complete) by tapping the **Downloads** button at the bottom right of the screen. When the download is complete, the item will show up in the correct area in your **iPad** icon.

> **NOTE:** Any file larger than 20MB cannot be downloaded over the 3G network; you must use Wi-Fi for larger files.

## Searching iTunes

Sometimes you have a good idea of what you want, but you are unsure where it is located or perhaps you don't feel like browsing or navigating all the menus. The **Search** tool is for you.

Up in the top right hand corner of the **iTunes** app, as in virtually every other iPad app, you have a search window.

Touch **Search**, and the search window and the on device keyboard will pop up. Once you start typing, the iPad will begin to try to match your entry with possibilities.

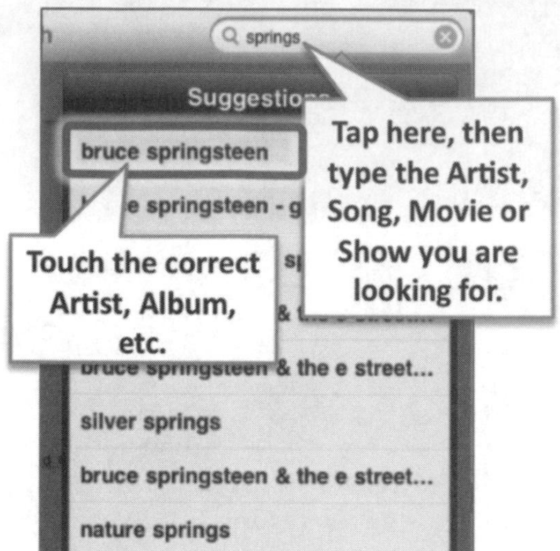


Type in the artist, song name, video name, podcast name, or album you are searching for, and the iPad will display detailed matches. Be as general or as specific as you would like. If you are just looking to browse all particular songs by an artist, type the artist's name. If you want a specific song or album, enter the full name of the song or album.

When you locate the song or album name, simply touch it and you will be taken to the purchase page.

## Purchasing or Renting Music, Videos, Podcasts, and More

Once you locate a song, video, TV show, or album, you can touch the **Buy** or (if you see it) **Rent** button. This will cause your media to start downloading. (If the content is free, then you will see **Free** button that you tap turn into a **Download** button.)

We suggest you view or listen to the preview, as well as check out the customer reviews first, unless you are absolutely sure you want to purchase the item.

## Previewing Music

Touch either the title of the song or its track number to the left of the song title; this will flip over the album cover will flip over and launch the preview window.

You will hear a representative clip of 30 seconds of the song.

Touch the **Stop** button and the track number will again be displayed.

## Check out Customer Reviews

Many items in iTunes offer customer reviews. The reviews range from a low of one star to a high of five stars.

> **CAUTION: YOU NEED TO BE AWARE THAT REVIEWS CAN HAVE EXPLICIT LANGUAGE.** Many of the reviews are clean; however some do contain explicit language that may not be caught by the iTunes store right away.

Reading the reviews might give you a fairly good idea of whether or not you would like to buy the item.

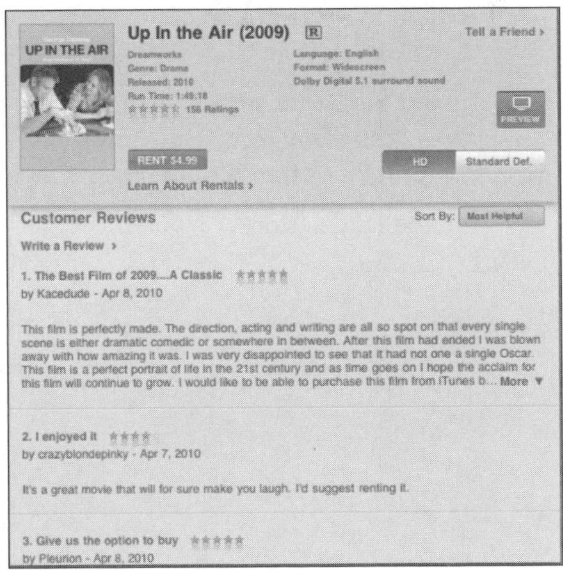

## Previewing a Video, TV Show, or Music Video

Pretty much everything on iTunes offers a preview. Sometimes you will see a **Preview** button, as with music videos and movies. TV shows are a little different; you tap the episode title in order to see the 30-second preview.

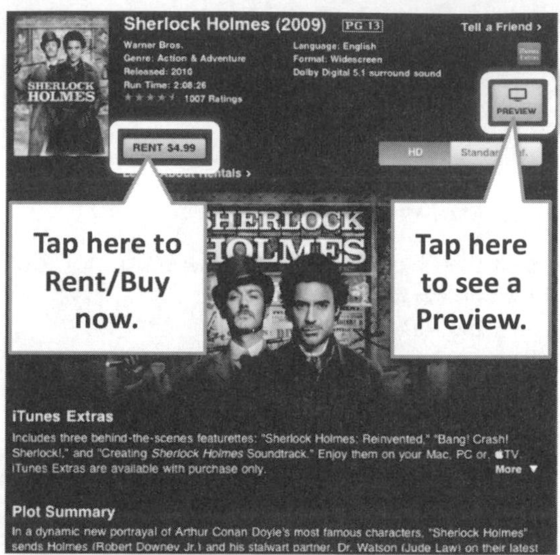


We do highly recommend checking out the reviews, as well as trying the preview before purchasing items on iTunes.

Typical movie previews or trailers will be longer than 30 seconds - some are 2 minutes 30 seconds or longer.

## Purchasing a Song, Video, or Other Item

Once you are sure you want to purchase a song, video, or other item, follow these steps to buy it.

1. Touch the **Price** button of the song or the **Buy** button.
2. The button will change and turn into a green **Buy Now**, **Buy Song**, **Buy Single**, or **Buy Album** button.
3. Tap the **Buy** button.

4. You will see an animated icon jump into the shopping cart. Type in your iTunes password and touch **OK** to complete the sale.

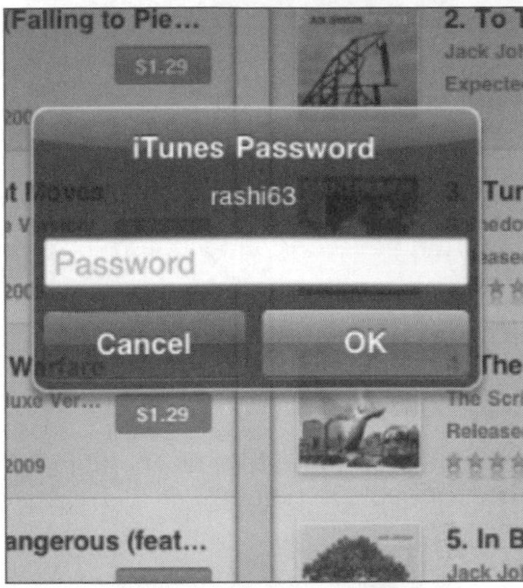


The song will then become part of your music library, and it will be synced with your computer the next time you connect your iPad to iTunes on your computer.

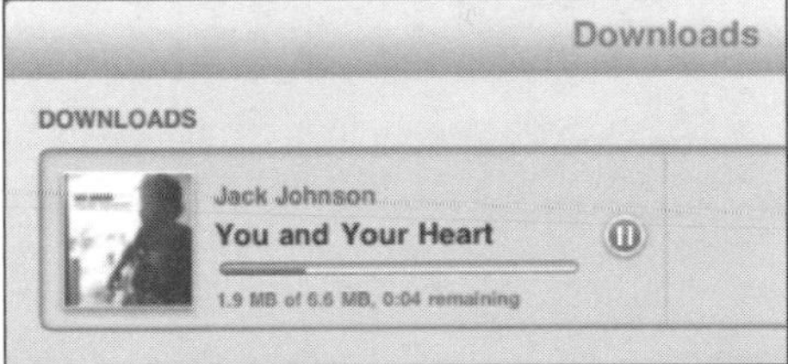


After the download is complete, you will see the new song, audiobook, podcast, or iTunes U podcast inside the correct category within your **iPod** icon.

**NOTE:** Purchased videos and iTunes U videos go into the **Videos** app, not the **iPod** app on your iPad.

# Podcasts in iTunes

Podcasts are usually a series of audio segments; these may be updated frequently (such as hourly news reports from National Public Radio) or not updated at all (such as a recording of a one-time lecture on a particular topic).

You can use the top three buttons to browse the podcasts in iTunes:

- **Featured**
- **Top Charts**
- **Categories**

## Downloading a Podcast

Podcasts are available in **Video** and **Audio** varieties. When you locate a podcast, just touch the title of the podcast (see Figure 19–6). Luckily, most podcasts are free. If it is free, you will see a **Free** button instead of the typical **Buy** button.

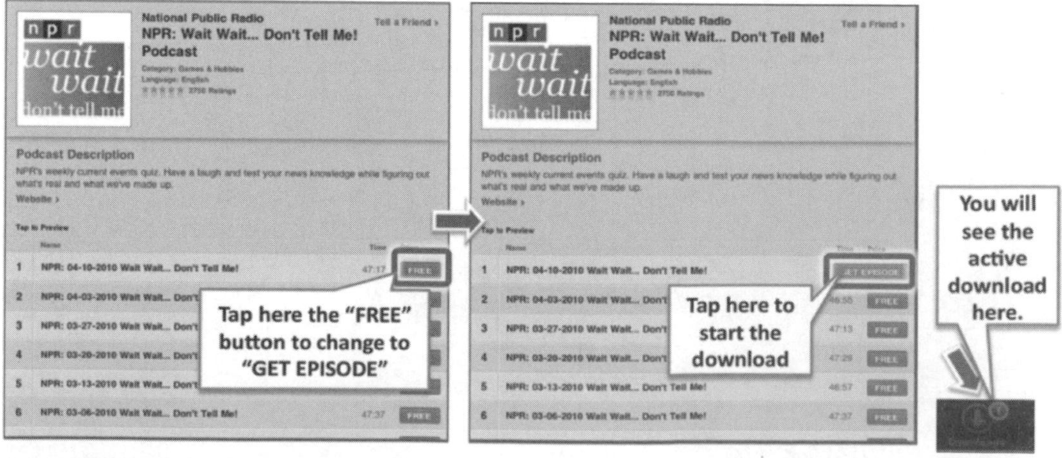


**Figure 19–6.** *Downloading a podcast*

When you touch the button, it turns into a green button that says **Download**. Touch **Download**, and an animated icon jumps into your **Downloads** icon at the bottom bar of soft keys. A small number displayed in red reflects the number of files downloading.

## The Download Icon – Stopping and Deleting Downloads

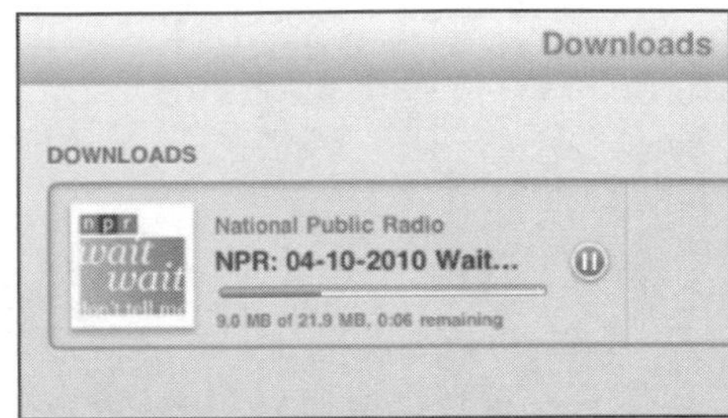


As you download items, they appear in your **Downloads** screen. This behavior is just like the behavior of iTunes on your computer.

You can touch the **Downloads** icon along the bottom row to see the progress of all your downloads.

## Where the Downloads Go

All of your downloads will be visible in either your **iPod** icon or your **Videos** icon, organized by category. In other words, if you download a podcast, you will need to go into your **iPod** icon and touch the **Podcasts** icon on the sidebar to see the downloaded podcast.

Sometimes, you decide that you do not want the all downloads you selected. If you want to stop a download and delete it, swipe your finger over the download to bring up the **Delete** button, and then tap **Delete** (see Figure 19–7).

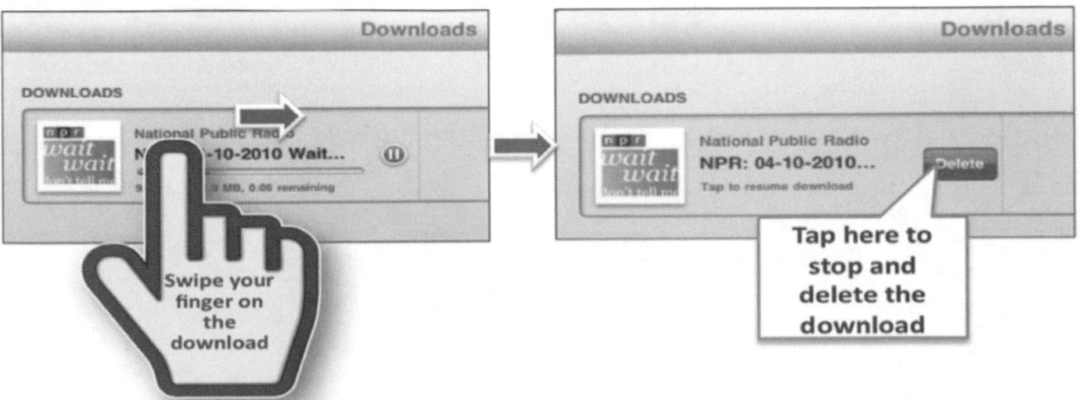


**Figure 19–7.** *Delete a file while downloading*

## Redeeming an iTunes Gift Card

One of the cool things about iTunes on your iPad is that, just as with iTunes on your computer, you can redeem a gift card and receive credit in your iTunes account for your purchases.

At the bottom of the **iTunes** screen, you should see the **Redeem** button (see Figure 19–8).

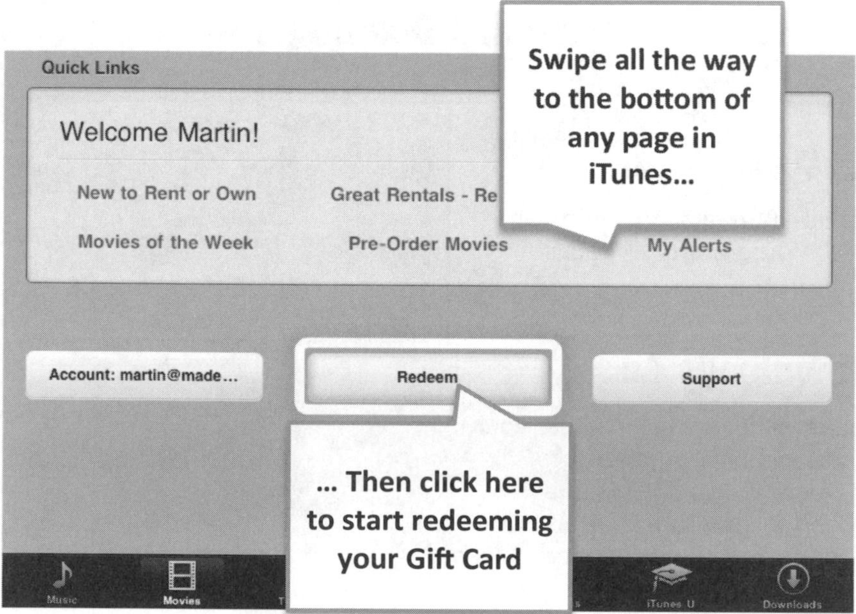


**Figure 19–8.** *Begin redeeming an iTunes gift card*

Tap the **Redeem** button to start the process of entering your iTunes **Gift Card Number** for an iTunes store credit.

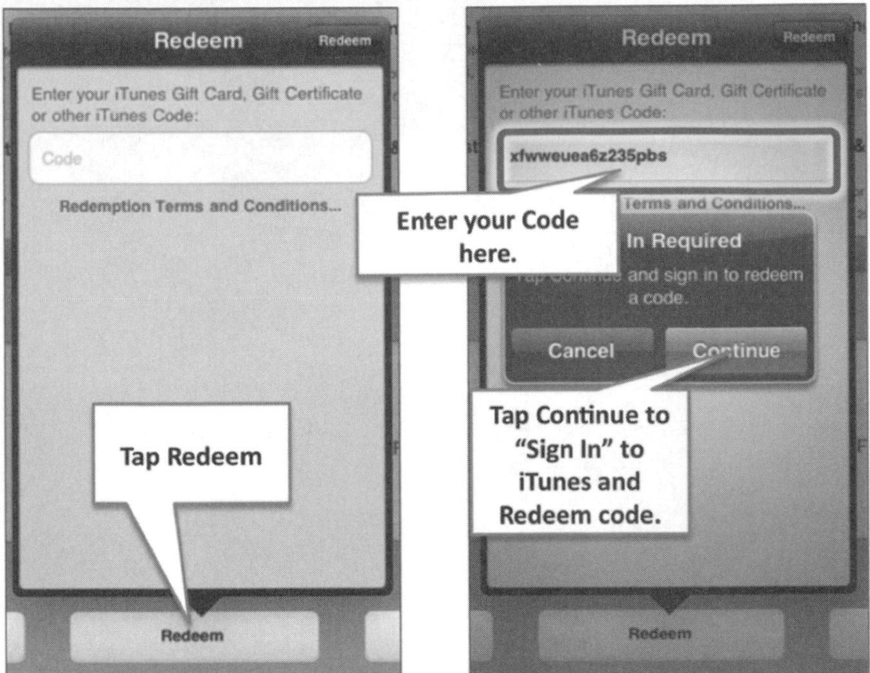


**Figure 19–9.** *Redeem an iTunes gift card*

You will then be prompted to enter your iTunes gift card info or gift certificate info in the box. Once you do this, you will have credit for downloads in the iTunes store – it is that easy!

**NOTE:** If you have more than one iTunes account, you can log in or out right in the **iTunes** app, as well.

Chapter 20

# The Amazing App Store

You have just seen how easy it is download music, videos, and podcasts from iTunes right on your iPad. We have also shown you how to download iBooks from the iBooks store.

It is just as easy to download new applications from Apple's amazing App store. Apps are available for just about any function you could think of—games, productivity tools, and social networking—whatever you can imagine. As the advertising says, "There's an app for that."

In this chapter, you will learn how to navigate the App store, how to search for Apps and how to download Apps. You will also learn how to maintain and update your Apps once they are downloaded onto your iPad.

**NOTE:** If you purchase a new iPad Wi-Fi or unlocked iPad 3G while travelling and bring it home to a country where it's not yet sold, there's a good chance your iTunes ID won't work to buy apps. The work-around is to buy iPad apps on desktop iTunes (which does work) and sync them over.

## Learning More About Apps and the App Store

In a very short amount of time, the App store has exploded in volume. There are Apps for just about anything you can imagine. Apps come in all prices, and, in many cases are free.

### App Store Facts and Figures

The following interesting App store statistics are provided courtesy of the 148apps.biz web site, from the web page, last updated on April 22, 2010.

In March 2010, there were over 600 apps submitted every day!

By the time you read this, there will likely be more than 200,000 apps in the store. Most of these are not iPad apps, but the number of iPad-specific apps is growing rapidly.

**COUNT OF ACTIVE APPLICATIONS IN THE APP STORE**

Total Active Apps (currently available for download): 188,977

Number of Active Publishers in the U.S. App Store: 36,753

**COUNT OF APPLICATION SUBMISSIONS**

This Month (Games): 2,270 (103/day )

This Month (Non-Games): 12,300 (559/day )

This Month (Total): 14,570 (662/day )

**APPLICATION PRICE DISTRIBUTION**

Current Average App Price: $3.04

Current Average Game Price: $1.39

Current Average Overall Price: $2.79

**APPLICATION CATEGORY DISTRIBUTION**

Most Popular Categories

1. Books (33,924 active)
2. Games (28,828 active)
3. Entertainment (22,411 active)
4. Education (14,092 active)
5. Utilities (11,323 active)

## Where to Find Apps News and Reviews

You certainly can find reviews in the App store itself, and we recommend you check out the App store reviews, but sometimes you would like more information from some experts. The blogs are a great place to find news and reviews.

Here is a list of apps and Apple iPad/iPhone/iPod touch-related blogs with reviews of apps:

The iPhone Blog: `www.tipb.co`

Touch Reviews: `www.touchreviews.net`

Touch My Apps: `www.touchmyapps.com`

The Unofficial Apple Weblog: www.tuaw.com

Cult of Mac: `www.cultofmac.com`

App Smile: `www.appsmile.com`

## App Store Basics

With a little time, you should find the **App Store** to be quite intuitive to navigate. There are some basics to familiarize yourself with so that the **App Store** experience can be that much more enjoyable.

## A Network Connection Is Required

After you setup your App store (iTunes) account, you still need to have the right network connectivity (either Wi-Fi or 3G/cellular) to access the App store and download apps. Check out Chapter 4: "Wi-Fi and 3G Connectivity" to learn how to tell if you are connected.

## Starting the App Store

The **App Store** icon should be on your first page of icons on the **Home** screen. Tap the icon to launch the App store.

## The App Store Home Page

Like iTunes, the **App store** has buttons on top and soft keys at the bottom, which help direct you in your purchases (see Figure 20–1).

Along the top, there are buttons for **New** apps and **What's Hot**. Along the bottom are icons for **Featured**, **Top Charts**, **Categories**, and **Update**.

Scrolling is handled the same way as in iTunes and in other programs—just move your finger up and down to scroll through the page.

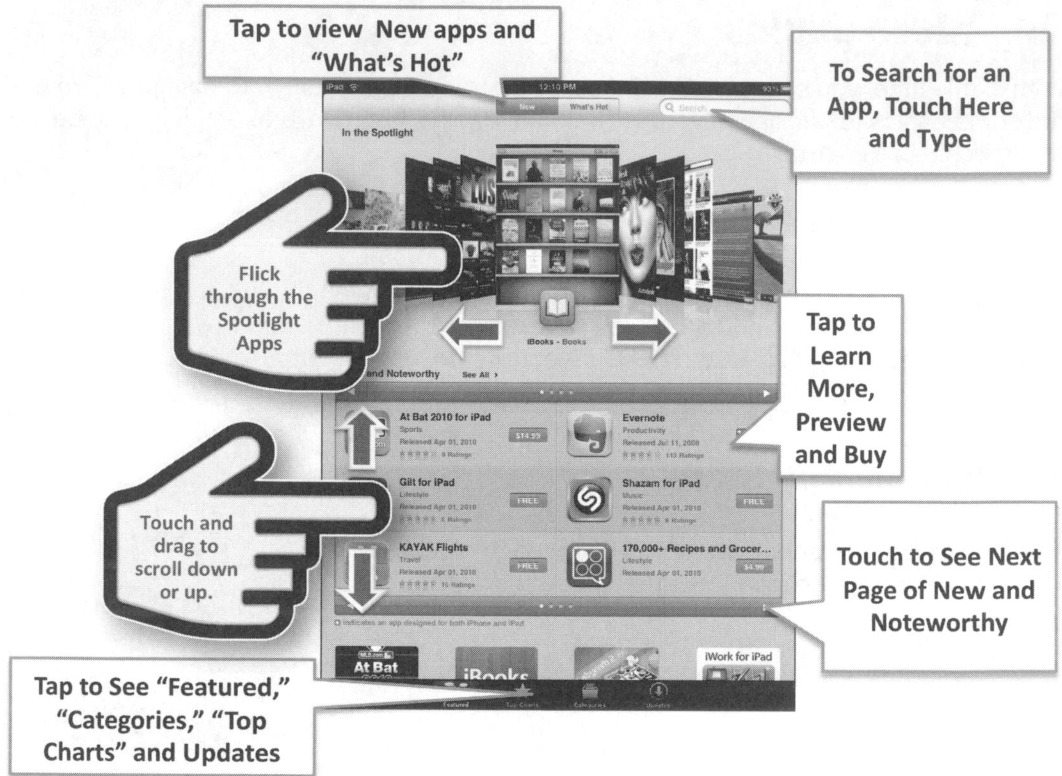
Tap to view New apps and "What's Hot"
To Search for an App, Touch Here and Type
Flick through the Spotlight Apps
Tap to Learn More, Preview and Buy
Touch and drag to scroll down or up.
Touch to See Next Page of New and Noteworthy
Tap to See "Featured," "Categories," "Top Charts" and Updates

**Figure 20–1.** *Layout of* ***App Store*** *home page*

You will notice that there are two main sections on the App store home page, **New and Noteworthy** and **Staff Favorites**. Each section has several pages. Just touch the arrows to advance through the pages or touch the **See All** tab.

> **NOTE:** Since the App store is essentially a web site, it will change frequently. Some of the details and nuances of the App store might be a bit different after this book goes to print.

## Viewing App Details

Once you find an App that interests you, there are many options to choose from so that you can be sure that a particular App is for you. Figure 20–2 shows you some of the options available.

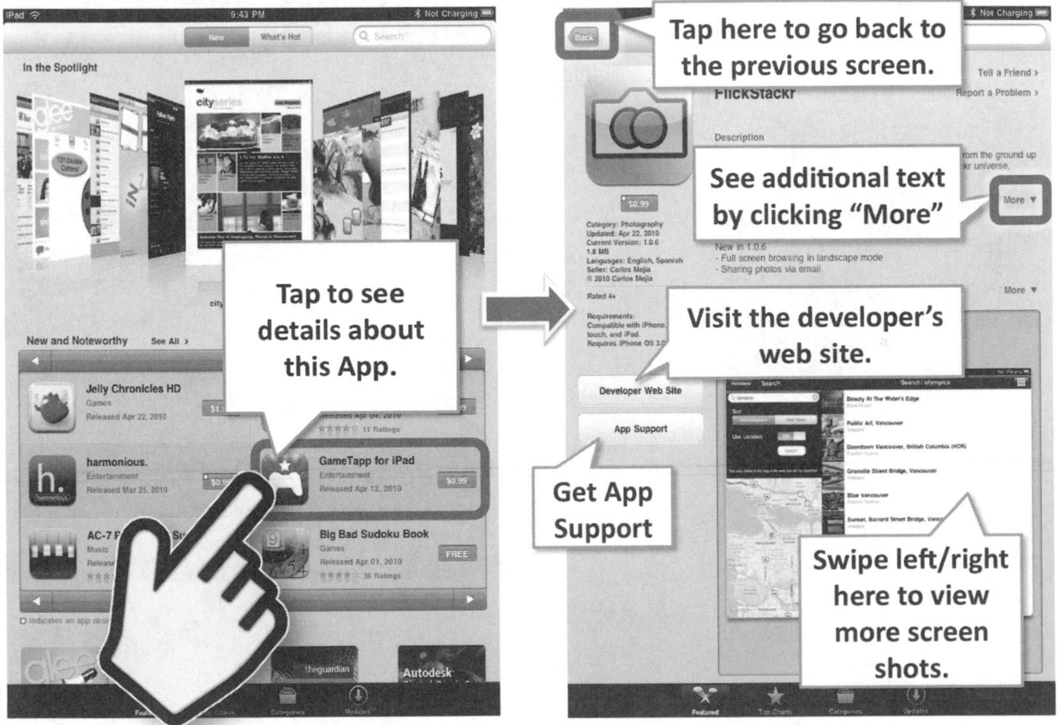


**Figure 20–2.** *Viewing details about an app*

# Finding an App to Download

Begin by looking around the default view, which shows the **Featured** apps. The App store loads with the **New Apps** at the top in a "coverflow" view. Just touch and "flip" through the apps at the top of the page.

> **NOTE:** Like with iTunes, you can download only apps under 20MB while on 3G. Bigger apps require a Wi-Fi connection.

## View What's Hot

Touch the **What's Hot** button on the top and the hottest apps in the store will now be visible on the screen. Again, just scroll through the "hot" apps to see if something catches your eye.

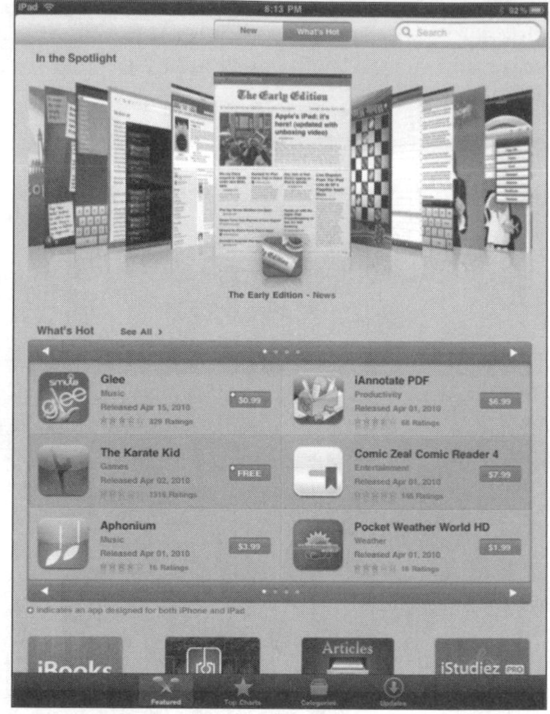


> **NOTE:** The fact that an app is in the "What's Hot" category does not necessarily mean you will also believe it is useful or fun. Check out the app descriptions and reviews carefully before you purchase anything.

## Using Categories

Sometimes, all the choices can be a bit overwhelming. If you have a sense of what type of app you are looking for, touch the **Categories** button along the bottom row of icons.

The apps are now in **Category** tabs, ranging from **Games** to **Finance** to **Medical** to **Photography** and all sorts of other possibilities.

> **NOTE:** It is possible that more categories will be added after the publication of this book.

Find the category of what you are searching for and touch the tab. So, if we were looking for a “weather” app, we would just touch the **Weather** tab. We can then browse the featured weather apps in “coverflow” at the top or touch **See All** to see all the weather apps.

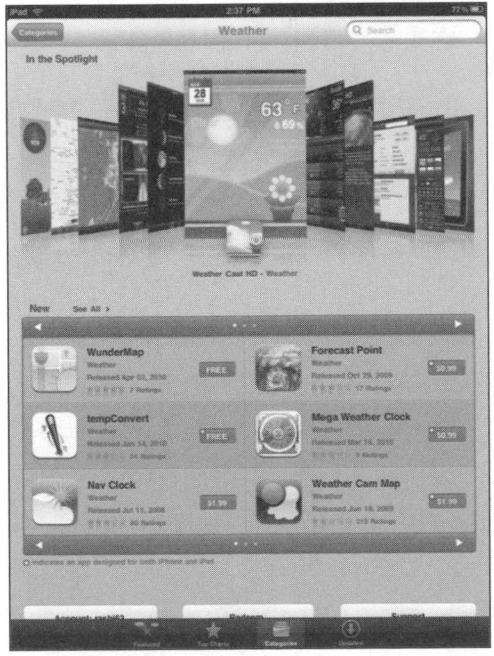

## Looking at the Top Charts

Touch the **Top Charts** icon along the bottom row and the App store will change the view again; this time showing you the top ten paid and top ten free apps. Just touch **Top Paid** or **Top Free** to switch between the views.

Scroll down to the bottom of the **Top Charts** page and you will see a second category, **Top Grossing**. For some, seeing how much an app grosses is important. To see a fuller list of either category of top apps touch, the **Show More** Show More ▼ tab.

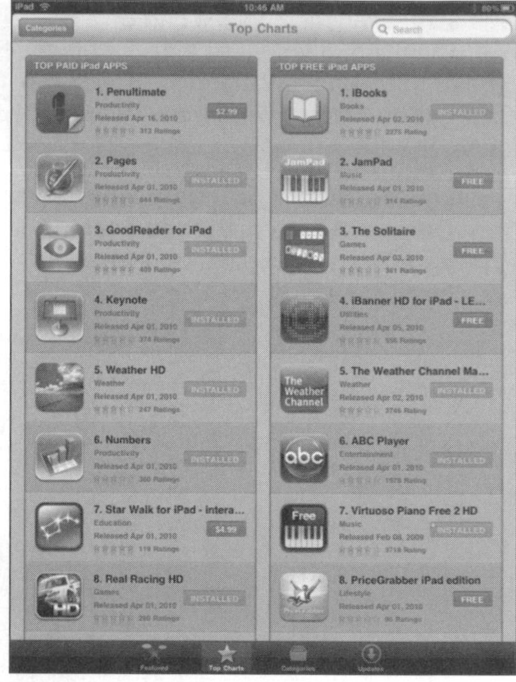

## Searching for an App

Let's say you have a specific idea of what you are looking for. Touch the **Search** icon and type in either the name of the program or the type of program you are looking for.

So, if you were looking for a golf scorecard program, just type in golf or golf scorecard and see what comes up. When you see something that resembles what you are searching for come up in the screen, just touch it.

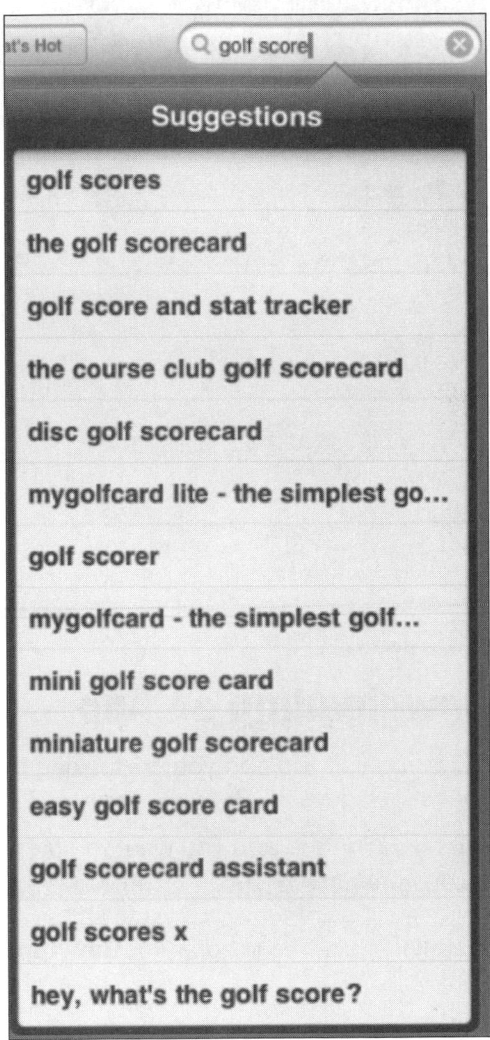

> **NOTE:** Because the iPad is new, you might touch on a program only to see that there is no iPad version. The App store will then show you all matching iPhone versions, which will still work, although the window will be small and the graphic quality not as good.

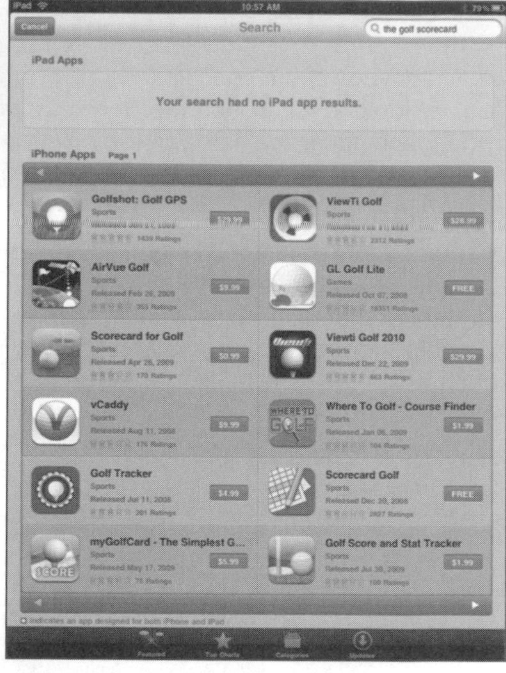


## Downloading an App

Once you find the app you are looking for, you can download it right onto your iPad, as shown in Figure 20–3.

After locating the app you want to buy, notice the small button that says either **Free** or **$9.99** (or whatever the price is). $9.99 Just touch that button, and it will change to say **Install** if it is a free program or **Buy App** if it is a paid program. BUY APP

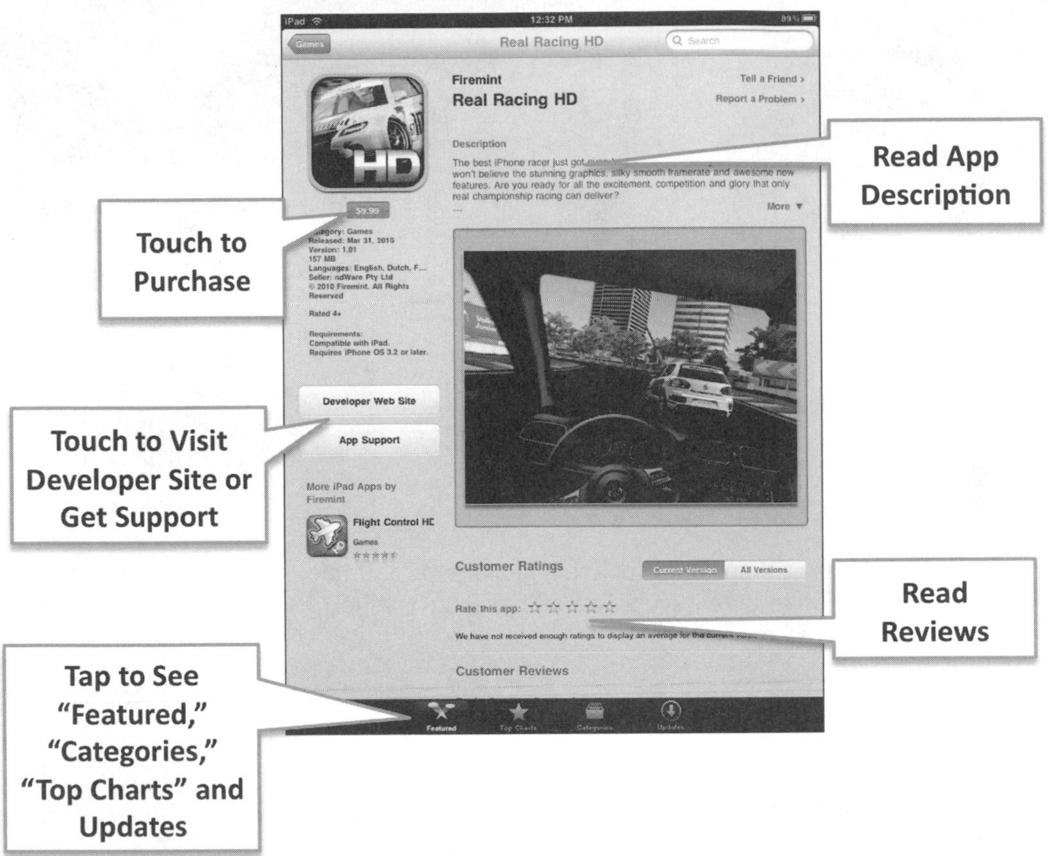


**Figure 20–3.** *Viewing details of an app*

Once you have read the reviews and the app description and perhaps visited the developer support site, go ahead and download or purchase the app. Once you tap the **Download App** button, you will be prompted to input your iTunes password.

Input your password and select **OK** and the app will be downloaded to your iPad, as shown in Figure 20–4.

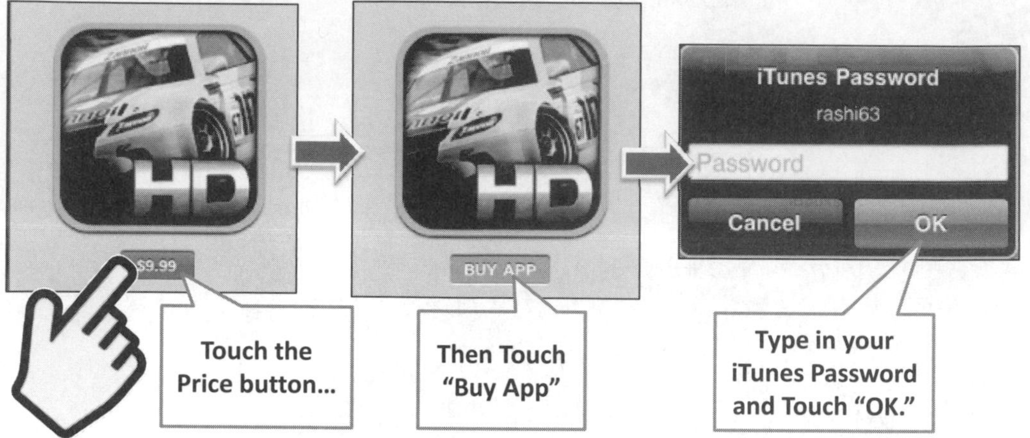


**Figure 20–4.** *Purchasing an app*

If you are sure that you want to purchase/install the app, touch the **Price** or **Free** button. You will be prompted to type in your iTunes password. When you are done, just touch **OK** and the app will start to download.

## Finding Free or Discounted Apps

After browsing around you will notice a couple of things about the App store. First, there are lots of *free* apps. Sometimes these are great applications. Other times, they are not so useful—but they can be fun!

The other thing that you will notice over time is that some of the apps will have sales, and some apps will become less expensive over time. So if you have a favorite app and it costs $6.99, it is likely that waiting a few weeks or a month might result in a lower price.

# Maintaining and Updating Your Apps

Quite often, developers will update their apps for the iPad. You don't even need to use your computer to perform the update—you can do it right on your iPad.

You can even tell if you have updates, and how many, by looking at the **App Store** icon. The one shown here has three updates.

Once you enter the App store, tap the icon to the farthest right on the bottom row. This is the **Updates** icon.

If you have apps that need to be updated, there will be a small number indicated in red. The number corresponds to the number of apps that require updates.

When you touch the **Update** button, the iPad shows you which apps need to update.

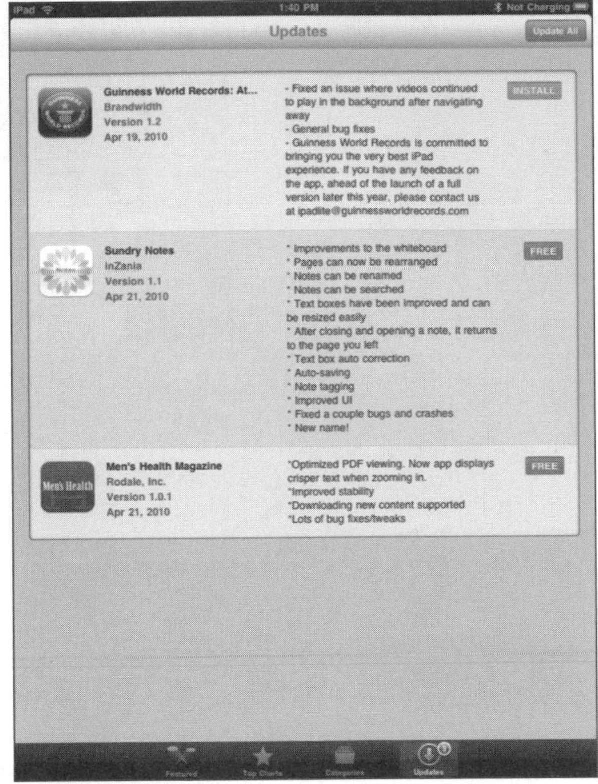


To get your updates, you could touch an individual app, but it is easier to touch the **Update All** button to have all your apps updated at once. The iPad will leave the App store and you can see the progress of the updates.

**NOTE:** You will need to re-launch the App store to get back in. The update process takes you completely out of the store.

Chapter 21

# Games and Fun

Your iPad excels at many things. It is a multimedia workhorse, and it can keep track of your busy life, as well. Two areas where the iPad really excels are as a gaming device and iPad-specific Apps that really take advantage of the large, high resolution touch screen. You can even find versions of popular games you might only expect to find on dedicated gaming consoles.

The iPad brings many advantages to portable gaming: the High Definition Screen makes for realistic visuals, the high quality audio provides great sound effects and the accelerometer allows you to really interact with your games. For example, in racing games, you can "steer" your car by turning the iPad as you hold it.

**NOTE:** We have written nine books on the BlackBerry smartphones, and we have many BlackBerry devices lying around the house. The BlackBerry smartphones don't disappear into our children's rooms; rather, the iPad is the device that our children (and our spouses) have decided is fun enough to grab. We regularly discover that the iPad has disappeared from its charger and have to yell out, "Where is my iPad? I need to finish this book!"

## The iPad As a Gaming Device

Thanks to the built in accelerometer – essentially a device that detects movement (acceleration) and tilt – the iPad is capable of doing thing that most portable game systems can't.

With literally thousands of gaming titles to choose from, you can play virtually any type of game you wish on your iPad.

**NOTE:** Some of these games do require that you have an active network connection, either Wi-Fi or 3G, to engage in multiplayer games.

With the iPad, you can play a driving game and use the iPad itself to steer – just by turning the device. You can touch the iPad to brake or tilt it forward to accelerate.

This game is so realistic that it might make someone car sick!

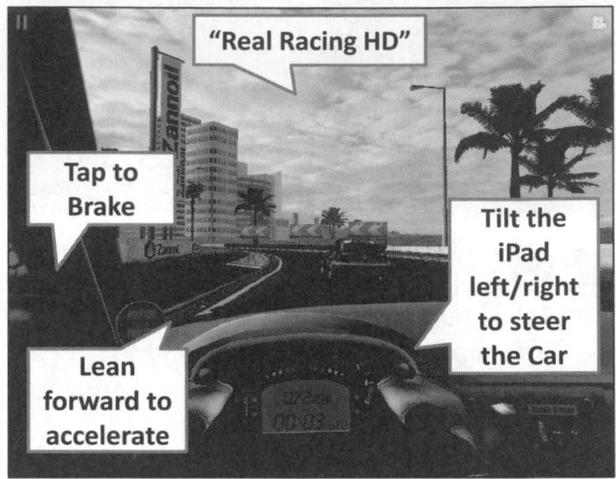


Or, you can try a fishing game, where you case and reel in fish from the perspective of being on a boat!

## Where to Get Games and Fun Apps

Games are found, like all iPad apps, at the App Store (see Figure 21–1). You can get them either through iTunes on your computer or on the device's App Store.

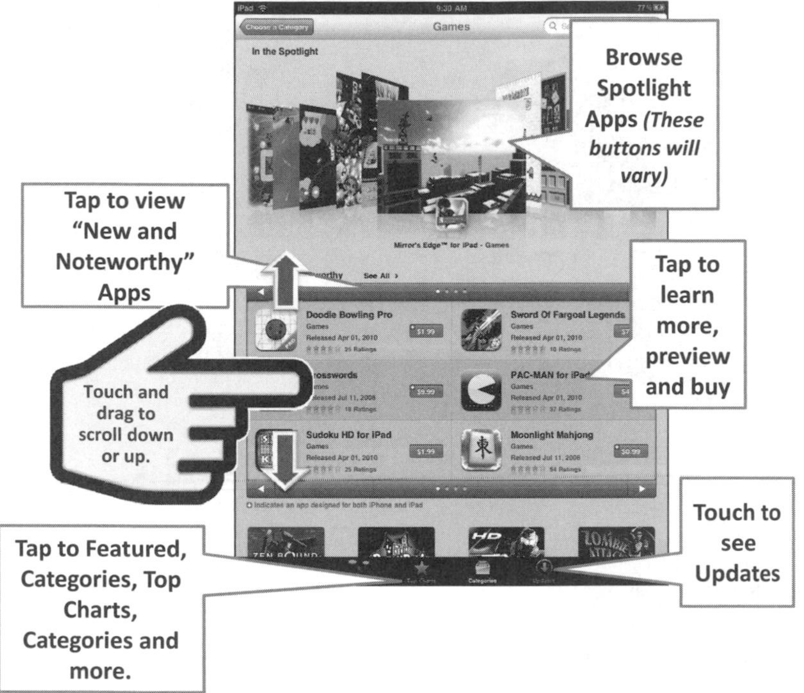
Browse Spotlight Apps *(These buttons will vary)*
Tap to view "New and Noteworthy" Apps
Tap to learn more, preview and buy
Touch and drag to scroll down or up.
Touch to see Updates
Tap to Featured, Categories, Top Charts, Categories and more.

**Figure 21–1.** *Layout of the App Store's* game section

To get a game, start up the App Store as you did in the last chapter, and then use the **Categories** icon to take you to the **Games** tab. You will also find many games in the **Featured** section of the App store, as well as in the **New and Notable** section. Figure 21–2 shows the app purchase page for a game available for the iPad.

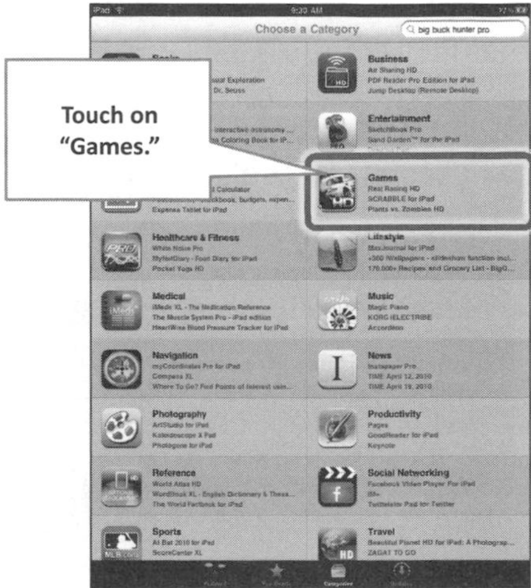
Touch on "Games."

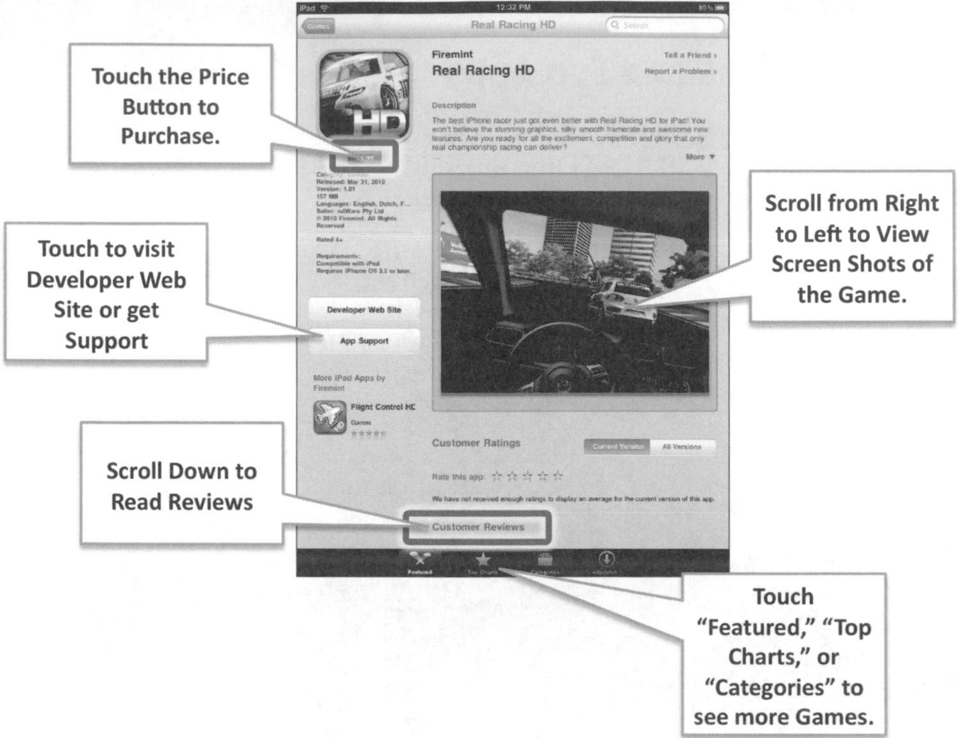


**Figure 21–2.** Layout of the app purchase page

## Read Reviews Before You Buy

Many of the games have user reviews that are worth perusing. Sometimes, you can get a good sense of the game before you buy it. If you find a game that looks interesting – don't be afraid to do a simple Google search on your computer to see if any mainstream media outlets have done a full review.

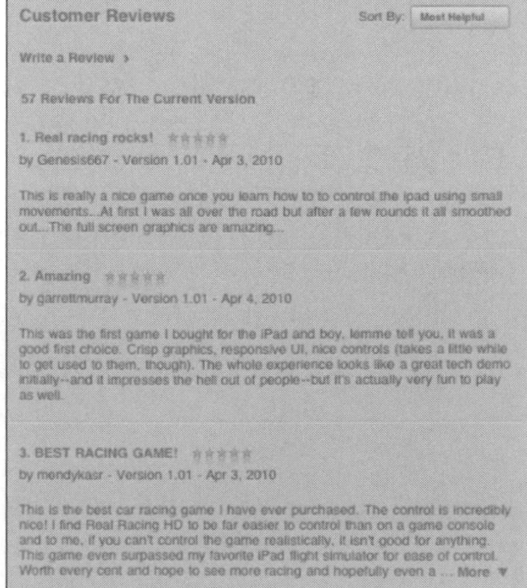


**CAUTION:** Beware that some reviews may contain explicit language.

## Look for Free Trials or Lite Versions

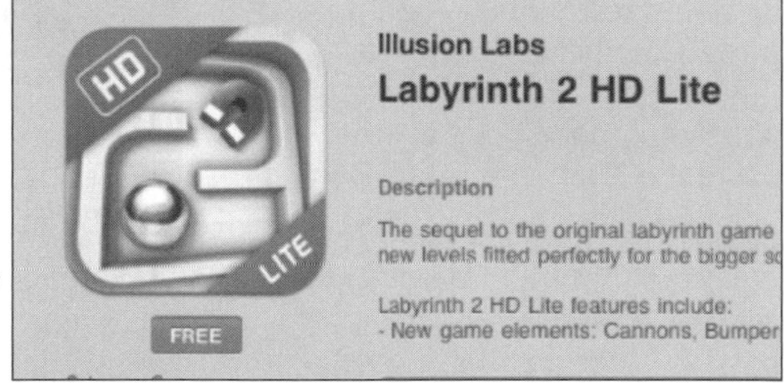
HD
LITE
FREE
Illusion Labs
Labyrinth 2 HD Lite
Description
The sequel to the original labyrinth game
new levels fitted perfectly for the bigger s
Labyrinth 2 HD Lite features include:
- New game elements: Cannons, Bumper

More and more frequently, game developers are giving users free trials of their games to see if they like them before they buy. You will find many games have both a Lite version and a Full version in the App Store.

Some games are "free," supported by the inclusion of ads within the App. Other apps are free to start, but require in-app purchases for continued play or additional features.

## Be Careful When You Play

Given the size of the iPad, some games have been modified from their iPhone/iPod Touch versions. You don't use the iPad to "cast" your line in a fishing game, as you would in the iPhone version; however, you can move around a bit in driving games and first person shooter games – so be mindful of your surroundings! For example, make sure you have a good grip on your device, so it doesn't slip out of your hand – we recommend a good silicone case to help with this.

**CAUTION:** Games like Real Racing can be quite addictive!

## Two Player Games

The iPad really opens up the possibility for two-player gaming. In this example, we are playing checkers against one another – using the iPad as a Game Board.

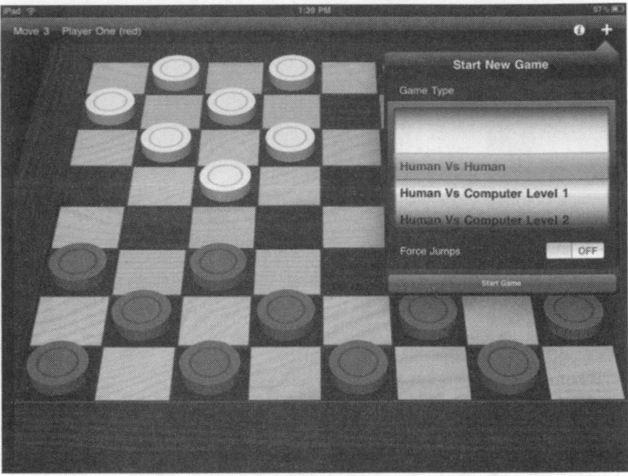


Similar two-person gaming can also be found for other board games, such as chess.

**TIP:** When playing a two-person game such as checkers, make sure you *lock* the screen orientation, just as you do when you read a book. Move the screen lock switch to the **locked** position.

## Online and Wireless Games

The iPad also allows online and wireless peer-to-peer play if the game supports it. Many new games are incorporating this technology. In **Scrabble**, for example, you can have multiple players on their own devices. You can even have the iPad as your game board and up to four individual iPhones as wireless "racks" to hold your letters. Just flick the letters off the rack, and they go onto the board – very cool!

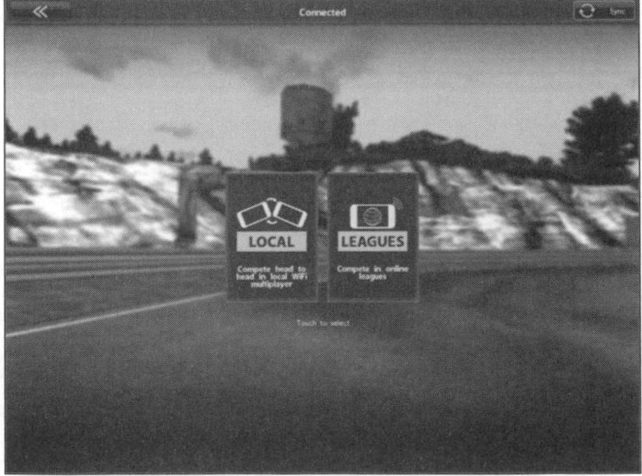


In this example, I selected **Online** from the Real Racing menu, and I now have the option to either play against another opponent via Wi-Fi or join an online league race.

> **NOTE:** If you just want to play against a friend who is nearby, select Wi-Fi mode for multi-player games. If you just want to play against new people, try going online for a league race or game.

## Playing Music with Your iPad

With its relatively large screen, you can even install a piano keyboard on your iPad and play music. There are a number of Apps available that are music related – check out the **Music** category in the iTunes Store.

One of the Apps that was in the Top 5 of the **Paid iPad** apps category when we were writing this book was **Magic Piano** – for just US $0.99.

Download the app and just have fun with it!

If you have children, they might enjoy it, as well.

> **NOTE:** This App is not meant to replace your priceless Steinway grand piano; however, it does provide a fun introduction to the piano.

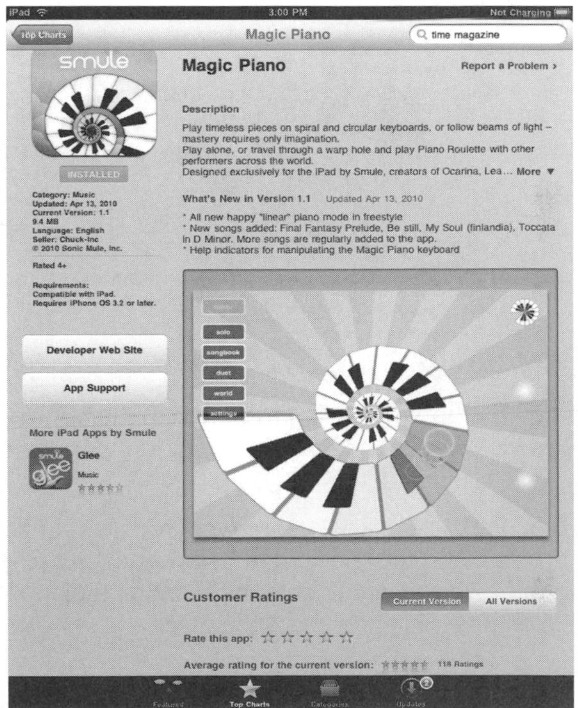


## Various Keyboards

You can play **Magic Piano** with a straight keyboard, a black (hidden keyboard), a spiral keyboard, or a circular keyboard (see Figure 21–3).

To change keyboard types, tap the **Keyboard** icon in the corner of the screen, and then keep tapping the icon to cycle through the various keyboards.

Use the pinch open or closed feature to give yourself more or fewer keys on the selected keyboard.

**Figure 21–3.** *Magic Piano's Various Keyboard Options*

## Play Songs from the Songbook

Begin by tapping the **Menu** button in the upper left-hand corner and select **Songbook**. Now you can choose from a number of popular songs, which **Magic Piano** will help you play (see Figure 21–4).

When you select a song, little green dots start floating down from the top of the screen. The idea is to tap the screen below each dot to get a feel for the relative position (left or right) of where your fingers might be on a piano keyboard to play the notes – note that this relative distance is not to scale.

> **TIP:** At first, try playing songs you are familiar with. Knowing the tempo of the song helps you get the hang of the app much more quickly!

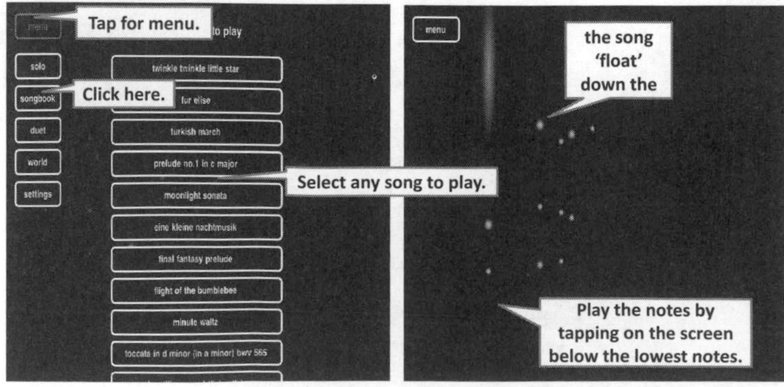


**Figure 21–4.** *Magic Piano playing songs from the Songbook*

## Duets with Others

Now tap the **Menu** button, select **Duet**, And then enter your piano name and a tagline to identify yourself. **Magic Piano** then searches the web for others seeking a duet and randomly pairs you up. Your partner may be in the same state, across the country, or across the world!

## The World View

Tap the **Menu** button and select **World** (Figure 21–5). This shows you a globe with people happily "tickling the ivories" in various places around the world. Sometimes you will see a duet.

If you like the way someone is playing, then hit the **Heart** icon.

If you do not like the music you are hearing, then hit the **Next** icon (the two right arrows).

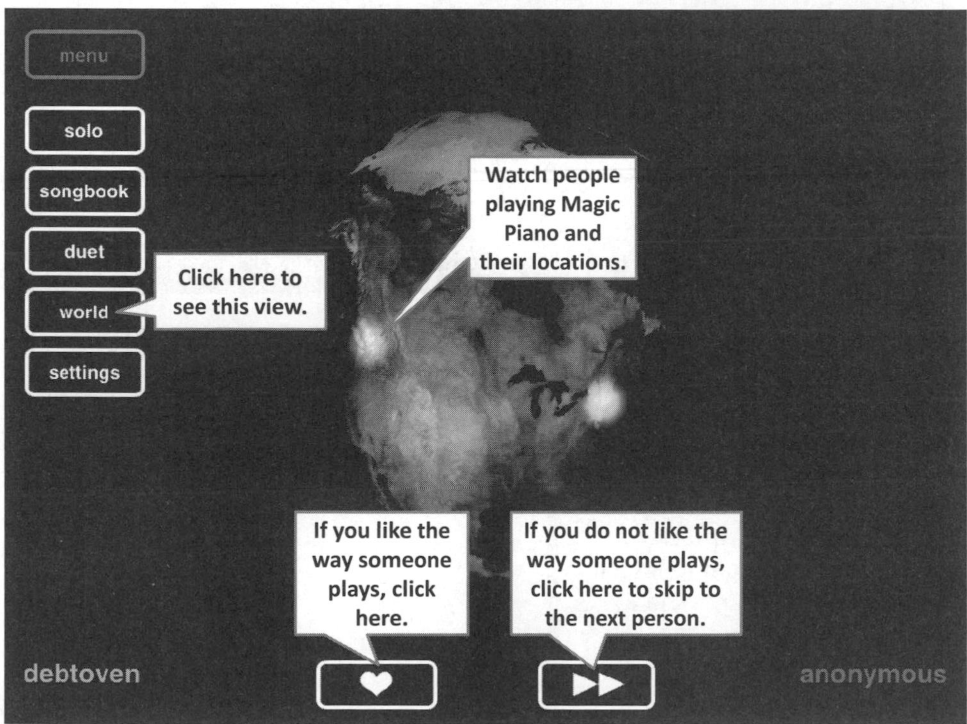


**Figure 21–5.** *Magic Piano world view – watching others play the piano*

# Other Fun Stuff: Baseball on the iPad

There are so many great apps that can provide users with endless hours of entertainment on the iPad. Since the iPad was released on opening day of the Major League Baseball season, it is appropriate to highlight an app that was honored as the first "App of the Week" in the iPad App Store.

**At Bat 2010 for iPad** is a US $14.99 application that is well worth the entry fee for any baseball fan. It also highlights the iPad's capabilities.

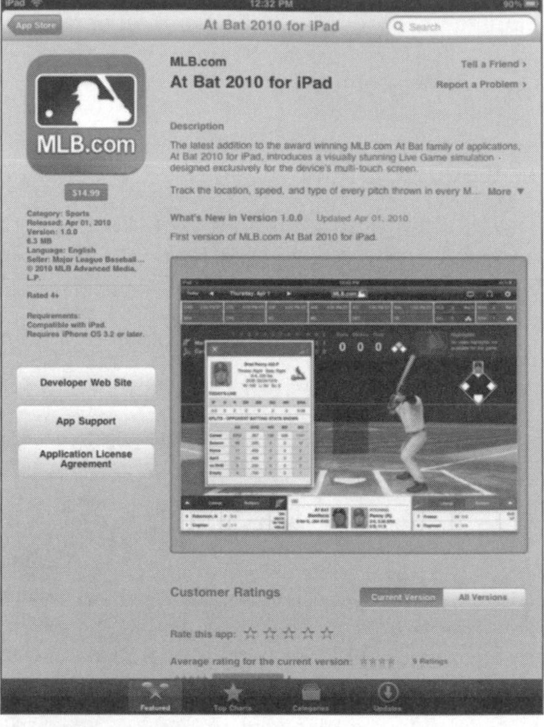


The main view of the app changes based on whether there are baseball games currently being played. When you first register the app, you pick your favorite team. The favorite team on the iPad in this example is set to the Red Sox. So, if they are playing, the view automatically goes to their game first. If they are not playing, a recap of the previous game is displayed.

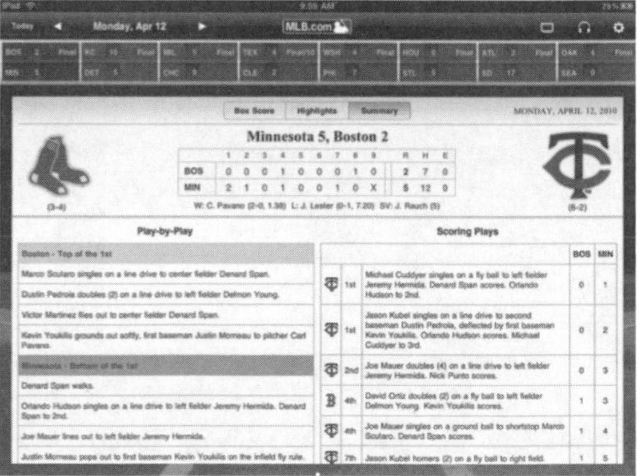


The main view during game time shows a batter at the plate (see Figure 21–6); this batter represents the real batter. Batters will switch sides of the plate, depending on whether the batter currently up hits from the left or right side of the plate. The current pitch count is shown above the plate, and the score is displayed at the top of the screen.

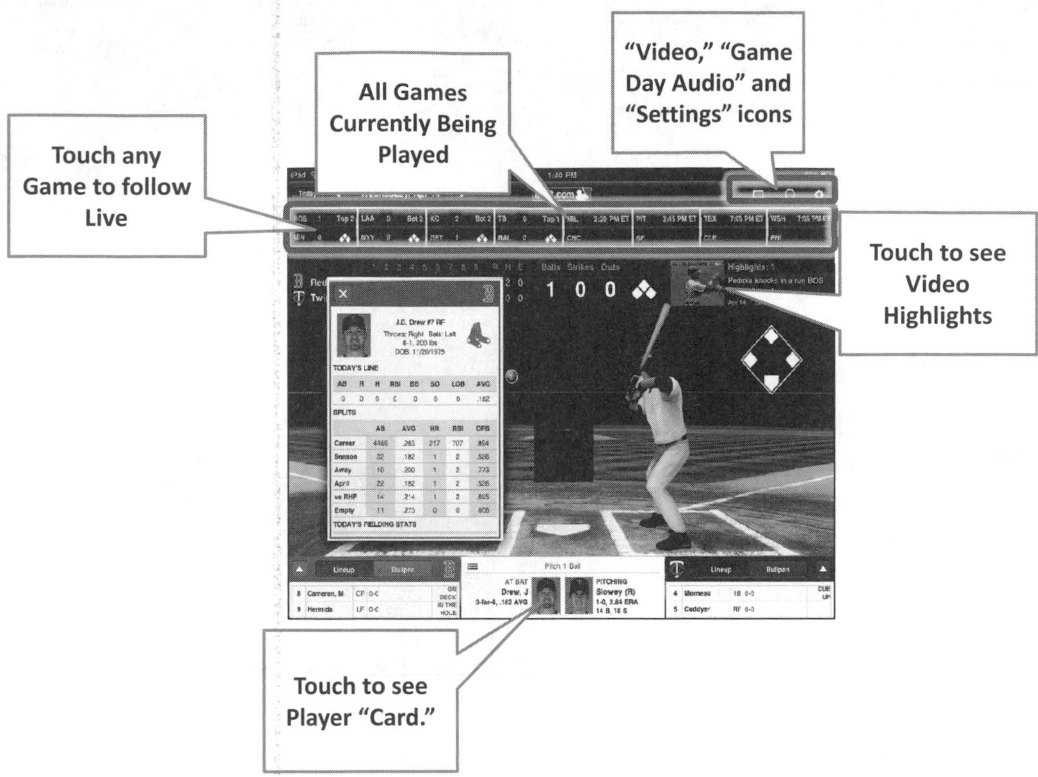


**Figure 21–6.** *At Bat 2010's layout*

When you see a player at the plate or on base, just touch the image and his baseball card pops up, enabling you to see his stats.

J.D. Drew #7 RF
Throws: Right Bats: Left
6-1, 200 lbs
DOB: 11/20/1975

TODAY'S LINE

| AB | R | H | RBI | BB | SO | LOB | AVG |
|---|---|---|---|---|---|---|---|
| 0 | 0 | 0 | 0 | 0 | 0 | 0 | .182 |

SPLITS

| | AB | AVG | HR | RBI | OPS |
|---|---|---|---|---|---|
| Career | 4469 | .283 | 217 | 707 | .894 |
| Season | 22 | .182 | 1 | 2 | .536 |
| Away | 10 | .200 | 1 | 2 | .773 |
| April | 22 | .182 | 1 | 2 | .536 |
| vs RHP | 14 | .214 | 1 | 2 | .695 |
| Empty | 11 | .273 | 0 | 0 | .606 |

TODAY'S FIELDING STATS

The three icons in the upper right-hand corner are the highlights of this app. Touch the image of the TV and you have the option of watching the game live.

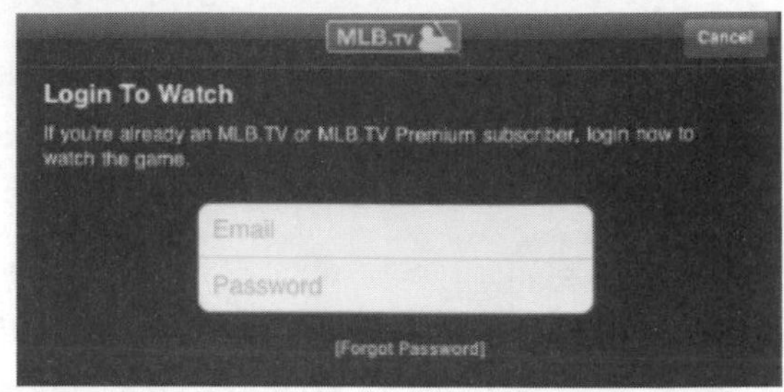


**Note**: You need to have a separate MLB TV account to be able to watch live games.

You can touch the **Headphones** icon to listen to game day audio from either of the two cities playing a particular game.

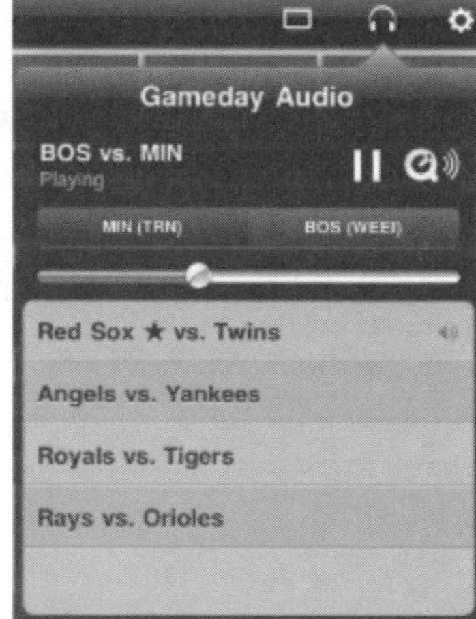


You can touch the **Settings** icon to adjust your favorite team, input your MLB TV subscription information (if you have one), or jump right to the MLB web site.

To see video highlights of key plays of the game, just touch the **Highlights** box in the right-hand corner.

To jump to any other game that is being played, you can touch on a game from the scoreboard, along the top.

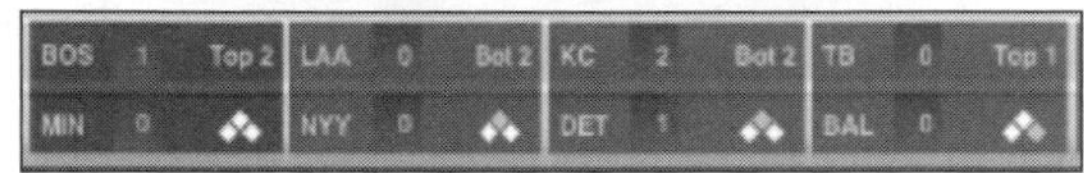


The options in this app are quite extensive, and the experience is immersive. This is a great way to follow your favorite teams, wherever you might be.

Chapter 22

# Social Networking

Your iPad can keep you in touch in many ways beyond e-mail and the Web. We will show you how you can turn your iPad into a big iPhone by using the Skype app.

Some of the most popular places to "connect" these days are those sites that are often called social networking sites—places that allow you to create your own page and connect with friends and family to see what is going in their lives. Some of the most popular web sites for social networking are Facebook, Twitter, and LinkedIn.

In this chapter, we will show you how to access these various sites. You will learn how to update your status, "tweet," and keep track of those who are both important or simply of interest to you.

## Phone Calls and More with Skype

Social Networking is all about keeping in touch with our friends and colleagues and family. While passive communication through sites like Facebook and MySpace are nice, sometimes there is just no substitute for hearing someone's voice.

Amazingly, from any iPad today, you can make phone calls using the **Skype** app. Calls to other Skype users anywhere in the world are free. A nice thing about Skype is that it works on computers and many mobile devices: iPads, iPhones, some BlackBerry smartphones and other mobile devices. You will be charged for calls to mobile phones and land lines , but rates are reasonable

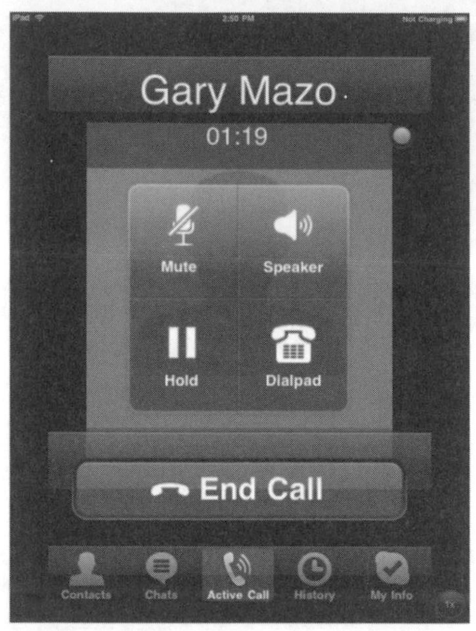

## Download the Skype App to Your iPad

Download the free **Skype** app from the **App Store** by searching for Skype and installing it. If you need help getting this done, please check out Chapter 20: "App Store."

> **NOTE:** As of publishing time, there was only an iPhone version of the App, but we expect to see an iPad version soon.

## Create Your Skype Account on Your iPad

If you need to setup your Skype account and have not already done it from your computer (see "Using Skype on your Computer" section), then follow the steps below to setup Skype on your iPad.

1. Tap the **Skype** icon from your Home Screen.
2. If you are using the iPhone **Skype** app, then tap the **2x** button in the lower right corner to expand the app to fill most of your iPad screen.
3. Tap the **Create Account** button.
4. Tap **Accept** if you accept the **No Emergency Calls** pop-up warning window to continue.

5. Enter your **Full Name**, **Skype Name**, **Password**, **E-Mail**, and decide whether you want to **Get News and Offers** by setting the switch at the bottom.
6. Tap the **Done** button to create your account.

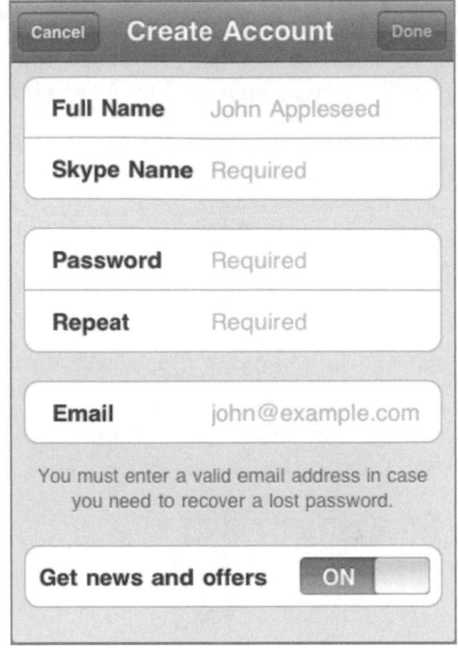


## Login to the Skype App

After you create your account, you are ready to login to Skype on your iPad. To do so, follow the steps below.

1. If you are not already in **Skype**, tap the **Skype** icon from your Home Screen.
2. Type your **Skype Name** and **Password**.
3. Tap the **Sign In** button in the upper right corner.
4. You should not have to enter this login information again, it is saved in **Skype**. Next time you tap **Skype**, it will automatically log you in.

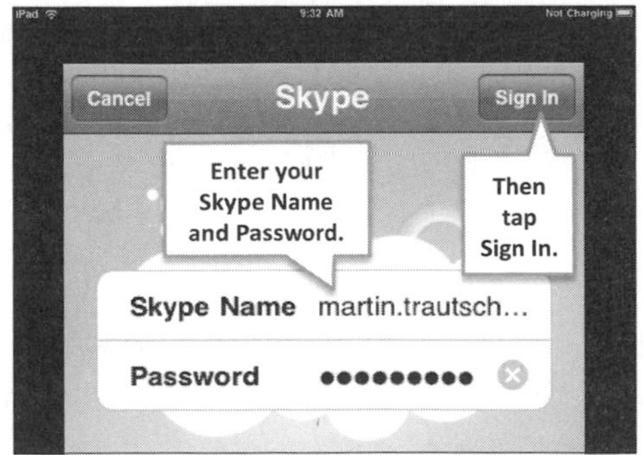

## Finding and Adding Skype Contacts

Once you have logged into the **Skype** app, then you will want to start communicating with people, so you have to find them and add then to your **Skype** contacts list.

1. If you are not already in **Skype**, tap the **Skype** icon from your Home Screen and login if asked.
2. Tap the **Contacts** soft key at the bottom.
3. Tap the **Search window** at the top and type someone's first and last name or Skype name. Tap **Search** to locate that person.
4. Once you see the person you want to add, tap their name.

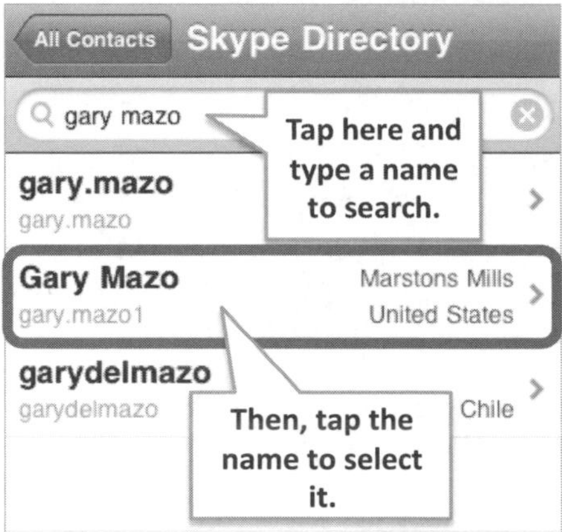


5. If you are not sure if this is the correct person, tap the **View Full Profile** button.
6. Tap **Add Contact** at the bottom.

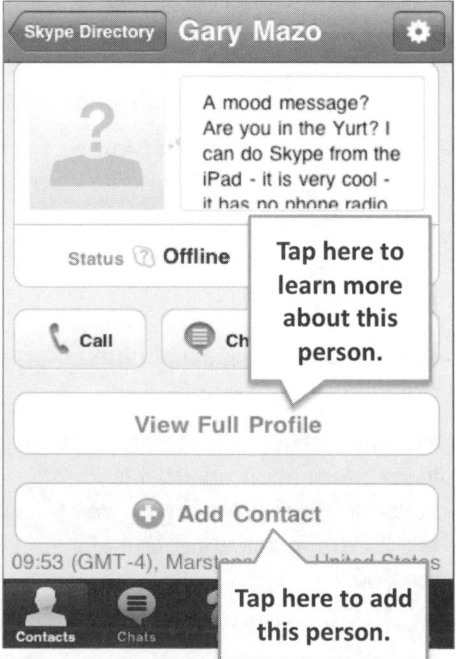

7. Adjust the invitation message and tap the **Send** button to send this person an invitation to become one of your Skype contacts.

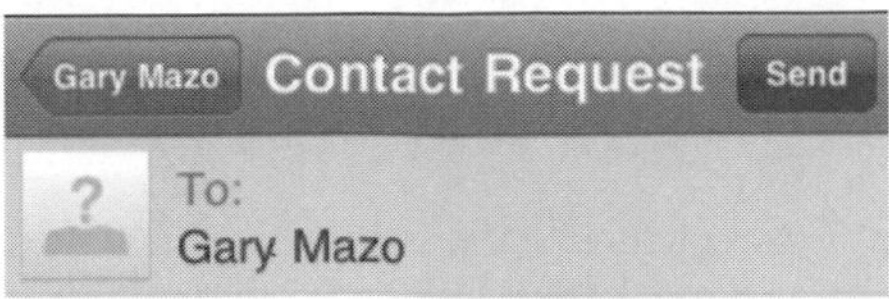


8. Repeat the procedure to add more contacts.
9. When you are done, tap the **Contacts** soft key at the bottom.
10. Tap **All Contacts** from the Groups screen to see all new contacts you have added.
11. Once this person accepts you as a contact, you will see them listed as a contact in your **All Contacts** screen.

**TIP:** Sometimes you want to get remove or block Skype contacts. You might want to do this if someone is annoying you or spamming you. To remove or block contacts you tapping their contact name in your list. Then, tap the settings icon (upper right corner) and select either **Remove from Contacts** or **Block**.

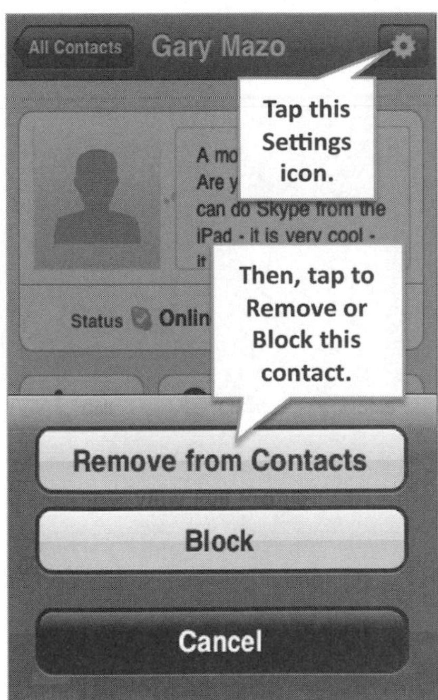

## Making Calls With Skype on Your iPad

Now that you have your account, have added contacts, you are ready to finally make that first call with **Skype** on your iPad.

1. If you are not already in **Skype**, tap the **Skype** icon from your Home Screen and login if asked.
2. Tap the **Contacts** soft key at the bottom.
3. Tap **All Contacts** to see your contacts.
4. Tap the contact name you wish to call. Figure 22–1.
5. Tap the **Call** button.
6. You may see a **Skype** button and a Mobile or other phone button. Press the **Skype** button to make the free call. Any other call requires you pay for it with Skype Credits.

**NOTE:** Please note that **Skype out** (placing calls to non-Skype phones) and **Skype in** (receiving calls from cell phones and landlines) are not available in all countries. Please consult the Skype website to learn which services are available in your area.

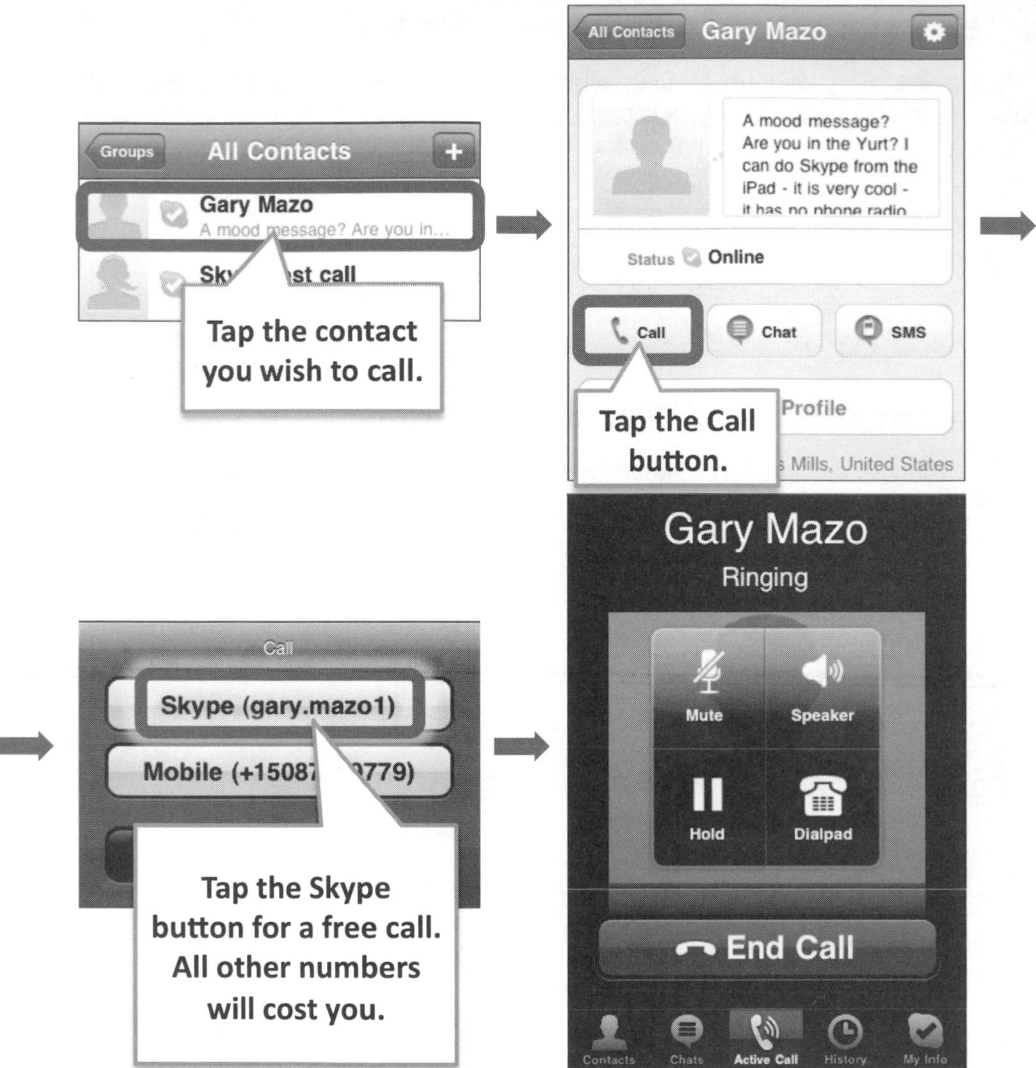


**Figure 22–1.** *Placing Calls from Skype on Your iPad.*

**NOTE:** You can call toll free numbers for free using Skype Out on your iPad. The following comes from the Skype Website:

The following countries and number ranges are supported and are free of charge to all users. France: +33 800, +33 805, +33 809. Poland: +48 800. UK: +44 500, +44 800, +44 808. USA: +1 800, +1 866, +1 877, +1 888. Taiwan: +886 80

## Receiving Calls with Skype on your iPad

Until the iPad handles multi-tasking, which will come with the OS 4.0 for iPad, the only way to receive a call with Skype is to have it open on your iPad. If someone calls you on Skype and the Skype app is not open, you will miss the call.

> **TIP:** If you want to call someone who you know is using Skype on their iPad, just send them a quick email or give them a quick call on their phone to alert them you would like to call them and to open up the Skype app.

### Buying Skype Credits or Monthly Subscription

Skype to Skype calls are free. However, if you want to call people on their land line or mobile phone from Skype, you will need to purchase Skype Credits or purchase a monthly subscription plan. If you try to purchase the credits or subscription from within the Skype app, it will take you to the Skype web site. So, we recommend using Safari on your iPad or using your computer's web browser.

> **TIP:** You may want to start with a limited amount of Skype Credits to try out the service before you sign up for a subscription plan. Subscription plans are the way to go if you plan on using Skype a lot for non-Skype callers (regular landlines and mobile phones).

1. Tap the **Safari** icon.
2. Type `www.skype.com` in the top address bar and tap **Go**.
3. Tap the **Sign In** link at the top of the page.
4. Enter your **Skype Name** and **Password**, tap **Sign me in.**
5. If you are not already on your Account screen, tap the **Account** tab in the right end of the Top Nav Bar.
6. Now you have the choice of buying credits or a subscription:
    a. Tap the **Buy pre-pay credit** button to purchase a fixed amount of credit.
    b. Tap the **Get a subscription** button to buy a monthly subscription account.
7. Finally, complete the payment instructions for either type of purchase.

## Chatting with Skype

In addition to phone calls, you can do a text chat with other Skype users from your iPad. Starting a Chat is very similar to starting a Call.

1. If you are not already in **Skype**, tap the **Skype** icon from your Home Screen and login if asked.
2. Tap the **Contacts** soft key at the bottom.
3. Tap **All Contacts** to see your contacts.
4. Tap the contact name you wish to chat with. Figure 22–2.
5. Tap the **Chat** button.
6. Type your chat text and press the **Send** button.
7. Your chat will appear in the top of the screen.

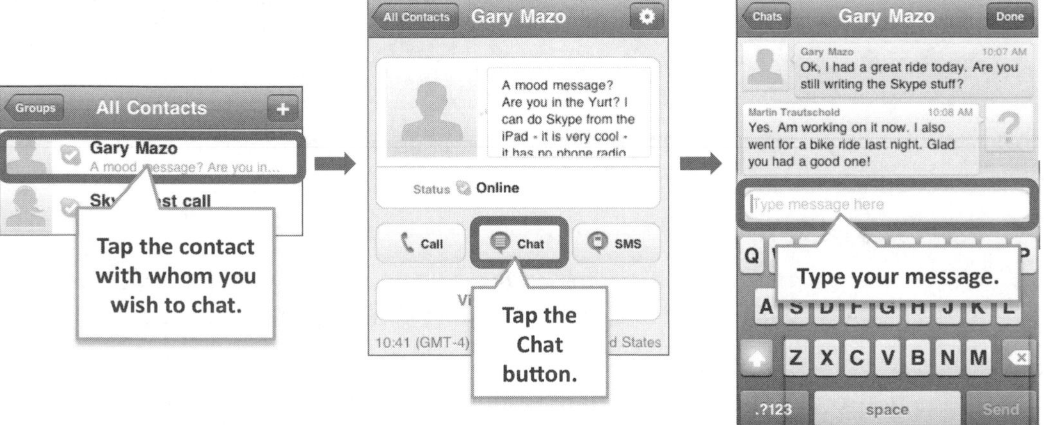


**Figure 22–2.** *Chatting with Skype on Your iPad.*

## Skype on your Computer - Create Account and Download Software

Since you can use Skype on your computer, we show you a little about how this works. In addition, with Skype on your computer (if you have a web cam), you can make video calls.

Note: When you call from your computer to an iPad or someone calls you from an iPad with Skype, you will not be able to do a video call. This is because Skype knows that the iPad does not have video capabilities.

To create a Skype account and download Skype software for your computer, follow these steps:

1. On your computer, open a web browser.
2. Go to: www.skype.com
3. Click the **Join** link at the top of the page.
4. Create your account by completing all required information and clicking the **Continue** button. Notice that you only have to enter information in the required fields noted with an asterisk. For example, your gender, birthdate and mobile phone are not required.
5. Now, you are done with the account setup process.
6. You are presented with the option of buying Skype Credit, but this is not required for the free Skype-to-Skype phone calls, video calls or chats.

**TIP:** You only need to pay for Skype if you want to call someone who is not using Skype. For example calls to phones on land lines or mobile phones (not using Skype) will cost you. At publishing time, pay-as-you-go rates were about 2.1 cents (U.S.) and monthly subscriptions ranged from about $3 - $14 for various calling plans.

7. Now, to download Skype to your computer, click the **Get Skype** link in the Top Nav Bar of the site.
8. Click the **Get Skype for Windows** or **Get Skype for Mac** button.
9. Follow the instructions to install the software. If you need assistance, we describe how to download and install software in the "Getting iTunes Software" section of Chapter 26: "iTunes Guide."
10. Once the software is installed, start it up and login using your Skype account.
11. You are ready to do phone calls, video calls and chats to anyone else using Skype and to all your friends with Skype on their iPads.

# Facebook

Facebook was founded in February of 2004. Since that time, it has served as the premier site for users to connect, re-connect, and share information with friends, co-workers, and family. Today, over 400 million people use Facebook as their primary source of "catching up" with the people who matter most to them.

> **NOTE:** You cannot play Facebook Games on your iPad. This may disappoint you if you are a big Facebook Game player. At publishing time, you could not play any Facebook games, such as Farmville and Mafia Wars on your iPad.

On your iPad, you have three primary ways of accessing your Facebook page as of publishing time:

1. Use Safari to go to the standard (full) web site: `www.facebook.com`.
2. Use Safari to go to the mobile site: touch.facebook.com.
3. Use the iPhone/iPad Touch Facebook app.

> **Note**: The authors expect an iPad Facebook app to be released in the coming months. The iPhone/iPad Touch app is more limited than the full site, but it is easier to navigate. Remember that since it is originally an iPhone/iPod Touch app, it will not fill up the screen. You can always touch the **2X** button to make it bigger—but it will not look as sharp and clear as the Facebook web page.

## Different Ways to Connect to Facebook

You can access Facebook by using the iPhone/iPod Touch app or using one of two Facebook web sites in your Safari browser.

## Downloading and Install the Facebook App

In order to find the app, use the **Search** feature in the App Store and simply type in **Facebook**.

You can also go to the Social Networking Category in the App Store and find the official **Facebook** app as well as many other Facebook-related apps.

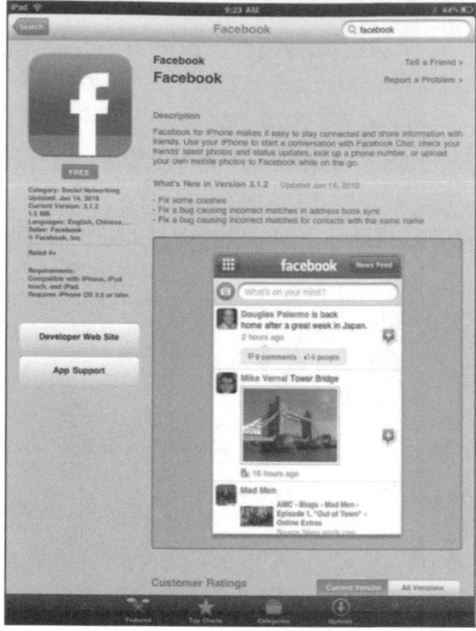


> **NOTE:** Some of the apps may look like "official" Facebook apps and they do cost money. The only "official" app is the iPhone/iPod app mentioned.

In order to connect to your account on Facebook, you will need to locate the icon you just installed and click on it. We use the example of Facebook here but the process is very similar for the rest of the apps.

Once Facebook is successfully downloaded, the icon should look something like this.

## Logging into facebook.com from Safari

To log in on the web-based app, just start up the Safari browser and go to `www.facebook.com`. Log in in just as you do on your computer.

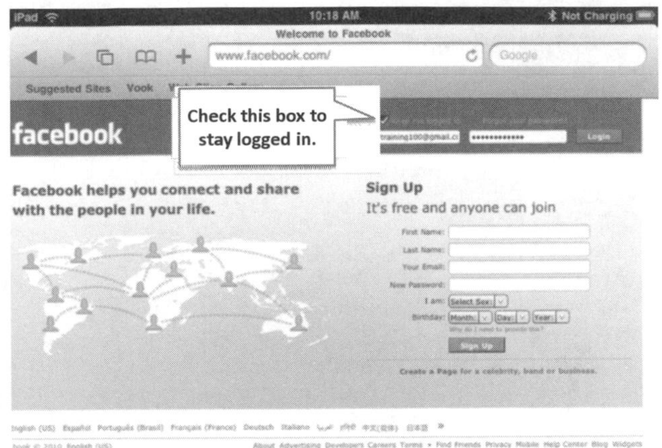


> **TIP:** For a full-featured Facebook experience, log in to touch.facebook.com or m.facebook.com to access the mobile site.

## Getting Around facebook.com

The nice thing about facebook.com is that you already know how to get around if you have ever used Facebook on your computer. It works essentially the same way.

Tap any of the links in the **Left Nav Bar** to get to your **News Feed**, **Messages**, **Events**, **Photos**, **Friends**, and more (see Figure 22–3).

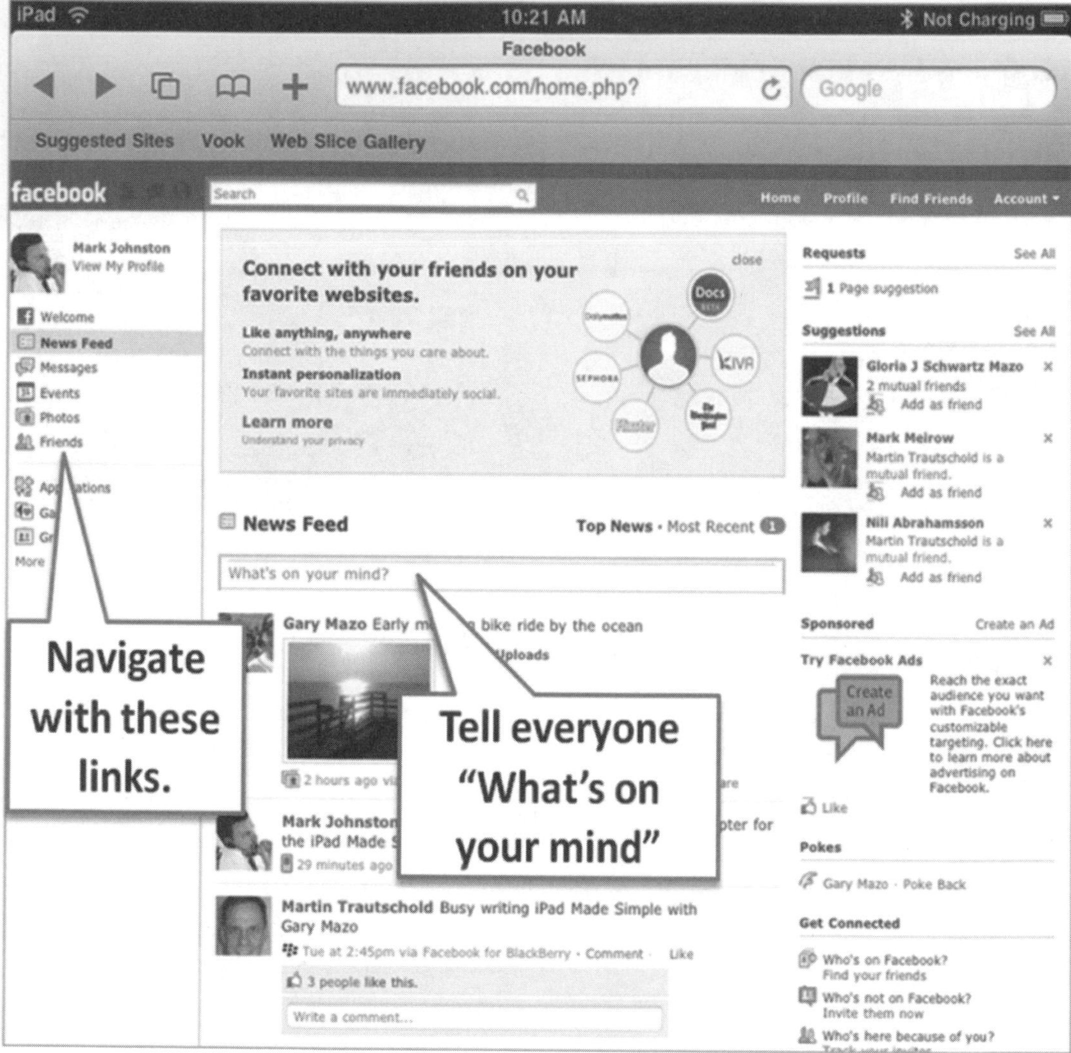


**Figure 22–3.** The facebook.com web page in the Safari browser

## Status Update/News Feed

Once you log on to the Facebook web site from Safari , you will have the option to write "What's on your mind" and see your News Feed from your friends.

## Finding Facebook Friends

In the web-based Facebook page, just touch the **Search** field and start typing in the name of the friend you are looking for.

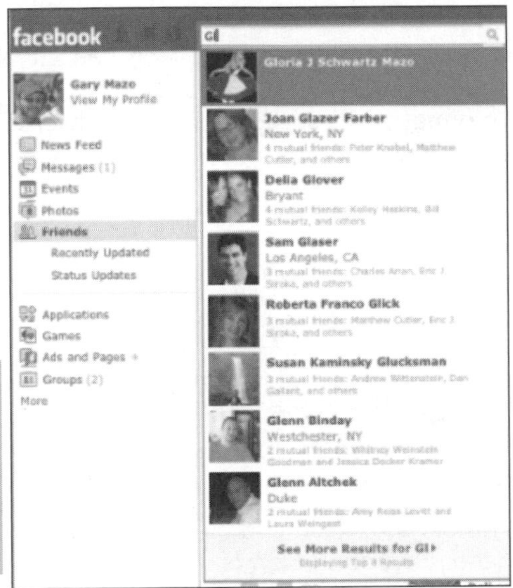


You can also touch the **Account** drop-down from your home page and then touch **All Connections** on the left side to see your friends.

Your friends are also listed under **Lists** along the left-hand sidebar.

> **NOTE:** if you are using either `touch.facebook.com` or `m.facebook.com`, you will have a **Friends** tab at the top to simply touch and see your listing of friends.

## Uploading a Photo to facebook.com

Unfortunately, at publishing time, the simple **Upload Photo** that you use from your computer did not work with the Safari browser. Instead, you are asked to send an e-mail to a uniquely generated e-mail address that appears in Facebook after you tap **Upload Photo**. Your subject of the e-mail becomes the text for the uploaded photo. One nice thing about uploading photos to Facebook by e-mail is that you can send a bunch of photos at one time and have them upload in the background. However, with the **acebook** app, you have to wait for each photo to upload before you do the next.

Instead of showing you these detailed steps, we recommend that you install the Facebook app and use it to upload photos. It is much easier. See the "Uploading Pictures with the Facebook App" section in this chapter for the upload steps.

# The Facebook App

As noted earlier, at publishing time, the full **Facebook** app for the iPad was not yet available. Here, we show you how to use the **Facebook** app that was designed for the iPhone/iPod touch. The screen is smaller, but you can press the **2x** button in the lower right corner to see it larger (but grainy). We anticipate that the iPad version of this app will have many similarities to its smaller cousin described here. So, much of what you learn here will be transferrable when the new software is released. To get the Facebook app installed on your iPad, start up the **App Store** and search for Facebook. Tap the **Install** button from the Facebook app listing.

## Facebook App Basics

Once Facebook is downloaded and installed, the first thing you will see is the log-in screen. Input your account information—your e-mail and password.

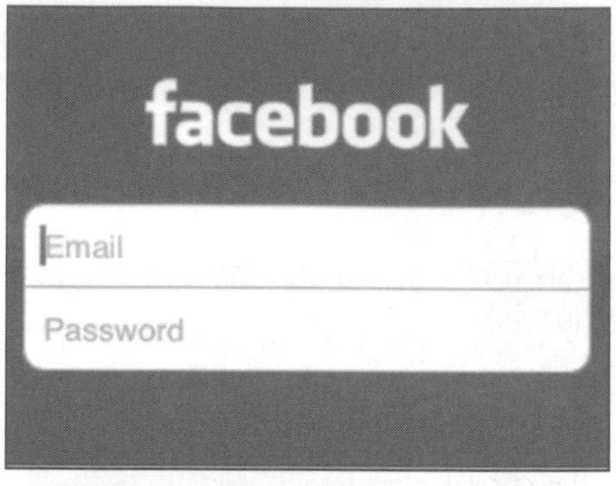


After you log-in the first time, you will see a **Push Notifications** warning message.

Click **OK** if you want to allow these messages, which can be pokes from other Facebook friends, notes, status update notifications, and more.

Once you login, you will see the Facebook screen shown in Figure 22–4. Tap the **Facebook** logo to navigate around the app.

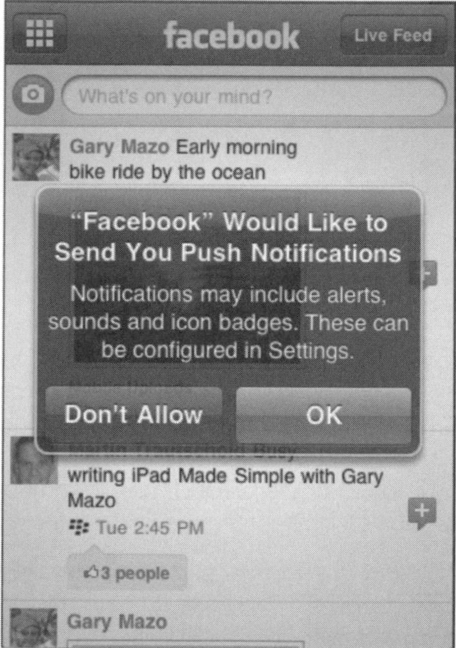

**Figure 22–4.** *Using the Facebook app*

## Expanding or Reducing the Size of the App

Since this **Facebook** app was designed for the smaller screen on the iPhone or iPod touch, you will notice it opens up as a smaller app in the center of the screen. To see a larger size app, tap the **2x** in the bottom right portion of the screen, as shown in Figure 22–5.

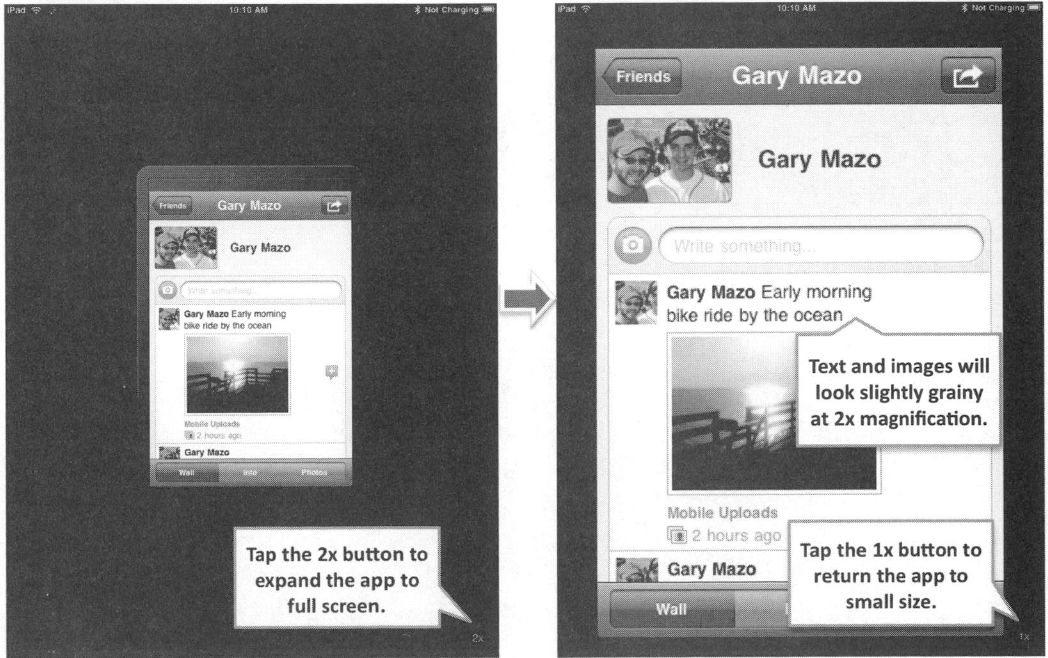


**Figure 22–5.** *Expand the app to full screen with the 2x button.*

## Navigating Around Facebook

Toggle between the **Navigation Icons** and your current location by tapping the word **Facebook** at the top of the page.

For example, if you are in the **News Feed** and tap **Facebook**, you will see all the icons. Tap **Facebook** again and you will return to the **News Feed**.

From the icons page, you can access your **News Feed, Profile, Notifications, Upload a Photo, Friends, Requests, Events, Chat,** or **Inbox**.

## Communicating with Your Friends

1. Tap **Facebook** at the top to see all the icons.
2. Tap the **Friends** icon and your list of friends is displayed.
3. Touch the Friend and you will go to their Facebook page where you can then write on their **Wall** and see their **Info** or **Photos**.

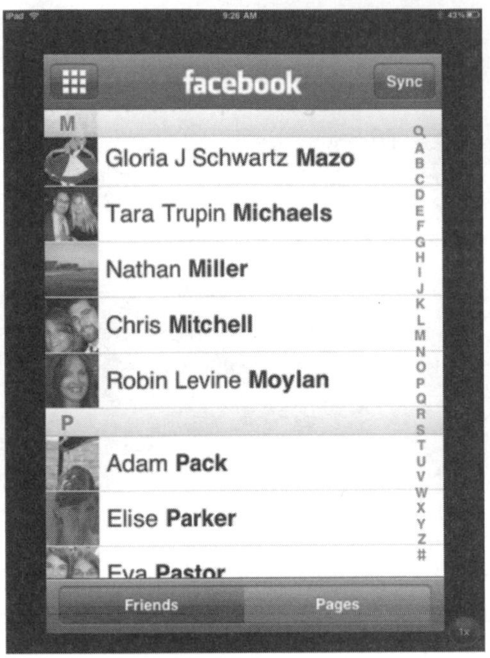


## Uploading Pictures with the Facebook App

An easy and fun thing to do with Facebook is to upload pictures. Below, we show you how to upload pictures in the **Facebook** app .

**NOTE:** The lack of a camera on the iPad means you need to have synced, copied, or e-mailed the photos to yourself and then saved them to the photo gallery. Or you could have saved them off the web, etc., first.

1. From the Facebook main icons, tap Photos.
2. Choose an album such as Mobile Uploads.
3. Tap the Camera icon in the upper right corner and navigate through the pictures on your iPad until you

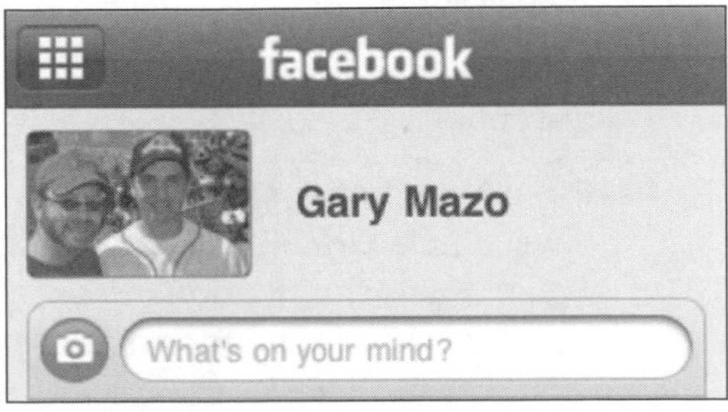

find the picture you wish to upload.

4. Next, tap **Write a caption...** to write a caption, if so desired.

5. To finish the upload, tap the blue **Upload** button and the photo will go into your "Mobile Uploads" folder.

> **Note**: Unfortunately, at the time of writing this book, the **Upload Photo** feature is not working with the Safari browser, only through the **Facebook** app shown here.

## Settings to Customize Your Facebook App

To adjust settings for the Facebook app:

1. Tap the **Settings** icon.
2. Tap **Facebook** in the left column.
3. You can now adjust various options:

   **Shake to Reload** feature, which reloads or updates the page when you shake your iPad;

   **Vibrate** feature, for when notifications are sent;

4. **Push Notifications -** These features have simple **ON/OFF** toggle switches. Touch **Push Notifications** to see the detailed switches on the next screen;.

Facebook
General
Shake to Reload ON
Chat
Vibrate ON
Push Notifications
Version 3.1.2

**Push Notifications** settings screen for the **Facebook** app;

Touch each switch to set it **ON** or **OFF**.

For each switch that is in the **ON** position, you will receive Push Notifications when something changes—for example when you receive a message when somebodyconfirms you as a friend, tags you in a photo, or comments on your wall.

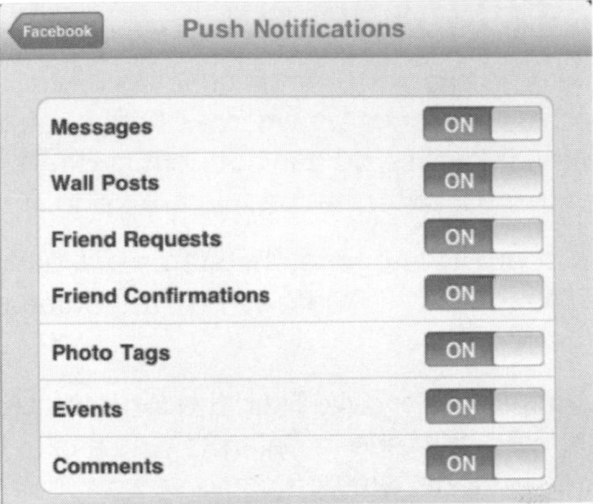


**TIP:** The latest version of the Facebook app will bring in Facebook profile pictures to your Contacts list. This can be quite humorous depending on the pictures.

# LinkedIn

LinkedIn has very similar core functionality to Facebook, but tends to be more business and career-focused, whereas Facebook is more personal friends and game-focused. With LinkedIn, you can connect and re-connect with past business associates, send messages, see what people are up to, have discussions, and more.

As of publishing time, the status of LinkedIn was very similar to Facebook. You can go to the regular LinkedIn site on the Safari browser, or download the **LinkedIn** app for the iPhone.

Which is better? We liked the **LinkedIn** App for the iPhone slightly better than the full LinkedIn.com site in Safari. It was easier to navigate using the **LinkedIn** app with the large buttons, but you could see more on the screen in the Safari version. We recommend giving both options a try and see which you like better—it is really a personal preference.

## LinkedIn.com on the Safari Browser

To get to LinkedIn on your browser, follow these steps:

1. Tap the **Safari** icon.
2. Tap the **Address** bar at the top of the browser.
3. Type in this address: `www.linkedin.com` Remember, if you see `www.linkedin.com` appear in the drop-down as you are typing it, then just touch the link to jump there.
4. Enter your LinkedIn username and password to log in and see the LinkedIn home page, as shown in Figure 22–6.

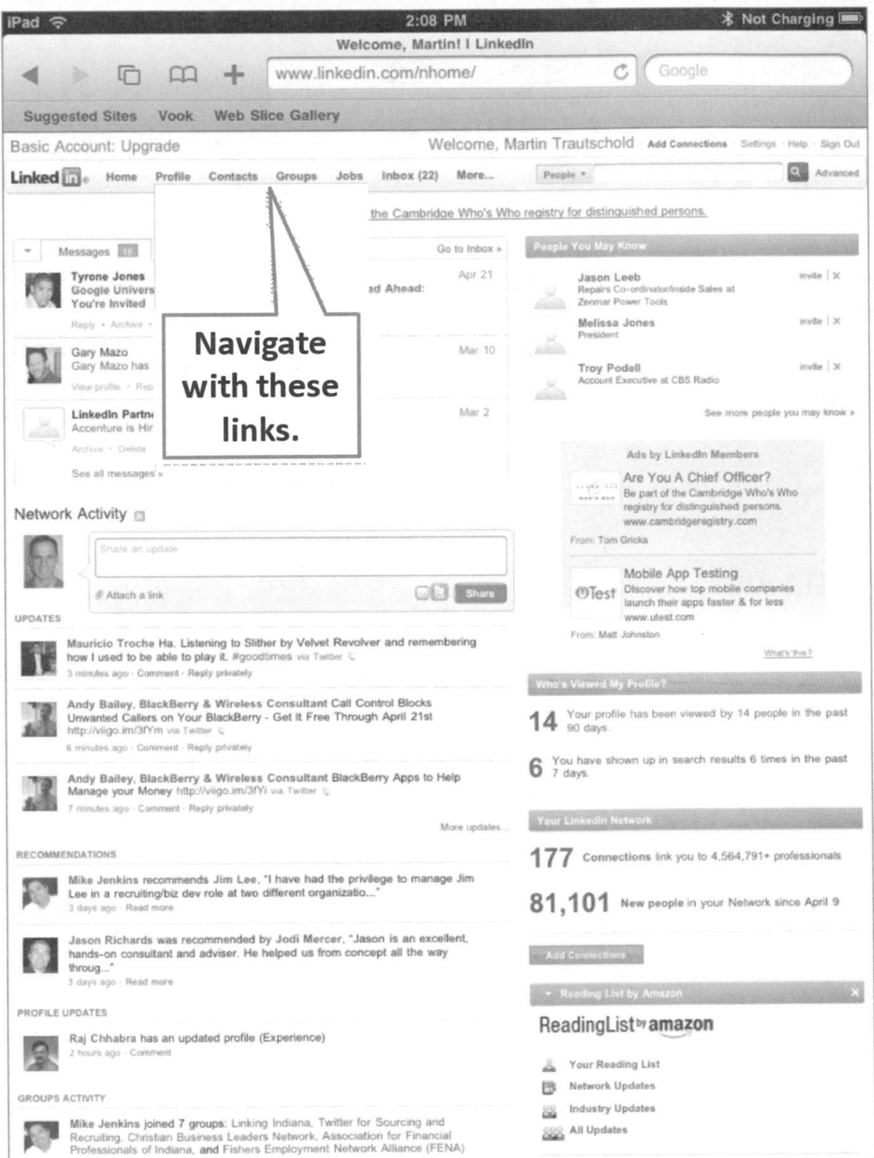


**Figure 22–6.** LinkedIn home page on your Safari web browser

> **TIP:** Remember to zoom using double-tap or pinching **open/closed** to see more of the web page.

You navigate around and interact with LinkedIn.com just as you would with your computer. The only difference is that you use your finger instead of the mouse to click links.

## LinkedIn App

As we mentioned earlier, this section describes the **LinkedIn** app for the iPhone since the iPad version was not yet available at publishing time.

### Download the App

Similar to downloading Facebook, start up the App Store on your iPad. Type **LinkedIn** in the search window and locate the app. It is free, so tap the **FREE** button to install it.

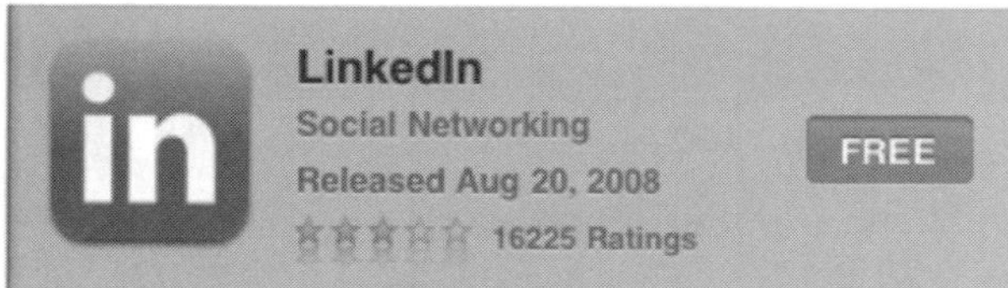


### Log in to LinkedIn App

Once the app is installed, click on the **LinkedIn** icon and enter your log in information.

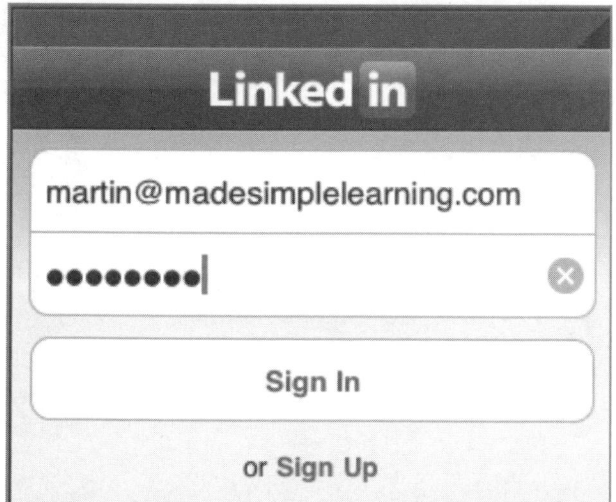


### Navigating around the LinkedIn App

LinkedIn has an icon-based navigation similar to Facebook. Tap any icon to move to that function, then tap the **Home** icon in the upper left corner to return back to the Home Screen. See Figure 22–7.

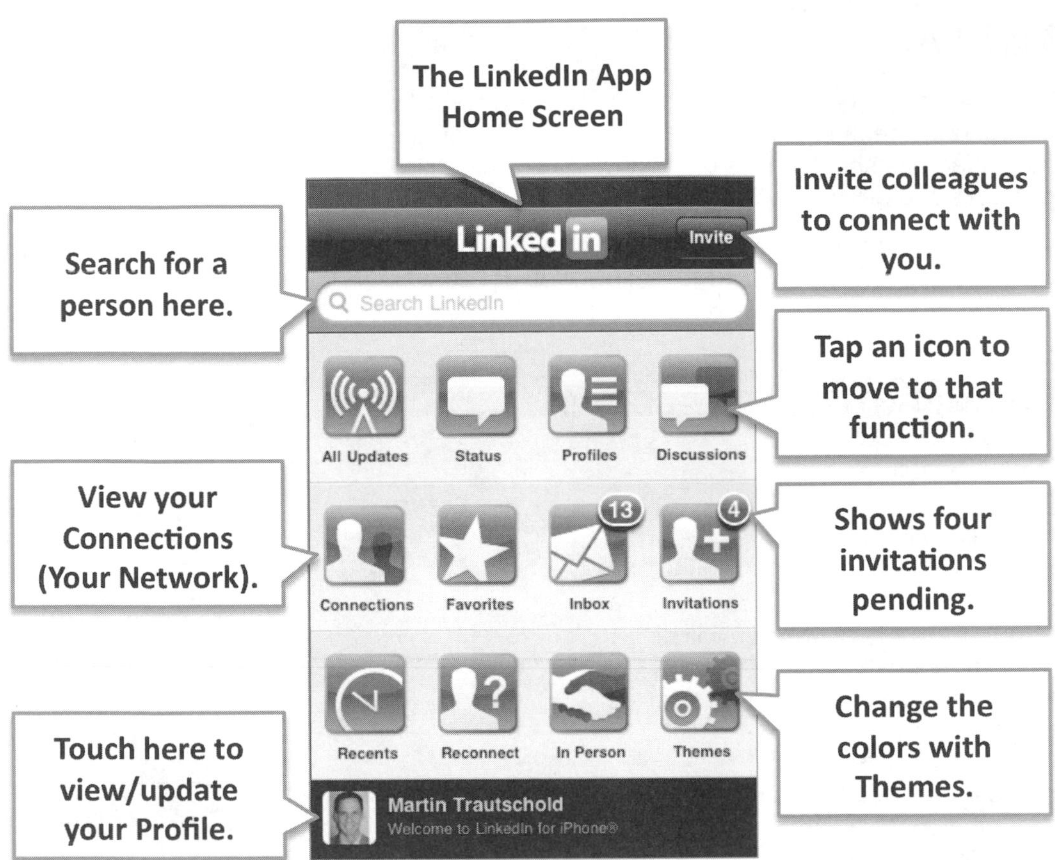


**Figure 22–7.** LinkedIn app home page

As you can see, when you compare LinkedIn on Safari (Figure 24-4) and the **LinkedIn** app home page (Figure 24-5), the icons are easier to use to navigate around quickly on the app.

Play around a bit with the app and the Safari version and you will get a feel for which version you like better. And we are sure you will soon see a **LinkedIn** app for the iPad, which will be better than both of the current options!

## Twitter

Twitter was started in 2006. Twitter is essentially an SMS (text message)-based social networking site. It is often referred to as a "micro-blogging" site where the famous and not so famous share what's on their mind. The catch is that you only have 140 characters to get your point across.

With Twitter, you subscribe to "follow" someone who "Tweets" messages. You might also find that people will start to "follow" you. If you want to follow us, we are: @garymadesimple on Twitter.

## Making a Twitter Account

Making a Twitter account is very easy. We do recommend that you first establish your Twitter account on the Twitter web site, `www.twitter.com`. When you establish your account, you will be asked to choose a unique user name—we use @garymadesimple—and a password.

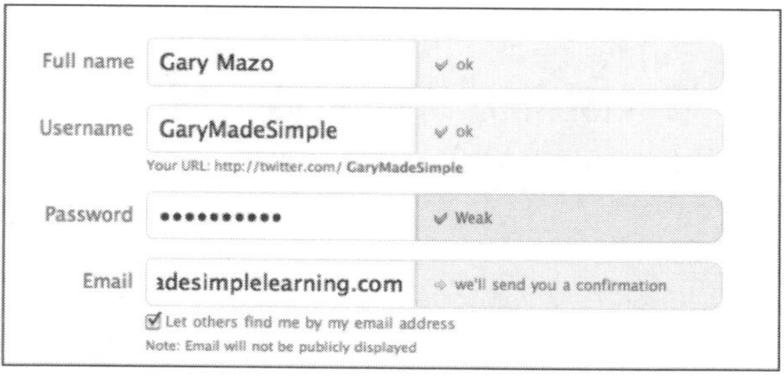


You will then be sent an e-mail confirmation. Click on the link in your e-mail and you will be taken back to the Twitter web site. You can choose people to "follow" or make "Tweets" on the web site and also read Tweets from your friends.

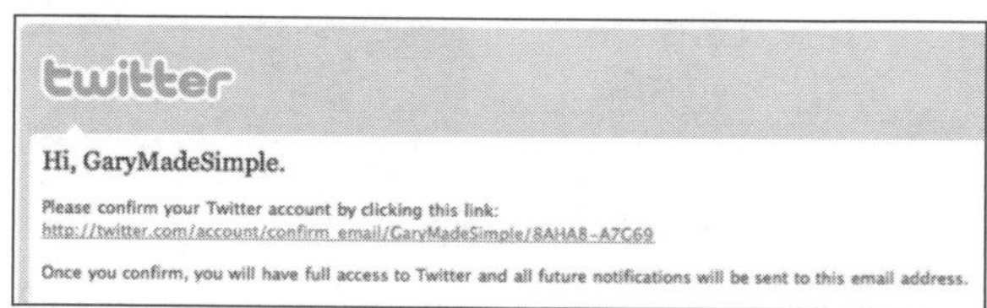


## Twitter Options for the iPad

There are many options for using twitter on the iPad. The easiest way to follow others and to tweet is to use one of the Twitter apps from the App Store.

There are many Twitter apps from which to choose. For purposes of this book, we are highlighting two specific Twitter apps, **TweetDeck** and **Twitterific**. Both are very well designed and easy to use.

**NOTE:** Twitter has recently purchased the makers of **Tweetie** and **Tweetie 2** and we expect that an "Official" Twitter client for the iPad will be released in the near future.

## Download Twitter App

Go to the App Store, touch **Categories**, and choose **Social Networking**. You should see both **TweekDeck** and **Twitterific** in the **Spotlight** section. If not, simply touch the **Search** window and type in either app name.

Download the app as you would any other app to the iPad.

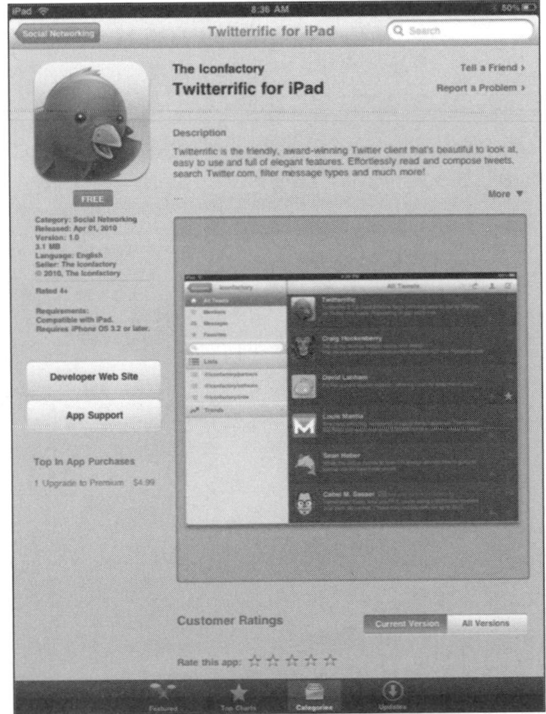

## Starting the Twitter App for the First Time

Touch either app icon and the program will start. The first time using either app will require you to sign in to Twitter. You user name was the one you picked when you first signed up for Twitter.

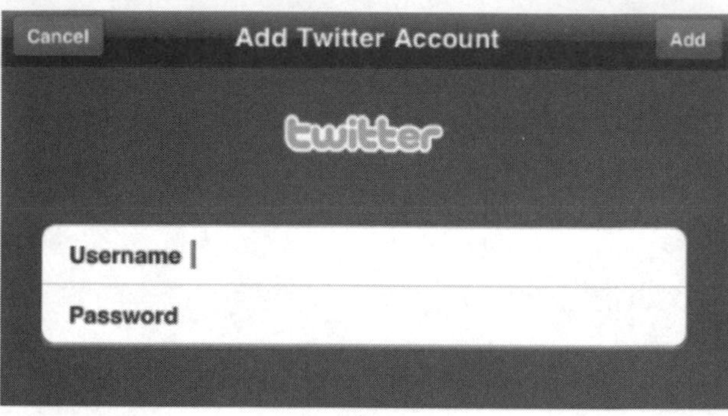


## Using TweetDeck

TweetDeck gives you a very clean home screen. You see the tweets from those you are following along the bottom left section of the screen under the **All Friends** label.

Usually, to the right are the **Mentions**, which are responses to your Tweets—almost like a text message conversation.

The controls for TweetDeck are in the upper right-hand corner. There are five icons available to you. See Figure 22–8.

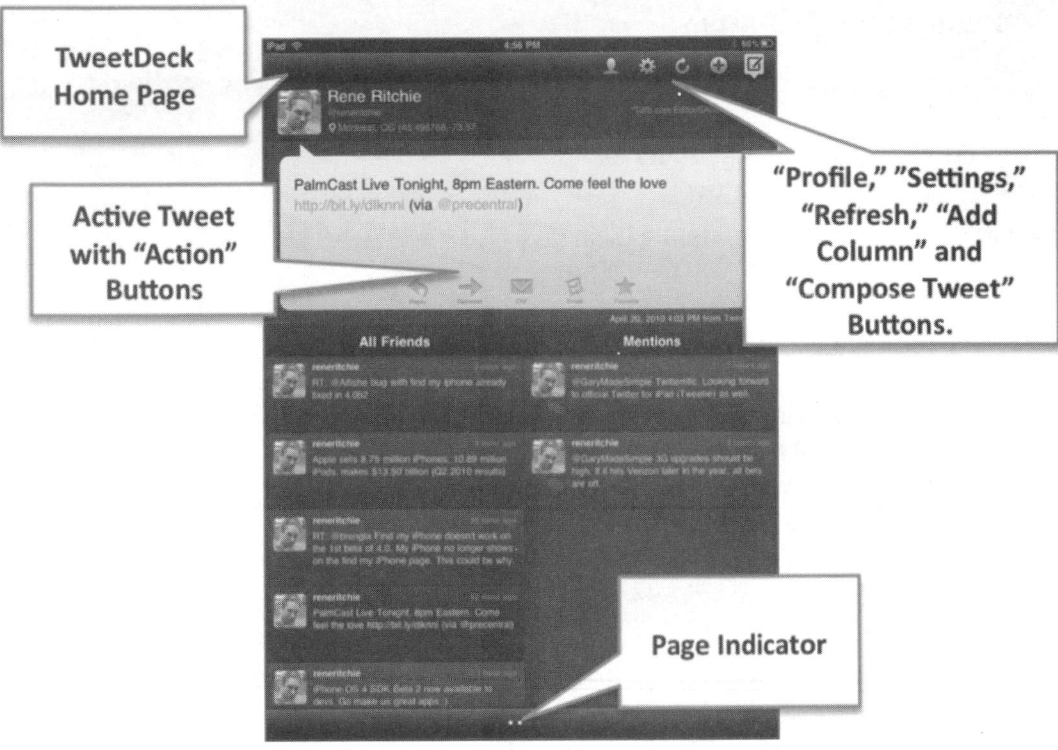


**Figure 22–8.** Layout of TweetDeck home page

## People

Tap the **Profile** icon (person) to see the he **Search** box and type in the name or username of the individual you are looking to follow.

In this example, I looked for my friend Kevin who goes by CrackBerryKevin. When you find the user, just touch the **View Profile** button to see their Twitter profile.

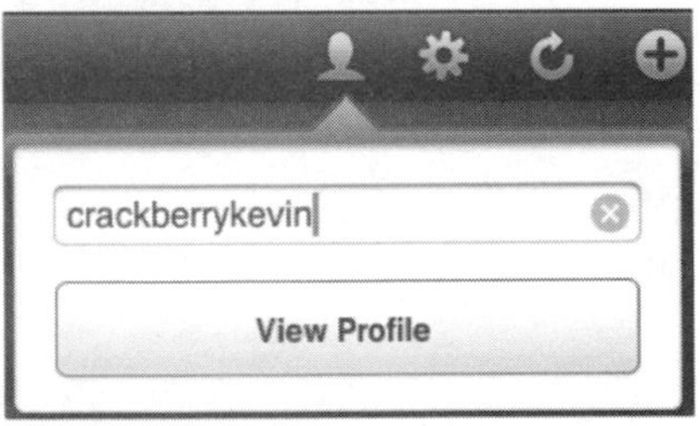

## Accounts and Settings

There are several adjustable fields in the **Accounts and Settings** section of the app. Touch the **Manage Accounts** tab to add or edit your Twitter account.

Touch the **Sign into an Account** to sign in to another Twitter account you may have. Just touch the tab and input your username and password.

Touch the **Settings** tab to adjust auto correction, auto capitalization, and sound options. You can also choose your picture service if you have a specific service for uploading pictures to Twitter.

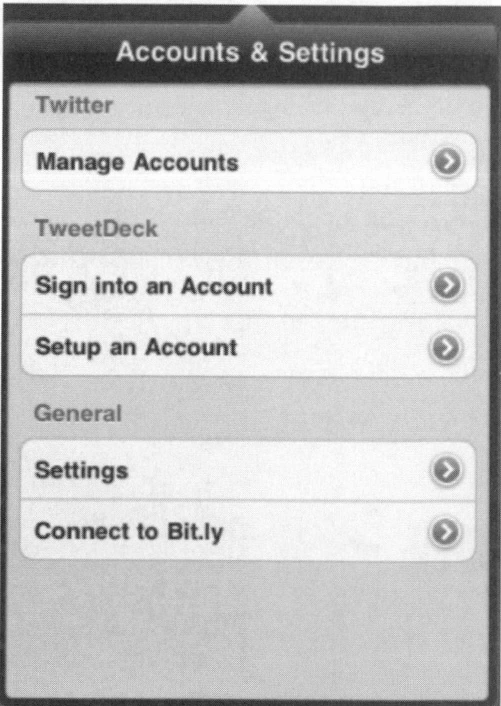


## Refresh

Touching the **Refresh** button simply refreshes your Tweets.

## Add Column

The **Add Column** button adds another column onto your Twitter home screen. Just slide from right to left to advance from one column to the next. The "dots" at the bottom indicate how many screens you have to move through. You can add a column for **Search**, **Direct Messages**, **Mentions**, **Favorites**, **Twitter Trends**, **Twitter Lists**, **Twitter Search**, and **All Friends**.

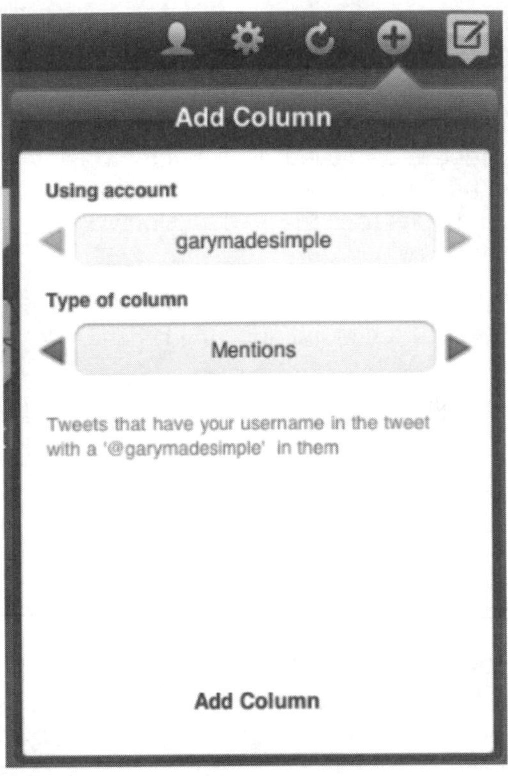

## Compose Tweet

Touch the **Compose Tweet** icon and the Tweet composition screen is displayed. Your Twitter ID is in the "From" line and you have 140 characters to express what is on your mind.

When you are done, just touch the **Send** button in the upper right-hand corner.

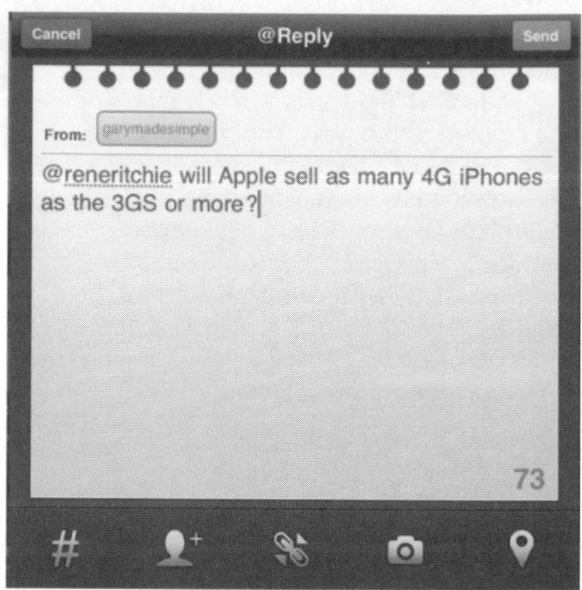


## Reading and Replying

Touch a Tweet to bring it to the main screen. In addition to the Tweet being nice and large, you can touch on a link within the Tweet to launch the web view. If you want to view the link in Safari, just touch the **View in Safari** button.

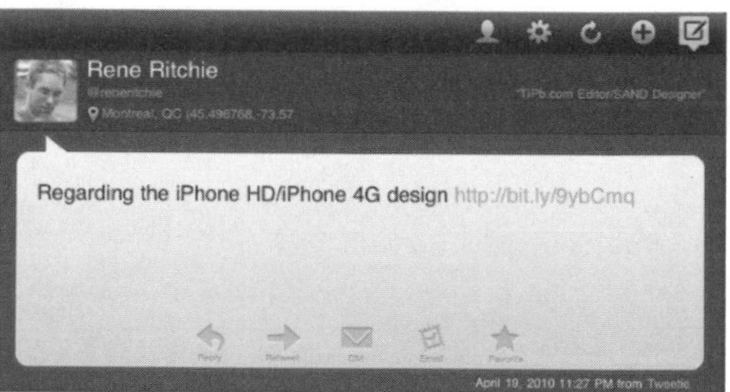


**NOTE:** When you view the link in Safari, you then need to close Safari and restart **TweetDeck**.

At the bottom of the Tweet window, you will see five icons; **Reply**, **Forward**, **DM**, **Email**, and **Favorite**.

Each will bring up an additional window and the onscreen keyboard for you to type your reply, forward the Tweet, Send a Direct Message to the author, Email the Tweet, or set it as a Favorite.

## Using Twitterific

Twitterific takes a streamlined approach to using Twitter. The home screen shows you the Tweets from those you are following. The full message is nice and large.

> **NOTE:** Twitterrific is free for a single account with ads. You can upgrade inside the app to a paid version with multiple accounts (for example, business and personal) and no ads.

The controls for Twitterific are in the top right-hand corner. See Figure 22–9.

**Figure 22–9.** *Layout of Twitterific home page*

## Refresh

To refresh your list of Tweets, just touch the **Refresh** button. You will also notice a sound notification as new Tweets are loaded. You can mute this if you prefer no sounds.

## Profile

Touch the **Profile** button and your Twitter profile is displayed. To see the most recent Tweets in your list, touch **Recent Tweets**.

To see those Tweets you have labeled as favorites, touch the **Favorites** tab.

To see those individuals whom you are following, touch the **Following** tab. Next to each individual you are following is an additional tab; touch this to see the profile of the individual. You can also see who they are following and see their most recent tweets.

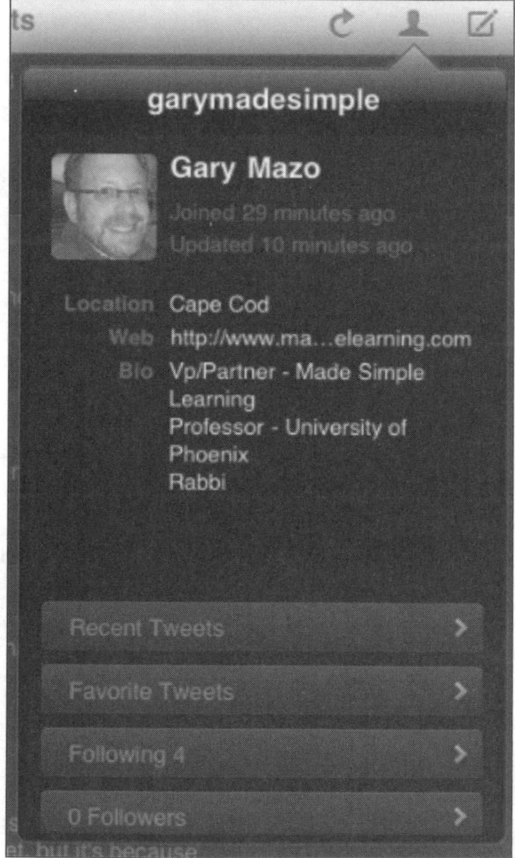

## Compose

Touch the **Compose** button and the **New Tweet** screen pops up. The character counter will count down from 140 as you type your message.

## Account Button

In the upper left-hand corner is the Account button. Touch it and you can access your **Messages**, **Favorites**, **Mentions**, or **All Tweets**.

The **Search** bar allows you to search for individuals, topic, and trends—just about anything. Touch a Trend and the Tweet window changes to show a list of Tweets from people on that trend.

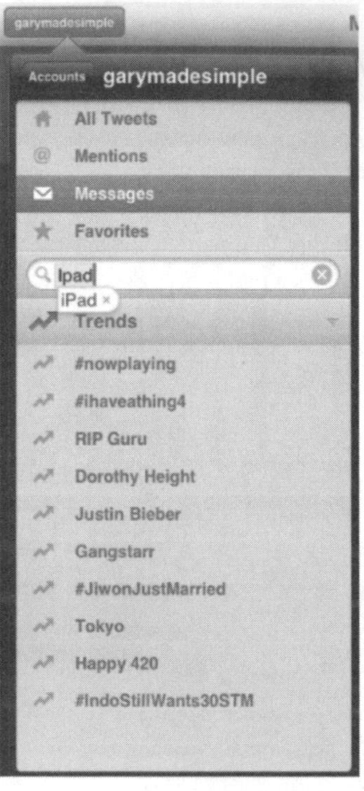


## Options from Within Tweet

From your Twitterific home screen, just touch one of your tweets for options. You can **Show the Conversation**, **Reply to the Author**, **Translate the Tweet**, or **Email the Tweet**. Just touch the corresponding button to launch the action.

Chapter 23

# New Media: Reading Newspapers, Magazines, and More

In Chapter 8, we spoke about how the iPad has revolutionized the world of reading. Not only is the iPad unparalleled in the realm of reading e-books, the iPad is also unparalleled in dealing with new media such as online newspapers and magazines, PDF files, and more.

In this chapter, we will explore how to enjoy new media with your iPad and its vivid screen and terrific touch interface. The iPad is even set to revitalize the comic book industry with comic books that look beautiful and are amazingly interactive.

## Newspapers on the iPad

Remember the days when newspapers were delivered to the house? Invariably, if there was one puddle in the sidewalk, that was where the newspaper landed! You took it out of that plastic bag, shook it off, and tried to make out what was in section two – the section that got soaked.

## Enter the iPad Interactive Newspaper

Well, those days may be gone forever. Users now have the opportunity to interact with their news and even get their paper delivered every day – but to their iPad instead of their driveway.

Many newspapers are developing apps for the iPad, with new apps seeming to appear every day. We will take a quick look at three apps from the largest newspapers in the United States and see how they revolutionize reading the news on the iPad (see Figure 23–1).

**Figure 23–1.** *The front pages of various newspaper apps*

## Popular Choices: The New York Times, The Wall Street Journal, and USA Today

Each of these three papers has a circulation of millions of readers, and each has taken a different approach to bringing you the news on the iPad.

> **NOTE:** You can always go and visit the dedicated web site for any news source. Some are optimized for the iPad, while others offer you a full web experience. Others will require registration and/or a paid subscription to view the paper's full content.

You must first follow several steps in the **App Store** to find, download, and install a news app on the iPad.

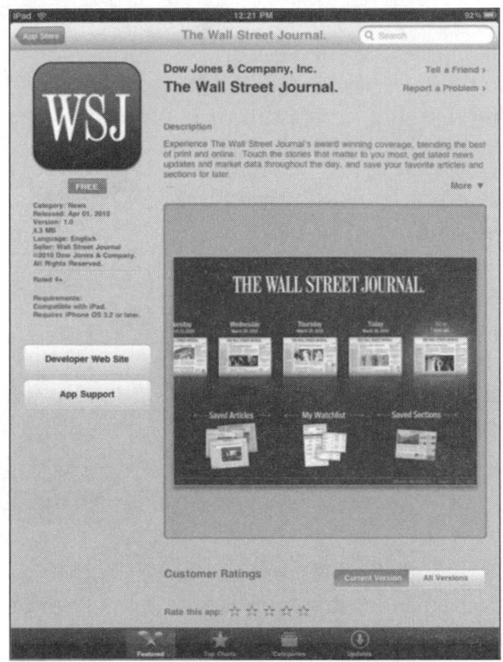


1. The first step is to locate your desired news app in the **App Store**. You may find one or more news apps in the **Featured** section.
2. Next, touch the **Categories** button at the bottom of the page and then touch the **News** icon. This will take you to all the news apps in the App Store. Browse or search for your desired news app, just as you would for any other app.
3. Once you locate the desired news app, download it as you would any other app.

**NOTE:** Many news apps are free. Some are free to try, but require you to buy them to continue receiving them. Others offer limited free content, but you need to subscribe to gain access to their full content.

4. Once the app is downloaded, touch its icon to start it.

*The New York Times* offers a slimmed-down version of the paper in its free iPad app, which it calls **Editors Choice**.

There are five soft keys at the bottom of the page for **News**, **Business**, **Technology**, **Opinion**, and **Features**. Each section carries a sampling of stories from those sections in today's paper.

EDITORS' CHOICE | NEWS

The New York Times

SATURDAY, APRIL 3, 2010

**Hurting U.S. Efforts to Win Minds, Taliban Disrupt Pay**

By RICHARD A. OPPEL Jr.

MARJA, Afghanistan — Since their offensive here in February, the Marines have flooded Marja with hundreds of thousands of dollars a week. The tactic aims to win over wary locals by paying them compensation for property damage or putting to work men who would otherwise look to the Taliban for support.

**At 89, Stevens Contemplates Law, and How to Leave It**

By ADAM LIPTAK

WASHINGTON — "There are still pros and cons to be considered," Justice John Paul Stevens said in his Supreme Court chambers on Friday afternoon, reflecting on his reluctance to leave a job he loves after almost 35 years. But his calculus seemed to be weighted toward departure, and he said his decision on the matter would come very

**Criticism of Chávez Is Stifled by Arrests**

By SIMON ROMERO

LOS TEQUES, Venezuela — When Judge María Lourdes Afiuni issued a ruling in December that irked President Hugo Chávez, he did little to contain his outrage. The president, contending on national television that she would have been put before a firing squad in earlier times, sent his secret intelligence police to arrest her.



Navigating **The New York Times** app is as simple as sliding screens from right to left. You can touch a section, and then slide the screen to the left to see additional pages in that section. Touch an article again, and then slide the screen to the left to continue reading additional pages in that article.

To go back to the **Home** page, touch the **News** button in the upper left-hand corner.

To e-mail an article, just touch the **E-mail Article** button in the upper right-hand corner. This button is only available when you are inside an article, not on the **Home** page.

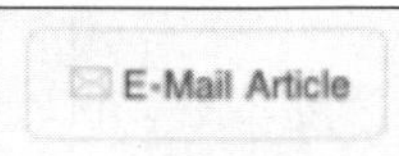


## Moving Through and Enjoying Content

After you play for a while with all these various newspapers, magazines, web sites, comics, and more – you will begin to realize that there is no real standard for moving around. This means you'll need to become familiar with each app and its own way of navigating articles, as well as how to return to the main screen. Here's a short guide for generally navigating these types of apps:

**Showing or Hiding Control buttons or Captions** –Tapping the screen once will usually show hidden controls or picture captions. You can tap them again to re-hide them.

**Getting to the Details of an Article** – Usually, you tap the article or its headline to see the next screen.

**Getting to the Next Page of an Article** – Usually you swipe right to read more. Sometimes you swipe up.

**Viewing a Video** – Tap A video to start playing IT. Usually, this plays the video in the same portion of the screen without expanding it.

**Expanding a Video or Image Size** – You can try pinching open in the video or image, and then double-tapping the video or image. Look for an **Expand** button; you may also try rotating to landscape mode.

**Reducing a Video or Image Size** –You can try pinching closed inside the video or image. Look for a **Close** or **Minimize** button; you may also try rotating back to portrait mode.

**The Wall Street Journal** app, however takes a different approach to delivering the news. Once the app is launched, you will be prompted to create an online account.

Once the account is created, you have access to a subset of content from *The Wall Street Journal*.

Material that is unavailable to free account users is marked with a small **Key** icon, indicating that material is locked.

If you fully subscribe to **The Wall Street Journal** app, all articles and tools become available.

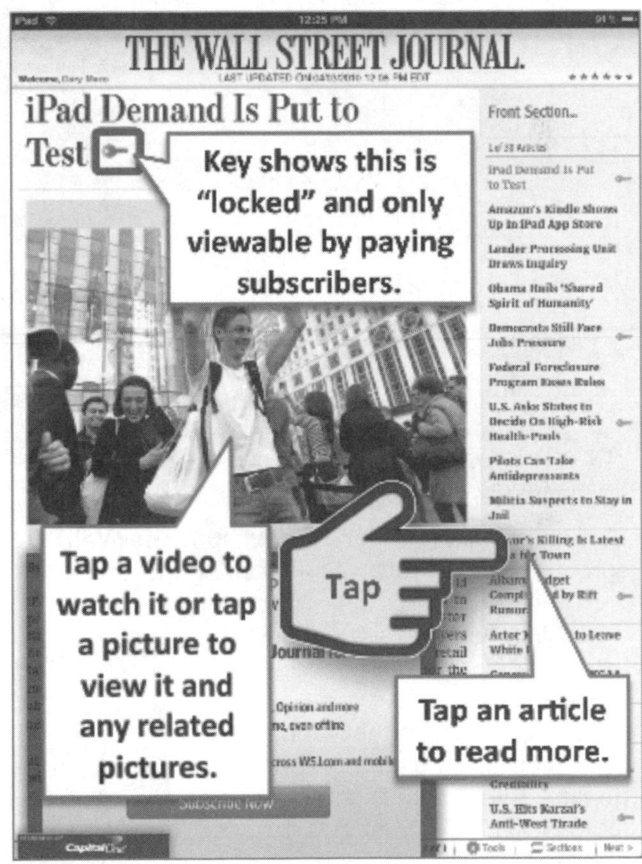

The home page of the app shows this week's newspapers along the top; it shows **Saved Articles**, **Saved Selections**, and **My Watchlists** below this week's newspapers.

In the free version of the app, only the **Now** section of the news along the top row is viewable. All other papers from the week have the **Key** icon next to them; this indicates they are locked and viewable only by paying subscribers.

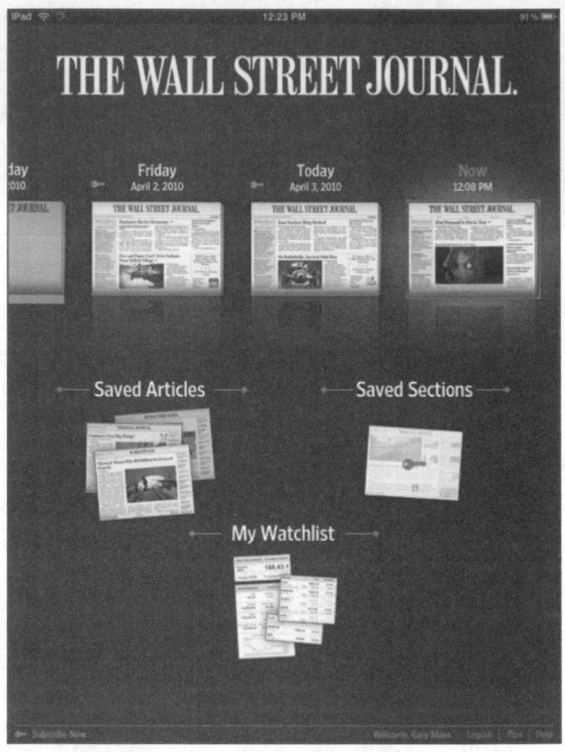


The articles that do not have a small "key" shown area available to read. Touch an article, and it loads onto the iPad.

Similar to **The New York Times** app, **The Wall Street Journal** app lets you slide the screen to the left to continue reading the article.

You will notice that some articles have a video clip embedded where you would normally find a photograph. Touch the video, and it will start playing right inside the paper – a very cool and interactive feature.

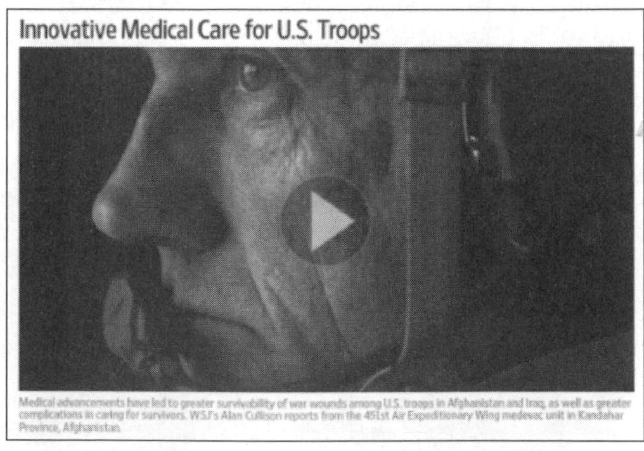

To access the other sections of the paper, touch the **Sections** button in the lower right-hand corner.

## Adjusting Options: Font Sizes and Share, E-mail, or Save an Article

In the various apps for reading newspapers and other content, you will usually find a button or icon to change font sizes. That same button or a button near it may also allow you to share, save, or e-mail an article to a friend. Some apps allow you to share the article with a social networking site, such as Facebook or Twitter.

> **TIP:** Almost all newspaper or magazine apps will allow you to change font sizes and e-mail or otherwise share an article. Look for a button or icon that says **Tools**, **Options**, **Settings**, or something similar. In some apps, the font-size adjustment option will show **Small A** and **Large A** icons.

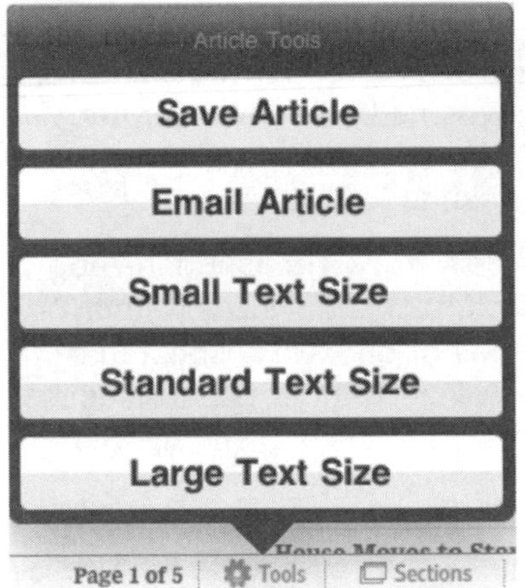


In the **Wall Street Journal** app, touch the **Tools** button in the lower right-hand corner to access options such as adjusting font sizes, or saving or e-mailing an article. This app gives you options to save or e-mail an article:

**Save Article** – This option shows up in the **Saved Articles** section on the **Start** screen.

**Email Article** – This option sends this article in an e-mail.

**The Wall Street Journal** app also gives you three choices for text sizes:

**Small Text Size**

**Standard Text Size**

**Large Text Size**

In the **USA Today** app, the **Font Sizes** and **Share** icons are separated, as shown to the right.

Touch the **Share** icon to e-mail an article or share it with a social networking site.

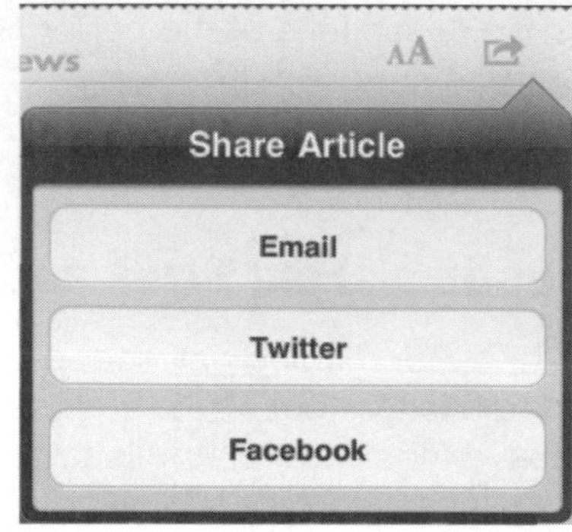


Similarly, you can touch the **Small A/Large A** icons to adjust font sizes.

Doing so brings up a slider that lets you slide from smaller to larger font sizes.

Tap the screen anywhere off the slider control to hide the control.

In the **New York Times Editor's Choice** app, you have one button in the upper right-hand corner of the article screen, but no way to change font sizes.

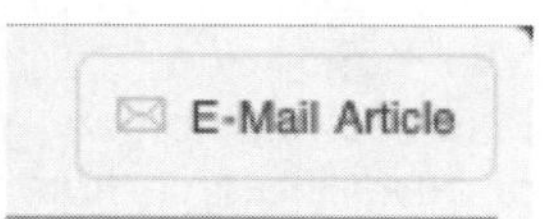


Since **The New York Times** iPhone app has a way to change font sizes (with a **T-** and **T+** at the bottom), we suspect that developers will add similar capabilities to the iPad version of the app shortly. Stay tuned!

To order the full subscription to the *Wall Street Journal* for the iPad, touch the **Subscribe Now** button along the bottom row to the left. At the time of publishing, subscription for weekly access was about US $4 a week or about US $17 a month.

The **USA Today** app has a very similar look and feel to the daily newspaper. Touch the **USA Today** icon, and you will be taken to the **Home** section of the paper. One of the first things you will notice is a group of rotating stories along the top of the screen.

The main stories are listed along the right-hand side. You can scroll through these stories; when you find a story you wish to view, just touch the headline.

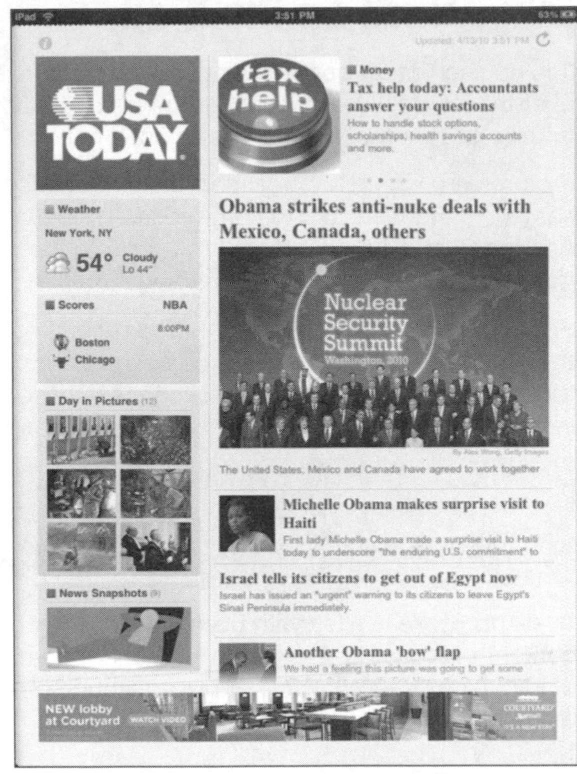


When you are in the **Article View** mode, you can adjust the font size by touching the **Font Size** icon in the upper right-hand corner. You can also e-mail the article by touching the **Share** icon and touch **E-mail** from the drop-down list.

If an article is more than one page long, you can scroll upwards to continue reading the article. Sliding the screen from right to left will advance you to the next article.

> **TIP:** If you touch the **Weather** box, you can customize it for your local weather by entering a city name or zip code.

To go to back to the **Home** screen, touch the **Newspaper** icon in the upper left-hand corner.

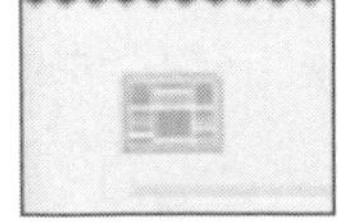

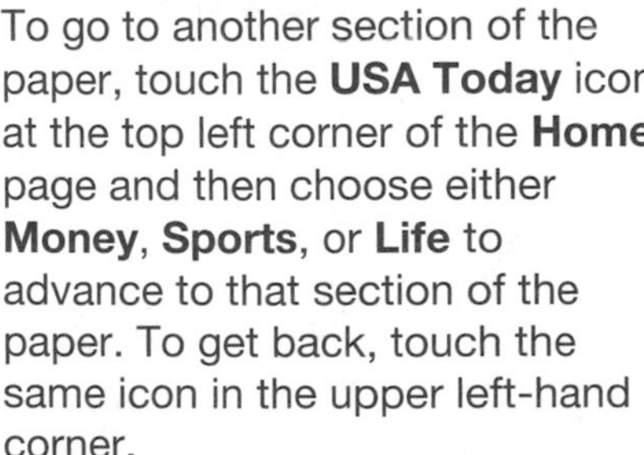

To go to another section of the paper, touch the **USA Today** icon at the top left corner of the **Home** page and then choose either **Money**, **Sports**, or **Life** to advance to that section of the paper. To get back, touch the same icon in the upper left-hand corner.

There are currently no locked articles or subscriptions required to use the **USA Today** app, but this is scheduled to change at some point in the future.

## Magazines on the iPad

It is no secret that both newspapers and magazines have suffered declines in readership over the last few years. The iPad offers a totally new way of reading magazines that might just give the industry the boost it needs.

Pictures are incredibly clear and brilliant on magazines for the iPad. Navigation is usually easy, and stories seem to come to life – much more so than in their print counterparts. Add video and sound integration right into the magazine, and you can see how the iPad truly enhances the magazine reading experience.

Some magazines, such as *Time Magazine*, also include links to live or frequently updated content. These might be called **Newsfeeds**, **Live Edition**, or **Updates**. Check for them in the magazine you purchase – these will give you the most up-to-date information.

**TIP:** Make sure to check the user ratings for a magazine or other app before you purchase it. Doing so may save you some grief and/or some money!

The **App Store** is filled with both individual magazines that can be purchased (or limited content that can be viewed for free) and magazine readers that provide a sample of many magazines, allowing you to subscribe to weekly or monthly delivery of a given magazine from your iPad.

Only a few magazines are available for free compared to newspapers. (*Men's Health* was one of the magazines available for free in the App Store, but at the time it did not have strong reviews.)

One magazine with strong reviews was **Time Magazine for the iPad**, which retailed for US $4.99 at the time of writing.

Unlike other media, you don't touch an article to read the magazine; instead, you simply slide from screen to screen paging through the magazine.

To make the text more viewable, **Pinch** and **Zoom** are both working in this and most magazine apps.

Many magazines are for sale in the App Store: *Popular Science*, *Men's Health*, *Outside*, *GQ*, *Time*, and others. Most are priced from $2.99 to $4.99 per issue.

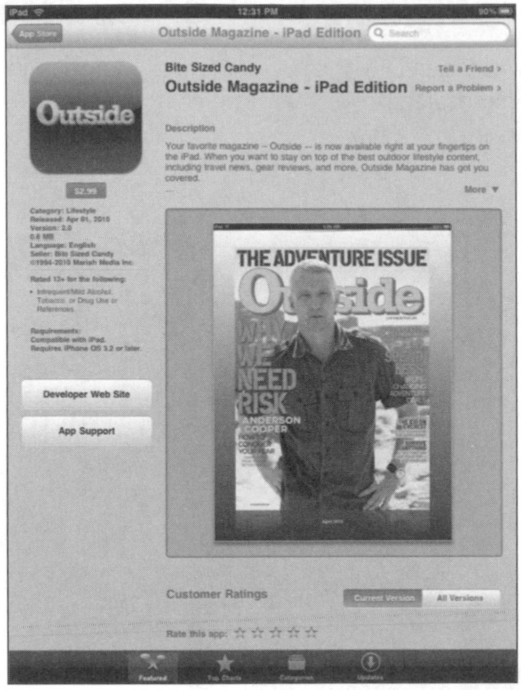

## Navigating Around Time Magazine

As Figure 23–2 shows, there are various ways to navigate around a magazine. This example shows the **Time Magazine** app.

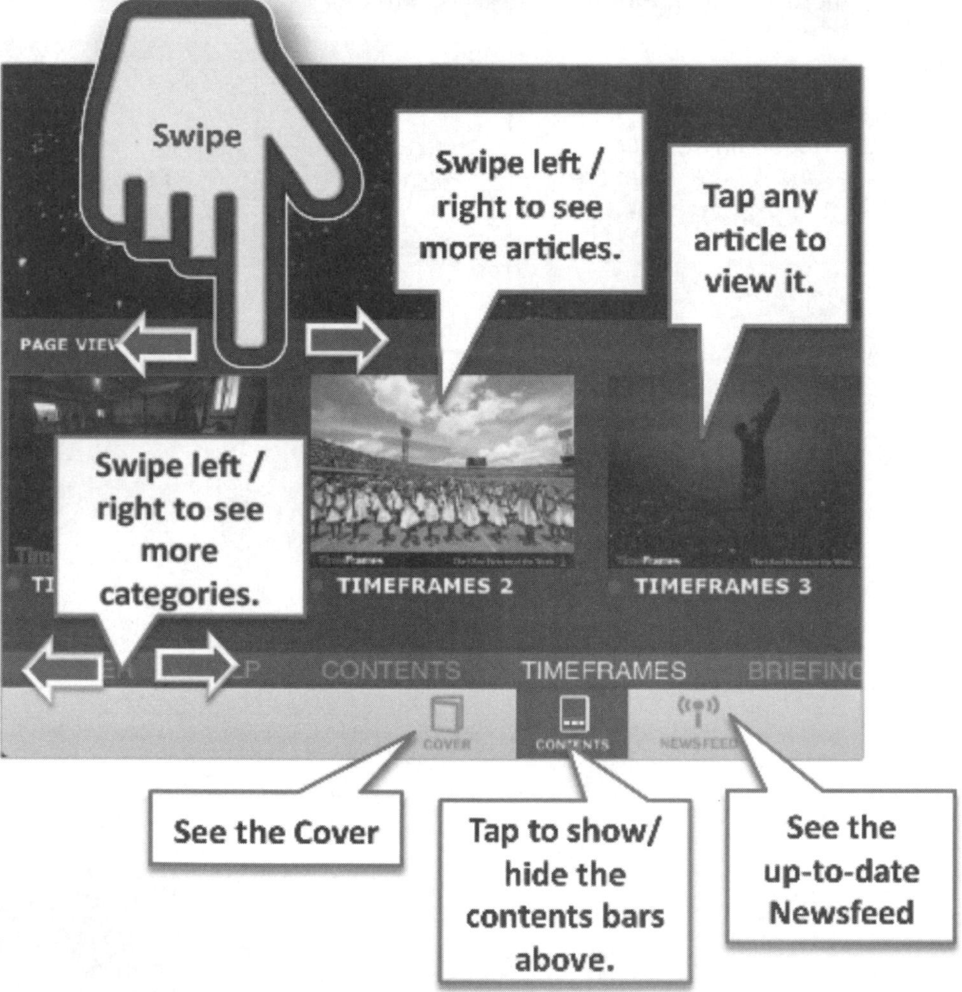


**Figure 23–2.** *Navigating around the Time Magazine app*

## Zinio Magazine App – A Sampler

One app called **Zinio** takes a unique approach. The **Zinio** app is free in the **App Store**, giving you a sampling of more than 20 magazines. Each sample has a few full articles to read. Reading an article in **Zinio** requires a few simple steps.

1. Begin by touching the cover of the magazine you wish to read.
2. Next, touch the screen, and you will see a sliding bar across the bottom that shows screen shots of the articles available for free.
3. To advance pages, slide the screen from right to left or touch the image along the bottom bar to jump to that page.
4. Some magazines will be giving away full, free issues. Just touch the **Read** button at the bottom to see what is available for the week. Touch the magazine cover to download the issue.

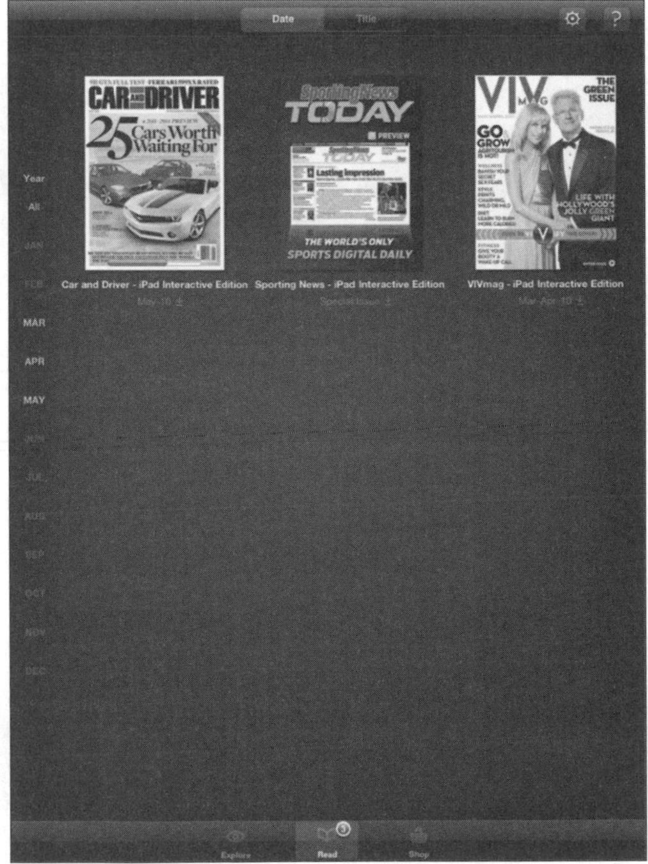

This image is from a free issue of *Car and Driver*, available for download in the week we composed this chapter.

To subscribe to any of the magazines featured in **Zinio**, touch the **Shop** button at the bottom right of the screen.

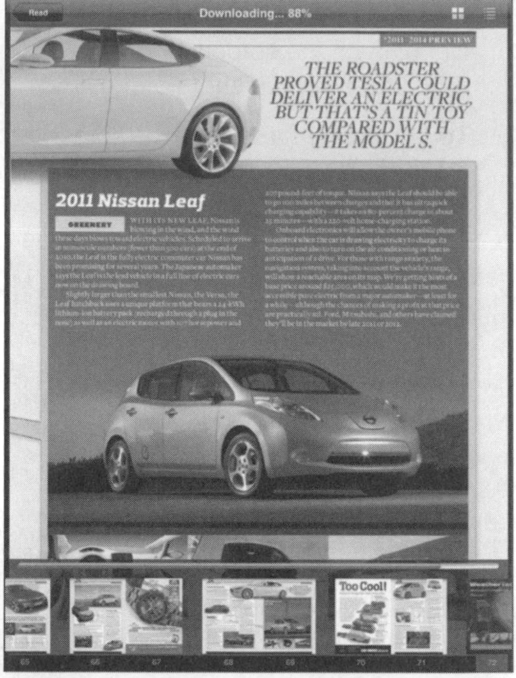


You can navigate magazines by category along the left-hand side, or you can slide the icons at the bottom to see available magazines.

There are many popular magazines from which you can choose. The categories cover everything from art to sports and more. Prices vary, but you will often find a price for a single issue and a price for a yearly subscription.

For example, the newest issue of *Popular Mechanics* was $1.99 on **Zinio**, with a yearly subscription of $7.99.

Some of the subscriptions make great sense. A single issue of *Bike Magazine* (one of my favorites) was $4.99 at the time of writing, but a yearly subscription was only $9.00.

A closer look showed me that there were more than 16 cycling magazines I could subscribe to.

# Comic Books on the iPad

One genre of "new media" poised for a comeback with the advent of the iPad is the comic book. The iPad, with its relatively large high-definition screen and powerful processor, makes the pages of comic books come alive.

There were already a few different comic book apps available when we wrote this book, but none from a company more famous than Marvel Comics.

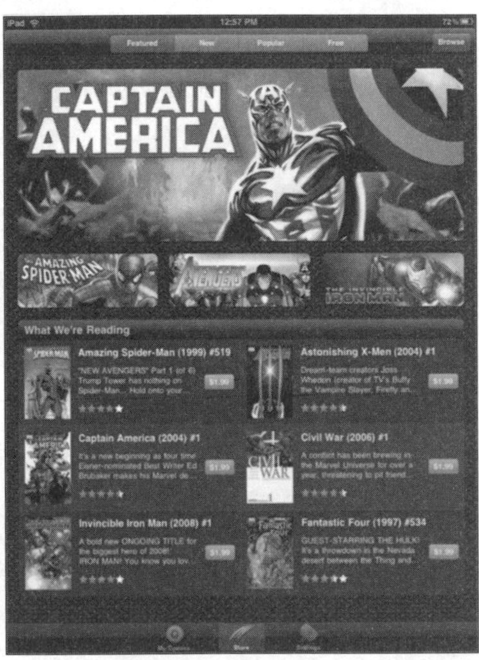


Locate the **Marvel Comics** app in the App Store. Go to **Categories** and then go to **Books**. The app is free, and comic books can be purchased from inside the app.

At the bottom of the **Home** screen are three buttons: **My Comics**, **Store**, and **Settings**. Purchases you make will be under the **My Comics** heading.

The App Store gives you the opportunity to download both free comics and individual issues for sale. Most sell for $1.99 per issue.

You can see four tabs along the top:

- **Featured**
- **New**
- **Popular**
- **Free**

Each tab takes you to a new list of comics to browse, much like the iTunes store.

Touch the **Browse** button to browse by **Genre**, **Creator**, **Storylines**, or **Series**. Or you can type in a search to find a particular comic.

Reading the comic book can be done in one of two ways. First, you can swipe through the pages and read one after the other. Second, you can double-tap a frame to **Zoom** in and then tap the screen to advance to the next frame in the comic strip. From there, you can just swipe from right to left to advance a frame; or, if you want to go back, swipe from left to right.

To return to the **Home** screen or see the on-screen options, just touch and hold anywhere on the screen for about a second and then release. You will see a **Settings** button in the top right-hand corner, a page thumbnail view (just like Photos) at the bottom, and a **Close** button in the upper left-hand corner that will take you to the **Home** screen.

**NOTE:** The makers of this app, **ComiXology**, also make the **Comics** app that contains the Marvel comics, as well as a bunch of others, including Archie, Image, and Top Cow.

# The iPad as a PDF Reader

In Chapter 12 we showed you how to open up attachments in your e-mail, including PDF files. While you can read just about any type of attached file, you don't have the option of saving PDF files on the iPad for future viewing.

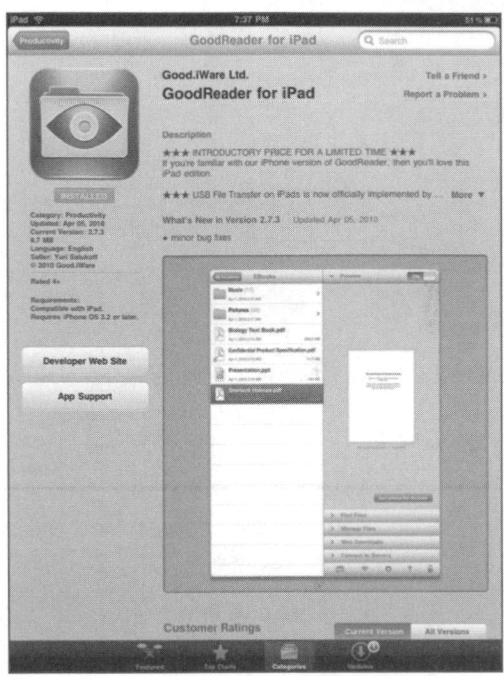


Fortunately, there are a few programs available that turn the iPad into a very capable PDF viewing program. One such program with multiple uses is **GoodReader**.

The **GoodReader** app is in the App Store in the **Productivity** section. At the time of publishing, this app was only US $0.99.

# Transferring Files to your iPad

One of the great things about the **GoodReader** app is that you can use it to wirelessly transfer large files from your Mac or PC to the iPad for viewing in the **GoodReader** app. You can also use **GoodReader** for document sharing in iTunes, as we discussed in Chapter 3. Follow these steps to transfer a file with **GoodReader**.

1. Touch the small **Wi-Fi** icon at the bottom, and the **Wi-Fi Transfer Utility** pops up. You are prompted to type in either an IP address into your browser or a Bonjour Address if you use the **Bonjour** service.

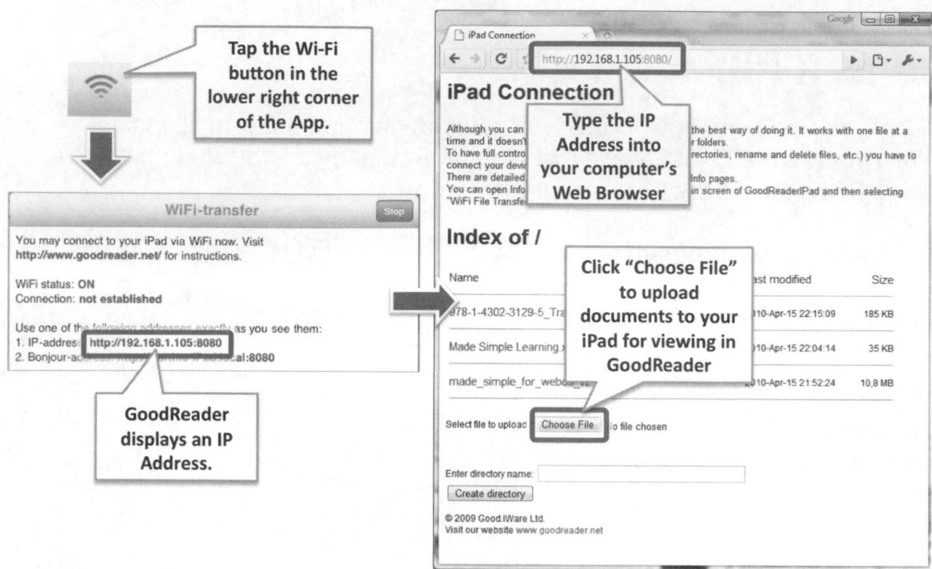


**Figure 23–3.** *Linking iPad and a computer to upload files*

2. Type the address shown in the pop-up window from the **GoodReader** into a web browser on your computer. Now, you can make your Computer act as a server. You will see that your computer and iPad are now connected (see Figure 23–3).

3. Click the **Choose File** button inside your web browser on your computer to locate files to upload to your iPad.

4. Once you have selected the file, click **Upload Selected File**, and the file will be automatically transferred to your iPad inside **GoodReader** (see Figure 23–4).

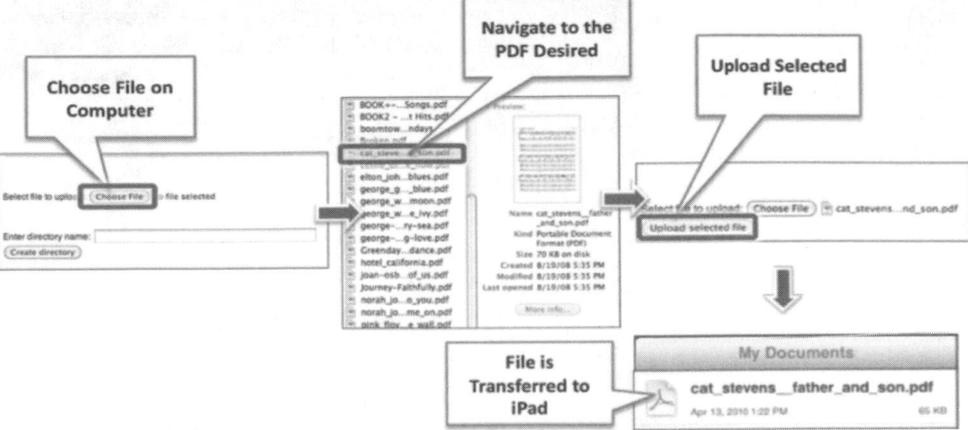


**Figure 23–4.** *Uploading a file to iPad*

Why is this useful? Well, for one of the authors (Gary,) the iPad has become a repository for more than 100 pieces of piano sheet music. This means no more downloading PDF files, printing them out, putting them into binders, and then trying to remember which song is in which binder. Now, all his music is catalogued on the iPad. All he has to do is put the iPad on the piano, and he has access to all his music in one place.

**NOTE:** You can also transfer **Word, Excel**, **and PowerPoint** files in the same manner. We believe that using the document transfer utility in iTunes, described in Chapter 18, might be a bit easier for this.

Navigating the **GoodReader** PDF viewer is quite easy. Tap the center of the screen quickly to bring up the onscreen controls. You can then go to your library or touch the **Turn Page** icon to turn the page.

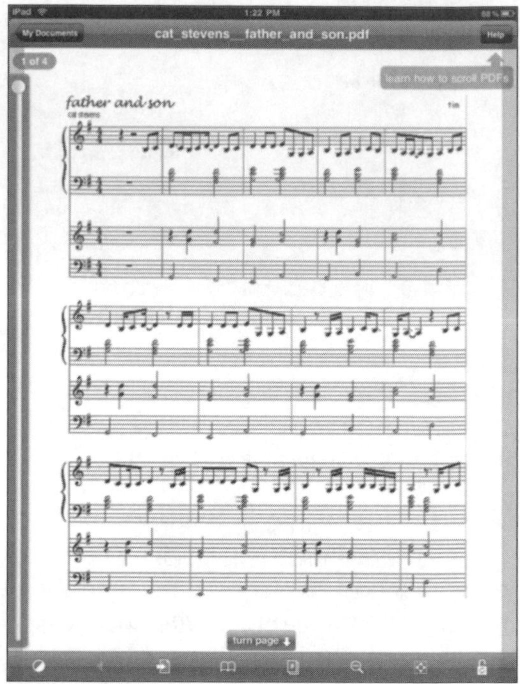


The easiest way to move through pages is to touch the lower right-hand side of the screen to advance a page and touch the upper left-hand side of the screen to go back a page. This becomes quite natural after a while.

You can also flick up or down to turn pages.

To go to another PDF file or another piece of sheet music, just touch the center of the iPad quickly and touch the **My Documents** button in the upper left-hand corner.

## Connecting to Google Docs and other Servers with GoodReader

You can also connect to **Google Docs** and other servers with **GoodReader**. Follow these steps to do so.

1. In the **Connect to Servers** tab on the right-hand side of the **GoodReader** screen, click the **Add** button.
2. Select **Google Docs**. (You can select a number of different servers: mail servers, MobileMe iDisk, Public iDisk, Dropbox, box.net, FilesAnywhere.com, MyDisk.se, WebDAV Server, and FTP Servers.)
3. Enter your **Google Docs** username and password to log in.
4. Once you have made the connection, a new **Google Docs Server** icon will appear under the **Connect to Server** tab on the right-hand side of the page.
5. Tap the new **Google** tab to connect to the server. (An internet connection is required to connect.)

6. Now you will see a list of all the documents you have stored on **Google Docs**. Tap any document and select the file type to download it. Usually PDF works well for this.
7. Once the file is downloaded, it will appear on the left-hand side of **GoodDocs**, and you will simply need to touch it to open it.

Chapter 24

# Other Sync Methods

In Chapter 3, "Sync Your iPad with iTunes," you learned how to connect your iPad to your computer and use iTunes to sync your personal information, music, videos, and more. In this chapter, we explore some alternative ways to wirelessly synchronize information to your iPad. The benefit with the wireless methods is that you don't need to connect your iPad to your computer to have the information updated. Everything happens over the air—and automatically. The two methods we cover are Apple's MobileMe Service and Google Sync .

## Wireless Sync of Your Google or Exchange Information

Using the steps we describe below, your iPad can wirelessly sync either a Microsoft Exchange account or a Google Account.

> **NOTE:** You cannot wirelessly sync both a Google account and a Microsoft Exchange account at the same time. At publishing time, you could only sync one account using the steps described in this chapter. So, if you have both Google and Exchange accounts, you will need to choose which you want to set up for wireless sync.

## Why do we say Google/Exchange?

We use the words Google and Exchange interchangeably here because you setup your Google sync using the Exchange setting on your iPad. We know it is a little confusing, but you set up both types of accounts in the identical manner, so we say Google/Exchange.

If you have a Microsoft Exchange account at work or elsewhere, you will follow the steps described below to setup your account.

If you have a Google account, you would also choose Microsoft Exchange as the Account Type during the setup process even though you do not have an Exchange account.

## If you Want a Google Account, Create One

If you do not have a Microsoft Exchange account, but you still want a wireless sync, then you should setup a free Google account to store your contacts and calendar. The account will allow you to start using Google Mail (Gmail), Contacts, and Calendar.

To set up your Google account, follow these steps:

1. From either your computer's web browser or Safari on your iPad, type in: `www.gmail.com`.
2. Press the **Create an account** button.

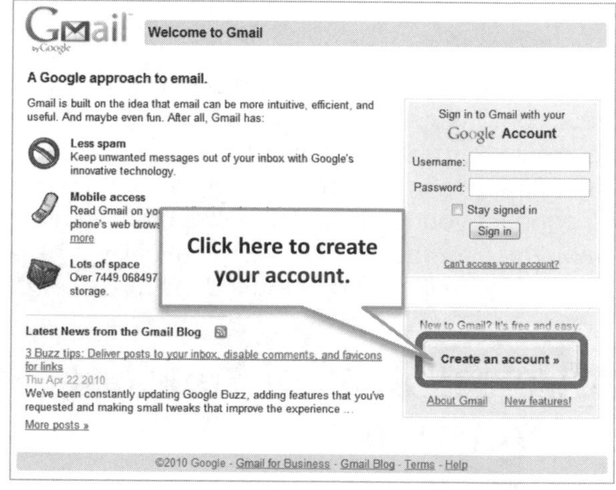

3. On the next screen, enter the information requested and click the button at the bottom of the page that says **I accept. Create my account.**
4. When that's successful, you'll see a screen that says **Congratulations!**
5. Click the **Show me my account>>** button to get started.

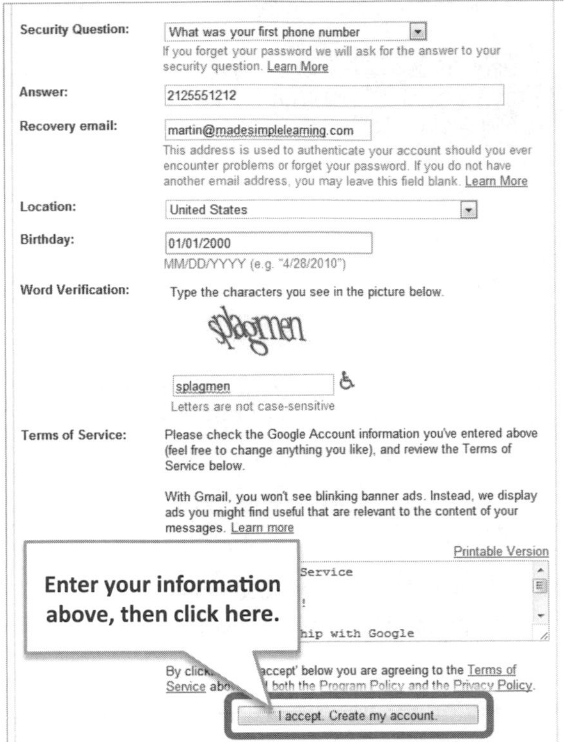


6. To see your Calendar, click the **Calendar** link in the upper left corner.
7. To see your Contacts, click the **Contacts** link in the left side of the Gmail inbox page.

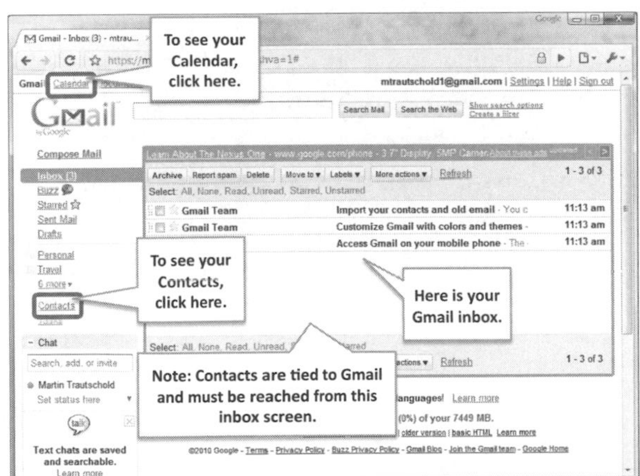


As soon as you set up the sync as shown below, you will begin to see all changes to contacts and calendar from Google magically appear on your iPad. The same goes for any changes or additions from your iPad, they will automatically appear in Google in moments.

**TIP:** It is extremely easy for your Google Contacts list grow into the thousands because it adds everyone you have ever emailed. You may want to clean up your list before you set up the sync to your iPad.

## Set Up your iPad to Access Your Google or Exchange Account

Use the following steps to set up the wireless sync for either your Exchange account or for your Google contacts and calendar:

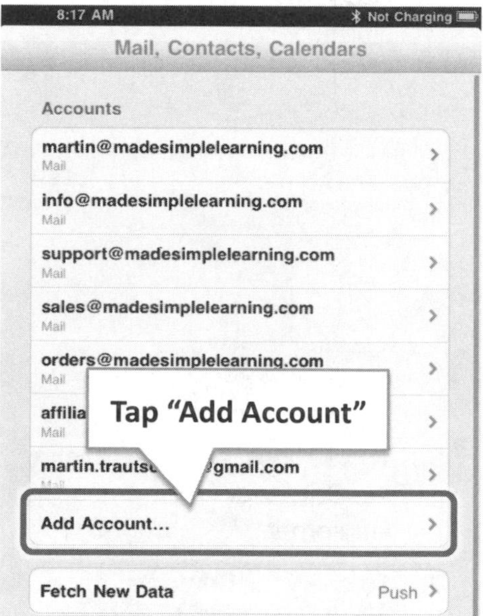


1. Touch the **Settings** icon on your iPad.
2. Touch **Mail, Contacts, and Calendars** in the left column.
3. You'll see a list of your e-mail accounts and, below that, the **Add Account** option.

   If you have no accounts set up, you will only see **Add Account**. In either case, tap **Add Account.**

**TIP:** To edit any account listed, just touch that account.

4. On the next screen, choose **Microsoft Exchange**.

**NOTE:** You should choose **Microsoft Exchange** if you want to have the wireless sync with your Google Contacts and Calendar.

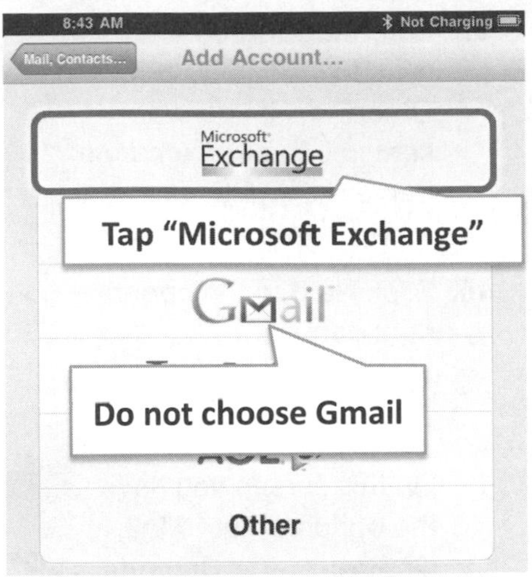


5. Type your **Email** address. Leave the **Domain** blank. Type your Google **Username and Password.** If you want, you can adjust the **Description** of the account, which defaults to your e-mail address.

6. Tap the **Next**

7. button in the upper right corner.

8. You may see an **Unable to Verify Certificate** screen as shown. If you do see it, click **Accept** to continue.

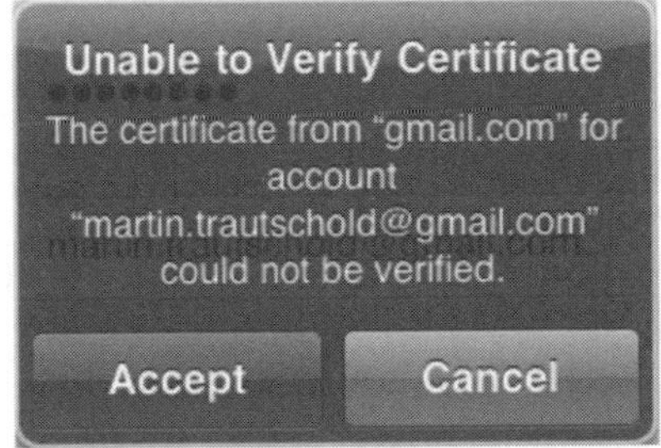

9. Enter **m.google.com** to sync to Google. Otherwise, if you are setting up your Exchange Server account, enter that server address.

10. Click **Next** in the upper right corner.

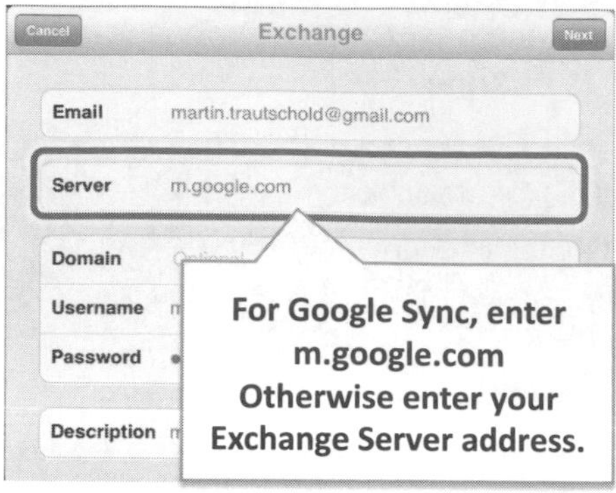


11. On this screen you have the option to turn **Mail, Contacts,** and **Calendars** wireless sync on or off. For each sync you'd like to turn on, tap the switch to change it to **ON**.

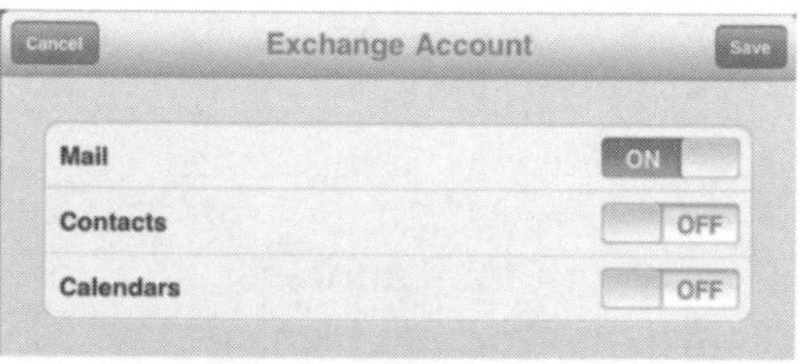


> **CAUTION:** If you already have contacts or calendar items on your iPad, you'll see a warning similar to the one shown to the right.

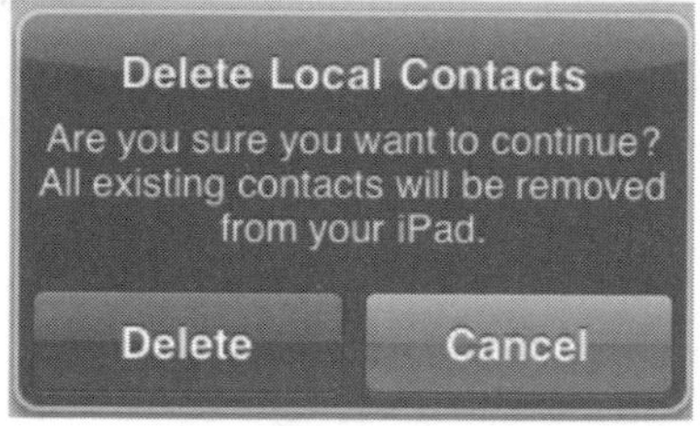


You may also be asked if you want to merge contacts or calendar items, which would combine all the existing items on your iPad together with the ones from Google or Exchange. So, for example, if you had John Smith on your iPad, he would be added to your Google or Exchange contacts if you selected **Merge**. If you happened to have John Smith already in your contact list on Google or Exchange, you'd end up with a duplicate. You may, therefore, want to l to make sure items won't be duplicated when you choose **Merge**.

Select **Keep on My iPad** if you want to merge or add these contacts or calendar items to your Google or Exchange account.

Select **Delete** if you already have these

contacts or calendar items in your Exchange or Google account and do not want to duplicate them.

12. If you turned on the sync for **Mail**, **Contacts**, and **Calendars**, you'll see a screen similar to the one to the right. Click Save to save your settings.

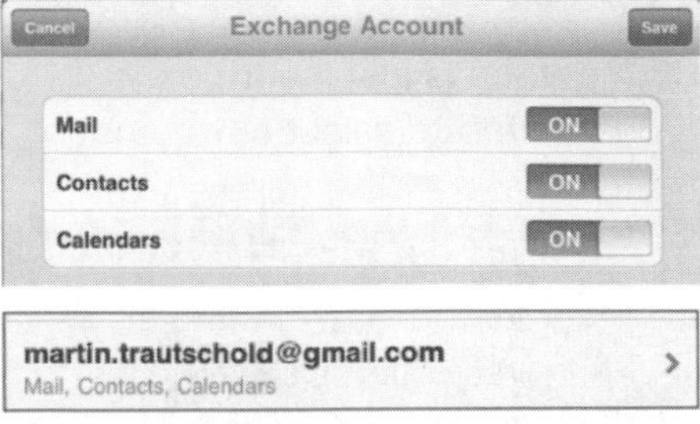


13. Then, on the **Settings** screen, you should see **Mail**, **Contacts**, **Calendars** below the account you just set up. Tap that e-mail account to see more configuration options.

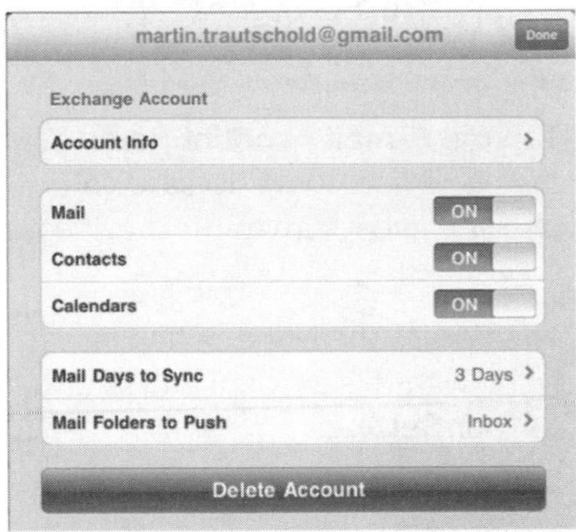


14. Tap **Mail Days to Sync** and adjust to suit your needs (you can go from **1 Day** to **No Limit** with 3 Days as the default).

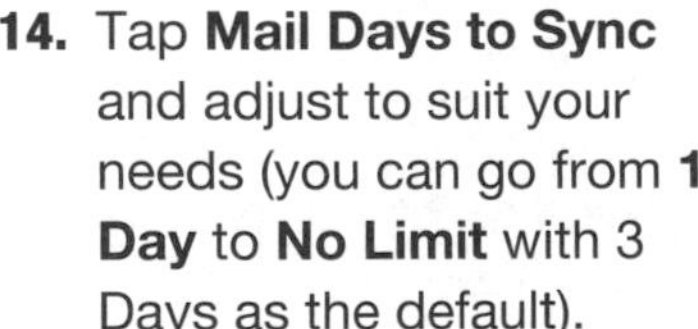

Tap the **E-mail Account Name** in the upper left corner to save your choices and return to the previous screen.

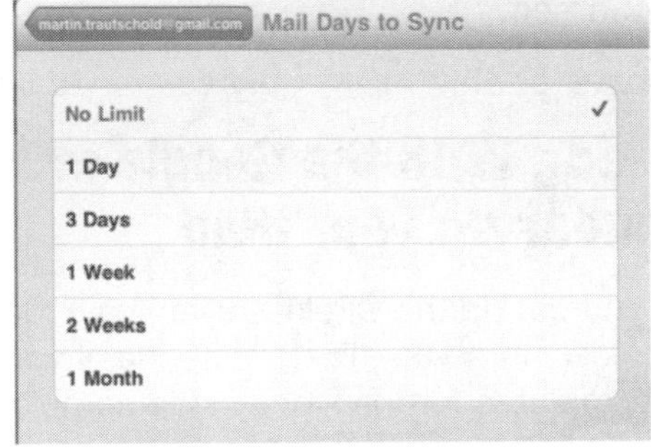

15. Tap **mail folders to push** to specify which mail folders should sync to your ipad.

    The default is just the **inbox**, but you can tap to select any number of folders.

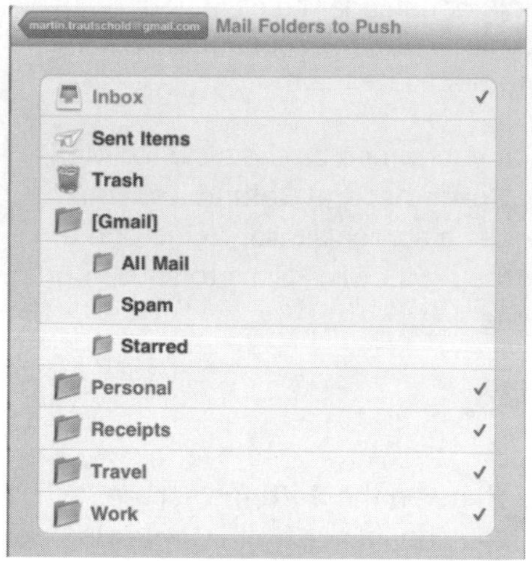


**TIP:** You can only move mail between these folders on your ipad if you have selected them here to sync.

16. Tap the **E-mail Account Name** in the upper left corner to save your choices and return to the previous screen.
17. Then press the **Done** button to finish with this account and return to your **Settings**.
18. Press the **Home** button to return to the Home Screen.

## Working With the Google or Exchange Contacts and Calendar on your iPad

Once you set up the wireless sync, your Google Contacts and Calendar information will flow quickly into your iPad. Note that if you have thousands of contacts, it could take several minutes for the first sync to complete.

You may want to go back and review Chapter 13 “Contacts” and Chapter 14 “Calendar” for details about working with both apps.

**NOTE:** Since the sync with Google or Exchange is wireless, you'll need to make sure you have an active network connection from your iPad. Check out Chapter 4, "Wi-Fi and 3G Connectivity," to learn more.

## Working with Multiple Address Books (Groups)

If you've added some contacts to your iPad or synced it at least once with iTunes, you may end up with two groups of contacts, as shown in Figure 24-1.

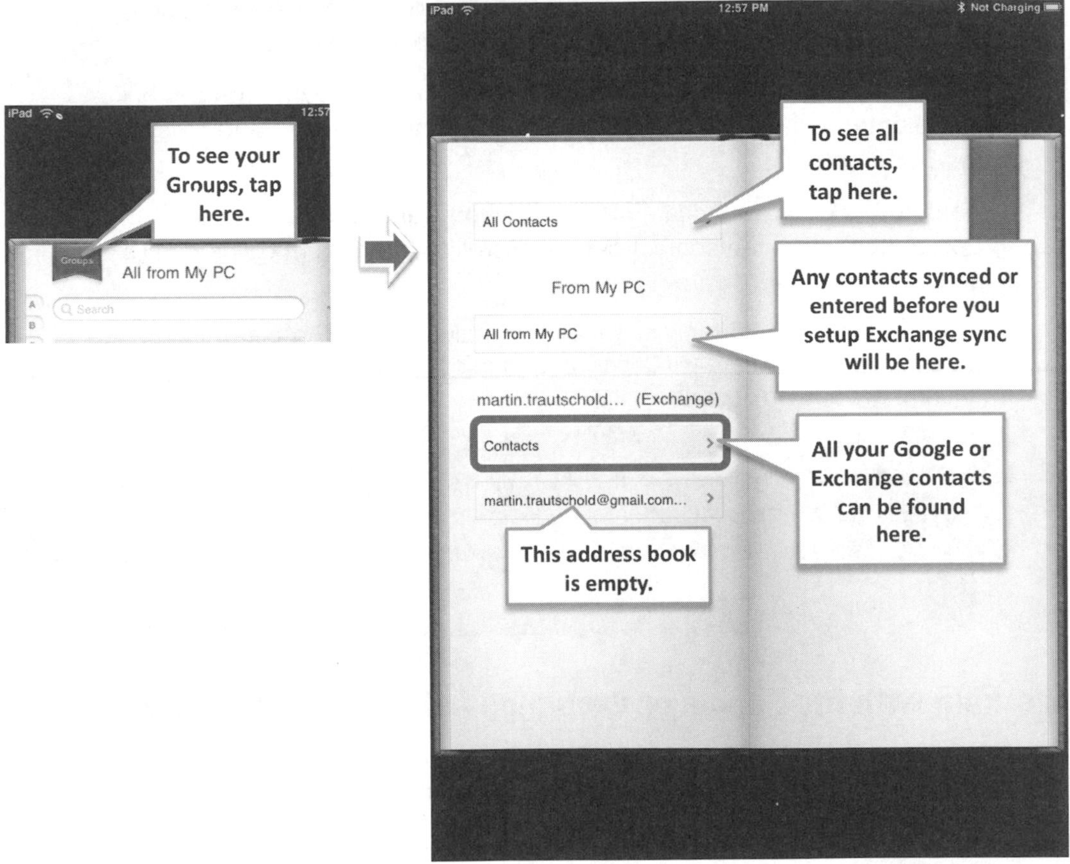


**Figure 24-1.** *You may see various groups in your Contacts.*

To view your Google or Exchange contacts:

1. Tap the **Contacts** icon.
2. Tap the **Groups** tab in the upper left corner.

3. If you've added new contacts or synced your address book, you'll see a **From My PC** or **From My Mac** group at the top. Under that you will see your Google or Exchange e-mail address with **(Exchange)** next to it.
4. Tap the **Contacts** listed under your Google or Exchange e-mail address to see all your synced contacts.

To add, edit, or delete contacts in your Google or Exchange contacts group:

1. Follow the steps to view your Google or Exchange contacts.
2. **To add a contact**: Tap the **+** button in the lower portion of the left column of the Contacts list view. Add contact details as we show you in Chapter 13, "Contacts." Touch **Done** in the upper right corner.
3. **To edit a contact**: Locate the contact in the list and tap the **Edit** button at the bottom under the contact details. Make any changes and press the **Done** button.
4. **To delete a contact**: Locate the contact you want to remove. Tap the **Edit** button under the contact details. Scroll to the bottom of the details and tap the **Delete Contact** button.

The amazing thing is that any changes you make to your Google or Exchange contacts on your iPad are wirelessly communicated and appear in your Google or Exchange account in seconds.

**NOTE:** To add, edit, or delete contacts in your other group (not the Google or Exchange group), first go to that group (**From My PC** or **From My Mac**), then make the changes you want. These additions, edits, or deletions will not affect your Google or Exchange contacts, they are kept separate.

## Working with the Google or Exchange Calendar on Your iPad

After you set up the sync with the Google or Exchange calendar on your iPad, all the calendar events will appear on your iPad. No wires or sync cable required!

Any event you change or update on your iPad will be wirelessly synced with Google or Exchange.

### Invite People to Meetings from your iPad

Now you can invite people to your calendar events. Here are the steps to follow:

1. Tap your **Calendar** icon to start your calendar.
2. Touch the **+** button in the lower right corner to schedule a new event.

3. On the **Add Event** screen, enter the meeting **Title** and **Location** and adjust the starting and ending time as required.
4. Tap the **Invitees** tab to invite people. (Refer to Figure 24-2.)
5. Type a few letters of a contact's first and last name separated by a space to instantly locate them. Or, tap the **blue plus sign** to find someone by browsing your contact list.
6. Touch the name and e-mail address you want to use. If someone has more than one e-mail address, you'll need to select one.
7. Add more invitees if you desire, then tap **Done** to exit the **Add Invitees** window.
8. Adjust any other items in the **Add Event** screen and tap **Done** to save.
9. The meeting invitation(s) will be sent via e-mail immediately to everyone you invited.

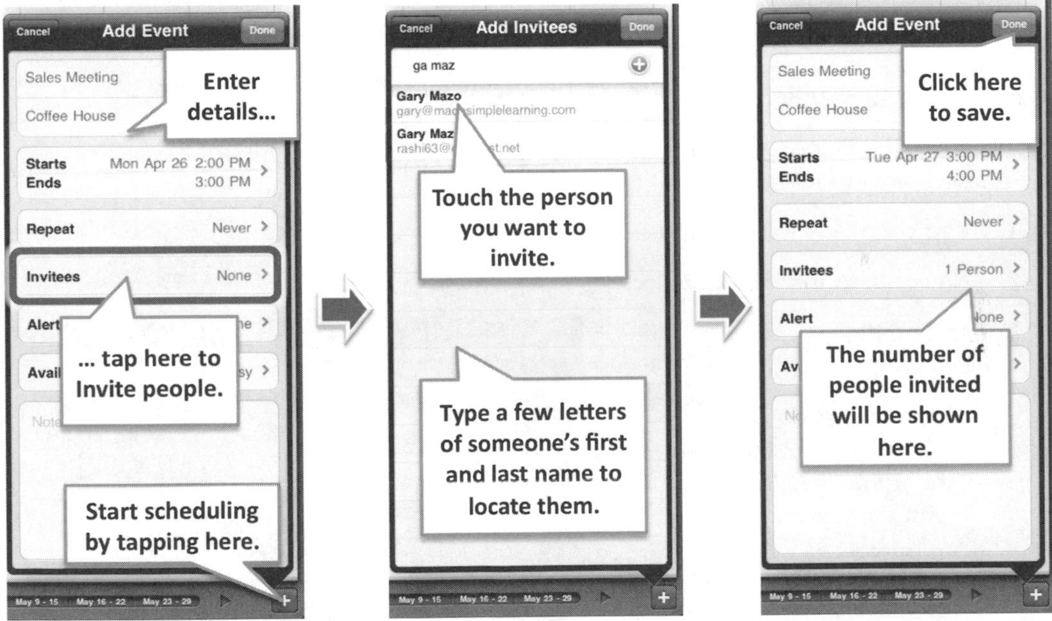


**Figure 24-2.** *How to invite people to meetings*

## Seeing the Status of Invitees on Your Calendar

You can see who has not replied, or who has accepted or rejected your invitations by touching the meeting in your calendar view.

As the image to the right shows, you can see when the status changes from **no reply** to **accepted**, **maybe**, or **declined**.

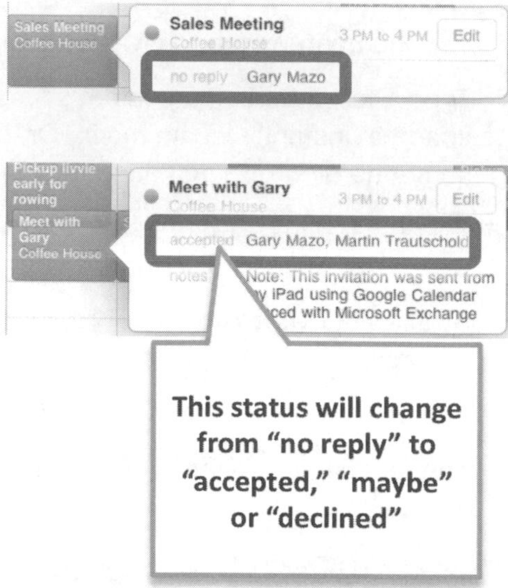


## Responding to Meeting Invitations from your iPad

If you are using Google Calendar with Exchange sync as we described above, you will be able to reply to meeting invitations in the **Mail** app on your iPad.

1. Tap your **Mail** icon to start the program.
2. Navigate to the **Inbox**, which has the meeting invitation.
3. Locate the invitation.

   Most invitations look something like the image to the right. Usually they start with the word **Invitation**.

**TIP:** To quickly find all meeting invitations in your inbox:

1. Type the word **meet** or **invitation** the search box.

2. Tap the **Subject** button to search only the message subjects as shown.

4. Tap the Google **Meeting Invitation** to open it.
5. Tap any of the responses next to **Going?** to reply to the invitation.
6. As soon as you tap the one of the choices, your reply will be sent. You may be shown a Google Calendar web page to type additional details.

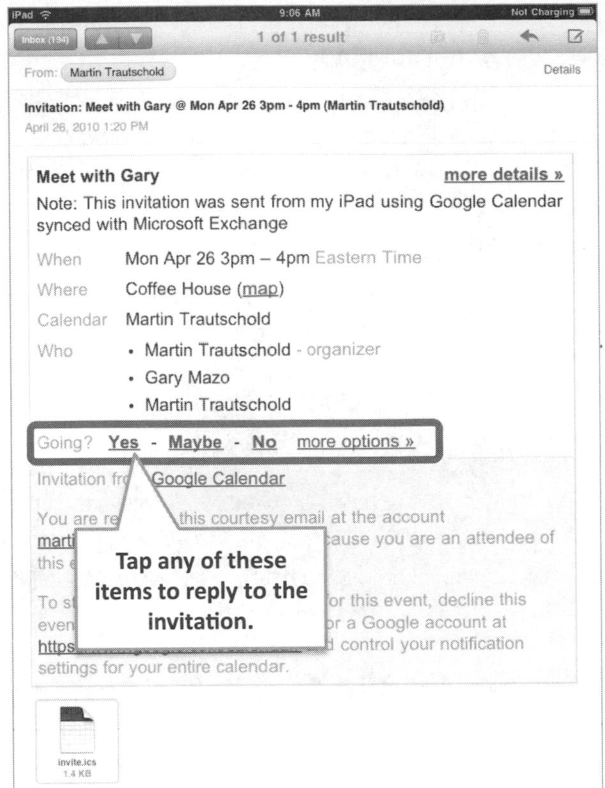


# Wireless Sync Using the MobileMe Service

Apple provides a great service to wirelessly sync your personal information between your computer (PC or Mac) and your iPad and other mobile devices such as an iPhone.

**The MobileMe Cloud:** The MobileMe service uses what is sometimes called a cloud to sync all your information. The MobileMe Cloud is a term used to describe the web servers where all your MobileMe information is stored on the Internet. The servers and the associated software you install on your computer (PC or Mac) and your mobile devices (iPad, iPhone, etc.) help keep all your mobile devices in sync with your computer. The idea is that changed information (a new calendar event, a new contact name) gets sent from your iPad to the cloud. Then the cloud disperses the changed information to all the devices in your MobileMe account. This could be your computer or possibly an iPhone or iPod touch.

Once you set up MobileMe from your computer and then set up access from your iPad, all your personal information (contacts, calendar, even bookmarks) will be shared wirelessly between your computer and your iPad.

In addition to the wireless sync of personal information, MobileMe lets you:

- Create a web-based photo gallery that you can access and add to from your iPad.
- Create an **iDisk** that allows you to share documents easily between your iPad and your computer. You can also use it to share files that are too large to e-mail. Most e-mail systems block files larger than about 5MB.
- Find your lost iPad using the **Find My iPad** feature.
- Erase all of the personal data on your lost iPad remotely using the **Remote Wipe** feature.

**NOTE:** As of publishing time, after your 60-day free trial, Apple charges $99/year for individual MobileMe service and $149/year for a family plan.

However, also at publishing time, there was a rumor floating around the web that apple may make the mobileme service a free service. Check with the mobileme web site (`www.mobileme.com`) to find out the latest information.

## Sign up for the MobileMe Service (PC or Mac)

Apple makes it easy for you to learn about MobileMe from iTunes after you register your iPad. As soon as you are done with registration, you'll see an ad for MobileMe with a **Try It Free** button.

If you use iTunes to sync your iPad, you will also see a **Learn More** button at the top of the info tab as shown below in Figure 24-3.

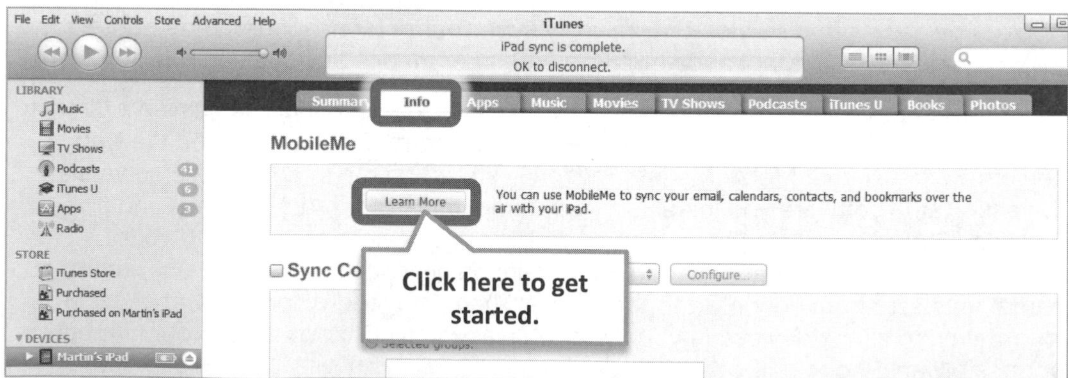


**Figure 24-3.** *Get started with MobileMe from the iTunes Info tab.*

1. You can also go straight to the MobileMe sign-up form by typing this web address into your computer or iPad's web browser: `www.me.com/signup`

2. Type your personal information to set up your account and click the **Continue** button.

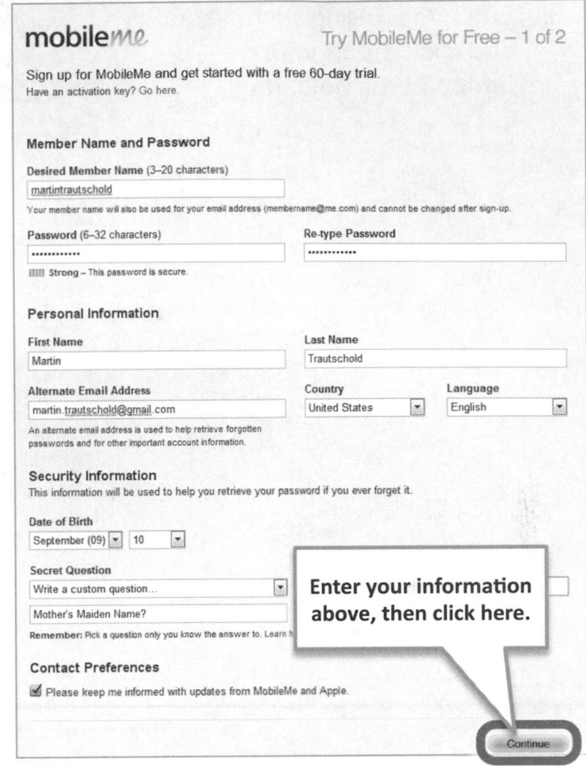

3. Enter your billing information and click the **Sign Up** button at the bottom.

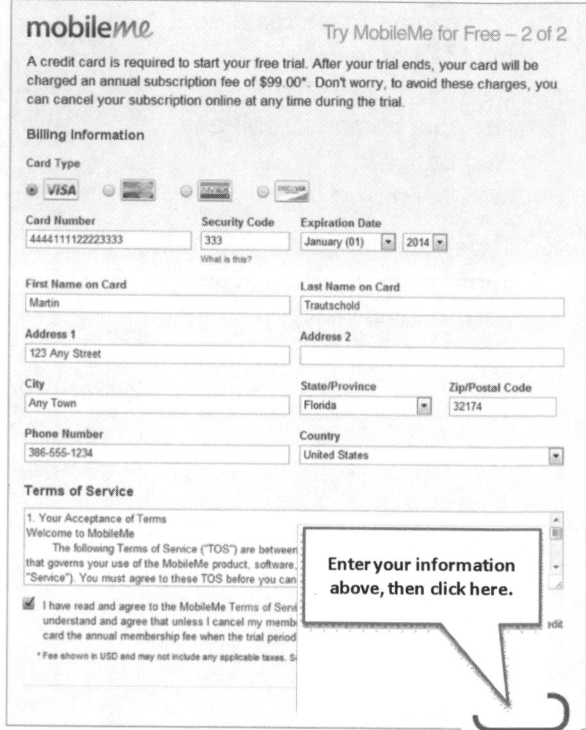


4. If everything was entered correctly, you'll see a **Signup Complete** screen similar to the one shown.

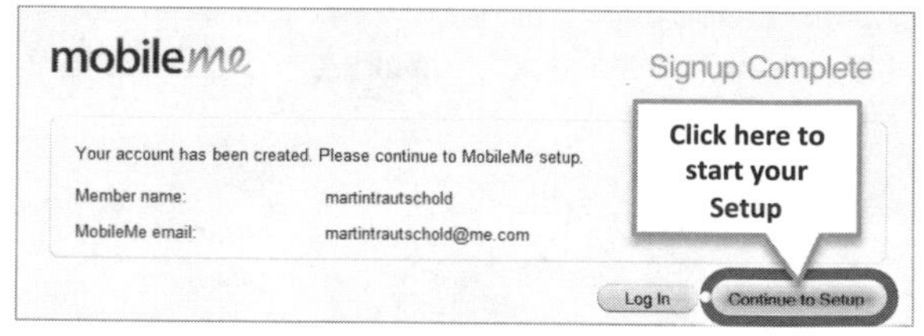


You have now created your MobileMe account. Now you'll set up MobileMe on your Mac or PC and your iPad.

If you are a Windows PC user, skip to the "Set Up MobileMe on Your PC" section .

## Set Up MobileMe on Your Mac

The MobileMe software that runs on your Mac is included in the latest version of the Mac Leopard (v10.5.8 or higher) or Snow Leopard (v10.6.3 or higher) operating systems.

If you don't have the latest version of the Mac system software, you'll have to install it and configure the MobileMe software it to sync to the MobleMe "cloud" to get started.

1. Click on the Apple menu and select **Software Update** as shown.

**TIP:** You'll find extensive step-by-step instructions showing you how to install or upgrade software on your Mac in Chapter 26: "Bonus iTunes User Guide."

2. Follow the steps to complete the software update.

3. After you have successfully installed the software update, click on the Apple menu and select **System Preferences**.

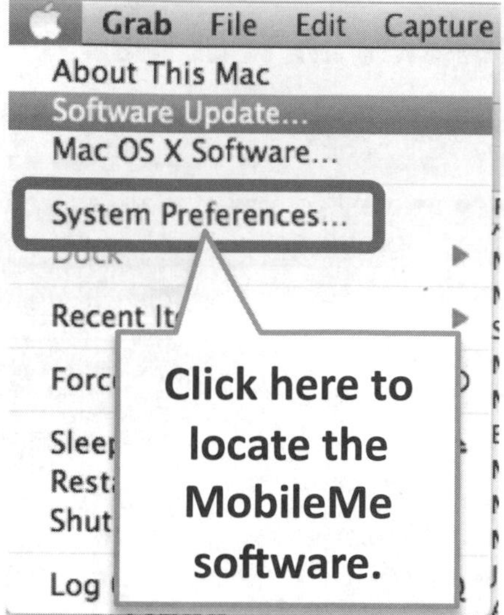


4. Click on the MobileMe icon in the Internet & Wireless section of System Preferences.

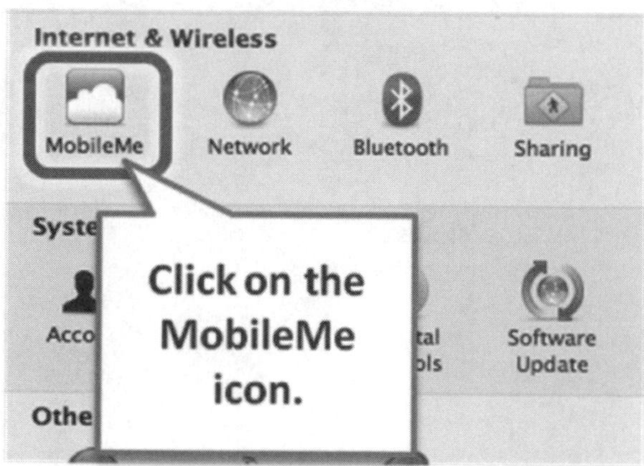


5. Enter your MobileMe **Member Name** and **Password**.
6. Click **Sign In**.

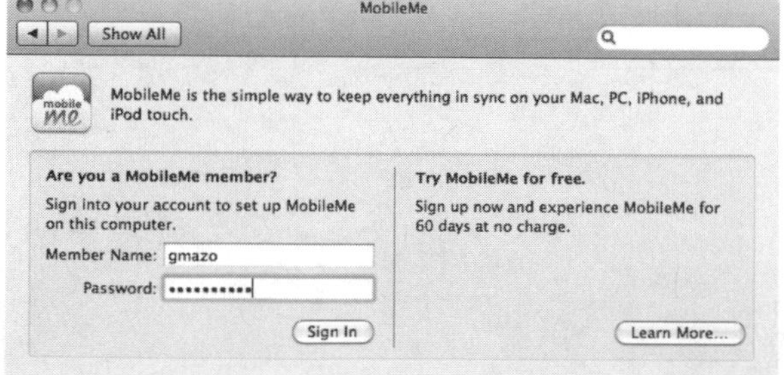

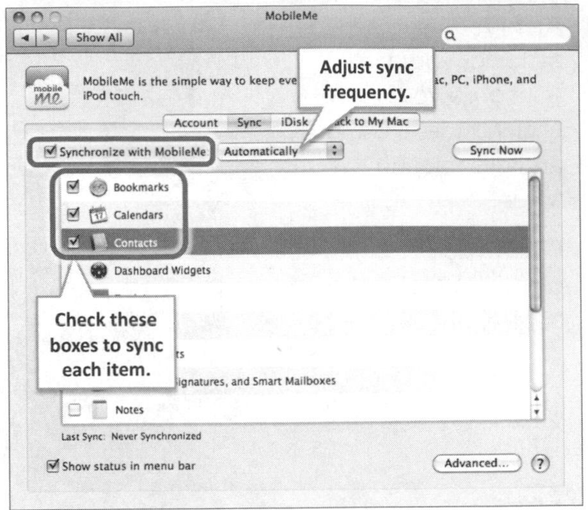


7. Click the **Sync** tab at the top to see the screen shown to the right.
8. Check the box next to **Synchronize with MobileMe.**
9. Next to this check box there's a drop-down for configuring the sync frequency. The default is **Automatically**, but you can sync every **Hour, Day, Week,** or **Manually**.
10. To sync bookmarks, check the box next to **Bookmarks** and select your computer's web browser.
11. To sync contacts, check the box next to **Contacts**.
12. To sync calendars, check the box next to **Calendars.**
13. You can also sync various other items by checking them.

14. After you have set up syncing, you can configure your iDisk by clicking the **iDisk** tab and completing this screen.
15. When you are done, close the **MobileMe** control panel.

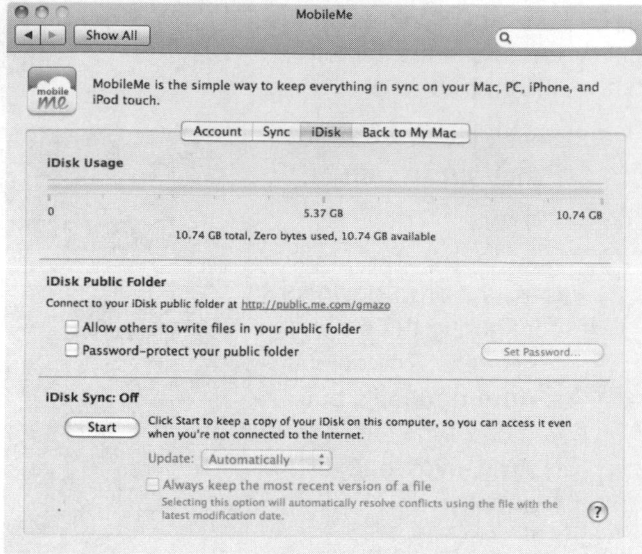


As soon as you close the MobileMe control panel, MobileMe will start sending your selected items—Contacts, Calendars and Bookmarks— to the MobileMe web site.

Now you can skip to the "Multiple Ways to Access MobileMe" section while we discuss how Windows users configure MobileMe.

# Set Up MobileMe on Your Windows PC

You need to install the latest version of iTunes and the MobileMe software on your PC and configure it to sync to the MobleMe "cloud" to get started.

1. On your computer's web browser, go to: `www.apple.com/mobileme/setup/pc.html`
2. If you don't have iTunes version 9.1 or later, click the **iTunes** link to download it.

> **TIP:** We give you extensive step-by-step instructions for installing or upgrading iTunes in Chapter 26 "Bonus, iTunes User Guide."

3. Click the link to download the MobileMe Control Panel for Windows.

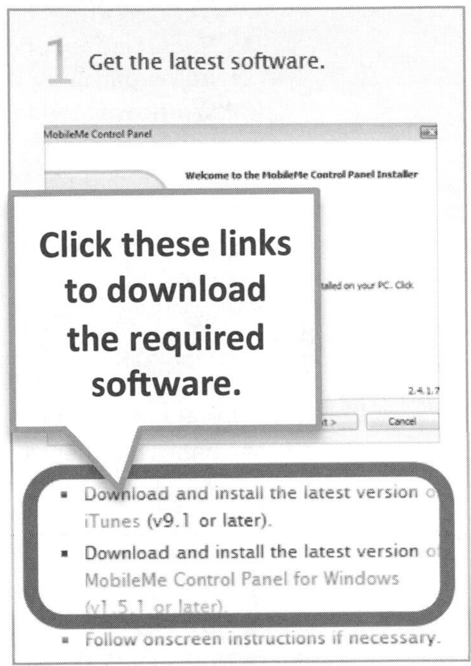


4. Click the **Download** button on this screen to download the installation file.
5. Follow the steps on the screen to install the software on your computer.

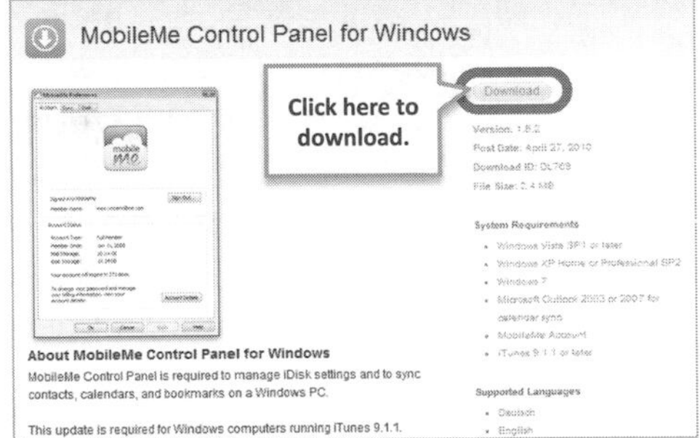

6. Once the software is installed, start it up by:
   - Clicking on the **MobileMe** icon on your Windows desktop, or by
   - Searching for and starting it from your **Start** button or **Windows** icon in the lower left corner. Type **MobileMe** and the icon should appear at the top of the Start Menu under **Programs**. Click it.

Programs
MobileMe
Finally, click here to start it.
First, click the Windows logo or Start button. Then, type "MobileMe" to search.
mobileme

7. Click the **Sync** tab at the top to see the screen shown to the right.
8. Check the box next to **Sync with MobileMe.**
9. Next to this check box you'll find a drop-down for the sync frequency. The default is **Automatically**, but you can choose to sync every **Hour, Day, Week** or **Manually**.
10. To sync contacts, check the box next to **Contacts** and select where your contacts are stored (such as **Outlook, Google Contacts, Yahoo!,** or **Windows Contacts**). For Google and Yahoo!, you will need to enter your username and password by clicking the **Options** button that appears.
11. To sync calendars, check the box next to **Calendars** and select where your Calendars are stored (e.g., **Outlook** or elsewhere.)
12. To sync bookmarks, check the box next to **Bookmarks** and select your computer's web browser (only Safari and Internet Explorer were supported for syncing bookmarks at publishing time).
13. Click **OK** when done.

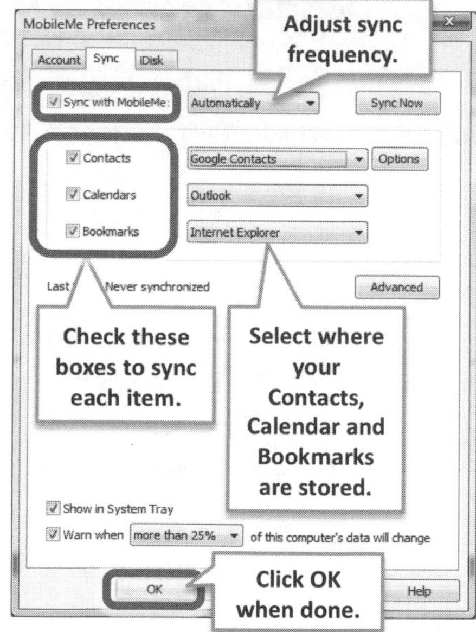

As soon as you click **OK**, **MobileMe** will start sending your selected items—Contacts, Calendars, and Bookmarks to the MobileMe web site.

## Multiple Ways to Access MobileMe

After the first sync, you will have at least three ways to access your synced information:

- The computer where you originally stored your contacts and calendar;
- The MobileMe web site;
- Your iPad (or other mobile device).

Since you already know how to get to the information on your computer, we will focus on how to access information from the MobileMe web site and your iPad.

## A Quick Tour of The MobileMe Web Site

1. Login to **MobileMe** from a web browser on your computer by going to `www.me.com`.
2. Type your username and password and click **Log In**.

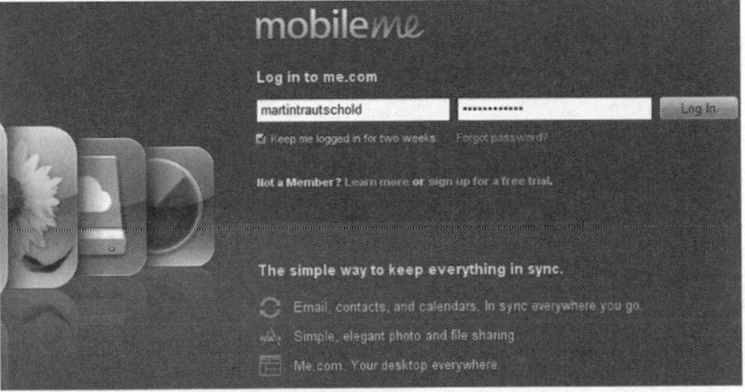


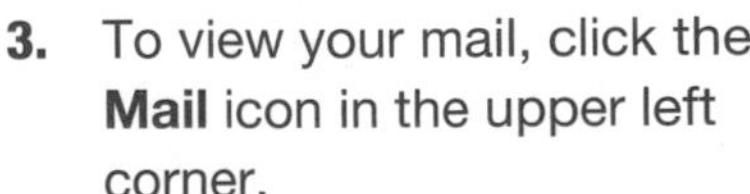

3. To view your mail, click the **Mail** icon in the upper left corner.

   This will show your MobileMe inbox for all e-mail going to `(membername)@me.com`

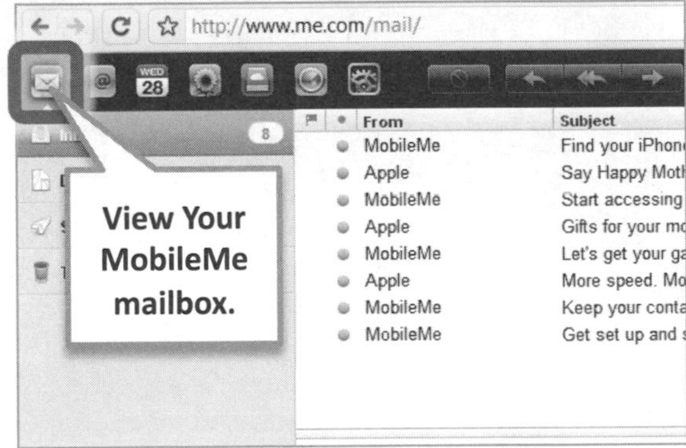

4. To view your contacts, click the **Contacts** icon next to Mail.

5. To view your calendar, click the **Calendar** icon.

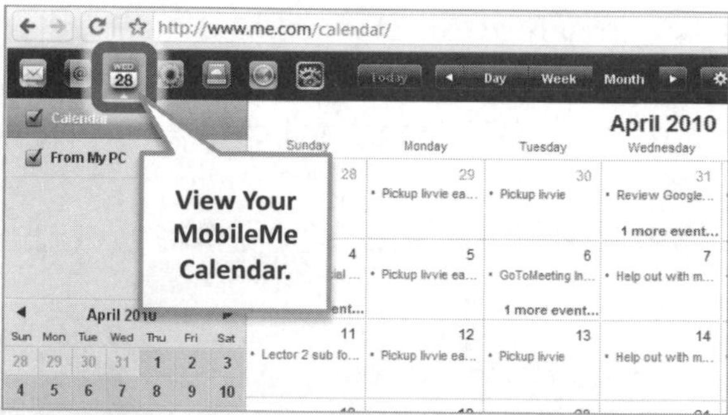


6. To view your photo albums, click the **Gallery** icon.
7. To create a new album, click the **+** in the lower left corner.

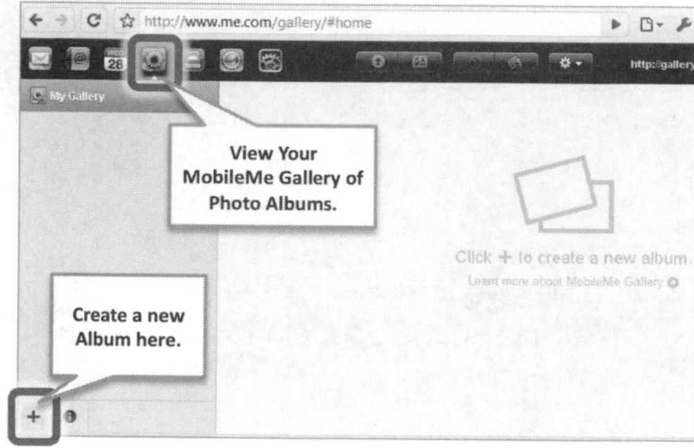

8. Enter your **Album Name**, and check the **Allow** and **Show** settings you want. Also, for Mac users, decide whether you want to sync with **iPhoto** or **Aperture**.
9. Click the **Create** button to create your new album.

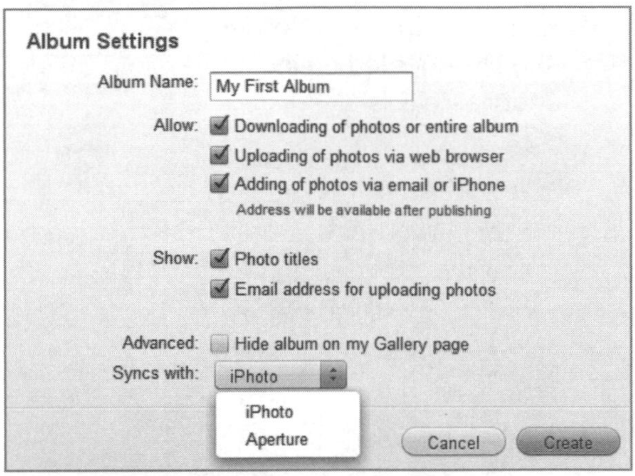


10. Click the **Upload Arrow** to select photos or videos to upload to your MobileMe album.
11. Navigate to the folder on your computer where your pictures are stored, click on the picture or video to select it, then click the **Open** button.

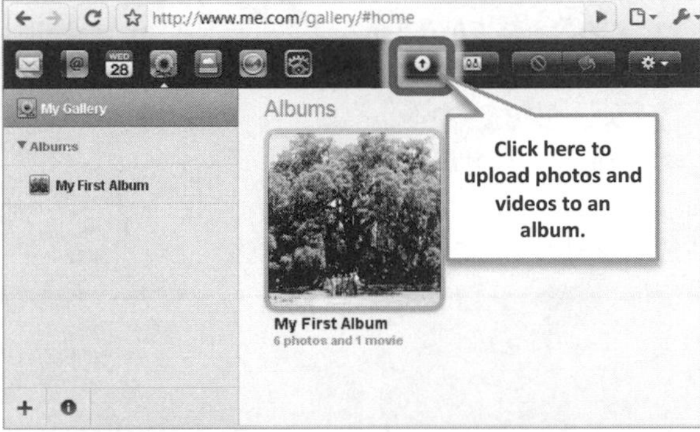


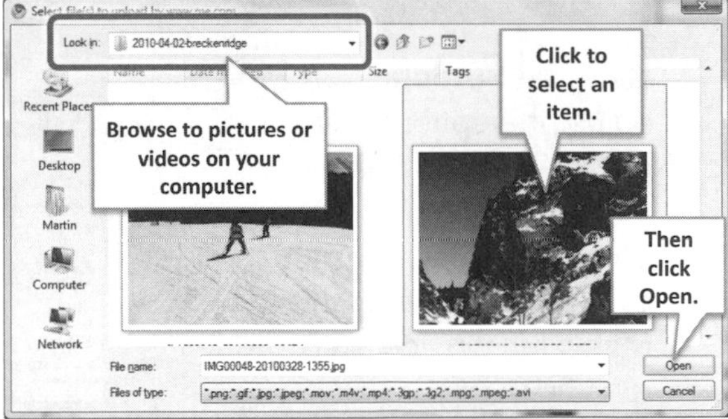


**NOTE:** The following image file formats are supported: .png, .gif, .jpg, .jpeg. The following video types are supported: .mov, .m4v, .mp4, .3gp, .3g2, .mpg, .mpeg, .avi.

12. Click the iDisk icon to view the files located on the MobileMe iDisk.

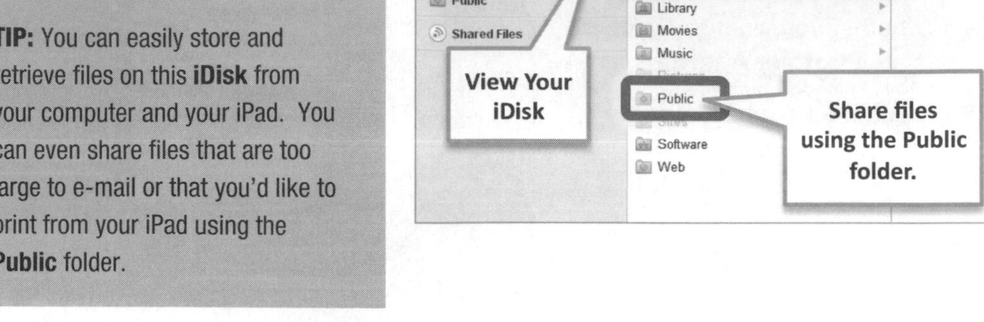

**TIP:** You can easily store and retrieve files on this **iDisk** from your computer and your iPad. You can even share files that are too large to e-mail or that you'd like to print from your iPad using the **Public** folder.

13. Click the **Find My iPhone/iPad** icon to locate your iPad. This assumes you have already logged into MobileMe from the **Settings** app on your iPad.

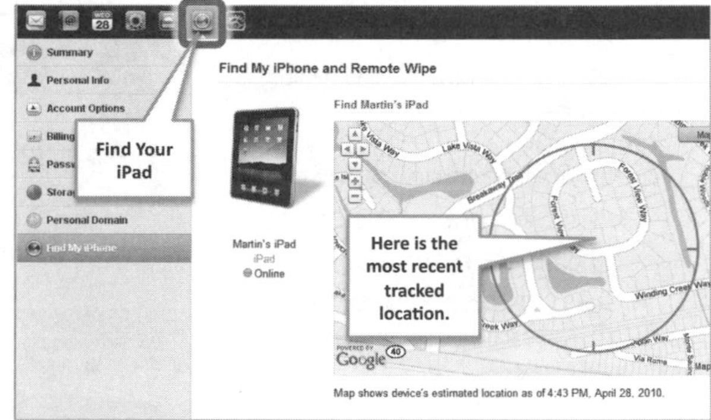


14. Click the **Settings** icon to adjust the options, see your account type and trial expiration date (if you are on a free trial), and get help, or to check whether the MobileMe service is up and running.

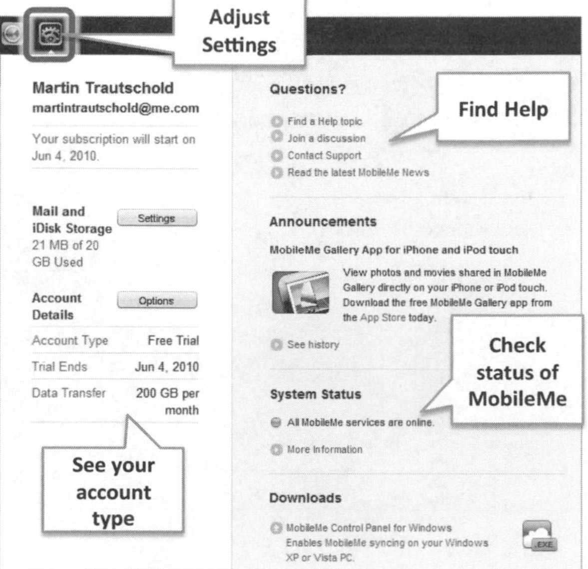

# Set Up Your iPad to Access Your MobileMe Account

Now that you've set up your MobileMe account, you are ready to sign into it from your iPad.

1. Tap your **Settings** icon.
2. Tap **Mail, Contacts, Calendars** in the left column.
3. Tap **Add Account...** in the right column

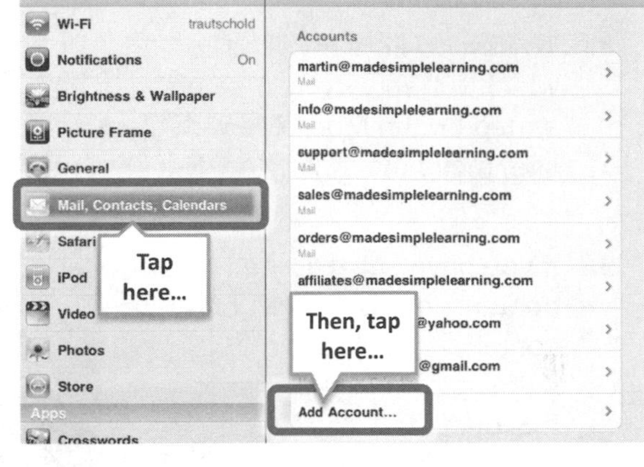


4. Tap **MobileMe** for the account type.

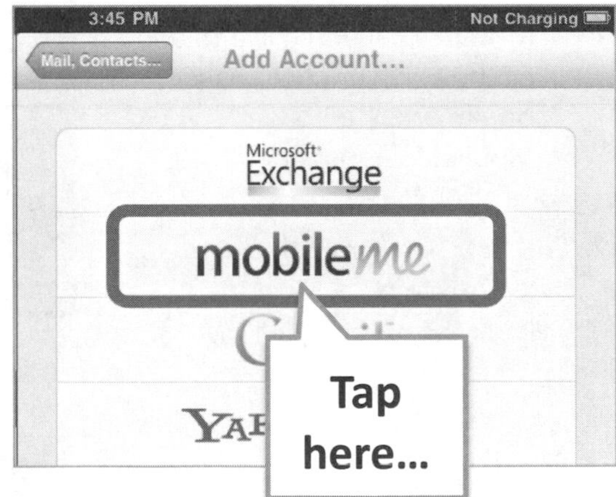


5. Enter your **Name** and your MobileMe e-mail **Address** and **Password,** then tap **Next**.

6. Now you'll see the MobileMe configuration screen showing your sync options.
7. To turn any synced item **ON** or **OFF**, tap the switch.
8. To turn on **Find My iPad**, which will show your iPad on a map on the MobileMe web site, move the switch to **ON**.

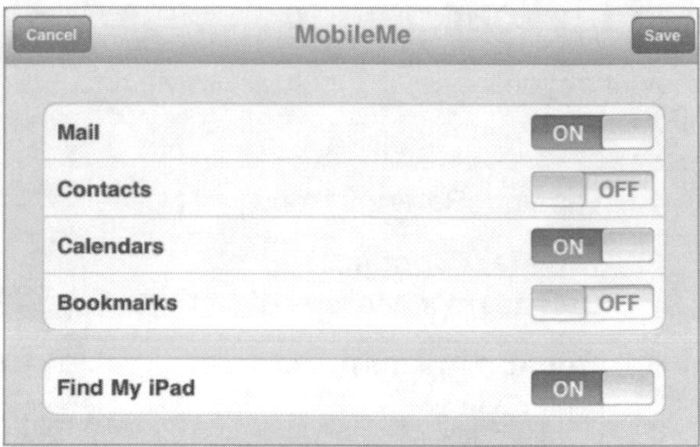


9. If you have any existing contacts or bookmarks on your iPad, you'll see a warning message similar to this one.

   Choose **Merge with MobileMe** if you'd like to add all the existing contacts (or bookmarks) to your MobileMe account.

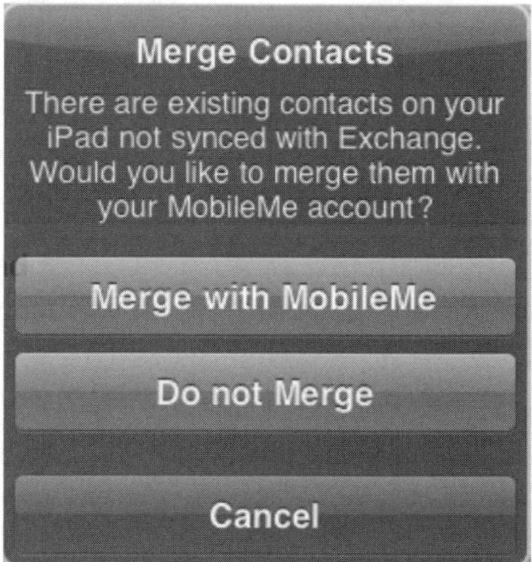


**CAUTION:** You could end up with duplicate contacts or bookmarks if you choose **Merge**. It would be safer to choose **Do not Merge.**

10. When you are done, tap **Save.** You should be brought back to the Settings screen and see your MobileMe account listed with the selected items turned **ON** for syncing.

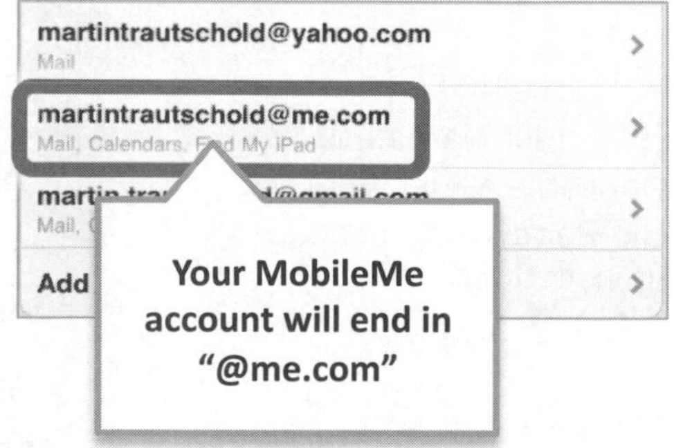

# Using MobileMe After Setup

Using MobileMe is fairly seamless once you get it set up. You update contacts and calendar on your iPad and the changes just appear on your computer. And, if you've set up other mobile devices such as an iPhone on the same account, the changes appear there, too. Everything is kept in sync wirelessly and automatically.

MobileMe has a few very cool features that we highlight below.

## Find My iPhone/iPad, Send Message, and Remote Wipe

From any web browser, you can locate your iPad using the **Find My iPhone** feature in MobileMe. You can send a message and play a loud sound to alert someone on your iPad, even if it is locked. You can remotely lock your iPad using a 4-digit code and remotely erase all information on your iPad.

1. Login to **MobileMe** from any web browser on your computer by going to `www.me.com`.
2. Type your **username** and **password** and click **Log In**.

3. the **Find My iPhone** icon in the top nav bar to display the current location of your iPad.

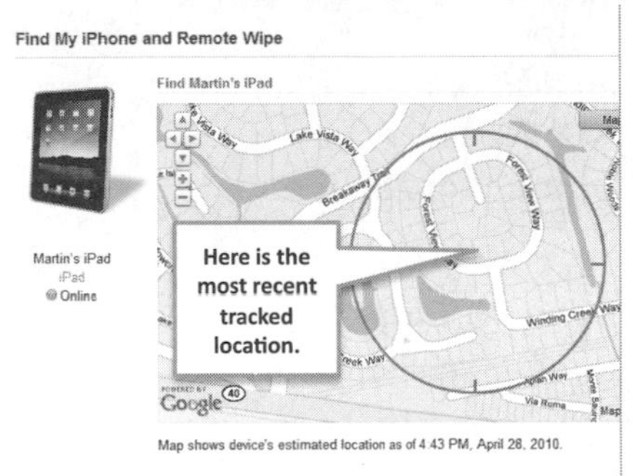


4. Click the **Display a Message** button to display a message on your iPad and play a loud sound for up to 2 minutes or until the screen is tapped.

5. You will see a small alert window pop up on the iPad and the sound will play.

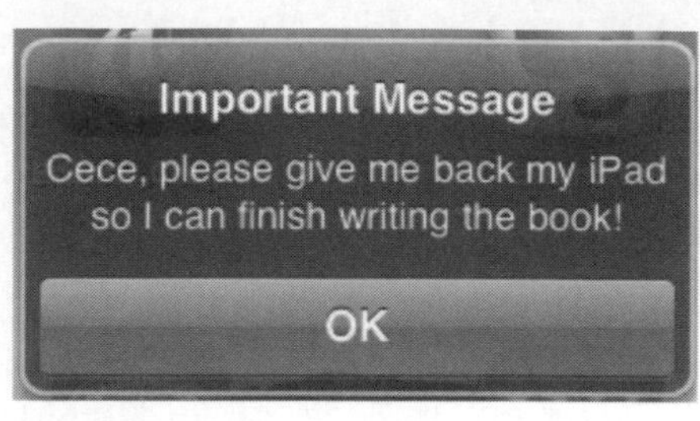


6. If you want to lock your iPad remotely, tap the **Remote Lock** button on the settings page.
7. Enter a new passcode twice to set it on your iPad. Your iPad will immediately be locked with this new passcode.

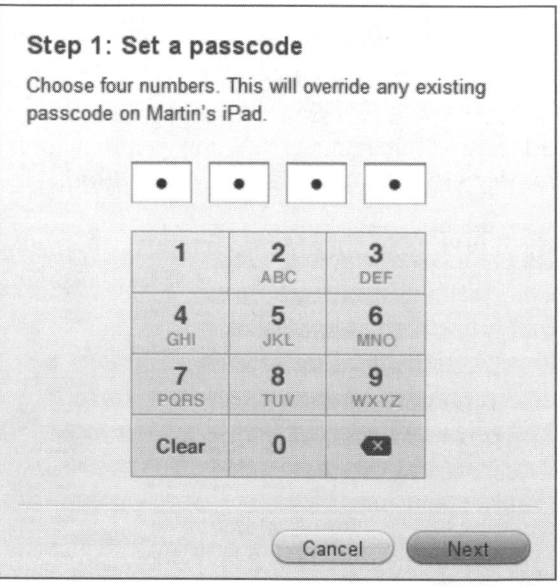


**TIP:** Since this overrides your existing passcode, you can also use this feature to unlock your iPad if you forget your original passcode. Just set a new one using **Remote Lock**.

8. You can also erase all data from your iPad by pressing the **Remote Wipe** button.
9. Mark the check box and click **Erase All Data**.

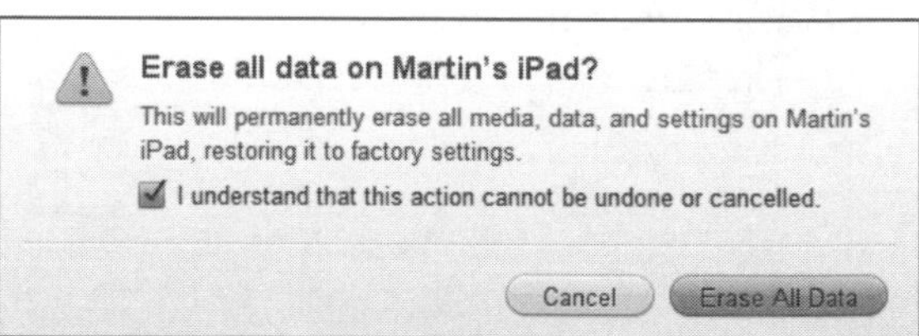


**CAUTION:** This will erase all data on your iPad and cannot be undone. All your data stored on MobileMe will automatically re-sync when you setup the account again. However, applications and other non-MobileMe information will have to be restored from your iTunes backup or from the App Store and iTunes.

# How to Cancel Your MobileMe Account

Should you decide that MobileMe is not for you, you can cancel your account. If you cancel your account within the first 60 days, you can avoid the $99.00 charge.

**10.** To cancel the service, login to MobileMe from any web browser on your computer by going to `www.me.com`.

**11.** Type your username and password and click **Log In**.

**12.** Click the **Settings** icon in the top row of icon.

**13.** Notice on the **Summary** tab the date your **Trial Ends**. In this image, the trial ends on June 4, 2010.

**14.** Click **Account Options** in the left column.

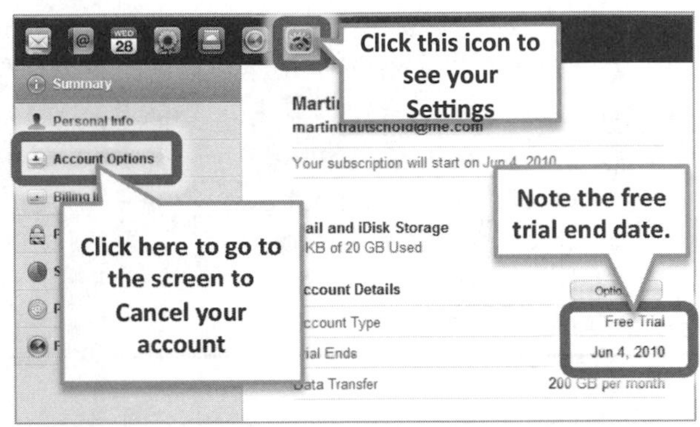


**15.** From the **Account Options** screen, click the **Cancel Account** button.

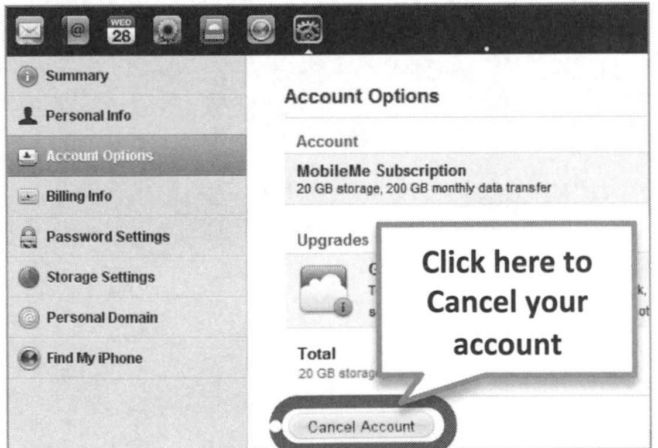


## Additional Settings for Google/Exchange or MobileMe

Once you set up the Google/Exchange or MobileMe sync, you may notice a few new options on your **Settings** screen in addition to the ones shown Chapter 13: "Contacts" and Chapter 14, "Calendar."

1. Tap the **Settings** icon.
2. Tap **Mail, Contacts, Calendars** in the left column.
3. Scroll down the right column to the bottom to see the image to the right.
4. The new option in the Contacts section is the **Default Account**. You can set this to either be your Exchange/Google account or your computer's account.
5. The new option in the Calendars section is **Sync,** which allows you to set how much of your calendar to sync (**2 weeks, 1 month, 3 months, 6 months** or **All events**).

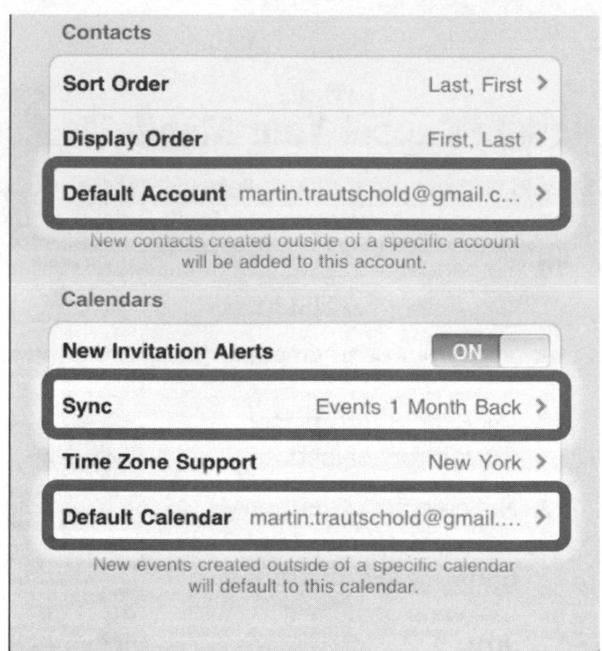

Chapter 25

# Troubleshooting

The iPad is usually highly reliable. Occasionally, like your computer or any complicated electronic device, you might have to reset the device or troubleshoot a problem. In this chapter we give you some useful tools to help get your iPad back up and running as quickly as possible. We start with some basic quick troubleshooting and move into more in-depth problems and resolutions later in the Advanced Troubleshooting section.

We also cover some other odds and ends related to your iPad and give you a list of resources where you can find more help with your iPad.

## Basic Troubleshooting

First, we will cover a few basic tips and tricks to get your iPad back up and running.

## What to Do If the iPad Stops Responding

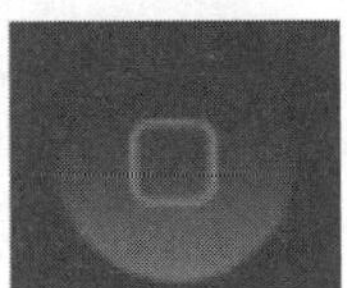

Sometimes, your iPad won't respond to your touch—it freezes in the middle of a program. If this happens, try these steps in order to see if the iPad will start responding (Figure 25–1).

1. Press the **Home** button to see if that exits to the **Home** screen.

2. If the iPad continues to be unresponsive, try pressing the **Sleep/Power** key until you see Slide to **Power Off**. Then press and hold the **Home** button until you return to the **Home** screen—this should quit the program.

3. Make sure your iPad isn't running out of power. Try plugging it in or attaching it to your computer (if it's plugged in) and see if it will start to respond.

4. If holding the **Home** button doesn't work, you will need to try to turn off your iPad by pressing and holding the **Power/Sleep** button for 3–4 seconds. Then slide the **Slide to Power Off** slider at the top of the screen. If you cannot power off the iPad, then see the following instructions about how to reset the iPad.

5. After you power off the iPad, wait a minute or so, and then turn on the iPad by holding the same **Power** button for a few seconds.

6. You should see the Apple logo appear on the screen. Wait until the iPad starts up, and you should be able to access your programs and data.

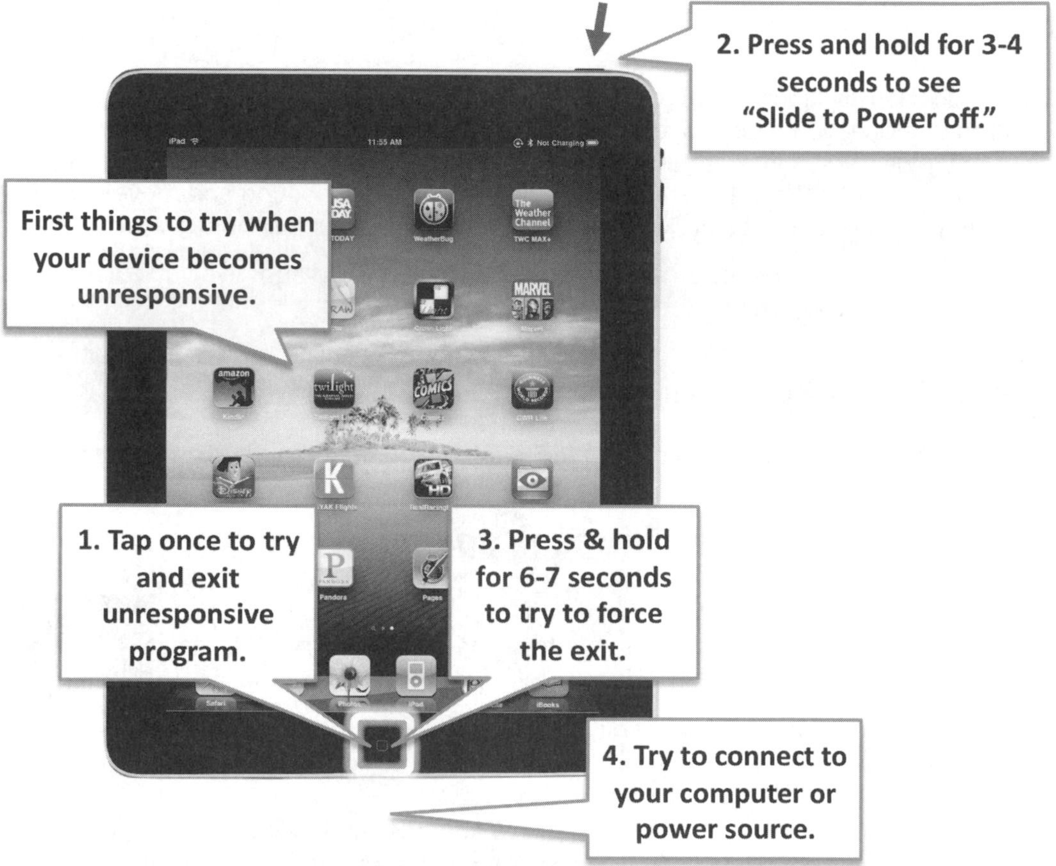

2. Press and hold for 3-4 seconds to see "Slide to Power off."
First things to try when your device becomes unresponsive.
1. Tap once to try and exit unresponsive program.
3. Press & hold for 6-7 seconds to try to force the exit.
4. Try to connect to your computer or power source.

**Figure 25–1.** *Basic troubleshooting steps*

If these steps don't work, you will need to reset your iPad.

## How to Hard-Reset Your iPad

Resetting your iPad is your last response to an unresponsive iPad. It is perfectly safe, and it usually fixes many problems. See Figure 25–2.

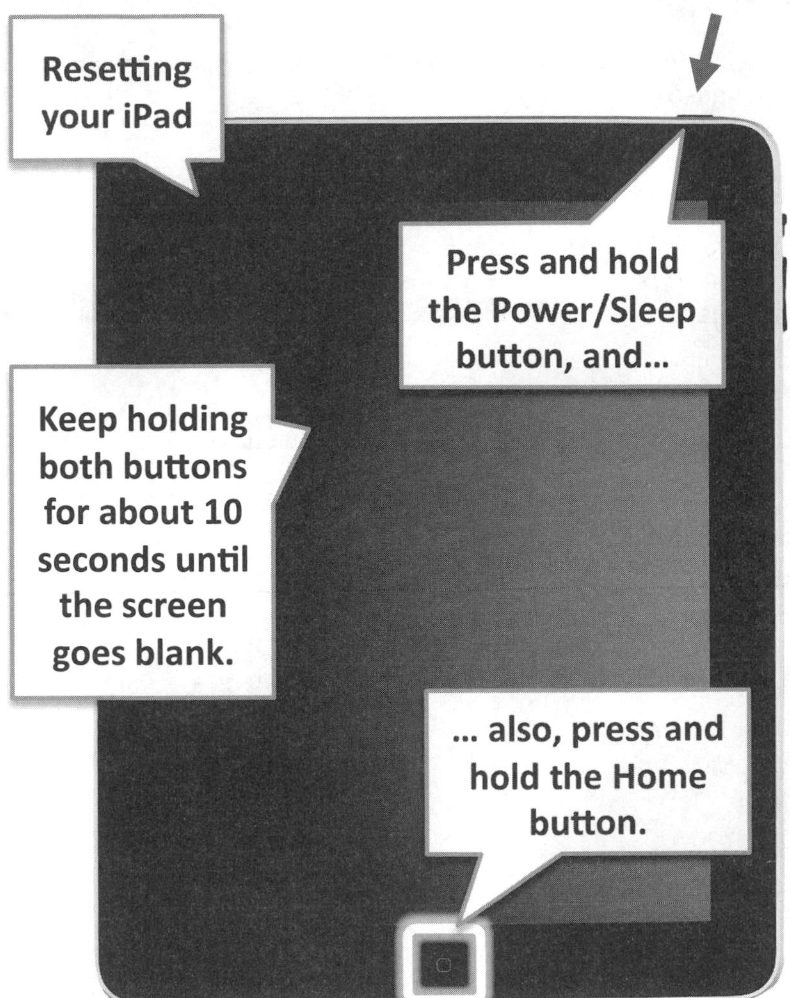


**Figure 25–2.** *Resetting your iPad*

The steps to hard-reset your iPad are

1. Using two hands, press and hold the **Home** button and the **Power/Sleep** button at the same time.
2. Keep both buttons held down for about 8–10 seconds. You will see the **Slide to Power Off** slider. Ignore that and keep holding both buttons until the screen goes blank.

3. After a few more seconds, you should see the Apple logo appear. When you see the logo, just release the buttons and your iPad will be reset.

## How to Soft-Reset Your iPad

There are various things you can reset in the **Settings** app, from the **Home** screen layout to the network settings to all data on your device.

1. Tap the **Settings** icon.
2. Tap **General** in the left column.
3. Tap **Reset** at the bottom of the right column.

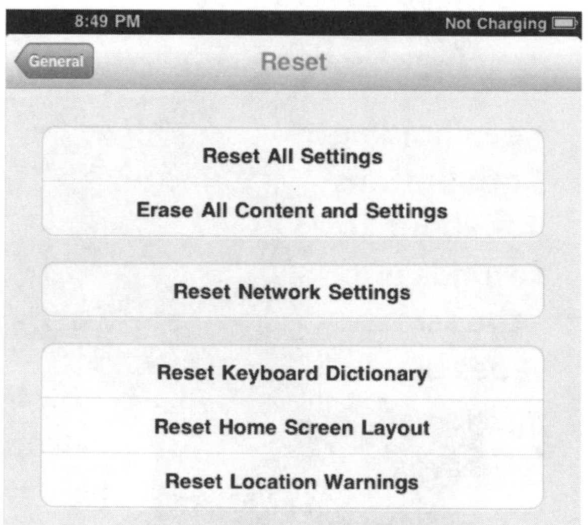


4. Tap **Reset All Settings** to reset network, keyboard, home screen layout, and location warnings. Tap **Reset** to confirm from the pop-up window.
5. Tap **Erase All Content and Settings** to erase absolutely everything from your iPad. Then tap **Erase** to confirm from the pop-up window.
6. Tap **Reset Network Settings** to clear out all your Wi-Fi (and 3G) network settings.
7. Tap **Reset Keyboard Dictionary** to reset the spelling dictionary.
8. Tap **Reset Home Screen Layout** to return to the factory layout, from when you first received your iPad.
9. Tap **Reset Location Warnings** to reset the warning messages you receive about allowing apps to use your current location.

## No Sound in Music or Video

There are few things more frustrating than hoping to listen to music or watch a video, only to find that no sound comes out of the iPad. Usually, there is an easy fix for this problem.

1. Check the volume by using the **Volume Up** key in the upper-right edge of your iPad. You might have accidentally lowered the volume all the way or muted it.
2. If you are using wired headphones from the headphone jack, unplug your headphones and then put them back in. Sometimes, the headset jack isn't connected well.
3. If you are using wireless Bluetooth headphones or a Bluetooth stereo setup:
   a. Check the volume setting (if available on the headphones or stereo).
   b. Check to make sure the Bluetooth device is connected. Go into the **Settings** icon. Tap **General** in the left column and **Bluetooth** in the right column. Make sure you see your device listed and that its status is **Connected**. If it is not connected, then touch it and follow the directions to pair it with the iPad.

> **NOTE:** Sometimes you may actually be connected to a Bluetooth device and not know it. If you are connected to a Bluetooth Stereo device, no sound will come out of the actual iPad.

4. Make sure the song or video is not in Pause mode.
5. Bring up the iPad music or video controls. Double-clicking the **Home** button should bring up the iPad music or video controls. Once you bring up the controls, verify the song is not paused or the volume is not turned down all the way, as shown here.

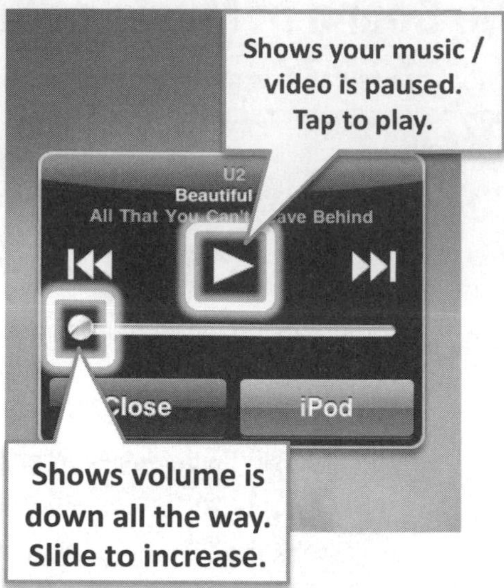
Shows your music / video is paused. Tap to play.
U2
Beautiful
iPod
Shows volume is down all the way. Slide to increase.

6. Check the **Settings** icon to see if you (or someone else) has set the **Volume Limit** on the iPad.
   a. Touch the **Settings** icon.
   b. Tap **iPod** in the left column.
   c. See if the **Volume Limit** is **ON**. Touch **Volume Limit** to check the setting level. If the limit is unlocked, simply slide the volume to a higher level. If it is locked, you need to unlock it first by tapping the **Unlock Volume Limit** button and entering the 4-digit code. See Figure 25–3.

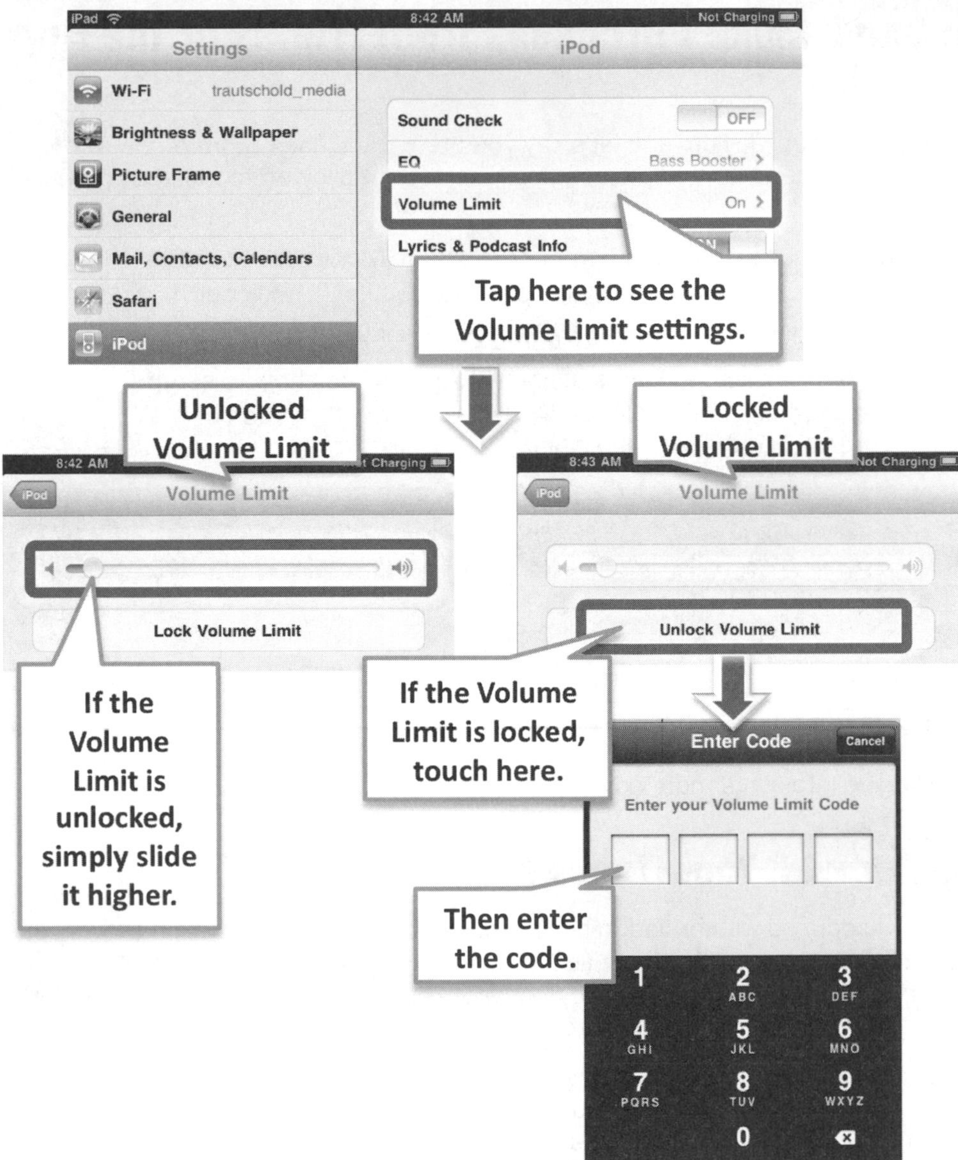


**Figure 25–3.** *Checking the volume limit in settings*

If none of these steps help, check out the "Additional Troubleshooting and Help Resources" section later in this chapter. If that doesn't help, then try to restore your iPad from a backup file using the steps found in the "Restore Your iPad from a Backup" section in the chapter. Finally, if that does not help, then contact the store or business that sold you your iPad for assistance.

## If You Can't Make Purchases from iTunes or the App Store

You have this new, cool device, and let's say you go to the iTunes Store or the App Store. What if you receive an error message or you are not allowed to make a purchase? What do you do now?

1. Both stores require an active internet connection. Make sure you have either a Wi-Fi connection or a cellular data connection. Check out Chapter 4, "Wi-Fi and 3G Connections," for assistance.
2. Verify you have an active **iTunes** account. We show you how to setup a new **iTunes** account in the "Create an iTunes Account" section of Chapter 26: "Bonus iTunes User Guide."

> **NOTE:** If you are traveling to a country where iPads are not yet sold, then you may not have an on-device App Store or **iTunes**. If this is the case, you will need to purchase items using **iTunes** on your computer and sync them to your iPad.

## Advanced Troubleshooting

Now we will delve into some more advanced troubleshooting steps.

### Re-register with Your iTunes Account

Every iPad is associated with or tied to an **iTunes** account. That association allows you to purchase **iTunes** music and videos, and apps from your iPad. It is also that association that allows you to play music from your **iTunes** account on your computer on your iPad.

Sometimes, your iPad might "lose" its registration and connection with **iTunes**. Usually, this is a very simple fix. Just connect your iPad to the computer via the USB cable and **iTunes** will walk you through the process of re-associating your iPad with your **iTunes** account. We show the detailed steps of how to do this in Chapter 1, "Getting Started."

If you have trouble registering your iPad through **iTunes**, then Apple provides an online resource that you can get to from your computer or iPad web browser.

Type this into your web browser:

`https://register.apple.com/cgi-bin/WebObjects/GlobaliReg.woa`

You should see a screen similar to the one shown here (Figure 25–4).

**Figure 25–4.** *The online registration site from Apple's login page*

1. Complete the information, enter your Apple ID and password, and click **Continue**.
2. Select whether you are registering **One product** or **More than one product**. In this case, we chose **One product** (Figure 25–5).

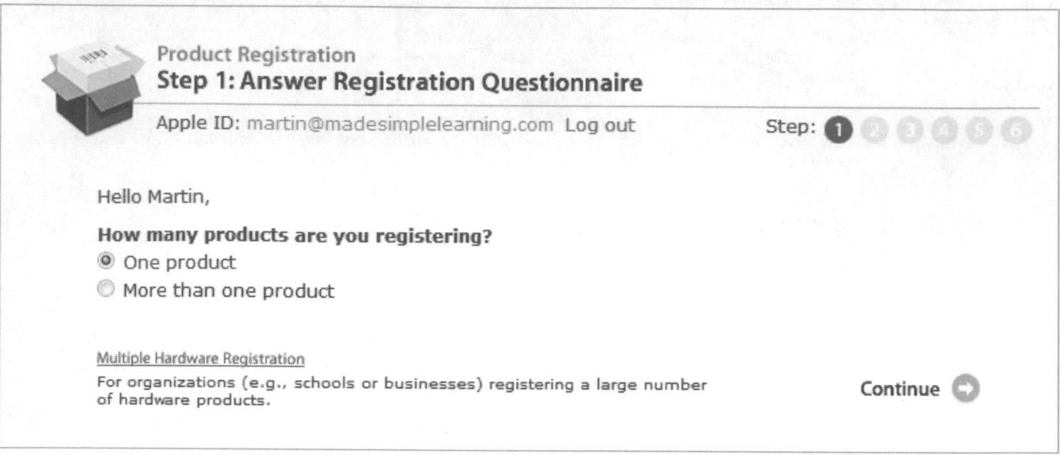


**Figure 25–5.** *Step 1 on Apple's online registration site*

1. Now, choose the category, product line, and product. In this case, we chose **iPad** category, **iPad** product line, and **iPad Wi-Fi**. This moved us through steps 2–4 at once (Figure 25–6).

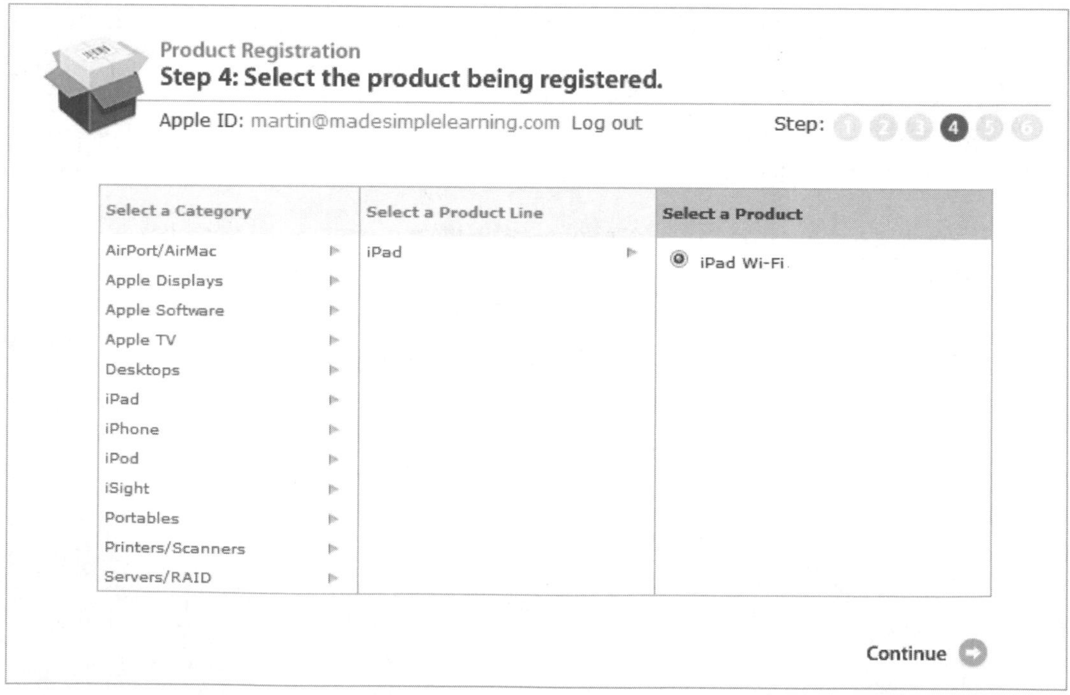


**Figure 25–6.** *Steps 2–4 on Apple's online registration site*

3. Now you need to enter your iPad serial number and other information about how you will use the iPad.

> **TIP:** To locate the serial number, connect your iPad to your computer and load up **iTunes**. Click your iPad in the left nav bar and click on **Summary** in the top nav bar. The serial number is at the top of the Summary screen, as shown in Figure 25–7.

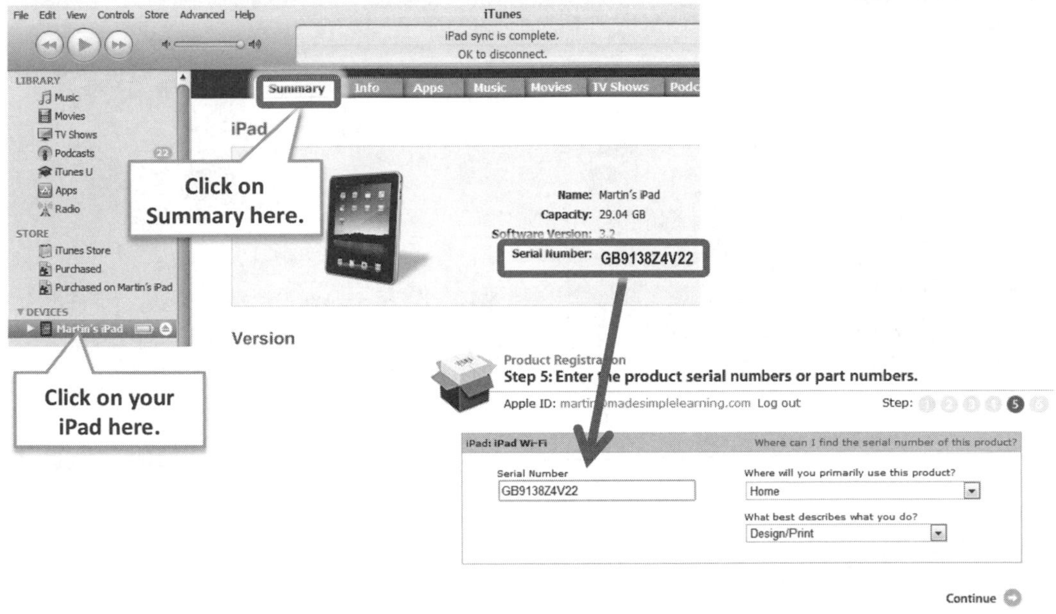


**Figure 25–7.** *Locating your iPad serial number in **iTunes** and Step 5 on Apple's online registration site*

4. Now click **Continue** and you should have successfully registered your iPad.

# iPad Does Not Show Up in iTunes

Occasionally, when you connect your iPad to your PC or Mac, your iPad may not be recognized in the **iTunes** screen.

In the first screen, this is what you should see—your iPad will be listed under DEVICES (Figure 25–8). In the second screen-shot, you will notice that there is no device shown, even though your iPad is connected to the computer.

**Figure 25–8.** *Verifying your iPad is listed in the left nav bar in **iTunes** when connected to your computer*

1. Check the battery charge of the iPad by looking at the battery level in the top right of the home screen. If you have let the battery run too far down, **iTunes** won't see it until the level of the battery rises a bit.
2. If the battery is charged, try connecting the iPad to a different USB port on the computer. Sometimes, if you have always used one USB port for the iPad and switch it to another port, the computer won't see it.
3. If this still does not fix the problem, try disconnecting the iPad and re-starting the computer. Then, reconnect the iPad to the USB port.
4. If this still does not work, download the latest update to **iTunes** or completely uninstall and re-install **iTunes** on the computer again. Just make sure if you choose this option that you back up all the information in **iTunes**.

5. We have included detailed steps showing you how to upgrade to the latest version of **iTunes** in the "Upgrade iTunes" section of Chapter 26: "Bonus iTunes User Guide."

## Synchronization Problems

Sometimes, you might be having errors when synchronizing your iPad with your computer (PC or Mac).

1. First, follow all the steps we outlined in the "iPad Does Not Show Up in iTunes" section.
2. If the iPad still will not sync, but you can see it in your **iTunes** left nav bar, go back to Chapter 3:, "Sync Your iPad with iTunes" and check your sync settings very carefully.

***Are you using Apple's Mobile Me program or Microsoft Exchange?***

**Microsoft Exchange** is a push e-mail and content program usually set up by an enterprise administrator. **Mobile Me** is Apple's own wireless sync program that you can set up (for a fee), which will keep your information wirelessly in sync. However, if you are using **Mobile Me** or **Exchange** to sync personal information, you won't be able to sync through **iTunes**.

On your iPad, go to your **Settings** icon; tap **Mail, Contacts and Calendars** in the left column.

If **Mobile Me** or **Exchange** is set up, it will show up in your list of **Accounts** at the top of the right column. If you don't see one of these on the list, then you are not using them to sync to your iPad.

If you do see one of these items listed, touch the account and then un-check any categories or items that you would prefer to sync through **iTunes**.

Now, when you go back into **iTunes**, those categories should show up as sync options.

> **NOTE:** If you do uncheck or de-select **Calendars** or **Contacts** in the **Mobile Me** or **Exchange** accounts, you won't be able to see that information anymore on the iPad until you set up the synchronization from the computer via **iTunes** (see Chapter 3, "Sync with iTunes").

# Reinstalling the iPad Operating System (With or Without a Restore)

Sometimes, you might have to do a clean install of your iPad operating system to get your iPad back up and running smoothly.

> **Tip**: This process is virtually identical to the process to update your iPad with a new version of the operating system.

During this process you will have three choices:

1. If you want to get the iPad back to its normal state with all your data, you will have to use the **iTunes** Restore function.
2. If you plan on getting a clean start and tying the iPad to an **iTunes** account, you would use the Setup a new iPad function at the end of this process.
3. If you plan on giving away or selling your iPad, then you would simply eject the iPad from **iTunes** at the end of this process (before doing a restore or new setup).

> **CAUTION:** This "restore process" will wipe your iPad totally clean.You will need to re-synchronize and re-install all of your apps and enter your account information, such as email accounts. This process could take 30 minutes or longer, depending on how much information you have synced to your iPad.

To reinstall the iPad operating system software with the option of restoring data to your iPad from a previous backup:

4. Connect your iPad to your computer and load up **iTunes**.
5. Click your **iPad** in the DEVICES category in the left nav bar.
6. Click on **Summary** in the top nav bar.
7. Now, you will see the iPad information screen. Click the **Restore** button in the middle screen, as shown here (Figure 25–9).

**Figure 25–9.** *Connecting your iPad and clicking the* ***Restore*** *button in* ***iTunes*** *in the Summary screen*

8. Now you will be asked if you want to backup. Click **Backup** just to be safe (Figure 25–10).

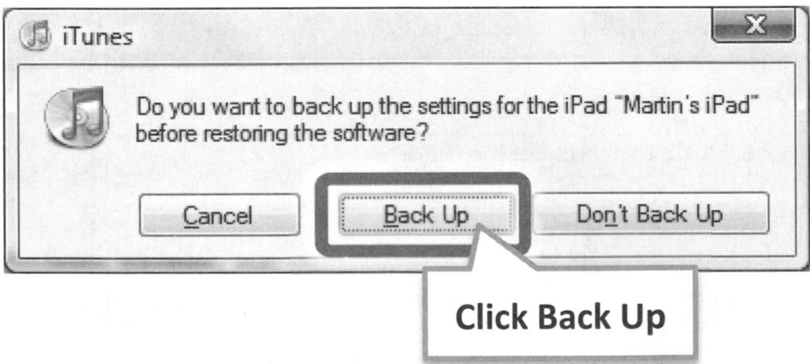


**Figure 25–10.** *Backing-up before you restore in* ***iTunes***

9. On the next screen you are warned that all data will be erased. Click **Restore** to continue (Figure 25–11).

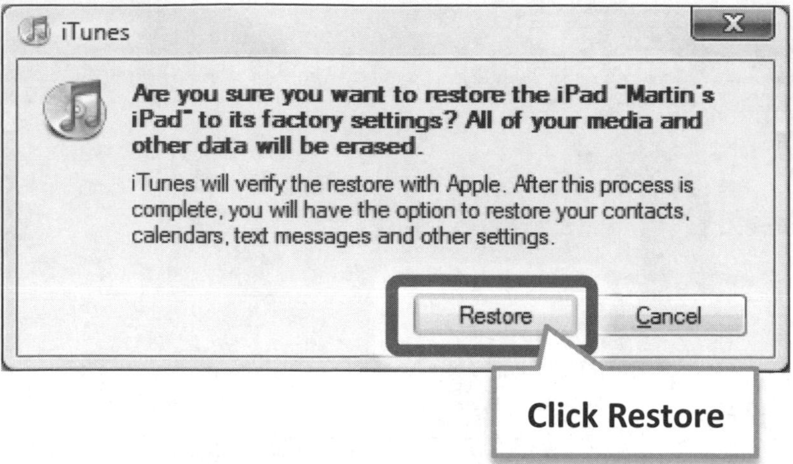


**Figure 25–11.** *Backing-up before you restore in* ***iTunes***

10. Then you will see an iPad Software Update screen. Click **Next >** to continue (Figure 25–12).

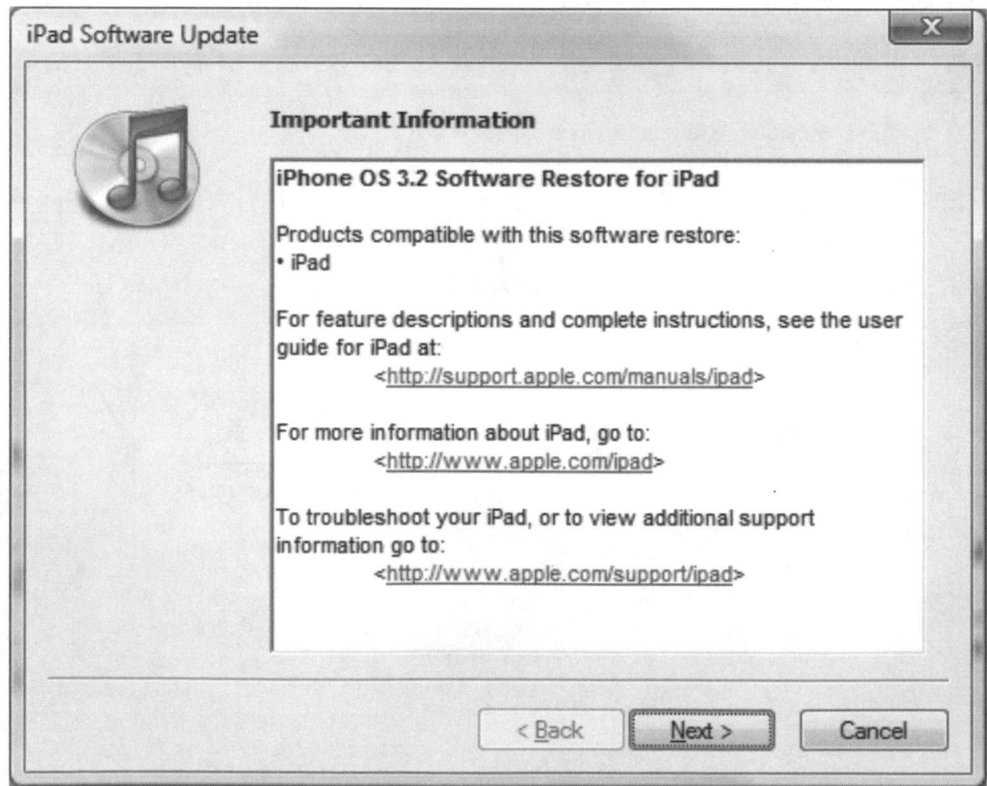


**Figure 25–12.** *Beginning of the software update/restore process*

11. Next, you will see the Software License Agreement screen. Click **Agree** to continue and start the process (Figure 25–13).

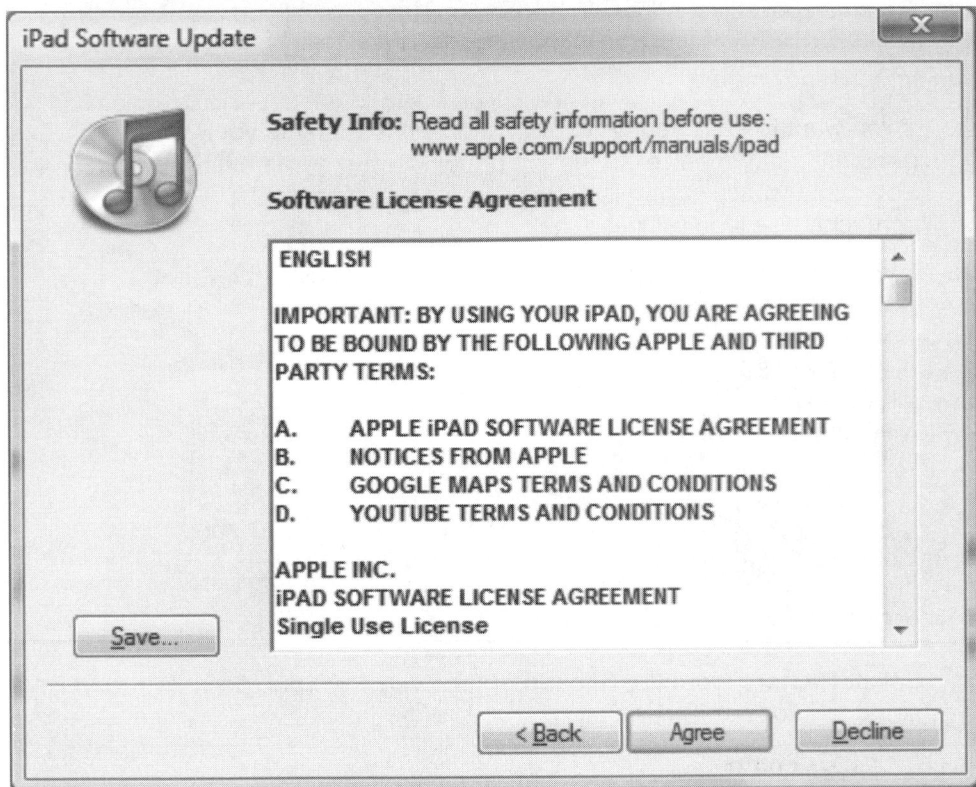


**Figure 25–13.** *Software update/restore process: license agreement*

12. Now, **iTunes** will download the latest iPad software, backup and sync your iPad, and then it will re-install the iPad software completely, erasing all data and restoring your iPad to its original "clean" state. You will see status messages at the top of **iTunes** similar to the one shown here (Figure 25–14).

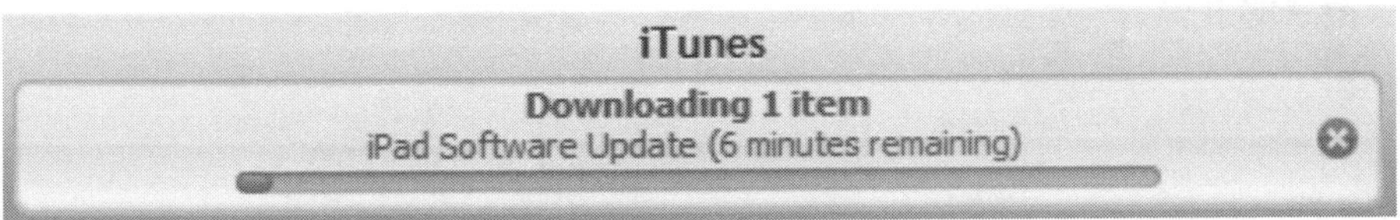


**Figure 25–14.** *Software update/restore process: status window at top of **iTunes***

13. After the backup and sync, your iPad screen will go black. Then the Apple logo will appear and you will see a status bar under the logo. Finally, a small pop-up window will appear in **iTunes** to tell you the update process is complete. Click **OK** to be brought to the Set Up your iPad screen, shown here.

    a. If you want to keep your iPad clean (i.e., without any of your personal data), then select the top option, **Setup as a new iPad**. You might want to use this option if you are setting up this iPad for someone else (you will need their Apple ID and password).

    b. If you are giving away or selling your iPad, simply click the **Eject** icon next to the iPad and you're done (Figure 25–15).

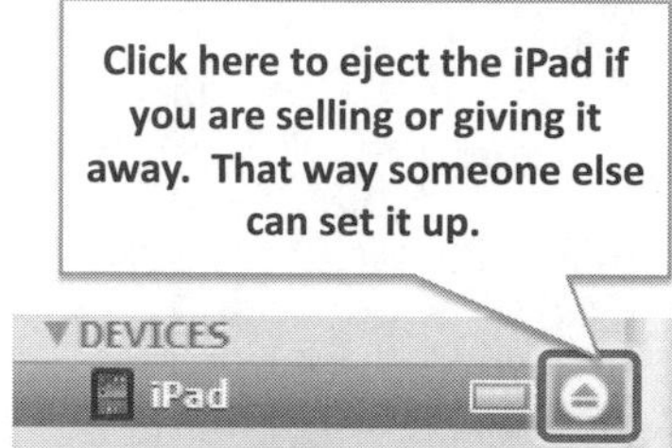


**Figure 25–15.** *Ejecting the iPad if you are giving it away or selling it*

    c. Select **Restore from the backup of:** and verify the pull-down is set to the correct device.

14. Finally, click **Continue** (Figure 25–16).

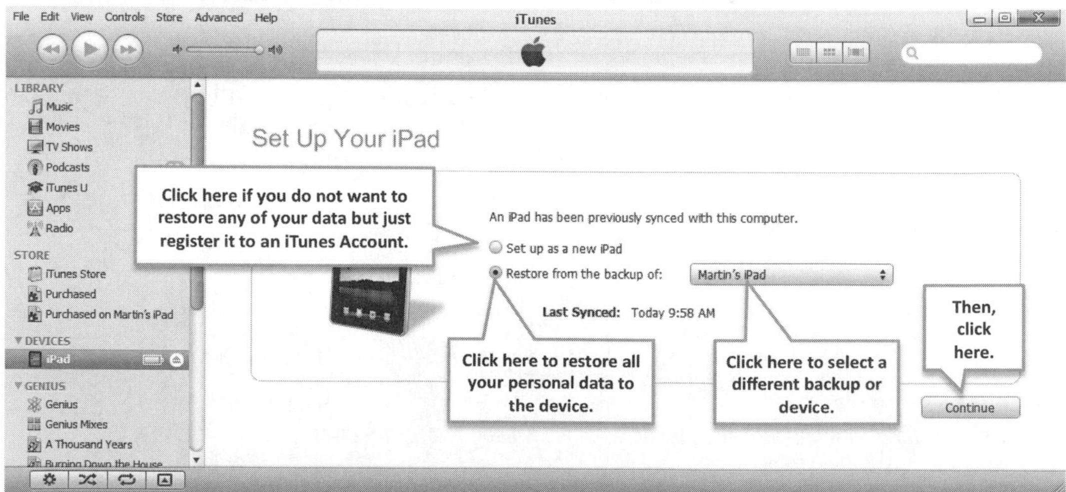


**Figure 25–16.** *Setting up as a new iPad or restoring from a backup file*

15. If you chose to restore, then after a little while you will see a "Restore in Progress" screen on your iPad and a status window in **iTunes** saying "Restoring iPad from backup…" with a time estimate.
16. Then you will see a little pop-up window saying "The settings for your iPad have been restored." In a few seconds you will see your iPad appear in the left nav bar under DEVICES in **iTunes**.
    a. If you sync your information with **iTunes**, all data will be synced now.
    b. If you use **MobileMe**, **Exchange**, or another sync process, you will probably have to re-enter passwords on your iPad to get those sync processes back up and running.

# Additional Troubleshooting and Help Resources

Sometimes you may encounter a particular issue or question that you cannot find an answer to in this book. Below we provide some good resources that you can access from the iPad itself and from your computer's web browser. The iPad on-device user guide is easy to navigate and may provide you some quick information you seek. The Apple knowledgebase is helpful if you are facing a troubleshooting problem that is proving especially difficult to resolve. The iPhone/iPad-related web blogs and forums are good places to locate answers and even ask unique questions you might be facing.

## On-Device iPad User Guide

Open up your Safari web browser to view the online user guide for your iPad.

Tap the **Bookmarks** button next to where you enter a web site address and select iPad User Guide.

If you don't see that bookmark, then type this into the Safari address bar on your iPad: `help.apple.com/ipad`

> **TIP:** To view the manual in PDF format from your computer, go to `http://support.apple.com/manuals/ipad/`.

Once you get to the guide on your iPad, you should see a screen similar to the one here (Figure 25–17).

The nice thing is that you already know how to navigate around the guide. Tap any topic in the left column to reveal that topic in the right column.

Read the topic or touch another link from the right column to learn more.

Tap the button at the top of the right column to back out one level.

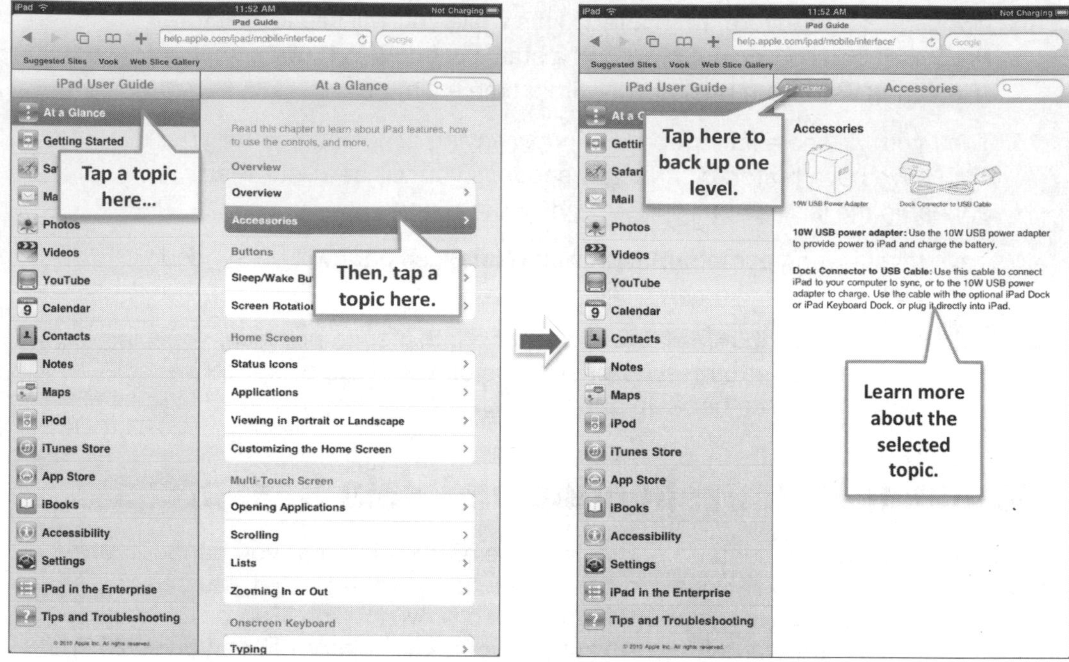


**Figure 25–17.** *Using the iPad manual from Safari on your iPad*

## Check out the Apple Knowledgebase for Helpful Articles

On your iPad or computer's web browser, go to this web page:

`http://www.apple.com/support/ipad/`

Then click on a topic in the left nav bar, as shown in Figure 25–18.

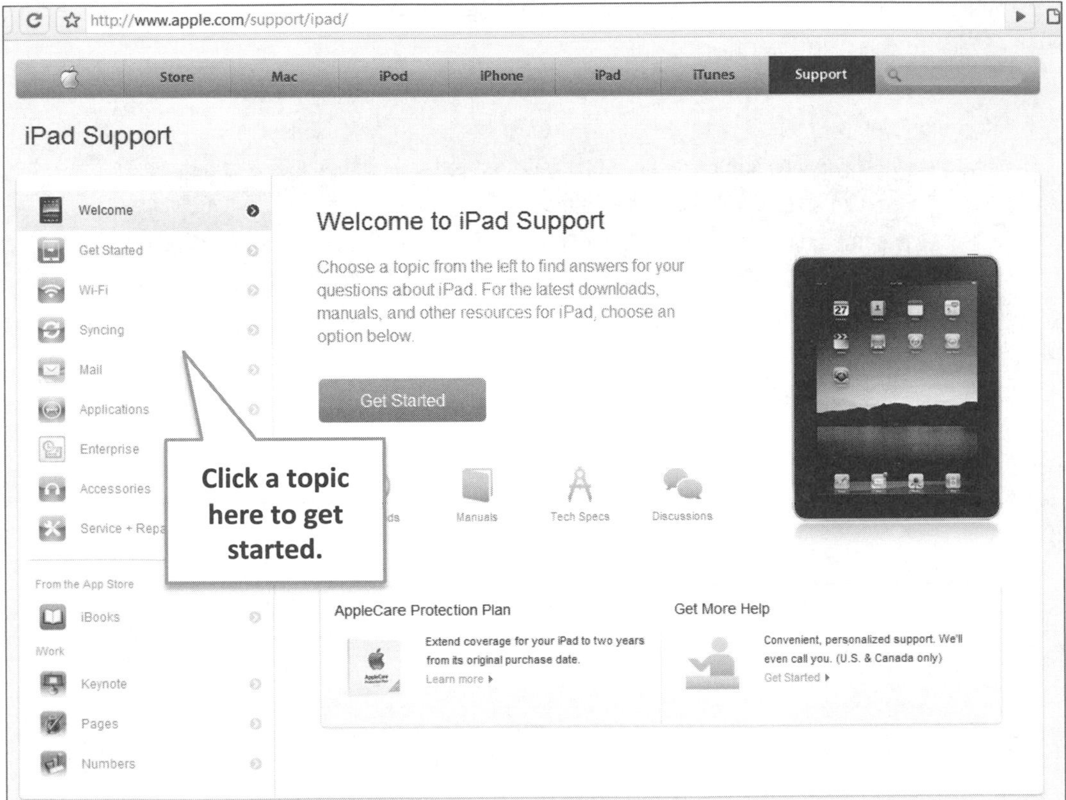


**Figure 25–18.** *Apple Knowlegebase web site for the iPad*

## iPad-Related Blogs

One of the great things about owning an iPad is that you immediately become a part of a worldwide camaraderie of iPad owners.

Many iPad owners would be classified as "enthusiasts" and are part of any number of iPad user groups. These user groups, along with various forums and web sites, serve as a great resource for iPad users.

Many of these resources are available right from your iPad, and others are web sites that you might want to visit on your computer.

Sometimes you might want to connect with other iPad enthusiasts, ask a technical question, or keep up with the latest and greatest rumors. The blogs are a great place to do that.

Here are a few popular iPad (and iPhone or iPod touch) blogs:

`www.tipb.com`

`www.iphonefreak.com`

`www.gizmodo.com` (iPad section)

> **TIP:** Before you post a new question on any of these blogs, please do a search on the blog to make sure your question has not already been asked and answered. Also, make sure you are posting your question on the right section (e.g. iPad) of the blog. Otherwise, you may incur the wrath of the community for not doing your homework first!

Also, do a web search for "iPad blogs" or "iPad news and reviews" to locate more blogs.

Part IV

# iPad's Soulmate: iTunes

Your iPad is inextricably tied to iTunes—the e-commerce center of Apple. iTunes is not only where you buy music, videos and apps, it's also where you organize all of the great content you can use on your iPad. We show you how to purchase exciting new content—and even how to find it for free. Learn something new with iTunes U or find related music and videos with the iTunes Genius feature. We even help you learn how to save money with iTunes Home Sharing.

Chapter 26

# Your iTunes User Guide

In this chapter, we will show you virtually everything you might want to do with iTunes. We help you get iTunes installed and updated. We will take you on a guided tour and describe all the great ways to view your music and videos.

Next, we'll also show you how to create normal playlists and smart playlists, and we will show you how to use the **Genius** feature in iTunes, as well as how to save some money by using the **Home Sharing** feature. We will also show you how to import music CDs, DVDs, and get album artwork for all your music. We will even teach you about the importance of authorizing computers to share content using iTunes. Finally, we will provide some useful iTunes troubleshooting tips.

> **NOTE:** If you are looking to set up your iPad the first time, please check out Chapter 1. If you are trying to sync your computer to your iPad using iTunes, please check out Chapter 3.

If you need to install iTunes on your computer, please jump to the "**Getting iTunes Software**" section later in this chapter. If you have iTunes installed, then go to the "**Getting iTunes Updated**" section to make sure you have the latest version.

> **TIP:** The App Store (see Figure 26–1) on your iPad is a separate icon, but on your computer it's included as a part of iTunes. You get to the App Store on your computer by clicking the **iTunes Store** in the **Left** navigation bar.

**Figure 26–1.** *The iTunes screen showing the iTunes App Store*

# The iTunes User Guide Contents

Since this chapter has so much great material, we will give you an outline of everything it includes. The table that follows outlines the order you will find the relevant sections in this chapter:

### Working with iTunes

What iTunes can do for you

Common questions

iTunes guided tour

Changing views in iTunes

Playing songs, videos, and more

Finding things in iTunes

Creating a new playlist

The iTunes Genius feature

Home Sharing

### iTunes Store and Account

Creating an iTunes account

Signing In to the iTunes store

Buying or getting free software from the App Store

Redeeming an iTunes gift card

### Getting Your Stuff into iTunes

Importing music CDs

Importing movies from DVDs

Getting album artwork

Authorizing and deauthorizing computers

### Getting & Updating iTunes

Getting iTunes software

Getting iTunes updated

### Troubleshooting iTunes

What to Do if iTunes AutoUpdate Fails?

Getting your Music Back if your computer crashes

## What iTunes Can Do

iTunes can do many things for you and your iPad, including the following tasks:

- *Organize your media*: It provides a way to organize your media (both purchased and your own) into playlists and more.
- *Load your music CDs*: It lets you load up all your music CDs into iTunes, manage them with playlists, and sync them to your iPad.
- *Buy media titles or download them for free*: In the **Media** sections of the iTunes store, you can purchase or download free music, movies, TV shows, podcasts, audiobooks, and educational content (with iTunes U).
- *Buy apps or download them for free*: In the App Store portion of the iTunes Store, you can purchase or download free applications (*apps*) for your iPad.
- *Share your media:* It lets you share your purchased music library (or portions of it) across all computers in your home network. This can be a great money saver if your family has similar tastes in music and videos.
- *Play your media:* It serves as a great media player for your computer to play all your media, including music, videos, TV shows, and podcasts.
- *Sync media to iPad*: It lets you transfer or synchronize your music, pictures, and video collections to your iPad (see Chapter 3).
- *Organize and sync your apps*: It lets you manage and sync your Apps on your iPad and arrange the app icons on your iPad's various screens.
- *Sync personal information to your iPad*: It lets you transfer or synchronize your personal information (e.g., addresses, calendar, and notes) between your computer and your iPad.
- *Backup and restore your iPad*: It lets you back up and restore your iPad data.

## Common Questions about iTunes

Here's a list of frequently asked questions about iTunes for the iPad, followed by short answers that address the core concern or issue raised by the question:

*Is iTunes on my computer the same as iTunes on my iPad?*

iTunes on your computer is actually much more than the equivalent iTunes app on the iPad. iTunes on your computer can do the job of five (or more) apps on your iPad. For example, iTunes on your computer handles the following tasks, all of which require different apps on the iPad: iTunes, iPod, Videos, App Store, and iBooks. The chart that follows gives you a quick overview of the differences between iTunes on your computer and iTunes on an iPad, explaining how these functions are split:

| You can do this with iTunes on your computer. | You use this app on your iPad for the same functionality. |
| --- | --- |
| Organize and play your music and audio podcasts. |   iPod |
| Organize and play videos, TV Shows, and video podcasts. |   Videos |
| Purchase music and videos, as well as download podcasts. |   iTunes |
| Purchase books. |   iBooks |
| Purchase or download free apps. |   App Store |

*I have an iPhone and/or another iPod; can I keep using my other iPod or iPhone?* Yes! You can definitely keep listening to all your music and sharing all your videos and even your apps on all of your devices (such as your iPhone, iPod touch, or other iPod) in addition to your new iPad.

*With my other iPhone and/or iPod, can I use my already existing iTunes software and account?* Yes! This is fine; you can use the same iTunes software already installed on your computer, as well as your existing iTunes account to set up your iPad.

*Can I use my purchased apps from my iPod touch or iPhone on my iPad?* Yes! However, you will notice that they initially show up in a small box in the center of the screen. You have to tap the **2x** button in the lower right corner to expand them so they fill most of the **iPad** screen. These iPhone/iPod touch apps do not rotate as you tilt your iPad. Some developers are creating new iPad versions that will show up under the **iPad** section in the App Store. Some iPad apps are known as "HD" versions of their iPhone apps.

**TIP:** If you are an Apple Mac user, it is likely that iTunes is already pre-installed on your computer, and it may already be in your **Bottom Dock**. If it is not there, then start your **Finder**, click **Applications** to locate the iTunes application, and start it.

## The iTunes Guided Tour

After you have iTunes installed or updated, you're ready to take a quick guided tour of the iTunes interface on your computer (both PC and Mac).

**NOTE:** If you need to install iTunes on your computer, please jump to the "**Getting iTunes Software**" section later in this chapter. If you have iTunes installed, then go to the "**Getting iTunes Updated**" section to make sure you have the latest version.

When you first start iTunes, you will see the main window with the top controls to play your music or videos (see Figure 26–2). You will also see the **Left** navigation bar (nav bar), which lets you select from your library, Store, iPad (when connected), shared media, **Genius** playlists, and your own playlists. The **Top** nav bar adjusts depending on what you have selected in the left nav bar. Also, the center main window adjusts depending on selections from the **Left** nav bar, **Top** nav bar, and what is inside the main window itself.

**Figure 26–2.** *The iTunes main window*

Starting from the top left of the main window, you can see the following menus, controls, windows, and other visual elements:

***Main menus***: These are just above the media controls and allow you to access all the actions iTunes can do through a logical and convenient set of menus. While a lot of the functionality in these menus is available in buttons and toolbars, these menus are where you'll find what you're looking for in a logical list.

***Media controls***: These buttons let you play, pause, or skip to the next song or video, as well as adjust the volume.

***Status window***: Located in the top, middle section of iTunes, this window shows you the status of what is currently going on (sync status, whether you're playing a song/video, or any other related messages).

***Adjust views***: These buttons allow you to adjust views between **List**, **Grid**, or **Cover Flow** views. (These are only active when you are in your own media libraries.)

***Search***: This box will search your library or the iTunes store for a particular song, video, TV show, anything based on the text you enter.

***Sign In***: Located just below the **Search** window, this button allows you to sign in or create a new Apple ID. (You use an Apple ID to purchase or download content from the iTunes store.)

***Left nav bar***: This nav bar allows you to view your library (e.g., music, videos, TV shows, and podcasts), the iTunes Store, any currently connected devices (your iPad, iPod, iPhone, and so on), shared libraries, **Genius** mixes, and your own playlists.

***Top nav bar***: This set of buttons is adjusted based on what you have selected in the **Left** nav bar. Click any of these buttons to change the content shown in the **Main** window.

***Main window***: This is where you see all the content based on your selections in the **Left** and **Top** nav bars. For example, if you selected your iPad in the **Left** nav bar and **Apps** in the **Top** nav bar, you would see a screen similar to the one shown in Figure 26–3.

**Figure 26–3.** *The iTunes Main window, which shows how the Main window changes based on Left and Top nav bar selections*

## Apple Video Tutorials for iTunes

In addition to all the information provided in this book, you can find some good video tutorials to help you start using iTunes from Apple. Check them out from within iTunes by following these steps:

1. Go to the **Help** menu item, then to **iTunes Tutorials**. (This is the same on a Mac or Windows PC.)
2. You should see a new window appear similar to the one shown in Figure 26–4. Tap any of the videos listed in the left column.
3. Press the **Click to Play** button in the center of the video in the Main window.

**Figure 26–4.** *The iTunes video tutorials*

In iTunes, you can also configure your iPad to sync with your personal information, data, and pictures, as we will explain later in this chapter. It is a good idea to familiarize yourself with the features of iTunes by going to `www.apple.com/itunes/tutorials/` and watching the various iTunes tutorials.

## Changing Views in iTunes

There are many ways to view your music, videos, and other media in iTunes on your computer. Getting familiar with these views on your computer will help you because you will notice that your iPad also has many of the same views. There are three customizable primary views: **List**, **Grid**, and **Cover Flow**.

### List View

Click the left-most icon of the three view icons to see **List** view (see Figure 26–5). You can re-sort the list by any column by clicking that column's heading. For example, to sort by name, you would click the **Name** column heading. To reverse the sort order, just click the same column heading again. This list view can be especially helpful to find all the songs by a particular artist or on a particular album.

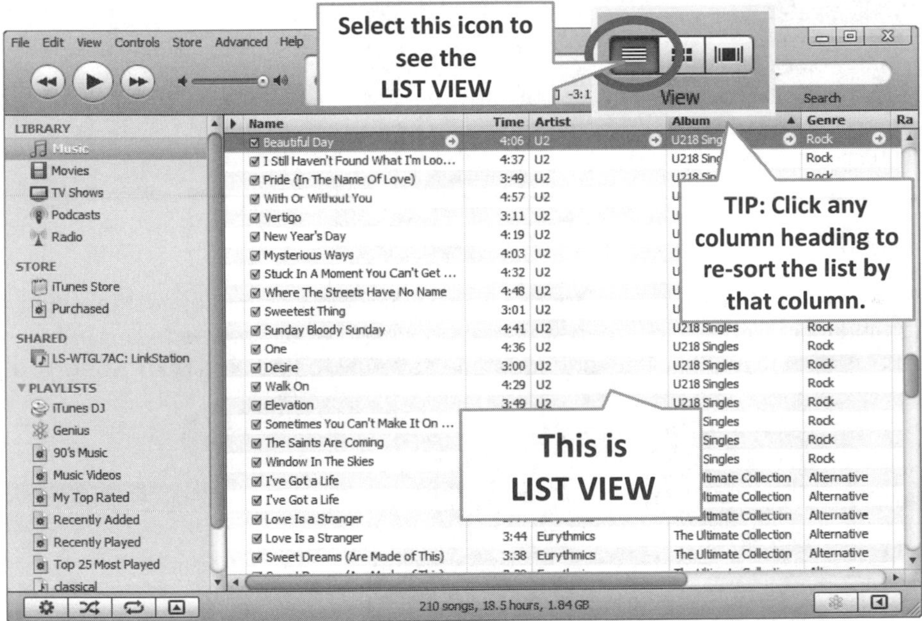


**Figure 26–5.** *The iTunes List view*

## Grid View

Click the middle icon to show **Grid** view (see Figure 26–6). This view is a very graphical view, and it is helpful if you want to quickly find album or poster art.

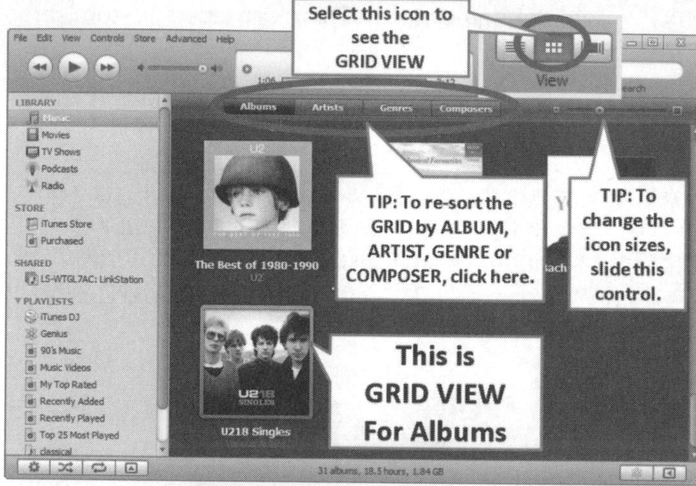


**Figure 26–6.** The *iTunes Grid view*

## Cover Flow View

Click the right-most icon to see **Cover Flow** view. This is a fun view because it is visual, and you can quickly flip through the images using the slider bar to browse through the covers. Like the **Album** view, this view provides an easy way to find an album when you know what the cover looks like.

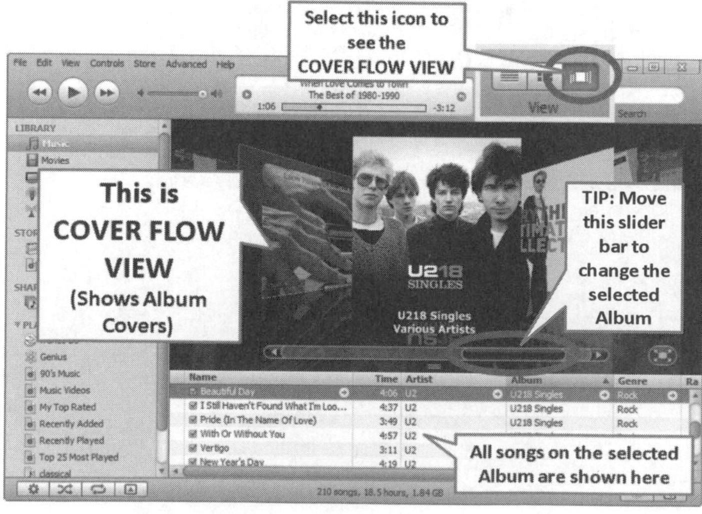


**Figure 26–7.** The *iTunes Cover Flow view*

## Playing Songs, Videos and More

If you are new to iTunes, these basic pointers can help you get around (see Figure 26–8):

*Playing a song, video, or podcast*: Double-click an item to start playing it.

*Controlling the song or video*: Use the **Rewind**, **Pause**, and **Fast Forward** buttons in addition to the **Volume** slider in the upper left corner to control the playback.

*Moving to a different part of the song or video*: Just click the diamond in the slider bar under the song name in the top of the window and drag it left or right as desired.

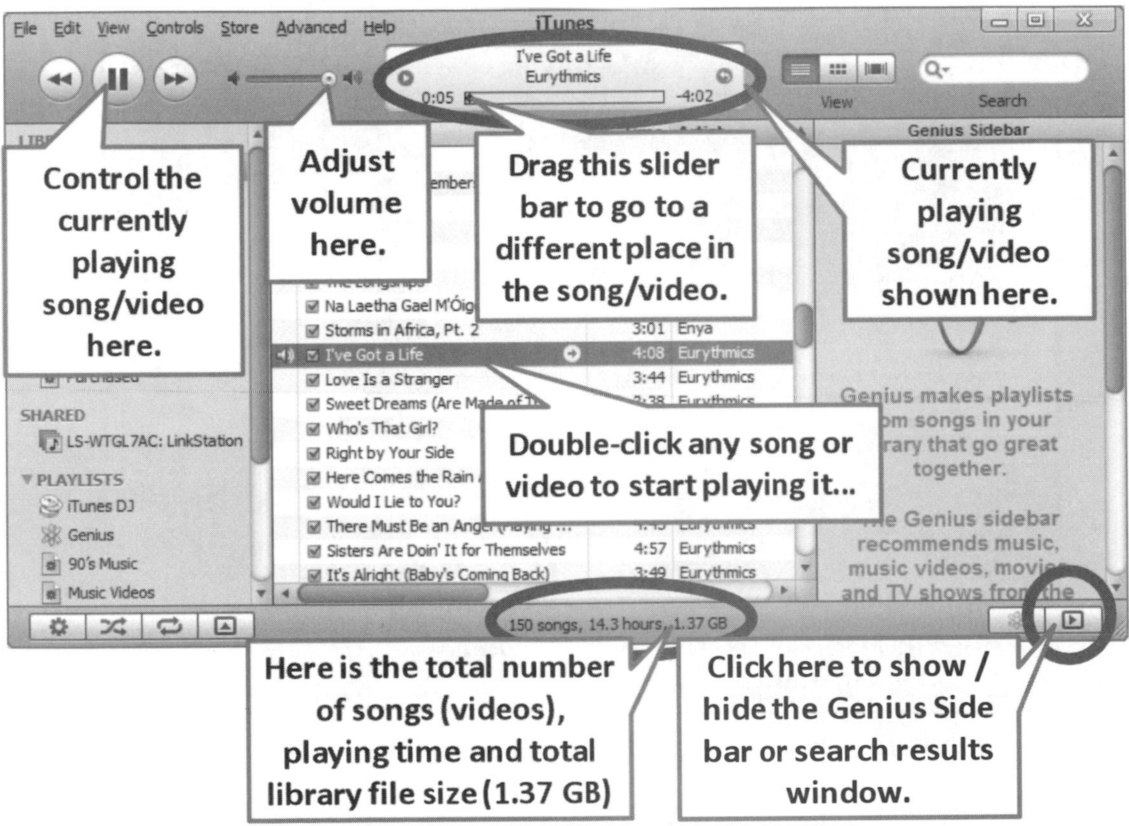


**Figure 26–8.** *Playing your songs, videos, and more in iTunes*

# Finding Things in iTunes

If your library does not already contain hundreds or thousands of songs and other media, it will soon! How do you quickly find that special song you are in the mood for right now? The quickest way to locate an individual song or video is to use the **Search** bar in the upper right corner of iTunes.

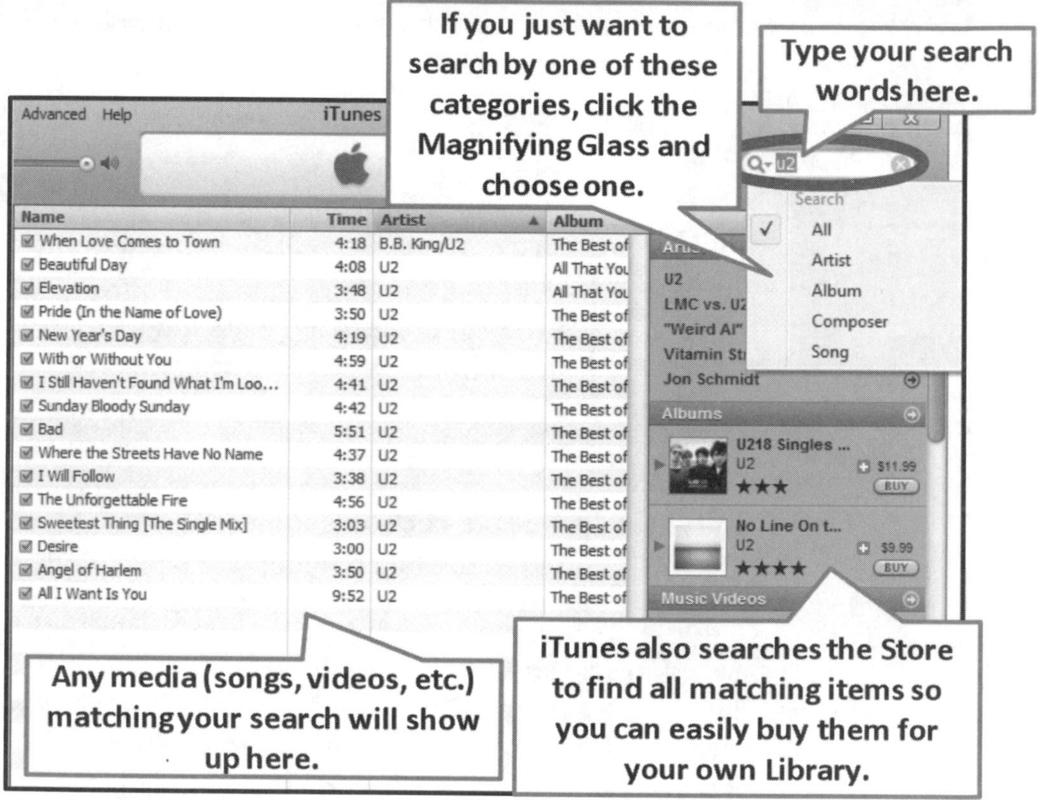


**Figure 26–9.** *Searching for media in iTunes*

In the **Search** window, just start typing any part of the following categories to find an item (see Figure 26–10):

- Artist name
- Album name
- Composer
- Song/video name

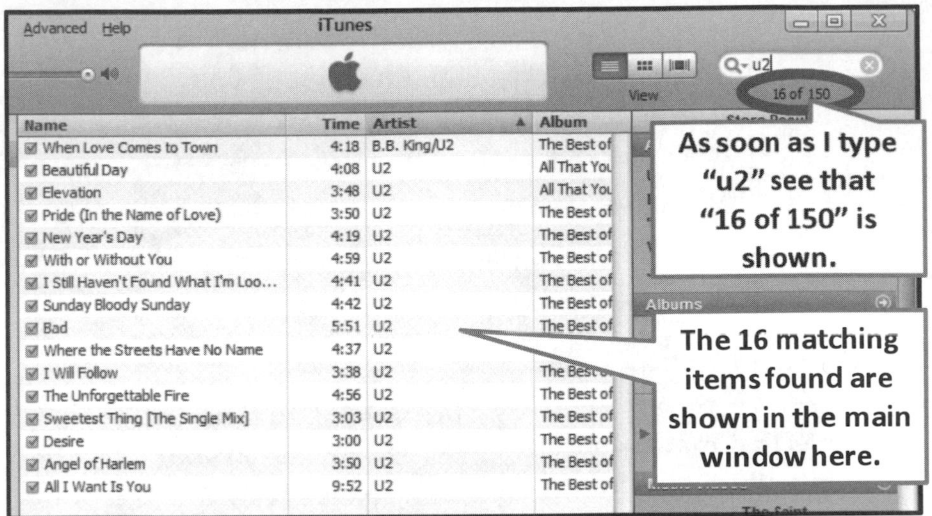


**Figure 26–10.** *Searching through results while looking for media in iTunes*

You will notice that, as soon as you type the first letter, iTunes will narrow your search results (shown in the **Main** window) by that letter. What it is doing is finding all matching songs/videos that have the letter (or series of letters) that match any part of the artist, album, composer or song/video name.

## Ways to Search iTunes

You can type any combination of words to match the item you are trying to find. For example, assume you know that the song has the word "love" in the title, and the song is by "U2." You could just type in those two words, separated by a space; "Love U2" will immediately show all matching items (see Figure 26–11). In this case, only two songs match, so you can quickly double-click the song you want to listen to. Search is also contextual. This means that if you are in your music library, the search function will search for music; whereas if you are in your apps library, the search will search only for apps. In every search, both your own library and the App Store will be searched.

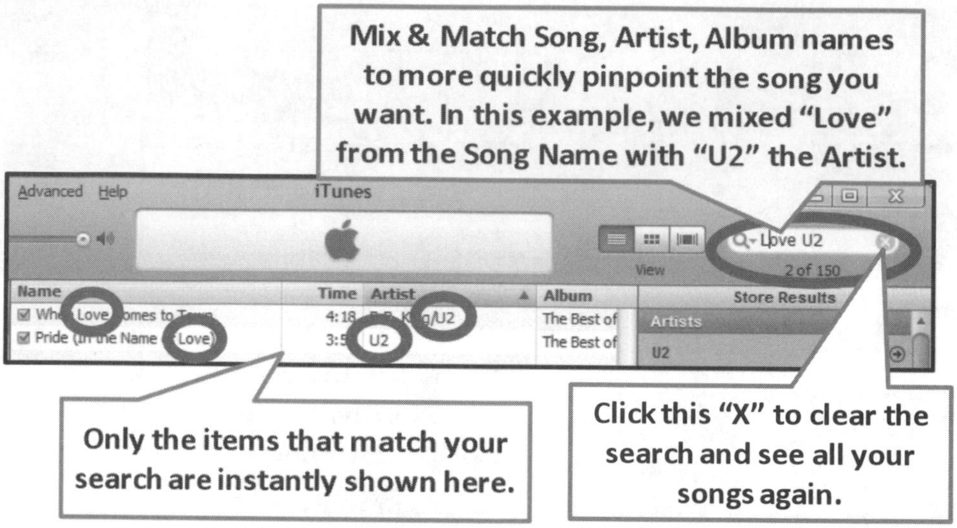
Mix & Match Song, Artist, Album names to more quickly pinpoint the song you want. In this example, we mixed "Love" from the Song Name with "U2" the Artist.
Advanced Help
iTunes
Love U2
View
2 of 150
Name
Time
Artist
Album
Store Results
Artists
U2
The Best of
The Best of
Only the items that match your search are instantly shown here.
Click this "X" to clear the search and see all your songs again.

**Figure 26–11.** *Use two or more words separated by spaces to quickly narrow the search results.*

When you are done searching, hit the little **X** in the circle next to the search words to clear out the search and see all your songs and videos again.

# Creating a New Playlist

You may be used to listening to all the music on a particular album, but you will soon find the benefits of creating your own custom playlists. These are lists of particular songs that you group together. You can create a **Normal** or a **Smart** playlist.

You can group playlists however you prefer, as in this example:

- Workout music
- Favorite U2 songs
- Traveling music

**TIP:** You can create playlists in your iTunes library or directly on your iPad. To create a playlist for your computer, click any existing playlist under the **Playlists** heading in the **Left** nav bar. To create a new playlist directly on your iPad, click your iPad listed under **Devices** in the **Left** nav bar. Depending on what you have highlighted in the **Left** nav bar, your new playlist will be created either on the computer or on the iPad.

## Creating a Normal Playlist

A Normal playlist is one in which you can drag and drop songs manually to your new playlist.

Once you have decided whether to create your playlist on your iPad or on your computer, you are ready to get started.

To create a new **Normal** Playlist, you can press **Ctrl + N** (or **Command + N** on a Mac) to select a **New Playlist** from the **File** menu, or you can simply click the **New Playlist** button in the lower left corner of iTunes, as shown to the right.

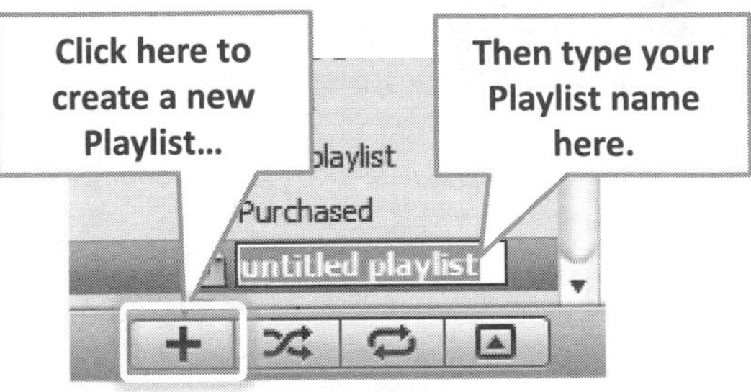


Next, type the name of your Playlist in the entry that appears in the **Left** nav bar.

Now you need to find music to add to your new playlist (see Figure 26–12). To select from your entire library, click **Music** under the **Library** tab.

To select songs from an existing playlist, click that Playlist.

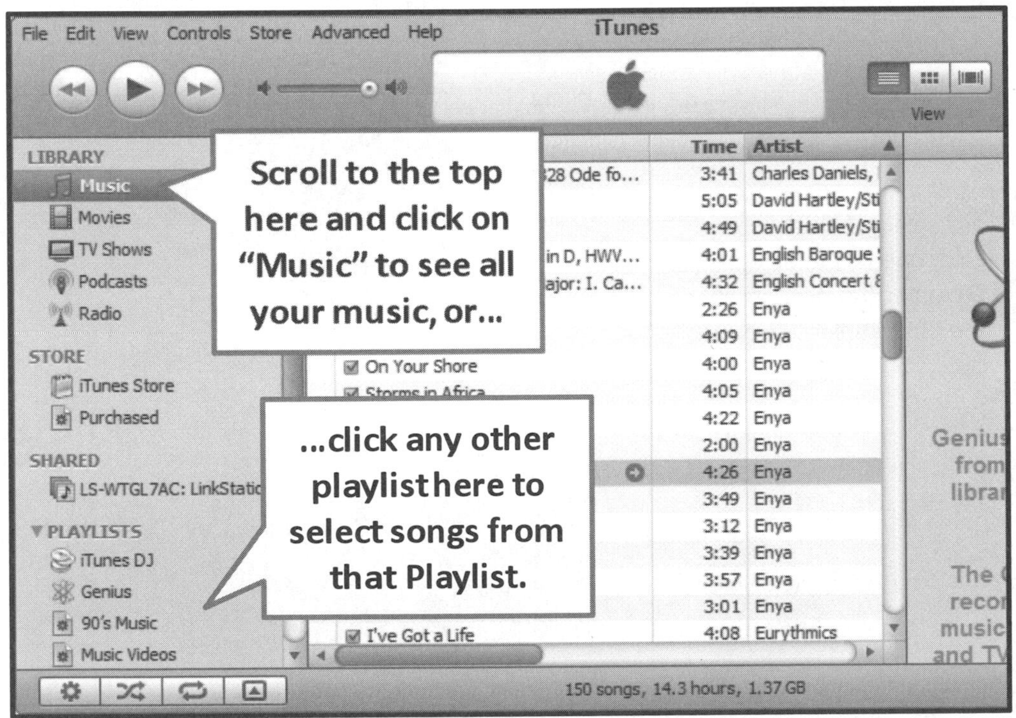


**Figure 26–12.** *Locating songs to add to a Playlist*

Here are some additional useful functions you can accomplish:

*Adding Individual Songs*: Click any individual song to select it, then keep holding down the **Mouse** key while you drag it over to your new Playlist. To put it into the Playlist, drop it by letting go of the **Mouse** key when the song name you are dragging is over the name of the Playlist.

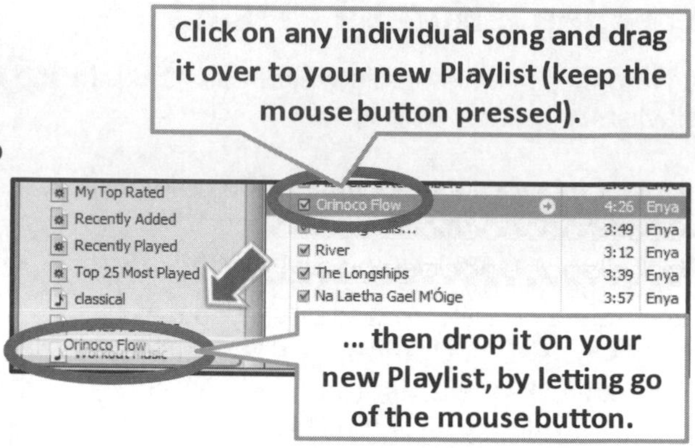

Click on any individual song and drag it over to your new Playlist (keep the mouse button pressed).

... then drop it on your new Playlist, by letting go of the mouse button.

*Adding Multiple Songs/Videos*: You can add multiple items in two simple steps.

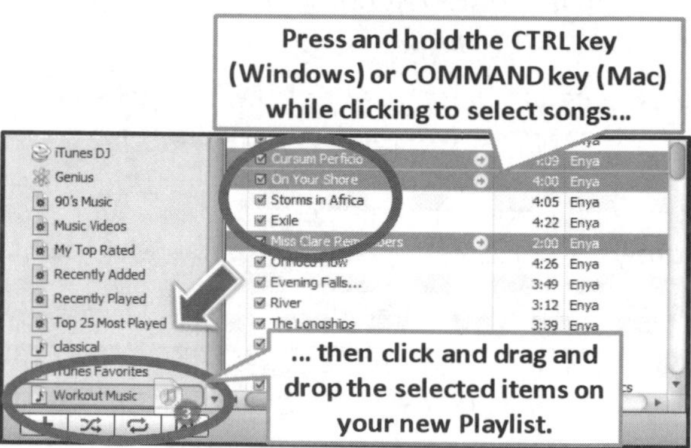

Press and hold the CTRL key (Windows) or COMMAND key (Mac) while clicking to select songs...
... then click and drag and drop the selected items on your new Playlist.


1. To add selected songs that are not listed sequentially, press and hold the **Ctrl** key (Windows) or **Command** key (Mac), then click the individual songs/videos. Once you are done selecting songs/videos, release the **Ctrl/Command** key.
2. After all the songs/videos are selected (highlighted), click one of the selected songs and drag-and-drop the entire selected group onto your Playlist.

*Adding a List of Songs/Videos*: You can also add a list of songs/videos using only a pair of simple steps:

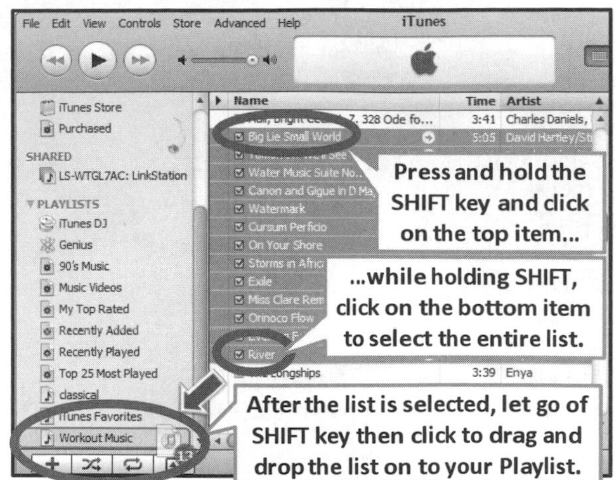


3. To add a list of songs/videos that are all together in a continuous list, press and hold the **Shift** key. While pressing the **Shift** key, click the top item in the list and then click the bottom item. All items will be selected.

4. After all the songs/videos are selected (highlighted), click one of the selected songs and drag-and-drop the entire selected group onto your Playlist.

# Creating a New Smart Playlist

A **Smart Playlist** is one that iTunes creates for you based on your selections. You can create a **Smart Playlist** for only those top 10 songs that you play all the time, only specific artists, a specific genre, or even limit the playlist to a certain size based on the number of songs or their size (MB or GB).

To start creating a **Smart Playlist**, select **File > New Smart Playlist**. Or, you can press **Ctrl + Alt+ N** (Windows) or **Command + Alt+ N** (Mac), and then select **New Smart Playlist** from the **File** menu.

Figure 26–13 illustrates that you have many options for creating a **Smart Playlist**. All of the default Playlists you see in iTunes are **Smart Playlists**. Default categories include **90's Music**, **Classical Music**, **Music Videos**, **My Top Rated**, **Recently Added**, **Recently Played**, and **Top 25 Most Played**.

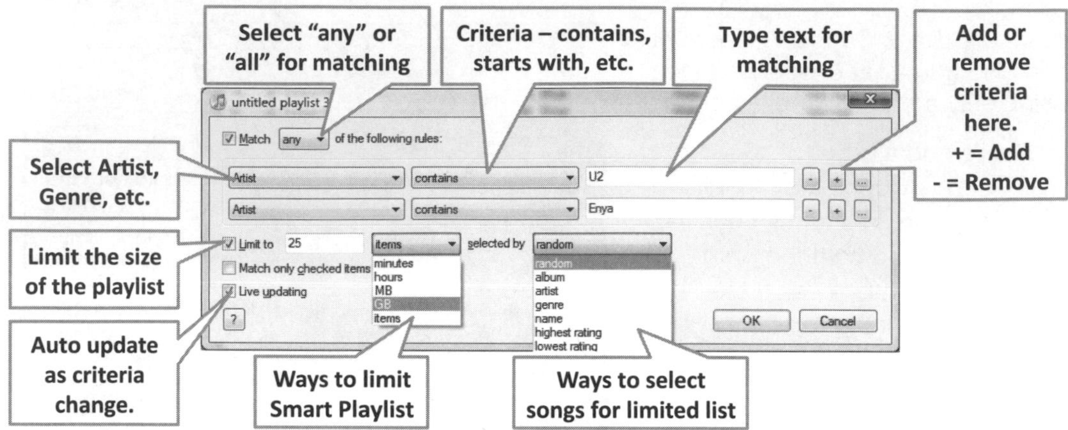


**Figure 26–13.** *The Smart playlist settings screen*

# Edit a Smart Playlist

Probably the best way to get a feel for how the **Smart Playlist** function works is to check out some of the pre-set **Smart Playlists**.

To edit a **Smart Playlist**, select **Edit Smart Playlist** from the **File** menu.

In Figure 26–14, you can see the **Smart Playlist** for **90's Music**; you can also see that it will pull all **Music** and **Music Videos** that are from 1990 to 1999. Check out a few other default **Smart Playlists** to start to learn how the myriad options interact to create a very powerful playlist function.

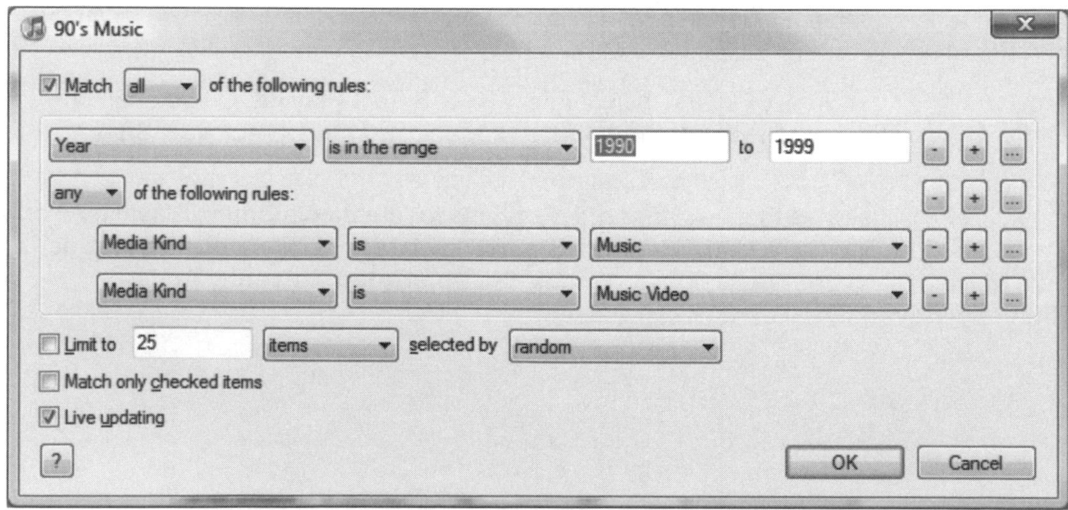


**Figure 26–14.** *The Smart Playlist settings screen for 90's Music*

> **NOTE:** The **Live Updating** feature of **Smart Playlists** allows them to scan whenever you play a song or add any new media (songs, videos, and so on) to your library; it then includes any new songs that it deems may fit the criteria of the **Smart Playlist**. This makes the Playlists really dynamic.

# The iTunes Genius Feature

The iTunes **Genius** feature can do all sorts of fun things to help enhance your music and video library in iTunes. You can take advantage of it by following these steps.

> **TIP:** You can use the **Genius** feature on your iPad, but only after you have enabled it on your computer using the steps that follow.

1. To get started, click **Genius** in the **Left** nav bar, then click the **Turn On Genius** button (see Figure 26–15).

**Figure 26–15.** *Starting up the Genius feature in iTunes*

2. If you are not already logged into the iTunes store, you will be asked to log in (see Figure 26–16). If you do not yet have an Apple ID, then please jump to the "Create an iTunes Account" section in this chapter to learn how to create one.

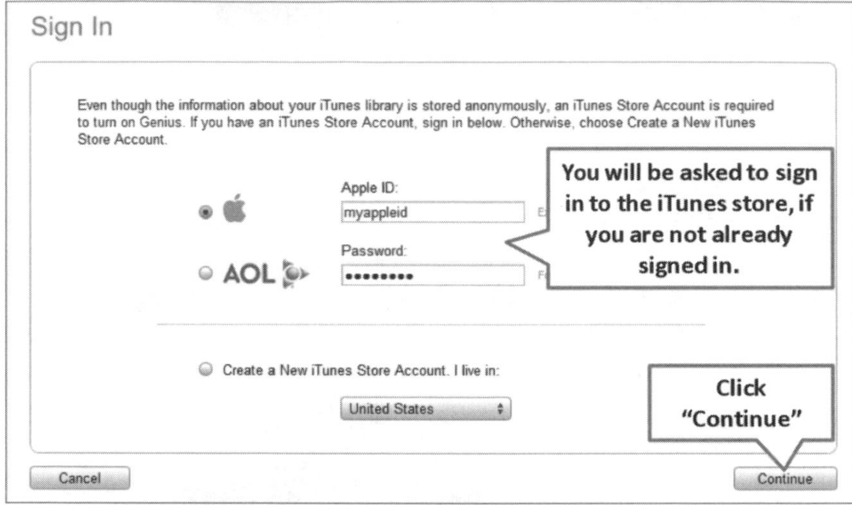


**Figure 26–16.** *Sign in using your Apple ID or AOL account to start the Genius feature in iTunes*

3. Read and agree to the **Genius** license agreement to continue (see Figure 26–17).

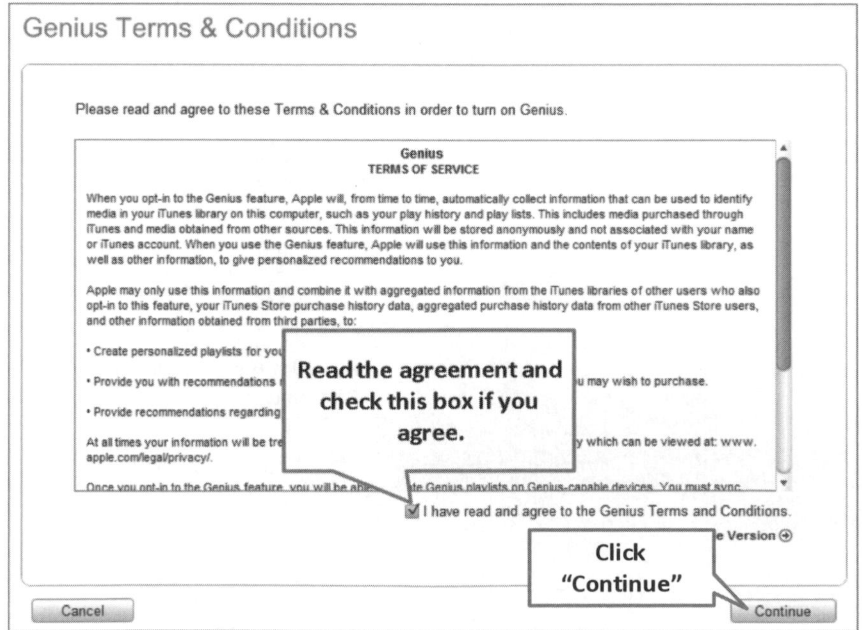


**Figure 26–17.** *The Genius license agreement in iTunes*

4. Next, you will see a window for some time (more if your library is large) on your screen that says the **Genius** feature is starting up (see Figure 26–18 below).

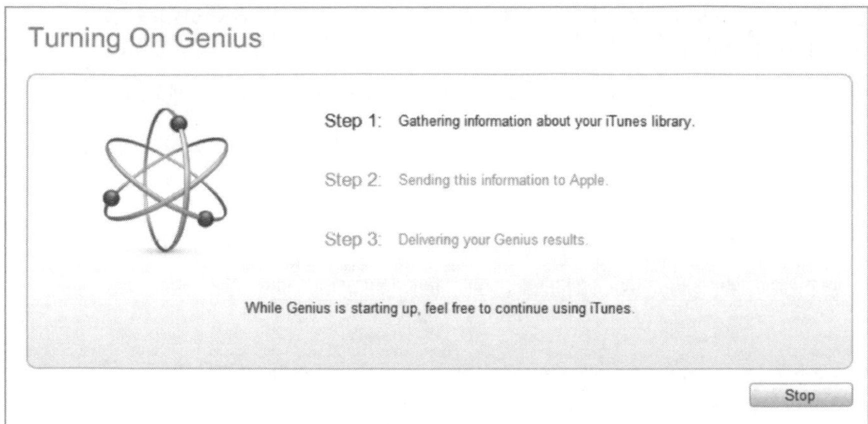


**Figure 26–18.** *The Genius feature getting turned on in iTunes*

5. In order for the **Genius** feature to work correctly, iTunes needs to understand the types of music and videos you have in your library. It will use this information to help make suggestions on similar artists or videos that you don't yet own, but might want to purchase. When this step is done, you will see a final success screen similar to the one shown in Figure 26–19. Now you are ready to start using the **Genius** feature!

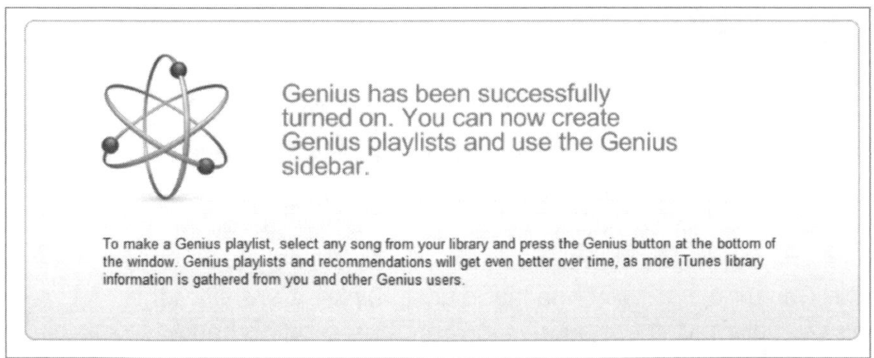


**Figure 26–19.** *The Genius feature successfully turned on in iTunes*

You can think of the Genius feature as your "personal shopper" who knows your tastes and makes good recommendations (**Genius** suggestions). You can also think of the **Genius** feature as your "personal DJ" who knows the music that goes well together and will create a great playlist for you (**Genius** playlists).

## Creating Genius Mixes and Playlists

To create a **Genius** mix and playlist, follow these steps.

1. Click a song in your library from that you would like to base the **Genius** mix and **Genius** playlist on.
2. Click the **Genius** button at the bottom of the **iTunes** screen, as shown in Figure 26–20.

**Figure 26–20.** *Start creating a Genius mix that can be saved as playlist*

3. After you click the **Genius** button, the screen will immediately change to show you the **Genius** mix of all songs that iTunes thinks fit or match the type of song you selected; these suggestions are based on computer algorithms and feedback from other iTunes users (see Figure 26–21). You may be surprised at the list of music or even artists that you would not normally put together into a play list.

**TIP: Genius** mixes and playlists provide a great way to keep your music library fresh, helping you to put together songs that go well together – often in combinations that you might not have thought about yourself.

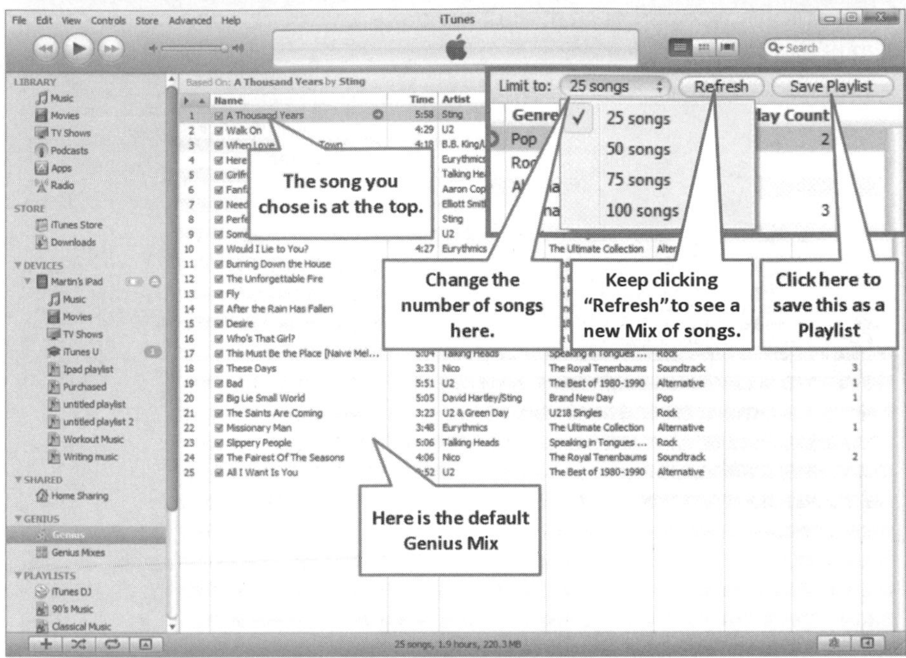


**Figure 26–21.** *The Genius Mix screen, showing options*

4. On the **Genius Mix** screen (see Figure 26–21), you have options to change to 25, 50, 75, or 100 songs. Click the **Refresh** button to see a new (usually slightly different) mix/playlist.

5. If you like the mix and want to save it as a Playlist, click the **Save Playlist** button in the upper right corner. Notice that the playlist is saved under the **Genius** section in the left column. The default name of the playlist is the name of the song you first clicked. You can change this name by double-clicking the playlist name. You will see it turn into editable text; from here, you can type a new name.

## The Genius Sidebar

The other thing the **Genius** sidebar can do for you is make suggestions of related songs or videos to purchase from the iTunes store based on the song or video you currently have highlighted from your library.

To view or hide the **Genius** sidebar, click the button in the lower left-hand corner of iTunes, as shown in Figure 26–22.

**Figure 26–22.** *The Genius sidebar, showing recommendations and similar songs*

Using the **Genius** sidebar, you can fill in your library with related songs or videos. If you get tired of the sidebar, then click the same button in the lower right corner to hide the **Genius** sidebar.

## Turn Off Genius

To turn off the **Genius** feature (which will disable the **Genius** sidebar) and remove all your **Genius** mixes and playlists, select **Store** from the iTunes menu, and then choose **Turn Off Genius**.

## Update Genius

If you have added a lot of music, videos, or other content to your iTunes library, periodically you will want to send an update to the **Genius** function in iTunes. To send this update, select **Store** from the iTunes menu, and then choose **Update Genius**.

# The Home Sharing Feature

If you have several people in your home that use iTunes, and they are all connected together on a home network, then the **Home Sharing** feature will help you share your content (music, videos and more) across your iTunes computers. Follow these steps to take advantage of the **Home Sharing** feature.

1. *Pick the account to use for the* ***Home Sharing*** *feature*: All computers connected to with the **Home Sharing** feature have to use the same iTunes account and password to log in and be connected. So usually, you will want to pick the account that has the most purchased content or the content you would like to share across all the computers.

**NOTE:** Even though you can see other peoples content and play it on iTunes on your computer, you need to import shared content into your own library if you want to enjoy it on your iPad (or iPod or iPhone). Keep in mind that shared content is for your personal enjoyment on your iTunes computer and your iPad.

2. Set up the **Home Sharing** feature and authorize each of the other computers: To get started with **Home Sharing,** as with the Genius feature, click **Home Sharing** under the **Shared** heading in the iTunes **Left** nav bar, as shown in Figure 26–23.

**NOTE:** Only rented movies purchased from iTunes are "DRM Protected." Such DRM Protected content cannot be synced to more than one mobile device (e.g. you cannot play this rented movie on another mobile device). Other purchased content videos and music can be authorized on up to five computers, and they can be synced to a large number of mobile devices as long as those mobile devices only sync to a single computer.

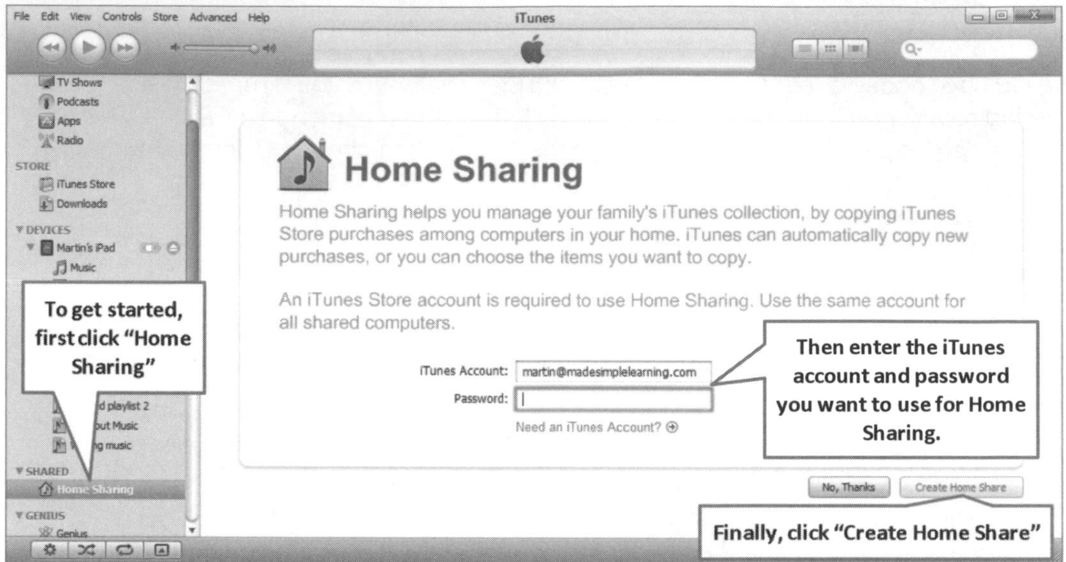


**Figure 26–23.** *Starting the Home Sharing feature*

Repeat this step on every computer you want to have access to your home shared content. Make sure to use the same iTunes account on every computer; this could be a little confusing at first, but it's important to use the same account. On the other computers, you will probably have to authorize the computer to play iTunes content. iTunes will notify you if you need to authorize the computer by popping up a window similar to the one shown below in Figure 26–24.

**NOTE:** There is a limit of up to five computer that can be authorized as **Home Sharing** computers.

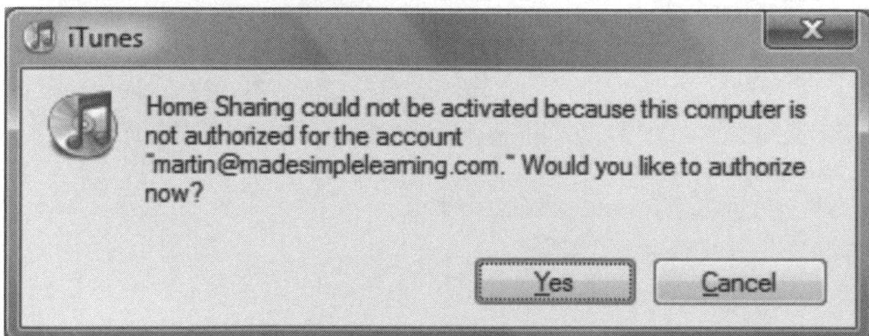


**Figure 26–24.** *A Home Sharing request for authorization*

Click **Yes** to continue. Once authorization is complete, you will see a screen showing how many of your five total authorizations have been used up (see Figure 26–25). To learn more about authorizing or deauthorizing computers, see the "Authorize and Deauthorize Computers" section later in this chapter.

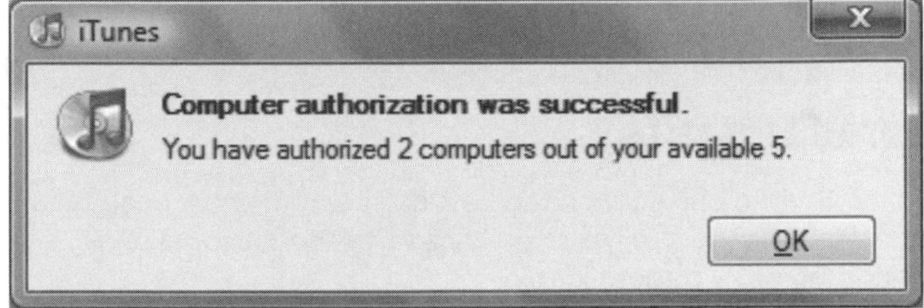


**Figure 26–25.** *A successful Home Sharing authorization*

3. *Start enjoying the shared content*: Once the **Home Sharing** feature is enabled on at least two computers, the second computer will then see the shared content underneath the **Shared** heading in the **Left** nav bar in iTunes. To start viewing, playing, and importing this shared content, click the shared library, as shown in Figure 26–26.

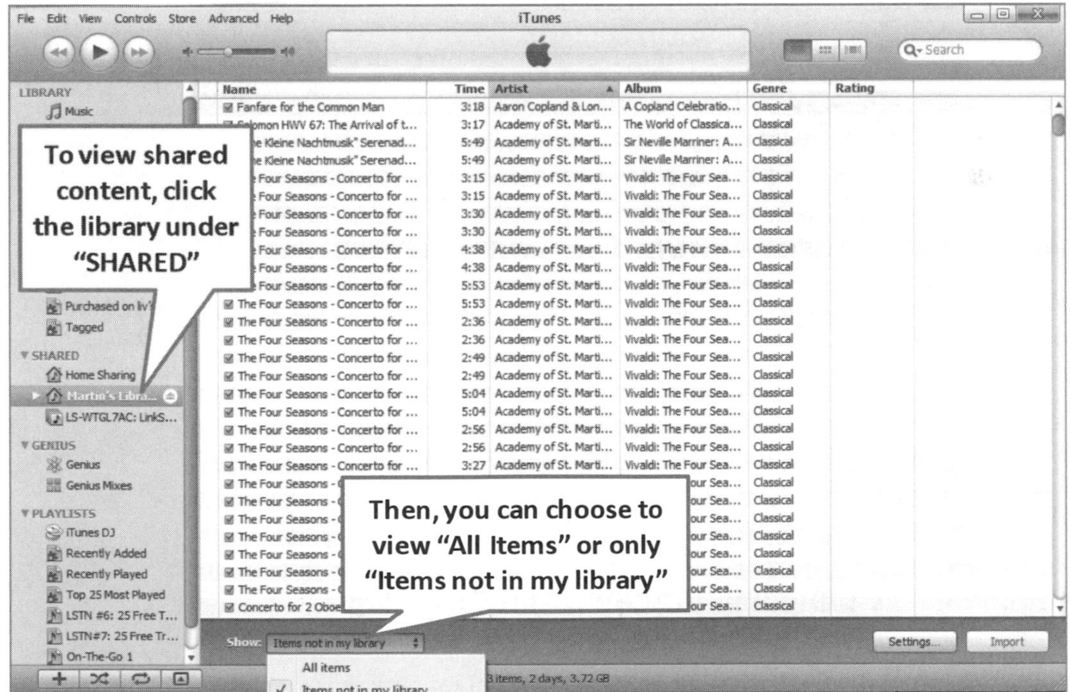


**Figure 26–26.** *Viewing a* ***Home Shared*** *library and filtering to view all items or those not in your own library*

## Filtering a Home Shared Library to Only Show Items Not in Your Library

Once you get up and running with a **Home Shared** library, notice that there is a switch in the bottom of the screen that allows you to show only those items that are not in your library (see Figure 26–26). This is a great way to quickly assess what you might need to add (i.e., "import") to your library from the shared library.

## Two Types of Shared Libraries

You will see two logos in the **Shared** category on the **Left** nav bar of iTunes. Each type of logo shows you whether the library is a fully shared library (the **House** logo) or a listen-only type of library (the **Stack of papers** icon).

|  Types of Shared Libraries | What this means |
| --- | --- |
| 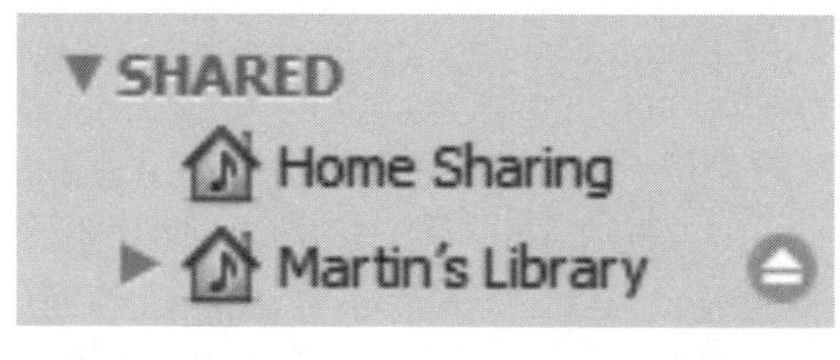  | (The **House** icon) "Martin's Library" is fully enabled for Home Sharing – you can view, listen, and import or add items from this library. |
|   | (The **Stack of papers** icon) "LS-WTGL7AC" is a listen-only and view-only library. You cannot import or add any songs from this library to your own library. |

## Importing Shared Content to Your Library

When you are viewing a **Home Shared** library, you can listen to anything in that library, as long as your computer has been authorized to do so. If you hit any authorization issues, please remember that in Chapter 3, '**Sync Your iPad with iTunes**' we show you how to authorize your computers for iTunes.

You can manually drag-and-drop content to your library, or you can set up the **Home Sharing** feature to automatically import all new purchases from the **Home Shared** iTunes account.

### Importing by Manually Dragging and Dropping

The drag-and-drop method for importing works well if you want to grab a few songs or videos from the shared library. Simply click the songs or videos to highlight them and drag them over to your library.

You can also click the songs/videos to highlight them and then click the **Import** button in the lower right corner to do the same thing.

## Automatic Import of New Purchases

If you want to automatically get all new purchases from the **Home Shared** iTunes account, follow these steps.

1. Click the **Home Sharing** library you would like to import from in the **Left** nav bar.
2. Click the **Settings** button in the lower right corner of the **iTunes** screen.

3. Now you will see a small window pop up similar to the one shown in Figure 26–27. Place a check next to the type of content you would like automatically transferred from the **Home Shared** library into your library. In Figure 26–27, all new music and movies purchased by the **Home Shared** iTunes account would automatically be imported and added to the iTunes account on this computer.
4. Click **OK** to save your Home Sharing settings.

**Figure 26–27.** *The Home Sharing Settings screen (automatically transfer purchases)*

# To Toggle Home Sharing Off or On

Once you have enabled the **Home Sharing** feature, you may want to turn it off. You do this by going to the iTunes **Advanced** menu and selecting **Turn Off Home Sharing**. To turn it back on, repeat this by going to the same **Advanced** menu and selecting **Turn On Home Sharing**.

## Troubleshooting Home Sharing

Sometime you will see a "Computer Not Authorized" error, even though your computer has already been authorized on the **Home Sharing** account. Usually this happens because the content (e.g., song or video) that you are trying to view or listen to from the **Home Sharing** account was purchased by an account other than the **Home Shared** iTunes account. To correct this problem, follow these steps.

1. Locate the person in your home who originally purchased this song.
2. Ask them to authorize your computer.
   (If you hit any authorization issues, then you'll find Chapter 3, '**Sync Your iPad with iTunes**' useful, where we show you how to authorize your computers for iTunes.)
3. Once your computer is authorized, you should be able to enjoy the music or video.

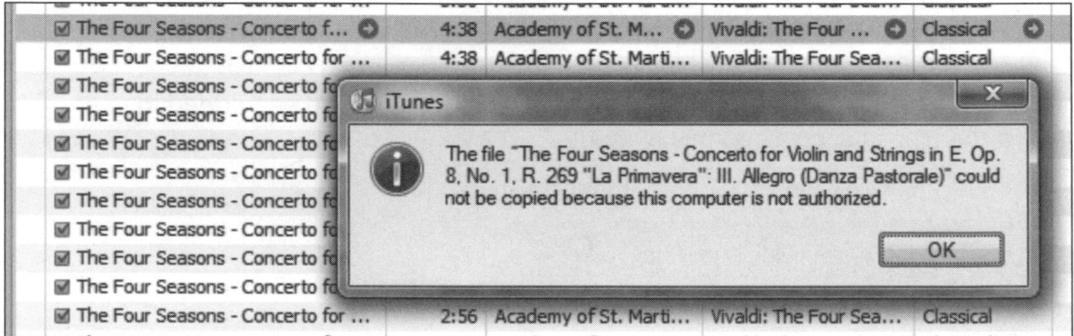


**Figure 26–28.** *The "not authorized" message*

# Create an iTunes Account

If you already have registered for an iTunes account using an Apple ID or AOL Screen Name, then you need to sign in (see the "Sign into the iTunes Store" section later in this chapter for information on how to do this).

If you want to buy or even download free songs, books, apps, videos, TV shows, and more, you will need to acquire them from the iTunes store. You can do so by following these steps.

Click the **Sign In** button in the upper right corner, as shown in Figure 26–29. If you do not yet have an iTunes account, then click the **Create New Account** button and follow the instructions to create your new account. If you already have an account, enter your Apple ID or AOL screen name and password, click the **Sign In** button, and skip ahead five or six pages to the section below called **Sign In to the iTunes Store**, where you'll go ahead and enter those details if you have them.

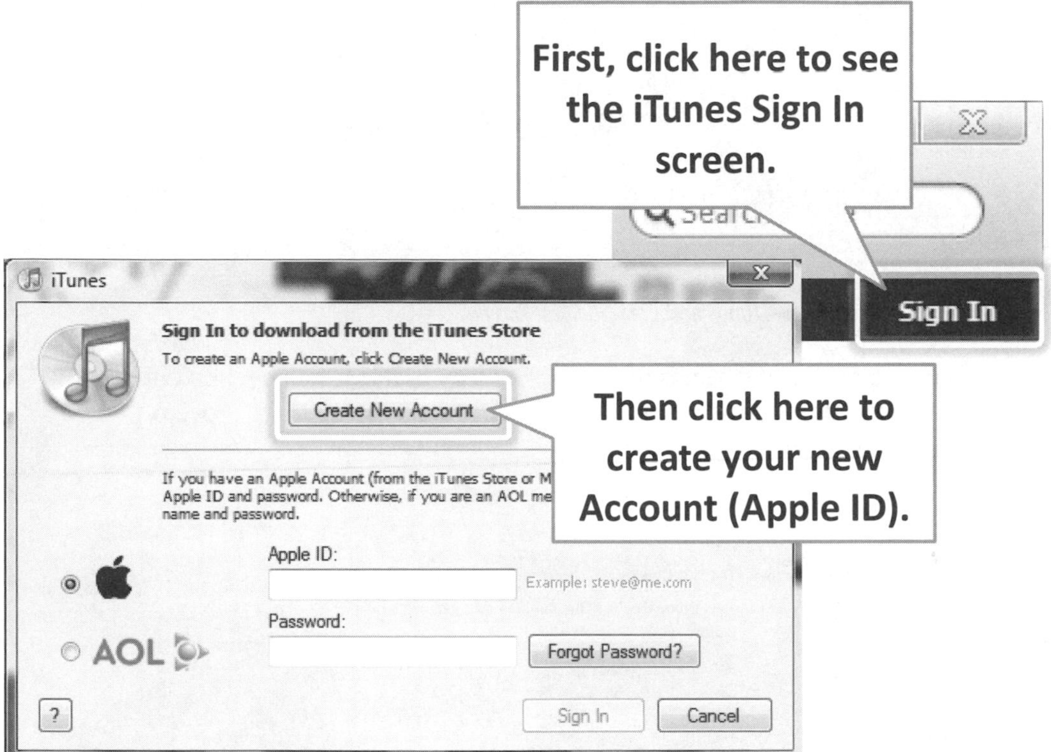


**Figure 26–29.** *The iTunes store Sign in screen – start creating a new account*

1. When you click the **Create New Account** button, you will see a screen similar to the one shown in Figure 26–30. Click **Continue** to move on.

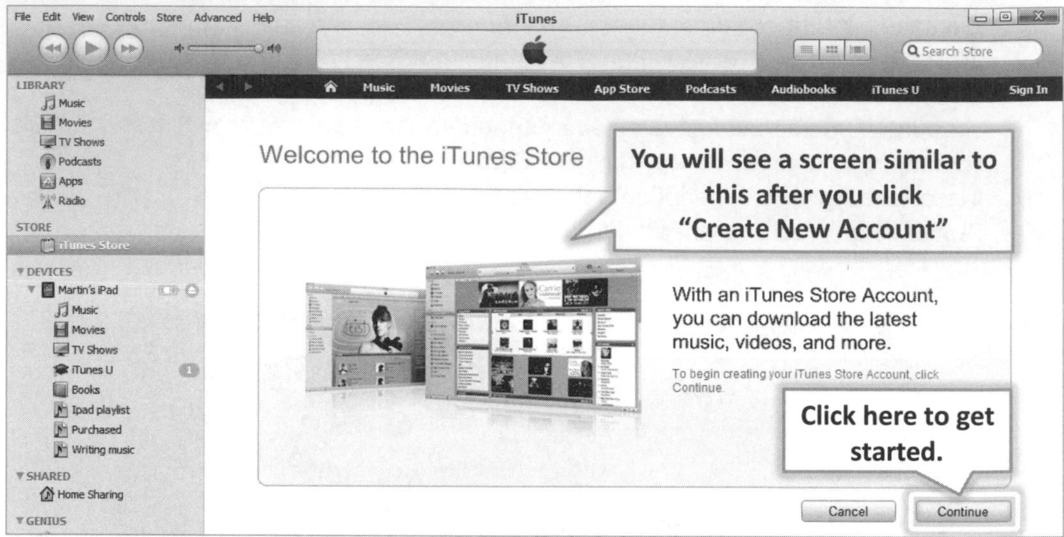


**Figure 26–30.** *Creating a new iTunes account – the first screen*

2. Read and accept the Terms and Conditions by clicking the checkbox at the bottom of this screen (see Figure 26–31). Click **Continue** to move on.

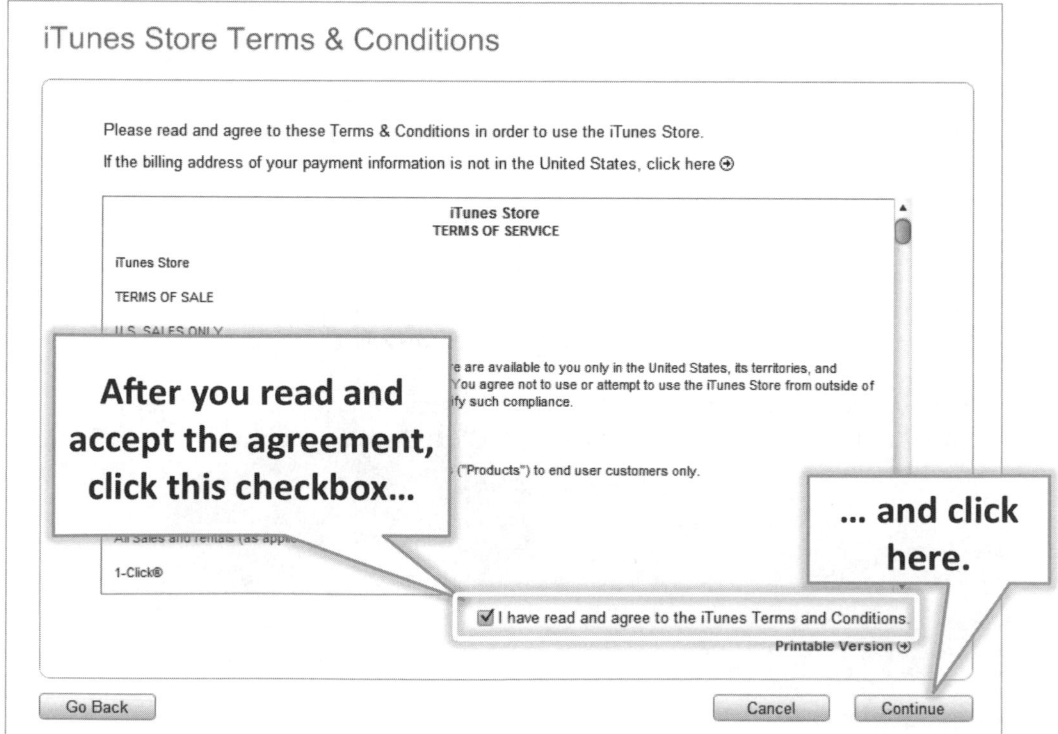


**Figure 26–31.** *Creating a new iTunes account – the Terms of Service screen*

3. On this next screen (see Figure 26–32), you set up your **Apple ID** (your login name for the iTunes store), your password, and your secret question and e-mail preferences. If you do not want e-mail notification, be sure to uncheck the boxes at the bottom of the page. Click **Continue** to move on.

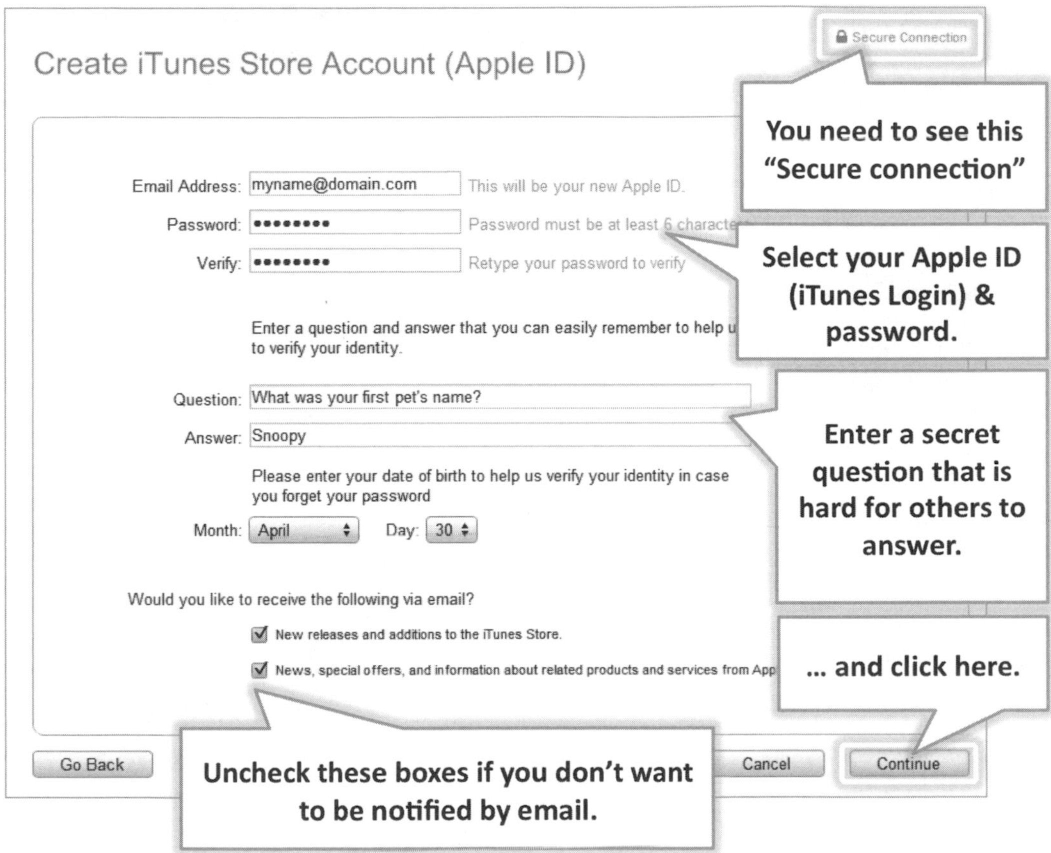


**Figure 26–32.** *Creating a new iTunes account – making an Apple ID account*

4. In the next screen (see Figure 26–33), you are asked to enter your billing information. Note that you can create a US-based account without billing information. Also, you can enter an iTunes gift card to receive credit, so you do not need to enter a credit card or PayPal account. This screen contains your preferred billing information, which will be used when you buy music, videos, and iPad apps (from the App Store on your iPad). Click **Continue** to move on. Please note that the contents of this screen may vary slightly, depending on the country in which you are located.

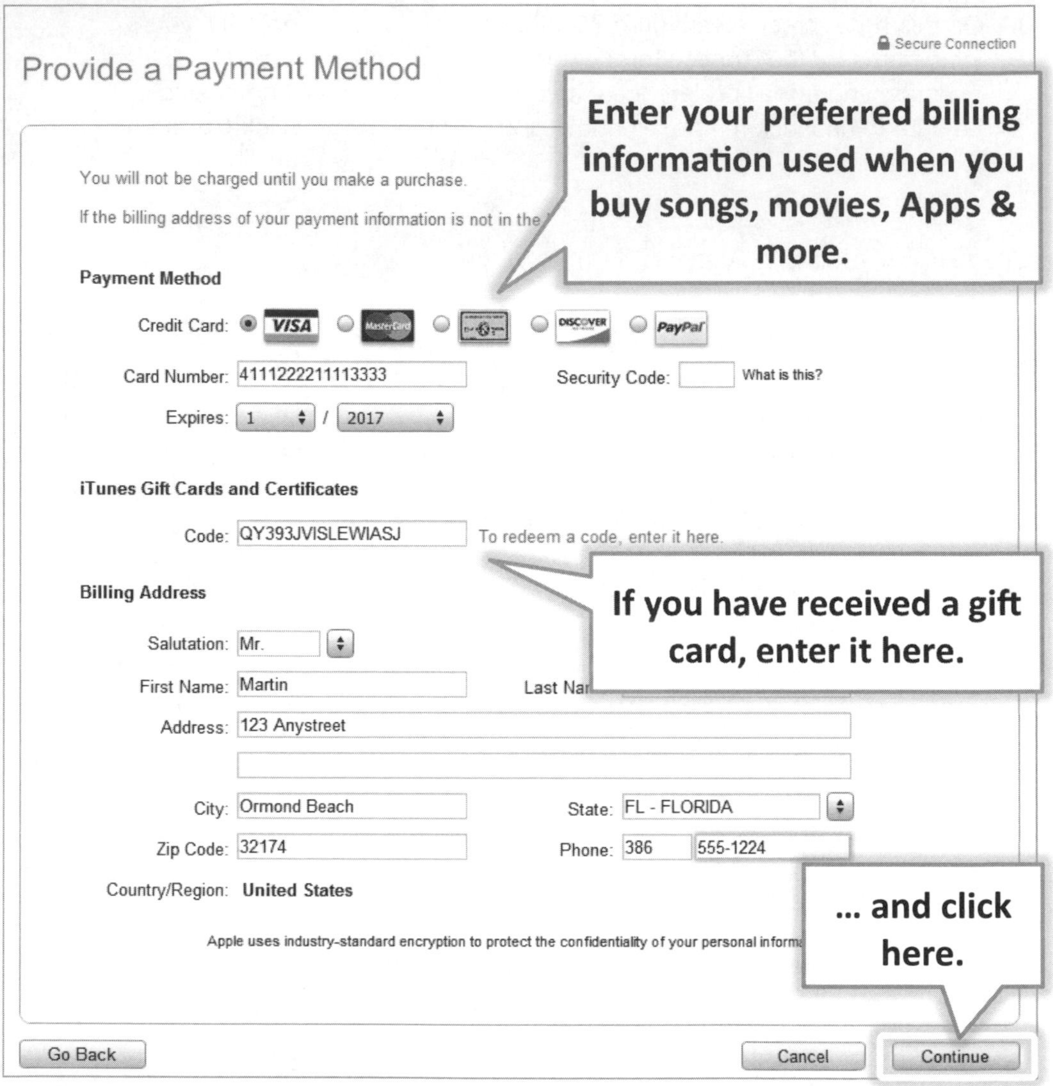

**Figure 26–33.** *Creating a new iTunes account – the Billing Information screen*

5. Depending on your locale, you may need to verify your county, province, or other local taxing authority (see Figure 26–34). Next, click **Done**.

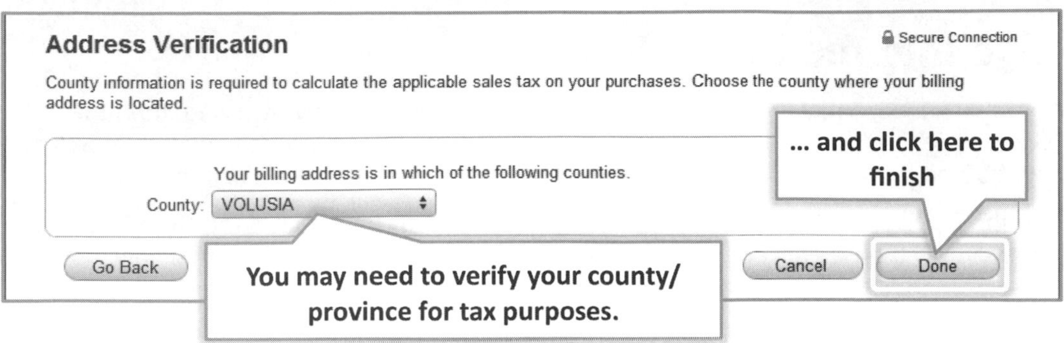


**Figure 26–34.** *Creating a new iTunes account – the Address Verification for Tax Purposes screen*

6. 7. Now you should see a screen similar to the one shown in Figure 26–35; this figure shows that you have correctly set up your iTunes account. Click **Done** to finish.

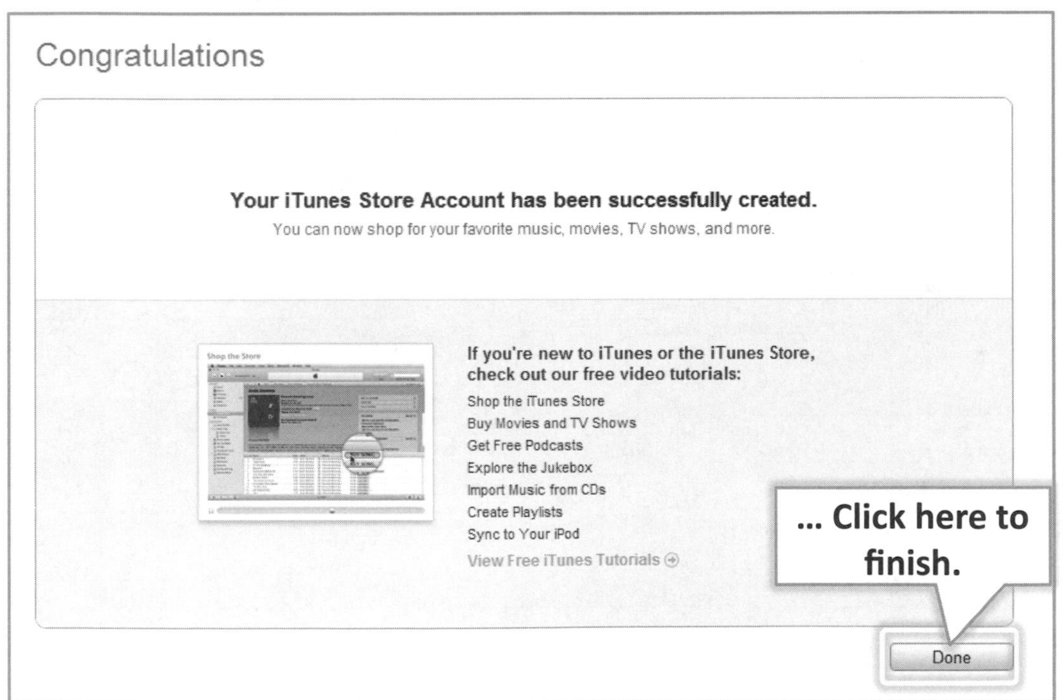


**Figure 26–35.** *Creating a new iTunes account – the Successful Completion screen*

## Sign Into the iTunes Store

If you've successfully created an iTunes account, or you already own one, then the wonders of the iTunes store are now yours to explore! The following sections show you most of the things you can do once you're signed in, but first – let's sign in.

To sign in, you first click on the iTunes **Sign In** button to take you to the **Sign In** screen, where you'll then be asked to enter your **Apple ID** and **Password.** Alternatively, you can enter your AOL Screen Name and Password:

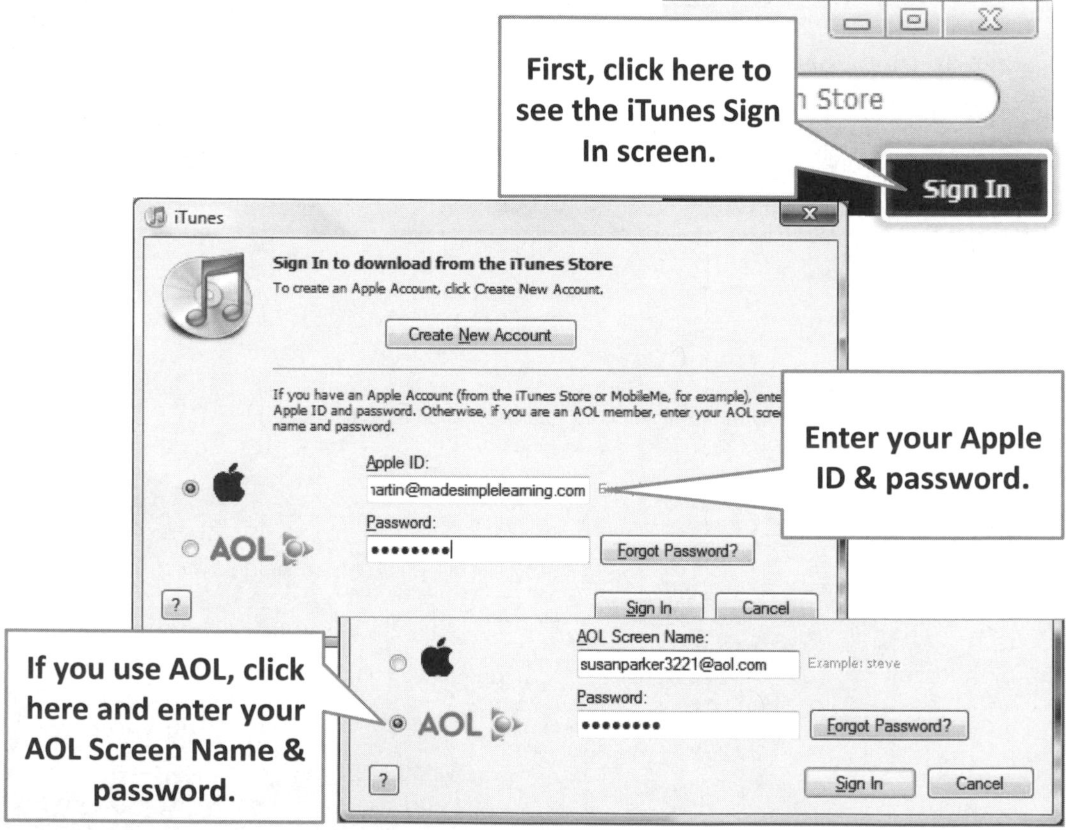


**Figure 26–36.** *Log in to iTunes using an Apple ID or an AOL screen name*

## How to Know If You're 'Logged In' to the Store

If you can see the **Sign In** button in the upper right corner of iTunes, you are not logged in.

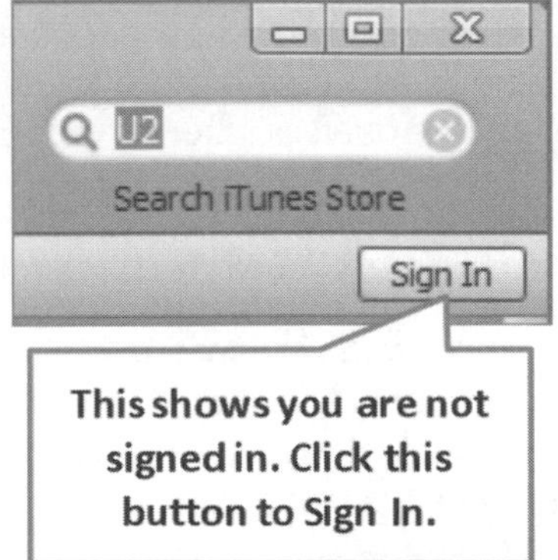
U2
Search iTunes Store
Sign In
This shows you are not signed in. Click this button to Sign In.

If you can see your Apple ID (usually your e-mail address) in the upper right corner instead of the **Sign In** button, then you are logged into the store.

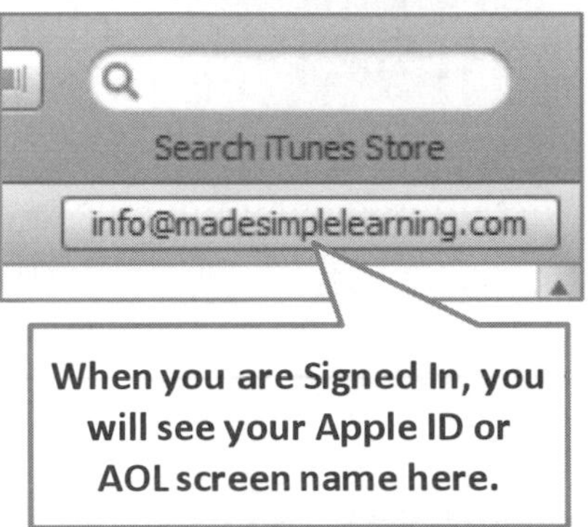
Search iTunes Store
info@madesimplelearning.com
When you are Signed In, you will see your Apple ID or AOL screen name here.

## Getting to the iTunes Store

You can always get back to the iTunes store by clicking the **iTunes Store** link under **Store** in the **Left** nav bar.

# Buy or Get Free Media from the iTunes Store

After signing in or creating a new account, you will be able to search the store for any artist, album, composer, or title.

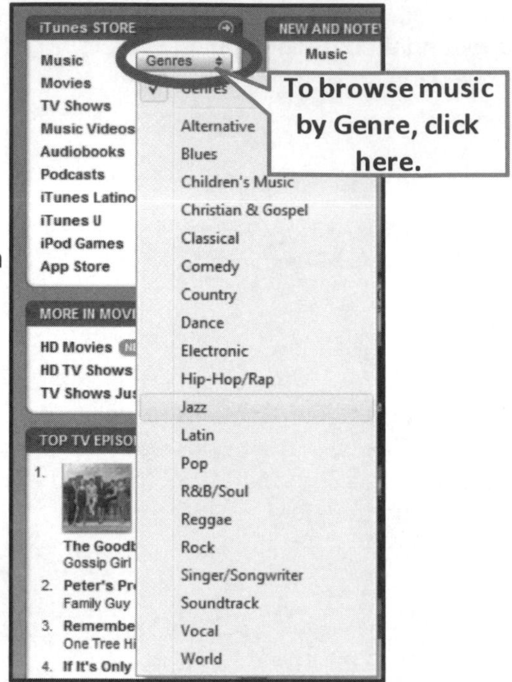


## Browse Store by Genre

If you prefer to browse by genre to locate songs, just click the **Genres** pull down button next to the **Music** option in the **iTunes Store** box. Select the genre you prefer.

The entire store will be tailored to show you songs from your selected genre.

To find all the songs by a particular artist, type that artist's name into the **Search** box in the upper right corner. You could also search by part or all of a particular song's name the same way. Once you press the **Enter** key, you will be presented with all the matching items from the iTunes store (see Figure 26–37).

You can then navigate around and purchase individual songs with the **Buy Song** buttons at the bottom.

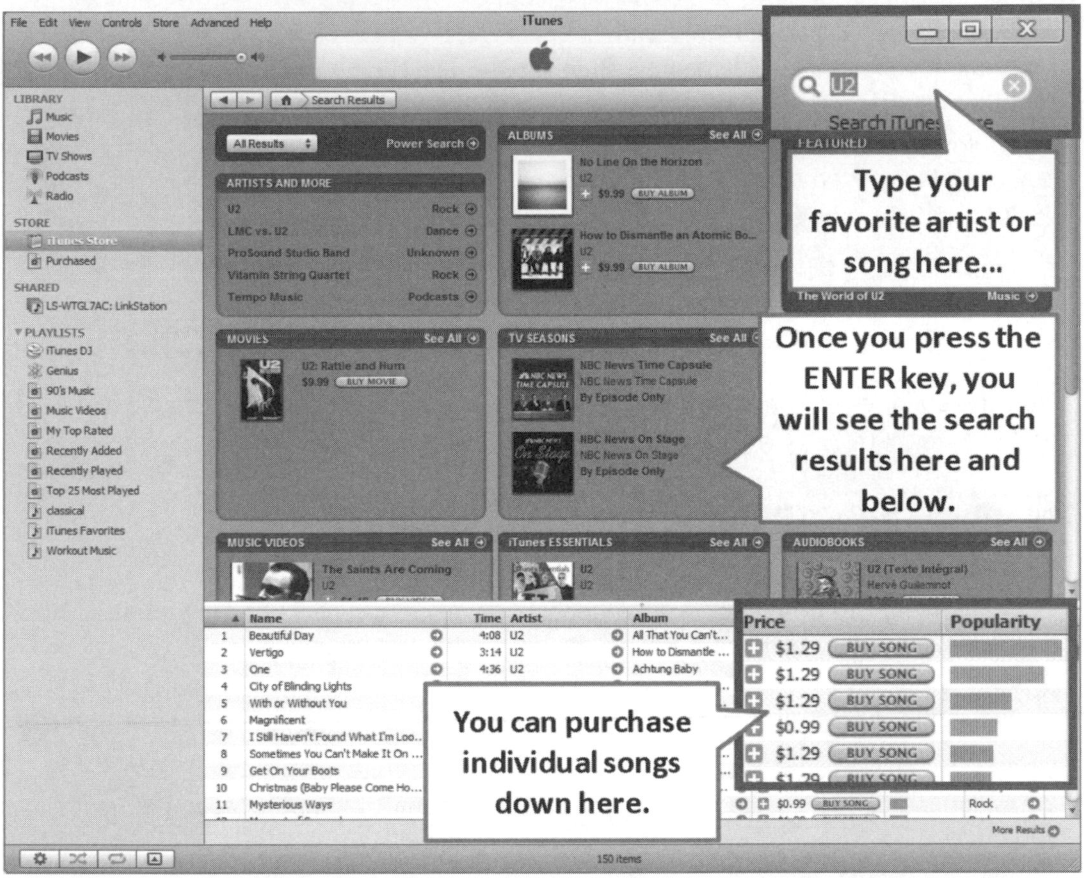

**Figure 26–37.** *Searching for and buying songs in the iTunes store*

After you click the **Buy Song** button, you will need to log in, unless you have previously instructed iTunes to keep you logged in for your purchases.

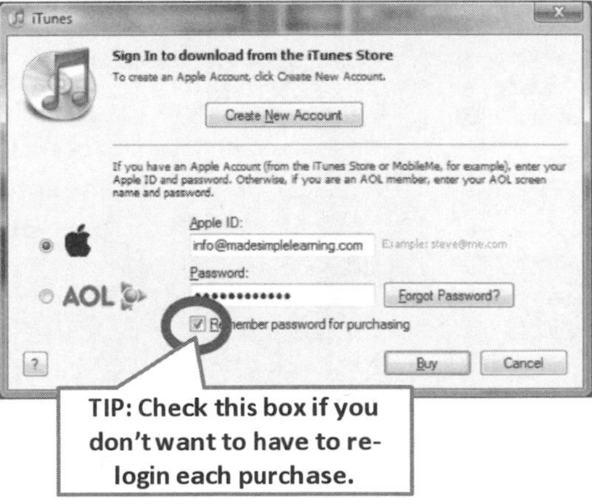


**CAUTION:** If you are at a public computer or are worried that anyone who might access your computer (e.g. your kids, spouse, or friends) would buy stuff without you knowing – then don't check the "Remember password for purchasing" box!

After you log in, you will see this warning message if you have just clicked the **Buy** button.

If you don't want to see this every time you buy something, then check the box at the bottom before clicking the **Buy** button.

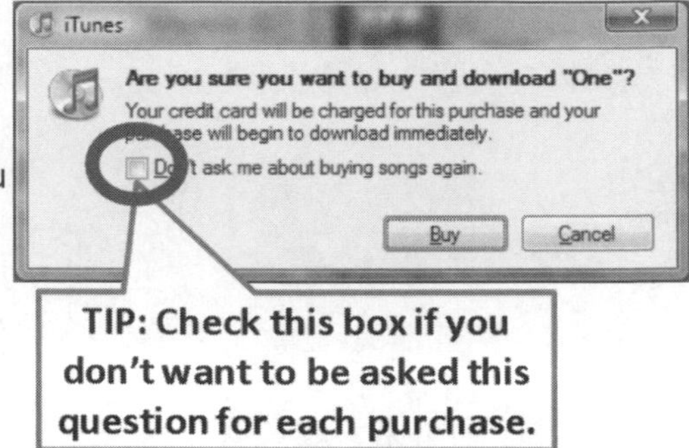


Now the song, video, or other item you purchased will be queued up to be downloaded to your local library in iTunes on your computer.

## Making Sure All Items Are Downloaded

After you purchase a song, video, app, or other item from the App Store – or if you have just authorized this computer on your account – you should click the **Downloads** link that appears under the **Store** category heading in the left column.

Any items currently being downloaded will show a status bar in the **Downloads** main window, showing "Done" when they are completely downloaded to your computer (see Figure 26–38).

You will need to see a status of "Done" before you can put the purchased item onto your iPad.

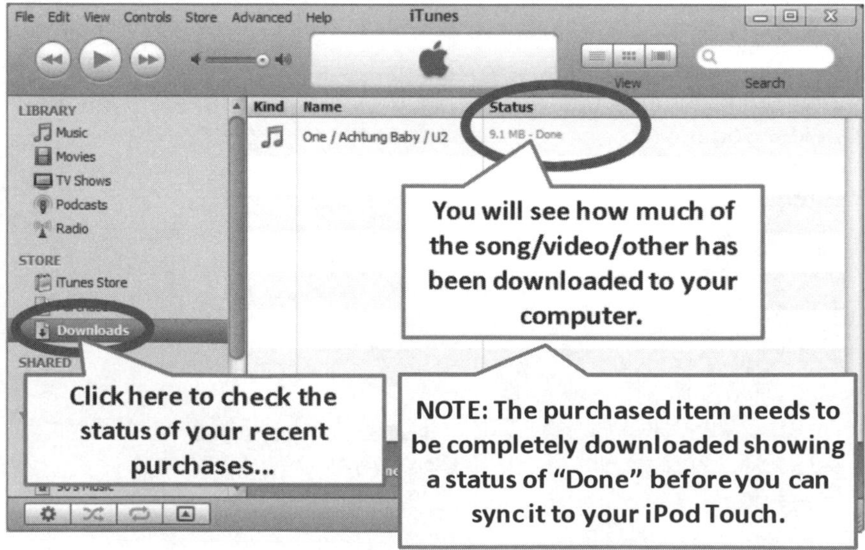


**Figure 26–38.** *The iTunes Store – see the status of items purchased or downloaded*

If you see a pop-up window asking if you want iTunes to download all your purchased items, then click **Yes**.

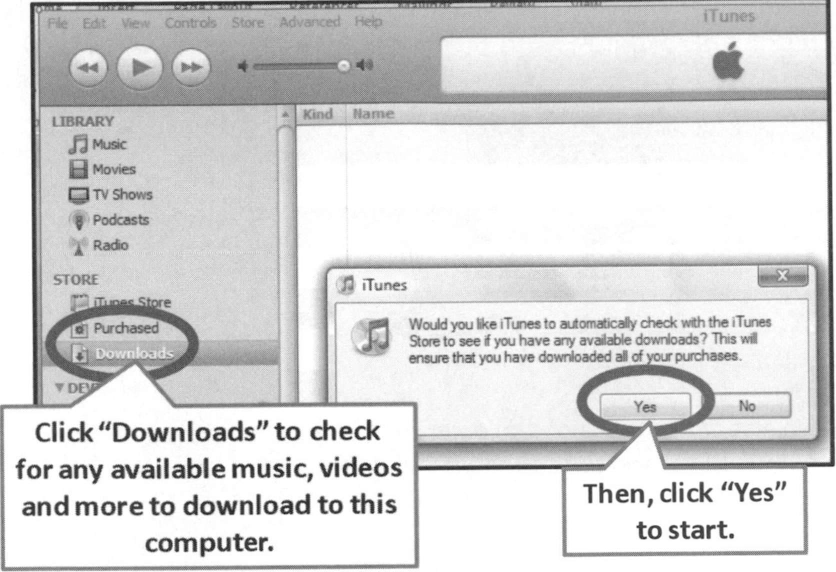


**Figure 26–39.** *iTunes asking to automatically check for downloaded items*

# Redeeming an iTunes Gift Card

At some point, you may receive an iTunes gift card; in this section. Follow these steps to learn how to add it to your iTunes account so you can buy music, videos, and more.

> **NOTE:** iTunes Gift Cards are country specific. In other words, a US gift card will only work for a US iTunes account.

1. Click the **iTunes Store** link in the **Left** nav bar.
2. Click the **Redeem** button in the **Quick Links** box on the right side.

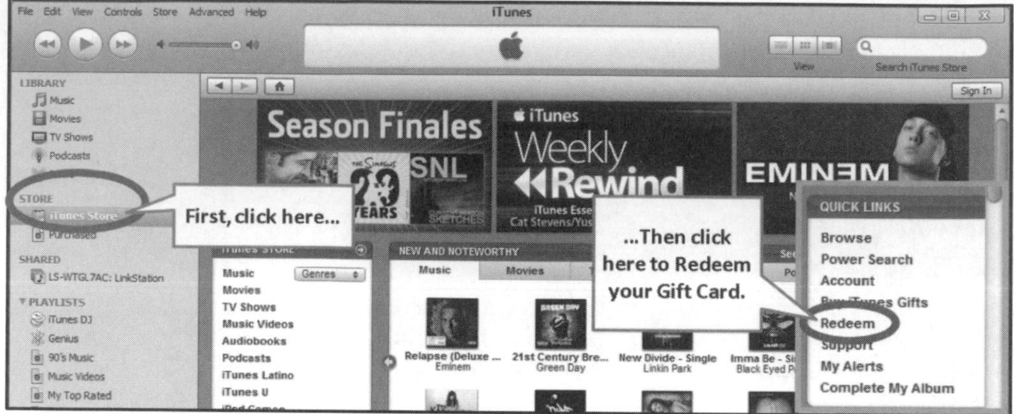


**Figure 26–40.** *Redeeming an iTunes gift card*

3. On the **Redeem** screen, you will need to enter the code from the back of the gift card. (You may need to scratch off the silver/gray covering to see the card's code.)

4. Click the **Redeem** button.

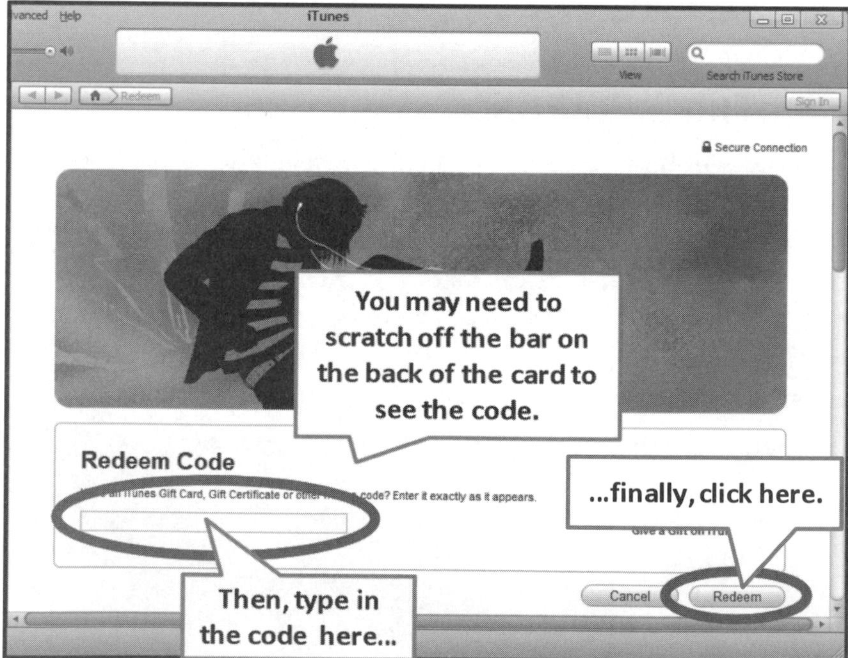


**Figure 26–41.** *The iTunes Redeem Gift Card screen.*

5. To verify that the gift card is being applied to the correct iTunes account, you will need to sign in or re-enter your password.
6. Click the **Sign In** or the **View Account** button (if you're already signed in).

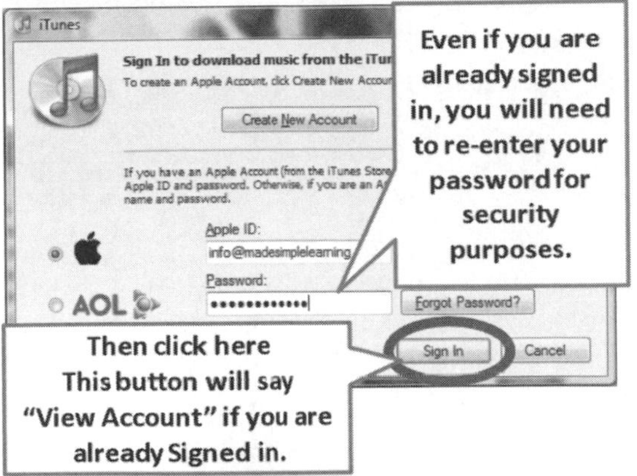
Even if you are already signed in, you will need to re-enter your password for security purposes.
Then click here
This button will say "View Account" if you are already Signed in.

7. Finally, when the gift card has been successfully applied to your account, you will see the total amount of the card in the upper right corner of the **iTunes** screen, right next to your sign-in name. Now you can use this gift card credit to buy stuff from iTunes.

# Import Music CDs

If you are of legal drinking age, then it's likely that you have a few music CDs in your home library. If you are over 40, that likelihood goes up to 100%. So... how do you get all your best CDs loaded onto your iPad? Accomplishing this is a two step process:

**Step 1** Load the CDs into iTunes,

**Step 2** Sync or manually transfer those CD songs to your iPad. Don't forget we show you how to Sync or Manually transfer with iTunes in Chapter 3 'Sync with iTunes'.

1. Need a quick reminder how to load a CD into iTunes? Here are the three steps to getting your lovely music from CDs into iTunes:Start up iTunes.
2. Insert the CD into your computer's CD drive. You may see a pop-up inside iTunes that asks if you would like to import the CD as shown.
3. Click **Yes** to import the CD.

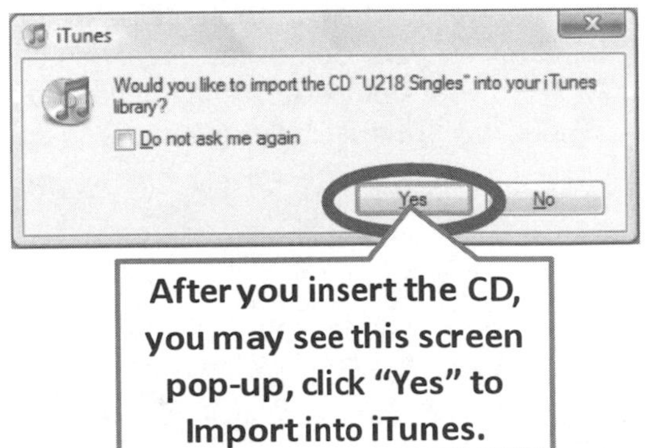
iTunes
Would you like to import the CD "U218 Singles" into your iTunes library?
Do not ask me again
Yes
No
After you insert the CD, you may see this screen pop-up, click "Yes" to Import into iTunes.

If you did not receive this pop-up window, then you can manually start the CD import into iTunes by clicking the **Import CD** button in the lower right corner. You will also notice that the CD has appeared under the **DEVICES** list in the left column (see Figure 26–42).

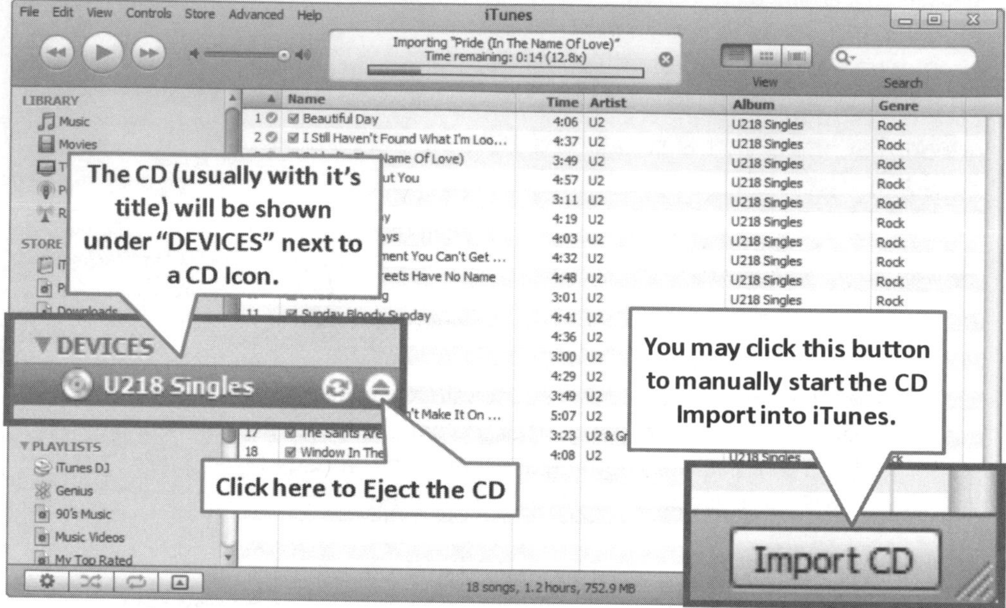


**Figure 26–42.** *Working with a music CD inside iTunes*

# Import Movies from DVDs

Some of the more recent DVDs and Blu-Rays you purchase have two versions of the movie: one for your DVD or Blu-Ray player and an extra digital copy that can be loaded automatically into iTunes.

Usually, you will see text on the outside of the DVD box that states there is an extra "Digital Copy for your Computer." You can check whether this copy exists by inserting the DVD into your computer's DVD drive and opening iTunes. If the digital copy exists, then iTunes will automatically detect it and ask if you would like to import the movie.

**CAUTION:** Most DVDs or Blu-Rays you own probably do not provide this extra digital version, which is meant to be loaded and watched on your computer or mobile devices. These standard DVDs or Blu-Rays are copy-protected and cannot normally be loaded into iTunes. However, if you do a web search for "load DVD into iTunes" you may find some software products that allow you to "rip" or "burn" your DVDs into iTunes. We strongly urge you to obey copyright laws; if you do this, you should only use the DVD on your own computer or iPad and never share the movie or otherwise violate the copyright agreement.

## Getting Album Artwork

iTunes may automatically get the album art for most songs and videos; however, if you need to manually retrieve this artwork, then follow these steps.

**NOTE:** You will need to already have an iTunes account and login for this to work correctly.

1. Start up iTunes.
2. Go to the **Advanced** menu.
3. Select **Get Album Artwork**.

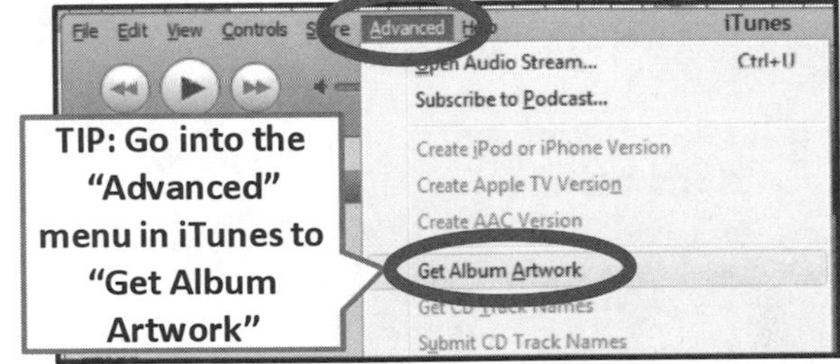


## Authorize and Deauthorize Computers to Play iTunes Media

You can authorize up to five different computers to play your iTunes media (e.g., music and movies).

Here's a question that you hear quite often: *Someone else has authorized my computer to play his songs; can I now load and listen to these "authorized songs" on my iPad?*

The short answer is "maybe."

The answer is "no" for all songs purchased on iTunes prior to January 2009 and for all songs purchased with DRM (*Digital Rights Management*) protection. These songs are tied specifically to one person's iPad/iPhone.

The answer is "yes" for all songs purchased without DRM Protection enabled. Early in 2009, iTunes announced that it would start selling some songs and videos without DRM Protection, which means they can be played on multiple iPods and iPads. Follow these steps to authorize or deauthorize a computer.

1. Start up iTunes.
2. To authorize a computer, go to the **Store** menu and select **Authorize Computer...**
3. To deauthorize a computer, go to the **Store** menu and select **Deauthorize Computer...**

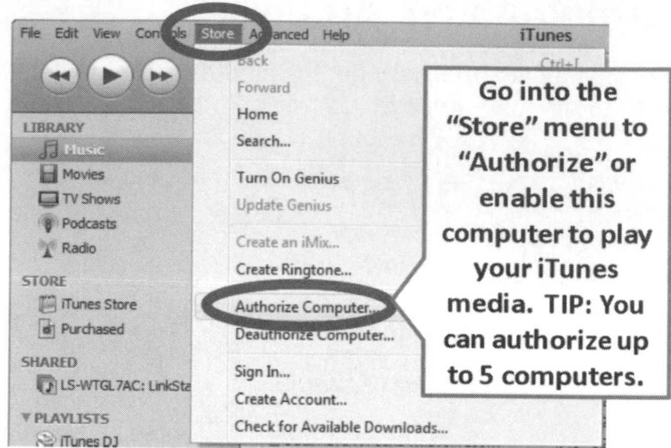

Go into the "Store" menu to "Authorize" or enable this computer to play your iTunes media. TIP: You can authorize up to 5 computers.


**NOTE:** You will need to know your iTunes or AOL username and password for this to work.

4. Enter your Apple ID or, if you prefer, click the radio button next to AOL and enter your **AOL** screen name and password.
5. Next, click the **Authorize** or **Deauthorize** button.

# Getting iTunes Software

If you have never installed iTunes before on your computer, you can download the software directly from the Apple's web site (`www.apple.com`) by following these steps.

1. Open a web browser on your computer, such as Safari, Internet Explorer, Chrome, or Firefox.
2. Type in this web address into the top of your browser: `www.itunes.com/download`, then press the **Enter** key. This web address works for both Windows PC and Mac users. If you typed the address correctly, then you will see a screen similar to the one shown in Figure 26–43.

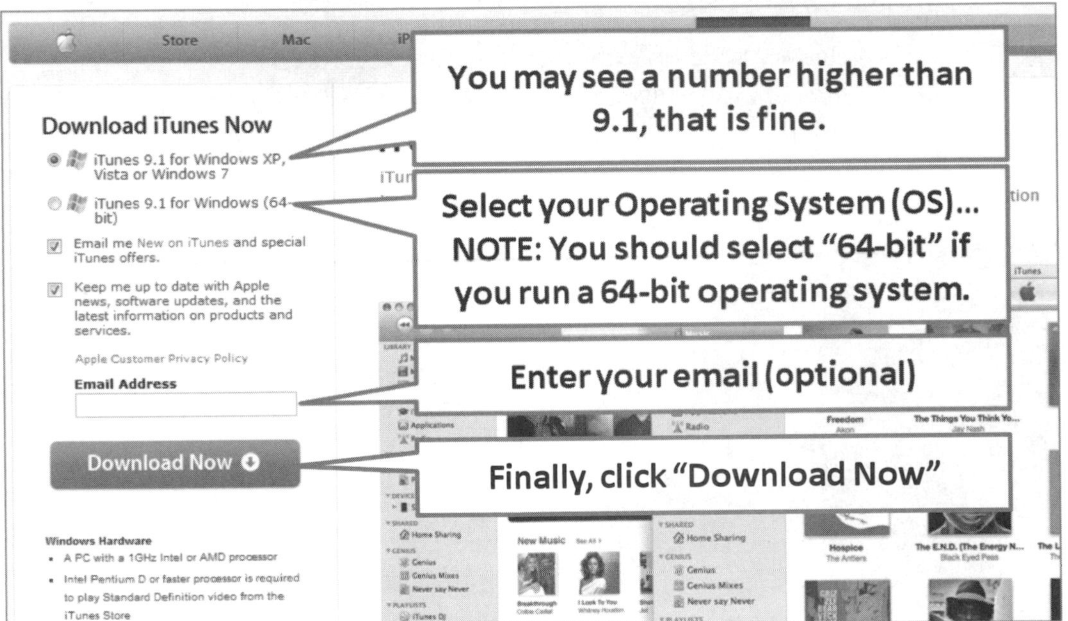


**Figure 26–43.** *The Apple iTunes software downloads web page*

3. On the web page shown in Figure 26–43, select the software that matches your computer's operating system, assuming that you're given a choice. (If you do not know what operating system version you are running, then please see the Determining Your Windows PC Computer Operating System sidebar later in this chapter for help.)

# Determining Your Windows or Mac Computer Operating System Version

The instructions in the sidebars that follows will help you determine what specific version the operating system your Windows- or Mac-based computer is running.

### Determining Your Computer's Windows Operating System

Follow these steps to determine which version of the Windows operating system your computer uses.

1. Click the **Start** button or the **Windows** logo in the lower left corner to bring up the **Start** menu.
2. Right-click **Computer** and select **Properties** from the pop-up menu.
3. You will then see a screen similar to the one shown in Figure 26–44. Notice that this computer is running "Windows Vista Home Premium" and that the System Type is a "64-Bit Operating System." So in the case of the iTunes download page, you would select "iTunes 9.1 for Windows (64-bit)."

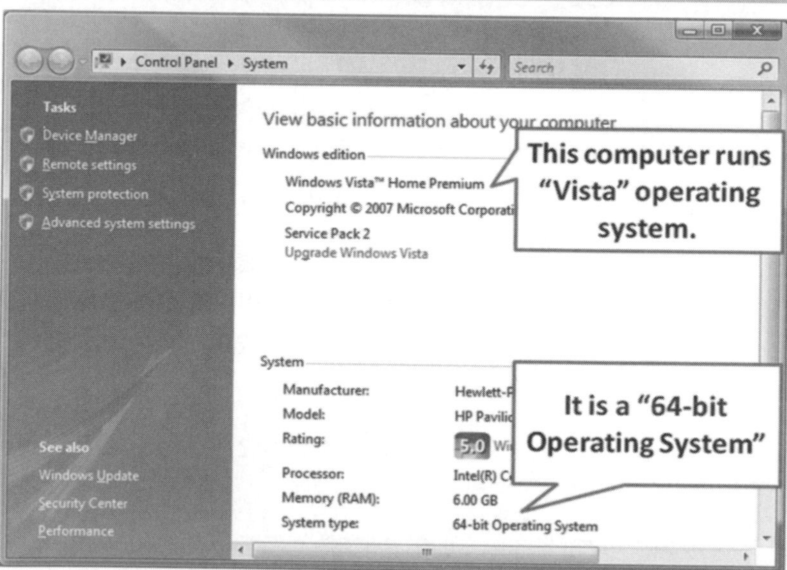


***Figure 26–44.*** *The Windows System properties page, which shows the operating system version*

**Determining Your Mac's Operating System**

Follow these steps to determine which version of the Mac operating system your computer uses.

1. Click the **Apple** logo in the upper right corner and select **About This Mac** from the menu.
2. You will then see a screen similar to the one shown in Figure 26–45. In this case, the Mac is running OS X Version 10.6.2. Note that you can check for updates by clicking the **Software Update** button.

**Figure 26–45.** *The About This Mac window, which shows the operating system version*

# How to Start the iTunes Installation

The next step is to install the iTunes application.

If you are on a Mac, then the install should start automatically; if it does not, then locate your downloads folder and double-click the file that says something like `iTunes_Install.dmg`. Then please skip further down this chapter to the Section called '**iTunes Installation Screens for a Mac**' where you'll find the step-by-step instructions.

If you're on a Windows PC, the steps you take to start the downloaded installation file vary a little, depending on your web browser. In the section that follows, we will walk you through the iTunes installation steps for four popular browsers: **Google Chrome**, **Microsoft Internet Explorer**, **Apple Safari**, and **Mozilla Firefox**.

If you are using **Google Chrome** browser, follow these steps to install iTunes on your Windows PC.

1. Click the **Save** button at the bottom of the web browser screen.

2. When the download is complete, double-click the `iTunesSetup.exe` or `iTunes64Setup.exe` shown at the bottom of the screen to start the iTunes installation.

> **CAUTION:** If you have previously downloaded an iTunes setup file, the more recently downloaded file name may have a number after it, such as `iTunes64Setup (1).exe`. You want to select the file with the highest number after it.

If you are using **Microsoft Internet Explorer** browser, follow these steps to install iTunes on your Windows PC.

1. Click the **Run** button in the **File Download-Security Warning** screen (see Figure 26–46).

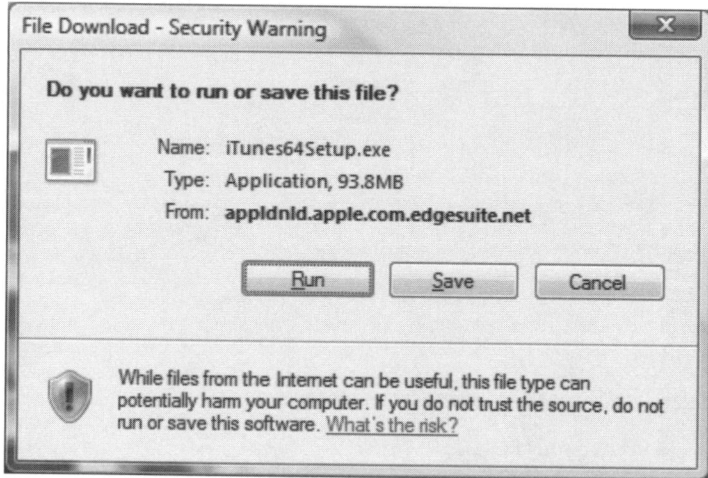


**Figure 26–46.** *The Internet Explorer File Download – Security Warning window*

2. To start the software installation of iTunes, you may need to answer another security question. If you see a window like the one shown in Figure 26–47, verify that the software name is "iTunes" and the Publisher is "Apple Inc."

3. Click the **Run** button.

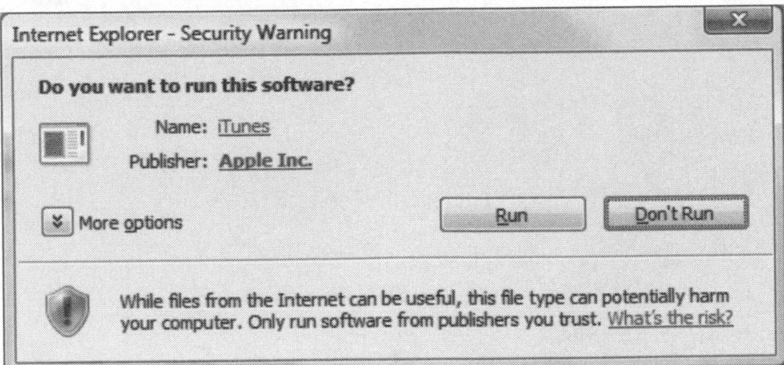


**Figure 26–47.** *The Internet Explorer File – Security Warning Pop-Up window*

If you are using **Apple Safari** browser on a Windows PC**,** follow these steps to install iTunes.

1. Click the **Run** button in the **File Download – Security Warning** pop-up window (see Figure 26–48).

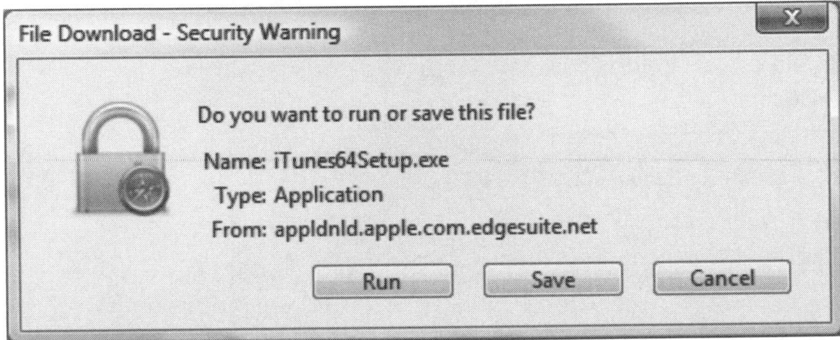


**Figure 26–48.** *The Apple Safari File Download – Security Warning window*

2. To start the installation of iTunes, you may need to answer another security question. If you see a window like the one shown in Figure 26–49, verify that the software name is `iTunesSetup.exe` or `iTunes64Setup.exe` and that the publisher is "Apple Inc."

3. Click the **Run** button.

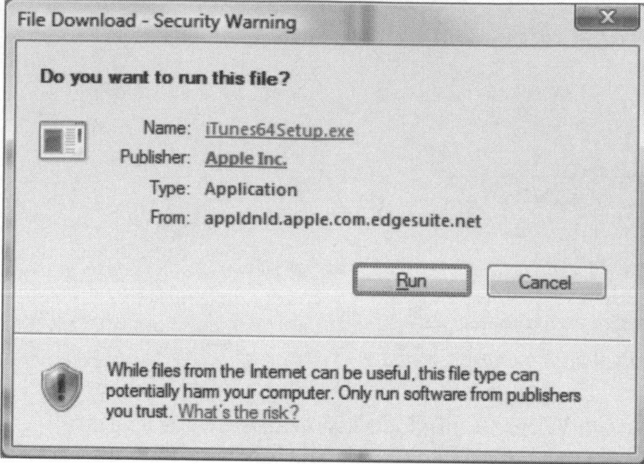


**Figure 26–49.** *The Apple Safari File Download-Security Warning window*

If you are using the **Firefox** browser, follow these steps to install iTunes on your Windows PC.

1. Click the **Save File** button in the `Opening iTunes.exe` pop-up window (see Figure 26–50).

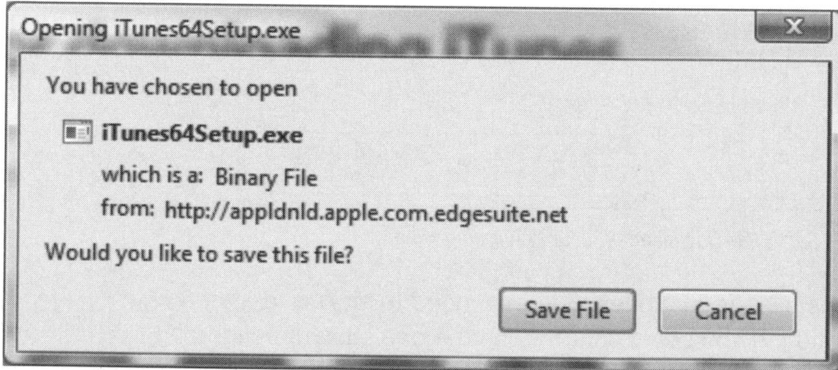


**Figure 26–50.** *The Firefox Opening File Pop-Up Window.*

2. To start the installation of iTunes, double-click on the iTunes setup file (it could be called `iTunesSetup.exe` or `iTunes64Setup.exe`) in the **Downloads** pop-up window, as shown in Figure 26–51.

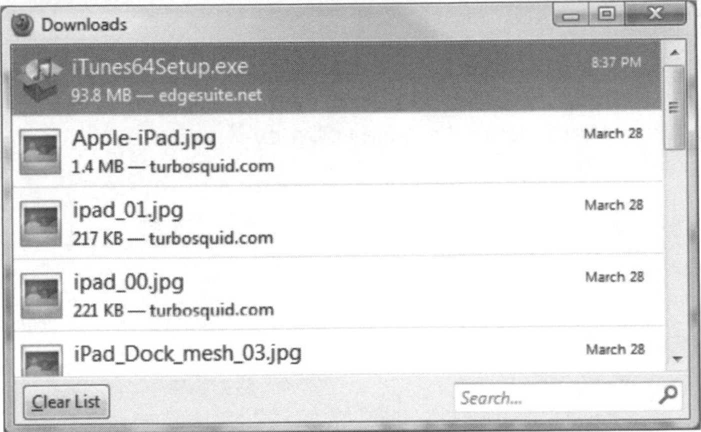


**Figure 26–51.** *The Firefox opening file pop-up window*

# The iTunes Installation Screens for a Windows PC

Now that you have successfully downloaded and started the installation file, you should see a screen similar to the one shown in Figure 26–52. This screen will have a main heading that says something like, "Welcome to the iTunes Installer." Follow these steps to complete the installation process.

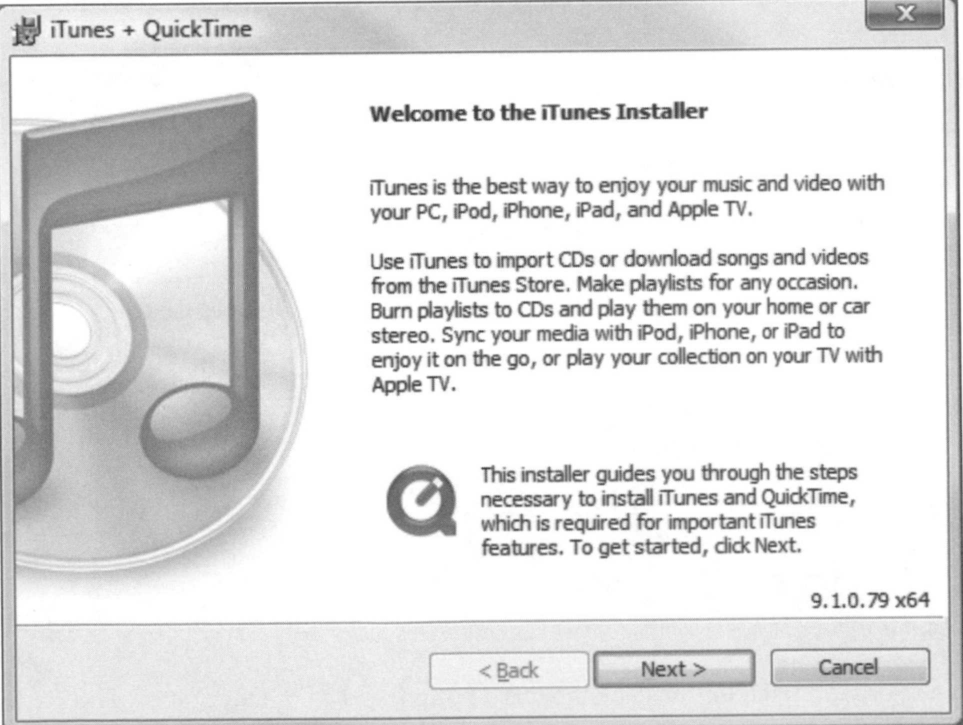

**Figure 26–52.** *The iTunes software installation first screen (Windows)*

1. Click the **Next>** button and follow the steps to get iTunes installed. If you see an error message about 32-bit or 64-bit versions, as shown below, please read the caution that follows because you may want to download another version of iTunes.

**CAUTION:** If you see a 64-bit warning message similar to this one, then please click the **No** button and return to the Apple site to download the 64-bit edition of iTunes better suited for your computer. You can grab the file at this URL: `www.itunes.com/download`.

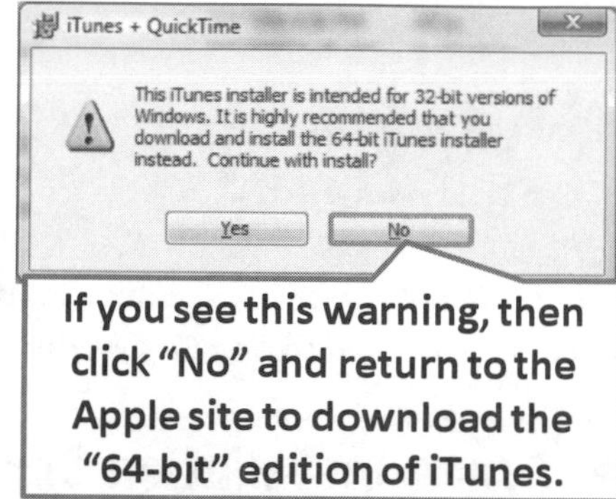


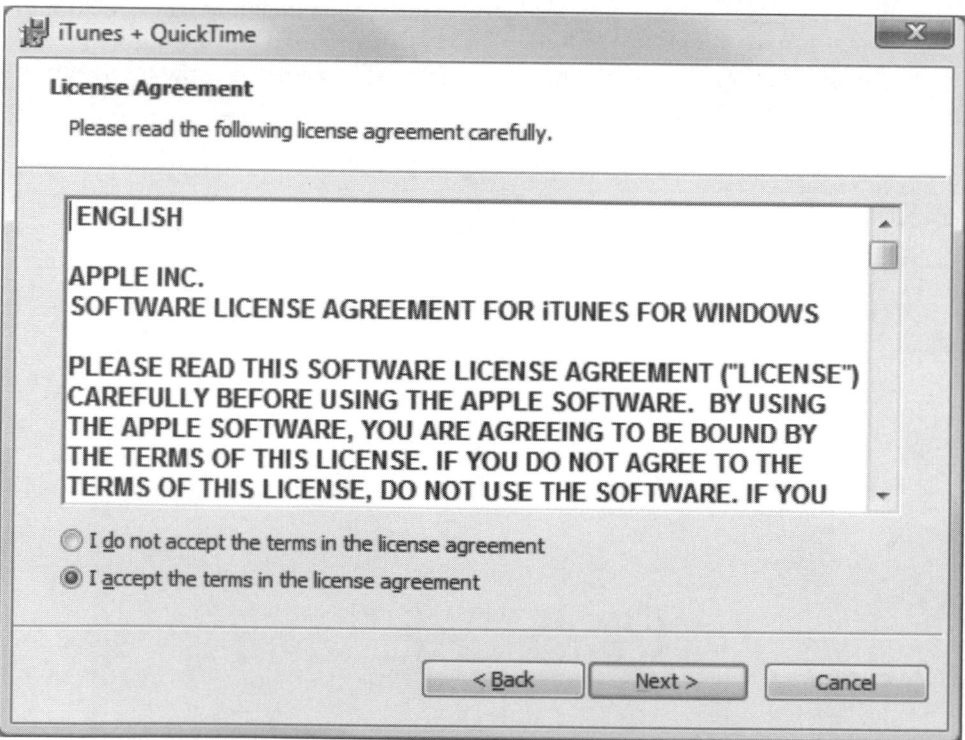


**Figure 26–53.** *The iTunes software installation software license screen (Windows).*

2. If you agree with the terms, click the radio button next to "I accept the terms in the license agreement" and click the **Next>** button.

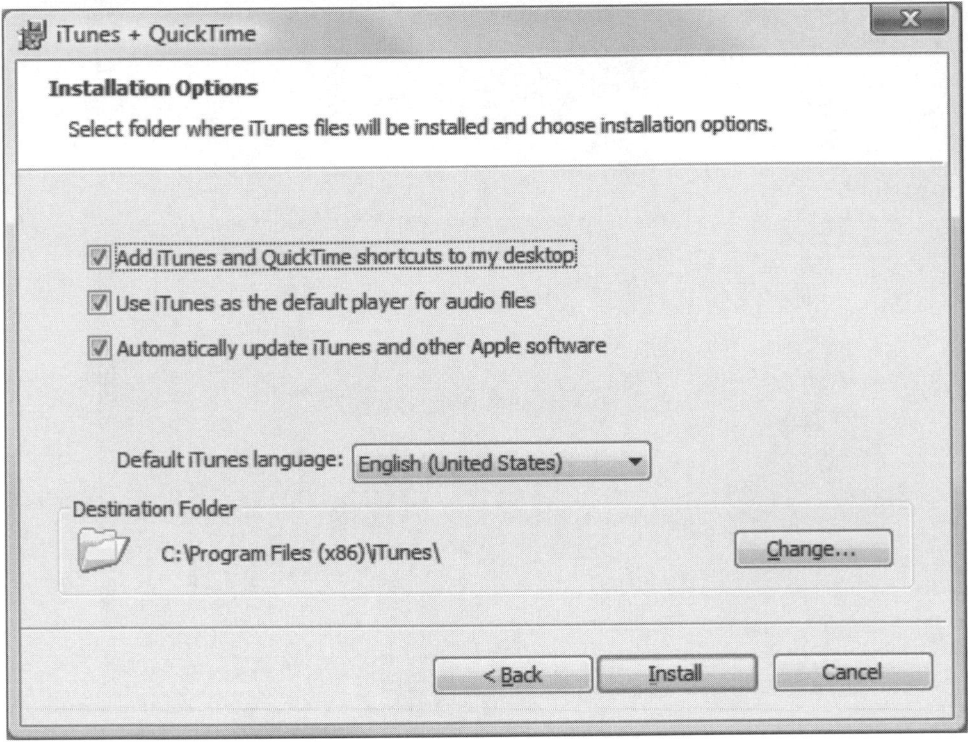


**Figure 26–54.** *The iTunes software Installation Options screen (Windows)*

3. Figure 26–54 is the final selection screen before the installation starts. Usually you can leave all the defaults alone, unless you have a specific reason to change them.
4. Click the **Install** button to start the installation.

**NOTE:** If you have Microsoft Outlook or another e-mail program running, you will be asked to stop it or re-start it after the installation completes. We recommend stopping Outlook before installing iTunes.

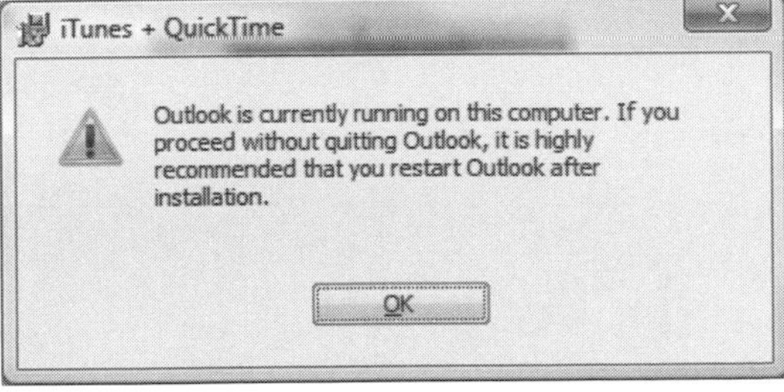


5. Once you have successfully installed iTunes, you will see a screen similar to the one shown in Figure 26–55. If you want to start up iTunes automatically, leave the box checked (again, see Figure 26–55).

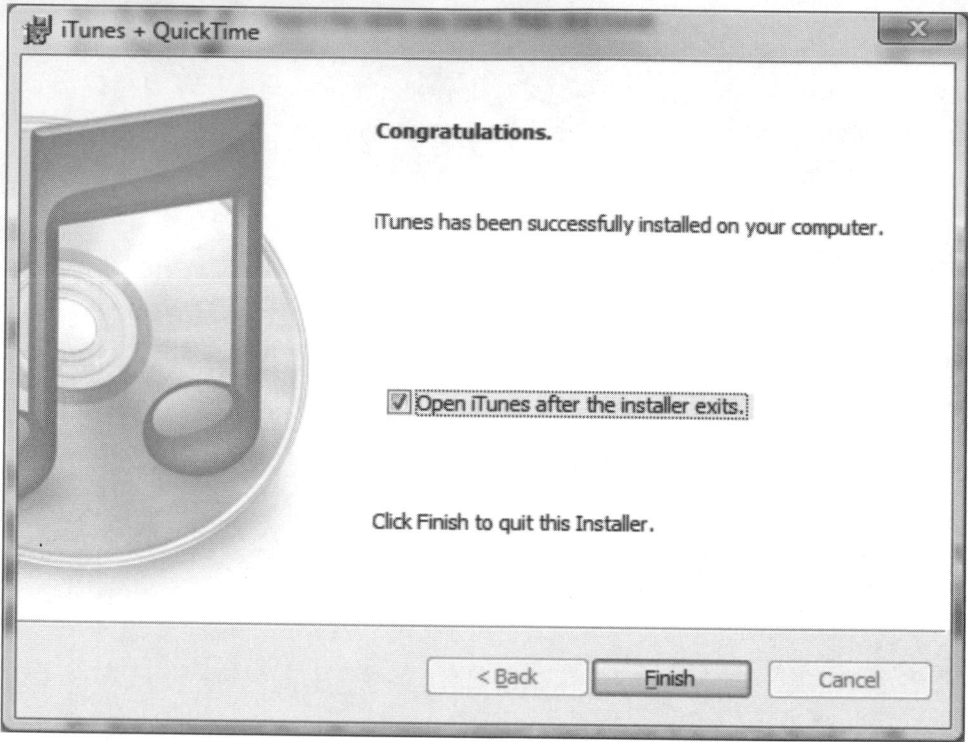


**Figure 26–55.** *The iTunes software installation final success screen (Windows)*

6. Click the **Finish** button to close the installer.

## iTunes Installation Screens for a Mac

Now that you have successfully downloaded and started the installation file on your Mac, you should see a screen similar to the one shown in Figure 26–56. This screen will have a main heading that says something like, "Welcome to the iTunes Installer." Follow these steps to complete the installation process.

**Figure 26–56.** *The iTunes software installation wizard's first screen (Apple Mac)*

1. Click the **Continue** button to bring up the **What's new** screen.

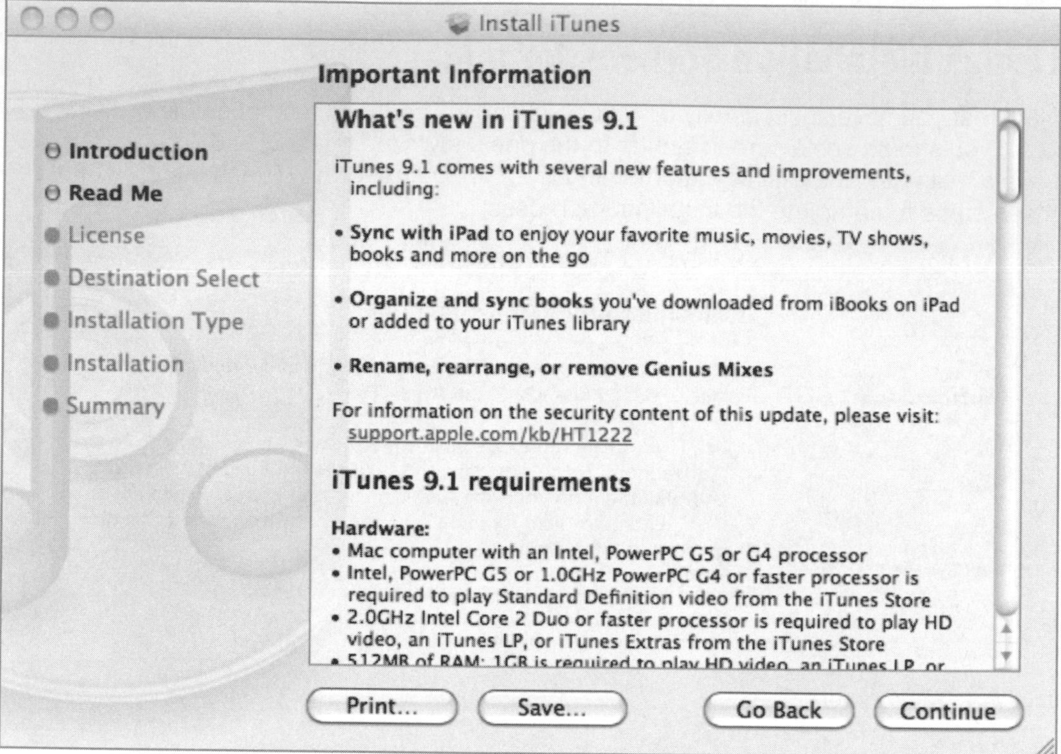


**Figure 26–57.** *The iTunes software installation What's new screen (Apple Mac)*

2. You can scroll down to check out what's new in the latest version of iTunes, as well as to see the system requirements (see Figure 26–58). Click **Continue** to move on.

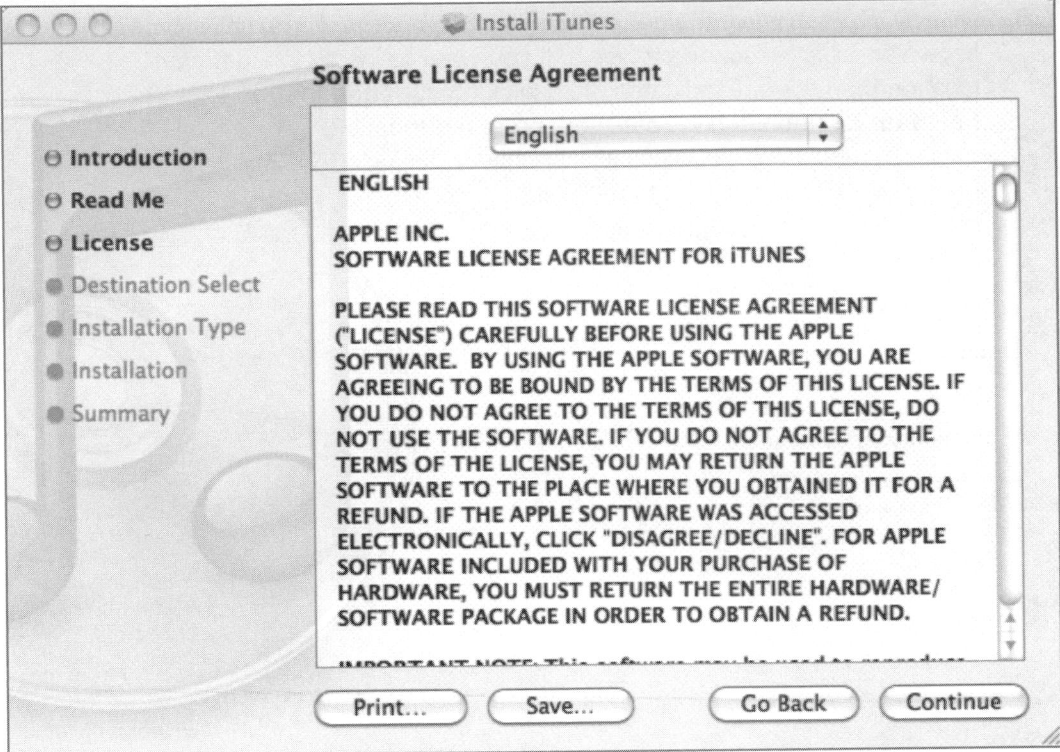


**Figure 26–58.** *The iTunes software installation Software License Agreement screen (Apple Mac)*

3. Read the license agreement and click the **Continue** button to bring up the screen that lets you accept or reject license agreement (see Figure 26–59).

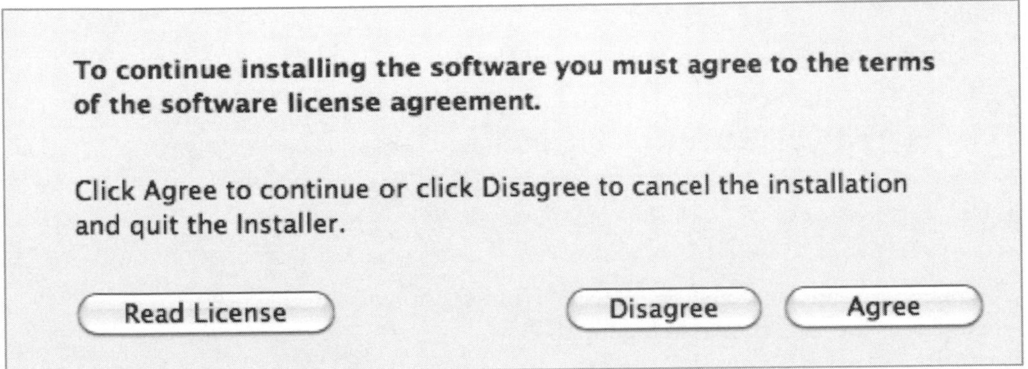


**Figure 26–59.** *The iTunes software installation agree to software license screen (Apple Mac)*

4. Now you need to confirm that you agree with the License by clicking the **Agree** button. Agreeing to the license terms bring up the final selection screen (see Figure 26–60).

5. Usually you can leave the default location information alone, unless you have a specific reason to change it. If you want to install to a different location than the one indicated, then click the **Change Install Location...** button and indicate your preferred location.

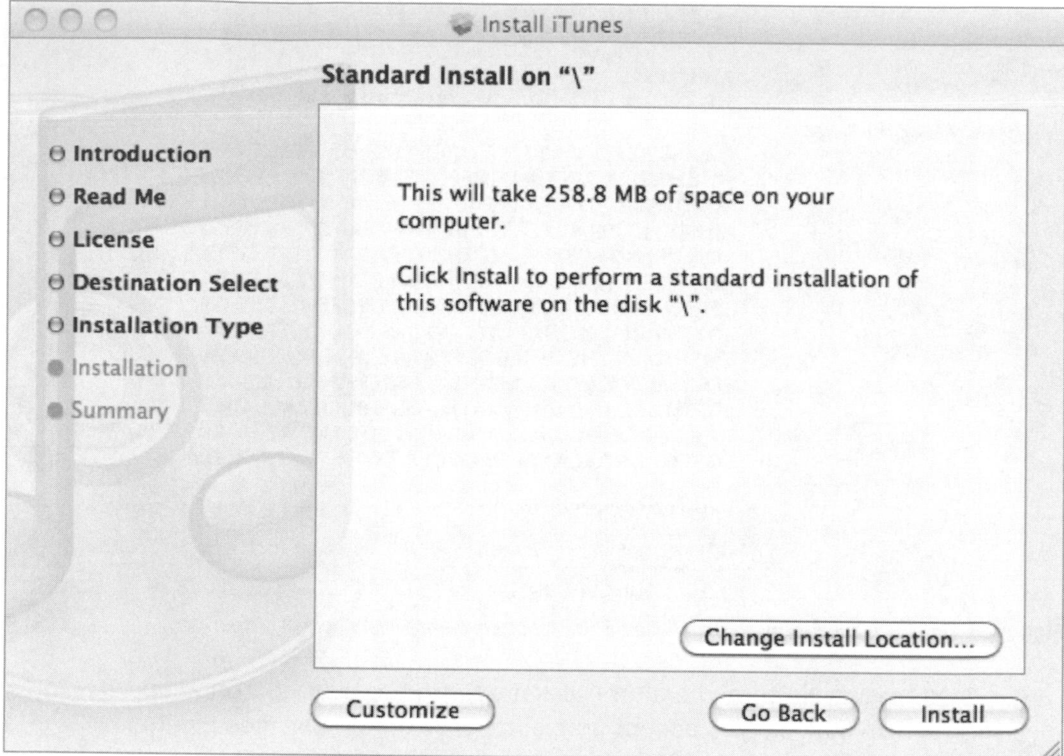


**Figure 26–60.** *iTunes software installation location screen (Apple Mac)*

6. Click the **Install** button to start the installation.

> **NOTE:** If you have iTunes, **Entourage**, **iCal** or another e-mail program running, you may be asked to stop it or re-start it after the installation completes. We recommend stopping your e-mail client before installing iTunes.

7. Once you have successfully installed iTunes, you will see a screen similar to the one shown in Figure 26–61.

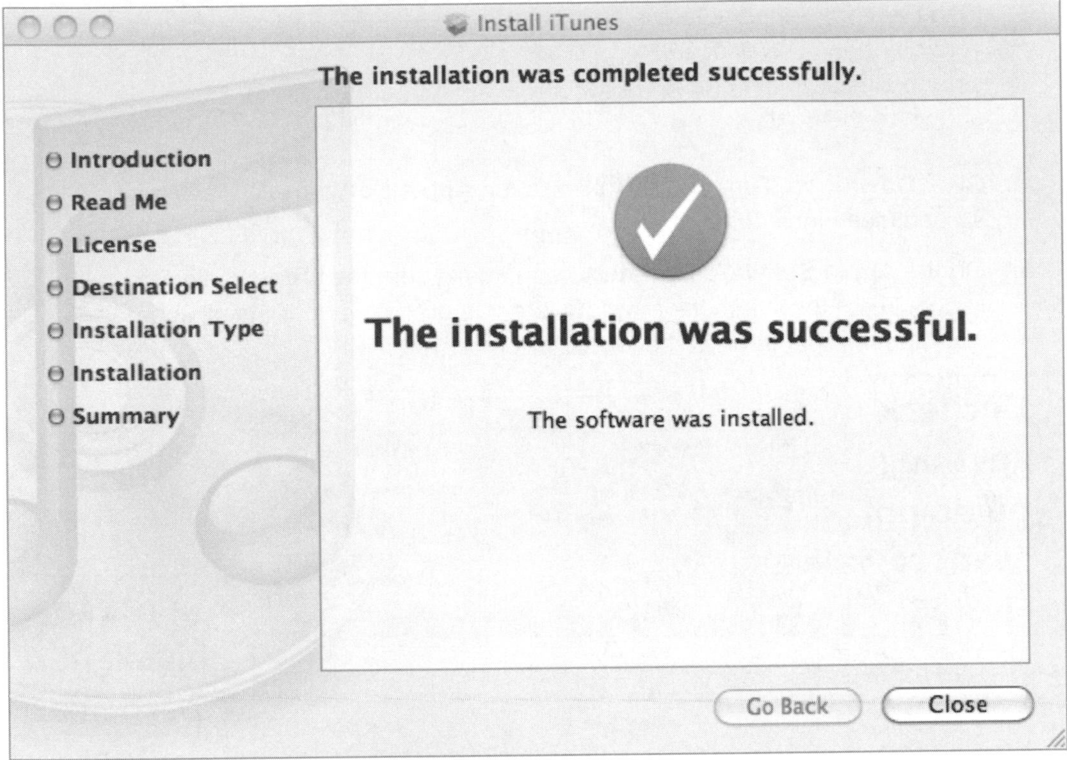


**Figure 26–61.** The *iTunes software installation final success screen*

8. Click the **Close** button to close the installer.

# Getting iTunes Updated

If you have previously installed iTunes on your computer, you should check for an updated version. Follow these steps to update your iTunes software.

> **NOTE:** You will need iTunes version 9.1 or higher in order to sync with your iPad. Next, we will show you how to make sure you have the most up-to-date version of iTunes on your computer.

1. Start the iTunes software.

2. Go to the **Help** menu (on your PC) or iTunes (the left-most menu on the Mac) and then select **Check for Updates**.

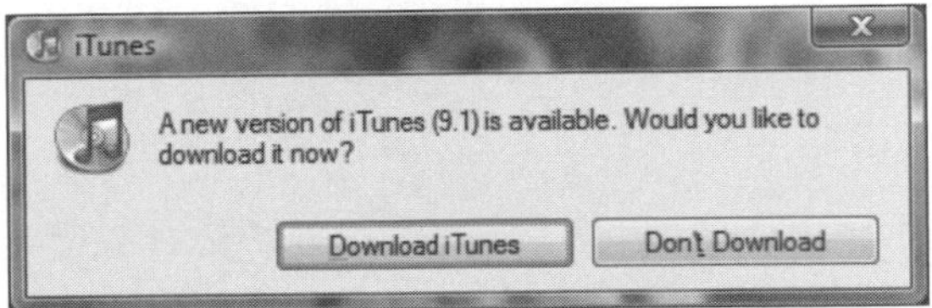

3. If you are not using the latest version, then you will see a screen similar to the one shown to the right.

4. Click **Download iTunes** to be taken to the **Apple Software Update** screen (see Figure 26–62).

5. On the **Apple Software Update** screen, make sure the **iTunes** selection is checked. Next, uncheck any software you do not want to install and click the **Install** button in the lower right corner.

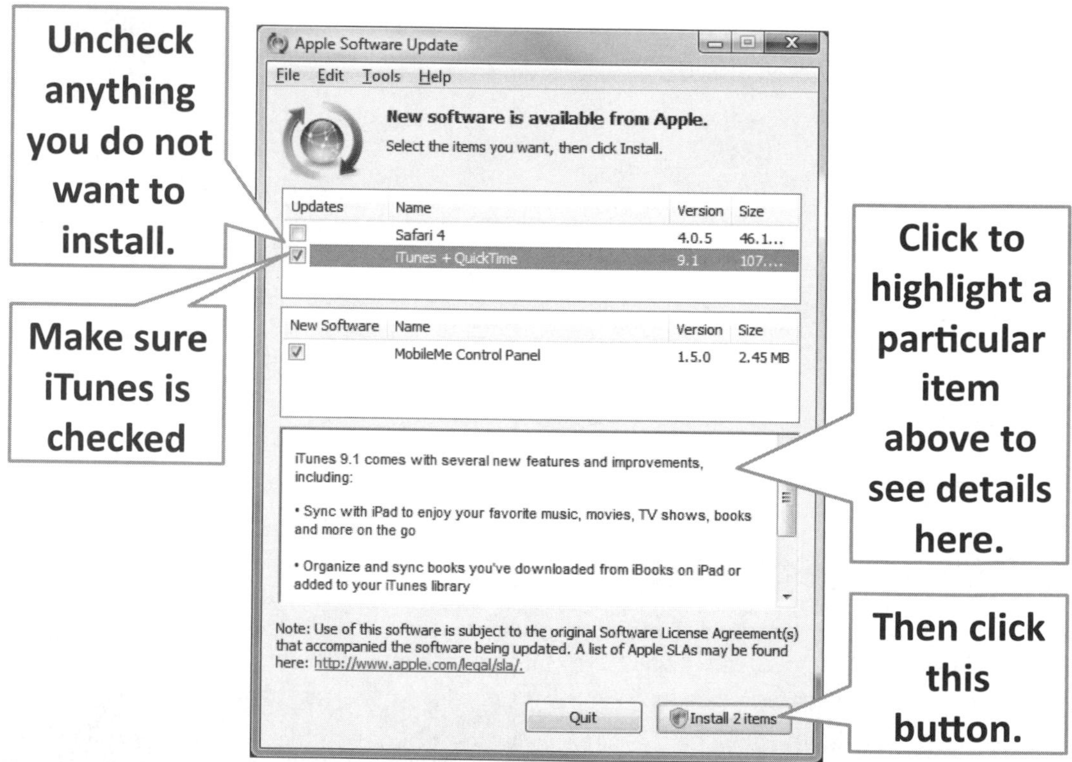


**Figure 26–62.** *The Apple Software Update screen*

6. You will then need to accept the Apple license agreement by clicking **Next** and **Accept** in order for the software update to start downloading (see Figure 26–63).

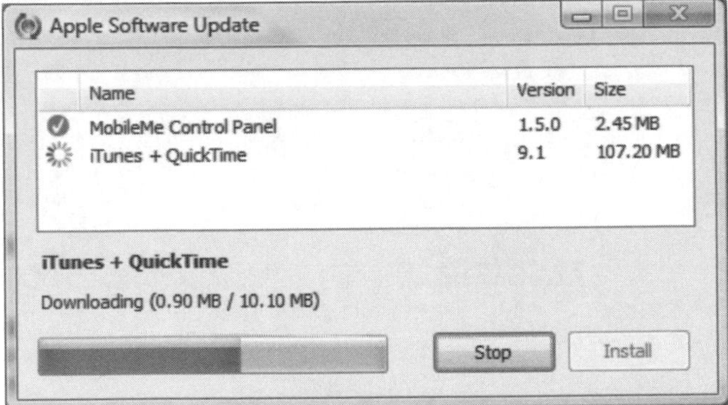


**Figure 26–63.** *The Apple Software Update download status screen*

> **TIP:** The software downloads can be 50 megabytes (MB) or more in size. We highly recommend doing the software downloads and updates from a high-speed Internet connection.

If everything goes smoothly, your iTunes and related software should be automatically updated with the latest version.

# iTunes Troubleshooting

In this section, we will provide a few tips and tricks to help you with some common issues you might encounter when using iTunes. We also have an entire chapter devoted to troubleshooting (see Chapter 25) if you cannot find answers to the problems you encounter in this section.

## What to Do If the iTunes Auto Update Fails

The automatic update may fail when you have the `About iTunes.rtf` text file open or you have another related file open that cannot be closed by the installer automatically. If you locate and close the problem file, you should be able to retry the automatic update.

If you see a message similar to the one shown to the right, you will have to manually install the update. Follow these steps to do so.

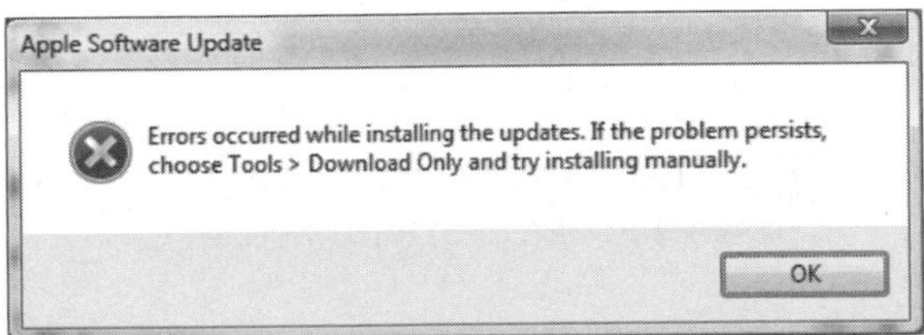

1. From the **Apple Software Update** screen, select the **Tools** menu and then **Download Only**.
2. You will see the download status screen shown in Figure 26–63.

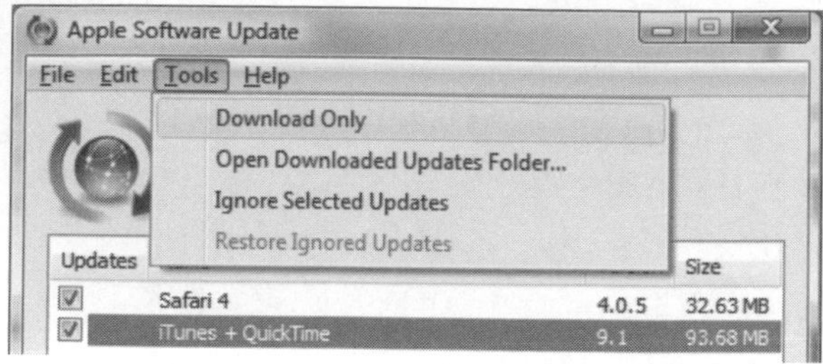


Once the download is finished, a new window should pop up, showing the downloaded files ready for you to manually install (see Figure 26–64).

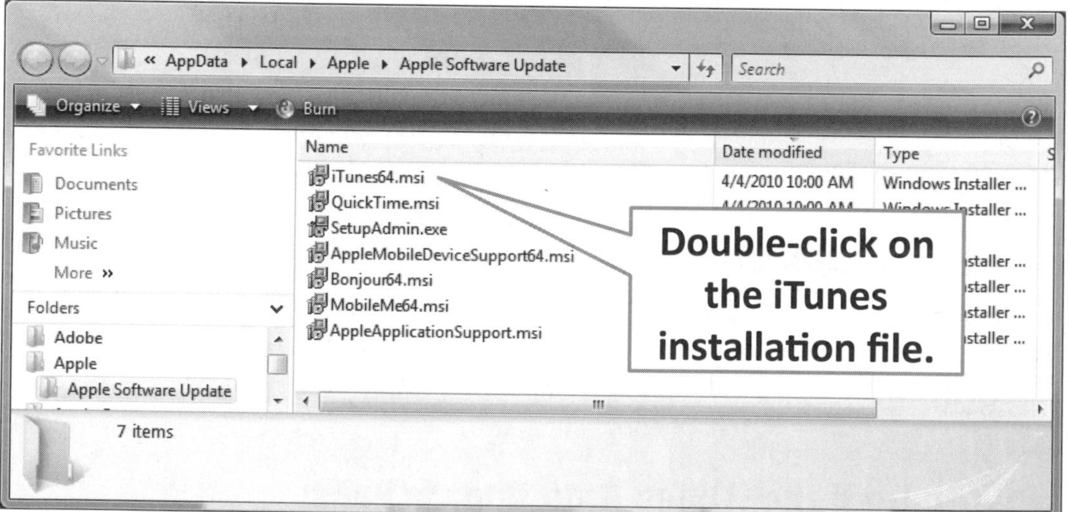


**Figure 26–64.** *Apple Software Update manual install folder (Windows PC)*

3. To manually start the install, double-click the **iTunes** installer file, as shown in Figure 26–64. The file may be slightly different than the one shown in the figure (e.g., `iTunes.msi` or `iTunes64.msi`), depending on the operating system on your computer.
4. From here, you need to follow the iTunes installation screens that were presented earlier in this chapter.

### Fixing the Apple ID Security Error

If you try to log in with your Apple ID, you might receive an error message at the top of the screen that looks similar to this one:

To use this Apple ID you must first login to the My Info Web page then provide additional security information.

If this happens, you will have to log in to the Apple Store web site and enter a Security Question/Answer and then add the month and day of your birth.

To correct this error, follow these steps.

1. Open up a web browser on your computer and go to `www.apple.com`.
2. Click on the **Store** link in the left portion of the **Top** nav bar, and then hover your mouse over the **Account** link in the upper right corner to see a drop-down list. Select **Account Information** from this list (see Figure 26–65).

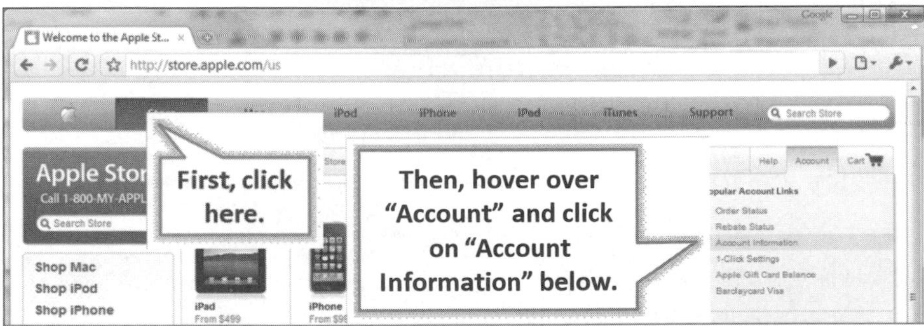


**Figure 26–65.** *Getting to your account information to correct your security information*

3. If you clicked **Account**, then you will need to select the **Change account information** link from the next screen.
4. Log in with your Apple ID and password (the one that caused the error above).
5. Most likely, your security question and answer or your birth month and birth date are blank. You need to add this information, type your password twice, scroll to the bottom of the screen, and then click the **Continue** button (see Figure 26–66).

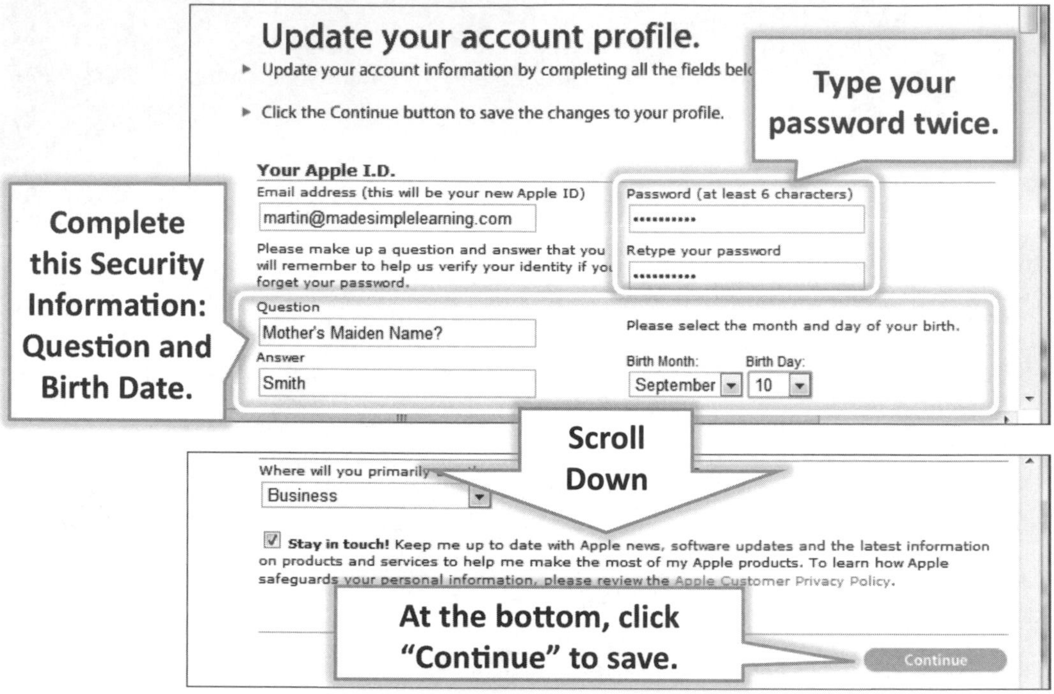

**Figure 26–66.** *Updating your Apple ID account's security information on the* `www.apple.com` *web site*

6. Now you should be able to use your Apple ID and password to register your iPad.

**CAUTION:** Apple will never send you an e-mail asking you for your password or asking you to log in and enter your password. If you receive such an e-mail, it might be a scam. Don't click on any links in such an e-mail. If you are concerned about your iTunes account, log in via iTunes to manage it.

## How Do I Get My Music Back if My Computer Crashes?

The good news is that you have a lot, or perhaps all, of your music on your iPad of course. We can't help you about getting your computer back up and running in this book, if the initial reboot isn't successful… but we can tell you about how you can get your music back from your iPad to iTunes, once your computer is running again!

So, if your only copy of your music, videos, and other content resides on your iPad, iPod, or iPhone, then you need to use a third-party tool to copy your music from that mobile device back into iTunes, once you've got your computer up and running again.

Do a web search for "copy iPod to iTunes" and you will find a number of both free and paid software tools to accomplish this.

We recommend using a free trial of any software before purchasing it to make sure it will meet your needs.

This solution will also help if you encounter the problem where all your iPad music is grayed-out when you view it from iTunes. In that case, you will need to copy all your iPad music to iTunes, then start fresh with the sync steps or manual transfer steps described in Chapter 3.

**CAUTION:** Please do not use this third-party software to create unauthorized copies of music, videos, or other content that you have not legitimately purchased.

# Index

## Special Characters and Numerics



## A

## D

## E

## G

## J



## K

## L



## M

## O



## P

## Q



## R

## T

## U

## V



## W

## Y

Z